THE PROSE READER

Annotated
Instructor's
Edition

*Essays for Thinking,
Reading, and Writing*

THIRD EDITION

■ ■ ■

Kim Flachmann
Michael Flachmann

California State University
Bakersfield

Prentice Hall, Englewood Cliffs, New Jersey 07632

Library of Congress Cataloging-in-Publication Data

The Prose reader : essays for thinking, reading, and writing /
  (compiled by) Kim Flachmann, Michael Flachmann. —3rd ed.
        p.   cm.
    Includes bibliographical references and index.
    ISBN 0-13-735879-2
    1. College readers.   2. English language—Rhetoric.
  I. Flachmann, Kim. II. Flachmann, Michael.
  PE1417.P847   1992b   92-33216
  808'.0427—dc20   CIP

Acquisition editor: Alison Reeves
Development editor: Karen Karlin
Editorial/production supervision and
    AIE page layout: Hilda Tauber
Prepress buyer: Herb Klein
Manufacturing buyer: Robert Anderson
Cover design: Bruce Kenselaar
Cover art: *The Soul of Seti This Way Passes*
    by Mark Ari. Private Collection/Superstock

 © 1993, 1990, 1987 by Prentice-Hall, Inc.
A Simon & Schuster Company
Englewood Cliffs, New Jersey 07632

Printed in the United States of America

10 9 8 7 6 5 4 3 2 1

ISBN 0-13-735887-3

Prentice-Hall International (UK) Limited, *London*
Prentice-Hall of Australia Pty. Limited, *Sydney*
Prentice-Hall Canada Inc., *Toronto*
Prentice-Hall Hispanoamericana, S.A., *Mexico*
Prentice-Hall of India Private Limited, *New Delhi*
Prentice-Hall of Japan, Inc., *Tokyo*
Simon & Schuster Asia Pte. Ltd., *Singapore*
Editora Prentice-Hall do Brasil, Ltda., *Rio de Janeiro*

For Our Parents

RHETORICAL CONTENTS

INTRODUCTION: *Thinking, Reading, and Writing*   1

THE GENERAL INTRODUCTION offers practical suggestions for approaching the tasks of thinking, reading, and writing—including several different examples of student writing in response to specific assignments.

CHAPTER 1

DESCRIPTION: *Exploring Through the Senses*   33

NOTES TO THE INSTRUCTOR appear throughout the margins of the **Annotated Instructor's Edition;** they include background information on each essay, definitions of difficult words, innovative teaching ideas, provocative questions, answers to the questions that follow each selection, additional essay topics, and instructor comments from throughout the United States on teaching different rhetorical modes. For those of you who want them, we offer readability levels calculated according to the Flesch and Dale indexes in the form of averge grade levels. These levels are generally accurate within one grade (e.g., an 8.4 readability level ranges from 7.4 to 9.4).

CHAPTER INTRODUCTIONS discuss the use of each rhetorical mode in daily life, define the rhetorical strategy, and show how to read and write essays based on that mode; followed by a sample student paragraph and a complete student essay that illustrate each rhetorical pattern and help bridge the gap between student writing and professional writing.

CHAPTER **2**

NARRATION: *Telling a Story*   87

PREREADING MATERIAL precedes each essay and consists of an extended biography and a list of informal questions that help students and instructors focus their attention on the subject of the selection.

CHAPTER 3

EXAMPLE: *Illustrating Ideas*   149

PREWRITING QUESTIONS precede each writing/discussion topic and are designed to help students and instructors focus their attention on the tasks that follow.

NEW

CHAPTER 4

PROCESS ANALYSIS: *Explaining Step by Step*
199

ALAN MONROE   *Characteristics of the Successful Speaker*
207

Cat got your tongue? Horrified of talking before large groups? Alan Monroe explains how to be a successful speaker—in just three easy lessons.

BETH WALD   *Let's Get Vertical*   213

Expert rock climber Beth Wald captures all the excitement, terror, and courage that accompany the ascent of a vertical rockface.

EDWIN BLISS   *Managing Your Time*   219

Feeling frantic and disorganized? Time-management expert Edwin Bliss reveals secrets of organization that will make your life much easier.

JESSICA MITFORD   *Behind the Formaldehyde Curtain*   226

In this chilling and macabre essay, celebrated "muckraker" Jessica Mitford exposes the greed and hypocrisy of the American mortuary business.

PAUL ROBERTS   *How to Say Nothing in Five Hundred Words*   236

Would you like to write a really *bad* essay in your freshman English class? Paul Roberts tells you how to get "F's" or "A's"—the choice is up to you!

APPARATUS
furnishes four types of questions after each selection that are designed to help students move from literal-level responses to interpretation and analysis: *Understanding Details; Analyzing Meaning; Discovering Rhetorical Strategies; and Ideas for Discussion/ Writing.*

CHAPTER 5

DIVISION/CLASSIFICATION: *Finding Categories*   251

NEW

CHAPTER 6

COMPARISON/CONTRAST: *Discovering*
Similarities and Differences 291

**READINGS THROUGHOUT THE
DISCIPLINES**
represent the major academic disciplines;
see the **Interdisciplinary Contents,** pages
xv–xxi, and a sample syllabus based on this
organization, in "Creating an Interdisciplinary Course" in the second chapter of the
Instructor's Resource Manual.

NEW

NEW

CHAPTER 8

CAUSE/EFFECT: *Tracing Reasons and Results*   385

CRITICAL THINKING
is taught through three strategies;
—Organization of the chapters from least to most difficult;
—Carefully sequenced questions after each essay;
—An expanded chapter on Argument and Persuasion, including essays demonstrating Opposing Viewpoints on timely issues.

CHAPTER 9

ARGUMENT AND PERSUASION: *Inciting People to Thought or Action* 425

DONALD DRAKEMAN *Religion's Place in Public Schools* 437

> To pray or not to pray? That is the question addressed by attorney Donald Drakeman within the emotionally charged context of today's public schools.

ELLEN GOODMAN *Putting In a Good Word for Guilt* 444

> Have you telephoned your mother lately? Do you know where your children are right now? Pulitzer-Prize-winning columnist Ellen Goodman gives us a fresh look at the value of guilt in our society.

NEW

SHELBY STEELE *Affirmative Action: The Price of Preference* 450

> Controversial author Shelby Steele examines the extent to which affirmative action programs perpetuate the "cultural myth of black inferiority."

NEW

ROBERT HUGHES *The N.R.A. in a Hunter's Sights* 462

> Hunting enthusiast Robert Hughes takes aim at the paranoia, rigid ideology, and bad faith of the powerful National Rifle Association.

NEW

BARBARA EHRENREICH *The Warrior Culture* 467

> Does our species have an inborn "murderous instinct"? Barbara Ehrenreich explains why America has always been a "primitive warrior culture."

CHAPTER 10

DOCUMENTED ESSAYS: *Reading and Writing from Sources* 501

OPPOSING VIEWPOINTS consists of four essays representing two different points of view on two critical issues for the 1990s—drug testing and homelessness; designed to help teach argument/persuasion and beginning research paper skills.

NEW

NEW

A NEW CHAPTER OF DOCUMENTED ESSAYS helps students learn research and documentation skills.

A FINAL CHAPTER
includes five essays that examine in detail the topics of thinking, reading, and writing that are the focus of this text.

A GLOSSARY OF USEFUL TERMS
defines and gives examples and page references for all relevant rhetorical terms used in the book.

AN INDEX OF AUTHORS AND TITLES
lists authors and essays with page numbers.

CHAPTER **11**

ESSAYS ON THINKING, READING, AND WRITING 535

INTERDISCIPLINARY CONTENTS

Behavioral Science

Black Studies

Business

Chicano and Latin-American Studies

Economics

Education

History

Language

Other Ethnic Studies

Philosophy and Religious Studies

Physical Education, Health, and Fitness

Political Science

Psychology

Science

Sociology

Women's Studies

Writing

PREFACE
TO THE INSTRUCTOR

The Prose Reader is based on the assumption that lucid writing follows lucid thinking, whereas poor written work is almost inevitably the product of foggy, irrational thought processes. As a result, our primary purpose in this book, as in the first two editions, is to help students *think* more clearly and logically—both in their minds and on paper.

Reading and writing are companion activities that involve students in the creation of thought and meaning—either as readers interpreting a text or as writers constructing one. Clear thinking, then, is the pivotal point that joins together these two efforts. Although studying the rhetorical strategies presented in *The Prose Reader* is certainly not the only way to approach writing, it does provide a productive means of helping students improve their abilities to think, read, and write on progressively more sophisticated levels.

The symbiosis we envision among thinking, reading, and writing is represented in this text by the following hierarchy of cognitive levels: (1) *literal*, which is characterized by a basic understanding of words and their meanings; (2) *interpretive*, which displays a knowledge of linear connections between ideas and an ability to make valid inferences based upon those ideas; and (3) *critical*, the highest level, which is distinguished by the systematic investigation of complex ideas and by the analysis of their relationship to the world around us.

How This Edition Is Organized

To help you bring about this improvement in student skills, *The Prose Reader* is organized on the assumption that our mental abilities are generally sequential. In other words, students cannot read or write analytically before they are able to perform well on the literal and interpretive levels. Accordingly, the book progresses from selections that require predominantly literal skills (Description, Narration, and Example) through readings involving more interpretation (Process Analysis, Division/Classification, Comparison/Contrast, and Definition) to essays that demand a high degree of analytical thought (Cause/Effect and Argument/ Persuasion). Depending upon the caliber of your students and your prescribed curriculum, these rhetorical modes can, of course, be studied in any order. In the Rhetorical Contents, each entry includes a one- or two-sentence synopsis of the selection so you can peruse the list quickly and decide which essays to assign. An alternate Interdisciplinary Contents lists selections by academic discipline, thereby responding to recent nationwide attempts to integrate reading and writing in content areas other than English through "Writing Across the Curriculum."

As in the earlier editions, the essays in *The Prose Reader* continue to represent a wide range of topics, such as discrimination of all types, ethnic identity, job opportunities, aging, education, sports, women's roles, prison life, time management, apartheid, AIDS, physical handicaps, and the writing process itself. They were selected on the basis of five criteria: (1) high interest level, (2) currency in the field, (3) moderate length, (4) readability, and (5) broad subject variety. Together, they portray the universality of human experience as expressed through the viewpoints of men and women, many different ethnic and racial groups, and a variety of ages and social classes.

Each of the nine rhetorical divisions in the text is introduced by an explanation of how to read and write in that particular rhetorical mode. These explanations are relatively brief so that the pedagogical emphasis in the text falls upon the discoveries students make as they work through the apparatus rather than upon a great deluge of material to be memorized. Each chapter introduction contains a sample paragraph and a complete student essay that illustrate each rhetorical pattern and help bridge the sometimes formidable gap between student and professional writing. After each student essay, the writer has provided a brief note explaining the most enjoyable, exasperating, or noteworthy aspects of writing that particular essay. We have found that this combination of student essays and commentaries makes the professional selections easier for students to read and more accessible as models of thinking and writing. Although each chapter focuses on one particular rhetorical strategy, students are continually encouraged to examine ways in which other modes help support the writers' main intentions.

The book ends with our popular chapter called "Thinking, Reading, and Writing," which includes essays on listening, reading fiction, understanding the process of writing, writing with style, and composing on the computer. Besides representing all the rhetorical modes at work, these essays provide a strong conclusion to the theoretical framework of this text, which focuses so intently on the interrelationships among thinking, reading, and writing.

Because our own experience suggests that students often produce their best writing when they are personally involved in the topics of the essays they read and in the human drama surrounding those essays, we precede each selection with thorough biographical information on the author and provocative prereading questions on the subject of the essay. The biographies explain the real experiences from which an essay emerges, whereas the prereading questions ("Preparing to Read") help students focus on the purpose, audience, and subject of the essay. These prereading questions also foreshadow the questions and writing assignments after each selection. Personalizing this preliminary material encourages students to identify with both the writer of the essay and the essay's subject matter—which, in turn, engages the students' attention and energizes their response to the selections they read.

The questions at the end of each selection are designed to help students move from various literal-level responses to interpretation and analysis as the topics become progressively more complex. Four different types of questions are appended to each essay: (1) those that test the students' understanding of what they have read on the literal and interpretive levels ("Understanding Details"), (2) those that require students to analyze various aspects of the essay ("Analyzing Meaning"), (3) those that investigate the author's rhetorical strategies ("Discovering Rhetorical Strategies"), and (4) those that supply writing and discussion topics for use inside or outside the classroom ("Ideas for Discussion/Writing"). These questions deliberately examine both the form and content of the essays so that your students can cultivate a similar balance in their own writing.

The writing assignments are preceded by prewriting questions ("Preparing to Write") designed to encourage students to express their feelings, thoughts, observations, and opinions on a certain topic. Questions about their own ideas and experiences help students produce writing that corresponds as closely as possible to the way they think. Then, the writing assignments themselves seek to involve the students in realistic situations by providing a specific purpose and audience for each essay topic. In this manner, student writers are drawn into rhetorical scenes that carefully focus their responses to a variety of questions or problems. The book concludes with a glossary of composition terms (along with examples and page references from the text) and an index of authors and titles.

What Is New

The third edition of *The Prose Reader* contains sixteen new essays. We have updated some of the selections, added new authors, and introduced new topics. The new essays feature such subjects as animal rights, divorce, date rape, fetal alcohol babies, gun control, homelessness, and deciding whether to have children.

Although multicultural and women's issues have always been well represented in *The Prose Reader*, this edition makes a renewed commitment to cultural and sexual diversity by including many new essays by women and ethnic-minority authors, among them Amy Tan, Bill Cosby, Jane Goodall, Beth Wald, Judith Wallerstein and Sandra Blakeslee, Elena Asturias, Nancy Gibbs, Michael Dorris, Alice Walker, Shelby Steele, Barbara Ehrenreich, and Annie Dillard.

We have added two essays to the chapter on argument/persuasion and developed a new chapter that focuses on writing from sources. Argument and Persuasion (Chapter 9) covers topics such as religion's place in public schools, affirmative action, gun control, and America's "warrior" culture and includes two sets of opposing viewpoint essays on drug testing and homelessness. Documented Essays: Reading and Writing from Sources (Chapter 10) features academic writing throughout the college curriculum in the form of research papers (on teenage pregnancy and group violence); these essays demonstrate the two most common documentation styles—Modern Language Association (MLA) and American Psychological Association (APA). By including essays of this kind, we intend to clarify some of the mysteries connected with research and documentation; we have also tried to provide interesting material for creating more elaborate writing assignments in accord with your own specific course goals. We offer a full range of apparatus for these two selections, including a list of Further Reading on each subject and suggested topics for longer, more sophisticated essays and research papers.

What Supplements Are Available

Available with *The Prose Reader* is a thorough ***Annotated Instructor's Edition*** designed to make your life in the classroom a little easier. We have filled the margins of the AIE with many different kinds of supplementary material, including background information about each essay, definitions of terms that might be unfamiliar to your students, a list of Related Readings from this text that can be taught profitably with each other, innovative teaching ideas, provocative quotations, specific answers to the questions after each selection, additional essay topics, and instructor comments on teaching different rhetorical modes.

Another part of the instructional package accompanying *The Prose Reader* is the ***Quiz Book,*** which consists of a series of objective questions designed to help you monitor your students' mastery of each essay's vocabulary and content. At the end of this supplement are the answers to the questions in the *Quiz Book.*

In addition to the *Annotated Instructor's Edition* and the *Quiz Book,* we have created a new supplement that we call the ***Instructor's Resource Manual.*** In it we identify and discuss some of the most widely used theoretical approaches to the teaching of composition; we then offer innovative options for organizing your course, specific suggestions for the first day of class, a summary of the advantages and disadvantages of using different teaching strategies, several successful techniques for responding to student writing, a series of student essays (one for each rhetorical strategy featured in the text) followed by the student writer's comments, and an annotated bibliography of books about thinking, reading, and writing.

This entire instructional package is intended to help your students discover what they want to say and prompt them to shape their ideas into a coherent form, thereby encouraging their intelligent involvement in the complex world around them.

Acknowledgments

We are pleased to acknowledge the kind assistance and support of a number of people who have helped us put together this third edition of *The Prose Reader.* For creative and editorial guidance at Prentice Hall, we thank Phil Miller, Editor in Chief; Joyce Perkins, Senior Development Editor for the Humanities; Karen Karlin, Development Editor; Hilda Tauber, Production Editor; Mark Tobey,

Supplements Editor; Heidi Moore and Kara Hado, Editorial Assistants; Gina Sluss, Senior Marketing Manager; and Tracy Augustine, Executive Marketing Manager. For reviews of the manuscript at various stages of completion, we are grateful to Terrence Burke, Cuyahoga Community College, Cleveland, Ohio; Ellen Dugan-Barrette, Brescia College, Owensboro, Kentucky; Lewis Emond, Dean Junior College, Franklin, Massachusetts; Jay Jernigan, Eastern Michigan University, Ypsilanti, Michigan; Nellie McCrory, Gaston College, Dallas, North Carolina; Leslie Shipp, Clark County Community College, Henderson, Nevada; and William F. Sutlife, Community College of Allegheny County, Monroeville, Pennsylvania; and for student essays and writing samples, Rosa Marie Augustine, Donel Crow, Dawn Dobie, Gloria Dumler, Jeff Hicks, Julie Anne Judd, Judi Koch, Dawn McKee, Paul Newberry, Joanne Silva-Newberry, JoAnn Slate, Peggy Stuckey, and Jan Titus.

Several writing instructors across the United States have been kind enough to help shape the third edition of *The Prose Reader* by responding to specific questions about their teaching experiences with the book: Charles Bordogna, Bergen Community College, Paramus, New Jersey; Mary G. Marshall and Eileen M. Ward, College of DuPage, Glen Ellyn, Illinois; Michael J. Huntington and Judith C. Kohl, Dutchess Community College, Poughkeepsie, New York; Ted Johnston, El Paso County Community College, El Paso, Texas; Koala C. Hartnett, Rick James Mazza, and William H. Sherman, Fairmont State College, Fairmont, West Virginia; Miriam Dick and Betty Krasne, Mercy College, Dobbs Ferry, New York; Elvis Clark, Mineral Area College, Flat River, Missouri; Dayna Spencer, Pittsburg State University, Pittsburg, Kansas; James A. Zarzana, Southwest State University, Marshall, Minnesota; Susan Reinhart Schneling and Trudy Vanderback, Vincennes University, Vincennes, Indiana; Carmen Wong, Virginia Commonwealth University, Richmond, Virginia; and John W. Hattman and Virginia E. Leonard, West Liberty State College, West Liberty, West Virginia. We want to extend special thanks to Sandra R. Woods, Fairmont State College, whose students' comments on the second edition were exceptionally valuable to us in making decisions for this edition.

We are also grateful to the following professors from our university who have offered useful advice about the book: Mary Allen, Charles Bicak, Ken Gobalet, Richard Graves, Bob Horton, Bruce Jones, Gary Kessler, Richard Noel, Warren Paap, Norman Prigge, Phil Silverman, and Jerry Stanley of the Writing Across the Curriculum Program; and Ed Barton, Robert Carlisle, Barbara Drushell, Don Green, Bonnie Greene, Solomon Iyasere, Victor Lasseter, Char Myers, Jeff Spencer, Susan Stone, and Emily Thiroux of the English and Communications Department at California State University, Bakersfield.

In preparing our *Annotated Instructor's Edition*, we owe special gratitude to the following writing instructors who have contributed their favorite techniques for teaching various rhetorical strategies: Mary P. Boyles, Pembroke State University; Terrence W. Burke, Cuyahoga Community College; Mary Lou Conlin, Cuyahoga Community College; Ellen Dugan-Barrette, Brescia College; Janet Eber, County College of Morris; Louis Emond, Dean Junior College; Peter Harris, West Virginia Institute of Technology, Montgomery; Jay Jernigan, Eastern Michigan University; Judith C. Kohl, Dutchess Community College; Joanne H. McCarthy, Tacoma Community College; Anthony McCrann, Peru State College; Nellie McCrory, Gaston College; Alan Price, Penn State University—Hazelton; Patricia A. Ross, Moorpark Colege; Leslie Shipp, Clark County Community College; Rodney Simard, California State University, San Bernadino; Elizabeth Wahlquist, Brigham Young University; John White, California State University, Fullerton; and Ted Wise, Porterville College. We also want to thank our graduate students and teaching assistants for suggesting instructional material to supplement the student text and for class-testing some of it as we were writing: Phyllis Agalos, Jeannette Bates, Charles Boland, Sarah Brothers, Diana Dominguez, Gloria Dumler, Brenda Frea-ney, Carol Heber, Marty Lechtreck, Frances Richardson, Cindy Shepherd, Martha Threewit, and Norma Walker. Finally, we appreciate the additional assistance on the AIE given to us by Gladys Stilwill, Dawn McKee, Cindy Shepherd, and Brenda Freaney.

Very special thanks are due to Kathryn Benauder, who served as a research and editorial assistant throughout the entire project; to Sue Keintz, who assisted us greatly on the AIE and the new *Instructor's Resource Manual*; and to Mette Kamstrup, who supported our efforts on this text in many important ways.

Our final and most important debt is to our students, who have taught us so much over the years about the writing process.

PREFACE
TO THE STUDENT

Accurate thinking is the beginning and fountain of writing.
—Horace

The Purpose of This Text

Have you ever had trouble expressing your thoughts? If so, you're not alone. Many people have this difficulty—especially when they are asked to write their thoughts down.

The good news is that this "ailment" can be cured. We've learned over the years that the more clearly students think about the world around them, the more easily they can express their ideas through written and spoken language. As a result, this textbook intends to improve your writing by helping you think clearly, logically, and critically about important ideas and issues that exist in our world today. You will learn to reason, read, and write about your environment in increasingly complex ways, moving steadily from a simple, literal understanding of topics to interpretation and analysis. Inspired by well-crafted prose models and guided by carefully worded questions, you can actually raise the level of your thinking skills while improving your reading and writing abilities.

The Prose Reader is organized on the assumption that as a college student you should be able to think, read, and write on three increasingly difficult levels: (1) *literal*, which involves a basic understanding of a selection and the ability to repeat or restate the material; (2) *interpretive*, which requires you to make associations and draw inferences from information in your reading; and (3) *analytical*, which demands that you systematically separate, explain, evaluate, and reassemble various important ideas discovered in your reading.

For example, students with a literal grasp of an essay would be able to understand the words on the page, cite details from the selection, and paraphrase certain sections of the essay. Students equipped with interpretive skills will see implicit relationships within a selection (such as comparison/contrast or cause/effect), make inferences from information that is supplied, and comprehend the intricacies of figurative language. Finally, students functioning analytically will be able to summarize and explain difficult concepts and generate plausible hypotheses from a series of related ideas. In short, this book leads you systematically toward higher levels of thinking and writing.

In order to stimulate your thinking on all levels, this text encourages you to participate in the making of meaning—as both a reader and a writer. As a reader, you have a responsibility to work with the author of each essay to help create sense out of the words on the page; as a writer, you must be conscious enough of your audience that they perceive your intended purpose clearly and precisely through the ideas, opinions, and details that you provide. Because of this unique relationship, we envision reading and writing as companion acts in which writer and reader are partners in the development of meaning.

To demonstrate this vital interrelationship between reader and writer, our text provides you with prose models that are intended to inspire your own thinking and writing. In the introduction to each chapter, we include a student paragraph and a student essay that feature the particular rhetorical strategy under discussion. The essay is highlighted by annotations and by underlining to illustrate how to write that type of essay and to help bridge the gap between student writing in the classroom and the professional selections in the text. After each essay, the student writer has drafted a personal note with some useful advice about generating that particular type of essay. The essays that follow each chapter introduction, selected from a wide variety of well-known contemporary authors, are intended to encourage you to improve your writing through a partnership with some of the best examples of professional prose available today. Just as musicians and athletes richly benefit from studying the techniques of the foremost people in their fields, so do we hope that you will grow in spirit and language use from your collaborative work with the writers in this collection.

How to Use This Text

The Prose Reader contains essays representing the four main purposes of writing: description, narration, exposition, and persuasion. Our primary focus within this framework is on exposition (which means "explanation"), because you will need to master this type of verbal expression to succeed in both the academic and the professional worlds. Although the essays in this text can be read in any order, we begin with description because it is a basic technique that often appears in other forms of discourse. We then move to narration, or storytelling, and next to the six traditional expository strategies—the established patterns of thought through which most educated people send and receive written ideas and information: example, process analysis, division/classification, comparison/contrast, definition, and cause/effect. The text continues with an expanded chapter on argument and persuasion, including two sets of opposing viewpoint essays. A new Chapter 10 discusses and presents documented research papers, and the anthology concludes with selections about thinking, reading, and writing.

"Pure" rhetorical types rarely exist, of course, and when they do, the result often seems artificial. Therefore, although each essay in this collection focuses on a single rhetorical mode as its primary strategy, other strategies are also at work in it. These selections concentrate on one primary technique at a time in much the same way a well-arranged photograph highlights a certain visual detail, though many other elements function in the background to make the picture an organic whole.

Each chapter begins with an explanation of a single rhetorical technique. These explanations are divided into four sections that move from the effect of this technique on our daily lives to its integral role in the writing process. The first section, called "Using ———" (for example, "Using Description"), catalogs the use of each rhetorical mode in our daily lives. The second section, "Defining ———"(e.g., "Defining Description"), offers a working definition of the technique and a sample paragraph so that we all have the same fundamental understanding of the term. A third section, called "Reading and Writing ——— Essays"(e.g., "Reading and Writing Descriptive Essays"), explains the processes of reading and writing an essay in each rhetorical mode, and a fourth section presents an annotated student essay showing this particular rhetorical method "at work," followed by comments from the student writer.

Prior to each reading selection, we have designed some material to focus your attention on a particular writer and topic before you begin reading the essay. This "prereading" segment begins with biographical information about the author and ends with a number of questions to whet your appetite for the essay that follows. This section is intended to help you discover interesting relationships among ideas in your reading and then anticipate various ways of thinking about and analyzing the essay. The prereading questions forecast not only the material in the essay, but also the questions and writing assignments that follow.

The questions following each reading selection are designed as guides for thinking about the essay. These questions are at the heart of the relationship represented in this book among thinking, reading, and writing. They are divided into four interrelated sections that move you smoothly from a literal understanding of what you have just read, to interpretation, and finally to analysis. The first set of questions, "Understanding Details," focuses on the basic facts and opinions in the selection. The second set of questions, "Analyzing Meaning," asks you to explain certain facts and evaluate various assumptions of the essay in an effort to understand the entire selection on an analytical level. The third set of questions, "Discovering Rhetorical Strategies," guides your thinking on how the author achieved certain effects through word choice, sentence structure, organization of ideas, and selection of details. This third series of questions often requires you to apply to your reading of an essay material you learned about a particular mode of writing in the chapter introduction.

The final section of questions consists of three "Ideas for Discussion/Writing." These topics are preceded by "prewriting" questions to help you generate new ideas. Most of the Discussion/Writing topics specify a purpose (a specific reason for writing the essay) and an audience (an identifiable person or group of people you should address in your essay) so that you can focus your work as precisely as possible. These assignments outline realistic scenes and roles for you to play in those scenes so that, as you write, your relationship to your subject and audience will be clear and precise.

The word "essay" (which comes from the Old French *essai*, meaning a "try" or an "attempt") is an appropriate label for these writing assignments, because they all ask you to grapple with an idea or problem and then try to give shape to your conclusions in some effective manner. Such "exercises" can be equated with the development of athletic ability in sports: The essay itself demonstrates that you can put together all the various skills you have learned; it proves that you can actually play the sport. After you have studied the different techniques at work in a reading selection, a specific essay assignment lets you practice them all in unison and allows you to discover for yourself even more secrets about the intricate details of effective communication.

INTRODUCTION
■ ■ ■
Thinking, Reading, and Writing

Thinking Critically

Thinking critically involves grappling with the ideas, issues, and problems that surround you in your immediate environment and in the world at large. It does not necessarily entail finding fault, which you might naturally associate with the word *critical*, but rather suggests continually questioning and analyzing the world around you. Thinking critically is the highest form of mental activity that human beings engage in; it is the source of success in college and in our professional and personal lives. Fortunately, all of us can learn how to think critically or can improve upon this ability.

Critical thinking means taking apart an issue, idea, or problem; examining its various parts; and reassembling the topic with a fuller understanding of its intricacies. Implied in this explanation is the ability to see the topic from one or more new perspectives. Using your mind in this way will help you find solutions to difficult problems, design creative plans of action, and ultimately live a life consistent with your opinions on important issues that we all must confront on a daily basis.

NOTES ON THE INTRODUCTION

The Introduction is carefully designed to shepherd your students through the process of thinking about a topic, reading an essay, and writing their own essays. We accomplish this by presenting a sample reading selection and apparatus in the same format as the instructional material that accompanies each of the 56 essays in this text. This Introduction actually shows students how to approach a specific selection, how to read and respond to it, and how to write about the issues raised by its author. Our overall goal is to assist students in learning a systematic approach to thinking, reading, and writing that can help them in all their college courses.

The first section of the Introduction, entitled "Thinking Critically," introduces students to various important preliminary materials that precede their reading assignments. In this text, the essay's title, the place of its first publication, extended biographi-

well-focused prereading material are furnished to help set the rhetorical scene and to encourage students to generate ideas on a particular subject.

The second part of the Introduction, "Reading Critically," leads students systematically through the process of reading and responding to a sample essay, with particular attention to answering three sets of questions that follow the selection: those that check literal and interpretive understanding (Understanding Details); those that ask analytical-level questions (Analyzing Meaning); and those that require students to explain how various rhetorical strategies work in a reading selection (Discovering Rhetorical Strategies). At the end of this section is an inventory of reading tasks that serves as a summary of the information here.

"Writing Critically," the third and last section of the Introduction, takes your students through the composition of an essay, from the initial preparation and invention of ideas to the proofreading of the final draft. We begin with prewriting questions related to the writing assignments that follow, thereby encouraging students to think about their topics before they begin writing about them. In this part of the Introduction, we have printed a student's prewriting activities (including brainstorming, clustering, and a journal entry) in response to the "Preparing to Write" questions. We also provide the same student's rough draft of a sample essay assignment and then a revised draft of the same theme, highlighting important changes made during the revising and editing/proofreading process. At the end of this section, we provide checklists that summarize the entire writing process.

This text, then, seeks to help your students refine their ability to think, read, and write skillfully on a variety of levels—in college and in their later lives. The reading and writing tasks, carefully interwoven with an emphasis on analytical thinking, will assist your students in meeting the many intellectual challenges that lie ahead of them as they confront our complex and exciting world. All that remains is for you to add to this material your own unique approach to the teaching of writing.

Recent psychological studies have shown that "thinking" and "feeling" are complementary operations. All of us have feelings that are automatic and instinctive. To feel pride after winning first place at a track meet, for example, or to feel anger at a spiteful friend is not behavior we have to study and master; such emotions come naturally to human beings. Thinking, on the other hand, is much less spontaneous than feeling; research suggests that study and practice are required for sustained mental development.

Actually, we can improve the way we think by exercising our brains on three sequential levels:

1. *Literal thinking* is the foundation of all human understanding; it entails knowing the meanings of words—individually and in relation to one another. In order for someone to comprehend the sentence "You must exercise your brain to reach your full mental potential" on the literal level, for example, that person would have to know the definitions of all the words in the sentence and understand the way those words work together to make meaning.

2. *Interpretation* requires the ability to make associations between details, draw inferences from pieces of information, and reach conclusions about the material. An interpretive understanding of the sample sentence in level 1 might be translated into the following thoughts: "Exercising the brain sounds a bit like exercising the body. I wonder if there's any correlation between the two. If the brain must be exercised, it is probably made up of muscles, much like the body is." None of these particular "thoughts" is made explicit in the sentence, but each is suggested in one way or another.

3. *Critical thinking*, the most sophisticated form of human thought, is a type of mental activity that is crucial for successful academic and professional work. A critical analysis of our sample sentence might proceed in the following way: "This sentence is talking to me. It actually addresses me with the word 'you.' I wonder what *my* mental potential is. Will I be able to reach it? Will I know when I attain it? Will I be comfortable with it? I certainly want to reach this potential, whatever it is. Reaching it will undoubtedly help me succeed scholastically and professionally. The brain is obviously an important tool for helping me achieve my goals in life, so I want to take every opportunity I have to develop and maintain this part of my body." Students who can take an issue or idea apart in this fashion and understand its various components more thoroughly after reassembling them are rewarded intrinsically with a clearer knowledge of life's complexities and the ability to generate creative, useful ideas. They are also rewarded extrinsically with good grades and are more likely to earn responsible jobs with higher pay, because their understanding of the world around them is perceptive and they are able to apply this understanding effectively to their professional and personal lives.

In this textbook, you will learn to think critically through reading essays written by intelligent, interesting authors and through writing your own essays on a variety of topics. The next several pages offer guidelines for approaching the reading and writing assignments in this book. These suggestions should also be useful to you in your other courses.

Reading Critically

Reading critically begins with developing a natural curiosity about an essay and nurturing that curiosity throughout the reading process. To learn as much as you can from an essay, you should first study any preliminary material you can find, then read the essay to get a general overview of its main ideas, and finally read the selection again to achieve a deeper understanding of its intent. The three phases of the reading process explained below—preparing to read, reading, and rereading—will help you develop this "natural curiosity" so you can approach any reading assignment with an active, inquiring mind; they should occur cyclically as you read each essay.

PREPARING TO READ

Focusing your attention is an important first stage in both the reading and writing processes. In fact, learning as much as you can about an essay and its "context" (the circumstances surrounding its development) before you begin reading can help you move through the essay with an energetic, active mind and then reach some degree of analysis before writing on the assigned topics. In particular, knowing where an essay was first published, studying the writer's background, and doing some preliminary thinking on the subject of a reading selection will help you understand the writer's ideas and form some valid opinions of your own.

As you approach any essay, you should concentrate on four specific areas that will begin to give you an overview of the material you are about to read. We use an essay by Lewis Thomas to demonstrate these techniques.

1. Title.   A close look at the title will usually provide important clues about the author's attitude toward the topic, the author's stand on an issue, or the mood of an essay. It can also furnish you with a sense of audience and purpose.

To Err Is Human

From this title, for example, we might infer that the author will discuss errors, human nature, and the extent to which mistakes influence human behavior. The title is half of a well-known proverbial quotation (Alexander Pope's "To err is human, to forgive, divine"), so we might speculate further that the author has written an essay intended for a well-read audience interested in the relationship between errors and humanity. After reading only four words of the essay—its title—you already have a good deal of information about the subject, its audience, and the author's attitude toward both.

2. Synopsis.   The Rhetorical Contents in this text contains a synopsis of each essay, very much like the following, so that you can find out more specific details about its contents before you begin reading.

> Physician Lewis Thomas explains how we can profit from our mistakes—especially if we trust human nature. Perhaps someday, he says, we can apply this same principle to the computer and magnify the advantages of these errors.

From this synopsis, you learn that Thomas' essay will be an analysis of human errors and of the way we can benefit from those errors. The synopsis also tells us the computer has the potential to magnify the value of our errors.

3. Biography. Learning as much as you can about the author of an essay will generally stimulate your interest in the material and help you achieve a deeper understanding of the issues to be discussed. From the biographies in this book, you can learn, for example, whether a writer is young or old, conservative or liberal, open- or closed-minded. You might also discover if the essay was written at the beginning, middle, or end of the author's career or how well versed the writer is on the topic. Such information will invariably provide a deeper, more thorough understanding of a selection's ideas, audience, and logical structure.

LEWIS THOMAS
(1913–   )

Lewis Thomas is a physician who is currently president emeritus of the Sloan-Kettering Cancer Center and scholar-in-residence at the Cornell University Medical Center in New York City. A graduate of Princeton University and Harvard Medical School, he was formerly head of pathology and dean of the New York University-Bellevue Medical Center and dean of the Yale Medical School. In addition to having written over two hundred scientific papers on virology and immunology, he has authored many popular scientific essays, some of which have been collected in *Lives of a Cell* (1974), *The Medusa and the Snail* (1979), *Late Night Thoughts on Listening to Mahler's Ninth Symphony* (1983), and *Etcetera, Etcetera* (1990). The memoirs of his distinguished career have been published in *The Youngest Science: Notes of a Medicine Watcher* (1983). Thomas likes to refer to his essays as "experiments in thought": "Although I usually think I know what I'm going to be writing about, what I'm going to say, most of the time it doesn't happen that way at all. At some point I get misled down a garden path. I get surprised by an idea that I hadn't anticipated getting, which is a little bit like being in a laboratory."

As this information indicates, Thomas is a prominent physician who has published widely on scientific topics. We know that he considers his essays "experiments in thought," which makes us expect a relaxed, spontaneous treatment of his subjects. From this biography, we can also infer that he is a leader in the medical world and that, because the positions he has held are generally elected, he is well respected in his professional life. Last, we can speculate that he has a clear sense of his audience because he is able to present difficult concepts in clear, everyday language.

4. Preparing to Read.   One other type of preliminary material will broaden your overview of the topic and enable you to approach the essay with an active, thoughtful mind. The "Preparing to Read" sections following the biographies are intended to focus your attention and stimulate your curiosity before you begin the essay. They will also get you ready to form your own opinions on the essay and its topic as you read. Keeping a journal to respond to these questions is an excellent idea, because you will then have a record of your thoughts on various topics related to the reading selection that follows.

Preparing to Read

The following essay, which originally appeared in the *New England Journal of Medicine* (January 1976), illustrates the clarity and ease with which Thomas explains complex scientific topics. As you prepare to read this essay, take a few moments to think about the role mistakes play in our lives: What are some memorable mistakes you have made in your life? Did you learn anything important from any of these errors? Do you make more or fewer mistakes than other people you know? Do you see any advantages to making mistakes? Any disadvantages?

Discovering where, why, and how an essay was first written will provide you with a context for the material you are about to read: Why did the author write this selection? Where was it first published? Who was the author's original audience? This type of information enables you to understand the circumstances surrounding the development of the selection and to identify any topical or historical references the author makes. All the selections in this textbook were published elsewhere first—in another book, a journal, or a magazine. Some are excerpts from longer works. The author's original audience, therefore, consisted of the readers of that particular publication.

From the "Preparing to Read" material, we learn that Thomas' essay "To Err Is Human" was originally published in the *New England Journal of Medicine,* a prestigious periodical read principally by members of the scientific community. Written early in 1976, the article plays upon its audience's growing fascination with computers and with the limits of artificial intelligence—subjects just as timely today as they were in the mid-1970s.

The questions here prompt you to consider your own ideas, opinions, or experiences in order to help you generate thoughts on the topic of errors in our lives. These questions are, ideally, the last step in preparing yourself for the active role you should play as a reader.

READING

People read essays in books, newspapers, magazines, and journals for a great variety of reasons. One reader may want to be stimulated intellectually, whereas another seeks relaxation; one person reads to keep up with the latest developments in his or her profession, whereas the next wants to learn why a certain event happened or how something can be done; some people read in order to be challenged by new ideas, whereas others find comfort principally in printed material that supports their own moral, social, or political opinions. The essays in this textbook variously fulfill all these expectations. They have been chosen, however, not only for these reasons, but for an additional, broader purpose: Reading them can help make you a better writer.

Every time you read an essay in this book, you will also be preparing to write your own essay concentrating on the same rhetorical pattern. For this reason, as you read you should pay careful attention to both the content (subject matter) and the form (language, sentence structure, organization, and development of ideas) of each essay. You will also see how effectively experienced writers use particular rhetorical modes (or patterns of thought) to organize and communicate their ideas. Each essay in this collection features one dominant pattern that is generally supported by several others. In fact, the more aware you are of each author's writing techniques, the more rapidly your own writing process will mature and improve.

The questions before and after each essay teach you a way of reading that can help you discover the relationship of a writer's ideas to one another as well as to your own ideas. These questions can also help clarify for you the connection between the writer's topic, his or her style or manner of expression, and your own composing process. In other words, the questions are designed to help you understand and generate ideas, then discover various choices the writers make in composing their essays, and finally realize the freedom you have to make related choices in your own writing. Such an approach to the process of reading takes reading and writing out of the realm of mystical creation and places them into the realistic world of the possible; a process of this sort takes some of the mystery out of reading and writing and makes them manageable tasks at which anyone can become proficient.

Three general guidelines, each of which is explained below in detail, will help you develop your own system for reading and responding to what you have read:

1. **Read the essay to get an overall sense of it.**
2. **Summarize the essay.**
3. **Read the questions and assignments that follow the essay.**

Guideline 1.   *First, read the essay to get an overall sense of it in relation to its title, purpose, audience, author, and publication information.* Write (in the margins, on a separate piece of paper or in a journal) your initial reactions, comments, and personal associations.

To illustrate, on the following pages is the Thomas essay with a student's comments in the margins, showing how the student reacted to the essay upon reading it for the first time.

LEWIS THOMAS
(1913–   )

■ ■ ■

To Err Is Human

Boy is this true!

Everyone must have had at least one personal experience with a computer error by this time. Bank balances are suddenly reported to have jumped from $379 into the millions, appeals for charitable contributions are mailed over and over to people with crazy sounding names at your address, department stores send the wrong bills, utility companies write that they're turning everything off, that sort of thing. If you manage to get in touch with someone and complain, you then get instantaneously typed, guilty letters from the same computer, saying, "Our computer was in error, and an adjustment is being made in your account." 1

last spring this happened to me.

exactly

These are supposed to be the sheerest, blindest accidents. Mistakes are not believed to be part of the normal behavior of a good machine. If things go wrong, it must be a personal, human error, the result of fingering, tampering, a button getting stuck, someone hitting the wrong key. The computer, at its normal best, is infallible. 2

How can it be?

I wonder whether this can be true. After all, the whole point of computers is that they represent an extension of the human brain, vastly improved upon but nonetheless human, superhuman maybe. A good computer can think clearly and quickly enough to beat you at chess, and some of them have even been programmed to write obscure verse. They can do anything we can do, and more besides. 3

In what way?

Can this be proven?

It is not yet known whether a computer has its own consciousness, and it would be hard to 4

find out about this. When you walk into one of *I expected this essay to be so much more stuffy than it is. I can even understand it.*
those great halls now built for the huge machines,
and stand listening, it is easy to imagine that the
faint, distant noises are the sound of thinking, and
the turning of the spools gives them the look of
In what way? wild creatures rolling their eyes in the effort to
concentrate, choking with information. But real
thinking, and dreaming, are other matters.

On the other hand, the evidences of something   5
like an *unconscious*, equivalent to ours, are all
around, in every mail. As extensions of the human   *good, clear comparison for the general reader*
brain, they have been constructed with the same
property of error, spontaneous, uncontrolled, and
rich in possibilities.

so true Mistakes are at the very base of human   6
great image thought, embedded there, feeding the structure like
root nodules. If we were not provided with the   *I don't understand this*
I agree! This is how we learn knack of being wrong, we could never get anything
useful done. We think our way along by choosing
between right and wrong alternatives, and the
wrong choices have to be made as frequently as
the right ones. We get along in life this way. We
are built to make mistakes, coded for error.

We learn, as we say, by "trial and error."   7 ?
Why do we always say that? Why not "trial and
rightness" or "trial and triumph"? The old phrase
puts it that way because that is, in real life, the
way it is done.

Another effective comparison for the general reader A good laboratory, like a good bank or a   8
corporation or government, has to run like a com-
puter. Almost everything is done flawlessly, by
the book, and all the numbers add up to the
predicted sums. The days go by. And then, if it   *Isn't this a contradiction?*
is a lucky day, and a lucky laboratory, somebody
makes a mistake: the wrong buffer, something in
one of the blanks, a decimal misplaced in reading
counts, the warm room off by a degree and a half,
a mouse out of his box, or just a misreading of
the day's protocol. Whatever, when the results
come in, something is obviously screwed up, and   *what?*
then the action can begin.

The misreading is not the important error; it   9
opens the way. The next step is the crucial one.   *aha!*
If the investigator can bring himself to say, "But
even so, look at that!" then the new finding,
whatever it is, is ready for snatching. What is

needed, for progress to be made, is <u>the move based on error.</u>

interest-ing idea

Whenever new kinds of thinking are about to be accomplished, or new varieties of music, there has to be an argument beforehand. With two sides debating in the same mind, haranguing, there is an amiable understanding that one is right and the other wrong. Sooner or later the thing is settled, but there can be no action at all if there are not the two sides, and the argument. <u>The hope is in the faculty of wrongness</u>, the tendency toward error. The capacity to leap across mountains of information to land lightly on the wrong side represents the highest of human endowments.

10

I believe Thomas here be-cause of his back-ground.

Could this be related to the human ability to think critically?

It may be that this is a uniquely human gift, perhaps even stipulated in our genetic instructions. Other creatures do not seem to have DNA sequences for making mistakes as a routine part of daily living, certainly not for programmed error as a guide for action.

11

Yes, but this is so frus-trating

We are at our human finest, <u>dancing with our minds,</u> when there are more choices than two. Sometimes there are ten, even twenty different ways to go, all but one bound to be wrong, and the richness of selection in such situations can lift us onto totally new ground. This process is called exploration and is based on human fallibility. If we had only a single center in our brains, capable of responding only when a correct decision was to be made, instead of the jumble of different, credulous, easily conned clusters of neurones that provide for being flung off into blind alleys, up trees, down dead ends, out into blue sky, along wrong turnings, around bends, we could only stay the way we are today, stuck fast.

12

nice mental image

This is a great sentence - it has a lot of feeling

I love the phrase "splendid freedom"

I never thought of mis-takes this way

<u>The lower animals do not have this splendid freedom.</u> They are limited, most of them, to absolute infallibility. Cats, for all their good side, never make mistakes. <u>I have never seen a mala-droit, clumsy, or blundering cat.</u> Dogs are sometimes fallible, occasionally able to make charming minor mistakes, but they get this way by trying to mimic their masters. <u>Fish are flawless in everything they do.</u> Individual cells in a tissue are mindless machines, perfect in their performance, as absolutely inhuman as bees.

13

see # "
look up "maladroit"

I like this idea

We should have this in mind as we become dependent on more complex computers for the arrangement of our affairs. Give the computers their heads, I say; let them go their way. If we can learn to do this, turning our heads to one side and wincing while the work proceeds, the possibilities for the future of mankind, and computerkind, are limitless. Your average good computer can make calculations in an instant which would take a lifetime of slide rules for any of us. Think of what we could gain from the near infinity of precise, machine-made miscomputation which is now so easily within our grasp. We would begin the solving of some of our hardest problems. How, for instance, should we go about organizing ourselves for social living on a planetary scale, now that we have become, as a plain fact of life, a single community? We can assume, as a working hypothesis, that all the right ways of doing this are unworkable. What we need, then, for moving ahead, is a set of wrong alternatives much longer and more interesting than the short list of mistaken courses that any of us can think up right now. We need, in fact, an infinite list, and when it is printed out we need the computer to turn on itself and select, at random, the next way to go. If it is a big enough mistake, we could find ourselves on a new level, stunned, out in the clear, ready to move again. 14

Thomas makes our technology sound really exciting

so true.

yes

We need to program computers to make deliberate mistakes so they can help our natural human tendency to learn thru error

So mistakes have value!

not a contradiction after all.

Guideline 2. *After you have read the essay for the first time, summarize its main ideas in some fashion.* The form of this task might be anything from a drawing of the main ideas as they relate to one another to a succinct summary. You could draw a graph or map of the topics in the essay (in much the same way that a person would draw a map of an area for someone unfamiliar with a particular route); outline the ideas to get an overview of the piece; or summarize the ideas to check your understanding of the main points of the selection. Any of these tasks can be completed from your original notes and underlining. Each will give you a slightly more thorough understanding of what you have read.

Guideline 3. *Next, read the questions and assignments following the essay to help focus your thinking for the second reading.* Don't answer the questions at this time; just read them to make sure you are picking up the main ideas from the selection and thinking about relevant connections among those ideas.

REREADING

Following your initial reading, read the essay again, concentrating this time on how the author achieved his or her purpose. The temptation to skip this stage of the reading process is often powerful, but this second reading is crucial to your development as a critical reader in all of your courses. This second reading could be compared to seeing a good movie for the second time: The first viewing would provide you with a general understanding of the plot, the characters, the setting, and the overall artistic accomplishment of the director; during the second viewing, however, you would undoubtedly notice many more details and see their specific contributions to the artistic whole. Similarly, the second reading of an essay allows a much deeper understanding of the work under consideration and prepares you to analyze the writer's ideas.

You should also be prepared to do some detective work at this point and look closely at the assumptions the essay is based on: For example, how does the writer move from idea to idea in the essay? What hidden assertions lie behind these ideas? Do you agree or disagree with these assertions? Your assessment of these unspoken assumptions will often play a major role in your critical response to an essay. In the case of Thomas' essay, do you accept the unspoken connection he makes between the workings of the human brain and the computer? What parts of the essay hinge upon your acceptance of this connection? What other assumptions are fundamental to Thomas' reasoning? If you accept his thinking along the way, you are more likely to agree with the general flow of Thomas' essay. If you discover a flaw in his premises or assumptions, your acceptance of his argument will start to break down.

Next, answer the questions that follow the essay. The "Understanding Details" questions will help you understand and remember what you have read on both the literal and interpretive levels. Some of the questions ask you to restate various important points the author makes (literal); others help you see relationships between the different ideas presented (interpretive).

UNDERSTANDING DETAILS

Literal   1. According to Thomas, in what ways are computers and humans similar? In what ways are they different?

Interpretive   2. What does Thomas mean by the statement, "If we were not provided with the knack of being wrong, we could never get anything useful done" (paragraph 6)?

Interpretive   3. According to Thomas, in what important way do humans and "lower" animals differ? What does this comparison have to do with Thomas' main line of reasoning?

The "Analyzing Meaning" questions require you to analyze and evaluate some of the writer's ideas in order to form valid opinions of your own. These questions demand a higher level of thought than the previous set and help you prepare more specifically for the discussion/writing assignments that follow the questions.

ANALYZING MEANING

Analytical   1. What is Thomas' main point in this essay? How do the references to computers help him make this point?

Analytical   2. Why does Thomas perceive human error as such a positive quality? What does "exploration" have to do with this quality (paragraph 12)?

Analytical   3. What could we gain from "The near infinity of precise, machine-made miscomputation" (paragraph 14)? In what ways would our civilization advance?

The "Discovering Rhetorical Strategies" questions ask you to look closely at what strategies the writer uses to develop his or her thesis and how those strategies work. The questions address features of the writer's composing process such as word choice, use of detail, transitions, statement of purpose, organization of ideas, sentence structure, and paragraph development. The intent of these questions is to raise various elements of the composing process to the conscious level so you can use them in creating your own essays. If you are able to understand and describe what choices a writer makes to create certain effects in his or her prose, you will more likely be able to perceive the range of choices available to you as you write and be aware of your ability to control your readers' thoughts and feelings.

DISCOVERING RHETORICAL STRATEGIES

1. Thomas begins his essay with a list of experiences most of us have had at one time or another. Do you find this an effective beginning? Why or why not?
2. Which main points in his essay does Thomas develop in most detail? Why do you think he chooses to develop these points so thoroughly?
3. Explain the simile Thomas uses in paragraph 6: "Mistakes are at the very base of human thought, embedded there, feeding the structure like root nodules." Is this comparison between "mistakes" and "root modules" useful in this context? Why or why not? Find another simile or metaphor in this essay, and explain how it works.

Because checklists can provide a helpful method of reviewing important information, we offer here a series of questions that represent the three stages of reading just discussed. All these guidelines can be generalized into a checklist for reading any academic assignment in any discipline.

READING INVENTORY

Preparing to Read

Title

1. What can I infer from the title of the essay about the author's attitude toward the subject or the general tone of the essay?
2. Who do I think is the author's audience? What is the principal purpose of the essay?

Synopsis

3. What is the general subject of the essay?
4. What is the author's approach to the subject?

Biography

5. What do I know about the author's age, political stance, general beliefs?
6. How qualified is the author to write on this subject?
7. When did the author write the essay? Under what conditions? In what context?
8. Why did the author write this selection?
9. Where was the essay first published?

Content

10. What would I like to learn about this topic?
11. What are some of my opinions on this subject?

Reading

1. What are my initial reactions, comments, and personal associations in reference to the ideas in this essay?
2. Did I summarize the essay's main ideas?
3. Did I read the questions and assignments following the essay?

Rereading

1. How does the author achieve his or her purpose in this essay?
2. What assumptions underlie the author's reasoning?
3. Do I have a clear literal understanding of this essay? What words do I need to look up in a dictionary? What do these words mean—by themselves and in their respective sentences?
4. Do I have a solid interpretive understanding of this essay? Do I understand the relationship among ideas? What conclusions can I draw from this essay?
5. Do I have an accurate analytical understanding of this essay? Which ideas can I take apart, examine, and put back together again? What is my evaluation of this material?
6. Do I understand the rhetorical strategies the writer uses and the way they work? Can I explain the effects of these strategies?

Writing Critically

The last stage of responding to the reading selections in this text offers you various "Ideas for Discussion/Writing" that will allow you to demonstrate the different skills you have learned in each chapter. You will be most successful if you envision each writing experience as an organic process that follows a natural cycle of prewriting, writing, and rewriting.

PREPARING TO WRITE

The prewriting phase involves exploring a subject, generating ideas, selecting and narrowing a topic, analyzing an audience, and developing a purpose. Preceding the writing assignments are "Preparing to Write" questions you should respond to before trying to structure your thoughts into a coherent essay. These questions will assist you in generating new ideas on the topics and may even stimulate new approaches to old ideas. Keeping a journal to respond to these questions is an excellent idea, because you will then have a record of your thoughts on various topics related to the writing assignments that follow. No matter what format you use to answer these questions, the activity of prewriting generally continues in various forms throughout the writing process.

Preparing to Write

Write freely about an important mistake you have made: How did the mistake make you feel? What (if anything) did you learn from this mistake? What did you fail to learn that you should have learned? Did this mistake have any positive impact on your life? What were its negative consequences? How crucial are mistakes in our lives?

Responses to these questions can be prompted by a number of different "invention" techniques and carried out by you individually, with another student, in small groups, or as a class project. Invention strategies can help you generate responses to these questions and discover related ideas through the various stages of writing your papers. Because you will undoubtedly vary your approach to different assignments, you should be familiar with the following choices available to you:

Brainstorming. The basis of brainstorming is free association. Ideally, you should get a group of students together and bounce ideas, words, and thoughts off one another until they begin to cluster around related topics. If you don't have a group of students handy, brainstorm by yourself or with a friend. In a group of students or with a friend, the exchange of thoughts usually starts orally but should transfer to paper when your ideas begin to fall into related categories. When you brainstorm by yourself, however, you should write down everything that comes to mind. The act of recording your ideas in this case becomes a catalyst for other thoughts; you are essentially setting up a dialogue with yourself on paper. Then, keep writing down words and phrases that occur to you until they begin to fall into logical subdivisions or until you stop generating new ideas.

Freewriting.   Freewriting means writing to discover what you want to say. Set a time limit of about 10 minutes, and just write by free association. Write about what you are seeing, feeling, touching, thinking; write about having nothing to say; recopy the sentence you just wrote—anything. Just keep writing, on paper, on a typewriter, or on a computer. After you have generated some material, locate an idea that is central to your writing assignment, put it at the top of another page, and start freewriting again.

Journal Entries.   Journal entries are much like freewriting, except you have some sense of an audience—probably either your instructor or yourself. In a journal, anything goes. You can respond to the "Preparing to Write" questions, jot down thoughts, paste up articles that spark your interest, write sections of dialogue, draft letters (the kind you never send), record dreams, or make lists. The possibilities are unlimited. An excellent way of practicing writing, the process of keeping a journal is also a wonderful means of dealing with new ideas—a way of fixing them in your mind and making them yours.

Direct Questions.   This technique involves asking a series of questions useful in any writing situation to generate ideas, arrange thoughts, or revise prose. One example of this strategy is to use the inquiries journalists rely on to check the coverage in their articles:

Who:	Who played the game?
	Who won the game?
What:	What kind of game was it?
	What happened in the game?
Why:	Why was the game played?
Where:	Where was the game played?
When:	When was the game played?
How:	How was the game played?

If you ask yourself extended questions of this sort on a specific topic, you will begin to produce thoughts and details that will undoubtedly be useful to you in the writing assignments that follow.

Clustering. Clustering is a method of drawing or mapping your ideas as fast as they come into your mind. Put a word, phrase, or sentence in a circle in the center of a blank page. Then, put every new idea that comes to you in a circle and show its relationship to a previous thought by drawing a line to the circle containing the previous thought. You will probably reach a natural stopping point for this exercise in about two to three minutes.

Although you can generate ideas in a number of different ways, the main principle behind the "Preparing to Write" questions in this text is to encourage you to do what is called "expressive writing" before you tackle any writing assignment. This is writing based on your feelings, thoughts, experiences, observations, and opinions. The process of answering questions about your own ideas and experiences makes you "think on paper," encouraging you to surround yourself with your own thoughts and opinions. From this reservoir, you can then choose the ideas you want to develop into an essay and begin writing about them one at a time.

As you use various prewriting techniques to generate responses to the "Preparing to Write" questions, you should know that these responses can (and probably will) appear in many different forms. You can express yourself in lists, outlines, random notes, sentences and paragraphs, charts, graphs, or pictures—whatever keeps the thoughts flowing smoothly and productively. One of our students used a combination of brainstorming and clustering to generate the following thoughts in response to the prewriting exercise following the Thomas essay:

Brainstorming

Mistakes:
- happen when I'm in a hurry
- make me feel stupid
- love
- relationships
- trip back east
  - pride
  - going in circles

- Bob
- learned a lot about people
- people aren't what they seem
- getting back on track
- parents
- corrections
- learning from mistakes
  - I am a better person
  - my values are clear
- mistakes help us change
  - painful
  - helpful
  - valuable

Clustering

From the free-flowing thoughts you generate, you next need to decide what to write about and how to limit your subject to a manageable length. Our student writer chose topic 2 from the "Choosing a Topic" list after the essay (see page 24). Her initial responses to the prewriting questions helped her decide to write on "A Time I Got Lost." She then generated more focused ideas and opinions in the form of a journal entry. It is printed here just as she wrote it, errors and all.

Journal Entry

> The craziest mistake I think I ever made was on a trip I took recently — — I was heading to the east coast from California and reached Durham, North Carolina. I was so excited because I was going to get to see the Atlantic Ocean for the first time in my life and Durham was one of my last towns before I reached the sea. In Durham I was going to have to change from a northeast direction to due east.
>
> ~~Unfortunately,~~ When I got there the highway was under construction. I took the detour, but got all skrewed up till I realized that I had gone the wrong direction. By this time I was lost somewhere in downtown Durham and didn't know which way was east. I stoped and asked a guy at a gas station and he explained how to get back on the east-bound highway. The way was through the middle of town. By the time I got to where I was supposed to turn right I could only turn left. So I started left and then realized I couldn't turn back the other way. I made a couple of other stops after that, and one jerk told me I "just couldn't get there from here." Eventually I found a truckdriver heading toward the same eastbound highway, and he told me to follow him. An hour and forty minutes after reaching Durham's city limits I finally managed

to leave going east. I felt as if I had spent an entire month there!

The thing I learned from this was just how egocentric I am. I would not have made this error if I had not been so damn cocky about my sense of direction. My mistake was made worse because I got flustered and didn't listen to the directions clearly. I find that the reason I most often make a mistake is because I don't listen carefully to instructions. This has been a problem all my life.

After I got over feeling really dum I decided this kind of thing was not going to happen again. It was too much a waste of time and gas, so I was going to be more careful of road signs and directions.

This all turned out to be a positive experience though. I learned that there are lots of friendly, helpful people. It was kind of reassuring to know that other folks would help you if you just asked.

I feel this and other mistakes are crucial not only to my life but to personal growth in general. It is the making of mistakes that helps people learn where they are misdirecting their energies. I think mistakes can help all of us learn to be more careful about some part of our lives. This is why mistakes are crucial. Otherwise, we would continue in the same old rut and never improve.

This entry served as the foundation upon which the student built her essay. Her next step was to consider *audience* and *purpose* (which are usually specified in the writing assignments in this text). The first of these features identifies the person or group of people you will address in your essay. The second is a declaration of your principal reason for writing the essay, which usually takes the form of a thesis statment (the statement of purpose or controlling idea of an essay). Together these pieces of information consciously or subconsciously help you make most of the decisions you are faced with as you write: what words to choose, what sentence structures to use, what order to present ideas in, which topics to develop, and which to summarize. Without a doubt, the more you know about your audience (age, educational background, likes, dislikes, biases, political persuasion, and social status) and your purpose (to inform, persuade, and/or entertain), the easier the writing task will be. In the rough draft and final draft of the essay in the section that follows, the student knew she was writing to a senior English class at her old high school in order to convince them that mistakes can be positive factors in their lives. This clear sense of audience and purpose helped her realize she should use fairly advanced vocabulary, call upon a variety of sentence structures, and organize her ideas chronologically to make her point most effectively to her intended audience.

At this stage of the writing process, some people benefit from assembling their ideas in the form of an outline. Others use an outline as a check on their logic and organization after the first draft has been written. Whether your outlines are informal (a simple list) or highly structured, they can help you visualize the logical relationship of your ideas to each other. We recommend using your outline throughout the prewriting and writing stages to ensure that your work is carefully and tightly organized.

WRITING

The writing stage asks you to draft an essay based upon the prewriting material you have assembled. Because you have already made the important preliminary decisions regarding your topic, your audience, and your purpose, the task of actually writing the essay should follow naturally. (Notice we did not say this task should necessarily be easy—just natural.) At this stage, you should look upon your essay as a way of solving a problem or answering a question: The problem/question is posed in your writing assignment, and the solution/answer is your essay. The three "Choosing a Topic" assignments that follow the prewriting questions in the text require you to consider issues related to the essay you just read. Although they typically ask you to focus on one rhetorical pattern, they draw on many rhetorical strategies (as do all writing assignments in the text) and require you to support your statements with concrete examples. These assignments refer to the Lewis Thomas essay and emphasize the use of example, his dominant rhetorical strategy.

Choosing a Topic

1. You have decided to write an editorial for your local newspaper concerning the impact of computers on our lives. Cite specific experiences you have had with computers to help make your main point.
2. You have been invited back to your high school to make a speech to a senior English class about how people can learn from their mistakes. Write your speech in the form of an essay explaining what you learned from a crucial mistake you have made. Use examples to show these students that mistakes can be positive factors in their lives.
3. In an essay for your writing class, explain one specific human quality. Use Thomas' essay as a model. Cite examples to support your explanation.

The following essay is our student's first-draft response to topic 2. After writing her journal entry, the student drafted a tentative thesis statement: "I know there are positive attitudes that can come from making a mistake because I recently had an opportunity to learn some valuable lessons in this way." This statement helped the student writer further develop and organize her ideas, as she focused finally on one well-chosen example to illustrate her thesis. At this point, the thesis is simply the controlling idea around which the other topics take shape; it is often revised several times before the final draft.

First Draft: A Time I Got Lost

Parents and teachers frequently pressure us to avoid committing errors. Meanwhile, our friends laugh at us when we make mistakes. With all these different messages, it is hard for us to think of mistakes as positive events. But if any of you take the time to think about what you have learned from mistakes, I bet you will realize all the good things that have come from these events. I know there are positive attitudes that can come from making a mistake because I recently had an opportunity to learn some valuable lessons in this way.

While traveling back east this last summer, I made the mistake of turning west on an interstate detour in order to reach the Atlantic Ocean. The adventure took me into the heart of Durham, North Carolina, where I got totally lost. I had to get directions several times until two hours later I was going in the right direction. As I was driving out of town, I realized that although I had made a dumb mistake, I had learned a great deal. Overall, the detour was actually a positive experience.

The first thing I remember thinking after I had gotten my wits together was that I had definitely learned something from making the mistake. I had the opportunity to see a new city, filled with new people--3,000 miles from my own hometown, but very much like it. I also became aware that the beach is not always toward the west, as it is in California. The entire experience was like getting a geography lesson firsthand.

As this pleasant feeling began to grow, I came to another realization. I was aware of how important other people can be in making a mistake into a positive experience. My first reaction was "Oh no, someone is going to know I made a mistake!" But the amazing part about this mistake was how supportive everyone was. The townspeople had been entirely willing to help someone they did not know. This mistake helped me to learn that people tend to be nicer than I imagined.

The final lesson I learned from getting lost in Durham was how to be more cautious about my actions so as not to repeat the same mistake. It was this internalization of all the information I gleaned from making the mistake that I see as the most positive part of the experience. I realized that in order to avoid such situations in the future I would have to be less egocentric in my decisions and more willing to listen to directions from other people. I needed to learn that my set way of doing things was not always the best way. If I had not made the mistake, I would not have been aware of my other options.

By making this mistake I learned that there is a more comprehensive manner of looking at the world. In the future, if we could all stop after making a mistake and ask ourselves "what can I learn from this?" we would be less critical of ourselves and have a great many more positive experiences. If I were not able to make mistakes, I would probably not be able to expand my knowledge of my environment, my understanding of people, and my choice of various actions.

REWRITING

The rewriting stage includes revising, editing, and proofreading. The first of these activities, *revising,* actually takes place during the entire writing process as you change words, recast sentences, and move whole paragraphs from one place to another. Making these linguistic and organizational choices means you will also be constantly adjusting your content to your purpose (what you want to accomplish) and your audience (the readers) in much the same way you alter your speech to communicate more effectively in response to the gestures, eye movements, or facial expressions of your listener. Revising is literally the act of "reseeing" your essay, looking at it through your readers' eyes to determine whether or not it achieves its purpose. As you revise, you should consider matters of both content and form. *In content,* do you have an interesting, thought-provoking title for your essay? Do you think your thesis statement will be clear to your audience? Does your introduction capture the readers' attention? Is your treatment of your topic consistent throughout the essay? Do you support your assertions with specific examples? Does your conclusion sum up your main points? *In form*, is your essay organized effectively? Do you use a variety of rhetorical strategies? Are your sentence structure and vocabulary varied and interesting?

If you compose on a word processor, you will certainly reap the benefits of it as you revise. Word processors remove much of the drudgery of rewriting and retyping your drafts. On a typewriter, you may not make as many major revisions as necessary, because of the length of time needed to retype the material. Word processors allow you to move paragraphs or whole sections of your paper from one position to another by pressing a few keys. Without the manual labor of cutting and pasting, you can immediately see if the new organization will improve the logic and coherence of your paper. You may then remove repetitions or insert words and sentences that will refine the transitions between sections.

You should also consider the value of the graphic design options available on computer software, because the way you present your papers generally affects how your instructor evaluates them. If they are clearly laid out without coffee stains or paw prints from your dog, you have a better chance of being taken seriously than if they are sloppily done. A computer can help in this regard, giving you access to boldface type, italics, boxes, bullets, and graphs of all sorts and letting you make a new copy if you do have an unexpected encounter with a coffee cup or a dog.

The *editing* process entails correcting mistakes in your writing so that your final draft conforms to the conventions of standard written English. Correct punctuation, spelling, and mechanics will help you make your points and will encourage your readers to move smoothly through your essay from topic to topic. At this stage, you should be concerned with such matters as whether your sentences are complete, whether your punctuation is correct and effective, whether you have followed conventional rules for using mechanics, and whether the words in your essay are spelled correctly.

The process of *proofreading* involves reading over your entire essay, slowly and carefully, to make certain you have not allowed any errors to slip into your draft. (Most college instructors don't look upon errors as kindly as Thomas does.) In general, good writers try to let some time elapse between writing the final draft and proofreading it (at least a few hours, perhaps a day or so). Otherwise, they find themselves proofreading their thoughts rather than their words. Some writers even profit from proofreading their papers backward—a technique that allows them to focus on individual words and phrases rather than on entire sentences.

Because many writers work well with checklists, we present here a set of guidelines that will help you review the entire writing process.

WRITING INVENTORY

Preparing to Write

1. Have I explored the prewriting questions through brainstorming, freewriting, journal entries, direct questions, or clustering?
2. Do I understand my topic or assignment?
3. Have I narrowed my topic adequately?
4. Do I have a specific audience for my essay? Do I know their likes and dislikes? Their education level? Their knowledge about the topic?
5. Do I have a clear and precise purpose for my essay?

Writing

1. Can I express my topic as a problem or question?
2. Is my essay a solution or answer to that problem or question?

Rewriting

Revising the Content

1. Does my essay have a clear, interesting title?
2. Will my statement of purpose (or thesis) be clear to my audience?
3. Does the introduction make my audience want to read the rest of my essay?
4. Do I pursue my topic consistently throughout the essay?
5. Have I included enough details to prove my main points?
6. Does my conclusion sum up my central points?
7. Will I accomplish my purpose with this audience?

Revising the Form

1. Have I organized my ideas as effectively as possible for this audience?
2. Do I use appropriate rhetorical strategies to support my main point?
3. Is my sentence structure varied and interesting?
4. Is my vocabulary appropriate for my topic, my purpose, and my audience?
5. Do I present my essay as effectively as possible, including useful graphic design techniques on the computer, if appropriate?

Editing and Proofreading

1. Have I written complete sentences throughout my essay?
2. Have I used punctuation correctly and effectively (check especially the use of commas, colons, and semicolons)?
3. Have I followed conventional rules for mechanics (capitalization, underlining or italics, abbreviations, and numbers)?
4. Are all the words in my essay spelled correctly? (Use a dictionary when in doubt.)

Following is the student's revised draft of her essay on making mistakes in life. The final draft of this typical freshman essay (written to high school seniors, as the assignment specifies) represents the entire writing process at work. We have made notes in the margin to highlight various effective elements in her essay, and we have underlined substantial changes in words and phrases from earlier drafts.

Mistakes and Maturity

Rapport with audience and point of view established

Parents and teachers frequently harp on us to correct our errors. Meanwhile, our friends laugh at us when we make mistakes. With all these negative messages, most of us have a hard time believing that problems can be positive experiences. But if we take the time to think about what we have learned from various blunders, we will realize all the good that has come from these events. I know making mistakes can have positive results because I recently learned several valuable lessons from one unforgettable experience.

Clear, stimulating introduction for high school seniors

Revised thesis statement

While I was traveling on the east coast last summer, I made the mistake of turning west on an interstate detour in an attempt to reach the Atlantic Ocean. This adventure took me into the center of Durham, North Carolina, where I became totally lost, bewildered, and angry at myself. I had to ask for directions several times, until two hours later when I finally found the correct highway toward the ocean. As I was driving out of town, I realized that although I had made a "dumb" mistake, I had actually learned a great deal. Overall, my adventure was quite positive.

Good brief summary of complex experience (see notes from Preparing to Read)

Background information

Good details

The first insight I remember having after my wits returned was that I definitely learned more about United States geography from making this mistake. I became intimately acquainted with a town 3,000 miles from home that greatly resembled my own city, and I became aware that the beach is not always toward the west, as it is in California. I also met some pleasant strangers. Looking at my confusion as a learning experience encouraged me to have positive feelings about the mistake.

First topic (Topics are in chronological order)

Adequate number of examples

Nice close to this paragraph

As I relaxed and let this happy feeling grow, I came to another realization. I became aware of how important other people can be in turning a mistake into a positive event. Although my first reaction was "Oh, no! Someone is going to know I'm lost," I was amazed by how supportive other people were during my panic and embarrassment. From an old man swinging on his front porch to an elementary school boy crossing the street with his bright blue backpack, I found that the townspeople of Durham were entirely willing to help someone they did not even know. I realized that people in general are nicer than I had previously thought.

Second topic

Clear explanation with details

Good summary statement

The final lesson I learned from making this mistake was how to be more cautious about my future decisions. This insight was, in fact, the most positive part of the entire experience. What I realized I must do to prevent similar errors in the future was to relax, not be so bullheaded in my decisions, and be more willing to listen to directions from other people. I might never have had these positive realizations if I had not made this mistake.

Third topic

Specific details

Thus, by driving in circles for two hours, I developed a more comprehensive way of looking at the world. If I were unable to make mistakes, I probably would not have had this chance to learn about my environment, improve my impressions of strangers, and reconsider the egocentric way in which I act in certain situations. Perhaps there's a lesson here for all of us. Instead of criticizing ourselves unduly, if each one of us could pause after we make an error and ask "How can I profit from this?" we would re-

Clear transition statement

Good summary of three topics without being repetitive

Concluding statement applicable to all readers

<u>alize   that   mistakes   can   often   be</u>   Nicely
<u>turned into positive events that will</u> focused
<u>help us become more confident and ma-</u> concluding
ture.   remark

As these various drafts of the student paper indicate, the essay assignments in this book encourage you to transfer to your own writing your understanding of how form and content work together. If you use the short-answer questions after each reading selection as a guide, the writing assignments will help you learn how to give shape to your own ideas and gain control of your readers' thoughts and feelings. In essence, they help you recognize the power you have through language over your life and your environment.

Conclusion

As you approach the essays in this text, remember that both reading and writing function most efficiently as processes of discovery. Through them, you educate and expand your own mind and the minds of your readers. They can provide a powerful means of discovering new information or clarifying what you already know. Reading and writing lead to understanding. And just as you can discover how to read through writing, so too can you become more aware of the details of the writing process through reading. We hope your time spent with this book is both pleasant and profitable as you refine your ability to discover and express effectively the good ideas within yourself.

CHAPTER 1

DESCRIPTION
■ ■ ■
Exploring Through the Senses

Using Description

All of us use description in our daily lives. We might, for example, try to convey the horrors of a recent history exam to our parents, or help a friend visualize someone we met on vacation, or describe an automobile accident for a police report. Whatever our specific purpose, description is fundamental to the act of communication: We give and receive descriptions constantly, and our lives are continually affected by this simple yet important rhetorical technique.

Defining Description

Description may be defined as the act of capturing people, places, events, objects, and feelings in words so that a reader (or listener) can visualize and respond to them. Unlike narration, which traditionally presents events in a clear time sequence, description essentially suspends its objects in time, making them exempt from such limits of chronology. Description is one of our primary forms of self-expression; it paints a verbal picture that helps the reader understand or share a sensory experience through the process of "showing" rather than "telling." *Telling* your friends, for example, that "the campgrounds were filled

To bridge the gap between the students' present abilities and the professional models, the introduction to this chapter ends with a student essay that "shows" us through sensory details the reminiscences the writer associates with her grandmother's house. The body of the chapter further demonstrates that students can approach description in a variety of ways. Before students read and again before they write, the exercises in each case help stimulate the senses and focus attention on the dominant impression (as explained in the chapter introduction) that each essay intends to create. Ray Bradbury's excerpt captures the essence of a family by describing its summer ritual of hanging a frontporch swing; the writing assignments following this description ask students to characterize people and places through the activities connected with them. Amy Tan describes her mother's way of escaping the horrors of war in the next essay, which is followed by questions that focus on each student's favorite retreats and lead up to writing assignments directly related to those environments. The third essay turns our attention from places to people: Through a description of two vivid backwoods personalities, John McPhee characterizes how different types of people react to their surroundings. The accompanying writing assignments ask students to make similar investigations of people and their environs. Changing focus, Kimberly Wozencraft describes her experiences in a Kentucky prison; her essay is accompanied by writing assignments that ask about awkward, difficult situations in life. This chapter ends with an essay by Malcolm Cowley that asks us to consider the satisfactions and traumas of the aging process and old age itself; the prereading questions, the prewriting exercises, and the writing assignments all request the students to consider their own process of aging and to think about old age in general. Students are even asked to interview an older person in preparation for one of the assignments.

with friendly, happy activities" is not as engaging as *showing* them by saying, "The campgrounds were alive with the smell of spicy baked beans, the sound of high-pitched laughter, and the sight of happy families sharing the warmth of a fire."

Descriptions range between two broad types: (1) totally objective reports, which we might find in a dictionary or an encyclopedia, and (2) very subjective accounts, which focus almost exclusively on personal impressions. The same horse, for instance, might be described by one writer as "a large, solid-hoofed herbivorous mammal having a long mane and a tail" and by another as "a magnificent and spirited beast flaring its nostrils in search of adventure." Most descriptive writing, however, falls somewhere between these two extremes: "a large, four-legged beast in search of adventure."

Objective description is principally characterized by its impartial, precise, and emotionless tone. Found most prominently in technical and scientific writing, such accounts might include a description of equipment to be used in a chemistry experiment, the results of a market survey for a particular consumer product, or a medical appraisal of a heart patient's physical symptoms. In situations like these, accurate, unbiased, and easily understandable accounts are of the utmost importance.

Subjective description, in contrast, is intentionally created to produce a particular response in the reader or listener. Focusing on feelings rather than on raw data, it tries to activate as many senses as possible, thereby leading the audience to a specific conclusion or state of mind. Examples of subjective descriptions could involve a parent's disapproving comments about one of your friends, a professor's glowing analysis of your most recent "A" paper, or a basketball coach's critique of his team's losing effort in last night's big game.

In most situations, the degree of subjectivity or objectivity in a descriptive passage depends to a large extent upon the writer's purpose and intended audience. In the case of the heart patient mentioned above, the person's physician might present the case in a formal, scientific way to a group of medical colleagues; in a personal, sympathetic way to the invalid's spouse; and in financial terms to a number of potential contributors in order to solicit funds for heart disease research.

The following paragraph describes one student's fond memories of visiting "the farm." As you read it, notice the writer's use of subjective description to communicate to her readers the multitude of contradictory feelings she connects with this rural retreat.

The shrill scream of the alarm shatters a dream. This is the last day of my visit to the place I call "the farm," an old ramshackle house in the country owned by one of my aunts. I want to go out once more in the peace of the early morning, walk in the crisp and chilly hour, and breathe the sweet air. My body feels jarred as my feet hit the hard-packed clay dirt. I tune out my stiff muscles and cold arms and legs and instead focus on two herons playing hopscotch on the canal bank: Every few yards I walk towards them, they fly one over the other an almost equal distance away from me. A kildeer with its piercing crystalline cry dips its body as it flies low over the water, the tip of its wing leaving a ring to reverberate outward. The damp earth has a strong, rich, musky scent. To the east, dust rises, and for the first time I hear the clanking and straining of a tractor as it harrows smooth the soil before planting. A crop duster rises close by just as it cuts off its release of spray, the acrid taste of chemical filtering down through the air. As the birds chatter and peck at the fields, I turn to escape to my life in the city.

Reading and Writing Descriptive Essays

All good descriptions share four fundamental qualities: (1) an accurate sense of audience and purpose, (2) a clear vision of the object being described, (3) a careful selection of details, and (4) a consistent point of view or perspective from which a writer composes. The dominant impression or main effect the writer wishes to leave with a specific audience dictates virtually all of the verbal choices in a descriptive essay. Although description is featured in this chapter, you should also pay close attention to how other rhetorical strategies (such as example, division/classification, and cause/effect) can effectively support the dominant impression.

HOW TO READ A DESCRIPTIVE ESSAY

Preparing to Read. As you approach the reading selections in this chapter, you should focus first on the author's title and try to make some initial assumptions about the essay that follows: Does Ray Bradbury reveal his attitude toward his subject in the title "Summer Rituals"? Can you guess what the general mood of "Notes from the Country Club" will be? Then, scan the essay to discover its audience and purpose: What do you think John McPhee's purpose is in "The Pines"? Whom is Malcolm Cowley addressing in "The View from 80"? You should also read the synopsis of each essay in the Rhetorical Contents, which will provide you with helpful information at this point in the reading process.

TEACHING DESCRIPTION: ONE INSTRUCTOR'S COMMENTS

Students appreciate vivid images in professional writing, but in their own essays they do not always appeal to the reader's senses. Early in the drafting stage, I ask students to work in groups of three to suggest sensory details for each other's paragraphs. Visual images are easy. More difficult are details that appeal to hearing, tasting, touching, and smelling. Fellow students in small groups can sometimes offer leads for sounds or textures that produce sharper, more memorable descriptions.

Alan Price
Penn State University
Hazleton, Pennsylvania

Description contains an implied narrative, but no real story has taken place. This is the hardest concept for the student to grasp about this strategy. To teach this concept, I ask each student to isolate one detail in a personal narrative and freeze time, just like the photographer stops the action in a picture. Have your students study the moment and describe each sensory detail surrounding the moment. An effective way of controlling the reader's focus is to use a frame. Tan's "The Joy Luck Club" begins by describing Kweilin and then focuses on various ways of escaping the horrors of that reality. In "The Pines," the narrator spies the pump amidst the junk at the beginning and concludes by remembering the pump and asking for water. A teaching technique I have used is to bring in an object for a frame. My favorite is the Hershey kiss. Each student is to use the kiss as the focus or the focal point, as in a painting. One student sees the silvery kiss and recalls her first love. She does not narrate the moment they met, but rather describes the delicate essence of that fragile, tender newness of love. Another student writes about the ebony black of a sweet jazz-filled night in Printer's Alley of Nashville, Tennessee. The past comes richly into focus around that sweet, shiny moment of his youth.

Leslie Shipp
Clark County Community College
North Las Vegas, Nevada

Next, learn as much as you can about the author and the conditions under which the essay was composed—information that is provided in the biographical statement before each essay. For a descriptive essay, the conditions under which the author wrote the essay, coupled with his or her purpose, can be very revealing: Can you determine when Amy Tan's essay was written? Does it describe her life now or in the past? When and under what conditions did Kimberly Wozencraft write "Notes from the Country Club"? What was her intention in writing the essay? Learning where the essay was first published will also give you valuable information about its audience.

Last, before you begin to read, try to do some brainstorming on the essay's title. In this chapter, respond to the Preparing to Read questions before each essay, which ask you to begin thinking and writing about the topic under consideration. Then, pose your own questions: What are some of the most important rituals in your life (Bradbury)? How do you envision your favorite retreat (Tan)? What would you like to learn from Cowley about the joys and frustrations of being eighty years old?

Reading. As you read each essay for the first time, jot down your initial reactions to it, and try to make connections and see relationships among the author's biography; the essay's title, purpose, and audience; and the synopsis. In this way, you will create a context or framework for your reading. See if you can figure out, for example, what Bradbury is implying about rituals in general in his essay "Summer Rituals" or why Wozencraft wrote an essay about her experiences in prison. Try to discover what the relationship is between purpose, audience, and publication information in Cowley's essay. Also determine at this point if the author's treatment of his or her subject is predominantly objective (generally free of emotion) or subjective (heavily charged with emotion). Or perhaps the essay falls somewhere between these two extremes. In addition, make sure you have a general sense of the dominant impression each author is trying to convey. Such an initial approach to reading these descriptive selections will give you a foundation upon which to analyze the material during your second, more in-depth reading. Finally, at the end of your first reading, take a look at the questions after each essay to make certain you can answer them.

Rereading. As you reread these descriptive essays, you should be discovering exactly what the author's dominant impression is and how he or she created it. Notice each author's careful selection of details and the way in which these details come together to leave you with this impression. Also try to determine how certain details add to and detract from that dominant impression and how the writer's point of view affects it: How does McPhee create a sense of complacency in "The Pines"? How does Wozencraft enable us to identify with her prison experiences when we have never been in prison? Try to find during this reading other rhetorical modes that support the description. Although the essays in this chapter describe various persons, places, or objects, all of the authors call upon other rhetorical strategies (especially example and comparison/contrast) to communicate their descriptions. How do these various rhetorical strategies work together in each essay to create a coherent whole? Finally, answering the questions after each essay will check your understanding of the author's main points and help you think critically about the essay in preparation for the discussion/writing assignments that follow.

For an inventory of the reading process, you may want to review the checklists on pages 15–16 of the Introduction.

HOW TO WRITE A DESCRIPTIVE ESSAY

Preparing to Write. Before you choose a writing assignment, use the prewriting questions that follow each essay to help you discover your own ideas and opinions about the general topic of the essay. Then, just as you do when you read an essay, you should determine the audience and purpose for your description (if these are not specified for you in the assignment). To whom are you writing? And why? Will an impartial, objective report be appropriate, or should you present a more emotional, subjective account to accomplish your task? In assessing your audience, you need to determine what they do and do not know about your topic. This information will help you make decisions about what you are going to say and how you will say it. Your purpose will be defined by what you intend your audience to know, think, or believe after they have read your descriptive essay. Do you want them to make up their own minds about summer rituals or old age, for example, based on an objective presentation of data, or do you hope to sway their opinion through a more subjective display of information? Or perhaps you will decide to blend the two techniques in order to achieve the impression of personal certainty based on objective evidence. What dominant impression do you want to leave with your audience? As you might suspect, decisions regarding audience and purpose are as important to writing descriptions as they are to reading descriptions and will shape your descriptive essay from start to finish.

The second quality of good description concerns the object of your analysis and the clarity with which you present it to the reader. Whenever possible, you should thoroughly investigate the person, place, moment, or feeling you wish to describe, paying particular attention to its effect upon each of your five senses. What can you see, smell, hear, taste, and touch as you examine it? If you want to describe your house, for example, begin by asking yourself a series of pertinent questions: How big is the house? What color is it? How many exterior doors does the house have? How many interior? Are any of the rooms wallpapered? If so, what is the color and texture of that wallpaper? How many different shades of paint cover the walls? Which rooms have constant noises (from clocks and other mechanical devices)? Are the kitchen appliances hot or cold to the touch? What is the quietest room in the house? The noisiest? What smells do you notice in the laundry? In the kitchen? In the basement? Most important, do any of these sensory questions trigger particular childhood memories? Although you will probably not use all of these details in your descriptive essay, the process of generating and answering such detailed questions will help reacquaint you with the object of your description as it also assists you in designing and focusing your paper. To help you generate some of these ideas, you might want to review the prewriting techniques introduced on pages 17–19.

Writing.   As you write, you must select the details of your description with great care and precision so that you leave your reader with a specific impression. If, for instance, you want your audience to feel the warmth and comfort of your home, you might concentrate on describing the plush carpets, the big upholstered chairs, the inviting scent of hot apple cider, and the crackling fire. If, on the other hand, you want to gain your audience's sympathy, you might prefer to focus on the sparse austerity of your home environment: the bare walls, the quietness, the lack of color and decoration, the dim lighting, and the frigid temperature. Your careful choice of details will help control your audience's reaction.

To make your impression even more vivid, you could use figurative language to fill out your descriptions. Using words "figuratively" means using them imaginatively rather than literally. The two most popular forms of figurative language are *simile* and *metaphor*. A *simile* is a comparison between two dissimilar objects or ideas introduced by *like* or *as:* "The rocking chairs sounded like crickets" (Bradbury). A *metaphor* is an implied comparison between two dissimilar objects or ideas that is not introduced by *like* or *as:* "Life for younger persons is still a battle royal of each against each" (Cowley). Besides enlivening your writing, figurative language helps your readers understand objects, feelings, and ideas that are complex or obscure by comparing them with things that are more familiar.

The last important quality of an effective descriptive essay is point of view, your physical perspective on your subject. Because the organization of your essay depends on your point of view, you need to choose a specific angle from which to approach your description. If you verbally jump around your home, referring first to a picture on the wall in your bedroom, next to the microwave in the kitchen, and then to the quilt on your bed, no reasonable audience will be able to follow your description. Nor will they want to. If, however, you move from room to room in some logical, sequential way, always focusing on the details you want your readers to know, you will be helping your audience form a clear, memorable impression of your home. Your vision will become their vision. In other words, your point of view plays a part in determining the organization of your description. Working spatially, you could move from side to side (from one wall to another in the rooms we have discussed), from top to bottom (from ceiling to floor), from near to far (from farthest to closest point in a room), or you might progress from large to small objects, from uninteresting to interesting, or from funny to serious. Whatever plan you choose should help you accomplish your purpose with your particular audience.

Rewriting. As you reread each of your descriptive essays, play the role of your audience and try to determine what dominant impression you receive by the end of your reading. Is this the impression you were trying to convey? How does the essay make you feel? What does it make you think about? Which senses does it stimulate? Are you "showing" rather than "telling" in your description? Which sections of the essay are most effective? What could you do to make the weaker sections more effective? Could you, for example, add more detailed information, reorganize some of the essay, or omit irrelevant material?

For additional suggestions on the writing process, you may want to consult the checklists on pages 27–28 of the Introduction.

Student Essay: Description at Work

In the following essay, a student relives some of her childhood memories through a subjective description of her grandmother's house. As you read it, pay particular attention to the different types of sensual details the student writer chooses in order to communicate to readers her dominant impression of her grandmother's home. Notice also her use of carefully chosen details to "show" rather than "tell" us about her childhood reminiscences.

Grandma's House

Writer's point of view or perspective — My most vivid childhood memories are set in my Grandma Goodlink's house, a curious blend of familiar and mysterious treasures. **Dominant impression** Grandma lived at the end of a dead-end street, in the same house she had lived in since the first day of her marriage. That was half a century and thirteen children ago. A set of crumbly steps made of concrete mixed with gravel led up to her front door. I remember a big gap between the house and the steps, **Comparison (simile)** as if someone had not pushed them up close enough to the house. Anyone who looked into the gap could see old toys **Sight** and books that had fallen into the crack behind the steps and had remained there, forever irretrievable.

Only a hook-type lock on the front door protected Grandma's many beautiful antiques. Her living room was set up **Comparison (simile)** like a church or schoolroom, with an old purple velvet couch against the far wall **Sight** and two chairs immediately in front of the couch facing the same direction. One-half of the couch was always buried in old clothes, magazines, and **Sight** newspapers, and a lone shoe sat atop the pile, a fin- **Comparison (metaphor)** ishing touch to some bizarre modern sculpture. To one side was an aged and tuneless upright piano **Sound** with yellowed keys. The ivory overlay was missing **Sight** so that the wood underneath showed through, and **Sight** many of them made only a muffled and frustrating **Sound** thump, no matter how hard I pressed them. On the wall facing the piano was the room's only window, draped with yellowed lace curtains. Grandma al- **Sight**

Smell ways left that window open. I remember sitting near it, smelling the rain while the curtains tickled Touch my face.

For no apparent reason, an old curtain hung in the door between the kitchen and the living room. In the kitchen, a large formica-topped table always held at least a half-dozen varieties of homemade Taste jelly, as well as a loaf of bread, gooseberry pies or cherry pies with the pits left in, boxes of cereal, and anything else not requiring refrigeration, as if the Compari- table served as a small, portable pantry. Grandma's son (simile) kitchen always smelled of toast, and I often won- Smell dered—and still do—if she lived entirely on toast. A hole had eaten through the kitchen floor, not just Sight the warped yellow linoleum, but all the way through the floor itself. My sisters and I never wanted to take a bath at Grandma's house, because we discovered that anyone who lay on the floor on his stomach and put one eye to the hole could see Sight the bathtub, which was kept in the musty basement Smell because the upstairs bathroom was too small.

The back bedroom was near the kitchen and adjacent to the basement stairs. I once heard one of my aunts call that room a firetrap, and indeed it was. The room was wallpapered with the old news- Sight papers Grandma liked to collect, and the bed was stacked high with my mother's and aunts' old clothes. There was no space between the furniture in that room, only a narrow path against one wall leading to the bed. A sideboard was shoved against the opposite wall; a sewing table was pushed up against the sideboard; a short chest of drawers lay against the sewing table; and so on. But no one could identify these pieces of forgotten furniture unless he dug through the sewing patterns, half-made dresses, dishes, and books. Any outsider would just think this was a part of the room where the floor had been raised to about waist-level, so thoroughly was the mass of furniture hidden.

Compari- Stepping off Grandma's sloping back porch son (simile) was like stepping into an enchanted forest. The grass and weeds were hip-level, with a tiny dirt Compari- path leading to nowhere, as if it had lost its way in son (simile) the jungle. A fancy white fence, courtesy of the Sight neighbors, bordered the yard in back and vainly at-tempted to hold in the gooseberries, raspberries, and blackberries that grew wildly along the side of

Grandma's yard. Huge crabapple, cherry, and wal-
nut trees shaded the house and hid the sky. I used
to stand under them and look up, pretending to be
deep in a magic forest. The ground was <u>cool and</u>   Touch
<u>damp</u> under my bare feet, even in the middle of the
day, and my head would fill with the <u>sweet fra-</u>   Smell
<u>grance of mixed spring flowers</u> and <u>throaty cooing</u>
Sound <u>of doves</u> I could never find but could always hear.
But, before long, the wind would shift, and the
Smell <u>musty aroma of petroleum</u> from a nearby refinery
would jerk me back to reality.

      Grandma's house is indeed a place for memo-
ries. Just as her decaying concrete steps store the
Dominant treasures of many lost childhoods, <u>her house still</u>
impression <u>stands, guarding the memories of generations of</u>
rephrased <u>children and grandchildren.</u>

Student Writer's Comments

      Writing this descriptive essay was easy and enjoyable for me. I
just picked a place I know well and brainstormed about it, being
sure to think of images from all five senses. After I had plenty of images, I organized my essay as if I were walking through Grandma's
house. I devoted one paragraph to each room, plus one for the yard.
In my rewriting, I looked for opportunities to use comparisons and
found plenty. My biggest problem was that I had too many memories and thus had to be selective. I hated leaving out anything!

Some Final Thoughts on Description

      Because description is one of the most basic forms of verbal
communication, you will find descriptive passages in most of the
reading selections throughout this textbook. Description provides
us with the means to capture our audience's attention and clarify
certain points in all of our writing. The examples chosen for the
following section, however, are predominantly descriptive—the
main purpose in each being to involve the readers' senses as
vividly as possible. As you read through each of these essays, try
to determine its intended audience and purpose, the object of the
description, the extent to which details are included or excluded,
and the author's point of view. Equipped with these four areas of
reference, you can become an increasingly sophisticated reader
and writer of descriptive prose.

RAY BRADBURY
(1920–   )

■ ■ ■

Summer Rituals

QUOTATION ON THINKING

"Previous to writing or speaking, we should obtain a clear view of the end to be aimed at; the problem to be proved, the goal at which we would arrive should be distinctly and precisely comprehended and announced; and holding this steadily in view, the style and reasoning should be adapted to it."

Hugh Blair

Ray Bradbury is one of America's best-known and best-loved writers of science fiction. His extensive publications include such popular novels as *The Martian Chronicles* (1950), *The Illustrated Man* (1951), *Fahrenheit 451* (1953), *Dandelion Wine* (1957), and *Something Wicked This Way Comes* (1962). He has also written dozens of short stories, poems, essays, plays, and radio and movie scripts (including the screenplay of John Huston's film version of *Moby Dick*). As a child, he escaped his strict Baptist upbringing through a steady diet of Jules Verne, H. G. Wells, and Edgar Rice Burroughs, along with Buck Rogers and Prince Valiant comic books: "I was a sucker for lies, beautiful, fabulous lies, which instruct us to better our lives as a result, but which don't tell the truth." A frequent theme in his many novels is the impact of science on humanity: "My stories are intended," he claims, "as much to forecast how to prevent dooms, as to predict them." Bradbury's recent publications include *"The Last Circus* (1981), *The Complete Poems of Ray Bradbury* (1982), *The Love Affair* (1983), *Dinosaur Tales* (1983), *A Memory for Murder* (1984), *Forever and the Earth* (1984), *Death Is a Lonely Business* (1985), and *The Toynbee Convector* (1989). The author lives in Cheviot Hills, California, where he enjoys painting and making ceramics.

Preparing to Read

"Summer Rituals," an excerpt from *Dandelion Wine*, describes the comfortable ceremony of putting up a front-porch swing in early summer. Focusing on the perceptions of Douglas, a young boy, the essay clearly sets forth the familiar yet deeply significant rhythms of life in a small town. Before you read this selection, take a few moments to consider the value of ritual in your own life: Can you think of any activities that you and your family have elevated to the level of ceremonial importance? What about holidays? Birthdays? Sporting events? Spring cleaning? When do these activities take place? Do the same people participate in them every year? Why do you repeat these rituals? What purpose do they have for you? For others whom you know? For society in general?

PREREADING

The purpose of this Preparing to Read material is to encourage students to think about rituals in general. To help your students focus their attention on rituals before responding to the questions here, you might discuss the meaning of the word and the various connotations of its synonyms, such as "ceremony," "rite," "custom," "tradition," or "formality." See pages 3–6 for other ways to generate thoughts on these questions.

BACKGROUND INFORMATION

Ray Bradbury's "Summer Rituals" is a slice of Americana, a Norman Rockwell canvas, a scene from an old Andy Hardy movie. Bradbury paints a nostalgic picture of a simple way of life when roles were clearly defined and tradition was revered.

READABILITY LEVEL

8.4

RELATED READING

Neighborhoods

Robert Ramirez, "The Barrio"   357

DEFINITIONS

Ahab (para. 2): captain of the whaling ship *Pequod* in Herman Melville's *Moby Dick*.
howdah (para. 4): a seat or covered pavilion on the back of an elephant or camel.
susurrant (para. 14): full of whispering sounds.

COLLABORATIVE LEARNING: CLASS ACTIVITY

Have the class members make up a story called "[Name a Season] Rituals" (e.g., Fall Rituals) by adding to the story orally one by one until they run out of ideas. Begin the story with "My favorite part of [season] is rituals."

COLLABORATIVE LEARNING: SMALL GROUP ACTIVITY

Have your students pair up with people they don't know very well. Then, tell them to take turns leading each other around campus. The person being led around should keep his or her eyes closed for the duration of the walk and should concentrate on what is happening to his or her other four senses. This exercise makes students aware of sensory stimuli that they didn't even know they responded to. Then, have your students report their discoveries to the class. Ask them to determine the extent to which writing an essay is like taking

Yes, summer was rituals, each with its natural time and place. The ritual of lemonade or ice-tea making, the ritual of wine, shoes, or no shoes, and at last, swiftly following the others, with quiet dignity, the ritual of the front-porch swing. 1

On the third day of summer in the late afternoon Grandfather reappeared from the front door to gaze serenely at the two empty eye rings in the ceiling of the porch. Moving to the geranium-pot-lined rail like Ahab surveying the mild mild day and the mild-looking sky, he wet his finger to test the wind, and shucked his coat to see how shirt sleeves felt in the westering hours. He acknowledged the salutes of other captains on yet other flowered porches, out themselves to discern the gentle ground swell of weather, oblivious to their wives chirping or snapping like fuzzball hand dogs hidden behind black porch screens. 2

"All right, Douglas, let's set it up." 3

In the garage they found, dusted, and carried forth the howdah, as it were, for the quiet summer-night festivals, the swing chair which Grandpa chained to the porch-ceiling eyelets. 4

Douglas, being lighter, was first to sit in the swing. Then, after a moment, Grandfather gingerly settled his pontifical weight beside the boy. Thus they sat, smiling at each other, nodding, as they swung silently back and forth, back and forth. 5

Ten minutes later Grandma appeared with water buckets and brooms to wash down and sweep off the porch. Other chairs, rockers and straight-backs, were summoned from the house. 6

"Always like to start sitting early in the season," said Grandpa, "before the mosquitoes thicken." 7

About seven o'clock you could hear the chairs scraping back from the tables, someone experimenting with a yellow-toothed piano, if you stood outside the dining-room window and listened. Matches being struck, the first dishes bubbling in the suds and tinkling on the wall racks, somewhere, faintly, a phonograph playing. And then as the evening changed the hour, at house after house on the twilight streets, under the immense oaks and elms, on shady porches, people would begin to appear, like those figures who tell good or bad weather in rain-or-shine clocks. 8

Uncle Bert, perhaps Grandfather, then Father, and some of the cousins; the men all coming out first into the syrupy evening, blowing smoke, leaving the women's voices behind in the cooling-warm kitchen to set their universe aright. Then the first male voices under the porch brim, the feet up, the boys fringed on the worn steps or wooden rails where sometime during the evening something, a boy or a geranium pot, would fall off. 9

At last, like ghosts hovering momentarily behind the door screen, Grandma, Great-grandma, and Mother would appear, and the men would shift, move, and offer seats. The women carried varieties of fans with them, folded newspapers, bamboo whisks, or perfumed kerchiefs, to start the air moving about their faces as they talked.

What they talked of all evening long, no one remembered next day. It wasn't important to anyone what the adults talked about; it was only important that the sounds came and went over the delicate ferns that bordered the porch on three sides; it was only important that the darkness filled the town like black water being poured over the houses, and that the cigars glowed and that the conversations went on, and on. The female gossip moved out, disturbing the first mosquitoes so they danced in frenzies on the air. The male voices invaded the old house timbers; if you closed your eyes and put your head down against the floor boards you could hear the men's voices rumbling like a distant, political earthquake, constant, unceasing, rising or falling a pitch.

Douglas sprawled back on the dry porch planks, completely contented and reassured by these voices, which would speak on through eternity, flow in a stream of murmurings over his body, over his closed eyelids, into his drowsy ears, for all time. The rocking chairs sounded like crickets, the crickets sounded like rocking chairs, and the moss-covered rain barrel by the dining-room window produced another generation of mosquitoes to provide a topic of conversation through endless summers ahead.

Sitting on the summer-night porch was so good, so easy and so reassuring that it could never be done away with. These were rituals that were right and lasting; the lighting of pipes, the pale hands that moved knitting needles in the dimness, the eating of foil-wrapped, chill Eskimo Pies, the coming and going of all the people. For at some time or other during the evening, everyone visited here; the neighbors down the way, the people across the street; Miss Fern and Miss Roberta humming by in their electric runabout, giving Tom or Douglas a ride around the block and then coming up to sit down and fan away the fever in their cheeks; or Mr. Jonas, the junkman, having left his horse and wagon hidden in the alley, and ripe to bursting with words, would come up the steps looking as fresh as if his talk had never been said before, and somehow it never had. And last of all, the children, who had been off squinting their way through a last hide-and-seek or kick-the-can, panting, glowing, would sickle quietly back like boomerangs along the soundless lawn, to sink

your reader on just such a "blind walk." How can each writer/leader best coax the reader/walker from point to point in their journey together?

ANSWERS TO QUESTIONS:
UNDERSTANDING DETAILS (p. 46)

1. Grandfather, in this essay, is an authority figure by virtue of age and position in the family, whereas Douglas is his devoted apprentice, learning life's rituals under the tutelage of the master. Douglas seems to be carrying on the traditions that Grandfather helped create. Douglas' youth adds vitality to this family and its customs. The reader is left with the feeling that someday Douglas will appear on that same porch with his own grandson at his side to test the wind of a summer day and see if the time is right to hang the front-porch swing.

2. The most important feature of Douglas' house is a large front porch, its generous dimensions suggested by the "other chairs, rockers and straight-backs" (para. 6) dragged onto the porch for their summer sojourn. While the author describes "the geranium-pot-lined rail" (para. 2), "the delicate ferns that bordered the porch on three sides" (para. 11), and the "immense oaks and elms" (para. 8) that lined the streets of the small town, he makes no specific reference to the number of trees and bushes surrounding this particular house. Likewise, other details, such as the color and style of the old house, must be drawn from the reader's imagination and experience.

3. Bradbury describes a patriarchal society in which the men wield the authority, protecting home and hearth, while the women serve the men. A partial list of qualities describing each sex follows:
Men:
—"acknowledged the salutes of other captains" (2)
—"the men would shift, move, and offer seats" (10)
—"The male voices invaded the old house timbers" (11)
Women:
—"wives chirping or snapping like fuzzball hand dogs" (2)

—"leaving the women's voices behind in the cooling-warm kitchen (9)

—"The women carried varieties of fans with them" (10)

The men in Douglas' childhood were charged not only with life's major decisions, from the declaration of war to the appropriate time to hang the front-porch swing, but also with a duty to respond with amused tolerance to the foibles of the "weaker" sex.

ANSWERS TO QUESTIONS:
ANALYZING MEANING (p. 46)

1. For Douglas' family, the front-porch ritual represents continuity, not only of family traditions, but of society as they know it. The passing down of the ritual gives them the comfort of assuming that their way of life will always continue.

2. Summer for Douglas was a time of ceremonies: "the ritual of lemonade or ice-tea making, the ritual of wine, shoes, or no shoes" (para. 1), "the lighting of pipes, the pale hands that moved knitting needles in the dimness, the eating of foil-wrapped, chill Eskimo Pies, the coming and going of all the people" (para. 13). These rituals, however, all originated with and revolved around the altar of the front-porch swing, where the family gathered on sultry evenings, confessions were shared, supplications made, and praises sung for summer nights. To Douglas and his family, these rites represent the salvation of a habitual way of life in a continually changing world.

3. Descriptive phrases evoking visual images might include "black water being poured over the houses" (para. 11) and "moss-covered rain barrel" (para. 12). The phrase "stream of murmurings" (para. 12) elicits an aural response, while a sense of feeling comes with "pontifical weight" (para. 5) and "cooling-warm kitchen" (para. 9).

beneath the talking talking talking of the porch voices which would weigh and gentle them down. . . .

Oh, the luxury of lying in the fern night and the grass night and the night of susurrant, slumbrous voices weaving the dark together. The grownups had forgotten he was there, so still, so quiet Douglas lay, noting the plans they were making for his and their own futures. And the voices chanted, drifted, in moonlit clouds of cigarette smoke while the moths, like late appleblossoms come alive, tapped faintly about the far street lights, and the voices moved on into the coming years. . . .

UNDERSTANDING DETAILS

1. What are the main similarities and differences between Douglas and Grandfather in this essay? How are their views of the world the same? How are their views different?

2. From the scattered details you have read in this essay, describe Douglas' house. How large do you think the front porch is? What color is the house? How many trees and shrubs surround it? What part of your description is based on facts in the essay? What part comes from inferences you have made on your own?

3. How do the men differ from the women in this excerpt? Divide a piece of paper into two columns; then list as many qualities of each gender as you can find. (For example, the narrator hears the men's voices "rumbling" like an "earthquake"; in contrast, the women move like "ghosts," their gossip "disturbing the . . . mosquitoes.") What other descriptive differences can you find between the men and women? What conclusions can you draw from these differences?

ANALYZING MEANING

1. A "ritual" may be briefly defined as "a customarily repeated act that expresses a system of values." Using this definition, explain why the ritual of the front-porch swing is important to Douglas' family. What important feelings or implicit values lie behind this particular ritual?

2. What other rituals are mentioned in this essay? How are they related to the front-porch swing? To summer? To Douglas and his family?

3. Bradbury helps us feel the comfort, warmth, and familiarity of the scene depicted in this essay through the use of a number of original descriptive details: for example, "summer-night festivals," "yellow-toothed piano," "rain-or-shine clocks," "syrupy evening," and "foil-wrapped, chill Eskimo Pies." Find at least five other descriptive words or phrases, and explain how each enables us to identify with

the characters and situations in this story. Which of the five senses does each of these details arouse in the reader?

DISCOVERING RHETORICAL STRATEGIES

1. Some of the author's sentences are very long and involved, whereas others are quite short. What effects do these changes in sentence length have upon you as a reader? Give a specific example of a shift in length from one sentence to another and explain its effect.
2. This descriptive essay is filled with many interesting similes (comparisons using the words *like* or *as*) and metaphors (comparisons without *like* or *as*). For example, Grandfather standing on the front porch looks *like* Ahab, the possessed sea captain from Melville's epic novel *Moby Dick* (paragraph 2). Later, Bradbury uses a metaphor to focus his readers on "the night of susurrant, slumbrous voices weaving the dark together" (paragraph 14). Find at least one other comparison, either a simile or a metaphor, and explain how it works within the context of its sentence or paragraph. What type of comparison is being made (a simile or a metaphor)? What do we learn about the object being described (for example, Grandfather or the night) through its association with the other reference (Ahab or voices weaving the dark together)?
3. What is the point of view of the author in this excerpt? Would the essay be more effective if it were reported from the standpoint of Douglas? Of Grandfather? Of the women? Why or why not? How does the author's point of view help Bradbury organize his description? Should the fact that Bradbury's middle name is Douglas have any bearing on our interpretation of this story?

IDEAS FOR DISCUSSION/WRITING

Preparing to Write

List some of the most important rituals in your life: How many times a year do these rituals occur? What purpose do they serve? How do rituals help create a strong social framework in your life? In your friends' lives? In society in general?

Choosing a Topic

1. Write a descriptive essay about a ritual that is significant in your life, addressing it to someone who has never experienced that particular activity. Include the people involved and the setting. Try to use all five senses in your description.
2. Choose a ritual that is part of your family life, and write an essay de-

ANSWERS TO QUESTIONS: DISCOVERING RHETORICAL STRATEGIES (p. 47)

1. The long and involved sentences provide a flow to the essay that gives a timelessness to the rituals of summer. In some places, they resemble a litany; in others, the drone of adult voices. The insertion of a short sentence into this stream of words forces the reader to pause and focus upon an immediate action required to implement the rite: "He acknowledged the salutes of other captains on yet other flowered porches, out themselves to discern the gentle ground swell of weather, oblivious to their wives chirping or snapping like fuzzball hand dogs hidden behind black porch screens" (para. 2), for example, emphasizes the repetitive nature of this preparatory portion of the ceremony. The short injunction that follows, "All right, Douglas, let's set it up," breaks the flow and turns the focus to the act itself.

2. Responses to this question will vary.

3. Bradbury tells his story very effectively from the third-person objective point of view with a focus upon Douglas. This perspective presents a more complete, although innocent, picture than Douglas, Grandfather, or the women would tell. From any one of these standpoints, such issues as the excitement of the moment, one's duty to tradition, or the injustice of role expectations might have overshadowed the focus on the ritual itself. In using the third-person objective point of view, the author is able to describe the ritual chronologically, from preparation to implementation to effect. Although the reader must be aware that the narrator of a story does not always reflect the point of view of the author, the fact that Bradbury's middle name is "Douglas" as well as that the relationship between the boy and his grandfather is warm and loving suggests that this nostalgic vignette might be drawn to some extent from the personal life of the author.

PREWRITING

In preparation for the writing assignments, the Preparing to Write questions ask students to put rituals into a specific context before writing an essay on a related topic.

See pages 16–23 for suggestions on generating ideas in response to these questions.

ADDITIONAL DISCUSSION/WRITING TOPIC

How do you benefit from rituals in your own life? How do you think society benefits from rituals in general? What would your life be like with no rituals or traditions whatsoever? In an essay for your classmates, describe a fictitious society that doesn't honor any rituals. Depict the people and their daily lifestyle in vivid detail. How are they different from you and me? If you feel particularly creative, name your society and tell your readers about its origin and history.

REVISING STRATEGY

The dominant impression you want to make generally determines your purpose in a descriptive essay. Choose one of your descriptive essays, name your dominant impression, and underline all parts of the essay that help you achieve that particular impression. Notice where your impression could be tighter or more focused. Then revise your paper, concentrating on communicating a consistent dominant impression to your intended audience.

scribing your feelings about this ceremonial event. Address it to someone outside your family. Use similes and metaphors to make your description as vivid as possible.

3. Explain to someone visiting the United States for the first time the value of a particular tradition in American society. Then help this person understand the importance of that tradition in your life.

AMY TAN
(1952–   )

■ ■ ■

The Joy Luck Club

In a very short time, Amy Tan has established herself as one of the foremost Chinese-American writers. Her first novel, *The Joy Luck Club* (1989), which was praised as "brilliant . . . a jewel of a book" by the *New York Times Book Review,* focuses on the lives of four Chinese women in pre-1949 China and their American-born daughters in modern-day California. Through a series of vignettes, Tan weaves together the dreams and sorrows of these mothers and daughters as they confront oppression in China and equally difficult cultural challenges in the new world of the United States. Like the protagonists in *The Joy Luck Club,* Tan's parents, a Baptist minister and a licensed vocational nurse, emigrated to America shortly before Tan's birth. She showed an early talent for writing when, at age eight, she won an essay contest (and a transistor radio) with a paper entitled "Why I Love the Library." Following the tremendous success of her first novel, Tan apparently had great difficulty writing her second book, *The Kitchen God's Wife* (1991). As she was working on it, she began grinding her teeth, which resulted in two broken molars and a sizable dental bill. "I am glad that I shall never again have to write a second book," the author has confessed. "Actually, I cannot recall any writer—with or without a splashy debut—who said the second book came easily."

Preparing to Read

In the following essay, excerpted from the beginning of *The Joy Luck Club,* Tan describes how the club began amid the horror and devastation of Japan's conquest of the Kweilin area of China during the 1930s. As you prepare to read Tan's description, take a few moments to think about a place that is particularly meaningful in your life: What physical characteristics does this place have? Do you remember it as pleasant or unpleasant? Are you happy or sad when you think about it? What are some sights, smells, tastes, sounds, or textures you associate with this place? Did you ever feel trapped or confined there? If so, how did you escape?

PREREADING

The purpose of this Preparing to Read material is to encourage students to think about a particularly meaningful place in their lives and so begin the process of understanding Amy Tan's mother's story about Kweilin. To begin this process, you might try discussing significant public places, including their actual histories, their functions, and various associations these places hold for individuals in the class. Then, help students focus their attention on important places in their own lives and the memories those places conjure up. See pages 3–6 for other ways to generate thoughts on these questions.

Tan's ability to paint a vivid picture with words is clearly illustrated in "The Joy Luck Club," an excerpt from her book of the same title. The book is a semiautobiographical collection of Tan's childhood memories as the daughter of a Chinese couple who sought political asylum in the United States. This excerpt describes Kweilin, a city in China that was the source of much beauty for the author's mother until she was trapped there with two babies when the Japanese invaded China during World War II. In every paragraph, the reader is immersed in the sights, sounds, smells, textures, and tastes of Tan's mother's experiences in Kweilin. Although many readers may be unfamiliar with the degree of terror and loneliness Tan describes, they should have no difficulty relating to the shattered dreams and insecurities that overpowered the beauty of Kweilin for her mother.

READABILITY LEVEL

7.8

RELATED READINGS

Cultural Diversity

Parent–Child Relationships

My mother started the San Francisco version of the Joy Luck Club in 1949, two years before I was born. This was the year my mother and father left China with one stiff leather trunk filled only with fancy silk dresses. There was no time to pack anything else, my mother had explained to my father after they boarded the boat. Still his hands swam frantically between the slippery silks, looking for his cotton shirts and wool pants. 1

When they arrived in San Francisco, my father made her hide those shiny clothes. She wore the same brown-checked Chinese dress until the Refugee Welcome Society gave her two hand-me-down dresses, all too large in sizes for American women. The society was composed of a group of white-haired American missionary ladies from the First Chinese Baptist Church. And because of their gifts, my parents could not refuse their invitation to join the church. Nor could they ignore the old ladies' practical advice to improve their English through Bible study class on Wednesday nights and, later, through choir practice on Saturday mornings. This was how my parents met the Hsus, the Jongs, and the St. Clairs. My mother could sense that the women of these families also had unspeakable tragedies they had left behind in China and hopes they couldn't begin to express in their fragile English. Or at least, my mother recognized the numbness in these women's faces. And she saw how quickly their eyes moved when she told them her idea for the Joy Luck Club. 2

Joy Luck was an idea my mother remembered from the days of her first marriage in Kweilin, before the Japanese came. That's why I think of Joy Luck as her Kweilin story. It was the story she would always tell me when she was bored, when there was nothing to do, when every bowl had been washed and the Formica table had been wiped down twice, when my father sat reading the newspaper and smoking one Pall Mall cigarette after another, a warning not to disturb him. This is when my mother would take out a box of old ski sweaters sent to us by unseen relatives from Vancouver. She would snip the bottom of a sweater and pull out a kinky thread of yarn, anchoring it to a piece of cardboard. And as she began to roll with one sweeping rhythm, she would start her story. Over the years, she told me the same story, except for the ending, which grew darker, casting long shadows into her life, and eventually into mine. 3

"I dreamed about Kweilin before I ever saw it," my mother began, speaking Chinese. "I dreamed of jagged peaks lining a curving river, with magic moss greening the banks. At the tops of these peaks were white mists. And if you could float down this 4

DEFINITIONS

river and eat the moss for food, you would be strong enough to climb the peak. If you slipped, you would only fall into a bed of soft moss and laugh. And once you reached the top, you would be able to see everything and feel such happiness it would be enough to never have worries in your life ever again.

"In China, everybody dreamed about Kweilin. And when I arrived, I realized how shabby my dreams were, how poor my thoughts. When I saw the hills, I laughed and shuddered at the same time. The peaks looked like giant fried fish heads trying to jump out of a vat of oil. Behind each hill, I could see shadows of another fish, and then another and another. And then the clouds would move just a little and the hills would suddenly become monstrous elephants marching slowly toward me! Can you see this? And at the root of the hill were secret caves. Inside grew hanging rock gardens in the shapes and colors of cabbage, winter melons, turnips, and onions. These were things so strange and beautiful you can't ever imagine them.

"But I didn't come to Kweilin to see how beautiful it was. The man who was my husband brought me and our two babies to Kweilin because he thought we would be safe. He was an officer with the Kuomintang, and after he put us down in a small room in a two-story house, he went off to the northwest, to Chungking.

"We knew the Japanese were winning, even when the newspapers said they were not. Every day, every hour, thousands of people poured into the city, crowding the sidewalks, looking for places to live. They came from the East, West, North, and South. They were rich and poor, Shanghainese, Cantonese, northerners, and not just Chinese, but foreigners and missionaries of every religion. And there was, of course, the Kuomintang and their army officers who thought they were top level to everyone else.

"We were a city of leftovers mixed together. If it hadn't been for the Japanese, there would have been plenty of reason for fighting to break out among these different people. Can you see it? Shanghai people with north-water peasants, bankers with barbers, rickshaw pullers with Burma refugees. Everybody looked down on someone else. It didn't matter that everybody shared the same sidewalk to spit on and suffered the same fast-moving diarrhea. We all had the same stink, but everybody complained someone else smelled the worst. Me? Oh, I hated the American air force officers who said habba-habba sounds to make my face turn red. But the worst were the northern peasants who emptied their noses into their hands and pushed people around and gave everybody their dirty diseases.

5 **Kweilin** (pronounced Gway-lin; also spelled Guilin) (para. 3): a scenic city in the Kwangsi province of China where mountain peaks rise from the flat terrain along the winding Li River; subject of numerous paintings and poems; considered by many to be the most scenic city in China.

Kuomintang (para. 6): also known as the Nationalist Party, which opposed the Chinese Communist Party; founded by Sun Yat-sen, who is known as the Father of modern China.

mah jong (para. 12): Chinese. A popular game played with tiles, similar to gin rummy but with more variations and a complex scoring system.

dyansyin (para. 13): Mandarin pronunciation of the Cantonese food "dim sum," a wide variety of individually made hot and cold hors d'oeuvres.

hong mu (para. 15): Chinese. Red wood.

pai (para. 15): Chinese. Tiles used in mah jong.

pung (para. 16): Chinese. Meet or run into; exclamation of a mah jong player who has a pair of tiles and wants to claim the third matching tile discarded by another player.

chr (para. 16): Chinese. Eat or gobble; exclamation of a mah jong player who has a pair of tiles and wants to claim the third matching tile discarded by the previous player.

yuan (para. 21): a unit of currency for both the People's Republic of China (mainland) and the Republic of China (Taiwan).

Have your students let the class know what their special place is like by doing one of the following activities: (1) draw an impression or replica of this place; (2) bring to class a collage of pictures representing this place; or (3) pantomime a game or activity they associate with this place. Forbidding the use of words is important in this exercise so that students are forced to explore other ways of expressing themselves.

COLLABORATIVE LEARNING: SMALL GROUP ACTIVITY

Put your students in groups of 3 or 4, and have them list five traits common to the places represented in their group. If you have time, put these lists on the chalkboard or on a transparency. This will encourage students to continue to generate ideas as they read, reread, and respond to Tan's essay.

ANSWERS TO QUESTIONS: UNDERSTANDING DETAILS (p. 54)

1. The Joy Luck Club was a "gathering of four women," all young, well mannered, and financially comfortable. "Each week one of us would host a party to raise money and to raise our spirits" (para. 13). The women "feasted" on special Chinese foods, played games, and told amusing anecdotes to escape from war and loneliness into a world that still followed the traditions and rituals to which they were accustomed.

2. The following are examples; answers to this question will vary.

Sights:
—"jagged peaks lining a curved river" (para. 4)
—"the clouds would move just a little" (para. 5)

Smells:
—"We all had the same stink" (para. 8)
—"there was no room for fresh air" (para. 11)

"So you can see how quickly Kweilin lost its beauty for me. I no longer climbed the peaks to say, How lovely are these hills! I only wondered which hills the Japanese had reached. I sat in the dark corners of my house with a baby under each arm, waiting with nervous feet. When the sirens cried out to warn us of bombers, my neighbors and I jumped to our feet and scurried to the deep caves to hide like wild animals. But you can't stay in the dark for so long. Something inside of you starts to fade and you become like a starving person, crazy-hungry for light. Outside I could hear the bombing. Boom! Boom! And then the sound of raining rocks. And inside I was no longer hungry for the cabbage or the turnips of the hanging rock garden. I could only see the dripping bowels of an ancient hill that might collapse on top of me. Can you imagine how it is, to want to be neither inside nor outside, to want to be nowhere and disappear? 9

"So when the bombing sounds grew farther away, we would come back out like newborn kittens scratching our way back to the city. And always, I would be amazed to find the hills against the burning sky had not been torn apart. 10

"I thought up Joy Luck on a summer night that was so hot even the moths fainted to the ground, their wings were so heavy with the damp heat. Every place was so crowded there was no room for fresh air. Unbearable smells from the sewers rose up to my second-story window and the stink had nowhere else to go but into my nose. At all hours of the night and day, I heard screaming sounds. I didn't know if it was a peasant slitting the throat of a runaway pig or an officer beating a half-dead peasant for lying in his way on the sidewalk. I didn't go to the window to find out. What use would it have been? And that's when I thought I needed something to do to help me move. 11

"My idea was to have a gathering of four women, one for each corner of my mah jong table. I knew which women I wanted to ask. They were all young like me, with wishful faces. One was an army officer's wife, like myself. Another was a girl with very fine manners from a rich family in Shanghai. She had escaped with only a little money. And there was a girl from Nanking who had the blackest hair I have ever seen. She came from a low-class family, but she was pretty and pleasant and had married well, to an old man who died and left her with a better life. 12

"Each week one of us would host a party to raise money and to raise our spirits. The hostess had to serve special *dyansyin* foods to bring good fortune of all kinds—dumplings shaped like silver money ingots, long rice noodles for long life, boiled 13 peanuts for conceiving sons, and of course, many good-luck oranges for a plentiful, sweet life.

"What fine food we treated ourselves to with our meager allowances! We didn't notice that the dumplings were stuffed mostly with stringy squash and that the oranges were spotted with wormy holes. We ate sparingly, not as if we didn't have enough, but to protest how we could not eat another bite, we had already bloated ourselves from earlier in the day. We knew we had luxuries few people could afford. We were the lucky ones.

"After filling our stomachs, we would then fill a bowl with money and put it where everyone could see. Then we would sit down at the mah jong table. My table was from my family and was of a very fragrant red wood, not what you call rosewood, but *hong mu*, which is so fine there's no English word for it. The table had a very thick pad, so that when the mah jong *pai* were spilled onto the table the only sound was of ivory tiles washing against one another.

"Once we started to play, nobody could speak, except to say *'Pung!'* or *'Chr!'* when taking a tile. We had to play with seriousness and think of nothing else but adding to our happiness through winning. But after sixteen rounds, we would again feast, this time to celebrate our good fortune. And then we would talk into the night until the morning, saying stories about good times in the past and good times yet to come.

"Oh, what good stories! Stories spilling out all over the place! We almost laughed to death. A rooster that ran into the house screeching on top of dinner bowls, the same bowls that held him quietly in pieces the next day! And one about a girl who wrote love letters for two friends who loved the same man. And a silly foreign lady who fainted on a toilet when firecrackers went off next to her.

"People thought we were wrong to serve banquets every week while many people in the city were starving, eating rats and, later, the garbage that the poorest rats used to feed on. Others thought we were possessed by demons—to celebrate when even within our own families we had lost generations, had lost homes and fortunes, and were separated, husband from wife, brother from sister, daughter from mother. Hnnnh! How could we laugh, people asked.

"It's not that we had no heart or eyes for pain. We were all afraid. We all had our miseries. But to despair was to wish back for something already lost. Or to prolong what was already unbearable. How much can you wish for a favorite warm coat that

Tastes:
—"stringy squash" (para. 14)
—"good-luck oranges for a plentiful, sweet life" (para. 13)

14 Sounds:
—"the sound of raining rocks" (para. 9)
—"the only sound was of ivory tiles washing against one another" (para. 15)

Textures:
—"slippery silks" (para. 1)
—"bed of soft moss" (para. 4)

15 The sensual details of Tan's mother's life before the war and after the war are sharply contrasted. The reader understands that Tan's mother needs the Joy Luck Club because she has gone from wearing silk and perfume to being surrounded by foul odors and eating stringy squash. The detail and description Tan uses help make this abrupt change in lifestyle vivid.

16 **3.** Women in Tan's mother's position in China after World War II no longer had money and cultural status to sustain them. "We could hope to be lucky. That hope was our only joy" (para. 20). They prayed, therefore, for "joy" and "luck": that their husbands might come home, that they might stay alive and in good health, that
17 they might once again be prosperous.

**ANSWERS TO QUESTIONS:
ANALYZING MEANING (p. 54)**

1. Tan's mother remembers Kweilin for both the sad and happy times she spent there. Though she still remembers its beauty, her age and wisdom have increased
18 her awareness of the pain and suffering that occurred there. After surviving through this troubled time in China's history, she recalls the emotional strife that she once tried so hard to ignore.

2. The varieties of food served at the Joy Luck Club meetings symbolized the richness of past tradition and hopefulness for the future. Their attempt to continue "feast-
19 ing" and having parties while others suffered was not malicious, but illustrates their resistance to change.

3. As Tan's mother grew older, she remembered not only the "joy" she felt in the Joy Luck Club, but the pain as well. She realizes the foolishness of packing only silk dresses and her own vanity in trying to preserve customs such as eating delicacies while others around her were starving. Her bitterness seems to rise from the discrepancy between the luck she hoped for and the reality she experienced.

ANSWERS TO QUESTIONS: DISCOVERING RHETORICAL STRATEGIES (p. 55)

1. Tan uses first-person narration when she relates her mother's story in her mother's voice and third-person narration when Tan herself adds detail or comments to her mother's tale. Even though Tan is the writer here, her mother's personality comes through in the way the story is told. Tan's protective and revealing comments also tell us a great deal about her mother.

2. *Senses and Words*

Sight	see
	beauty
	dark corners
	fade
	dripping bowels
	crazy-hungry for light
Touch	climbed
	baby under each arm
	nervous feet
	jumped
	scurried
Hearing	sirens cried out
	hear the bombing
	Boom! Boom!
	raining rocks
Taste	starving person
	crazy-hungry for light
	no longer hungry for the cabbage or the turnips

3. Tan changes the tone here in several ways:

— Questions allow her to involve the reader while changing from a bright, hopeful story to a dismal tale just as her mother does.

— Exclamations help the reader feel her nervousness and the overwhelming violence of war.

hangs in the closet of a house that burned down with your mother and father inside of it? How long can you see in your mind arms and legs hanging from telephone wires and starving dogs running down the streets with half-chewed hands dangling from their jaws? What was worse, we asked among ourselves, to sit and wait for our own deaths with proper somber faces? Or to choose our own happiness?

"So we decided to hold parties and pretend each week had become the new year. Each week we could forget past wrongs done to us. We weren't allowed to think a bad thought. We feasted, we laughed, we played games, lost and won, we told the best stories. And each week, we could hope to be lucky. That hope was our only joy. And that's how we came to call our little parties Joy Luck." 20

My mother used to end the story on a happy note, bragging about her skill at the game. "I won many times and was so lucky the others teased that I had learned the trick of a clever thief," she said. "I won tens of thousands of *yuan*. But I wasn't rich. No. By then paper money had become worthless. Even toilet paper was worth more. And that made us laugh harder, to think a thousand-*yuan* note wasn't even good enough to rub on our bottoms." 21

UNDERSTANDING DETAILS

1. What is the Joy Luck Club and why was it formed?
2. List two sights, two smells, two tastes, two sounds, and two textures that Tan's mother recalls in her Kweilin story. How are these senses used throughout the story? How do these sensual details help the reader experience the place described by the author?
3. How are joy and luck related to the naming of the "Joy Luck Club"?

ANALYZING MEANING

1. Why does Kweilin hold a special meaning for Tan's mother? Did it keep its positive associations in her memory? Explain your answer.
2. What significance did the varieties of food and the process of eating have at the Joy Luck Club meetings?
3. Why do you think the ending of the author's mother's Kweilin story "grew darker" (paragraph 3) over the years?

DISCOVERING RHETORICAL STRATEGIES

1. This descriptive essay contains two different voices. How do we know which voice is speaking/writing? What special characteristics does each voice have?
2. Using vivid details throughout her description, Tan's mother engages our senses as often as possible. Look, for example, at the following sentences: "So when the bombing sounds grew farther away, we would come back out like newborn kittens scratching our way back to the city. And always, I would be amazed to find the hills against the burning sky had not been torn apart" (paragraph 10). These sentences stimulate our senses of hearing ("bombing sounds"), seeing ("the hills," "the burning sky"), and touching ("scratching"). Reread paragraph 9. Then list in one column all the senses mentioned and in another the words that arouse those senses.
3. How does Tan use words and details to change the tone of her writing at key points in this excerpt?

IDEAS FOR DISCUSSION/WRITING

Preparing to Write

Write freely for a few minutes about a place that is special to you: What are some of the strongest memories of the sights, smells, tastes, sounds, and textures you associate with this place? Who else is involved with this place? What are your feelings about this place?

Choosing a Topic

1. Based on your sensory memories, write a descriptive essay about this special place for a friend of yours who has never been there. Decide on a specific impression you want to communicate to your friend and a perspective that will help create that impression.
2. Describe for your classmates your favorite game. How many can play? What are the rules? When is the game most exciting? Why do you like this game?
3. Using your imagination, travel back in time to a particular moment or event in your past. Write an essay describing in detail what you were seeing, smelling, tasting, hearing, and touching at that time in your life. Where were you? How old were you? What was happening at this precise moment in your past? What exactly were you doing? How did you feel while you were engaged in this activity? Who else was in the scene with you? Did you feel safe? Secure? Happy? Sad? Anxious to escape?

—Alliteration in "raining rocks" and onomatopoeia in "scurried" and "dripping" both add to the reader's involvement in this scene.

—The images of animals and wildness help change Tan's tone from that of a listener to that of a participant. The term "crazy-hungry" is especially effective, because it appeals to our sense of fear as well as hunger.

PREWRITING

Prior to the writing assignments, the Preparing to Write questions ask students to focus their attention as specifically as possible on the sights, smells, tastes, sounds, and textures they connect with their special place. See pages 16–23 for other suggestions on generating ideas in response to these questions.

ADDITIONAL DISCUSSION/WRITING TOPIC

Learn the details about another class member's special place by interviewing that person. Ask this person questions that will help you imagine the entire environment through your five senses: hearing, seeing, smelling, tasting, and touching. In an essay written for your classmates, describe this person's special place as vividly and clearly as possible. (If your students have responded to essay topic #1, have them exchange papers and compare these two descriptions of the same place.)

REVISING STRATEGY

Frequent references to our senses make our writing easy for our readers to imagine. In one of your descriptive essays, underline all words or phrases that represent one of the five senses: hearing, seeing, smelling, tasting, and touching. Notice the pattern of these references and the vitality of your writing when you engage these senses. Then revise your paper, concentrating only on sensory perceptions. Increase your references to some senses and decrease references to others so that you create a paper with a more balanced representation of the five senses than your previous draft.

JOHN McPHEE
(1931–   )

■ ■ ■

The Pines

The range of subjects investigated by author John McPhee is quite astounding. In his twenty books and numerous articles, he has written about sports, food, art, geology, geography, science, history, education, and a variety of other topics. One of the most famous of these "non-fictional, book-length narratives," as he calls them, is *A Sense of Where You Are* (1965), a study of former basketball great Bill Bradley; another is *Levels of the Game* (1969), a chronicle of the epic 1968 U.S. Open semifinal tennis match between Arthur Ashe and Clark Graebner. Most of McPhee's essays have appeared first in *The New Yorker,* a prestigious literary magazine for which he has been a staff writer since 1965. His most recent publications include *In Suspect Terrain* (1983), *La Place de la Concorde Suisse* (1984), *Table of Contents* (1985), *Rising from the Plains* (1986), *The Control of Nature* (1989), and *Looking for a Ship* (1990). "What all these pieces of writing have in common," according to the author, "is that they are about real people and real places. All the different topics are just milieus in which to sketch people and places." McPhee lives in New Jersey near Princeton University, where he teaches a seminar entitled "The Literature of Fact." His hobbies include going on long bike rides, fishing for shad and pickerel, and skiing.

PREREADING

Because the following excerpt focuses on the interaction of people rather than on a sequence of action, this Preparing to Read material encourages students to think about different character types they have encountered. To help students focus their attention in this way before they respond to the questions here, you might have them begin by classifying the various types of people in their composition class. See pages 3–6 for other ways to generate thoughts on these questions.

Preparing to Read

The following essay, "The Pines," is a small section from a longer piece called *The Pine Barrens* (1968), which describes a remote wilderness in southern New Jersey. Like many of McPhee's narrative essays, "The Pines" is structured around a single colorful character—in this case, Fred Brown, a talkative backwoods native whose simple surroundings and quaint mannerisms speak well for the solitary life. In contrast, Brown's friend Bill Wasovwich is almost painfully shy; he is a person (like McPhee himself, some critics tell us) who speaks little, listens intently, and observes the world around him with great care. Both men worry openly about the encroaching civilization that threatens their unique way of life. As you prepare to read this essay, think for a moment about the different types of people you know: Do you have talkative friends? Quiet friends? Which type of person is most appealing to you? Which type are you? Have you ever lived in the woods? What are the principal advantages of living in a rural environment rather than in a big city? What are the disadvantages?

Fred Brown's house is on an unpaved road that curves along the edge of a wide cranberry bog. What attracted me to it was the pump that stands in his yard. It was something of a wonder that I noticed the pump, because there were, among other things, eight automobiles in the yard, two of them on their sides and one of them upside down, all ten years old or older. Around the cars were old refrigerators, vacuum cleaners, partly dismantled radios, cathode-ray tubes, a short wooden ski, a large wooden mallet, dozens of cranberry picker's boxes, many tires, an orange crate dated 1946, a cord or so of firewood, mandolins, engine heads, and maybe a thousand other things. The house itself, two stories high, was covered with tarpaper that was peeling away in some places, revealing its original shingles, made of Atlantic white cedar from the stream courses of the surrounding forest. I called out to ask if anyone was home, and a voice inside called back, "Come in. Come in. Come on the hell in."

I walked through a vestibule that had a dirt floor, stepped up into a kitchen, and went on into another room that had several overstuffed chairs in it and a porcelain-topped table, where Fred Brown was seated, eating a pork chop. He was dressed in a white sleeveless shirt, ankle-top shoes, and undershorts. He gave me a cheerful greeting and, without asking why I had come or what I wanted, picked up a pair of khaki trousers that had been tossed onto one of the overstuffed chairs and asked me to sit down. He set the trousers on another chair, and he apologized for being in the middle of his breakfast, explaining that he seldom drank much but the night before he had had a few drinks and this had caused his day to start slowly. "I don't know what's the matter with me, but there's got to be something the matter with me, because drink don't agree with me anymore," he said. He had a raw onion in one hand, and while he talked he shaved slices from the onion and ate them between bites of the chop. He was a muscular and well-built man, with short, bristly white hair, and he had bright, fast-moving eyes in a wide-open face. His legs were trim and strong, with large muscles in the calves. I guessed that he was about sixty, and for a man of sixty he seemed to be in remark-

1 **BACKGROUND INFORMATION**

John McPhee's "The Pines" is predominantly a visual essay, offering the reader a fascinating glimpse of life in a fast-disappearing pocket of wilderness, the New Jersey Pine Barrens. Yet this essay is not merely a tour of the woods or of the ramshackle home of one of its more picturesque residents. The two characters in the piece reflect the paradox of the Pine Barrens—the struggle between change and continuity that will eventually result in the death of a unique way of life.

READABILITY LEVEL

6.8

2 **RELATED READING**

Environment

Jane Goodall, "The Mind of the Chimpanzee" 172

DEFINITIONS

cathode-ray tube (para. 1): a vacuum tube in which cathode-rays, which consist of streams of electrons, are projected on a fluorescent screen to produce a luminous image; used for television sets and computer monitors.

rotogravure (para. 4): a photographic process by which an impression is made with a rotary printing press.

jerry can (para. 17): a narrow, flatsided, 5-gallon container.

Have your students as a class define "civilization," then discuss the advantages and disadvantages of civilization itself. Ask your students why some people welcome "progress" and others shun it. To initiate this discussion, you might want your class to create a cluster based on the word "civilization"; have your students call out their personal associations with this word as you draw a map of the group's impressions on the chalkboard or on a transparency. (See pages 19 and 20 for more information on clustering.)

Divide your students into groups of 3 or 4. Then, have each person try to get his or her group to name the character from McPhee's essay he or she is thinking of by giving one-word clues. See which student can get his or her group to guess the character with the fewest number of clues.

ably good shape. He was actually seventy-nine. "My rule is: Never eat except when you're hungry," he said, and he ate another slice of the onion.

In a straight-backed chair near the doorway to the kitchen sat a young man with long black hair, who wore a visored red leather cap that had darkened with age. His shirt was coarse-woven and had eyelets down a V neck that was laced with a thong. His trousers were made of canvas, and he was wearing gum boots. His arms were folded, his legs were stretched out, he had one ankle over the other, and as he sat there he appeared to be sighting carefully past his feet, as if his toes were the outer frame of a gunsight and he could see some sort of target in the floor. When I had entered, I had said hello to him, and he had nodded without looking up. He had a long, straight nose and high cheekbones, in a deeply tanned face that was, somehow, gaunt. I had no idea whether he was shy or hostile. Eventually, when I came to know him, I found him to be as shy a person as I have ever had a chance to know. His name is Bill Wasovwich, and he lives alone in a cabin about half a mile from Fred. First his father, then his mother left him when he was a young boy, and he grew up depending on the help of various people in the pines. One of them, a cranberry grower, employs him and has given him some acreage, in which Bill is building a small cranberry bog of his own, "turfing it out" by hand. When he is not working in the bogs, he goes roaming, as he puts it, setting out cross-country on long, looping journeys, hiking about thirty miles in a typical day, in search of what he calls "events"—surprising a buck, or a gray fox, or perhaps a poacher or a man with a still. Almost no one who is not native to the pines could do this, for the woods have an undulating sameness, and the understory—huckleberries, sheep laurel, sweet fern, high-bush blueberry—is often so dense that a wanderer can walk in a fairly tight circle and think that he is moving in a straight line. State forest rangers spend a good part of their time finding hikers and hunters, some of whom have vanished for days. In his long, pathless journeys, Bill always emerges from the woods near his cabin—and about when he plans to. In the fall, when thousands of hunters come into the pines, he sometimes works as a guide. In the evenings, or in the daytime when he is not working or roaming, he goes to Fred Brown's house and sits there for hours. The old man is a widower whose seven children are long since gone from Hog Wallow, and he is as expansively talkative and worldly as the young one is withdrawn and wild. Although there are fifty-three years between their ages, it is obviously fortunate for each of them to be the other's neighbor.

That first morning, while Bill went on looking at his outstretched toes, Fred got up from the table, put on his pants, and said he was going to cook me a pork chop, because I looked hungry and ought to eat something. It was about noon, and I was even hungrier than I may have looked, so I gratefully accepted his offer, which was a considerable one. There are two or three small general stores in the pines, but for anything as fragile as a fresh pork chop it is necessary to make a round trip from Fred's place of about fifty miles. Fred went into the kitchen and dropped a chop into a frying pan that was crackling with hot grease. He has a fairly new four-burner stove that uses bottled gas. He keeps water in a large bowl on a table in the kitchen and ladles some when he wants it. While he cooked the meat, he looked out a window through a stand of pitch pines and into the cranberry bog. "I saw a big buck out here last night with velvet on his horns," he said. "Them horns is soft when they're in velvet." On a nail high on one wall of the room that Bill and I were sitting in was a large meat cleaver. Next to it was a billy club. The wall itself was papered in a flower pattern, and the wallpaper continued out across the ceiling and down the three other walls, lending the room something of the appearance of the inside of a gift box. In some parts of the ceiling, the paper had come loose. "I didn't paper this year," Fred said. "For the last couple months, I've had sinus." The floor was covered with old rugs. They had been put down in random pieces, and in some places as many as six layers were stacked up. In winter, when the temperature approaches zero, the worst cold comes through the floor. The only source of heat in the house is a wood-burning stove in the main room. There were seven calendars on the walls, all current and none with pictures of nudes. Fading into pastel on one wall was a rotogravure photograph of President and Mrs. Eisenhower. A framed poem read:

> God hath not promised
> Sun without rain
> Joy without sorrow
> Peace without pain.

Noticing my interest in all this, Fred reached into a drawer and showed me what appeared to be a postcard. On it was a photograph of a woman, and Fred said with a straight face that she was his present girl, adding that he meets her regularly under a juniper tree on a road farther south in the pines. The woman, whose

---

1. The narrator is attracted to Fred Brown's house by the pump that stands amid the clutter in Fred's yard. The paradox of "God's water" being provided by means of a mechanical device reflects the struggle between nature and civilization embodied in this story. The pump, however, is only one of the tokens of civilization in Fred's yard that reflect the persistent intrusion of the modern world into the tranquility of the forest. Like the pump, Fred is a paradox, continually seduced by the mechanisms that will eventually destroy the unique lifestyle he cherishes.

2. The symbiotic relationship that appears to exist between Fred and Bill makes the fact that the two men are "each other's neighbors" indeed a "fortunate coincidence." In a friendship based on mutual acceptance and respect, the most obvious needs met by the relationship are that of the gregarious elderly man's desire for companionship in his old age and the youth's craving for acceptance after his early abandonment by both parents. On another level, however, the pair represents various tensions that exist throughout the Pine Barrens: the pull of change versus continuity, civilization versus wilderness, the new versus the old. Together they form a balance that helps them survive.

3. The interior of Fred's house, though weathered and worn, provides a curious monument to comfort and convenience in the midst of his primitive surroundings. As the narrator passes through the "vestibule that had a dirt floor" (para. 2), his attention is arrested by the "overstuffed chairs" (para. 2). McPhee focuses upon Fred's pride in his modern conveniences, not only in the machines and appliances in and around the house, but particularly in the "seven calendars on the walls, all current and none with pictures of nudes" (para. 4) as well as the "rotogravure photograph of President and Mrs. Eisenhower" (para. 4). Although he must be aware of the threat to his way of life posed by the intrusion of civilization, he accepts this inevitability as he accepts everything else in life, his philosophy being best expressed by the framed poem that hangs on the flowered wall of the kitchen: "God hath not promised / Sun without rain / Joy without sorrow / Peace without pain" (para. 4).

ANSWERS TO QUESTIONS: ANALYZING MEANING (p. 61)

1. The narrator explains to Fred that he is hiking through "the pines" because he "found it hard to believe that so much unbroken forest could still exist so near the big Eastern cities" (para. 9) and because he "wanted to see it while it was still there" (para. 9). The narrator views the pines as someone would a relic that is soon to be destroyed. His respect for the way of life in the pines is obvious through his descriptions of Bill's ability to journey through the pines and Fred's easygoing mannerisms that the narrator seems to admire. The narrator also values the idea that the land and water belong to God and that Fred and Bill respect and appreciate the land and water rather than attempting to own or control it.

2. To Bill, these woods represent a special kind of freedom. The society of the pines is such that he is able to wander or stay home, to speak or remain silent, and to accept only the trappings of civilization that he chooses. With the opening of a jetport in the area, not only would much of the forest be destroyed, but a new society would intrude upon the serenity of the pines, bringing with it the regulations and restrictions that accompany any such influx of people. Bill views the narrator as an outsider. Though the narrator perceives him as shy, Bill's refusal to speak shows his passive resistance to the changes he sees coming to the pines. To Bill, the narrator represents the society that is trying to modernize the pines; his avoidance of speaking directly to the narrator helps him get a feeling of control in a situation that has been thrust upon him—much like the change that was forced on him when his parents deserted him.

3. The references to God in this essay express the spirituality and harmony embodied in the pines, which have a significance far exceeding that of the city; though people can create cities, they cannot create forests in perfect balance and harmony with the other parts of the universe. The conver-

appearance suggested strongly that she had never been within a great many miles of the Pine Barrens, was wearing nothing at all.

I asked Fred what all those cars were doing in his yard, and he said that one of them was in running condition and the rest were its predecessors. The working vehicle was a 1956 Mercury. Each of the seven others had at one time or another been his best car, and each, in turn, had lain down like a sick animal and had died right there in the yard, unless it had been towed home after a mishap elsewhere in the pines. Fred recited, with affection, the history of each car. Of one old Ford, for example, he said, "I upset that up to Speedwell in the creek." And of an even older car, a station wagon, he said, "I busted that one up in the snow. I met a car on a little hill, and hit the brake, and hit a tree." One of the cars had met its end at a narrow bridge about four miles from Hog Wallow, where Fred had hit a state trooper, head on.   6

The pork was delicious and almost crisp. Fred gave me a potato with it, and a pitcher of melted grease from the frying pan to pour over the potato. He also handed me a loaf of bread and a dish of margarine, saying, "Here's your bread. You can have one piece or two. Whatever you want."   7

Fred apologized for not having a phone, after I asked where I would have to go to make a call, later on. He said, "I don't have no phone because I don't have no electric. If I had electric, I would have had a phone in here a long time ago." He uses a kerosene lamp, a propane lamp, and two flashlights.   8

He asked where I was going, and I said that I had no particular destination, explaining that I was in the pines because I found it hard to believe that so much unbroken forest could still exist so near the big Eastern cities, and I wanted to see it while it was still there. "Is that so?" he said, three times. Like many people in the pines, he often says things three times. "Is that so? Is *that* so?"   9

I asked him what he thought of a plan that has been developed by Burlington and Ocean Counties to create a supersonic jetport in the pines, connected by a spur of the Garden State Parkway to a new city of two hundred and fifty thousand people, also in the pines.   10

"They've been talking about that for three years, and they've never given up," Fred said.   11

"It'd be the end of these woods," Bill said. This was the first time I heard Bill speak. I had been there for an hour, and he had not said a word. Without looking up, he said again, "It'd be the end of these woods, I can tell you that."   12

Fred said, "They could build ten jetports around me. I wouldn't give a damn."

"You ain't going to be around very long," Bill said to him. "It would be the end of these woods."

Fred took that as a fact, and not as an insult. "Yes, it would be the end of these woods," he said. "But there'd be people here you could do business with."

Bill said, "There ain't no place like this left in the country, I don't believe—and I travelled around a little bit, too."

Eventually, I made the request I had intended to make when I walked in the door. "Could I have some water?" I said to Fred. "I have a jerry can and I'd like to fill it at the pump."

"Hell, yes," he said. "That isn't my water. That's God's water. That's God's water. That right, Bill?"

"I *guess* so," Bill said, without looking up. "It's good water, I can tell you that."

"That's God's water," Fred said again. "Take all you want."

UNDERSTANDING DETAILS

1. What attracted McPhee to Fred Brown's house? In what ways is this object representative of Fred's yard? Of Fred's life?
2. In paragraph 3, McPhee comments that, despite the wide difference in age between Fred and Bill, "it is obviously fortunate for each of them to be the other's neighbor." In what ways do the two characters need each other?
3. Describe in your own words the inside of Fred's house. Which details does McPhee stress in his description? Why does he focus on these and not on others?

ANALYZING MEANING

1. Why is McPhee visiting "the pines"? What do you think his opinion of "the pines" is? What specific references reveal his opinions?
2. Why does Bill believe a jetport would be "the end of these woods" (paragraph 12)? Why do you think these were the first words Bill spoke since the author arrived? Explain your answer.
3. Why do you think McPhee ends this piece with several references to God? How does the dialogue about "God's water" help us understand Fred and Bill even more specifically?

sation between Fred and Bill illustrates the harmonious relationship they have achieved with nature. In their belief, God owns not only the land and water but all of the pines, because he made them. To destroy the pines would be equivalent to destroying something that belongs only to God.

ANSWERS TO QUESTIONS:
DISCOVERING RHETORICAL
STRATEGIES (p. 62)

1. The author uses a variety of sensual details in recreating Fred's house, concentrating primarily on visual description. In an analysis of paragraph 2, a partial response might include the following:

Sight	overstuffed chairs
	porcelain-topped table
	white sleeveless shirt
Sound	cheerful greeting
	explaining
Taste	eating a pork chop
	raw onion

For some readers, however, certain phrases might stimulate more than one sensual response, such as the pungent smell of a raw onion as well as its sharp taste, or the sight and sound of a pork chop sizzling in a hot frying pan.

2. A sense of foreboding pervades the essay, a mood created initially by the incongruence of Fred's accumulation of automobiles, calendars, and overstuffed chairs in the natural environment of the forest. This mood is affirmed and intensified in the final paragraphs of the essay by his open apprehensiveness about the intrusion of a jetport into the pines.

3. Although the essay is written in the first person, the narrator's point of view is objective (impartial, emotionless; see page 34), revealing the scene before him as through the lens of a camera. Neither Fred nor Bill could have presented his story as effectively as an outside narrator does: Fred's obsession with all things modern would have distorted his perceptions, and Bill's story would have been colored by his fears about the future of the Pine Barrens. In presenting the description from an objective viewpoint, McPhee allows the readers to draw their own conclusions, giving greater legitimacy to any sympathy aroused in the reader.

In preparation for the writing assignments, the Preparing to Write questions ask students to begin to analyze the character types they have been observing and reading about and the places where these people live. See pages 16–23 for suggestions on generating ideas in response to these questions.

ADDITIONAL DISCUSSION/WRITING TOPIC

Write an essay describing your best friend for your classmates so that they feel as if they know this person. Pay special attention to your choice of details and to the effect these details create.

REVISING STRATEGY

A clear, carefully controlled point on view is vital to a well-written descriptive essay. In one of your descriptive essays, underline all the pronouns and take a few minutes to notice the pattern of these references. Locate any inconsistencies (for example, an unwarranted shift from "I" to "he" or "she"); then revise your essay, paying close attention to your vantage point (relation-ship with your subject) and your mood (attitude) throughout the essay. See the Glossary if you need more thorough definitions for any of these rhetorical terms.

DISCOVERING RHETORICAL STRATEGIES

1. Which senses does McPhee concentrate on most in this description? Choose one paragraph to analyze. In one column, write down all the senses the description arouses; in another, record the words and phrases that activate these senses.
2. What "tone" or "mood" is McPhee trying to create in this excerpt? Is he successful? Explain your answer.
3. What is the author's "point of view" in this essay? How would the method of description change if the story were told from Fred's vantage point? From Bill's? How does this particular point of view help the author organize his description?

IDEAS FOR DISCUSSION/WRITING

Preparing to Write

Write freely about someone you know who represents a specific personality "type": What distinguishes this type from other types you know? What do people of this type have in common? What are their looks, values, needs, desires, living conditions, and so on? What do you have in common with the type of person you have just described? How are you different?

Choosing a Topic

1. Give a name (either real or fictitious) to the person you have just described in the prewriting exercise, and write an essay depicting the house, apartment, or room in which this person lives. Try to make your description as vivid and as well organized as McPhee's portrait of Fred Brown. Imagine that the audience for your description is someone who has never met this person and has never seen where the person lives.
2. Write an essay describing for your classmates some of the "junk" you have collected over the years. Why are certain items junk to some people and treasures to others? What makes the things you are describing special to you?
3. Describe the inside of your house, apartment, or room, explaining to your class what the decorations say about you as a person. If someone in your class were to see where you live, could he or she make any accurate deductions about your political, social, or moral values based upon the contents and arrangement of the place you call "home"?

KIMBERLY WOZENCRAFT
(1954–   )

■ ■ ■

Notes from the Country Club

Kimberly Wozencraft grew up in Dallas, Texas, and dropped out of college when she was twenty-one to become a police officer. Her first assignment, prior to training at the police academy, was a street-level undercover narcotics investigation. Like many narcotics agents, Wozencraft became addicted to drugs, which impaired her judgment and resulted in a 1981 conviction for violating the civil rights of a reputed child pornographer. After serving an eighteen-month sentence in the Federal Correctional Institution at Lexington, Kentucky, she moved to New York City, where she has lived since her release. She holds a Master of Fine Arts degree from Columbia University, and her essays, poems, and short stories have appeared in a variety of magazines, including *Northwest Review, Quarto, Big Wednesday,* and *Witness*. Her first novel, *Rush*, was made into a movie in 1992.

Preparing to Read

Originally published in *Witness*, "Notes from the Country Club" was selected for inclusion in *The Best American Essays of 1988*, edited by Annie Dillard. Through carefully constructed prose, the author describes her prison environment and the anxiety caused by living for more than a year in such an alien, difficult place. As you prepare to read this essay, take a moment to think about your own behavior in difficult situations: What kind of person do you become? How do you act toward other people? How is this behavior different from the way you usually act? How do you know when you're in a difficult situation? What do you generally do to relieve the tension?

QUOTATION ON THINKING

"Beneath the content of every message is intent. And form embodies that intent. Intuitively or not, an author chooses his techniques according to his meaning."

James Moffett

PREREADING

The purpose of this Preparing to Read material is to get students to write freely about their behavior in difficult situations. To help your students focus their attention before they respond to the questions here, have them discuss as a class various sets of circumstances that could be classified as "difficult." Then, you might have them discuss in pairs their individual reactions to such problems. See page 3–6 for other ways to generate thoughts on these questions.

The ironically titled "Notes from the Country Club" describes Kimberly Wozencraft's vivid experience as an inmate in a minimum-security prison in Lexington, Kentucky. After providing her readers with a geographic tour of the facility, the author challenges the notion that prison life rehabilitates criminals. She concludes with some important observations about America's drug laws and its criminal justice system.

READABILITY LEVEL

10.4

RELATED READINGS

Crime

Societal Problems

DEFINITIONS

concertina wire (para. 1): coiled barbed wire used as an obstacle.
AIDS (para. 1): the acronym for Acquired Immune Deficiency Syndrome, a lack of cells that reject foreign tissue in the human immune system, resulting in infection, cancer, and nervous-system degeneration.
Cabernet Sauvignon (para. 11): a fine red wine made from a single variety of grape; usually very expensive.
goyim (para. 13): Yiddish. Plural for "goy," meaning Gentile or non-Jew.
alter kokers (para. 13): Yiddish. Plural for an elderly but active old man, usually one who is stubborn or shrewd.

They had the Haitians up the hill, in the "camp" section where they used to keep the minimum security cases. The authorities were concerned that some of the Haitians might be diseased, so they kept them isolated from the main coed prison population by lodging them in the big square brick building surrounded by eight-foot chain-link with concertina wire on top. We were not yet familiar with the acronym AIDS.

One or two of the Haitians had drums, and in the evenings when the rest of us were in the Big Yard, the drum rhythms carried over the bluegrass to where we were playing gin or tennis or softball or just hanging out waiting for dark. When they really got going some of them would dance and sing. Their music was rhythmic and beautiful, and it made me think of freedom.

There were Cubans loose in the population, spattering their guttural Spanish in streams around the rectangular courtyard, called Central Park, at the center of the prison compound. These were Castro's Boat People, guilty of no crime in this country, but requiring sponsors before they could walk the streets as free people.

Walking around the perimeter of Central Park was like taking a trip in microcosm across the United States. Moving leftward from the main entrance, strolling along under the archway that covers the wide sidewalk, you passed the doorway to the Women's Unit, where I lived, and it was how I imagined Harlem to be. There was a white face here and there, but by far most of them were black. Ghetto blasters thunked out rhythms in the sticky evening air, and folks leaned against the window sills, smoking, drinking Cokes, slinking and nodding. Every once in a while a joint was passed around, and always there was somebody pinning, checking for hacks on patrol.

Past Women's Unit was the metal door to the Big Yard, the main recreation area of three or four acres, two sides blocked by the building, two sides fenced in the usual way—chain-link and concertina wire.

Past the Big Yard you entered the Blue Ridge Mountains, a sloping grassy area on the edge of Central Park, where the locals, people from Kentucky, Tennessee, and the surrounding environs, sat around playing guitars and singing, and every once in a while passing around a quart of hooch. They make it from grapefruit juice and a bit of yeast smuggled out of the kitchen. Some of the inmates who worked in Cable would bring out pieces of a black foam rubber substance and wrap it around empty Cremora jars to make thermos jugs of sorts. They would mix the grapefruit juice and yeast in the containers and stash them in some out-of-the-way spot for a few weeks until presto! you had hooch, bitter and tart and sweet all at once, only mildly alcoholic, but entirely suitable for evening cocktails in Central Park.

Next, at the corner, was the Commissary, a tiny store tucked inside the entrance to Veritas, the second women's unit. It wasn't much more than a few shelves behind a wall of Plexiglas, with a constant line of inmates spilling out of the doorway. They sold packaged chips, cookies, pens and writing paper, toiletries, some fresh fruit, and the ever-popular ice cream, sold only in pints. You had to eat the entire pint as soon as you bought it, or else watch it melt, because there weren't any refrigerators. Inmates were assigned one shopping night per week, allowed to buy no more than seventy-five dollars' worth of goods per month, and were permitted to pick up a ten-dollar roll of quarters if they had enough money in their prison account. Quarters were the basic spending unit in the prison; possession of paper money was a shippable offense. There were vending machines stocked with junk food and soda, and they were supposedly what the quarters were to be used for. But we gambled, we bought salami or fried chicken sneaked out by the food service workers, and of course people sold booze and drugs. The beggars stood just outside the Commissary door. Mostly they were Cubans, saying "Oyez! Mira! Mira! Hey, Poppy, one quarter for me. One cigarette for me, Poppy?"

There was one Cuban whom I was specially fond of. His name was Shorty. The name said it, he was only about five-two, and he looked just like Mick Jagger. I met him in Segregation, an isolated section of tiny cells where prisoners were locked up for having violated some institutional rule or another. They tossed me in there the day I arrived; again the authorities were concerned, supposedly for my safety. I was a police woman before I became a convict, and they weren't too sure that the other inmates would like that. Shorty saved me a lot of grief when I went into Seg. It didn't matter if you were male or female there, you got stripped and handed a tee shirt, a pair of boxer shorts and a set of Peter Pans—green canvas shoes with thin rubber soles designed to prevent you from running away. As if you could get past three steel doors and a couple of hacks just to start with. When I was marched down the hall between the cells the guys started whistling and hooting and they didn't shut up even after I was locked down. They kept right on screaming until finally I yelled out, "Yo no comprendo!" and they all moaned and said,

shabot shiksa (para. 13): Yiddish. A Gentile woman who performs duties during the Jewish Sabbath (sunset Friday to sunset Saturday) for Jews who observe the custom that forbids work during this period.

ludes (para. 14): slang for quaalude, a drug used as a sedative.

7 **"Borracho Me Acosté a Noche"** (para. 15): a popular song in Spanish ("I Went to Bed Drunk Last Night").

op-ed page (para. 20): the opinion and editorial page of a newspaper.

oxymoron (para. 28): a combination of contradictory or incongruous words (e.g., jumbo shrimp).

8

Have your class pool their knowledge of prisons by sharing what they know about prison life. Direct or indirect experience, observation, and hearsay might produce different parts of the puzzle.

"Another . . . Cuban," and finally got quiet. Shorty was directly across from me, I could see his eyes through the rectangular slot in my cell door. He rattled off a paragraph or two of Spanish, all of which was lost on me, and I said quietly, "Yo no comprendo bien español. Yo soy de Texas, yo hablo inglés?" I could tell he was smiling by the squint of his eyes, and he just said, "Bueno." When the hacks came around to take us out for our mandatory hour of recreation, which consisted of standing around in the Rec area while two guys shot a game of pool on the balcony above the gym, Shorty slipped his hand into mine and smiled up at me until the hack told him to cut it out. He knew enough English to tell the others in Seg that I was not really Spanish, but he kept quiet about it, and they left me alone.

Beyond the Commissary, near the door to the dining hall, was 9 East St. Louis. The prison had a big portable stereo system which they rolled out a few times a week so that an inmate could play at being a disc jockey. They had a good-sized collection of albums and there was usually some decent jazz blasting out of there. Sometimes people danced, unless there were uptight hacks on duty to tell them not to.

California was next. It was a laid back kind of corner near the 10 doors to two of the men's units. People stood around and smoked hash or grass or did whatever drugs happened to be available and there was sometimes a sort of slow-motion game of handball going on. If you wanted drugs, this was the place to come.

If you kept walking, you would arrive at the Power Station, 11 the other southern corner where the politicos-gone-wrong congregated. It might seem odd at first to see these middle-aged government mavens standing around in their Lacoste sport shirts and Sans-a-belt slacks, smoking pipes or cigars and waving their arms to emphasize some point or other. They kept pretty much to themselves and ate together at the big round tables in the cafeteria, sipping cherry Kool-Aid and pretending it was Cabernet Sauvignon.

That's something else you had to deal with—the food. It was 12 worse than elementary school steam table fare. By the time they finished cooking it, it was tasteless, colorless, and nutritionless. The first meal I took in the dining room was lunch. As I walked toward the entry, a tubby fellow was walking out, staggering really, rolling his eyes as though he were dizzy. He stopped and leaned over, and I heard someone yell, "Watch out, he's gonna puke!" I ducked inside so as to miss the spectacle. They were serving some rubbery, faint pink slabs that were supposed to be ham, but I didn't even bother to taste mine. I just slapped at it a few times to watch the fork bounce off and then ate my potatoes and went back to the unit.

Shortly after that I claimed that I was Jewish, having gotten the word from a friendly New York lawyer who was in for faking some of his clients' immigration papers. The kosher line was the only way to get a decent meal in there. In fact, for a long time they had a Jewish baker from Philadelphia locked up, and he made some truly delicious cream puffs for dessert. They sold for seventy-five cents on the black market, but once I had established myself in the Jewish community I got them as part of my regular fare. They fed us a great deal of peanut butter on the kosher line; every time the "goyim" got meat, we got peanut butter, but that was all right with me. Eventually I was asked to light the candles at the Friday evening services, since none of the real Jewish women bothered to attend. I have to admit that most of the members of our little prison congregation were genuine *alter kokers*, but some of them were amusing. And I enjoyed learning first hand about Judaism. The services were usually very quiet, and the music, the ancient intoning songs, fortified me against the screeching pop-rock vocal assaults that were a constant in the Women's Unit. I learned to think of myself as the *shabot shiksa*, and before my time was up, even the rabbi seemed to accept me.

I suppose it was quite natural that the Italians assembled just "down the street" from the offending ex-senators, judges, and power brokers. Just to the left of the main entrance. The first night I made the tour, a guy came out of the shadows near the building and whispered to me. "What do you need, sweetheart? What do you want, I can get it. My friend Ahmad over there, he's very rich, and he wants to buy you things. What'll it be, you want some smoke, a few ludes, vodka, cigarettes, maybe some kosher salami fresh from the kitchen? What would you like?" I just stared at him. The only thing I wanted at that moment was out, and even Ahmad's millions, if they existed at all, couldn't do that. The truth is, every guy I met in there claimed to be wealthy, to have been locked up for some major financial crime. Had I taken all of them up on their offers of limousines to pick me up at the front gate when I was released and take me to the airport for a ride home in a private Lear jet, I would have needed my own personal cop out front just to direct traffic.

Ahmad's Italian promoter eventually got popped for zinging the cooking teacher one afternoon on the counter in the home economics classroom, right next to the new Cuisinart. The assistant

13

14

15

COLLABORATIVE LEARNING: SMALL GROUP ACTIVITY

Divide your class into ten groups—one for each part of Lexington prison that Wozencraft describes in detail: "camp" section, Central Park, Women's Unit, Big Yard, Blue Ridge Mountains, Veritas, Segregation, East St. Louis, California, and the Power Station. Have each group draw a different part of the prison. Groups should feel free to put characters and scenery in their pictures. Then, have one person from each group explain the picture to the class.

warden walked in on the young lovebirds, and before the week
was up, even the Cubans were walking around singing about it.
They had a whole song down, to the tune of "Borracho Me Acosté
a Noche."

At the end of the tour, you would find the jaded New   16
Yorkers, sitting at a picnic table or two in the middle of the park,
playing gin or poker and bragging about their days on Madison
Avenue and Wall Street, lamenting the scarcity of good deli, even
on the kosher line, and planning where they would take their first
real meal upon release.

If you think federal correctional institutions are about the   17
business of rehabilitation, drop by for an orientation session one
day. There at the front of the classroom, confronting rows of
mostly black faces, will be the warden, or the assistant warden, or
the prison shrink, pacing back and forth in front of the blackboard and asking the class, "Why do you think you're here?" This
gets a general grumble, a few short, choked laughs. Some well-
meaning soul always says it—rehabilitation.

"Nonsense!" the lecturer will say. "There are several reasons   18
for locking people up. Number one is incapacitation. If you're in
here, you can't be out there doing crime. Secondly, there is deter-
rence. Other people who are thinking about doing crime see that
we lock people up for it and maybe they think twice. But the real
reason you are here is to be punished. Plain and simple. You done
wrong, now you got to pay for it. Rehabilitation ain't even part of
the picture. So don't be looking to us to rehabilitate you. Only
person can rehabilitate you is you. If you feel like it, go for it, but
leave us out. We don't want to play that game."

So that's it. You're there to do time. I have no misgivings   19
about why I went to prison. I deserved it. I was a cop, I got strung
out on cocaine, I violated the rights of a pornographer. My own
drug use as an undercover narcotics agent was a significant factor
in my crime. But I did it and I deserved to be punished. Most of
the people I met in Lexington, though, were in for drugs, and the
majority of them hadn't done anything more than sell an ounce of
cocaine or a pound of pot to some apostle of the law.

It seems lately that almost every time I look at the *New York*   20
Times op-ed page, there is something about the drug problem. I
have arrested people for drugs, and I have had a drug problem
myself. I have seen how at least one federal correctional institution functions. It does not appear that the practice of locking people up for possession or distribution of an insignificant quantity
of a controlled substance makes any difference at all in the

amount of drug use that occurs in the United States. The drug laws are merely another convenient source of political rhetoric for aspiring officeholders. Politicians know that an antidrug stance is an easy way to get votes from parents who are terrified that their children might wind up as addicts. I do not advocate drug use. Yet, having seen the criminal justice system from several angles, as a police officer, a court bailiff, a defendant, and a prisoner, I am convinced that prison is not the answer to the drug problem, or for that matter to many other white-collar crimes. If the taxpayers knew how their dollars were being spent inside some prisons, they might actually scream out loud.

There were roughly 1,800 men and women locked up in Lex,   21
at a ratio of approximately three men to every woman, and it did get warm in the summertime. To keep us tranquil they devised some rather peculiar little amusements. One evening I heard a commotion on the steps at the edge of Central Park and looked over to see a rec specialist with three big cardboard boxes set up on the plaza, marked 1, 2, and 3. There were a couple of hundred inmates sitting at the bottom of the steps. Dennis, the rec specialist, was conducting his own version of the television game show *Let's Make a Deal!* Under one of the boxes was a case of soda, under another was a racquetball glove, and under a third was a fly swatter. The captive contestant picked door number 2, which turned out to contain the fly swatter, to my way of thinking the best prize there. Fly swatters were virtually impossible to get through approved channels, and therefore cost as much as two packs of cigarettes on the black market.

Then there was the Annual Fashion Show, where ten or   22
twenty inmates had special packages of clothing sent in, only for the one evening, and modeled them on stage while the baddest drag queen in the compound moderated and everyone else ooohed and aahhed. They looked good up there on stage in Christian Dior and Ralph Lauren instead of the usual fatigue pants and white tee shirts. And if such activities did little to prepare inmates for a productive return to society, well, at least they contributed to the fantasyland aura that made Lexington such an unusual place.

I worked in Landscape, exiting the rear gate of the compound   23
each weekday morning at about nine after getting a half-hearted frisk from one of the hacks on duty. I would climb on my tractor to drive to the staff apartment complex and pull weeds or mow the lawn. Landscape had its prerogatives. We raided the gardens regularly and at least got to taste fresh vegetables from time to

1.

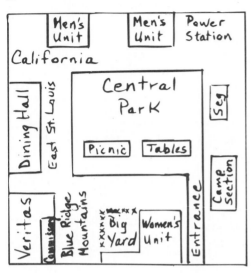

Wozencraft begins her tour of the prison with a view of the "camp" section, an area made up of Haitians who have been segregated from the rest of the population because of suspected disease; these Haitians are housed in a brick building surrounded by an 8-foot fence. In the middle of the complex is Central Park, made up mostly of Castro's Boat People, who require sponsors before they can be released. Next to the entrance is the Women's Unit, the building Wozencraft lives in; this facility seems to be filled with music and drugs. Clockwise, the Big Yard, a three-to-four-acre recreation site for the inmates, follows. This site is fenced on two sides and blocked in by buildings on the other two, presumably for greater security. Just above the Big Yard is the Blue Ridge Mountains, a grassy place where the Kentucky and Tennessee natives spend time making music. Veritas, a second women's unit, follows the Blue Ridge area and contains the Commissary near its entrance. This store sells many of the comforts nonprisoners enjoy, such as chips, cookies, and ice cream, and is populated by a group of beggars who plead with other inmates to give them change. Continuing the tour from this corner of the prison, Wozencraft does

time. I had never eaten raw corn before, but it could not have tasted better. We also brought in a goodly supply of real vodka, and a bit of hash now and then, for parties in our rooms after lights out. One guy strapped a six-pack of Budweiser to his arms with masking tape and then put on his prison-issue Army field jacket. When he got to the rear gate, he raised his arms straight out at shoulder level, per instructions, and the hack patted down his torso and legs, never bothering to check his arms. The inmate had been counting on that. He smiled at the hack and walked back to his room, a six-pack richer.

I was fortunate to be working Landscape at the same time as Horace, a fellow who had actually lived in the city of Lexington before he was locked up. His friends made regular deliveries of assorted contraband, which they would stash near a huge elm tree near the outer stone fence of the reservation. Horace would drive his tractor over, make the pickup, and the rest of us would carry it, concealed, through the back gate when we went back inside for lunch or at the end of the day. "Contraband" included everything from drugs to blue eye shadow. The assistant warden believed that female inmates should wear no cosmetics other than what she herself used—a bit of mascara and a light shade of lipstick. I have never been a plaything of Fashion, but I did what I could to help the other women prisoners in their never-ending quest for that Cover Girl look.   24

You could depend on the fact that most of the hacks would rather have been somewhere else, and most of them really didn't care *what* the inmates did, as long as it didn't cause any commotion. Of course, there were a few you had to look out for. The captain in charge of security was one of them. We tried a little experiment once, after having observed that any time he saw someone laughing, he took immediate steps to make the inmate and everyone around him acutely miserable. Whenever we saw him in the area, we immediately assumed expressions of intense unhappiness, even of despair. Seeing no chance to make anyone more miserable than they already appeared to be, the captain left us alone.   25

Almost all of the female hacks, and a good number of the males, had outrageously large derrières, a condition we inmates referred to as "the federal ass." This condition may have resulted from the fact that most of them appeared, as one inmate succinctly described it, simply to be "putting in their forty a week to stay on the government teat." Employment was not an easy thing to find in Kentucky.   26

Despite the fact that Lexington is known as a "country club" prison, I must admit that I counted days. From the first moment that I was in, I kept track of how many more times I would have to watch the sun sink behind eight feet of chain-link, of how many more days I would have to spend eating, working, playing and sleeping according to the dictates of a "higher authority." I don't think I can claim that I was rehabilitated. If anything I underwent a process of dehabilitation. What I learned was what Jessica Mitford tried to tell people many years ago in her book *Kind and Usual Punishment*. Prison is a business, no different from manufacturing tires or selling real estate. It keeps people employed and it provides cheap labor for NASA, the U.S. Postal Service, and other governmental or quasi-governmental agencies. For a short time, before I was employed in Landscape, I worked as a finisher of canvas mailbags, lacing white rope through metal eyelets around the top of the bags and attaching clamps to the ropes. I made one dollar and fourteen cents for every one hundred that I did. If I worked very hard, I could do almost two hundred a day.

It's not about justice. If you think it's about justice, look at the newspapers and notice who walks. Not the little guys, the guys doing a tiny bit of dealing, or sniggling a little on their income tax, or the woman who pulls a stunt with welfare checks because her husband has skipped out and she has no other way to feed her kids. I do not say that these things are right. But the process of selective prosecution, the "making" of cases by D.A.s and police departments, and the presence of some largely unenforceable statutes currently on the books (it is the reality of "compliance": no law can be forced on a public which chooses to ignore it, hence, selective prosecution) make for a criminal justice system which cannot realistically function in a fair and equitable manner. Criminal justice—I cannot decide if it is the ultimate oxymoron or a truly accurate description of the law enforcement process in America.

In my police undercover capacity, I have sat across the table from an armed robber who said, "My philosophy of life is slit thy neighbor's throat and pimp his kids." I believe that the human animals who maim and kill people should be dealt with, as they say, swiftly and surely. But this business of locking people up, at enormous cost, for minor, nonviolent offenses does not truly or effectively serve the interest of the people. It serves only to promote the wasteful aspects of the federal prison system, a system that gulps down tax dollars and spews up *Let's Make a Deal!*

not give the exact location of Segregation, the block of isolation cells, but suggests its placement by the order of her description. 27 East St. Louis, an entertainment center where inmates can dance and "play" at being disc jockeys, is just outside the doors of the dining hall. In the next corner is California, so named for its drug trade and relaxed atmosphere. Finally, after passing two men's units, which Wozencraft does not describe in any detail, she ends the tour with the Power Station, a corner where those accused of political crimes wear very expensive clothing and avoid other inmates.

2. The author liked Shorty because he protected her from the other male inmates and did not divulge the fact that she was not Cuban and could not speak Spanish. She appreciated him even more because he held her hand and became someone she could trust at a time when, more than anything, she needed that security.

3. The author openly admits she committed a crime by violating the rights of a 28 pornographer. She also confesses that her mistake was partly the result of a drug dependency she developed while working as a narcotics officer.

ANSWERS TO QUESTIONS: ANALYZING MEANING (p. 73)

1. One characteristic of Wozencraft's relationships with the inmates is her lack of prejudice or judgment. The author does not criticize inmates because of their crimes, their religious affiliations, or their illegal activities while in prison; in fact, she accepts them without questions because she wants neither to condemn herself through association with them nor to invite their scorn and anger. Treating other inmates with respect 29 allows the author to establish a rapport with them, an equal relationship based on her acceptance of the prisoners and participation in the criticism of the prison employees whom she deceived much as the other inmates did. Thus Wozencraft had many types of relationships within the prison— some based on honesty, some based on deception, but all of them based primarily on the need to survive.

2. The author cites many wastes that occur within the prison walls, but perhaps none is as important as the wasting of human lives. The prison system Wozencraft describes "gulps down tax dollars and spews up *Let's Make A Deal*" (para. 29). This is alarming not only because it wastes money on unnecessary and potentially harmful programs rather than productive ones, but also because it ignores both punishment and rehabilitation, two major issues within this essay.

One example of this waste, both of public funds and of human life, is apparent in the Annual Fashion Show, in which inmates model the clothes of great designers. This show wastes money, but, even worse, it wastes the minds of people who participate. Rather than preparing inmates to go out and face the real world upon their release, fashion shows create a "fantasyland aura" (para. 22) that does little good in rehabilitating the prisoners who participate in them.

3. Lexington is known as a "country club" prison because its inmates have committed primarily "white-collar" crimes. In addition, the rules within the prison are more lax than those of most other prisons; prisoners manage to take drugs, drink alcohol, and smuggle in forbidden goods without getting caught. Prisoners are also given the opportunity to participate in dances, games, and other enjoyable activities that create a "club" atmosphere.

**ANSWERS TO QUESTIONS:
DISCOVERING RHETORICAL
STRATEGIES (p. 73)**

1. The success of Wozencraft's essay depends on the reader's belief in her firsthand knowledge of the prison system. The prison jargon she uses adds to the authenticity of her essay by assuring the reader that she has had the experiences she writes about and that she understands prison from an inmate's perspective. Devoid of prison terminology, this essay would seem superficial and insincere instead of emotional and informative.

2. The ending Wozencraft provides is effective for two reasons. First, her acceptance of and compliance with this tradition reveal

I think about Lexington almost daily. I will be walking up 30 Broadway to shop for groceries, or maybe riding my bike in the original Central Park and suddenly I'm wondering who's in there now, at this very moment, and for what inane violations, and what they are doing. Is it chow time, is the Big Yard open, is some inmate on stage in the auditorium singing "As Time Goes By" in a talent show? It is not a fond reminiscence, or a desire to be back in the Land of No Decisions. It is an awareness of the waste. The waste of tax dollars, yes, but taxpayers are used to that. It is the unnecessary trashing of lives that leaves me uneasy. The splitting of families, the enforced monotony, the programs which purport to prepare an inmate for re-entry into society but which actually succeed only in occupying a few more hours of the inmate's time behind the walls. The nonviolent offenders, such as small-time drug dealers and the economically deprived who were driven to crime out of desperation, could remain in society under less costly supervision, still undergoing "punishment" for their crime, but at least contributing to rather than draining the resources of society.

Horace, who was not a subtle sort of fellow, had some tee 31 shirts made up. They were delivered by our usual supplier out in Landscape, and we wore them back in over our regular clothes. The hacks tilted their heads when they noticed, but said nothing. On the front of each shirt was an outline of the state of Kentucky, and above the northwest corner of the state were the words "Visit Beautiful Kentucky!" Inside the state boundary were:

- Free Accommodations
- Complimentary Meals
- Management Holds Calls
- Recreational Exercise

In small letters just outside the southwest corner of the state was: "Length of Stay Requirement." And in big letters across the bottom:

Take Time to Do Time
F.C.I. Lexington

I gave mine away on the day I finished my sentence. It is a 32 time-honored tradition to leave some of your belongings to friends who have to stay behind when you are released. But you must never leave shoes. Legend has it that if you do, you will come back to wear them again.

UNDERSTANDING DETAILS

1. Draw Lexington prison and put the names on the sections of the facility. Then, describe each section in your own words.
2. Why was Wozencraft especially fond of Shorty? What secret did they share at the beginning of the author's prison term?
3. Does the author feel she was unfairly punished by being sent to prison? What did she do wrong?

ANALYZING MEANING

1. What was Wozencraft's attitude toward other people in Lexington prison? Why do you think she felt this way? What types of relationships did she have with inmates and staff members?
2. Why does the author say "If the taxpayers knew how their dollars were being spent inside some prisons, they might actually scream out loud" (paragraph 20)? What exactly is she referring to? What is she implying? Give some examples.
3. Why do you think Lexington is known as a "country club" prison? What features of the prison might have brought about its nickname?

DISCOVERING RHETORICAL STRATEGIES

1. Wozencraft uses specific prison jargon throughout this essay. In what way does this jargon add to or detract from the essay? What effect would the essay have without this jargon?
2. Wozencraft ends her essay with an explanation of "a time-honored tradition." Is this an effective ending for the piece? Why or why not?
3. Though spatial description is the dominant rhetorical strategy the author uses in this essay to accomplish her purpose, what other strategies help make the essay effective? Give examples of these strategies.

IDEAS FOR DISCUSSION/WRITING

Preparing to Write

Write freely about your memories of a recent difficult or awkward situation in your life: What were the circumstances? What did you do? What did others do? How did you relate to others in this situation? Why was the situation so difficult? How did you get out of it?

an understanding and sincerity that lend credibility to the rest of her essay. Second, the tee shirt provides a lasting symbol of the prison system. The inmates' ability to sneak the tee shirts into the complex shows that the prison is lax in its enforcement of rules. The description of the prison on the tee shirt is accurate in questioning how money is being spent and whether or not the punishment in this prison is really effective. In fact, one of the main questions in the essay—do prisons rehabilitate inmates?—is answered through this tee shirt. The response is a resounding "no."

3. The author uses example, narration, and argument/persuasion, in addition to spatial description, to make her essay effective. This essay works on several levels: It is a description of Lexington prison supported by narration that tells the story of Wozencraft's stay at Lexington; various examples of the problems within the penal system convince her readers that prisons are just warehouses where society stores those it has no better way of dealing with. Narration helps the readers understand prison life because Wozencraft relates stories, such as the legend about leaving something behind, that help us identify with Wozencraft and with the situation she is in. Examples make Wozencraft's ideas about the penal system credible because in each case she illustrates her point with one or more specific references. Perhaps her most effective examples are the tee shirt and *Let's Make A Deal*, both of which symbolize the failure of the system. Finally, persuasion is especially evident in paragraph 18, which presents a lecturer who shows the meaninglessness of the typical prison term. Most people assume that a prison rehabilitates, yet this lecturer and the examples in this essay bring this assumption into serious doubt.

PREWRITING

In preparation for the writing assignments, the Preparing to Write questions ask your students to begin thinking analytically about an awkward situation in their lives. Ask them to focus on a single event from their own past before they begin writing on a related topic. See pages 16–23 for other suggestions on generating ideas in response to these questions.

Describe for your classmates a difficult situation you were in. How did you respond to this situation? How do you wish you had responded?

REVISING STRATEGY

The order in which you present material in an essay governs its overall effect. Choose one of your descriptive essays, and list all the details in the order they appear. Review this list along with your paper, and decide which details would be more effective in a different place in the essay. Then revise your paper, paying close attention to the flow of details from one point in the essay to another.

Choosing a Topic

1. Write an essay describing for your peers a difficult or awkward situation you have been in recently. Why was it awkward? Explain the specific circumstances so that your classmates can clearly imagine the setting and the difficulty or problem. Then, discuss your reaction to the situation.
2. A friend of yours has just been sentenced to prison for one year. Write a letter to this person describing what you think his or her biggest adjustments will be.
3. Wozencraft describes many problems within the prison system. With these problems in mind, write a letter to the editor of your local newspaper discussing whether prisons actually rehabilitate "criminals." Use examples from Wozencraft's essay to help make your point.

MALCOLM COWLEY
(1898–1989)

■ ■ ■

The View from 80

Malcolm Cowley had a long and distinguished career as a literary historian, critic, editor, and poet. After receiving his bachelor's degree at Harvard, he served in the American Ambulance Corps during World War I, then pursued graduate studies in literature at the University of Montpellier in France. In 1929, he became associate editor of *The New Republic*, presiding over the magazine's literary department for the next fifteen years. Perhaps his most important book of literary criticism is *Exile's Return* (1934), a study of the "lost generation" of expatriate Americans living in Paris in the 1920s, which included Hemingway, Pound, Fitzgerald, and Hart Crane. Cowley returned to the same topic in 1973 with *A Second Flowering: Works and Days of the Lost Generation.* He has also published editions of such authors as Hemingway, Faulkner, Hawthorne, Whitman, and Fitzgerald; two collections of his own poetry, *Blue Juniata* (1929) and *The Dry Season* (1941); and numerous other translations, editions, and books of criticism. Recent publications include *The Flower and the Leaf: A Contemporary Record of American Writing Since 1941* (1985) and *Conversations with Malcolm Cowley* (1986). Asked the secret of his amazing productivity, Cowley replied: "Writers often speak of 'saving their energy,' as if each man were given a nickel's worth of it, which he is at liberty to spend. To me, the mind of the poet resembles Fortunatus' purse: The more spent, the more it supplies."

Preparing to Read

The following essay was originally commissioned by *Life* magazine (1978) for inclusion in a series of articles on aging. Cowley later converted the piece into the first chapter of a book with the same title: *The View from 80* (1980). Through a combination of vivid personal experience and well-researched documentation, the author has crafted an essay that helps us experience what life is like for an eighty-year-old man. As you prepare to read Cowley's description of "the country of age," take some time to think about age in general: How many people over the age of sixty do you know? Over the age of seventy? How do

PREREADING

The purpose of this Preparing to Read material is to encourage students to explore their thoughts on age. They might begin by discussing as a class various facts, fears, and misconceptions we share about old age before they respond to the questions here. Then, you might try to enumerate the most striking differences between youth and old age. Before you begin, ask your students to identify the age at which someone becomes "old." See pages 3–6 for other ways to generate thoughts on these questions.

BACKGROUND INFORMATION

In "The View from 80," Malcolm Cowley takes the reader on a unique journey into the "unfamiliar country" of old age. With the use of colorful metaphors and striking examples, he presents a sympathetic picture of the frustrations of the elderly, the sadness that accompanies the surrender to one's infirmities, and the joy that comes from successfully meeting each new daily challenge.

READABILITY LEVEL

7.9

DEFINITIONS

bar mitzvah (para. 2): a Jewish ceremony celebrating the age of religious duty and responsibility (13 years).
rite de passage (para. 2): French. Rite of passage, ceremony, or ritual (often casual) marking a stage of development or maturity.
cantor (para. 2): a synagogue official who sings or chants music and leads the congregation in prayer.
snapper (para. 4): the punch line of a joke.
André Gide (1869–1951) (para. 9): a French novelist, critic, and essayist.
nirvana (para. 17): a state of oblivion achieved by detachment from external reality.
Renoir (para. 22): Pierre-Auguste Renoir (1841–1919), a French Impressionist painter.
Goya (para. 22): Francisco José de Goya (1746–1828), a prominent 18th-century Spanish painter.
Paul Claudel (1868–1955) (para. 23): a French diplomat, poet, and dramatist; associated with the symbolist school of poetry.

they behave? Do you think these older people see themselves in the same way you see them? Do you think they consider themselves "old"? What clues remind them of their advancing age? What events and attitudes remind you of your age? In what ways will you be different than you are now when you reach the age of eighty.

They gave me a party on my 80th birthday in August 1978. First there were cards, letters, telegrams, even a cable of congratulation or condolence; then there were gifts, mostly bottles; there was catered food and finally a big cake with, for some reason, two candles (had I gone back to very early childhood?). I blew the candles out a little unsteadily. Amid the applause and clatter I thought about a former custom of the Northern Ojibwas when they lived on the shores of Lake Winnipeg. They were kind to their old people, who remembered and enforced the ancient customs of the tribe, but when an old person became decrepit, it was time for him to go. Sometimes he was simply abandoned, with a little food, on an island in the lake. If he deserved special honor, they held a tribal feast for him. The old man sang a death song and danced, if he could. While he was still singing, his son came from behind and brained him with a tomahawk. 1

That was quick, it was dignified, and I wonder whether it was any more cruel, essentially, than some of our civilized customs or inadvertencies in disposing of the aged. I believe in rites and ceremonies. I believe in big parties for special occasions such as an 80th birthday. It is a sort of belated bar mitzvah, since the 80-year-old, like a Jewish adolescent, is entering a new stage of life; let him (or her) undergo a *rite de passage*, with toasts and a cantor. Seventy-year-olds, or septuas, have the illusion of being middle-aged, even if they have been pushed back on a shelf. The 80-year-old, the octo, looks at the double-dumpling figure and admits that he is old. The last act has begun, and it will be the test of the play. 2

To enter the country of age is a new experience, different from what you supposed it to be. Nobody, man or woman, knows the country until he has lived in it and has taken out his citizenship papers. Here is my own report, submitted as a road map and guide to some of the principal monuments. 3

The new octogenarian feels as strong as ever when he is sitting back in a comfortable chair. He ruminates, he dreams, he re- 4 members. He doesn't want to be disturbed by others. It seems to him that old age is only a costume assumed for those others; the true, the essential self is ageless. In a moment he will rise and go for a ramble in the woods, taking a gun along, or a fishing rod, if it is spring. Then he creaks to his feet, bending forward to keep his balance, and realizes that he will do nothing of the sort. The body and its surroundings have their messages for him, or only one message: "You are old." Here are some of the occasions on which he receives the message:

- when it becomes an achievement to do thoughtfully, step by step, what he once did instinctively
- when his bones ache
- when there are more and more little bottles in the medicine cabinet, with instructions for taking four times a day
- when he fumbles and drops his toothbrush (butterfingers)
- when his face has bumps and wrinkles, so that he cuts himself while shaving (blood on the towel)
- when year by year his feet seem farther from his hands
- when he can't stand on one leg and has trouble pulling on his pants
- when he hesitates on the landing before walking down a flight of stairs
- when he spends more time looking for things misplaced than he spends using them after he (or more often his wife) has found them
- when he falls asleep in the afternoon
- when it becomes harder to bear in mind two things at once
- when a pretty girl passes him in the street and he doesn't turn his head
- when he forgets names, even of people he saw last month ("Now I'm beginning to forget nouns," the poet Conrad Aiken said at 80)
- When he listens hard to jokes and catches everything but the snapper
- when he decides not to drive at night anymore
- when everything takes longer to do—bathing, shaving, getting dressed or undressed—but when time passes quickly, as if he were gathering speed while coasting downhill. The year from 79 to 80 is like a week when he was a boy.

Those are some of the intimate messages. "Put cotton in your ears and pebbles in your shoes," said a gerontologist, a member of that new profession dedicated to alleviating all maladies of old people except the passage of years. "Pull on rubber gloves. Smear Vaseline over your glasses, and there you have it: instant aging." 5

COLLABORATIVE LEARNING: CLASS ACTIVITY

Have your students collectively list features of old age they are particularly afraid of. Record these on the chalkboard or on a transparency. If the occasion warrants, venture into a discussion of why these fears exist and how we can cope with them. To make your discussion more concrete, you might have a few student volunteers put on rubber gloves and smear Vaseline on their glasses (see para. 5) and then share their reactions with the class.

Have your students individually ask people over 75 years old if Cowley's list of symptoms of aging (para. 4) is accurate. Which signals do these people find most telling? Then, divide your students into groups of 3 or 4; have them discuss their findings and then come up with a list of the five most common symptoms. Finally, have your students compare their lists and see which items appear most frequently.

Not quite. His formula omits the messages from the social world, which are louder, in most cases, than those from within. We start by growing old in other people's eyes, then slowly we come to share their judgment.

I remember a morning many years ago when I was backing 6 out of the parking lot near the railroad station in Brewster, New York. There was a near collision. The driver of the other car jumped out and started to abuse me; he had his fists ready. Then he looked hard at me and said, "Why, you're an old man." He got back into his car, slammed the door, and drove away, while I stood there fuming. "I'm only 65," I thought. "He wasn't driving carefully. I can still take care of myself in a car, or in a fight, for that matter."

My hair was whiter—it may have been in 1974—when a 7 young woman rose and offered me her seat in a Madison Avenue bus. That message was kind and also devastating. "Can't I even stand up?" I thought as I thanked her and declined the seat. But the same thing happened twice the following year, and the second time I gratefully accepted the offer, though with a sense of having diminished myself. "People are right about me," I thought while wondering why all those kind gestures were made by women. Do men now regard themselves as the weaker sex, not called upon to show consideration? All the same it was a relief to sit down and relax.

A few days later I wrote a poem, "The Red Wagon," that be- 8 longs in the record of aging:

> For his birthday they gave him a red express wagon
> with a driver's high seat and a handle that steered.
> His mother pulled him around the yard.
> "Giddyap," he said, but she laughed and went off
> to wash the breakfast dishes.
>
> "I wanta ride too," his sister said,
> and he pulled her to the edge of a hill.
> "Now, sister, go home and wait for me,
> but first give a push to the wagon."
> He climbed again to the high seat,
> this time grasping that handle-that-steered.
> The red wagon rolled slowly down the slope,
> then faster as it passed the schoolhouse
> and faster as it passed the store,
> the road still dropping away.
> Oh, it was fun.

But would it ever stop?
Would the road always go downhill?

The red wagon rolled faster.
Now it was in strange country.
It passed a white house he must have dreamed about,
deep woods he had never seen,
a graveyard where, something told him, his sister
was buried.

Far below
the sun was sinking into a broad plain.

The red wagon rolled faster.
Now he was clutching the seat, not even trying to steer.
Sweat clouded his heavy spectacles.
His white hair streamed in the wind.

Even before he or she is 80, the aging person may undergo   9
another identity crisis like that of adolescence. Perhaps there had
also been a middle-aged crisis, the male or the female
menopause, but the rest of adult life he had taken himself for
granted, with his capabilities and failings. Now, when he looks in
the mirror, he asks himself, "Is this really me?"—or he avoids the
mirror out of distress at what it reveals, those bags and wrinkles.
In his new makeup he is called upon to play a new role in a play
that must be improvised. Andre' Gide, that long-lived man of letters, wrote in his journal, "My heart has remained so young that I
have the continual feeling of playing a part, the part of the 70-
year-old that I certainly am; and the infirmities and weaknesses
that remind me of my age act like a prompter, reminding me of
my lines when I tend to stray. Then, like the good actor I want to
be, I go back into my role, and I pride myself on playing it well."

In his new role the old person will find that he is tempted by   10
new vices, that he receives new compensations (not so widely
known), and that he may possibly achieve new virtues. Chief
among these is the heroic or merely obstinate refusal to surrender
in the face of time. One admires the ships that go down with all
flags flying and the captain on the bridge.

Among the vices of age are avarice, untidiness, and vanity,   11
which last takes the form of a craving to be loved or simply admired. Avarice is the worst of those three. Why do so many old
persons, men and women alike, insist on hoarding money when
they have no prospect of using it and even when they have no

heirs? They eat the cheapest food, buy no clothes, and live in a single room when they could afford better lodging. It may be that they regard money as a form of power; there is a comfort in watching it accumulate while other powers are dwindling away. How often we read of an old person found dead in a hovel, on a mattress partly stuffed with bankbooks and stock certificates! The bankbook syndrome, we call it in our family, which has never succumbed.

Untidiness we call the Langley Collyer syndrome. To explain, 12 Langley Collyer was a former concert pianist who lived alone with his 70-year-old brother in a brownstone house on upper Fifth Avenue. The once fashionable neighborhood had become part of Harlem. Homer, the brother, had been an admiralty lawyer, but was now blind and partly paralyzed; Langley played for him and fed him on buns and oranges, which he thought would restore Homer's sight. He never threw away a daily paper because Homer, he said, might want to read them all. He saved other things as well and the house became filled with rubbish from roof to basement. The halls were lined on both sides with bundled newspapers, leaving narrow passageways in which Langley had devised booby traps to catch intruders.

On March 21, 1947, some unnamed person telephoned the 13 police to report that there was a dead body in the Collyer house. The police broke down the front door and found the hall impassable; then they hoisted a ladder to a second-story window. Behind it Homer was lying on the floor in a bathrobe; he had starved to death. Langley had disappeared. After some delay, the police broke into the basement, chopped a hole in the roof, and began throwing junk out of the house, top and bottom. It was 18 days before they found Langley's body, gnawed by rats. Caught in one of his own booby traps, he had died in a hallway just outside Homer's door. By that time the police had collected, and the Department of Sanitation had hauled away, 120 tons of rubbish, including, besides the newspapers, 14 grand pianos and the parts of a dismantled Model T Ford.

Why do so many old people accumulate junk, not on the 14 scale of Langley Collyer, but still in a dismaying fashion? Their tables are piled high with it, their bureau drawers are stuffed with it, their closet rods bend with the weight of clothes not worn for years. I suppose that the piling up is partly from lethargy and partly from feeling that everything once useful, including their own bodies, should be preserved. Others, though not so many, have such a fear of becoming Langley Collyers that they strive to be painfully neat. Every tool they own is in its place, though it will never be used again; every scrap of paper is filed away in alphabetical order. At last their immoderate neatness becomes another vice of age, if a milder one.

The vanity of older people is an easier weakness to explain, and to condone. With less to look forward to, they yearn for recognition of what they have been: the reigning beauty, the athlete, the soldier, the scholar. It is the beauties who have the hardest time. A portrait of themselves at twenty hangs on the wall, and they try to resemble it by making an extravagant use of creams, powder, and dyes. Being young at heart, they think they are merely revealing their essential persons. The athletes find shelves for their silver trophies, which are polished once a year. Perhaps a letter sweater lies wrapped in a bureau drawer. I remember one evening when a no-longer athlete had guests for dinner and tried to find his sweater. "Oh, that old thing," his wife said. "The moths got into it and I threw it away." The athlete sulked and his guests went home early. 15

But there are also pleasures of the body, or the mind, that are enjoyed by a greater number of older persons. Those pleasures include some that younger people find hard to appreciate. One of them is simply sitting still, like a snake on a sunwarmed stone, with a delicious feeling of indolence that was seldom attained in earlier years. A leaf flutters down; a cloud moves by inches across the horizon. At such moments the older person, completely relaxed, has become a part of nature—and a living part, with blood coursing through his veins. The future does not exist for him. He thinks, if he thinks at all, that life for younger persons is still a battle royal of each against each, but that now he has nothing more to win or lose. He is not so much above as outside the battle, as if he had assumed the uniform of some small neutral country, perhaps Liechtenstein or Andorra. From a distance he notes that some of the combatants, men or women, are jostling ahead—but why do they fight so hard when the most they can hope for is a longer obituary? He can watch the scrounging and gouging, he can hear the shouts of exultation, the moans of the gravely wounded, and meanwhile he feels secure; nobody will attack him from ambush. 16

Age has other physical compensations besides the nirvana of dozing in the sun. A few of the simplest needs become a pleasure to satisfy. When an old woman in a nursing home was asked what she really liked to do, she answered in one word: "Eat." She might have been speaking for many of her fellows. Meals in a 17 nursing home, however badly cooked, serve as climactic moments of the day. The physical essence of the pensioners is being renewed at an appointed hour; now they can go back to meditating or to watching TV while looking forward to the next meal. They can also look forward to sleep, which has become a definite pleasure, not the mere interruption it once had been.

Here I am thinking of old persons under nursing care. Others   18
ferociously guard their independence, and some of them suffer less than one might expect from being lonely and impoverished. They can be rejoiced by visits and meetings, but they also have company inside their heads. Some of them are busiest when their hands are still. What passes through the minds of many is a stream of persons, images, phrases, and familiar tunes. For some that stream has continued since childhood, but now it is deeper; it is their present and their past combined. At times they conduct silent dialogues with a vanished friend, and these are less tiring—often more rewarding—than spoken conversations. If inner resources are lacking, old persons living alone may seek comfort and a kind of companionship in the bottle. I should judge from the gossip of various neighborhoods that the outer suburbs from Boston to San Diego are full of secretly alcoholic widows. One of those widows, an old friend, was moved from her apartment into a retirement home. She left behind her a closet in which the floor was covered wall to wall with whiskey bottles. "Oh, those empty bottles!" she explained. "They were left by a former tenant."

Not whiskey or cooking sherry but simply giving up is the   19
greatest temptation of age. It is something different from a stoical acceptance of infirmities, which is something to be admired.

The givers-up see no reason for working. Sometimes they lie   20
in bed all day when moving about would still be possible, if difficult. I had a friend, a distinguished poet, who surrendered in that fashion. The doctors tried to stir him to action, but he refused to leave his room. Another friend, once a successful artist, stopped painting when his eyes began to fail. His doctor made the mistake of telling him that he suffered from a fatal disease. He then lost interest in everything except the splendid Rolls-Royce, acquired in his prosperous days, that stood in the garage. Daily he wiped the dust from its hood. He couldn't drive it on the road any longer, but he used to sit in the driver's seat, start the motor, then back the Rolls out of the garage and drive it in again, back twenty feet and forward twenty feet; that was his only distraction.

I haven't the right to blame those who surrender, not being   21
able to put myself inside their minds or bodies. Often they must

have compelling reasons, physical or moral. Not only do they suffer from a variety of ailments, but also they are made to feel that they no longer have a function in the community. Their families and neighbors don't ask them for advice, don't really listen when they speak, don't call on them for efforts. One notes that there are not a few recoveries from apparent senility when that situation changes. If it doesn't change, old persons may decide that efforts are useless. I sympathize with their problems, but the men and women I envy are those who accept old age as a series of challenges.

For such persons, every new infirmity is an enemy to be outwitted, an obstacle to be overcome by force of will. They enjoy each little victory over themselves, and sometimes they win a major success. Renoir was one of them. He continued painting, and magnificently, for years after he was crippled by arthritis; the brush had to be strapped to his arm. "You don't need your hand to paint," he said. Goya was another of the unvanquished. At 72 he retired as an official painter of the Spanish court and decided to work only for himself. His later years were those of the famous "black paintings" in which he let his imagination run (and also of the lithographs, then a new technique). At 78 he escaped a reign of terror in Spain by fleeing to Bordeaux. He was deaf and his eyes were failing; in order to work he had to wear several pairs of spectacles, one over another, and then use a magnifying glass; but he was producing splendid work in a totally new style. At 80 he drew an ancient man propped on two sticks, with a mass of white hair and beard hiding his face and with the inscription "I am still learning."

"Eighty years old!" the great Catholic poet Paul Claudel wrote in his journal. "No eyes left, no ears, no teeth, no legs, no wind! And when all is said and done, how astonishingly well one does without them!"

UNDERSTANDING DETAILS

1. Name five ways, according to Cowley, that people begin to realize they are "old." How did Cowley himself learn that he was old?
2. List three vices of old age, and explain them as Cowley sees them. What are three compensations of advancing age?
3. What does Cowley mean in paragraph 15 by "the vanity of older people"? How do older people manifest this vanity?

ANSWERS TO QUESTIONS: UNDERSTANDING DETAILS (p. 83)

1. Cowley claims that the mere fact of being 80 years old destroys any remaining illusion of youth, but he lists in paragraph 4 some of the other specific signs of old age. Cowley first became aware that he was old when an irate driver with whom he had been involved in a near collision drew back with the comment, "Why, you're an old man" (para. 6). This perception was affirmed a number of years later when young women began offering him seats on the bus.

2. Cowley sees the following vices of old age: avarice, which he describes as the sacrifices of the normal needs of life in the interest of hoarding money; untidiness, which comes with the irrational accumulation of sentimental miscellany; and vanity, based on the need for recognition (often reaching back to the achievements of youth for this acclaim). The compensations of age, however, are physical: the pleasant indolence of sitting in the sun; the satisfaction of a meal, whether savory or unpalatable; and the gratification of sleep.

3. "The vanity of older people" is less involved in the present than in the past. It is characterized by demands of recognition for achievements of long ago. This vanity manifests itself in such acts as the overapplication of powder and rouge to hide the increasing bumps and wrinkles, the ostentatious display of tarnished athletic trophies, and the periodic modeling of a moth-eaten letter sweater.

ANSWERS TO QUESTIONS: ANALYZING MEANING (p. 84)

1. Cowley's poem about a ride in a red wagon provides a visual image of the aging process. It expresses through both imagery and poetic structure the increasing speed of time as one ages. This poem reinforces Cowley's statement that "The year from 79 to 80 is like a week when he was a boy" (para. 4) and provides symbolic representation of age as an unfamiliar country.

2. In Cowley's opinion, people who surrender to old age are characterized by lethargy and a complete lack of interest in life, prompting them to give in and give up. This renunciation of life frequently pro-

vokes an escape into the "whiskey or cooking sherry" (para. 19). People who view life as a challenge, conversely, believe "every new infirmity is . . . an obstacle to be overcome by force of will" (para. 22). These individuals do the best they can with both their talents and ills. Cowley uses the examples of several famous painters whom he admires to show how determination can often overcome the difficulties of age.

3. Cowley seems to have mixed feelings about "the country of age" (para. 3). On the one hand, it presents a new experience, a unique stage of life never before encountered; as such, it is a cause for celebration. On the other hand, as an octogenarian he has often felt abandoned, neglected, and ignored by the rest of society because of his advanced age and growing physical infirmities. In the final analysis, he describes old age as "a series of challenges" (para. 21) to be met with courage and ingenuity.

ANSWERS TO QUESTIONS: DISCOVERING RHETORICAL STRATEGIES (p. 84)

1. Cowley considers old age a "challenge" (although "adventure," "struggle," or "battle" might also be appropriate metaphors). In using this central comparison, he gives the challenge definition through a description of its frustrations and its compensations; he then offers distressing examples of those who have surrendered to the adversities of old age as well as heartening examples of others who have successfully met the challenge.

2. The reflection at the end of the first paragraph on the traditional treatment of their elderly tribesmen by the Ojibwas immediately defines the problem to be addressed in the essay: whether or not old age has sufficient compensations to make it worth living. This vivid example immediately engages the sympathy and attention of the reader.

3. The metaphors Cowley uses to describe old age each help us to understand a different aspect of aging. The metaphor of old age as a "role" suggests not only that the outward performance does not necessarily reflect the inner being, but that the actor has some control over his or her role and can

Chapter 1 • Description

ANALYZING MEANING

1. What does the wagon symbolize in the author's poem about aging (paragraph 8)? What purpose does this poem serve in the essay?
2. According to this essay, what qualities characterize those people who "surrender" (paragraph 21) to old age and those who "accept old age as a series of challenges" (paragraph 21)? Why do you think Cowley has more respect for the latter group?
3. What is Cowley's general attitude toward "the country of age"? Why does he feel that way about this stage of life?

DISCOVERING RHETORICAL STRATEGIES

1. After reading this essay, try to summarize in a single word or phrase Cowley's impressions of old age. How does this dominant impression help the author organize the many different details presented in his essay?
2. Why did Cowley include the reference to the Ojibwas at the end of the first paragraph? What effect does that anecdote have on our sympathies as readers?
3. Cowley uses a number of distinct metaphors in describing old age. He equates being old, for example, with acting out a certain "role" in life. He also portrays aging as a "rite of passage," a "challenge," and an "unfamiliar country" through which we must travel. In what sense is each of these metaphors appropriate? How does each help us understand the process of growing old?

IDEAS FOR DISCUSSION/WRITING

Preparing to Write

Write freely about your impressions of one or more older people in your life: Who are they? What characteristics do they share? How are they different from each other? Different from you? Similar to you? How do you know they are "old"?

Choosing a Topic

1. Cowley explains at the outset of his essay that "the country of age is a new experience, different from what you supposed it to be. Nobody, man or woman, knows the country until he has lived in it and has taken out his citizenship papers" (paragraph 3). Interview an older person to discover his or her view of "the country of age." Then write an essay for your peers describing that person's opinions.

2. In his essay, Cowley describes the signals he receives from his body and his environment that tell him he is "old." What messages did you receive when you were young that indicated you were a "child"? What messages do you receive now that remind you of your present age? How are these messages different from those you received when you were a child? Describe these signals in a well-developed essay addressed to your classmates.
3. Do you think that Americans treat their aged with enough respect? Explain your answer in detail to an older person. Describe various situations that support your opinion.

determine whether it will be played as a comedy or a tragedy. Age as a "rite of passage" portrays aging as merely another stage of life. Cowley's positive attitude is present in his treatment of this waning period of life as a "challenge." Finally, the description of the later years as an "unfamiliar country" reflects the idea that no one can look back upon old age—the final transition to death.

PREWRITING

In preparation for the writing assignments, the Preparing to Write questions ask students to concentrate on specific older people in their lives. You might encourage your students to interview these people before writing on a related topic. One instructor has had success asking his students to interview two people of different ages and then explain how their views differ. See pages 16–23 for other suggestions on generating ideas in response to these questions.

ADDITIONAL DISCUSSION/WRITING TOPIC

In an essay written for your classmates, describe your greatest fears about growing old. How do you think you will cope with these anxieties when you are eighty years old?

REVISING STRATEGY

A good descriptive essay *shows* rather than *tells* its readers what it wants them to know or feel. In one of your descriptive essays, label all the words and sentences that show or tell your readers what to think or feel. Notice how some of the telling could be converted to showing. Then revise your paper so that it shows rather than tells in as many places as possible.

CHAPTER 2

NARRATION

■ ■ ■

Telling a Story

Using Narration

A good story is a powerful method of getting someone's attention. The excitement that accompanies a suspenseful ghost story, a lively anecdote, or a vivid joke easily attests to this effect. In fact, narration is one of the earliest verbal skills we all learn as children, providing us with a convenient, logical, and easily understood means of sharing our thoughts with other people. Storytelling is powerful because it offers us a way of dramatizing our ideas so that others can identify with them.

Defining Narration

Narration involves telling a story that is often based on personal experience. Stories can be oral or written, real or imaginary, short or long. A good story, however, always has a point or purpose. It can be the dominant mode (as in a novel or short story), supported by other rhetorical strategies, or it can serve the purpose of another rhetorical mode (as in a persuasive essay, a historical survey, or a scientific report).

In its subordinate role, narration can provide examples or explain ideas. If asked why you are attending college, for example, you might turn to narration to make your answer clear, beginning

INTRODUCTORY NOTES

Some instructors postpone teaching narration and personal experience essays because students often have difficulty distancing themselves enough from their own activities to gain significant insights into them; other instructors insist on teaching narration at the beginning of a composition course because everyone has had some experiences to draw from. Whenever you introduce narration, you will find that the task of storytelling itself teaches several abilities that are invaluable in development of good writing skills in any mode: (1) a keen awareness of purpose and audience; (2) a clear writing voice; and (3) the importance of organization and timing in the unfolding of a tale. Stories, more than other types of writing, are told to or written for a certain person or group of people to accomplish a specific purpose. For this reason, writers may be more aware than others of their own perspective on a subject and of their ability to control their audience's reaction to that subject. Making readers laugh at an experience, for example, might require the writer to draw out one part of a tale instead of another. Anticipating audience reactions helps students (1) make important decisions about timing and (2) develop a new awareness about writer–reader relationships that they can then use in other forms of writing

The student essay at the end of the chapter introduction uses narration for its own sake to tell a story about an unusual family vacation; the student's pacing of the events in the story reveals the humor of the experience. The five essays in the chapter use narration for a specific purpose within a larger context. The prereading questions, prewriting exercises, and writing assignments then help students discover how narration actually works in these particular essays. In "For My Indian Daughter," Lewis Sawaquat writes a narrative about his ethnic identity to warn his daughter of inevitable problems in her future; the exercises accompanying this selection ask the students to consider their own ethnic identity and then relate various stories about their heritage to achieve different purposes for different audiences. George Orwell in "Shooting an Elephant" recounts an unpleasant experience in Burma to express his discontent with England's imperialism in the 1920s; the exercises in this case ask students to reveal times in their own lives when they were forced to do something against their wills. "Graduation" by Maya Angelou presents the author's memory of her eighth-grade graduation, which reveals the frustrating and destructive gap between ambition and reality for an African-American female growing up in Stamps, Arkansas; the exercises ask the students to think and write about various events and the impact they had on people's lives. Russell Baker uses narration in "The Saturday Evening Post" to develop a fascinating character study revealing the origin of his interest in journalism; before and after the selection, the apparatus stresses various perspectives of the writer's own professional development. "Passport to Knowledge" by Mark Mathabane recounts the author's first few days in school and the way that experience began to change his life forever; the exercises ask students to consider various pressures in their lives and the effects of those pressures.

with a story about your family's hardships in the past. The purpose of telling such a story would be to help your listeners appreciate your need for higher education by encouraging them to understand and identify with your family history.

Unlike description, which generally portrays people, places, and objects in *space*, narration asks the reader to follow a series of actions through a particular *time* sequence. Description often complements the movement of narration, though. People must be depicted, for instance, along with their relationships to one another, before their actions can have any real meaning for us; similarly, places must be described so that we can picture the setting and understand the activities in a specific scene. The organization of the action and the time spent on each episode in a story should be based principally on a writer's analysis of the interests and needs of his or her audience.

To be most effective, narration should prolong the exciting parts of a story and shorten the routine facts that simply move the reader from one episode to another. If you were robbed on your way to work, for example, a good narrative describing the incident would concentrate on the traumatic event itself rather than on such mundane and boring details as what you had for breakfast and what clothes you had put on prior to the attack. Finally, just like description, narration *shows* rather than *tells* its purpose to the audience. The factual statement "I was robbed this morning" could be made much more vivid and dramatic through the addition of some simple narration: "As I was walking to work at 7:30 A.M., a huge and angry-looking man ran up to me, thrust a gun into the middle of my stomach, and took my money, my new wristwatch, all my credit cards, and my pants—leaving me penniless and embarrassed."

The following paragraph written by a student recounts a recent parachuting experience. As you read this narrative, notice especially the writer's use of vivid detail to *show* rather than *tell* her message to the readers.

> I have always needed occasional "fixes" of excitement in my life, so when I realized one spring day that I was more than ordinarily bored, I made up my mind to take more than ordinary steps to relieve that boredom. I decided to go parachuting. The next thing I knew, I was stuffed into a claustrophobically small plane with five other terrified people, rolling down a bumpy, rural runway, droning my way to 3,500 feet and an exhilarating experience. Once over the jump area, I waited my turn, stepped onto the strut, held my breath, and then kicked off into the cold, rushing air as my heart pounded heavily. All I could think was, "I hope this damn parachute opens!"

The sensation of falling backwards through space was unfamiliar and disconcerting till my chute opened with a loud "pop," momentarily pulling me upwards toward the distant sky. After several minutes of floating downward, I landed rudely on the hard ground. Life, I remembered happily, could be awfully exciting. And a month later, when my tailbone had stopped throbbing, I still felt that way.

Reading and Writing Narrative Essays

To read a narrative essay most effectively, you should spend your time concentrating on the writer's main story line and use of details. To create an effective story, you have some important decisions to make before you write and certain variables to control as you actually draft your narrative. During the prewriting stage, you need to generate ideas and choose a point of view through which your story will be presented. Then, as you write, the preliminary decisions you have made regarding the selection and arrangement of your details (especially important in a narrative) will allow your story to flow more easily. Carefully controlled organization, along with appropriate timing and pacing, can influence your audience's reactions in very powerful ways.

HOW TO READ A NARRATIVE ESSAY

Preparing to Read. As you prepare to read the narratives in this chapter, try to guess what each title tells you about its essay's topic and about the author's attitude toward that topic: Can you tell, for example, what Lewis Sawaquat feels toward his daughter from his title "For My Indian Daughter" or what George Orwell's attitude is toward the events described in "Shooting an Elephant"? Also, scan the essay and read its synopsis in the Rhetorical Table of Contents to help you anticipate as much as you can about the author's purpose and audience.

The more you learn from the biography about the author and the circumstances surrounding the composition of a particular essay, the better prepared you will be to read the essay. For a narrative essay, the writer's point of view or perspective toward the story and its characters is especially significant. From the biographies, can you determine Orwell's reason for writing his essay or Maya Angelou's attitude toward graduation exercises at Lafayette County Training school? What is Russell Baker's opinion of his mother in "The Saturday Evening Post"?

TEACHING NARRATION:
ONE INSTRUCTOR'S COMMENTS

I introduce narrative writing by first defining and explaining what it involves. At the same time, I assign readings which exemplify narration. Next, we discuss the readings for both content and organization. Since narration lends itself well to writing about personal experience, I ask students to bring to class five thesis statements (prompted by one of the readings) that could be developed into essays. In short one-to-one conferences, the student and I decide which one he or she will later expand into an essay. A favorite method of organization I use is chronological development with an emphasis upon dialogue. Thus I relate narrative writing to the use of quotations. Then, as I do with practically all of my assignments, I select several papers from the group to be read to the class by the students who wrote them.

Nellie McCrory
Gaston College
Dallas, North Carolina

We tell stories to validate experience; conveying personal experience (and the wisdom which so often shines through it) reaffirms the meaning of the experience. Regardless of the story or experience, it wasn't for naught. Both narrator and audience are wiser for having shared it.

In teaching narration, I emphasize the "how" of relating personal experience. Since many students apparently feel that their own experiences are not significant or dramatic enough, I suggest to them that just about any experience will suffice, providing the narration is well told.

Structure is important, but the story must "find itself," its own natural shape. In an attempt to help the story find itself, I often ask students to *tell* their story first, using a cassette recorder, then transcribe it onto paper. In keeping with oral tradition, this method allows the story to take its early form naturally. I point out that its naive to suppose that we retell any experience exactly as it happened. Storytellers usually select a key event and focus on a moment of intensity, a conflict, a dramatic peak, or, in the case of a lighter narration, perhaps an anticlimactic moment. In most cases, the story then revolves around this focal point. Orwell's actual shooting of the elephant (in "Shooting an Elephant") is a superb example. Telling the story into the cassette can help reveal the crucial moment. Reviewing the elements of fiction and showing how they work in a model essay like Orwell's also seems to help.

In my opinion, narration is probably the most abused of the modes because many students allow it to take over virtually any other type of essay when other rhetorical strategies would be more effective. I find that eventually some students need to be weaned away from narration in order to write credible academic essays.

Ted Wise
Porterville College
Porterville, California

Last, before you begin to read, answer the Preparing to Read questions and then try to generate some of your own inquiries on the general subject of the essay: What do you want to know about being a Native American (Sawaquat)? What childhood experience greatly affected your life (Baker)? What do you think of apartheid in South Africa (Mathabane)?

Reading. As you read a narrative essay for the first time, simply follow the story line and try to get a general sense of the narrative and of the author's general purpose. Is Orwell's purpose to make us feel sympathetic or antagonistic toward his role in shooting the elephant? Is Baker trying to encourage us all to be writers or simply to help us understand why he writes? Record your initial reactions to each essay as they occur to you. Based on the biographical information preceding the essay and on the essay's tone, purpose, and audience, try to create a context for the narrative as you read. How do such details help you understand your reading material more thoroughly? A first reading of this sort, along with a survey of the questions that follow the essay, will help prepare you for a critical understanding of the material when you read it for the second time.

Rereading. As you reread these narrative essays, notice the author's selection and arrangement of details. Why does Orwell organize his story one way and Baker another? What effect does their organization create? Also, pay attention to the timing and the pacing of the story line. What do the inactive, pensive moments add to Angelou's "Graduation"? What does the quick pace of Mathabane's narrative communicate? In addition, consider at this point what other rhetorical strategies the authors use to support their narratives. Which writers use examples to supplement their stories? Which use definitions? Which use comparisons? Why do they use these strategies? Finally, when you answer the questions after each essay, you can check your understanding of the material on different levels before you tackle the discussion/writing topics that follow.

For a general checklist of reading guidelines, please see pages 15–16 of the Introduction.

HOW TO WRITE A NARRATIVE ESSAY

Preparing to Write. First, you should answer the prewriting questions to help you generate thoughts on the subject at hand. Next, as in all writing, you should explore your subject matter and discover as many specific details as possible. (See pages 16–23 of the Introduction for a discussion of prewriting techniques.) Some writers rely on the familiar journalistic checklist of Who, What, When, Where, Why, and How to make sure they cover all aspects of their narrative. If you were using the story of a basketball game at your college to demonstrate the team spirit of your school, for example, you might want to consider telling your readers *who* played in the game and/or *who* attended; *what* happened before, during, and after the game; *when* and *where* it took place; *why* it was being played (or *why* these particular teams were playing each other or *why* the game was especially important); and *how* the winning basket was shot. Once you have generated these ideas, you should always let your purpose and audience ultimately guide your selection of details, but the process of gathering such journalistic information gives you some material from which to choose. You will also need to decide whether or not to include dialogue in your narrative. Again, the difference here is between *showing* and *telling:* Will your audience benefit from reading what was actually said, word for word, during a discussion, or will a brief description of the conversation be sufficiently effective? In fact, all the choices you make at this stage of the composing process will give you material with which to create emphasis, suspense, conflict, and interest in your subject.

Next, you must decide upon the point of view that will most readily help you achieve your purpose with your specific audience. Point of view includes the (1) person, (2) vantage point, and (3) attitude of your narrator. *Person* refers to who will tell the story: an uninvolved observer, a character in the narrative, or an omniscient (all-seeing) narrator. This initial decision will guide your thoughts on *vantage point*, which is the frame of reference of the narrator: close to the action, far from the action, looking back on the past, or reporting on the present. Finally, your narrator will naturally have an *attitude* or *personal feeling* about the subject: accepting, hostile, sarcastic, indifferent, angry, pleased, or any of a number of similar emotions. Once you adopt a certain perspective in a story, you must follow it for the duration of the narrative. This consistency will bring focus and coherence to the story.

Writing. After you have explored your topic and adopted a particular point of view, you need to write a thesis statement and select and arrange the details of your story coherently so that the narrative has a clear beginning, middle, and end. The most natural way to organize the events of a narrative, of course, is chronologically. In your story about the school basketball game, you would probably narrate the relevant details in the order they occurred (i.e., sequentially, from the beginning of the game to its conclusion).

More experienced writers may elect to use flashbacks: An athlete might recall a significant event that happened during the game, or a coach might recollect the contest's turning point. Your most important consideration is that the elements of a story must follow some sort of time sequence aided by the use of clear and logical transitions (e.g., "then," "next," "at this point," "suddenly") that help the reader move smoothly from one event to the next.

Rewriting.   As you reread the narrative you have written, pretend you are a reader and make sure you have told the story from the most effective point of view, considering both your purpose and your audience. Will your readers identify with your narrator? To what extent does this narrator help you achieve your purpose? Is the narrator's attitude appropriate to your subject?

Further, as you reread, make certain you can follow the events of the story as they are related. Does one event lead naturally to the next? Are all the events relevant to your purpose? Will these events interest your audience? Have you chosen appropriate details to enhance the story? Do you show rather than tell your message?

For more advice on writing and editing, see pages 27–28.

Student Essay: Narration at Work

The following essay characterizes the writer's mother by telling a story about an unusual family vacation. As you read it, notice how the student writer states her purpose clearly and succinctly in the first paragraph. She then becomes an integral part of her story as she carefully selects examples and details that help convey the passage of time.

A Vacation with My Mother

First-person narrator   I had an interesting childhood—not because of where I grew up and not because I ever did anything particularly adventuresome or thrilling. In fact, I don't think my life seemed especially interesting to me at the time. But now, telling friends about my supposedly ordinary childhood, I notice an array of responses ranging from astonishment to hilarity. The source of their surprise and amusement is my mother—gracious, charming, sweet, and totally out of synchronization with the rest of the world. One strange family trip we took when I was eleven captures the essence of her zaniness.

General subject

Focused subject

Thesis statement

My two sets of grandparents lived in Colorado and North Dakota, respectively, and my parents decided we would spend a few weeks driving to those states and seeing all the sights along the relaxed and rambling way. <u>My eight-year-old brother, David, and I had some serious reservations.</u> If Dad had ever had Mom drive him to school, we reasoned, he'd never even consider letting her help drive us anywhere out of town, let alone out of California. If we weren't paying attention, we were as likely to end up at her office or the golf course as we were to arrive at school. Sometimes she'd drop us off at a friend's house to play and then forget where she'd left us. The notion of going on a long trip with her was really unnerving.

How can I explain my mother to a stranger? Have you ever watched reruns of the old "I Love Lucy" with Lucille Ball? I did as a child, and I thought Lucy Ricardo was normal. I lived with somebody a lot like her. Now, Mom wasn't a redhead (not usually, anyway), and Dad wasn't a Cuban nightclub owner, but <u>at home we had the same situation of a loving but bemused husband trying to deal with the off-the-wall logic and enthusiasm of a frequently exasperating wife. We all adored her, but we had to admit it: Mom was a flaky, absent-minded, genuine eccentric.</u>

As the first day of our trip approached, David and I reluctantly said goodbye to all of our friends. Who knew if we'd ever see any of them again? Finally, the moment of our departure arrived, and we loaded suitcases, books, games, some packing gear, and a tent into the car and bravely drove off. We bravely drove off again two hours later after we'd returned home to get the purse and traveler's checks that Mom had forgotten.

David and I were always a little nervous when using gas station bathrooms if Mom was driving while Dad napped. "You stand outside the door and play lookout while I go, and I'll stand outside the door and play lookout while you go." I had terrible visions: "Honey, where are the kids?" "What?! Oh, gosh . . . I thought they were being awfully quiet. Uh . . . Idaho?" We were never actually abandoned in a strange city, but we weren't about to take any chances.

Margin annotations:
Narrator's attitude
Examples
Transition
Narrator's vantage point
Transition
Careful selection of details
Use of dialogue
Examples

Transition   On the fourth or fifth night of the trip, we had trouble finding a motel with a vacancy. After driving futilely for an hour, Mom suddenly had a great idea: Why didn't we find a house with a **Example** likely-looking back yard and ask if we could pitch our tent there? To her, the scheme was eminently reasonable. Vowing quietly to each other to hide in the back seat if she did it, David and I groaned in anticipated mortification. To our profound relief, Dad vetoed the idea. Mom never could understand our objections. If a strange family showed up on her front doorstep, Mom would have been delighted. She thinks everyone in the world is as nice as she is. We finally found a vacancy in the next town. David and I were thrilled—the place featured bungalows in the shape of Native-American tepees.

Transition   The Native-American motif must have reminded my parents that we had not as yet used the brand-new tent, Coleman stove, portable mattress, and other camping gear we had brought. We headed to a national park the next day and found a campsite by a lake. It took hours to figure out how to get the tent up—it was one of those deluxe models with mosquito-net windows, canvas floors, and **Careful selection of details** enough room for three large families to sleep in. It was after dark before we finally got it erected, and the night had turned quite cold. We fixed a hurried campfire dinner (chicken burned on the outside and raw in the middle) and prepared to go to sleep. That was when we realized that Mom had forgotten to bring along some important pieces of equipment—our sleeping bags. The four of us huddled together on our thin mattresses under the carpet from the station-wagon floor. That ended our camping days. Give me a stucco tepee any time.

We drove through several states and saw lots of great sights along the way: the Grand Canyon, **Examples (spatial order)** Carlsbad Caverns, caves, mountains, waterfalls, even a haunted house. David and I were excited and amazed at all the wonders we found, and Mom was just as enthralled as we were. Her constant pleasure and sense of the world as a beautiful, magical place was infectious. I never realized until I grew up how really childlike—in the best sense of the word—my mother actually is. She is innocent, optimistic, and always ready to be entertained.

Transition Looking back on that long-past family vaca- Narrator's
tion, I now realize that my childhood was more attitude
special because I grew up with a mother who
wasn't afraid to try anything and who taught me to
look at the world as a series of marvelous opportunities to be explored. What did it matter that she
thought England was bordered by Germany? We
were never going to try to drive there. So what if Examples
she was always leaving her car keys in the refrigerator or some other equally inexplicable place? In
Concluding the end, we always got where we were going—and
remark we generally had a grand time along the way.

Student Writer's Comments

The hardest thing about writing this narrative was trying to decide what material to use and what to leave out. I enjoyed writing
about this childhood vacation because of all the memories it brought
back. I soon realized, though, that I could not include everything
that came to mind. I learned how important careful, judicious editing really is. I took the raw material of a very lengthy first draft and
forced myself to choose the story that best captured my mother and
what life was like growing up under the care of such a lovely but
daffy individual. I made myself ruthlessly eliminate anything that
interfered with the overall effect I was trying to create, including
any unnecessary words and phrases.

Some Final Thoughts on Narration

Just as with other modes of writing, all decisions regarding
narration should be made with a specific purpose and an intended audience constantly in mind. As you will see, each narrative in this section is directed at a clearly defined audience.
Notice, as you read them, how each writer manipulates the various features of narration so that the readers are simultaneously
caught up in the plot and deeply moved to feel, act, think, and believe the writer's personal opinions.

LEWIS SAWAQUAT
(1935–   )

■ ■ ■

For My Indian Daughter

Lewis Sawaquat is a Native American who recently retired from his thirty-year job as a surveyor for the Soil Conservation Service of the United States Department of Agriculture. He was born in Harbor Springs, Michigan, where his great-grandfather was the last official "chief" of the region. After finishing high school, Sawaquat entered the army, graduated with honors from Army Survey School, and then completed a tour of duty in Korea. Upon returning to America, he enrolled in the Art Institute of Chicago to study commercial art. Sawaquat now lives in Interlochen, Michigan, where his hobbies include gardening, swimming, and walking in the woods. He also helps support the Native American Scholarship Program at the Pathfinder's School in his home town and serves as a pipe-carrier and cultural/spiritual adviser to his Ottawa tribe. Now that he is retired, he hopes to write a book entitled *Dreams: The Universal Language*, which will investigate the Native-American approach to dream interpretation.

PREREADING

The purpose of this Preparing to Read material is to get students to consider their own cultural heritage so they have a framework for understanding Lewis Sawaquat's observations about his own identity. Although some discussion may be warranted, this topic more than others tends to trigger fairly personal memories and is handled best as a private freewriting assignment or journal entry. Depending on the tenor of the class, volunteers might share their entries *after* they are written. See pages 3–6 for other ways to generate thoughts on these questions.

BACKGROUND INFORMATION

In "For My Indian Daughter," Sawaquat has written a poignant essay revealing the

Preparing to Read

"For My Indian Daughter" originally appeared in the "My Turn" column of *Newsweek* magazine (September 5, 1983) under the author's former name, Lewis Johnson. In his article the author speaks eloquently of prejudice, ethnic pride, and growing cultural awareness. Before reading this selection, think for a few minutes about your own heritage: What is your ethnic identity? Are you content with this background? Have you ever gone through an identity crisis? Do you anticipate facing any problems because of your ancestry? If so, how will you handle these problems when they occur?

My little girl is singing herself to sleep upstairs, her voice mingling with the sounds of the birds outside in the old maple trees. She is two and I am nearly 50, and I am very taken with her.

1

She came along late in my life, unexpected and unbidden, a startling gift.

Today at the beach my chubby-legged, brown-skinned daughter ran laughing into the water as fast as she could. My wife and I laughed watching her, until we heard behind us a low guttural curse and then an unpleasant voice raised in an imitation war whoop.

I turned to see a fat man in a bathing suit, white and soft as a grub, as he covered his mouth and prepared to make the Indian war cry again. He was middle-aged, younger than I, and had three little children lined up next to him, grinning foolishly. My wife suggested we leave the beach, and I agreed.

I knew the man was not unusual in his feelings against Indians. His beach behavior might have been socially unacceptable to more civilized whites, but his basic view of Indians is expressed daily in our small town, frequently on the editorial pages of the county newspaper, as white people speak out against Indian fishing rights and land rights, saying in essence, "Those Indians are taking our fish, our land." It doesn't matter to them that we were here first, that the U.S. Supreme Court has ruled in our favor. It matters to them that we have something they want, and they hate us for it. Backlash is the common explanation of the attacks on Indians, the bumper stickers that say, "Spear an Indian, Save a Fish," but I know better. The hatred of Indians goes back to the beginning when white people came to this country. For me it goes back to my childhood in Harbor Springs, Mich.

Theft. Harbor Springs is now a summer resort for the very affluent, but a hundred years ago it was the Indian village of my Ottawa ancestors. My grandmother, Anna Showanessy, and other Indians like her, had their land there taken by treaty, by fraud, by violence, by theft. They remembered how whites had burned down the village at Burt Lake in 1900 and pushed the Indians out. These were the stories in my family.

When I was a boy my mother told me to walk down the alleys in Harbor Springs and not to wear my orange football sweater out of the house. This way I would not stand out, not be noticed, and not be a target.

I wore my orange sweater anyway and deliberately avoided the alleys. I was the biggest person I knew and wasn't really afraid. But I met my comeuppance when I enlisted in the U.S. Army. One night all the men in my barracks gathered together and, gang-fashion, pulled me into the shower and scrubbed me down with rough brushes used for floors, saying, "We won't

torment suffered by a Native American trying to reconcile his ethnic heritage in a hostile White society. The essay is particularly moving because it is addressed to the author's "chubby-legged, brown-skinned daughter" (para. 2), whose future pain can only be anticipated.

READABILITY LEVEL

7.0

RELATED READINGS

Cultural Diversity

Prejudice

Raising Children

COLLABORATIVE LEARNING: CLASS ACTIVITY

Let your students discuss the various racial and ethnic groups they represent. Then have them consider the advantages and disadvantages of nurturing a separate minority/cultural heritage within society.

Divide your students into groups of 3 or 4 and have them research the status of Native Americans in the United States today. This investigation should focus on the treatment of Native Americans in your area. The students' sources could range from encyclopedia information to firsthand interviews. After the students gather this information, have one person from each group summarize the group's findings for the class.

ANSWERS TO QUESTIONS: UNDERSTANDING DETAILS (p. 99)

1. The principal point of this essay is to expose the extent of modern prejudice against Native Americans. Sawaquat incorporates into his essay six short prejudicial anecdotes from his own life to make this point.

2. Sawaquat attributes the hatred of White people toward Native Americans to the fact that "we have something they want, and they hate us for it" (para. 4). For his own tribe, that "something" was, in the past, "the Indian village of my Ottawa ancestors" (para. 5); at present, it is the U.S. Supreme Court ruling concerning Native American fishing rights on land that has been theirs for centuries (para. 4).

3. From his first powwow, Sawaquat learned that he didn't know his own cultural heritage.

ANSWERS TO QUESTIONS: ANALYZING MEANING (p. 99)

1. The story of Sawaquat's daughter helps the reader feel the emotions of a victim of prejudice; it is especially poignant because Sawaquat's two-year-old daughter is unaware of the trials to come. Beyond this point, student opinions will vary.

2. The cruel behavior directed toward his daughter at the beach recalls sharply for Sawaquat the suffering he has experienced as a Native American in his youth and throughout much of his adulthood. Denial of his ethnicity neither protected him from attack nor eased his pain. Only when he returned to his Ottawa heritage and began to

have any dirty Indians in our outfit." It is a point of irony that I was cleaner than any of them. Later in Korea I learned how to kill, how to bully, how to hate Koreans. I came out of the war tougher than ever and, strangely, white.

I went to college, got married, lived in La Porte, Ind., worked   8 as a surveyor and raised three boys. I headed Boy Scout groups, never thinking it odd when the Scouts did imitation Indian dances, imitation Indian lore.

One day when I was 35 or thereabouts I heard about an   9 Indian powwow. My father used to attend them and so with great curiosity and a strange joy at discovering a part of my heritage, I decided the thing to do to get ready for his big event was to have my friend make me a spear in his forge. The steel was fine and blue and iridescent. The feathers on the shaft were bright and proud.

In a dusty state fairground in southern Indiana, I found white   10 people dressed as Indians. I learned they were "hobbyists," that is, it was their hobby and leisure pastime to masquerade as Indians on weekends. I felt ridiculous with my spear, and I left.

It was years before I could tell anyone of the embarrassment   11 of this weekend and see any humor in it. But in a way it was that weekend, for all its silliness, that was my awakening. I realized I didn't know who I was. I didn't have an Indian name. I didn't speak the Indian language. I didn't know the Indian customs. Dimly I remembered the Ottawa word for dog, but it was a baby word, *kahgee,* not the full word, *muhkahgee,* which I was later to learn. Even more hazily I remembered a naming ceremony (my own). I remembered legs dancing around me, dust. Where had that been? Who had I been? "Sawaquat," my mother told me when I asked, "where the tree begins to grow."

That was 1968, and I was not the only Indian in the country   12 who was feeling the need to remember who he or she was. There were others. They had powwows, real ones, and eventually I found them. Together we researched our past, a search that for me culminated in the Longest Walk, a march on Washington in 1978. Maybe because I now know what it means to be Indian, it surprises me that others don't. Of course there aren't very many of us left. The chances of an average person knowing an average Indian in an average lifetime are pretty slim.

Circle. Still, I was amused one day when my small, four-   13 year-old neighbor looked at me as I was hoeing in my garden and said, "You aren't a real Indian, are you?" Scotty is little, talkative, likable. Finally I said, "I'm a real Indian." He looked at me for a moment and then said, squinting into the sun, "Then where's your horse and feathers?" The child was simply a smaller, whiter version of my own ignorant self years before. We'd both seen too much TV, that's all. He was not to be blamed. And so, in a way, the moronic man on the beach today is blameless. We come full circle to realize other people are like ourselves, as discomfiting as that may be sometimes.

As I sit in my old chair on my porch, in a light that is fading so the leaves are barely distinguishable against the sky, I can picture my girl asleep upstairs. I would like to prepare her for what's to come, take her each step of the way saying, there's a place to avoid, here's what I know about this, but much of what's before her she must go through alone. She must pass through pain and joy and solitude and community to discover her own inner self that is unlike any other and come through that passage to the place where she sees all people are one, and in so seeing may live her life in a brighter future.

UNDERSTANDING DETAILS

1. What is the principal point of this essay by Sawaquat? How many different stories does the author tell to make this point?
2. What does Sawaquat see as the origin of the hatred of Native Americans in the United States?
3. What does Sawaquat learn from his first powwow (paragraphs 9 and 10)?

ANALYZING MEANING

1. Why did Sawaquat begin this essay with the story about his daughter on the beach? How does the story make you feel?
2. Why did thoughts about his daughter prompt Sawaquat's memories of his own identity crisis? What does the author's identity have to do with his daughter?
3. Why do you think Sawaquat says that his daughter "must pass through pain and joy and solitude and community to discover her own inner self" (paragraph 14)? To what extent do we all need to do this in our lives?

appreciate his ethnic traditions was he able to transform his resentment to pride. Because attitudes toward Native Americans have changed little over the years, he is already beginning to anticipate the pain his daughter will experience as she grows older.

3. The narrator is aware that his attempts to assimilate, to live a "White" life, to follow his parents' injunction to "not stand out, not be noticed, and not be a target" (para. 6) did not work for him. Consolation came only when he truly accepted his heritage. Likewise, his daughter must find her own way, suffer the pain of wrong choices and the confusion of a thousand voices pulling her in a thousand directions, and, finally, withdraw into herself to find the best path for the future (as we all have to do in our lives to some extent).

ANSWERS TO QUESTIONS: DISCOVERING RHETORICAL STRATEGIES (p. 100)

1. The brief bits of dialogue confirm the distorted attitude of some members of the White population toward Native Americans. Comments such as "Those Indians are taking our fish, our land" (para. 4); "We won't have any dirty Indians in our outfit" (para. 7); and "You aren't a real Indian, are you? . . . Then where's your horse and feathers?" (para. 13) express more powerfully than merely "telling" the distorted feelings aimed at the Native American.

2. The narrator of the story is a fifty-year-old Ottawa Indian who attempted to assimilate into White society until about fifteen years ago, when he and many other Native Americans began to feel the need to remember their heritage. Both the first-person point of view and the vantage point—that of a father who has been through the pain and is now beginning to predict the same suffering for his small daughter—make the essay very personal, eliciting from the reader strong emotional responses to the injustices experienced by Sawaquat and his daughter. The narrator's acceptance of his anger appears to have transformed itself into sad resignation and a determination to find peace within himself.

3. Sawaquat's essay is designed as a lengthy flashback, framed at the beginning and at the end by reflections on the fate of his small daughter. The greater portion of the essay, subtitled "Theft," deals with the author's early life and his reconciliation with his ethnic heritage, which helps us establish a clear perspective for the rest of the essay. The focus on his daughter throughout the essay emphasizes both the change and the lack of change in the plight of the Native American in the years since he was a boy. The subtitle of the third section, "Circle," further stresses the feeling that Native Americans are trapped within a tight circle of prejudice.

PREWRITING

In preparation for the writing assignments, the focus in the Preparing to Write questions is on each student's identity and the changes that identity has undergone. See pages 16–23 for suggestions on generating ideas in response to these questions.

ADDITIONAL DISCUSSION/WRITING TOPIC

Use a fable (a symbolic story about animals) to explain an identity crisis you have had. Direct your fable to a group of elementary school children.

REVISING STRATEGY

The point of view of the writer is one of the most important features of a good narrative. From the chapter introduction, you learned that point of view includes (1) the person who will tell the story, (2) the vantage point of that person, and (3) the person's attitude or feeling about the subject. In one of your narrative essays, underline all clues to the narrator's point of view. See if you can discern any inconsistencies in those references (for example, an unjustified change in tone or point of view). Then revise your paper, concentrating on making the narrator's voice more appropriate and consistent.

DISCOVERING RHETORICAL STRATEGIES

1. Sawaquat occasionally uses dialogue to help make his points. What does the dialogue add to the various narratives he cites here?
2. Describe as thoroughly as possible the point of view of Sawaquat's narrator. Include in your answer a discussion of person, vantage point, and attitude.
3. Why do you think Sawaquat divided his essay into three sections? Why do you think he spends most of his time in the second part?

IDEAS FOR DISCUSSION/WRITING

Preparing to Write

Write freely about your own identity: What is your cultural heritage? How do you fit into your immediate environment? Has your attitude about yourself and your identity changed over the years? Do you know your own inner self? How do you plan to continue learning about yourself?

Choosing a Topic

1. Write a narrative essay that uses one or more stories from your past in order to describe to a group of friends the main features of your identity.
2. Explain to your children (whether real or imaginary) in narrative form some simple but important truths about your heritage. Take care to select your details well, choose an appropriate point of view, and arrange your essay logically so that you keep your readers' interest throughout the essay.
3. Have you recently experienced any social traumas in your life that you would like to prepare someone else for? Write a letter to the person you would like to warn. Use narration to explain the situation, and suggest ways to avoid the negative aspects you encountered.

GEORGE ORWELL
(1903–1950)

■ ■ ■

Shooting an Elephant

QUOTATION ON THINKING

"How do I know what I think until I see what I say?"

E. M. Forster

"George Orwell" was the pseudonym of English writer Eric Arthur Blair. Born in India, where his father was a British civil servant, Orwell moved to England in 1907 to attend Eton School, then returned to Burma to serve as an officer in the Indian Imperial Police. From 1927 to 1935 he lived an impoverished existence in Paris and London until his persistence as a writer brought him critical praise. After a series of modestly successful novels, Orwell wrote the classic *Animal Farm* (1945), his best-known work, a prose satire of Stalinism and totalitarianism. Collections of his essays include *Inside the Whale* (1940), *Critical Essays* (1946), and *Shooting an Elephant* (1950). In his later years, ill with tuberculosis, Orwell wrote his darkly horrifying *Nineteen Eighty-Four* (1949), which predicted a world where unorthodox thought was prohibited, love was condemned, and three superpowers controlled the entire planet.

Preparing to Read

"Shooting an Elephant," as essay from Orwell's collection of the same title, chronicles one of the author's autobiographical experiences as a policeman in Burma in the 1920s. Full of anti-imperialist sentiment, the story uses the death of an elephant as an emblem of Orwell's frustration with his role in England's colonial domination of India. As you prepare to read this essay, take a few moments to consider the many influences that shape your life: What forces have power over you? Have you ever done something you didn't want to do because of these forces? Have you ever been ashamed of the extent to which social or ethical pressures have governed your life? Why did you allow these forces to control you? How did you feel while all this was going on? Can you think of a specific situation in which you resisted these outside forces? What was the result?

PREREADING

The purpose of this Preparing to Read material is to get students to reminisce about influences that have had an uncanny control over them. You might help your class get started on this exercise by having them brainstorm aloud about such influences before they respond to the questions here. After a few minutes of free association as a class, have the students explore their individual thoughts in response to these questions. See pages 3–6 for other ways to generate thoughts on these questions.

In "Shooting an Elephant," George Orwell presents a dramatic account of the questionable destruction of a frenzied working elephant in a village in the former British colony of Burma. Having already concluded that "imperialism was an evil thing" (para. 2), the author felt that being forced into killing the elephant substantiated his belief that "when the white man turns tyrant it is his own freedom that he destroys" (para. 7).

READABILITY LEVEL

7.9

RELATED READINGS

Violence

In Moulmein, in Lower Burma, I was hated by large numbers of people—the only time in my life that I have been important enough for this to happen to me. I was sub-divisional police officer of the town, and in an aimless, petty kind of way anti-European feeling was very bitter. No one had the guts to raise a riot, but if a European woman went through the bazaars alone somebody would probably spit betel juice over her dress. As a police officer I was an obvious target and was baited whenever it seemed safe to do so. When a nimble Burman tripped me up on the football field and the referee (another Burman) looked the other way, the crowd yelled with hideous laughter. This happened more than once. In the end the sneering yellow faces of young men that met me everywhere, the insults hooted after me when I was at a safe distance, got badly on my nerves. The young Buddhist priests were the worst of all. There were several thousands of them in the town and none of them seemed to have anything to do except stand on street corners and jeer at Europeans.

All this was perplexing and upsetting. For at that time I had already made up my mind that imperialism was an evil thing and the sooner I chucked up my job and got out of it the better. Theoretically—and secretly, of course—I was all for the Burmese and all against their oppressors, the British. As for the job I was doing, I hated it more bitterly than I can perhaps make clear. In a job like that you see the dirty work of Empire at close quarters. The wretched prisoners huddling in the stinking cages of the lock-ups, the grey, cowed faces of the long-term convicts, the scarred buttocks of the men who had been flogged with bamboos—all these oppressed me with an intolerable sense of guilt. But I could get nothing into perspective. I was young and ill-educated and I had had to think out my problems in the utter silence that is imposed on every Englishman in the East. I did not even know that the British Empire is dying, still less did I know that it is a great deal better than the younger empires that are going to supplant it. All I knew was that I was stuck between my hatred of the empire I served and my rage against the evil-spirited little beasts who tried to make my job impossible. With one part of my mind I thought of the British Raj as an unbreakable tyranny, as something clamped down, *in saecula saeculorum*, upon the will of prostrate peoples; with another part I thought that the greatest joy in the world would be to drive a bayonet into a Buddhist priest's guts. Feelings like these are the normal by-products of imperialism; ask any Anglo-Indian official, if you can catch him off duty.

One day something happened which in a roundabout way was enlightening. It was a tiny incident in itself, but it gave me a better glimpse than I had had before of the real nature of imperialism—the real motives for which despotic governments act. Early one morning the sub-inspector at a police station at the other end of the town rang me up on the phone and said that an elephant was ravaging the bazaar. Would I please come and do something about it? I did not know what I could do, but I wanted to see what was happening and I got on to a pony and started out. I took my rifle, an old .44 Winchester and much too small to kill an elephant, but I thought the noise might be useful *in terrorem*. Various Burmans stopped me on the way and told me about the elephant's doings. It was not, of course, a wild elephant, but a tame one which had gone "must." It had been chained up, as tame elephants always are when their attack of "must" is due, but on the previous night it had broken its chain and escaped. Its mahout, the only person who could manage it when it was in that state, had set out in pursuit, but had taken the wrong direction and was now twelve hours' journey away, and in the morning the elephant had suddenly reappeared in town. The Burmese population had no weapons and were quite helpless against it. It had already destroyed somebody's bamboo hut, killed a cow and raided some fruit-stalls and devoured the stock; also it had met the municipal rubbish van and, when the driver jumped out and took to his heels, had turned the van over and inflicted violences upon it.

The Burmese sub-inspector and some Indian constables were waiting for me in the quarter where the elephant had been seen. It was a very poor quarter, a labyrinth of squalid bamboo huts, thatched with palm-leaf, winding all over a steep hillside. I remember that it was a cloudy, stuffy morning at the beginning of the rains. We began questioning the people as to where the elephant had gone and, as usual, failed to get any definite information. That is invariably the case in the East; a story always sounds clear enough at a distance, but the nearer you get to the scene of events the vaguer it becomes. Some of the people said that the elephant had gone in one direction, some said that he had gone in another, some professed not even to have heard of any elephant. I had almost made up my mind that the whole story was a pack of lies, when we heard yells a little distance away. There was a loud, scandalized cry of "Go away, child! Go away this instant!" and an old woman with a switch in her hand came round the corner of a hut, violently shooing away a crowd of naked children. Some more women followed, clicking their tongues and exclaiming; ev-

DEFINITIONS

betel juice (para. 1): juice from the leaf of a plant that is combined with a palm nut and lime and chewed by the natives of India.
football (para. 1): the game that Americans call soccer.
British Raj (para. 2): the British governing body that ruled colonial India.
in saecula saeculorem (para. 2): Latin. For ages of ages, or forever and ever.
despotic government (para. 3): a government that exercises power abusively or tyrannically.
in terrorem (para. 3): Latin. An object of terror or dread.
attack of "must" (para. 3): a period of excitement in male elephants.
mahout (para. 3): a keeper or driver of an elephant.
Dravidian (para. 4): a native of India, Ceylon, or Pakistan.
coolie (para. 4): an unskilled laborer or porter hired for low wages.
sahib (para. 7): sir or master, form of address traditionally used by Hindus and Muslims in colonial India when speaking to a European.
dah (para. 13): a large, heavy knife used by the Burmese.
Coringhee (para. 14): a person from the city of Coringa, a port in India, called Kakinada since 1949.

3

4

Have your students act out as a class the scene in this story immediately following the shooting of the elephant. An effective way to carry out this activity is in the form of psychodrama: First, have one student begin the process by sitting in the center of a circle made up of class members. That person becomes the narrator and must answer all questions as he or she thinks the narrator would. Start the questions by asking the student anything that is on your mind from the story. Then, the class members in the circle can ask their own questions. As the "drama" continues, bring one student at a time (up to 4 or 5) into the center of the circle to play members of the crowd. These students must also answer the class's questions as the crowd would. The important feature of this exercise is to create a dramatic environment. To do this, the members of the class on the outskirts of the circle can ask anything that is on their minds; the students in the center of the circle must answer each question addressed to them as the characters they have been assigned would respond. From this activity, students often get intensely involved in the topic and are able to experience different points of view.

idently there was something that the children ought not to have seen. I rounded the hut and saw a man's dead body sprawling in the mud. He was an Indian, a black Dravidian coolie, almost naked, and he could not have been dead many minutes. The people said that the elephant had come suddenly upon him round the corner of the hut, caught him with its trunk, put its foot on his back and ground him into the earth. This was the rainy season and the ground was soft, and his face had scored a trench a foot deep and a couple of yards long. He was lying on his belly with arms crucified and head sharply twisted to one side. His face was coated with mud, the eyes wide open, the teeth bared and grinning with an expression of unendurable agony. (Never tell me, by the way, that the dead look peaceful. Most of the corpses I have seen looked devilish.) The friction of the great beast's foot had stripped the skin from his back as neatly as one skins a rabbit. As soon as I saw the dead man I sent an orderly to a friend's house nearby to borrow an elephant rifle. I had already sent back the pony, not wanting it to go mad with fright and throw me if it smelt the elephant.

The orderly came back in a few minutes with a rifle and five cartridges, and meanwhile some Burmans had arrived and told us that the elephant was in the paddy fields below, only a few hundred yards away. As I started forward practically the whole population of the quarter flocked out of the houses and followed me. They had seen the rifle and were all shouting excitedly that I was going to shoot the elephant. They had not shown much interest in the elephant when he was merely ravaging their homes, but it was different now that he was going to be shot. It was a bit of fun to them, as it would be to an English crowd; besides they wanted the meat. It made me vaguely uneasy. I had no intention of shooting the elephant—I had merely sent for the rifle to defend myself if necessary—and it is always unnerving to have a crowd following you. I marched down the hill, looking and feeling a fool, with the rifle over my shoulder and an ever-growing army of people jostling at my heels. At the bottom, when you got away from the huts, there was a metalled road and beyond that a miry waste of paddy fields a thousand yards across, not yet ploughed but soggy from the first rains and dotted with coarse grass. The elephant was standing eight yards from the road, his left side towards us. He took not the slightest notice of the crowd's approach. He was tearing up bunches of grass, beating them against his knees to clean them and stuffing them into his mouth.

I had halted on the road. As soon as I saw the elephant I knew

5

6

with perfect certainty that I ought not to shoot him. It is a serious matter to shoot a working elephant—it is comparable to destroying a huge and costly piece of machinery—and obviously one ought not to do it if it can possibly be avoided. And at that distance, peacefully eating, the elephant looked no more dangerous than a cow. I thought then and I think now that his attack of "must" was already passing off; in which case he would merely wander harmlessly about until the mahout came back and caught him. Moreover, I did not in the least want to shoot him. I decided that I would watch him for a little while to make sure that he did not turn savage again, and then go home.

But at that moment I glanced round at the crowd that had followed me. It was an immense crowd, two thousand at the least and growing every minute. It blocked the road for a long distance on either side. I looked at the sea of yellow faces above the garish clothes—faces all happy and excited over this bit of fun, all certain that the elephant was going to be shot. They were watching me as they would watch a conjurer about to perform a trick. They did not like me, but with the magical rifle in my hands I was momentarily worth watching. And suddenly I realized that I should have to shoot the elephant after all. The people expected it of me and I had got to do it; I could feel their two thousand wills pressing me forward, irresistibly. And it was at this moment, as I stood there with the rifle in my hands, that I first grasped the hollowness, the futility of the white man's dominion in the East. Here was I, the white man with his gun, standing in front of the unarmed native crowd—seemingly the leading actor of the piece; but in reality I was only an absurd puppet pushed to and fro by the will of those yellow faces behind. I perceived in this moment that when the white man turns tyrant it is his own freedom that he destroys. He becomes a sort of hollow, posing dummy, the conventionalized figure of a sahib. For it is the condition of his rule that he shall spend his life in trying to impress the "natives," and so in every crisis he has got to do what the "natives" expect of him. He wears a mask, and his face grows to fit it. I had got to shoot the elephant. I had committed myself to doing it when I sent for the rifle. A sahib has got to act like a sahib, he has got to appear resolute, to know his own mind and do definite things. To come all that way, rifle in hand, with two thousand people marching at my heels, and then to trail feebly away, having done nothing—no, that was impossible. The crowd would laugh at me. And my whole life, every white man's life in the East, was one long struggle not to be laughed at.

COLLABORATIVE LEARNING: SMALL GROUP ACTIVITY

British imperialism as it was practiced in early twentieth-century India was marred by serious problems:

> India was governed by a Viceroy, appointed by the English parliament, who was responsible for the 11 British provinces established. Although Indians could participate in internal government on a regional or local level, they had no political power compared to the British. This situation led to resentment on the part of the Indians toward the British and eventually toward the British and eventually to revolution. The English view of the Indian people was that they were inferior and incapable of running their own country.

Provide your students with this information. Then, divide them into groups of 3 or 4, and have them compare British imperialism with American democracy. To focus their comparison, you might encourage the groups to make two lists: one of the similarities between these two forms of government and one of the differences. Another approach would be to ask your students if they see any similarities between British imperialism in early twentieth-century India and the doctrine of apartheid in modern South Africa.

But I did not want to shoot the elephant. I watched him beat-   8
ing his bunch of grass against his knees, with that preoccupied
grandmotherly air that elephants have. It seemed to me that it
would be murder to shoot him. At that age I was not squeamish
about killing animals, but I had never shot an elephant and never
wanted to. (Somehow it always seems worse to kill a *large* animal.) Besides, there was the beast's owner to be considered.
Alive, the elephant was worth at least a hundred pounds; dead,
he would only be worth the value of his tusks, five pounds, possibly. But I had got to act quickly. I turned to some experienced-
looking Burmans who had been there when we arrived, and
asked them how the elephant had been behaving. They all said
the same thing: he took no notice of you if you left him alone, but
he might charge if you went too close to him.

It was perfectly clear to me what I ought to do. I ought to   9
walk up to within, say, twenty-five yards of the elephant and test
his behavior. If he charged, I could shoot; if he took no notice of
me, it would be safe to leave him until the mahout came back. But
also I knew that I was going to do no such thing. I was a poor shot
with a rifle and the ground was soft mud into which one would
sink at every step. If the elephant charged and I missed him, I
should have about as much chance as a toad under a steam-roller.
But even then I was not thinking particularly of my own skin,
only of the watchful yellow faces behind. For at that moment,
with the crowd watching me, I was not afraid in the ordinary
sense, as I would have been if I had been alone. A white man
mustn't be frightened in front of "natives"; and so, in general, he
isn't frightened. The sole thought in my mind was that if anything went wrong those two thousand Burmans would see me
pursued, caught, trampled on and reduced to a grinning corpse
like that Indian up the hill. And if that happened it was quite
probable that some of them would laugh. That would never do.
There was only one alternative. I shoved the cartridges into the
magazine and lay down on the road to get a better aim.

The crowd grew very still, and a deep, low, happy sigh, as of   10
people who see the theatre curtain go up at last, breathed from in-
numerable throats. They were going to have their bit of fun after
all. The rifle was a beautiful German thing with cross-hair sights.
I did not then know that in shooting an elephant one would shoot
to cut an imaginary bar running from ear-hole to ear-hole. I
ought, therefore, as the elephant was sideways on, to have aimed
straight at his ear-hole; actually I aimed several inches in front of
this, thinking the brain would be further forward.

When I pulled the trigger I did not hear the bang or feel the kick—one never does when a shot goes home—but I heard the devilish roar of glee that went up from the crowd. In that instant, in too short a time, one would have thought, even for the bullet to get there, a mysterious, terrible change had come over the elephant. He neither stirred nor fell, but every line of his body had altered. He looked suddenly stricken, shrunken, immensely old, as though the frightful impact of the bullet had paralyzed him without knocking him down. At last, after what seemed a long time—it might have been five seconds, I dare say—he sagged flabbily to his knees. His mouth slobbered. An enormous senility seemed to have settled upon him. One could have imagined him thousands of years old. I fired again into the same spot. At the second shot he did not collapse but climbed with desperate slowness to his feet and stood weakly upright, with legs sagging and head drooping. I fired a third time. That was the shot that did for him. You could see the agony of it jolt his whole body and knock the last remnant of strength from his legs. But in falling he seemed for a moment to rise, for as his hind legs collapsed beneath him he seemed to tower upward like a huge rock toppling, his trunk reaching skywards like a tree. He trumpeted, for the first and only time. And then down he came, his belly towards me, with a crash that seemed to shake the ground even where I lay.

I got up. The Burmans were already racing past me across the mud. It was obvious that the elephant would never rise again, but he was not dead. He was breathing very rhythmically with long rattling gasps, his great mount of a side painfully rising and falling. His mouth was wide open—I could see far down into caverns of pale pink throat. I waited a long time for him to die, but his breathing did not weaken. Finally I fired my two remaining shots into the spot where I thought his heart must be. The thick blood welled out of him like red velvet, but still he did not die. His body did not even jerk when the shots hit him, the tortured breathing continued without a pause. He was dying, very slowly and in great agony, but in some world remote from me where not even a bullet could damage him further. I felt that I had got to put an end to that dreadful noise. It seemed dreadful to see the great beast lying there, powerless to move and yet powerless to die, and not even to be able to finish him. I sent back for my small rifle and poured shot after shot into his heart and down his throat. They seemed to make no impression. The tortured gasps continued as steadily as the ticking of a clock.

11   **1.** Orwell hates his job as a sub-divisional police officer in Burma because of the insults and abuses directed at him as a representative of the British oppressors and because, from his position, "you see the dirty work of Empire at close quarters" (para. 2). Although "no one had the guts to raise a riot" (para. 1), as a result of British imperialism foreigners were subjected to frequent affronts: the spitting of betel juice on a dress, the tripping of a European player on the football field, and continual jeers from the street corners.

2. During its attack of "must," the elephant had "destroyed somebody's bamboo hut, killed a cow, and raided some fruit-stalls and devoured the stock" (para. 3). Then, upon encountering a municipal rubbish van, it had "turned the van over and inflicted violences upon it" (para. 3). Finally, coming upon a Black Dravidian coolie, it "caught him with its trunk, put its foot on his back and ground him into the earth" (para. 4).

3. After the bullet reaches the elephant's head, he does not fall immediately but appears to shrink and grow old, then sags to his knees, slobbering. With the second shot, 12   he struggles to his feet again, and with the third, crashes to the ground. He breathes in great gasps with his mouth open, blood streaming from the holes where the bullets had entered. Despite additional shots in an attempt to relieve the beast's misery, death does not occur until a half hour after Orwell leaves the scene.

1. The crowd sees the killing of the elephant as a diversion, a form of entertainment, a supply of fresh meat, and not as a reluctant act of violence performed for its protection. Orwell feels that he must shoot the elephant, not because it remains a danger to the communtiy, but because the crowd expects him to do so. If he does not shoot the elephant, the crowd will laugh at him; and if the crowd laughs at him, the authority of the British Empire in the East will be compromised. The incident reveals for

Orwell a paradox: "when the white man turns tyrant it is his own freedom that he destroys" (para. 7).

2. Orwell describes imperialism as "an evil thing" (para. 2) that is losing power over the East. Orwell, a police officer in Burma, is threatened by the crowd not because he fears for his life, but because he fears being mocked. Laughter and mockery are weapons the Burmese people use to subvert the rule of the British Empire and show the weaknesses that characterize this rule. Thus, when Orwell becomes involved in controlling the elephant, he is presented with a dilemma: If he shoots, he is allowing the crowd to determine his actions; if he does not, they will mock him aloud. He realizes that he is a puppet being controlled by the will of the people despite his gun and government position.

3. Although the owner of the elephant was angry and not all of the spectators agreed with the decision to destroy the animal merely for killing a coolie, the British officials ruled the slaughter justifiable because of the death of the Indian. Perhaps Orwell should have followed his inclinations and walked away, but he was not courageous enough to "look a fool."

ANSWERS TO QUESTIONS: DISCOVERING RHETORICAL STRATEGIES (p. 108)

1. In this autobiographical essay, the point of view is first person, with the narrator as protagonist. This perspective allows the reader to view events through the mind of the protagonist, experience his thoughts and emotions as the plot progresses, and understand the thought processes that lead to the actions. In this way, the narrator helps the reader to the conclusion that imperialism is evil.

2. Contradictions in the essay include "All I knew was that I was stuck between my hatred of the empire I served and my rage against the evil-spirited little beasts who tried to make my job impossible" (para. 2) and "For at that moment, with the crowd watching me, I was not afraid in the ordinary sense, as I would have been if I had been alone. A white man mustn't be frightened in front of 'natives'; and so, in general,

In the end I could not stand it any longer and went away. I 13 heard later that it took him half an hour to die. Burmans were bringing *dahs* and baskets even before I left, and I was told they had stripped his body almost to the bones by the afternoon.

Afterwards, of course, there were endless discussions about 14 the shooting of the elephant. The owner was furious, but he was only an Indian and could do nothing. Besides, legally I had done the right thing, for a mad elephant has to be killed, like a mad dog, if its owner fails to control it. Among the Europeans opinion was divided. The older men said I was right, the younger men said it was a damn shame to shoot an elephant for killing a coolie, because an elephant was worth more than any damn Coringhee coolie. And afterwards I was very glad that the coolie had been killed; it put me legally in the right and it gave me a sufficient pretext for shooting the elephant. I often wondered whether any of the others grasped that I had done it solely to avoid looking a fool.

UNDERSTANDING DETAILS

1. Why does Orwell hate his job? According to the author, what is the relationship between British imperialism in Burma and the treatment of foreigners?
2. What has the elephant done during its attack of "must"?
3. In your own words, describe the shooting of the elephant from the time the first bullet hits its mark to the actual death.

ANALYZING MEANING

1. Why does the crowd want to see the elephant killed? Why does Orwell feel he has to shoot the animal?
2. In paragraph 7, Orwell says, "And my whole life, every white man's life in the East, was one long struggle not to be laughed at." Why was not being laughed at so important for him (and other imperialists)? What political overtones does this desire to save face carry?
3. What are the consequences of the elephant's death? Do you think Orwell took the right action? What else could he have done?

DISCOVERING RHETORICAL STRATEGIES

1. From what point of view is Orwell's narrative written? How does this

particular point of view help us understand Orwell's attitude toward the experience? How does this point of view help the author accomplish his purpose?

2. Orwell tends to second-guess himself throughout the story. Look, for example, at the following:

> It was perfectly clear to me what I ought to do. I ought to walk up to within, say, twenty-five yards of the elephant and test his behavior. If he charged, I could shoot; if he took no notice of me, it would be safe to leave him until the mahout came back. But also I knew that I was going to do no such thing. [paragraph 9]

Find at least two other such contradictions in the essay. What effect does this verbal strategy have on us as readers?

3. How does Orwell organize the details of this narrative? At what point in the story does the climax occur? When does the passage of time seem slowest to you? How does the author create this change of pace?

IDEAS FOR DISCUSSION/WRITING

Preparing to Write

Write freely about a time in your life when you were forced to do something you didn't want to do: What were the circumstances? How did you feel? What were the motivating forces for what you did? What were your alternatives? Were you satisfied with the outcome? How do you feel about this experience now?

Choosing a Topic

1. Write a narrative essay telling your classmates about a time when you were forced to do something you didn't want to do. Make a special effort to communicate your feelings regarding this experience. Remember to choose your details and point of view with an overall purpose in mind.

2. What is America's system of social classes? Where do you fit into the structure? Does our system allow for mobility? Write a narrative essay for your classmates explaining your understanding of the American class system. Use yourself and/or a friend as an example.

3. Explain in a coherent essay written for the general public why you think we are all sometimes motivated by forces that work against our better judgment. Refer to the Orwell essay or to experiences of your own to support your explanation.

he isn't frightened" (para. 9). These paradoxes not only reflect the confusion in the mind of the narrator about his position in this strange society, but suggest the irrationality of the concept of British imperialism.

3. Once Orwell has described the mood of the country and his responses to his position there, he presents "Shooting an Elephant" chronologically, the climax occurring with the entry of the first bullet into the elephant's head. The passage of time feels slowest during that period after the bullet has hit the beast and the narrator is waiting for him to die. This retardation of time is accomplished in two long paragraphs, with many descriptive phrases and frequent pauses created by means of periods and dashes. Repeated references to "slowness" and "tortured breathing" affirm the illusion of slowly passing time.

PREWRITING

In preparation for the writing assignments, the Preparing to Write questions ask students to think about one specific instance in which they were forced to do something they didn't want to do. The prompts ask the students to explain the incidents and then respond to them from a bit more distance before writing on a related topic. See pages 16–23 for suggestions on generating ideas in response to these questions.

ADDITIONAL DISCUSSION/WRITING TOPIC

Tell your classmates about a time when you were forced to do something you didn't want to do. Use carefully chosen details to communicate the facts and your feelings about this experience.

REVISING STRATEGY

A clear sense of purpose is important to any essay. In one of your narrative essays, write out your purpose, and then underline all parts of your essay that help achieve that purpose. Notice where your purpose could be clearer or better focused. Then revise your paper so that it communicates a consistent purpose to your intended audience.

MAYA ANGELOU
(1928–   )

■ ■ ■

Graduation

Maya Angelou was born Marguerite Johnson on April 4, 1928, in St. Louis, Missouri. Nicknamed "Maya" by her brother, she moved with her family to California; then, at age three, she was sent to live with her grandmother in Stamps, Arkansas, where she spent the childhood years later recorded in her autobiographical novel *I Know Why the Caged Bird Sings* (1970). After a brief marriage, she embarked upon an amazingly prolific career in dance, drama, and writing. During the past thirty-five years, Angelou has been at various times a nightclub performer specializing in calypso songs and dances, an actress, a playwright, a civil-rights activist, a newspaper editor, a television writer and producer, a poet, and a screenwriter. She has also written several television specials, including "Three Way Choice" (a five-part miniseries) and "Afro-Americans in the Arts," both for PBS. Her most recent work has included a BBC-TV documentary entitled "Trying to Make It Home" (1988); a stage production of Errol John's *Moon on a Rainbow Shawl*, which she directed in London (1988); and a novel, *I Shall Not Be Moved* (1990). A tall, graceful, and imposing woman, Angelou was once described as conveying "pride without arrogance, self-esteem without smugness."

PREREADING

The purpose of this Preparing to Read material is to get students to conjure up the details of an important day in their lives and then reminisce freely about their expectations before, during, and after that day. Before the students record their individual testimonials, you might ask them to tell the class what important day they are thinking of. These shared ideas will stimulate memories in some students who could not immediately think of an important day in their lives. All other responses to the Preparing to Read questions are best handled as individual exercises. See pages 3–6 for other ways to generate thoughts on these questions.

Preparing to Read

Like other excerpts from Angelou's popular *I Know Why the Caged Bird Sings*, "Graduation" presents a poignant memory from the author's early childhood in Arkansas—graduation from the eighth grade. Rich in the texture of rural southern custom, the story presents an image of the innocence and exuberance of youth set against the brutal reality of White racial stereotyping. Before you read Angelou's autobiographical narrative, take a few minutes to think about an important day in your life: What occurred on that day? How did you feel as the day approached? On that day? After it was over? Did the events of that day go as you expected they would? How well do you remember the day in retrospect? Why are such times so meaningful in our lives?

The children in Stamps trembled visibly with anticipation. Some adults were excited too, but to be certain the whole young population had come down with graduation epidemic. Large classes were graduating from both the grammar school and the high school. Even those who were years removed from their own day of glorious release were anxious to help with preparations as a kind of dry run. The junior students who were moving into the vacating classes' chairs were tradition-bound to show their talents for leadership and management. They strutted through the school and around the campus exerting pressure on the lower grades. Their authority was so new that occasionally if they pressed a little too hard it had to be overlooked. After all, next term was coming, and it never hurt a sixth grader to have a play sister in the eighth grade, or a tenth-year student to be able to call a twelfth grader Bubba. So all was endured in a spirit of shared understanding. But the graduating classes themselves were the nobility. Like travelers with exotic destinations on their minds, the graduates were remarkably forgetful. They came to school without their books, or tablets or even pencils. Volunteers fell over themselves to secure replacements for the missing equipment. When accepted, the willing workers might or might not be thanked, and it was of no importance to the pregraduation rites. Even teachers were respectful of the now quiet and aging seniors, and tended to speak to them, if not as equals, as beings only slightly lower than themselves. After tests were returned and grades given, the student body, which acted like an extended family, knew who did well, who excelled, and what piteous ones had failed.

Unlike the white high school, Lafayette County Training School distinguished itself by having neither lawn, nor hedges, nor tennis court, nor climbing ivy. Its two buildings (main classrooms, the grade school and home economics) were set on a dirt hill with no fence to limit either its boundaries or those of bordering farms. There was a large expanse to the left of the school which was used alternately as a baseball diamond or basketball court. Rusty hoops on swaying poles represented the permanent recreational equipment, although bats and balls could be borrowed from the P.E. teacher if the borrower was qualified and if the diamond wasn't occupied.

Over this rocky area relieved by a few shady tall persimmon trees the graduating class walked. The girls often held hands and no longer bothered to speak to the lower students. There was a sadness about them, as if this old world was not their home and

BACKGROUND INFORMATION

In "Graduation," Maya Angelou shares an excerpt from her moving autobiography, *I Know Why the Caged Bird Sings*. This narrative recounts a time during her impoverished childhood when the magic of her eighth-grade graduation was quickly dashed by a White politician who implied that she and her Black classmates were the maids and gardeners of the future. Despite the despair that enveloped the students in the auditorium of the Lafayette County Training School, Angelou illustrates the manner in which one small voice was able to remind the crowd that they were survivors.

READABILITY LEVEL

7.8

RELATED READINGS

Black Issues

Mark Mathabane, "Passport to Knowledge"   133
Harry Edwards, "Triple Tragedy in Black Society"   161
Shelby Steele, "Affirmative Action: The Price of Preference"   450

Growing Up

Russell Baker, "The Saturday Evening Post"   124
Mark Mathabane, "Passport to Knowledge"   133
Elena Asturias, "Growing Up in the U.S."   325
Eudora Welty, "Listening"   536

Prejudice

Lewis Sawaquat, "For My Indian Daughter"   96
Harry Edwards, "Triple Tragedy in Black Society"   161
Harold Krents, "Darkness at Noon"   167
Alleen Pace Nilsen, "Sexism in English: A 1990s Update"   183
Shelby Steele, "Affirmative Action: The Price of Preferenece"   450

School

Mark Mathabane, "Passport to Knowledge"   133
Garrison Keillor, "School"   278

Negro National Anthem (para. 29): "Lift Every Voice and Sing."

Booker T. Washington (1856–1915) (para. 32): an American educator.

Jesse Owens, Joe Lewis (para. 40): famous American athletes.

white-goddom (para. 41): apparently a portmanteau (a word coined from two others) combining "white-god" and "kingdom."

George Washington Carver (1864–1943) (para. 41): an American botanist.

decasyllabic (para. 46): consisting of ten syllables.

Gabriel Prosser (1775?–1800) (para. 46): an American slave and the leader of an unsuccessful slave revolt in Virginia in 1800.

Nat Turner (1800–1831) (para. 46): an American slave and leader of a slave rebellion in Virginia in 1831.

Harriet Tubman (1820–1913) (para. 46): an American slave and abolitionist who led several parties of slaves north to freedom; suffered a head injury in her youth that left her subject to periodic loss of consciousness, making her expeditions more dangerous.

James Weldon Johnson (1871–1938) (para. 55): an American poet and lawyer, the first African American to be admitted to the Florida bar; American consul to Nicaragua and Venezuela; one of the founders of the NAACP (National Association for the Advancement of Colored People).

J. Rosamond Johnson (1873–1954) (para. 55): an American composer and actor; brother of James Weldon Johnson.

they were bound for higher ground. The boys, on the other hand, had become more friendly, more outgoing. A decided change from the closed attitude they projected while studying for finals. Now they seemed not ready to give up the old school, the familiar paths and classrooms. Only a small percentage would be continuing on to college—one of the South's A & M (agricultural and mechanical) schools, which trained Negro youths to be carpenters, farmers, handymen, masons, maids, cooks and baby nurses. Their future rode heavily on their shoulders, and blinded them to the collective joy that had pervaded the lives of the boys and girls in the grammar school graduating class.

4 Parents who could afford it had ordered new shoes and ready-made clothes for themselves from Sears and Roebuck or Montgomery Ward. They also engaged the best seamstresses to make the floating graduating dresses and to cut down second-hand pants which would be pressed to a military slickness for the important event.

5 Oh, it was important, all right. Whitefolks would attend the ceremony, and two or three would speak of God and home, and the Southern way of life, and Mrs. Parsons, the principal's wife, would play the graduation march while the lower-grade graduates paraded down the aisles and took their seats below the platform. The high school seniors would wait in empty classrooms to make their dramatic entrance.

6 In the Store I was the person of the moment. The birthday girl. The center. Bailey had graduated the year before, although to do so he had had to forfeit all pleasures to make up for his time lost in Baton Rouge.

7 My class was wearing butter-yellow piqué dresses, and Momma launched out on mine. She smocked the yoke into tiny crisscrossing puckers, then shirred the rest of the bodice. Her dark fingers ducked in and out of the lemony cloth as she embroidered raised daisies around the hem. Before she considered herself finished she had added a crocheted cuff on the puff sleeves, and a pointy crocheted collar.

8 I was going to be lovely. A walking model of all the various styles of fine hand sewing and it didn't worry me that I was only twelve years old and merely graduating from the eighth grade. Besides, many teachers in Arkansas Negro schools had only that diploma and were licensed to impart wisdom.

9 The days had become longer and more noticeable. The faded beige of former times had been replaced with strong and sure colors. I began to see my classmates' clothes, their skin tones, and

the dust that waved off pussy willows. Clouds that lazed across the sky were objects of great concern to me. Their shiftier shapes might have held a message that in my new happiness and with a little bit of time I'd soon decipher. During that period I looked at the arch of heaven so religiously my neck kept a steady ache. I had taken to smiling more often, and my jaws hurt from the unaccustomed activity. Between the two physical sore spots, I suppose I could have been uncomfortable, but that was not the case. As a member of the winning team (the graduating class of 1940) I had outdistanced unpleasant sensations by miles. I was headed for the freedom of open fields.

Youth and social approval allied themselves with me and we trammeled memories of slights and insults. The wind of our swift passage remodeled my features. Lost tears were pounded to mud and then to dust. Years of withdrawal were brushed aside and left behind, as hanging ropes of parasitic moss. 10

My work alone had awarded me a top place and I was going to be one of the first called in the graduating ceremonies. On the classroom blackboard, as well as on the bulletin board in the auditorium, there were blue stars and white stars and red stars. No absences, no tardinesses, and my academic work was among the best of the year. I could say the preamble to the Constitution even faster than Bailey. We timed ourselves often: Wethepeopleofthe UnitedStatesinordertoformamoreperfectunion. . . ." I had memorized the Presidents of the United States from Washington to Roosevelt in chronological as well as alphabetical order. 11

My hair pleased me too. Gradually the black mass had lengthened and thickened, so that it kept at last to its braided pattern, and I didn't have to yank my scalp off when I tried to comb it. 12

Louise and I had rehearsed the exercises until we tired out ourselves. Henry Reed was class valedictorian. He was a small, very black boy with hooded eyes, a long, broad nose and an oddly shaped head. I had admired him for years because each term he and I vied for the best grades in our class. Most often he bested me, but instead of being disappointed I was pleased that we shared top places between us. Like many Southern Black children, he lived with his grandmother, who was as strict as Momma and as kind as she knew how to be. He was courteous, respectful and soft-spoken to elders, but on the playground he chose to play the roughest games. I admired him. Anyone, I reckoned, sufficiently afraid or sufficiently dull could be polite. But to be able to operate at a top level with both adults and children was admirable. 13

COLLABORATIVE LEARNING: CLASS ACTIVITY

Most likely all of your students (even your international students) have attended some form of high school graduation. To recreate the excitement of that day, have your students collectively make a list of chores and preparations they can recall from their own graduation day. The students, working through free association, should spontaneously call out random items for the list as you write them on the chalkboard or on a transparency. Then, as a class, discuss the feelings aroused by these recollections.

Have your students in groups of 3 or 4 discuss the various manifestations of prejudice they have experienced in their lifetimes. From these examples, have each group prepare a statement about the nature and degree of prejudice at this point in America's development. The statement should represent the group's feelings about prejudice, supported by appropriate examples. One person from each group should read this statement to the rest of the class.

His valedictory speech was entitled "To Be or Not to Be." The rigid tenth-grade teacher had helped him write it. He'd been working on the dramatic stresses for months. 14

The weeks until graduation were filled with heady activities. A group of small children were to be presented in a play about buttercups and daisies and bunny rabbits. They could be heard throughout the building practicing their hops and their little songs that sounded like silver bells. The older girls (nongraduates, of course) were assigned the task of making refreshments for the night's festivities. A tangy scent of ginger, cinnamon, nutmeg and chocolate wafted around the home economics building as the budding cooks made samples for themselves and their teachers. 15

In every corner of the workshop, axes and saws split fresh timber as the woodshop boys made sets and stage scenery. Only the graduates were left out of the general bustle. We were free to sit in the library at the back of the building or look in quite detachedly, naturally, on the measures being taken for our event. 16

Even the minister preached on graduation the Sunday before. His subject was, "Let your light so shine that men will see your good works and praise your Father, Who is in Heaven." Although the sermon was purported to be addressed to us, he used the occasion to speak to backsliders, gamblers, and general ne'er-do-wells. But since he had called our names at the beginning of the service we were mollified. 17

Among Negroes the tradition was to give presents to children going only from one grade to another. How much more important this was when the person was graduating at the top of the class. Uncle Willie and Momma had sent away for a Mickey Mouse watch like Bailey's. Louise gave me four embroidered handkerchiefs. (I gave her crocheted doilies.) Mrs. Sneed, the minister's wife, made me an undershirt to wear for graduation, and nearly every customer gave me a nickel or maybe even a dime with the instruction "Keep on moving to higher ground," or some such encouragement. 18

Amazingly the great day finally dawned and I was out of bed before I knew it. I threw open the back door to see it more clearly, but Momma said, "Sister, come away from that door and put your robe on." 19

I hoped the memory of that morning would never leave me. Sunlight was itself young, and the day had none of the insistence maturity would bring it in a few hours. In my robe and barefoot in the backyard, under cover of going to see about my new beans, I gave myself up to the gentle warmth and thanked God that no 20 matter what evil I had done in my life He had allowed me to live to see this day. Somewhere in my fatalism I had expected to die, accidentally, and never have the chance to walk up the stairs in the auditorium and gracefully receive my hard-earned diploma. Out of God's merciful bosom I had won reprieve.

21   Bailey came out in his robe and gave me a box wrapped in Christmas paper. He said he had saved his money for months to pay for it. It felt like a box of chocolates, but I knew Bailey wouldn't save money to buy candy when we had all we could want under our noses.

22   He was as proud of the gift as I. It was a soft-leather-bound copy of a collection of poems by Edgar Allan Poe, or, as Bailey and I called him, "Eap." I turned to "Annabel Lee" and we walked up and down the garden rows, the cool dirt between our toes, reciting the beautifully sad lines.

23   Momma made a Sunday breakfast although it was only Friday. After we finished the blessing, I opened my eyes to find the watch on my plate. It was a dream of a day. Everything went smoothly and to my credit. I didn't have to be reminded or scolded for anything. Near evening I was too jittery to attend to chores, so Bailey volunteered to do all before his bath.

24   Days before, we had made a sign for the Store, and as we turned out the lights Momma hung the cardboard over the door-knob. I read clearly: CLOSED, GRADUATION.

25   My dress fitted perfectly and everyone said that I looked like a sunbeam in it. On the hill, going toward the school, Bailey walked behind with Uncle Willie, who muttered, "Go on, Ju." He wanted him to walk ahead with us because it embarrassed him to have to walk so slowly. Bailey said he'd let the ladies walk together, and the men would bring up the rear. We all laughed, nicely.

26   Little children dashed by out of the dark like fireflies. Their crepe-paper dresses and butterfly wings were not made for running and we heard more than one rip, dryly, and the regretful "uh uh" that followed.

27   The school blazed without gaiety. The windows seemed cold and unfriendly from the lower hill. A sense of ill-fated timing crept over me, and if Momma hadn't reached for my hand I would have drifted back to Bailey and Uncle Willie, and possibly beyond. She made a few slow jokes about my feet getting cold, and tugged me along to the now-strange building.

28   Around the front steps, assurance came back. There were my fellow "greats," the graduating class. Hair brushed back, legs oiled, new dresses and pressed pleats, fresh pocket handkerchiefs

and little handbags, all homesewn. Oh, we were up to snuff, all right. I joined my comrades and didn't even see my family go in to find seats in the crowded auditorium.

The school band struck up a march and all classes filed in as had been rehearsed. We stood in front of our seats, as assigned, and on a signal from the choir director, we sat. No sooner had this been accomplished than the band started to play the national anthem. We rose again and sang the song, after which we recited the pledge of allegiance. We remained standing for a brief minute before the choir director and the principal signaled to us, rather desperately I thought, to take our seats. The command was so unusual that our carefully rehearsed and smooth-running machine was thrown off. For a full minute we fumbled for our chairs and bumped into each other awkwardly. Habits change or solidify under pressure, so in our state of nervous tension we had been ready to follow our usual assembly pattern: the American national anthem, then the pledge of allegiance, then the song every Black person I knew called the Negro National Anthem. All done in the same key, with the same passion and most often standing on the same foot. 29

Finding my seat at last, I was overcome with a presentiment of worse things to come. Something unrehearsed, unplanned, was going to happen, and we were going to be made to look bad. I distinctly remember being explicit in the choice of pronoun. It was "we," the graduating class, the unit, that concerned me then. 30

The principal welcomed "parents and friends" and asked the Baptist minister to lead us in prayer. His invocation was brief and punchy, and for a second I thought we were getting on the high road to right action. When the principal came back to the dais, however, his voice had changed. Sounds always affected me profoundly and the principal's voice was one of my favorites. During assembly it melted and lowed weakly into the audience. It had not been in my plan to listen to him, but my curiosity was piqued and I straightened up to give him my attention. 31

He was talking about Booker T. Washington, our "late great leader," who said we can be as close as the fingers on the hand, etc. . . . Then he said a few vague things about friendship and the friendship of kindly people to those less fortunate than themselves. With that his voice nearly faded, thin, away. Like a river diminishing to a stream and then to a trickle. But he cleared his throat and said, "Our speaker tonight, who is also our friend, came from Texarkana to deliver the commencement address, but due to the irregularity of the train schedule, he's going to, as they 32 say, 'speak and run.'" He said that we understood and wanted the man to know that we were most grateful for the time he was able to give us and then something about how we were willing always to adjust to another's program, and without more ado—"I give you Mr. Edward Donleavy."

Not one but two white men came through the door offstage. 33
The shorter one walked to the speaker's platform, and the tall one moved to the center seat and sat down. But that was our principal's seat, and already occupied. The dislodged gentleman bounced around for a long breath or two before the Baptist minister gave him his chair, then with more dignity than the situation deserved, the minister walked off the stage.

Donleavy looked at the audience once (on reflection, I'm sure 34 that he wanted only to reassure himself that we were really there), adjusted his glasses and began to read from a sheaf of papers.

He was glad "to be here and to see the work going on just as 35 it was in the other schools."

At the first "Amen" from the audience I willed the offender 36 to immediate death by choking on the word. But Amens and Yes, sir's began to fall around the room like rain through a ragged umbrella.

He told us of the wonderful changes we children in Stamps 37 had in store. The Central School (naturally, the white school was Central) had already been granted improvements that would be in use in the fall. A well-known artist was coming from Little Rock to teach art to them. They were going to have the newest microscopes and chemistry equipment for their laboratory. Mr. Donleavy didn't leave us long in the dark over who made these improvements available to Central High. Nor were we to be ignored in the general betterment scheme he had in mind.

He said that he had pointed out to people at a very high level 38 that one of the first-line football tacklers at Arkansas Agricultural and Mechanical College had graduated from good old Lafayette County Training School. Here fewer Amen's were heard. Those few that did break through lay dully in the air with the heaviness of habit.

He went on to praise us. He went on to say how he had 39 bragged that "one of the best basketball players at Fisk sank his first ball right here at Lafayette County Training School."

The white kids were going to have a chance to become 40 Galileos and Madame Curies and Edisons and Gauguins, and our boys (the girls weren't even in on it) would try to be Jesse Owenses and Joe Louises.

Owens and the Brown Bomber were great heroes in our   41
world, but what school official in the white-goddom of Little
Rock had the right to decide that those two men must be our only
heroes? Who decided that for Henry Reed to become a scientist
he had to work like George Washington Carver, as a bootblack, to
buy a lousy microscope? Bailey was obviously always going to be
too small to be an athlete, so which concrete angel glued to what
country seat had decided that if my brother wanted to become a
lawyer he had to first pay penance for his skin by picking cotton
and hoeing corn and studying correspondence books at night for
twenty years?

The man's dead words fell like bricks around the auditorium   42
and too many settled in my belly. Constrained by hard-learned
manners I couldn't look behind me, but to my left and right the
proud graduating class of 1940 had dropped their heads. Every
girl in my row had found something new to do with her handkerchief. Some folded the tiny squares into love knots, some into tri-
angles, but most were wadding them, then pressing them flat on
their yellow laps.

On the dais, the ancient tragedy was being replayed.   43
Professor Parsons sat, a sculptor's reject, rigid. His large, heavy
body seemed devoid of will or willingness, and his eyes said he
was no longer with us. The other teachers examined the flag
(which was draped stage right) or their notes, or the windows
which opened on our now-famous playing diamond.

Graduation, the hush-hush magic time of frills and gifts and   44
congratulations and diplomas, was finished for me before my
name was called. The accomplishment was nothing. The meticu-
lous maps, drawn in three colors of ink, learning and spelling
decasyllabic words, memorizing the whole of *The Rape of
Lucrece*—it was for nothing. Donleavy had exposed us.

We were maids and farmers, handymen and washerwomen,   45
and anything higher that we aspired to was farcical and presumptuous.

Then I wished that Gabriel Prosser and Nat Turner had killed   46
all whitefolks in their beds and that Abraham Lincoln had been
assassinated before the signing of the Emancipation Proclama-
tion, and that Harriet Tubman had been killed by that blow on
her head and Christopher Columbus had drowned in the *Santa
Maria*.

It was awful to be a Negro and have no control over my life.   47
It was brutal to be young and already trained to sit quietly and
listen to charges brought against my color with no chance of de-

fense. We should all be dead. I thought I should like to see us all dead, one on top of the other. A pyramid of flesh with the white-folks on the bottom, as the broad base, then the Indians with their silly tomahawks and teepees and wigwams and treaties, the Negroes with their mops and recipes and cotton sacks and spiri-tuals sticking out of their mouths. The Dutch children should all stumble in their wooden shoes and break their necks. The French should choke to death on the Louisiana Purchase (1803) while silkworms ate all the Chinese with their stupid pigtails. As a species, we were an abomination. All of us.

Donleavy was running for election, and assured our parents   48
that if he won we could count on having the only colored paved playing field in that part of Arkansas. Also—he never looked up to acknowledge the grunts of acceptance—also, we were bound to get some new equipment for the home economics building and the workshop.

He finished, and since there was no need to give any more   49
than the most perfunctory thank-you's, he nodded to the men on the stage, and the tall white man who was never introduced joined him at the door. They left with the attitude that now they were off to something really important. (The graduation cere-monies of Lafayette County Training School had been a mere pre-liminary.)

The ugliness they left was palpable. An uninvited guest who   50
wouldn't leave. The choir was summoned and sang a modern arrangement of "Onward Christian Soldiers," with new words pertaining to graduates seeking their place in the world. But it didn't work. Elouise, the daughter of the Baptist minister, recited "Invictus," and I could have cried at the impertinence of "I am the master of my fate, I am the captain of my soul."

My name had lost its ring of familiarity and I had to be   51
nudged to go and receive my diploma. All my preparations had fled. I neither marched up to the stage like a conquering Amazon, nor did I look in the audience for Bailey's nod of approval. Marguerite Johnson, I heard the name again, my honors were read, there were noises in the audience of appreciation, and I took my place on the stage as rehearsed.

I thought about colors I hated: ecru, puce, lavender, beige and   52
black.

There was shuffling and rustling around me, then Henry   53
Reed was giving his valedictory address, "To Be or Not to Be." Hadn't he heard the whitefolks? We couldn't *be,* so the question was a waste of time. Henry's voice came out clear and strong. I

1. With the irrational optimism of youth, the graduates of Angelou's eighth-grade class are convinced that their graduation certificates will open doors, not to the menial jobs of their parents and grandparents, but to wonderful opportunities beyond imagination.

2. Angelou was amazed and grateful just to be alive on her graduation day. Up until that special morning, she had lived with the fatalistic conviction that God would call her to Him before she ever had the opportunity to "walk up the stairs in the auditorium and gracefully receive my hard-earned diploma" (para. 20). In addition, Angelou also wanted to remember the innocent pride that enveloped her, pride that would be bruised later at the ceremony she had awaited for such a long time.

3. As Angelou and her family trudge up the hill to school, the somber changes that are about to occur in the ceremony are foreshadowed by her observation that "The school blazed without gaiety" (para. 27), accompanied by a feeling of "ill-fated timing" (para. 27). The illusion the graduates had created of sparkling beauty, extraordinary talent, and infinite worlds to conquer was shattered by Donleavy's patronizing praise of Black athletes as models for the children (instead of the scientists or writers of White children's dreams) and by his pledge, if he won at the polls, of a paved playground and perhaps some new home economics and workshop equipment (rather than the art and chemistry supplies promised to the White school). Through his eyes, the graduates instantly saw themselves for what they were: a cluster of Black adolescents in homemade dresses and secondhand trousers, the new generation of "maids and farmers, handymen and washerwomen, and anything higher that we aspired to was farsical and presumptuous" (para. 45).

feared to look at him. Hadn't he got the message? There was no "nobler in the mind" for Negroes because the world didn't think we had minds, and they let us know it. "Outrageous fortune"? Now, that was a joke. When the ceremony was over I had to tell Henry Reed some things. That is, if I still cared. Not "rub," Henry, "erase." "Ah, there's the erase." Us.

Henry had been a good student in elocution. His voice rose on tides of promise and fell on waves of warnings. The English teacher had helped him to create a sermon winging through Hamlet's soliloquy. To be a man, a doer, a builder, a leader, or to be a tool, an unfunny joke, a crusher of funky toadstools. I marveled that Henry could go through with the speech as if we had a choice. 54

I had been listening and silently rebutting each sentence with my eyes closed; then there was a hush, which in an audience warns that something unplanned is happening. I looked up and saw Henry Reed, the conservative, the proper, the A student, turn his back to the audience and turn to us (the proud graduating class of 1940) and sing, nearly speaking, 55

> "Lift ev'ry voice and sing
> Till earth and heaven ring
> Ring with the harmonies of Liberty . . ."

It was the poem written by James Weldon Johnson. It was the music composed by J. Rosamond Johnson. It was the Negro national anthem. Out of habit we were singing it.

Our mothers and fathers stood in the dark hall and joined the hymn of encouragement. A kindergarten teacher led the small children onto the stage and the buttercups and daisies and bunny rabbits marked time and tried to follow: 56

> "Stony the road we trod
> Bitter the chastening rod
> Felt in the days when hope, unborn, had died.
> Yet with a steady beat
> Have not our weary feet
> Come to the place for which our fathers sighed?"

Each child I knew had learned that song with his ABC's and along with "Jesus Loves Me This I Know." But I personally had never heard it before. Never heard the words, despite the thousands of times I had sung them. Never thought they had anything to do with me. 57

On the other hand, the words of Patrick Henry had made such an impression on me that I had been able to stretch myself tall and trembling and say, "I know not what course others may take, but as for me, give me liberty or give me death."

And now I heard, really for the first time:

> "We have come over a way that with tears
> has been watered,
> We have come, treading our path through
> the blood of the slaughtered."

While echoes of the song shivered in the air, Henry Reed bowed his head, said "Thank you," and returned to his place in the line. The tears that slipped down many faces were not wiped away in shame.

We were on top again. As always, again. We survived. The depths had been icy and dark, but now a bright sun spoke to our souls. I was no longer simply a member of the proud graduating class of 1940; I was a proud member of the wonderful, beautiful Negro race.

Oh, Black known and unknown poets, how often have your auctioned pains sustained us? Who will compute the lonely nights made less lonely by your songs, or the empty pots made less tragic by your tales?

If we were a people much given to revealing secrets, we might raise monuments and sacrifice to the memories of our poets, but slavery cured us of that weakness. It may be enough, however, to have it said that we survive in exact relationship to the dedication of our poets (including preachers, musicians and blues singers).

UNDERSTANDING DETAILS

1. How were the graduates of Angelou's eighth-grade class "like travelers with exotic destinations on their minds" (paragraph 1)?
2. Explain in your own words how the author felt on graduation morning. Why did she hope the memory of that morning would never leave her?
3. At what point in the narrative does Angelou begin to prepare us for abrupt changes that are about to occur at the ceremony? What does she mean when she says, "Donleavy had exposed us" (paragraph 44)?

ANSWERS TO QUESTIONS: ANALYZING MEANING (p. 122)

58 **1.** The overriding purpose of this eassay is to show the ability of human beings to survive despite all odds. The excerpt revolves not only around the tension between Blacks and Whites of Stamps, Arkansas, but 59 around the audacity of Angelou's dreams in contrast with the social expectations for her people in that time and place.

2. Donleavy's condescending speech about the sports opportunities and lack of other opportunities available to the graduates defeats the hopes for greatness that the author had prior to the ceremony. Though she 60 thought her diploma would bring her success in the world, Donleavy's speech limits the possibilities for male graduates and completely denies the female students any 61 hope of achievement.

3. Realizing the absurdity of his pretentious valedictory address after the disheartening comments of Donleavy, Henry Reed turns and begins to sing the Negro National Anthem, originally eliminated from the 62 program because of the presence of "whitefolks." Joined by the graduating class and the entire audience, he leads the song that says they will continue to survive.

63 ### ANSWERS TO QUESTIONS: DISCOVERING RHETORICAL STRATEGIES (p. 122)

1. Angelou develops an atmosphere of euphoric anticipation by devoting almost half the essay to the spirited preparation for the big day—first offering a panoramic view of the frenzied activity of the school, then turning the focus upon herself to create a very personal response to the celebration. As graduation day grows closer, she gives loving attention to each individual detail, retarding time and building anticipation by stretching out each description, culminating with an impatient dispute about who should lead as they climb the hill to the school because it embarrasses Uncle Willie "to have to walk so slowly" (para. 25). The intensity of the excitement provides a stark contrast to the crushing revelations by Donleavy. The author's shift from omniscient to first-person narration in paragraph 6 begins for us the identification between writer and reader that will grow stronger and then reach a climax during the Donleavy speech.

2. Although no overt hostility is present in paragraph 40, the passage becomes sarcastic in tone, contemptuously noting the equation of the "white kids" with mental achievement, the Black boys with physical prowess, and the Black girls with nothing at all. A subtle difference in connotation also exists between the phrase "have a chance," which is used in conjunction with the White children and suggests the possibility of success, and "try," which describes the Black boys and hints at improbability.

3. The writer spends 18 paragraphs discussing the preparation for graduation day and 45 (beginning with "Amazingly the great day finally dawned and I was out of bed before I knew it") describing the activities on graduation day itself. Spending over twice as long on graduation day emphasizes the agonizing movement from joy to sorrow to survival that Angelou felt, and it also underscores the resignation she leaves us with at the end of the essay.

PREWRITING

In preparation for the writing assignments, the Preparing to Write questions focus on a single event that each student anticipated for a long time. The questions encourage students to analyze the event, now that it is over, before they write on a related topic. See pages 16–23 for suggestions on generating ideas in response to these questions.

ADDITIONAL DISCUSSION/WRITING TOPIC

Your high school has asked you to speak at its graduation ceremony on the extent to which you think rituals such as graduation are important in our lives. Write a speech explaining your thoughts on this issue, citing stories from your own life whenever possible.

ANALYZING MEANING

1. What is the overriding purpose of this narrative? In what way is the essay based on opposing forces?
2. Why is Donleavy's reference to the successful football and basketball players so devastating to the author? Why does Angelou say, "Graduation . . . was finished for me before my name was called" (paragraph 44)?
3. What action by Henry Reed serves to unite and encourage the class at the conclusion of his commencement speech? Why does it do so?

DISCOVERING RHETORICAL STRATEGIES

1. How does Angelou build up the atmosphere of euphoric anticipation connected with graduation at Lafayette County Training School? How does this sense of excitement help make the narrative especially effective? Why does Angelou shift from an omniscient point of view to first-person narrator after paragraph 5?
2. The tone of paragraphs 40 and 41 becomes sharply angry, frustrated, and self-aware when Angelou realizes exactly what the keynote speaker is saying. How does the author's use of language help her achieve this change in tone from optimism to despair? Give specific examples to explain your answer.
3. This essay could easily be divided into two parts: preparation for graduation day and the day itself. On which section does the author spend most of her time? Why do you think she creates this imbalance?

IDEAS FOR DISCUSSION/WRITING

Preparing to Write

Write freely about a day you looked forward to for a long time: What was the occasion? Were the preparations elaborate? How did you feel as the day approached? On the day itself? After the day was over? Did everything turn out as you had expected it would? How do you look upon this experience now?

Choosing a Topic

1. Write a narrative essay for the general public about a big event in your life or in the life of someone important to you. Take time to choose an appropriate point of view. Then choose and arrange your details in such a way that your readers will be interested in the essay.
2. Some events don't quite turn out the way we hoped they would, but we can often learn a great deal from such experiences. In narrative

form, explain one experience of yours that was very different from the way you had imagined it.

3. In Angelou's narrative, Donleavy imposed a limit on the heights to which the graduates could aspire. Write a narrative essay in which you tell about a time you overcame the odds against you or you exceeded the boundaries imposed on you by others.

REVISING STRATEGY

The careful selection of details is important in the development of any essay, but especially so in a narrative essay, because these details create the substance of the paper. In one of your narrative essays, underline the details. Do they all support a more general "topic" sentence (either explicit or implied)? Do you have enough details to explain all your generalities? Are these details as specific as possible so the readers can understand your narrative clearly? Locate any problem areas in your essay and revise them, concentrating on making your details as precise as you can.

RUSSELL BAKER
(1925–   )

■ ■ ■

The Saturday Evening Post

Russell Baker is one of America's foremost satirists and humorists. Born in Virginia, he grew up in New Jersey and Maryland, graduated from Johns Hopkins University, and then served for two years as a pilot in the Navy. Following the service, he became a newspaper reporter for the *Baltimore Sun*, which sent him to England as its London correspondent. He subsequently joined the staff of the *New York Times* as a member of its Washington bureau. Since 1962, he has written his widely syndicated "Observer" column in the *Times*, which blends wry humor, a keen interest in language, and biting social commentary about the Washington scene. His books include *An American in Washington* (1961), *No Cause for Panic* (1964), and *Poor Russell's Almanac* (1972), plus two collections of early essays, *So This Is Depravity* (1980) and *The Rescue of Miss Yaskell and Other Pipe Dreams* (1983). *Growing Up* (1982), a bestseller vividly recounting his own childhood, earned him the 1983 Pulitzer Prize for biography. His most recent publications include *The Good Times* (1989), which continues his life story from approximately age twenty until he began working for the *New York Times* in the early 1960s, and *There's a Country in My Cellar: The Best of Russell Baker* (1990), a collection of his most recent newspaper columns.

PREREADING

The purpose of this Preparing to Read material is to help students capture the essence of their childhood personalities. Having each student create a cluster (see pages 19 and 20) from the word "childhood" is a good way to begin this process of free association. See pages 3–6 for other ways to generate thoughts on these questions.

Preparing to Read

The following skillfully written essay is an excerpt from Baker's autobiography, *Growing Up*. In it, the author recalls enduring memories from his youth that clearly project the experiences and emotions of his coming of age in 1920s rural Virginia. As you prepare to read this excerpt, think for a moment about some of your own childhood memories: What were your strengths as a child? Your weaknesses? Have these character traits changed as you've matured? How are you like or unlike various members of your family? How do you react to these similarities and/or differences? What are your main goals in life? How do your character traits affect these goals?

I began working in journalism when I was eight years old. It was my mother's idea. She wanted me to "make something" of myself and, after a levelheaded appraisal of my strengths, decided I had better start young if I was to have any chance of keeping up with the competition.

The flaw in my character which she had already spotted was lack of "gumption." My idea of a perfect afternoon was lying in front of the radio rereading my favorite Big Little Book, *Dick Tracy Meets Stooge Viller*. My mother despised inactivity. Seeing me having a good time in repose, she was powerless to hide her disgust. "You've got no more gumption than a bump on a log," she said. "Get out in the kitchen and help Doris do those dirty dishes."

My sister Doris, though two years younger than I, had enough gumption for a dozen people. She positively enjoyed washing dishes, making beds, and cleaning the house. When she was only seven she could carry a piece of short-weighted cheese back to the A&P, threaten the manager with legal action, and come back triumphantly with the full quarter-pound we'd paid for and a few ounces extra thrown in for forgiveness. Doris could have made something of herself if she hadn't been a girl. Because of this defect, however, the best she could hope for was a career as a nurse or schoolteacher, the only work that capable females were considered up to in those days.

This must have saddened my mother, this twist of fate that had allocated all the gumption to the daughter and left her with a son who was content with Dick Tracy and Stooge Viller. If disappointed, though, she wasted no energy on self-pity. She would make me make something of myself whether I wanted to or not. "The Lord helps those who help themselves," she said. That was the way her mind worked.

She was realistic about the difficulty. Having sized up the material the Lord had given her to mold, she didn't overestimate what she could do with it. She didn't insist that I grow up to be President of the United States.

Fifty years ago parents still asked boys if they wanted to grow up to be President, and asked it not jokingly but seriously. Many parents who were hardly more than paupers still believed their sons could do it. Abraham Lincoln had done it. We were only sixty-five years from Lincoln. Many a grandfather who walked among us could remember Lincoln's time. Men of grandfatherly age were the worst for asking if you wanted to grow up to be President. A surprising number of little boys said yes and meant it.

1

2

3

4

5

6

BACKGROUND INFORMATION

Russell Baker's autobiographical essay "The Saturday Evening Post" recreates with gentle humor the feelings of an eight-year-old child who is torn between the desire to please his zealous mother and his total ineptitude as a salesman. Despite his mother's continual injunction to "have a little gumption, Russell" (para. 9) and his realization that he would never make anything of himself by "pursuing a life in business" (para. 63), Baker does not look upon his mother's obsession with success with bitterness or anger. He treats her idiosyncrasies with amused affection, crediting this period of his life with influencing positively his eventual choice of careers.

READABILITY LEVEL

7.4

RELATED READINGS

chasuble (para. 30): a sleeveless outer garment worn by the priest officiating at Catholic mass.

I was asked many times myself. No, I would say, I didn't 7 want to grow up to be President. My mother was present during one of these interrogations. An elderly uncle, having posed the usual question and exposed my lack of interest in the Presidency, asked, "Well, what *do* you want to be when you grow up?"

I loved to pick through trash piles and collect empty bottles, 8 tin cans with pretty labels, and discarded magazines. The most desirable job on earth sprang instantly to mind. "I want to be a garbage man," I said.

My uncle smiled, but my mother had seen the first distress- 9 ing evidence of a bump budding on a log. "Have a little gumption, Russell," she said. Her calling me Russell was a signal of unhappiness. When she approved of me I was always "Buddy."

When I turned eight years old she decided that the job of 10 starting me on the road toward making something of myself could no longer be safely delayed. "Buddy," she said one day, "I want you to come home right after school this afternoon. Somebody's coming and I want you to meet him."

When I burst in that afternoon she was in conference in the 11 parlor with an executive of the Curtis Publishing Company. She introduced me. He bent low from the waist and shook my hand. Was it true as my mother had told him, he asked, that I longed for the opportunity to conquer the world of business?

My mother replied that I was blessed with a rare determina- 12 tion to make something of myself.

"That's right," I whispered. 13

"But have you got the grit, the character, the never-say-quit 14 spirit it takes to succeed in business?"

My mother said I certainly did. 15

"That's right," I said. 16

He eyed me silently for a long pause, as though weighing 17 whether I could be trusted to keep his confidence, then spoke man-to-man. Before taking a crucial step, he said, he wanted to advise me that working for the Curtis Publishing Company placed enormous responsibility on a young man. It was one of the great companies of America. Perhaps the greatest publishing house in the world. I had heard, no doubt, of the *Saturday Evening Post*?

Heard of it? My mother said that everyone in our house had 18 heard of the *Saturday Post* and that I, in fact, read it with religious devotion.

Then doubtless, he said, we were also familiar with those two 19 monthly pillars of the magazine world, the *Ladies Home Journal* and the *Country Gentleman*.

Indeed we were familiar with them, said my mother.

Representing the *Saturday Evening Post* was one of the weightiest honors that could be bestowed in the world of business, he said. He was personally proud of being a part of the great corporation.

My mother said he had every right to be.

Again he studied me as though debating whether I was worthy of a knighthood. Finally: "Are you trustworthy?"

My mother said I was the soul of honesty.

"That's right," I said.

The caller smiled for the first time. He told me I was a lucky young man. He admired my spunk. Too many young men thought life was all play. Those young men would not go far in this world. Only a young man willing to work and save and keep his face washed and his hair neatly combed could hope to come out on top in a world such as ours. Did I truly and sincerely believe that I was such a young man?

"He certainly does," said my mother.

"That's right," I said.

He said he had been so impressed by what he had seen of me that he was going to make me a representative of the Curtis Publishing Company. On the following Tuesday, he said, thirty freshly printed copies of the *Saturday Evening Post* would be delivered at our door. I would place these magazines, still damp with the ink of the presses, in a handsome canvas bag, sling it over my shoulder, and set forth through the streets to bring the best in journalism, fiction, and cartoons to the American public.

He had brought the canvas bag with him. He presented it with reverence fit for a chasuble. He showed me how to drape the sling over my left shoulder and across the chest so that the pouch lay easily accessible to my right hand, allowing the best in journalism, fiction, and cartoons to be swiftly extracted and sold to a citizenry whose happiness and security depended upon us soldiers of the free press.

The following Tuesday I raced home from school, put the canvas bag over my shoulder, dumped the magazines in, and, tilting to the left to balance their weight on my right hip, embarked on the highway of journalism.

We lived in Belleville, New Jersey, a commuter town at the northern fringe of Newark. It was 1932, the bleakest year of the Depression. My father had died two years before, leaving us with a few pieces of Sears, Roebuck furniture and not much else, and my mother had taken Doris and me to live with one of her

20
21
22
23
24
25
26
27
28
29
30
31
32

COLLABORATIVE LEARNING:
SMALL GROUP ACTIVITY
Divide your students into groups of 3 or 4
and have them list and discuss the ways in
which writing plays a part in the working
world. If you have enough time, you might
ask these groups to turn their lists into ads
to recruit English majors.

younger brothers. This was my Uncle Allen. Uncle Allen had made something of himself by 1932. As salesman for a soft-drink bottler in Newark, he had an income of $30 a week; wore pearl-gray spats, detachable collars, and a three-piece suit; was happily married; and took in threadbare relatives.

With my load of magazines I headed toward Belleville   33
Avenue. That's where the people were. There were two filling stations at the intersection with Union Avenue, as well as an A&P, a fruit stand, a bakery, a barber shop, Zuccarelli's drugstore, and a diner shaped like a railroad car. For several hours I made myself highly visible, shifting position now and then from corner to corner, from shop window to shop window, to make sure everyone could see the heavy black lettering on the canvas bag that said THE SATURDAY EVENING POST. When the angle of the light indicated it was suppertime, I walked back to the house.

"How many did you sell, Buddy?" my mother asked.   34

"None."   35

"Where did you go?"   36

"The corner of Belleville and Union Avenues."   37

"What did you do?"   38

"Stood on the corner waiting for somebody to buy a *Saturday*   39
Evening Post."

"You just stood there?"   40

"Didn't sell a single one."   41

"For God's sake, Russell!"   42

Uncle Allen intervened. "I've been thinking about it for some   43
time," he said, "and I've about decided to take the *Post* regularly. Put me down as a regular customer." I handed him a magazine and he paid me a nickel. It was the first nickel I earned.

Afterwards my mother instructed me in salesmanship. I   44
would have to ring doorbells, address adults with charming self-confidence, and break down resistance with a sales talk pointing out that no one, no matter how poor, could afford to be without the *Saturday Evening Post* in the home.

I told my mother I'd changed my mind about wanting to suc-   45
ceed in the magazine business.

"If you think I'm going to raise a good-for-nothing," she   46
replied, "you've got another think coming." She told me to hit the streets with the canvas bag and start ringing doorbells the instant school was out next day. When I objected that I didn't feel any aptitude for salesmanship, she asked how I'd like to lend her my leather belt so she could whack some sense into me. I bowed to superior will and entered journalism with a heavy heart.

My mother and I had fought this battle almost as long as I   47
could remember. It probably started even before memory began,
when I was a country child in northern Virginia and my mother,
dissatisfied with my father's plain workman's life, determined
that I would not grow up like him and his people, with calluses
on their hands, overalls on their backs, and fourth-grade educations in their heads. She had fancier ideas of life's possibilities.
Introducing me to the *Saturday Evening Post*, she was trying to
wean me as early as possible from my father's world where men
left with their lunch pails at sunup, worked with their hands until
the grime ate into the pores, and died with a few sticks of mail-
order furniture as their legacy. In my mother's vision of the better
life there were desks and white collars, well-pressed suits,
evenings of reading and lively talk, and perhaps—if a man were
very, very lucky and hit the jackpot, really made something important of himself—perhaps there might be a fantastic salary of
$5,000 a year to support a big house and a Buick with a rumble
seat and a vacation in Atlantic City.

And so I set forth with my sack of magazines. I was afraid of   48
the dogs that snarled behind the doors of potential buyers. I was
timid about ringing the doorbells of strangers, relieved when no
one came to the door, and scared when someone did. Despite my
mother's instructions, I could not deliver an engaging sales pitch.
When a door opened I simply asked, "Want to buy a *Saturday
Evening Post*?" In Belleville few persons did. It was a town of
30,000 people, and most weeks I rang a fair majority of its doorbells. But I rarely sold my thirty copies. Some weeks I canvassed
the entire town for six days and still had four or five unsold magazines on Monday evening; then I dreaded the coming of
Tuesday morning, when a batch of thirty fresh *Saturday Evening
Posts* was due at the front door.

"Better get out there and sell the rest of those magazines   49
tonight," my mother would say.

I usually posted myself then at a busy intersection where a   50
traffic light controlled commuter flow from Newark. When the
light turned red I stood on the curb and shouted my sales pitch at
the motorists.

"Want to buy a *Saturday Evening Post*?"   51

One rainy night when car windows were sealed against me I   52
came back soaked and with not a single sale to report. My mother
beckoned to Doris.

"Go back down there with Buddy and show him how to sell   53
these magazines," she said.

1. Baker's ideal day is one of blissful indolence, "lying in front of the radio rereading my favorite Big Little Book, *Dick Tracy Meets Stooge Viller*" (para. 2). In contrast, his aggressive and energetic younger sister, Doris, is happiest "washing dishes, making beds, and cleaning the house" (para. 3).

2. According to Baker's mother, the main flaw in his character is his lack of gumption, the type of shrewdness and initiative required for success in the business world. His choice of writing as a career grows from his relieved realization that "writers didn't have to have any gumption at all" (para. 67).

3. Baker's least favorite of his mother's maxims is "if at first you don't succeed, try, try again." This admonition invariably precedes her insistence that he return to the street to peddle the remainder of the hated magazines.

1. By opening this excerpt with a comparison between his retiring personality and the energetic spirit of his younger sister, Baker introduces his shortcomings in the eyes of his mother. This contrast, emphasized throughout the essay, accentuates the conflict in Baker's life, the struggle between meeting his mother's expectations for him and meeting his own needs.

2. In her insistence that Baker work as a salesman for the *Saturday Evening Post*, the author's mother is attempting to wean him away from his father's world, "where men left with their lunch pails at sunup, worked with their hands until the grime ate into the pores, and died with a few sticks of mail-order furniture as their legacy" (para. 47). From this experience, she hopes he will develop the business sense and salesmanship that will help him flourish in a genteel profession. What he does learn from his *Saturday Evening Post* job is that he is not fit for salesmanship.

Brimming with zest, Doris, who was then seven years old, returned with me to the corner. She took a magazine from the bag, and when the light turned red she strode to the nearest car and banged her small fist against the closed window. The driver, probably startled at what he took to be a midget assaulting his car, lowered the window to stare, and Doris thrust a *Saturday Evening Post* at him. 54

"You need this magazine," she piped, "and it only costs a nickel." 55

Her salesmanship was irresistible. Before the light changed half a dozen time she disposed of the entire batch. I didn't feel humiliated. To the contrary. I was so happy I decided to give her a treat. Leading her to the vegetable store on Belleville Avenue, I bought three apples, which cost a nickel, and gave her one. 56

"You shouldn't waste money," she said. 57

"Eat your apple." I bit into mine. 58

"You shouldn't eat before supper," she said. "It'll spoil your appetite." 59

Back at the house that evening, she dutifully reported me for wasting a nickel. Instead of a scolding, I was rewarded with a pat on the back for having the good sense to buy fruit instead of candy. My mother reached into her bottomless supply of maxims and told Doris, "An apple a day keeps the doctor away." 60

By the time I was ten I had learned all my mother's maxims by heart. Asking to stay up past normal bedtime, I knew that a refusal would be explained with, "Early to bed and early to rise, makes a man healthy, wealthy, and wise." If I whimpered about having to get up early in the morning, I could depend on her to say, "The early bird gets the worm." 61

The one I most despised was, "If at first you don't succeed, try, try again." This was the battle cry with which she constantly sent me back into the hopeless struggle whenever I moaned that I had rung every doorbell in town and knew there wasn't a single potential buyer left in Belleville that week. After listening to my explanation, she handed me the canvas bag and said, "If at first you don't succeed . . . ." 62

Three years in that job, which I would gladly have quit after the first day except for her insistence, produced at least one valuable result. My mother finally concluded that I would never make something of myself by pursuing a life in business and started considering careers that demanded less competitive zeal. 63

One evening when I was eleven I brought home a short "composition" on my summer vacation which the teacher had 64 graded with an A. Reading it with her own schoolteacher's eye, my mother agreed that it was top-drawer seventh grade prose and complimented me. Nothing more was said about it immediately, but a new idea had taken life in her mind. Halfway through supper she suddenly interrupted the conversation.

"Buddy," she said, "maybe you could be a writer."

I clasped the idea to my heart. I had never met a writer, had shown no previous urge to write, and hadn't a notion how to become a writer, but I loved stories and thought that making up stories must surely be almost as much fun as reading them. Best of all, though, and what really gladdened my heart, was the ease of the writer's life. Writers did not have to trudge through the town peddling from canvas bags, defending themselves against angry dogs, being rejected by surly strangers. Writers did not have to ring doorbells. So far as I could make out, what writers did couldn't even be classified as work.

I was enchanted. Writers didn't have to have any gumption at all. I did not dare tell anybody for fear of being laughed at in the schoolyard, but secretly I decided that what I'd like to be when I grew up was a writer.

UNDERSTANDING DETAILS

1. How does Baker's ideal day differ from that of his sister?
2. According to the author's mother, what is the main flaw in his character? How does this flaw eventually affect his choice of a career?
3. Which of his mother's maxims does the author dislike the most? Explain his reaction.

ANALYZING MEANING

1. Why does Baker begin this selection with a comparison between his personality and his sister's? What does this comparison have to do with the rest of the excerpt?
2. Why did the author's mother insist that he work for the *Saturday Evening Post?* What did she think he would gain from the experience? What did he actually learn?
3. Why was Baker so delighted with the idea of becoming a writer when he grew up? How was this notion compatible with his personality?

3. Baker was delighted with the idea of becoming a writer because of what he says "was the ease of the writer's life" (para. 66). This job, which required no assertiveness, no walking through the streets, no real *work*, seemed the perfect profession to Baker.

ANSWERS TO QUESTIONS: DISCOVERING RHETORICAL STRATEGIES (p. 132)

1. The author devotes a substantial portion of the piece to his uneasy interview with the executive from the Curtis Publishing Company, who was at his home to assess the boy's potential as a *Saturday Evening Post* salesman and to impart to him the tricks of the trade. Then, using a few specific examples and many generalizations, Baker describes his three long years as a faint-hearted businessman. Finally, he introduces the "A" composition that rescued him from life as a reluctant salesman. The method of organization places the emphasis on the pain suffered by Baker in his attempts to live up to his mother's expectations and the relief he feels when he discovers a profession that would satisfy both of them. A different arrangement would have given the story a much different focus.

2. Baker's narrative appears to be addressed to an audience made up of "ordinary" middle-class Americans, a group that might appreciate a traditional American success story—the tale of a quiet boy who overcomes poverty and the manipulations of an overambitious mother to become a prosperous writer. This conclusion is supported by the unsophisticated language of the story as well as by its gentle humor.

3. The climax of the narrative occurs with Baker's presentation of the "A" composition to his mother, an achievement resulting in the new notion that perhaps her son should not become a businessman after all, but a writer instead. Baker leads up to the climax with repeated examples of his ineffective salesmanship and his dread of each new shipment of magazines. Finally, his mother's realization that he would never be a businessman prepares the reader for the change of plan. As the narrative reaches its climax, the focus turns from the aspirations of Baker's mother to the dreams of Baker himself.

In preparation for the writing assignments, the Preparing to Write questions ask students to consider their aspirations in light of their immediate family environment. Responses to these queries will vary greatly and are probably handled most productively as private freewriting assignments or journal entries. See pages 16–23 for suggestions on generating ideas in response to these questions.

ADDITIONAL DISCUSSION/WRITING TOPIC

In *Growing Up*, Baker explains that his mother used to say to him, "You've got no more gumption than a bump on a log." Write a narrative essay explaining the amount of gumption you have. What gives you your gumption? How do you maintain it?

REVISING STRATEGY

The arrangement of details in an essay, along with the pacing or timing of those details, has an important effect on the essay's overall impact on its readers. Choose one of your narrative essays, and list all the details or examples in the order they occur. Review this list, and decide which details would be more effective in a different place in the essay. Then revise your paper, paying close attention to the flow and the timing of the details from one point of the essay to another.

DISCOVERING RHETORICAL STRATEGIES

1. How does Baker arrange the details in this excerpt? Why do you think he organizes them in this way? How would a different arrangement have changed the essay?
2. Who do you think is Baker's intended audience? Describe them in detail. How did you come to this conclusion?
3. What is the climax of Baker's narrative? How does he lead up to and develop this climactic moment? What stylistic traits tell us this is the most exciting point in the story?

IDEAS FOR DISCUSSION/WRITING

Preparing to Write

Write freely about yourself in relation to your aspirations: What type of person are you? What do you think about? What are your ideals? Your hopes? Your dreams? Your fears? What do you enjoy doing in your spare time? How are you different from other members of your family? Is anyone in your family a model for you? How have members of your immediate family affected your daily life—past and present? Your career goals? How do you anticipate your family will affect your future?

Choosing a Topic

1. Write a narrative essay introducing yourself to your English class. To explain and define your identity, include descriptions of family members whenever appropriate.
2. Write a narrative that helps explain to a friend how you got involved in a current interest of yours. To expand upon your narrative, refer whenever possible to your long-term goals and aspirations.
3. Ten years from now, your local newspaper decides to devote an entire section to people getting started in careers. You are asked to submit the story of how you got involved in your profession (whatever it may be). Write a narrative that might appear in your hometown newspaper ten years from now; be sure to give the article a catchy headline.

MARK MATHABANE
(1960–   )

■ ■ ■

Passport to Knowledge

QUOTATION ON THINKING

"Reading furnished the mind only with materials of knowledge; it is thinking that makes what we read ours."

John Locke

Born in a Black ghetto section of Johannesburg, South Africa, Mark Mathabane grew up persecuted by a racist political structure and dominated by an illiterate, angry father who hated education and bullied his son into following ancient tribal customs. At the insistence of his mother, Mathabane reluctantly began school, where he slowly discovered not only the excitement of learning but also the game of tennis, which he had always seen as a "White man's sport." As his studies progressed, so did his tennis skills, which garnered him success in local tournaments and brought him to the attention of Wimbledon champion Stan Smith, who helped arrange a scholarship for him at Dowling College in New York. At Dowling, he was number one on the tennis team and earned a degree in economics. Now a freelance writer in New York, Mathabane has chronicled his struggle to escape South Africa's dehumanizing, repressive environment in a bestselling biography entitled *Kaffir Boy* (1986). A sequel, *Kaffir Boy in America*, was published in 1989.

Preparing to Read

The following essay, taken from Mathabane's autobiography, narrates the author's first experience with school when he was seven years old and illustrates the fierce power struggle between his father and mother over whether their son would receive an education. The word *kaffir*, an Arabic term meaning "infidel," is a name disparagingly applied to Blacks in South Africa. As you prepare to read this essay, take a few minutes to think about the various types of pressure in your life: What different kinds of pressure are you under right now? What is the most obvious pressure? The most subtle, unspoken pressure? How do you generally respond to such influence? Have you ever been forced to do something you didn't want to do? What were the circumstances? Who applied the pressure? How did you react to the situation? Could you have avoided the experience? How do you feel about the event now? Did you learn anything useful from it?

PREREADING

The purpose of this Preparing to Read material is to encourage students to explore various forms of pressure in their lives. This topic works well as a class discussion before students write, because as they talk they clarify the word "pressure." Rather than limiting the scope of inquiry, this preliminary discussion becomes a generative process for most students before they respond to the questions here. See pages 3–6 for other ways to generate thoughts on these questions.

BACKGROUND INFORMATION

This narrative by Mark Mathabane relates the author's traumatic introduction to school when he was seven years old. It also sets into contrast his brutal father's distrust of "a useless white man's education" (para. 99) and his mother's hope that the experience would give her son the necessary academic skills to escape the repressive, racist world of their South African ghetto.

READABILITY LEVEL

7.5

RELATED READINGS

Black Issues

Cultural Diversity

Growing Up

Parent–Child Relationships

1   When my mother began dropping hints that I would soon be going to school, I vowed never to go because school was a waste of time. She laughed and said, "We'll see. You don't know what you're talking about." My philosophy on school was that of a gang of ten-, eleven- and twelve-year-olds whom I so revered that their every word seemed that of an oracle.

2   These boys had long left their homes and were now living in various neighborhood junkyards, making it on their own. They slept in abandoned cars, smoked glue and benzene, ate pilchards and brown bread, sneaked into the white world to caddy and, if unsuccessful, came back to the township to steal beer and soda bottles from shebeens, or goods from the Indian traders on First Avenue. Their life-style was exciting, adventurous and full of surprises; and I was attracted to it. My mother told me that they were no-gooders, that they would amount to nothing, that I should not associate with them, but I paid no heed. What does she know? I used to tell myself. One thing she did not know was that the gang's way of life had captivated me wholly, particularly their philosophy on school: They hated it and considered an education a waste of time.

3   They, like myself, had grown up in an environment where the value of an education was never emphasized, where the first thing a child learned was not how to read and write and spell, but how to fight and steal and rebel; where the money to send children to school was grossly lacking, for survival was first priority. I kept my membership in the gang, knowing that for as long as I was under its influence, I would never go to school.

4   One day my mother woke me up at four in the morning.

5   "Are they here? I didn't hear any noises," I asked in the usual way.

6   "No," my mother said. "I want you to get into that washtub over there."

7   "What!" I balked, upon hearing the word *washtub*. I feared taking baths like one feared the plague. Throughout seven years of hectic living the number of baths I had taken could be counted on one hand with several fingers missing. I simply had no natural inclination for water; cleanliness was a trait I still had to acquire. Besides, we had only one bathtub in the house, and it constantly sprung a leak.

8   "I said get into that tub!" My mother shook a finger in my face.

9   Reluctantly, I obeyed, yet wondered why all of a sudden I had to take a bath. My mother, armed with a scrobrush and a

piece of Lifebuoy soap, purged me of years and years of grime till I ached and bled. As I howled, feeling pain shoot through my limbs as the thistles of the brush encountered stubborn callouses, there was a loud knock at the door.

Instantly my mother leaped away from the tub and headed, on tiptoe, toward the bedroom. Fear seized me as I, too, thought of the police. I sat frozen in the bathtub, not knowing what to do.

"Open up, Mujaji [my mother's maiden name]," Granny's voice came shrilling through the door. "It's me."

My mother heaved a sigh of relief; her tense limbs relaxed. She turned and headed to the kitchen door, unlatched it and in came Granny and Aunt Bushy.

"You scared me half to death," my mother said to Granny. "I had forgotten all about your coming."

"Are you ready?" Granny asked my mother.

"Yes—just about," my mother said, beckoning me to get out of the washtub.

She handed me a piece of cloth to dry myself. As I dried myself, questions raced through my mind: What's going on? What's Granny doing at our house this ungodly hour of the morning? And why did she ask my mother, "Are you ready?" While I stood debating, my mother went into the bedroom and came out with a stained white shirt and a pair of faded black shorts.

"Here," she said, handing me the togs, "put these on."

"Why?" I asked.

"Put them on I said!"

I put the shirt on; it was grossly loose-fitting. It reached all the way down to my ankles. Then I saw the reason why: It was my father's shirt!

"But this is Papa's shirt," I complained. "It don't fit me."

"Put it on," my mother insisted. "I'll make it fit."

"The pants don't fit me either," I said. "Whose are they anyway?"

"Put them on," my mother said. "I'll make them fit."

Moments later I had the garments on; I looked ridiculous. My mother started working on the pants and shirt to make them fit. She folded the shirt in so many intricate ways and stashed it inside the pants, they too having been folded several times at the waist. She then choked the pants at the waist with a piece of sisal rope to hold them up. She then lavishly smeared my face, arms and legs with a mixture of pig's fat and vaseline. "This will insulate you from the cold," she said. My skin gleamed like the morning star and I felt as hot as the center of the sun and I smelled God

DEFINITIONS

benzene (para. 2): a flammable, toxic liquid used as a solvent and a motor fuel.
pilchards (para. 2): herrings or sardines.
shebeen (para. 2): an unlicensed or illegally operated tavern.
scropbrush (para. 9): a variation of scrub brush.
veld (para. 36): open grassland, usually with scattered shrubs or trees.
scuttle (para. 38): a broad, open basket used for carrying grain and vegetables.
tsotsi (para. 40): a street thug, member of a gang.
Pretoria (para. 64): capital of the Republic of South Africa.
Pitori (para. 65): the grandmother's mispronunciation of "Pretoria."
Shangaan (para. 68): a tribe of Zulu origin; also the language of the Shangaan people.
Venda (para. 69): a Bantu language of the Venda people of the northern Transvaal (northeastern province of South Africa between the Vaal and Limpopo rivers).
Zulu (para. 73): a Bantu language of the Zulu people of Natal (eastern province of South Africa).
Sisotho (para. 73): the language of the Basotho or Basuto people.
taboo (para. 104): prohibited.
mores (para. 106): morally binding customs, attitudes, habits, or manners.
Louis Trichardt (para. 111): a city in the northwest corner of South Africa.

At the beginning of *Kaffir Boy*, Mathabane quotes Nobel Peace Prize winner Albert Luthuli as saying " 'apartheid' or 'separate development' . . . is unforgivable. It seems utterly indifferent to the suffering of individual persons, who lose their land, their homes, their jobs, in pursuit of what surely is the most terrible dream in the world." Have your students speculate on the nature of the dream Luthuli refers to: What might it consist of? Why is it so terrible? Then, bring the whole class back to a discussion of apartheid and its relationship to this "terrible dream."

knows like what. After embalming me, she headed to the bedroom.

"Where are we going, Gran'ma?" I said, hoping that she would tell me what my mother refused to tell me. I still had no idea I was about to be taken to school. 26

"Didn't your mother tell you?" Granny said with a smile. "You're going to start school." 27

"What!" I gasped, leaping from the chair where I was sitting as if it were made of hot lead. "I am not going to school!" I blurted out and raced toward the kitchen door. 28

My mother had just reappeared from the bedroom and guessing what I was up to, she yelled, "Someone get the door!" 29

Aunt Bushy immediately barred the door. I turned and headed for the window. As I leaped for the windowsill, my mother lunged at me and brought me down. I tussled, "Let go of me! I don't want to go to school! Let me go!" but my mother held fast onto me. 30

"It's no use now," she said, grinning triumphantly as she pinned me down. Turning her head in Granny's direction, she shouted, "Granny! Get a rope quickly!" 31

Granny grabbed a piece of rope nearby and came to my mother's aid. I bit and clawed every hand that grabbed me, and howled protestations against going to school; however, I was no match for the two determined matriarchs. In a jiffy they had me bound, hands and feet. 32

"What's the matter with him?" Granny, bewildered, asked my mother. "Why did he suddenly turn into an imp when I told him you're taking him to school?" 33

"You shouldn't have told him that he's being taken to school," my mother said. "He doesn't want to go there. That's why I requested you come today, to help me take him there. Those boys in the streets have been a bad influence on him." 34

As the two matriarchs hauled me through the door, they told Aunt Bushy not to go to school but stay behind and mind the house and the children. 35

The sun was beginning to rise from beyond the veld when Granny and my mother dragged me to school. The streets were beginning to fill with their everyday traffic: Old men and women, wizened, bent and ragged, were beginning their rambling; workless men and women were beginning to assemble in their usual coteries and head for shebeens in the backyards where they discussed how they escaped the morning pass raids and contemplated the conditions of life amidst intense beer drinking and 36 vacant, uneasy laughter; young boys and girls, some as young as myself, were beginning their aimless wanderings along the narrow, dusty streets in search of food, carrying bawling infants piggyback.

As we went along some of the streets, boys and girls who shared the same fears about school as I were making their feelings known in a variety of ways. They were howling their protests and trying to escape. A few managed to break loose and make a mad dash for freedom, only to be recaptured in no time, admonished or whipped, or both, and ordered to march again.

As we made a turn into Sixteenth Avenue, the street leading to the tribal school I was being taken to, a short, chubby black woman came along from the opposite direction. She had a scuttle overflowing with coal on her *doek*-covered (cloth-covered) head. An infant, bawling deafeningly, was loosely swathed with a piece of sheepskin onto her back. Following closely behind the woman, and picking up pieces of coal as they fell from the scuttle and placing them in a small plastic bag, was a half-naked, potbellied and thumb-sucking boy of about four. The woman stopped abreast. For some reason we stopped too.

"I wish I had done the same to my oldest son," the strange woman said in a regretful voice, gazing at me. I was confounded by her stopping and offering her unsolicited opinion.

"I wish I had done that to my oldest son," she repeated and suddenly burst into tears; amidst sobs, she continued, "before . . . the street claimed him . . . and . . . turned him into a *tsotsi.*"

Granny and my mother offered consolatory remarks to the strange woman.

"But it's too late now," the strange woman continued, tears now streaming freely down her puffy cheeks. She made no attempt to dry them. "It's too late now," she said for the second time, "he's beyond help. I can't help him even if I wanted to. *Uswile* [He is dead]."

"How did he die?" my mother asked in a sympathetic voice.

"He shunned school and, instead, grew up to live by the knife. And the same knife he lived by ended his life. That's why whenever I see a boy-child refuse to go to school, I stop and tell the story of my dear little *mbitsini* [heartbreak]."

Having said that, the strange woman left as mysteriously as she had arrived.

"Did you hear what that woman said!" my mother screamed into my ears. "Do you want the same to happen to you?"

I dropped my eyes. I was confused.

One of the critical issues in American schools today is the accommodation of students from different cultural backgrounds. Have your students discuss this issue in groups of 3 or 4. They should come to some consensus and then report their opinions and their reasoning to the class.

37
38
39
40
41
42
43
44
45
46
47

"Poor woman," Granny said ruefully. "She must have truly   48
loved her son."

Finally, we reached the school and I was ushered into the   49
principal's office, a tiny cubicle facing a row of privies and a
patch of yellowed grass.

"So this is the rascal we'd been talking about," the principal,   50
a tall, wiry man, foppishly dressed in a black pin-striped suit,
said to my mother as we entered. His austere, shiny face, in-
scrutable and imposing, reminded me of my father. He was sitting behind a brown table upon which stood piles of dust and
cobweb-covered books and papers. In one upper pocket of his
jacket was arrayed a variety of pens and pencils; in the other nes-
tled a lily-white handkerchief whose presence was more decora-
tive than utilitarian. Alongside him stood a disproportionately
portly black woman, fashionably dressed in a black skirt and a
white blouse. She had but one pen, and this she held in her hand.
The room was hot and stuffy and buzzing with flies.

"Yes, Principal," my mother answered, "this is he."   51

"I see he's living up to his notoriety," remarked the principal,   52
noticing that I had been bound. "Did he give you too much
trouble?"

"Trouble, Principal," my mother sighed. "He was like an imp."   53

"He's just like the rest of them, Principal," Granny sighed.
"Once they get out into the streets, they become wild. They take   54
to the many vices of the streets like an infant takes to its mother's
milk. They begin to think that there's no other life but the one
shown them by the *tsotsis*. They come to hate school and forget
about the future."

"Well," the principal said. "We'll soon remedy all that. Untie   55
him."

"He'll run away," my mother cried.   56

"I don't think he's that foolish to attempt that with all of us   57
here."

"He *is* that foolish, Principal," my mother said as she and   58
Granny began untying me. "He's tried it before. Getting him here
was an ordeal in itself."

The principal rose from his seat, took two steps to the door   59
and closed it. As the door swung closed, I spotted a row of canes
of different lengths and thicknesses hanging behind it. The principal, seeing me staring at the canes, grinned and said, in a manner
suggesting that he had wanted me to see them, "As long as you
behave, I won't have to use any of those on you."

Use those canes on me? I gasped. I stared at my mother—she   60 smiled; at Granny—she smiled too. That made me abandon any inkling of escaping.

"So they finally gave you the birth certificate and the papers," the principal addressed my mother as he returned to his chair. 61

"Yes, Principal," my mother said, "they finally did. But what a battle it was. It took me nearly a year to get all them papers together." She took out of her handbag a neatly wrapped package and handed it to the principal. "They've been running us around for so long that there were times when I thought he would never attend school, Principal," she said. 62

"That's pretty much standard procedure, Mrs. Mathabane," the principal said, unwrapping the package. "But you now have the papers and that's what's important. 63

"As long as we have the papers," he continued, minutely perusing the contents of the package, "we won't be breaking the law in admitting your son to this school, for we'll be in full compliance with the requirements set by the authorities in Pretoria." 64

"Sometimes I don't understand the laws from Pitori," Granny said. "They did the same to me with my Piet and Bushy. Why, Principal, should our children not be allowed to learn because of some piece of paper?" 65

"The piece of paper you're referring to, Mrs. Mabaso [Granny's maiden name]," the principal said to Granny, "is as important to our children as a pass is to us adults. We all hate passes; therefore, it's only natural we should hate the regulations our children are subjected to. But as we have to live with passes, so our children have to live with the regulations, Mrs. Mabaso. I hope you understand, that is the law of the country. We would have admitted your grandson a long time ago, as you well know, had it not been for the papers. I hope you understand." 66

"I understand, Principal," Granny said, "but I don't understand," she added paradoxically. 67

One of the papers caught the principal's eye and he turned to my mother and asked, "Is your husband a Shangaan, Mrs. Mathabane?" 68

"No, he's not, Principal," my mother said. "Is there anything wrong? He's Venda and I'm Shangaan." 69

The principal reflected for a moment or so and then said, concernedly, "No, there's nothing seriously wrong. Nothing that we can't take care of. You see, Mrs. Mathabane, technically, the fact that your child's father is a Venda makes him ineligible to attend this tribal school because it is only for children whose parents are 70 of the Shangaan tribe. May I ask what language the children speak at home?"

"Both languages," my mother said worriedly, "Venda and Shangaan. Is there anything wrong?" 71

The principal coughed, clearing his throat, then said, "I mean which language do they speak more?" 72

"It depends, Principal," my mother said, swallowing hard. "When their father is around, he wants them to speak only Venda. And when he's not, they speak Shangaan. And when they are out at play, they speak Zulu and Sisotho." 73

"Well," the principal said, heaving a sigh of relief. "In that case, I think an exception can be made. The reason for such an exception is that there's currently no school for Vendas in Alexandra. And should the authorities come asking why we took in your son, we can tell them that. Anyway, your child is half-half." 74

Everyone broke into a nervous laugh, except me. I was bewildered by the whole thing. I looked at my mother, and she seemed greatly relieved as she watched the principal register me; a broad smile broke across her face. It was as if some enormously heavy burden had finally been lifted from her shoulders and her conscience. 75

"Bring him back two weeks from today," the principal said as he saw us to the door. "There're so many children registering today that classes won't begin until two weeks hence. Also, the school needs repair and cleaning up after the holidays. If he refuses to come, simply notify us, and we'll send a couple of big boys to come fetch him, and he'll be very sorry if it ever comes to that." 76

As we left the principal's office and headed home, my mind was still against going to school. I was thinking of running away from home and joining my friends in the junkyard. 77

I didn't want to go to school for three reasons: I was reluctant to surrender my freedom and independence over to what I heard every school-going child call "tyrannous discipline." I had heard many bad things about life in tribal school—from daily beatings by teachers and mistresses who worked you like a mule to long school hours—and the sight of those canes in the principal's office gave ample credence to rumors that school was nothing but a torture chamber. And there was my allegiance to the gang. 78

But the thought of the strange woman's lamentations over her dead son presented a somewhat strong case for going to school: I didn't want to end up dead in the streets. A more com- 79

pelling argument for going to school, however, was the vivid rec-
ollection of all that humiliation and pain my mother had gone
through to get me the papers and the birth certificate so I could
enroll in school. What should I do? I was torn between two
worlds.

But later that evening something happened to force me to go   80
to school.

I was returning home from playing soccer when a neighbor   81
accosted me by the gate and told me that there had been a bloody
fight at my home.

"Your mother and father have been at it again," the neighbor,   82
a woman, said.

"And your mother left."   83

I was stunned.   84

"Was she hurt badly?"   85

"A little bit," the woman said. "But she'll be all right. We took 86
her to your grandma's place."

I became hot with anger.   87

"Is anyone in the house?" I stammered, trying to control my   88
rage.

"Yes, your father is. But I don't think you should go near the   89
house. He's raving mad. He's armed with a meat cleaver. He's
chased out your brother and sisters, also. And some of the neighbors who tried to intervene he's threatened to carve them to
pieces. I have never seen him this mad before."

I brushed aside the woman's warnings and went. Shattered   90
windows convinced me that there had indeed been a skirmish of
some sort. Several pieces of broken bricks, evidently broken after
being thrown at the door, were lying about the door. I tried opening the door; it was locked from the inside. I knocked. No one answered. I knocked again. Still no one answered, until, as I turned
to leave:

"Who's out there?" my father's voice came growling from inside.

"It's me, Johannes," I said.

"Go away, you bastard!" he bellowed. "I don't want you or
that whore mother of yours setting foot in this house. Go away
before I come out there and kill you!"

"Let me in!" I cried. "Dammit, let me in! I want my things!"

"What things? Go away, you black swine!"

I went to the broken window and screamed obscenities at my   91
father, daring him to come out, hoping that if he as much as ever
stuck his black face out, I would pelt him with the half-a-loaf

brick in my hand. He didn't come out. He continued launching a tirade of obscenities at my mother and her mother, calling them whores and bitches and so on. He was drunk, but I wondered where he had gotten the money to buy beer because it was still the middle of the week and he was dead broke. He had lost his entire wage for the past week in dice and had had to borrow bus fare.

"I'll kill you someday for all you're doing to my mother," I 92 threatened him, overwhelmed with rage. Several nosey neighbors were beginning to congregate by open windows and doors. Not wanting to make a spectacle of myself, which was something many of our neighbors seemed to always expect from our family, I backtracked away from the door and vanished into the dark street. I ran, without stopping, all the way to the other end of the township where Granny lived. There I found my mother, her face swollen and bruised and her eyes puffed up to the point where she could scarcely see.

"What happened, Mama?" I asked, fighting to hold back the 93 tears at the sight of her disfigured face.

"Nothing, child, nothing," she mumbled, almost apologeti- 94 cally, between swollen lips. "Your papa simply lost his temper, that's all."

"But why did he beat you up like this, Mama?" Tears came 95 down my face. "He's never beaten you like this before."

My mother appeared reluctant to answer me. She looked 96 searchingly at Granny, who was pounding millet with pestle and mortar and mixing it with sorghum and nuts for an African delicacy. Granny said, "Tell him, child, tell him. He's got a right to know. Anyway, he's the cause of it all."

"Your father and I fought because I took you to school this 97 morning," my mother began. "He had told me not to, and when I told him that I had, he became very upset. He was drunk. We started arguing, and one thing led to another."

"Why doesn't he want me to go to school?"   98

"He says he doesn't have money to waste paying for you to 99 get what he calls a useless white man's education," my mother replied. "But I told him that if he won't pay for your schooling, I would try and look for a job and pay, but he didn't want to hear that, also. 'There are better things for you to work for,' he said. 'Besides, I don't want you to work. How would I look to other men if you, a woman I owned, were to start working?' When I asked him why shouldn't I take you to school, seeing that you were now of age, he replied that he doesn't believe in schools. I told him that school would keep you off the streets and out of trouble, but still he was belligerent."

"Is that why he beat you up?"   100

"Yes, he said I disobeyed his orders."   101

"He's right, child," Granny interjected. "He paid *lobola* [bride   102
price] for you. And your father ate it all up before he left me."

To which my mother replied, "But I desperately want to leave   103
this beast of a man. But with his *lobola* gone I can't do it. That
worthless thing you call your husband shouldn't have sold
Jackson's scrawny cattle and left you penniless."

"Don't talk like that about your father, child," Granny said.   104
"Despite all, he's still your father, you know. Anyway, he asked
for *lobola* only because he had to get back what he spent raising
you. And you know it would have been taboo for him to let you
or any of your sisters go without asking for *lobola.*"

"You and Papa seemed to forget that my sisters and I have   105
minds of our own," my mother said. "We didn't need you to tell
us whom to marry, and why, and how. If it hadn't been for your
interference, I could have married that schoolteacher."

Granny did not reply; she knew well not to. When it came to   106
the act of "selling" women as marriage partners, my mother was
vehemently opposed to it. Not only was she opposed to this one
aspect of tribal culture, but to others as well, particularly those involving relations between men and women and the upbringing
of children. But my mother's sharply differing opinion was an exception rather than the rule among tribal women. Most times,
many tribal women questioned her sanity in daring to question
well-established mores. But my mother did not seem to care; she
would always scoff at her opponents and call them fools in letting
their husbands enslave them completely.

Though I disliked school, largely because I knew nothing   107
about what actually went on there, and the little I knew had
painted a dreadful picture, the fact that a father would not want
his son to go to school, especially a father who didn't go to school,
seemed hard to understand.

"Why do you want me to go to school, Mama?" I asked, hop-   108
ing that she might, somehow, clear up some of the confusion that
was building in my mind.

"I want you to have a future, child," my mother said. "And,   109
contrary to what your father says, school is the only means to a
future. I don't want you growing up to be like your father."

The latter statement hit me like a bolt of lightning. It just   110
about shattered every defense mechanism and every pretext I

1. Mathabane was captivated by the gang's exciting lifestyle of stealing, taking drugs, and sneaking around in the "white world" (para. 2). The dangers of gang life did not occur to him at first. He saw the rewards (food, comradery, goods that he could not afford), but he did not realize that the gang's lifestyle was dangerous or that their disregard for school was the same force that caused his family to live in ignorance and poverty.

2. This is a story about a young boy whose life changes in a matter of a few days. Mathabane at first is interested in gang life and is quite happy just to survive. However, when his mother decides he should go to school, he is forced to make decisions that will affect his entire life. In fact, when Mathabane is taken to school, he has to be tied up like an animal. His views change because of a fight between his mother and father. Like most seven-year-olds, Mathabane feels the need to choose a side. His choice is between his father (who drinks, acts ignorantly and cruelly, and cares little for Mathabane) and his mother (who, despite personal sacrifice, registers Mathabane in school so that his life might be better than her own). At the end of this story, Mathabane understands that his mother is striving to help him live a better life. This decision divides the family but will eventually save Mathabane.

3. The author promises to stay in school "forever" because through this decision he could truly show support for his mother, who had sacrificed so much for him. He realizes his mother cares for him enough to give him the chance to learn, whereas his father wants him to remain ignorant.

had against going to school.

"Your father didn't go to school," she continued, dabbing her puffed eyes to reduce the swelling with a piece of cloth dipped in warm water, "that's why he's doing some of the bad things he's doing. Things like drinking, gambling and neglecting his family. He didn't learn how to read and write; therefore, he can't find a decent job. Lack of any education has narrowly focused his life. He sees nothing beyond himself. He still thinks in the old, tribal way, and still believes that things should be as they were back in the old days when he was growing up as a tribal boy in Louis Trichardt. Though he's my husband, and your father, he doesn't see any of that." 111

"Why didn't he go to school, Mama?" 112

"He refused to go to school because his father led him to believe that an education was a tool through which white people were going to take things away from him, like they did black people in the old days. And that a white man's education was worthless insofar as black people were concerned because it prepared them for jobs they can't have. But I know it isn't totally so, child, because times have changed somewhat. Though our lot isn't any better today, an education will get you a decent job. If you can read or write you'll be better off than those of us who can't. Take my situation: I can't find a job because I don't have papers, and I can't get papers because white people mainly want to register people who can read and write. But I want things to be different for you, child. For you and your brother and sisters. I want you to go to school, because I believe that an education is the key you need to open up a new world and a new life for yourself, a world and life different from that of either your father's or mine. It is the only key that can do that, and only those who seek it earnestly and perseveringly will get anywhere in the white man's world. Education will open doors where none seem to exist. It'll make people talk to you, listen to you and help you; people who otherwise wouldn't bother. It will make you soar, like a bird lifting up into the endless blue sky, and leave poverty, hunger and suffering behind. It'll teach you to learn to embrace what's good and shun what's bad and evil. Above all, it'll make you a somebody in this world. It'll make you grow up to be a good and proud person. That's why I want you to go to school, child, so that education can do all that, and more, for you." 113

A long, awkward silence followed, during which I reflected upon the significance of my mother's lengthy speech. I looked at my mother; she looked at me. 114

Finally, I asked, "How come you know so much about school, Mama? You didn't go to school, did you?"

"No, child," my mother replied. "Just like your father, I never went to school." For a second time that evening, a mere statement of fact had a thunderous impact on me. All the confusion I had about school seemed to leave my mind, like darkness giving way to light. And what had previously been a dark, yawning void in my mind was suddenly transformed into a beacon of light that began to grow larger and larger, until it had swallowed up, blotted out, all the blackness. That beacon of light seemed to reveal things and facts, which, though they must have always existed in me, I hadn't been aware of up until now.

"But unlike your father," my mother went on, "I've always wanted to go to school, but couldn't because my father, under the sway of tribal traditions, thought it unnecessary to educate females. That's why I so much want you to go, child, for if you do, I know that someday I too would come to go, old as I would be then. Promise me, therefore, that no matter what, you'll go back to school. And I, in turn, promise that I'll do everything in my power to keep you there."

With tears streaming down my cheeks and falling upon my mother's bosom, I promised her that I would go to school "forever." That night, at seven and a half years of my life, the battlelines in the families were drawn. My mother on the one side, illiterate but determined to have me drink, for better or for worse, from the well of knowledge. On the other side, my father, he too illiterate, yet determined to have me drink from the well of ignorance. Scarcely aware of the magnitude of the decision I was making or, rather, the decision which was being emotionally thrusted upon me, I chose to fight on my mother's side, and thus my destiny was forever altered.

UNDERSTANDING DETAILS

1. What various pressures and rewards drew Mathabane into the gang he belonged to? What did the gang members think about school?
2. Retell in your own words the basic story of this narrative. At what point are "the battlelines in the family" drawn?
3. Why does the author decide to stay in school "forever"(paragraph 118)?

ANSWERS TO QUESTIONS:
ANALYZING MEANING (p. 146)

115 **1.** Mathabane shows the importance of education in two ways in this essay. First, he 116 illustrates the opportunities education can bring to a person's life by the comparison between himself at seven and the boys in the gang. Second, he uses the example of his own father to demonstrate the negative effects a lack of education can have on a person's life. His narrative effectively shows the reader that getting an education is one of the most important steps a person can take in planning for the future.

2. For Mathabane's father, schools symbolize the governmental system that restricts 117 and subjugates the Blacks in South Africa to a life of poverty. He thinks that, even with an education, his son will not be able to find a good job or be treated fairly. Mathabane's father, who agrees with the gang that schools are a waste of time, fears that his son might learn to accept the system that teaches Blacks subservience. Mathabane's mother believes quite the opposite. She sees small improvements in society and thinks 118 that, even though there may not be great opportunities for her son, he will have a better chance of success if he is educated. Though she resents the government's restrictions herself, she does not let them control her life as Mathabane's father does.

3. Mathabane chose to fight on his mother's side because she had hope for him and was willing to make a sacrifice to see him have a chance to better himself, whereas his father did not encourage him at all. Obviously Mathabane's destiny was altered by this; he is now a very successful writer. If Mathabane had not made this decision at such a young age, he probably would have been killed in the streets of South Africa.

1. Besides narration, the author uses vivid descriptions such as his depiction of the bruises his mother acquired in her fight for Mathabane's education; comparison/contrast as he describes the differences between the lifestyle and beliefs of the gang members and those his mother is trying to instill in him; and example in the portrayal of his father, who is obviously a product of the type of lifestyle that Mathabane decides to avoid.

2. Responses to this question will vary. •

3. Responses to this question will vary.

PREWRITING

In preparation for the writing assignments, the focus of the Preparing to Write questions is on the pros and cons of various types of pressure in our lives. The questions ask the students whether or not they can see any difference between positive and negative pressures in their lives. See pages 16–23 for suggestions on generating ideas in response to these questions.

ADDITIONAL DISCUSSION/WRITING TOPIC

Fill in the following blank with a word that interests you: "Passport to_____." Then, use this phrase as the title of a narrative essay describing for your classmates a journey you took to a special place or state of mind. Choose your details carefully, and explain your experience as fully as possible.

ANALYZING MEANING

1. What is Mathabane's main purpose in this essay? Do you think he achieves it?

2. Why doesn't Mathabane's father believe in schools? What do schools symbolize for him? What do they symbolize for the author's mother?

3. In the last paragraph of this essay, Mathabane says that at age seven and a half, "scarcely aware of the magnitude of the decision I was making or, rather, the decision which was being emotionally thrusted upon me, I chose to fight on my mother's side, and thus my destiny was forever altered." Why does he choose to fight on his mother's side? In what ways was his destiny "forever altered"?

DISCOVERING RHETORICAL STRATEGIES

1. Explain the rhetorical strategies, besides narration, that the author uses to help develop his story.

2. In this essay, Mathabane uses dialogue effectively to recreate his feelings about going to school. Find an example of dialogue that seems to work especially well, and explain its effectiveness.

3. Mathabane cites many vivid details of his preparation for the first day of school. Which details seem most vivid to you? Why do you think they are particularly effective?

IDEAS FOR DISCUSSION/WRITING

Preparing to Write

Write freely about your views on the various pressures in your life: What forms of pressure do you see around you? What forms of pressure play an active role in your life? Which types of pressure are unpleasant for you? Pleasant for you? Are there any forms of pressure that you fear? If so, what are they? Do you think pressure can ever be a productive force in our lives? Why or why not?

Choosing a Topic

1. For a group of sociologists trying to classify the various types of social pressures in the world today, you have been asked to write a narrative essay about one specific pressure you were subjected to and its effect on your life.

2. Write a narrative essay for a group of high school students in which you explain the value of a good education. Use stories from your own life to illustrate your main points.

3. You have been asked by the president of your college or university to serve as a student representative on a campus-wide committee charged with investigating some of the pressures students face today. Each of the committee members is obliged to present a coherent statement on one of these pressures. Present yours in narrative form.

REVISING STRATEGY

A good narrative essay *shows* rather than *tells* its readers what it wants them to know or feel. In one of your narrative essays, label all the points at which you show or tell your readers what to think or feel. Notice how some of the telling could be converted to showing. Then revise your paper so that it shows rather than tells in as many places as possible.

CHAPTER 3

EXAMPLE
■ ■ ■
Illustrating Ideas

Using Examples

Citing an example to help make a point is one of the most instinctive techniques we use in communication. If, for instance, you state that being an internationally ranked tennis player requires constant practice, a friend might challenge that assertion and ask what you mean by "constant practice." When you respond "about three hours a day," your friend might ask for more specific proof. At this stage in the discussion, you could offer the following illustrations to support your statement: When not on tour, Steffi Graf practices three hours per day; Monica Seles, four hours; and André Agassi, two hours. Your friend's doubt will have been answered through your use of examples.

Defining Examples

Well-chosen examples and illustrations are an essay's building blocks. They are drawn from your experience, your observations, and your reading. They help you *show* rather than *tell* what you mean, usually by supplying concrete details (references to what we can see, smell, taste, hear, or touch) to support abstract ideas (such as faith, hope, understanding, love), by providing specifics (I like chocolate) to explain generalizations (I like sweets), and by giving definite references (turn left at the second

INTRODUCTORY NOTES

Ideally, you and your students should be functioning from a common definition of "example" before you assign the reading selections in this chapter. Most students, however, do not really understand what examples and details are. Therefore, they have difficulty choosing and arranging them. Distinguishing between levels of generality is where this chapter must begin:

General:	food
More specific:	meat
More specific:	beef
More specific:	steak
More specific:	rare New York steak

Of the five levels of generality above, many students think "meat" (level two) is an example, not realizing that examples such as "rare New York steak" are more specific. Showing students these levels and having them practice moving back and forth from details to generalities, like warming up before an athletic event, will help students comprehend the refinements in language and thought necessary for verbal clarity. One helpful approach involves giving students general words, such as "book," "residence," "job," or "gift," and letting them generate various levels of specificity.

The student author of the writing sample at the end of this chapter introduction uses examples to illustrate her parents' behavior with their grandchildren during the Christmas holidays. Similarly, the professional essays in the chapter each make a specific claim and then show how examples can support that contention. The exercises connected to each selection help students discover how examples function in the larger context, whereas the writing assignments ask students to use examples to prove thesis statements of their own. In "The Baffling Question," Bill Cosby explains that he and his wife decided to have children before they knew exactly what this decision entailed; the exercises ask students to think about and use detailed examples to explain various aspects of having children and growing up. Harry Edwards, in "Triple Tragedy in Black Society," quotes statistics and examples from sports to prove that African Americans are as exploited in athletics as they are in society in general; the apparatus helps students consider and discuss various issues related to racism. Harold Krents uses examples in "Darkness at Noon" to show how handicapped people are often unfairly judged; the assignments before and after this essay ask students to furnish examples in a discussion of topics related to handicaps in general. Next, in an essay entitled "The Mind of the Chimpanzee," Jane Goodall examines in detail the cognitive abilities of chimps; the apparatus in this case prompts students to look closely at the role of learning and education in their own lives. Finally, "Sexism in English: A 1990s Update" by Alleen Pace Nilsen shows how language influences culture through a study of words associated with males and females in our society; the exercises encourage students to explore from a number of different perspectives the topic of sexual bias.

stoplight) to clarify vague statements (turn in a few blocks). Though illustrations take many forms, writers often find themselves indebted to description or narration (or some combination of the two) in order to supply enough relevant examples to achieve their rhetorical intent.

As you might suspect, examples are important ingredients in producing exciting, vivid prose. Just as crucial is the fact that carefully chosen examples can often encourage your readers to feel one way or another about an issue being discussed. If you tell your parents, for instance, that living in a college dormitory is not conducive to academic success, they may doubt your word, perhaps thinking that you are simply attempting to coerce money out of them for an apartment. You can help dispel this notion, however, by giving them specific examples of the chaotic nature of dorm life: the party down the hall that broke up at 2:00 A.M. when you had a chemistry exam that same morning at 8 o'clock; the stereo next door that seems to be stuck on its highest decibel level all hours of the day and night; and the new "friend" you recently acquired who thinks you are the best listener in the world—especially when everyone else has the good sense to be asleep. After such a detailed and well-documented explanation, your parents could hardly deny the strain of this difficult environment on your studies. Examples can be very persuasive.

The following paragraphs written by a student use examples to explain how he reacts to boredom in his life. As you read this excerpt, notice how the writer shows rather than tells the readers how he copes with boredom by providing exciting details that are concrete, specific, and definite.

We all deal with boredom in our own ways. Unfortunately, most of us have to deal with it far too often. Some people actually seek boredom. Being bored means that they are not required to do anything; being boring means that no one wants anything from them. In short, these people equate boredom with peace and relaxation. But for the rest of us, boredom is not peaceful. It produces anxiety.

Most people deal with boredom by trying to distract themselves from boring circumstances. Myself, I'm a reader. At the breakfast table over a boring bowl of cereal, I read the cereal box, the milk carton, the wrapper on the bread. (Have you ever noticed how many of those ingredients are unpronounceable?) Waiting in a doctor's office, I will gladly read weekly news magazines of three years ago, a book for five-year-olds, advertisements for drugs, and even the physician's odd-looking diplomas on the walls. Have you ever been

Example 151

so bored you were reduced to reading through all the business cards in your wallet? Searching for names similar to yours in the phone book? Browsing through the *National Enquirer* while waiting in the grocery line? At any rate, that's my recipe for beating boredom. What's yours?

Reading and Writing Essays that Use Examples

A common criticism of college-level writers is that they often base their essays on unsupported generalizations, such as "all sports cars are unreliable." The guidelines discussed here will help you avoid this problem and use examples effectively to support your ideas. As you read the essays in this chapter, take time to notice the degree of specificity the writers use to make various points. To a certain extent, the more examples in your essays, the clearer your ideas will be and the more your readers will understand and be interested in what you are saying. Notice also that these writers know when to stop—when "more" becomes too much and boredom sets in for the reader. Most college students err by using too few examples, however, so we suggest that when in doubt about whether or not to include another illustration, you should go ahead and add it.

HOW TO READ AN ESSAY THAT USES EXAMPLES

Preparing to Read. Before you begin reading the essays in this chapter, take some time to think about each author's title: What can you infer about Bill Cosby's attitude toward having children from his title "The Baffling Question"? What do you think Harry Edwards' view of African-American society is? In addition, try to discover the writer's audience and purpose at this point in the reading process; scanning the essay and surveying its synopsis in the Rhetorical Contents will provide you with useful information for this task.

Also important as you prepare to read is information about the author and about how a particular essay was written. Most of this material is furnished for you in the biography preceding each essay. From it, you might learn why Jane Goodall is qualified to write about the minds of chimpanzees or why Alleen Pace Nilson published "Sexism in English: A 1990s Update."

Finally, before you begin to read, take time to answer the Preparing to Read questions and to make some associations with

TEACHING EXAMPLE:
ONE INSTRUCTOR'S COMMENTS

The first rhetorical pattern I teach in freshman composition is example, and I make the point that example very likely will form the basis of individual paragraphs in all rhetorical modes. Specifically, I try to impress upon my students that very few people, including intelligent students, have original *general* ideas. Thus, the only way we can make our shared generalizations original is to present them with specific examples that others may not have considered and that come from our own experiences.

On a practical level, I am constantly asking students to isolate in an essay sentences that contain specific details. ("The $300 walk-up flat was just ten minutes from Manhattan.") I also find the opposite exercise very useful, asking students to find sentences that do not contain many examples or details ("The old lady had a bad accident.") and to rephrase them specifically ("The ninety-year-old spinster fell down a flight of stairs.").

Terrence Burke
Cuyahoga Community College
Cleveland, Ohio

Many students assume readers will understand and respond to flaccid generalizations that lack adequate supporting details or examples. I tell them communication just doesn't happen that way, as most good writers know, because good prose is packed with specifics—with concrete examples and detailed illustrations. What students too often fail to recognize is the basic teleology of communication. A writer has to "get" to his reader through a conscious appeal to the five senses.

To impress this upon my students, I first discuss how we know what we know. I do this through the concept of the SELF—not Descartes' "I think therefore I am," but the symbiosis of the ME and the NOT ME. How does the SELF—the "spirit," the ME—know about the outside—the SELF, the "material," the NOT ME? Most of us rely heavily upon our senses to know things.

After I present this concept, I then move on to its application to writing. For example, I ask my class to supply details that will make the building we're in more "real" to an audience. I give them a generalization, like "our classroom is traditionally institutional," then ask them how they could make that generalization clearer to an audience. We note the faint smell of chalk dust, the blackboard across one end with "TEKs Are Nerds" scratched in its upper right-hand corner, the slightly quavering white of neon lights, the pebbled uniformity of concrete block walls, the windowless claustrophobic-inducing ventilation, the battered Merriam Webster Unabridged on its sprung shelf, and so on.

Jay Jernigan
Eastern Michigan University
Ypsilanti, Michigan

the general subject of the essay: What do you want to know about blindness (Harold Krents)? What are some of your opinions on sexism in the English language (Alleen Pace Nilsen)?

Reading. As you first read these essays, record any thoughts that come to mind. Make associations freely with the content of each essay, its purpose, audience, and the facts about its publication. For example, try to learn why Cosby writes about having children or why Krents titles his essay "Darkness at Noon." At this point, you will probably be able to make some pretty accurate guesses about the audience each author is addressing. Creating a context for your reading—including the writer's qualifications; the essay's tone, purpose, and audience; and publication data—is an important first step toward being able to analyze your reading material in any mode. Finally, after you have read an essay in this section once, preview the questions after the selection before you read it again.

Rereading. As you read the essays in this chapter for a second time, focus on the examples each writer uses to make his or her point: How relevant are these examples to the thesis and purpose of each essay? How many examples do the writers use? Do they vary the length of these examples to achieve different goals? Do the authors use examples their readers can easily identify with and understand? How are these examples organized in each case? Does this arrangement support each writer's purpose? For example, how relevant are Cosby's examples to his central idea? How many examples does Edwards use to make each point? Does Krents vary the length of each of his examples to accomplish different purposes? How does Goodall organize her examples? Does this arrangement help her accomplish her purpose? In what way? Does Nilsen use examples that men as well as women can identify with? How effective are her examples? As you read, consider also how other rhetorical modes help each writer accomplish his or her purpose. What are these modes? How do they work along with examples to help create a coherent essay? Last, answering the questions after each essay will let you check your grasp of its main points and will lead you from the literal to the analytical level in preparation for the discussion/writing assignments that follow.

For a thorough summary of reading tasks, you might want to consult the checklists on pages 15–16 of the Introduction.

Example 153

HOW TO WRITE AN ESSAY THAT USES EXAMPLES

Preparing to Write. Before you can use examples in an essay, you must first think of some. One good way to generate ideas is to use some of the prewriting techniques explained in the Introduction as you respond to the Preparing to Write questions that appear before the writing assignments for each essay. You should then consider these thoughts in conjunction with the purpose and audience specified in your chosen writing assignments. Out of these questions should come a number of good examples for your essay.

Writing. In an example essay, a thesis statement or controlling idea will help you begin to organize your paper. The examples you use should always be relevant to the thesis and purpose of your essay. If, for instance, the person talking about tennis players cited the practice schedules of only unknown players, her friend certainly would not be convinced of the truth of her statement about how hard internationally ranked athletes work at their games. To develop a topic principally with examples, you can use one extended example or several shorter examples, depending on the nature and purpose of your assertion. If you are attempting to prove that Americans are more health-conscious now than they were twenty years ago, citing a few examples from your own neighborhood will not provide enough evidence to be convincing. If, however, you are simply commenting on a neighborhood health trend, you can legitimately refer to these local cases. Furthermore, always try to find examples with which your audience can identify so that they can follow your line of reasoning. If you want your parents to help finance an apartment, citing instances from the lives of current rock stars will probably not prove your point, because your parents may not sympathize with these particular role models.

The examples you choose must also be arranged as effectively as possible in order to encourage audience interest and identification. If you are using examples to explain the imaginative quality of Disneyland, for instance, the most logical approach would probably be to organize your essay by degrees (i.e., from least to most imaginative or most to least original). But if your essay uses examples to help readers visualize your bedroom, a spatial arrangement of the details (moving from one item to the next) might be easiest for your readers to follow. If the subject concerned a series of important events, like graduation weekend, the illustrations might most effectively be organized chronologically. As you will learn from reading the selections that follow, careful organization of examples can lead quite easily to unity (a sense of wholeness or interrelatedness) and coherence (clear, logical development) in your essays. Unity and coherence produce good writing—and that, of course, helps foster confidence and accomplishment in school and in your professional life.

Rewriting.   As you reread your example essays, look closely at the choice and arrangement of details in relation to your purpose and audience. Have you included enough examples to develop each of your topics adequately? Are the examples you have chosen relevant to your thesis? Have you selected examples that your readers can easily understand? Have you arranged these examples in a logical manner that your audience can follow?

For more detailed information on writing, see the checklists on pages 27–28 of the Introduction.

Student Essay: Examples at Work

In the following essay, a student uses examples to explain and analyze her parents' behavior as they prepare for and enjoy their grandchildren during the Christmas holidays. As you read it, study the various examples the student writer uses to convince us that her parents truly undergo a transformation each winter.

Mom and Dad's
Holiday Disappearing Act

General topic   Often during the winter holidays, people find surprises: Children discover the secret contents of brightly wrapped packages that have teased them for weeks; cooks are astonished by the wealth of smells and memories their busy kitchens can bring about; workaholics stumble upon the true joy of a few days' rest. **Background information** My surprise over the past few winters has been the personality transformation my parents go through around mid-December as they change from Dad and Mom into Poppa and Granny. Yes, they become grandparents and are completely different from the people I know the other eleven and a half months of the year. **Details to capture holiday spirit** **Thesis statement**

The first sign of my parents' metamorphosis is the delight they take in visiting toy and children's clothing stores. These two people, who usually despise anything having to do with shopping malls, **First point**

Example 155

Examples relevant to thesis — become crazed consumers. While they tell me to budget my money and shop wisely, they are buying every doll, dump truck, and velvet outfit in sight. And this is only the beginning of the holidays!

Transition — When my brother's children arrive, Poppa and Granny come into full form. First they throw out all ideas about a balanced diet for the grandkids. — Second point

While we were raised in a house where everyone had to take two bites of broccoli, beets, or liver (foods that appeared quite often on our table despite constant groaning), the grandchildren never have to eat anything that does not appeal to them. Granny carries marshmallows in her pockets to bribe the littlest ones into following her around the house, while Poppa offers "surprises" of candy and cake to them all day long. Boxes of chocolate-covered cherries disappear while the bran muffins get hard and stale. The kids love all the sweets, and when the sugar revs up their energy levels, Granny and Poppa can always decide to leave and do a bit more shopping or go to bed while my brother and sister-in-law try to deal with their supercharged, hyperactive kids. — Humorous examples (organized from most to least healthy)

Transition — Once the grandchildren have arrived, Granny and Poppa also seem to forget all of the responsibility lectures I so often hear in my daily life. If little Tommy throws a fit at a friend's house, he is "overwhelmed by the number of adults"; if Mickey screams at his sister during dinner, he is "developing his own personality"; if Nancy breaks Granny's vanity mirror (after being told twice to put it down), she is "just a curious child." But, if I track mud into the house while helping to unload groceries, I become "careless"; if I scold one of the grandkids for tearing pages out of my calculus book, I am "impatient." If a grandchild talks back to her mother, Granny and Poppa chuckle at her spirit. If I mumble one word about all of this dotage, Mom and Dad reappear to have a talk with me about petty jealousies. — Third point / Examples in the form of comparisons

When my nieces and nephews first started appearing at our home for the holidays a few years ago, I probably was jealous, and I complained a lot. But now I spend more time simply sitting back and watching Mom and Dad change into what we call the "Incredible Huggers." They enjoy their time with these grandchildren so much that I easily forgive them their Granny and Poppa faults. — Transition to conclusion

Writer's attitude

<u>I believe their personality change is due to the</u> <u>lack of responsibility they feel for the grandkids</u>: In their role as grandparents, they don't have to worry about sugar causing cavities or temporary failures of self-discipline turning into lifetime faults. Those problems are up to my brother and sister-in-law. All Granny and Poppa have to do is enjoy and love their grandchildren. They have all the fun of being parents without any of the attendant obligations. And you know what? <u>I think they've earned the right to</u> <u>make this transformation—at least once a year.</u>

Writer's analysis of situation

Specific reference to introduction

Concluding remark

Student Writer's Comments

To begin this essay, I scratched out an outline by first listing examples of my parents' behavior, then figuring out how they fit together. Once I sat down to write, I was stumped. I wanted the introduction to be humorous, but I also wanted to maintain a respectable tone (so I wouldn't sound like a whiny kid!). Finally, I just decided to write down *anything* to get started and come back to the beginning later on. All those examples and anecdotes were swimming around in my head wanting to be committed to paper. I found I needed my thesaurus and dictionary from the very beginning; they helped to take the pressure off to come up with the perfect word every time I was stuck. As I neared the middle of the paper, the introduction popped into my head, so I jotted down my thoughts and continued with the flow of ideas I needed for the body of my paper. Writing my conclusion helped me put my experiences with my parents into perspective. I had never really tried to analyze how I felt toward them or why they acted as they do during the Christmas holidays. They were glad to hear I had figured them out!

Some Final Thoughts on Examples

Although examples are often used to supplement and support other methods of development—such as cause/effect, comparison/contrast, and process analysis—the essays in this section are focused principally on examples. A main idea is expressed in the introduction of each, and the rest of the essay provides examples to bolster that contention. As you read these essays, pay close attention to each author's choice and arrangement of examples; then try to determine which organizational techniques are most persuasive for each specific audience.

BILL COSBY
(1937–)

■ ■ ■

The Baffling Question

Comedian, actor, recording artist, and author Bill Cosby is undoubtedly one of America's best-loved entertainers. From his beginnings on the "I Spy" television series through his "Fat Albert" years and his work on "Sesame Street," his eight Grammy awards for comedy albums, his commercials for everything from Kodak film to Jell-O pudding, and his portrayal of the affable obstetrician Cliff Huxtable on the immensely popular "Cosby Show," he has retained his public persona of an honest and trustworthy storyteller intrigued with the ironies in our everyday lives. "When I was a kid," he has explained, "I always used to pay attention to things that other people didn't even think about. I'd remember funny happenings, just little trivial things, and then tell stories about them later. I found I could make people laugh, and I enjoyed doing it because it gave me a sense of security. I thought that if people laughed at what you said, that meant they liked you." After a series of hit movies in the 1970s, Cosby returned to prime-time television in 1984 because of his concern over his family's viewing habits. "I got tired of seeing TV shows that consisted of a car crash, a gunman, and a hooker talking to a Black pimp. It was cheaper to do a series than to throw out my family's six television sets."At the peak of its success, "The Cosby Show" was seen weekly by over sixty million viewers. Cosby lives with his wife, Camille, in Los Angeles, where he relaxes by playing an occasional game of tennis.

Preparing to Read

The following excerpt is from one of the author's six books, *Fatherhood* (1986), which details the joys and frustrations of raising children. Before reading this selection, pause to consider the effect parenthood has had or might have on your life: How did/would you make the decision whether or not to have children? What variables were/would be involved in this decision? What are/would be some of the difficulties involved in raising children? Some of the joys? How did your parents react to you when you were a child? What memories do you have of your own childhood?

QUOTATION ON READING

"To read without reflecting is like eating without digesting."

Edmund Burke

PREREADING

The purpose of this Preparing to Read material is to encourage students to consider the effect of parenthood on their lives. Your students have had actual experience with this role—either as parents or as children. To help them turn their attention to this issue, you might begin by discussing the image of parents as presented in the media. What movies have your students seen that examine the role of parents? How are parents depicted on TV? What impressions of parenthood do your students get from newspapers and magazines? See pages 3–6 for other ways to generate thoughts.

BACKGROUND INFORMATION

Taking a lighthearted, satiric view of the important issue of deciding whether or not to have children, Cosby writes about his own deliberations on the topic. He approaches the subject by citing several reasons he and his wife did not consider; then he creates humor by making fun of his wife and himself because they did not take these important considerations into account, reminding us occasionally of Cosby's persona as Dr. Huxtable on his television show.

READABILITY LEVEL

7.9

RELATED READINGS

Childbirth

Germaine Greer, "A Child Is Born"   308
Michael Dorris, "The Broken Cord"   400
Betty Gittman, "Pregnant Teenagers: A
   Challenge"   516

Parent–Child Relationships

Amy Tan, "The Joy Luck Club"   49
Russell Baker, "The Saturday Evening
   Post"   124

DEFINITIONS

Menninger Clinic (para. 17): a psychiatric clinic in Topeka, Kansas, named after Karl Augustus Menninger (1893–1990), a well-known American psychiatrist.

COLLABORATIVE LEARNING: CLASS ACTIVITY

To understand the complexities involved in deciding whether or not to have children, your students might benefit from a formal debate. Assign two students to speak in favor of (affirmative) and two students against (negative) having children. Let them take turns speaking, reacting to each other's points according to the following format:

Opening statement, affirmative	5 min.
Cross-examination, negative	2 min.
Opening statement, negative	5 min.
Cross-examination, affirmative	2 min.
Second statement, affirmative	4 min.
Cross-examination, negative	1 min.
Second statement, negative	4 min.
Cross-examination, affirmative	1 min
Negative rebuttal	2 min.
Affirmative rebuttal	2 min.
Negative rebuttal	2 min.
Affirmative rebuttal	2 min.

The most important feature of a debate is the credibility and quality of the evidence. Here, an example from family life today is more effective than one from twenty years ago. Then, have the class vote for the winner based on the validity of the evidence.

1 **S**o you've decided to have a child. You've decided to give up quiet evenings with good books and lazy weekends with good music, intimate meals during which you finish whole sentences, sweet private times when you've savored the thought that just the two of you and your love are all you will ever need. You've decided to turn your sofas into trampolines and to abandon the joys of leisurely contemplating reproductions of great art for the joys of frantically coping with reproductions of yourselves.

2 Why?

3 Poets have said the reason to have children is to give yourself immortality; and I must admit I did ask God to give me a son because I wanted someone to carry on the family name. Well, God did just that and I now confess that there have been times when I've told my son not to reveal who he is.

4 "You make up a name," I've said. "Just don't tell anybody who you are."

5 Immortality? Now that I have had five children, my only hope is that they all are out of the house before I die.

6 No, immortality was not the reason why my wife and I produced these beloved sources of dirty laundry and ceaseless noise. And we also did not have them because we thought it would be fun to see one of them sit in a chair and stick out his leg so that another one of them running by was launched like Explorer I. After which I said to the child who was the launching pad, "Why did you do that?"

7 "Do what?" he replied.

8 "Stick out your leg."

9 "Dad, I didn't know my leg was going out. My leg, it does that a lot."

10 If you cannot function in a world where things like this are said, then you better forget about raising children and go for daffodils.

11 My wife and I also did not have children so they could yell at each other all over the house, moving me to say, "What's the problem?"

12 "She's waving her foot in my room," my daughter replied.

13 "And something like that *bothers* you?"

14 "Yes, I don't *want* her foot in my room."

15 "Well," I said, dipping into my storehouse of paternal wisdom, "why don't you just close the door?"

16 "Then I can't see what she's doing!"

17 Furthermore, we did not have the children because we

thought it would be rewarding to watch them do things that should be studied by the Menninger Clinic.

"Okay," I said to all five one day, "go get into the car."

All five then ran to the same car door, grabbed the same handle, and spent the next few minutes beating each other up. Not one of them had the intelligence to say, "Hey, *look*. There are three more doors." The dog, however, was already inside.

And we did not have the children to help my wife develop new lines for her face or because she had always had a desire to talk out loud to herself: "Don't tell *me* you're *not* going to do something when I tell you to move!" And we didn't have children so I could always be saying to someone, "Where's my change?"

Like so many young couples, my wife and I simply were unable to project. In restaurants we did not see the small children who were casting their bread on the water in the glasses the waiter had brought; and we did not see the mother who was fasting because she was both cutting the food for one child while pulling another from the floor to a chair that he would use for slipping to the floor again. And we did not project beyond those lovely Saturdays of buying precious little things after leisurely brunches together. We did not see that *other* precious little things would be coming along to destroy the first batch.

UNDERSTANDING DETAILS

1. According to Cosby, exactly what is "the baffling question"? Why is this question "baffling"?
2. If everyone felt as Cosby does about raising children, what kinds of people would have children?
3. From Cosby's point of view, in what important ways do children change a couple's life?

ANALYZING MEANING

1. Why do you think Cosby focuses on the problems children create in a couple's life? What effect does this approach have on his main point?
2. Following Cosby's logic, why did he and his wife have children? What examples lead you to this conclusion?
3. In what way is the last sentence in this essay a good summary statement? What specific thoughts does it summarize?

1. In the first paragraph, Cosby juxtaposes life without children against life with children. The reader is immediately introduced to the humor Cosby finds in the way kids act and his obvious affection for and frustration with his own children. This conflict leads to an effective conclusion in which these feelings are successfully resolved.

2. This approach is likely to make those who do not have children think twice about having them, whereas readers who already have children will more fully appreciate the frustrations and joys he describes.

3. Cosby creates humor by describing the antics of his children from *their* view as well as his own. Cosby's humor emphasizes his affection for children and his positive outlook on child-rearing, despite the negative situations he describes.

PREWRITING

In preparation for the writing assignments, the Preparing to Write questions ask students to focus on the problems and joys they associate with parenthood—from observation or from experience as parents or children—before they write an essay on a related topic. See pages 16–23 for suggestions on generating ideas in response to these questions.

ADDITIONAL DISCUSSION/WRITING TOPIC

Write an essay using examples to explain an important decision you have recently made. Make sure these examples have a focus and a specific purpose.

REVISING STRATEGY

A clear background statement is especially useful in an example essay, because it focuses the readers' attention. Reread the introduction to one of your example essays. Make sure it develops a clear frame of reference for your essay. Mark parts of the introduction that could provide fuller explanations. Then revise your paper, concentrating on developing the introduction so that it prepares readers for the rest of the essay.

DISCOVERING RHETORICAL STRATEGIES

1. How does the first paragraph set the tone for the rest of the essay?
2. Cosby's primary strategy in this essay is irony. That is, he suggests reasons for having children by listing reasons *not* to have children. What effect is this approach likely to have on his readers?
3. How does Cosby use specific examples to create humor? Is his humor effective? Explain your answer.

IDEAS FOR DISCUSSION/WRITING

Preparing to Write

Write freely about the art of parenthood: From your observations or experience, what are some of the principal problems and joys of parenthood? How is being a parent different from babysitting? What pleasant babysitting experiences have you had? What unpleasant experiences? What kind of child were you? What specific memories lead you to this conclusion?

Choosing a Topic

1. Write an essay for the general public explaining one particular problem or joy of parenthood. In your essay, mimic Cosby's humorous approach to his topic. Use several specific examples to make your point.
2. Write an editorial for your local newspaper on your own foolproof techniques for doing one of the following: (a) babysitting, (b) raising children, or (c) becoming a model child. Use specific examples to explain your approach.
3. Interview one or two relatives who are older than you; ask them about the type of child you were. Have them recall some particularly memorable details that characterize your behavior. Then write an essay explaining their predominant impressions of you. Use examples to support these impressions.

HARRY EDWARDS
(1942–)

■ ■ ■

Triple Tragedy in Black Society

Harry Edwards is a prominent sports sociologist who has risen from an impoverished childhood in East St. Louis to a professorship in sociology at the University of California at Berkeley. His first book, *The Revolt of the Black Athlete* (1969), effectively challenged the myth of the American sports establishment as a model of racial harmony and ethnic fair play. Edwards next wrote *Sociology in Sports* (1973), an analysis of the many complex issues that affect sports in modern society, and *The Struggle That Must Be* (1980), an autobiography recounting his personal experiences with racism, his organization of the Black Athletes' Protest at the 1968 Olympics, and his predictions about the future of race relations in America. Edwards is most emphatic when describing an athletic system that, he believes, entraps and exploits African-American youths by falsely promising them social equality through sports. In addition to performing his academic duties, he currently serves as special assistant to the commissioner of Major League Baseball and as staff consultant and player personnel consultant for the San Francisco 49ers and the Golden State Warriors.

Preparing to Read

"Triple Tragedy in Black Society," which originally appeared in *Ebony* magazine in August 1988, argues that the "obsessive pursuit of sports" among African-American youths prevents them from advancing in other areas of American society. It decries the "talent drain" toward athletics and away from important careers in such fields as medicine, law, politics, and education. As you prepare to read this essay, take a few moments to consider your own observations on the role of African Americans in society today: To what extent does racial discrimination still exist in American society? Have you ever experienced prejudice? Have any of your friends experienced it? Do you think racism exists in sports today? If so, which sports seem most racist? Which are least so? What can be done to relieve racism in the world of sports? In all aspects of American society?

QUOTATION ON WRITING

"Composition is the supplying at the right time and place of whatever the developing meaning then and there requires."

I. A. Richards

PREREADING

The purpose of this Preparing to Read material is to encourage students to think about the relationship between sports and racism. Before your students respond to the questions here, you might discuss the role of athletes in our society, from high school to professional sports. See pages 3–6 for other ways to generate thoughts on these questions.

BACKGROUND INFORMATION

In "Triple Tragedy in Black Society," prominent sociologist Harry Edwards indicts African-American athletes and their families for "the single-minded pursuit of sports fame and fortune" at a time when fewer than 1 out of 1,000 high school athletes end up as successful professional competitors in their sport. Instead of allowing themselves to be systematically exploited by the American sports establishment, African-American youngsters should actively consider careers in other important areas that will provide better opportunities for a successful and satisfying professional life.

READABILITY LEVEL

13.7

RELATED READINGS

Black Issues

Prejudice

DEFINITIONS

beneficence (para. 2): the quality of doing good.

unconscionable (para. 4): shockingly unfair or unjust.

Irv Cross (1944–) (para. 6): a sports commentator and former professional football player.

Ahmad Rashad (1950–) (para. 6): a sports commentator and former professional football player.

Tom Jackson (1951–) (para. 6): a sports commentator and former football player.

Bill Russell (1934–) (para. 6): a former professional basketball player, coach, and sports commentator.

O. J. Simpson (1947–) (para. 6): an actor, former professional football player, and sports commentator.

Paul Robeson (1898–1976) (para. 12): a college football player at Princeton and a stage and screen actor and singer.

Joe Louis (1914–1981) (para. 12): a professional boxer.

Jesse Owens (1913–1980) (para. 12): a track-and-field athlete.

Jackie Robinson (1919–1972) (para. 12): a professional baseball player.

Althea Gibson (1927–) (para. 12): a former professional tennis player.

Larry Doby (1923–) (para. 12): a former professional baseball player.

Roy Campanella (1921–) (para. 12): a former professional baseball player.

Jim Brown (1936–) (para. 12): an actor and a former professional football player.

Curt Flood (1938–) (para. 12): a former professional baseball player.

Tommie Smith (1944–) (para. 12): a former track athlete.

John Carlos (1945–) (para. 12): a former track athlete.

Muhammad Ali (1942–) (para. 12): a former professional boxer.

Arthur Ashe (1943–) (para. 12): a former professional tennis player.

The single-minded pursuit of sports fame and fortune is today approaching an institutionalized *triple tragedy* in Black society: The tragedy of thousands and thousands of Black youths in obsessive pursuit of sports goals foredoomed to elude the vast and overwhelming majority of them; the tragedy of the personal and cultural underdevelopment that afflicts so many among both successful and unsuccessful Black sports aspirants; and the tragedy of cultural and institutional underdevelopment in Black society overall, partially as a consequence of the *talent drain* toward sports and away from other critically vital areas of occupational and career emphasis (medicine, law, economics, politics, education, the technical fields, etc.). 1

Our circumstances in sports are inextricably intertwined with the broader Black experience in America. Notwithstanding sports' reputation in Black society for beneficence and for providing extraordinary, if not exemplary, social and economic mobility opportunities, the reality is that in sports, no less than in society, Black advancement has been achieved at the price of persistent, vigilant, intelligent reflection and determined individual and collective struggle. Nowhere is this perspective more clearly evident than when we consider the challenges and prospects confronting Black youths aspiring to sports stardom. 2

Owing largely to (1) a longstanding, widely held and—at its root—*racist* presumption of innate race-linked Black athletic superiority, to (2) media propaganda about sports as a broadly accessible route to Black social and economic mobility, and finally to (3) a lack of comparably visible, high-prestige Black role models beyond the sports arena, Black families are four times more likely than White families to push their children toward sports-career aspirations—often to the neglect and detriment of other critically important areas of personal and cultural development. 3

Only *five percent* of high school athletes go on to compete in their sports at the collegiate level—including those who participate in junior college—which is to say that over 95% of all athletes must face the realities of life after sports at the conclusion of their last high-school athletic competition. Of those Black athletes who do attend four-year institutions on athletic scholarships or grants-in-aid, 65 to 75 percent *never* graduate from the schools they represent in sports. Of the 25 to 35 percent who do graduate, an unconscionable proportion graduate in what are for Blacks often less marketable academic majors riddled with "keep 'em eligible" less-competitive "jock courses" of dubious educational value and occupational relevance. What passes for "physical edu- 4 cation" and "communications" majors at many colleges are prime examples.

Even in sports where Blacks predominate as athletes, we are routinely passed over as candidates for top coaching and sports-administration jobs—often despite having the combination of both academic preparation in physical education and substantial practical experience at the *assistant* level in major athletic programs. Hence, there are only two Black athletic directors, four Black head football coaches, and fewer than 30 Black head basketball coaches at major Division I, NCAA colleges and universities. There are no Black head baseball coaches at such institutions today. And in the professional ranks, circumstances relative to Black access to top positions are even more dismal.

Similarly, notwithstanding Black athletes' preparation in communications, the press box and the broadcast booth remain the most racially segregated corners of the sports arena. Of 664 beat writers in basketball, football, and baseball, only 28 are Black. And those few Blacks who have found their way into the broadcast booths of major television and radio networks have done so owing more to their athletic prominence than to their academic preparation. (For example, Irv Cross at CBS, Ahmad Rashad at NBC, Tom Jackson at ESPN, Bill Russell formerly at WTBS and O. J. Simpson formerly at ABC).

What all of this amounts to is a *plantation system* of occupational relationships in sport—one having Whites holding a virtual monopoly on power and decision-making positions, with a few Blacks in mid-level *assistant* positions, and with the majority of Blacks in the lowest level production and labor roles, i.e., that of athlete. In essence, Blacks have advanced from the cotton fields to the football fields, but the structure of occupational relations remains strikingly similar.

Of the Black athletes who participate in collegiate football, basketball or baseball, only 1.6 percent ever sign a professional contract—less than *two out of 100*. And within three and a half years, over 60 percent of those who do sign such contracts are out of professional sports, more often than not financially destitute or in debt, and on the street without either the credentials or the skills to make their way productively in our extremely competitive high-tech society.

Despite efforts by a broad array of media, academic, civil rights and sports interests to draw attention to and rectify the tragedies of Black sports involvement, the fact remains that it is Black families and Black athletes who must assume principal re-

1. According to Edwards, athletic programs are representative of society as a whole because African Americans have had to struggle together against the myths of great opportunity that are even less true in sports than they are in society in general. Athletic programs sometimes help African Americans by providing opportunities for a few talented youths; however, this avenue of success has become highly overrated, and, in fact, most young African Americans gain little success from athletics.

2. Edwards asserts that racism shows up in athletics primarily in (1) the assumption that Blacks are somehow racially or genetically superior to other races in athletic ability (and thus intellectually inferior) and (2) the difference between the number of African Americans on the field or court and those in high-level coaching or press positions.

3. Responses to this question will vary.

ANSWERS TO QUESTIONS:
DISCOVERING RHETORICAL
STRATEGIES (p. 166)

1. Edwards' main points are as follows:
   —The single-minded pursuit of sports goals leads to a "triple tragedy."
   —Many Black youths attempt to achieve greatness solely through athletics.
   —This one-dimensional behavior contributes to a lack of personal and cultural development.
   —Blacks have achieved a great deal through individual and collective battles.
   —The myth that the majority of Black youths can achieve greatness through sports is racist.
   —Only Black families and communities can bring about change.
   —Black athletes should demand that they receive a quality education.

Edwards presents his thesis at the beginning of his essay and follows it with examples that sustain his theory. He encourages African Amerians by listing what they have done well and then introduces some current problems that need to be solved.

sponsibility for remedying the situation. It is now undeniable that through a blind belief in the beneficence and accessibility of sports as a socioeconomic mobility vehicle, Black families have unwittingly become accessories to, and major perpetrators of, the tragedies of Black sports involvement. We have, in effect, set up our children for personal and cultural underdevelopment, academic victimization, and athletic exploitation by our encouragement of the primacy of sports achievement over all else. We have then bartered away the services of the more competitive among our children to the highest bidders among collegiate athletic recruiters in exchange for what are typically extremely hollow promises of ethical educational opportunities or, even worse, promises of sports fame, fortune, and *fat city* forever.

Black families have the responsibility to inform themselves about the realities of Black sports involvement—its advantages and liabilities, its triumphs and its tragedies. As a culture and as a people, we simply can no longer permit many among our most competitive and gifted youths to sacrifice a wealth of human potential on the altar of athletic aspiration, to put playbooks ahead of textbooks. This does not mean that Blacks should abandon sports, but that we *must* learn to deal with the realities of sports more intelligently and constructively. Black parents must insist upon the establishment and pursuit of high academic standards and personal development goals by their children. And here we must be crystal clear: *our children's allegiance to high goals and standards will be principally established and enforced not on the campus but in the home.* 10

And, finally, it must be stated unequivocally that it is Black athletes themselves who must shoulder a substantial portion of the responsibility for improving Black circumstances and outcomes in American sports. Black athletes must insist upon intellectual discipline no less than athletic discipline among themselves, and upon educational integrity in athletic programs rather than, as is all too often the case, merely seeking the easiest route to maintaining athletic eligibility. If Black athletes fail to take a conscious, active and informed role in changing the course and character of Black sports involvement, nothing done by any other party to this tragic situation is likely to be effective or lasting—if for no other reason than the fact that *a slave cannot be freed against his will.* 11

In the 1930s, Paul Robeson, Joe Louis and Jesse Owens led the fight for *Black legitimacy* as athletes. In the late 1940s, and into the 1950s, Jackie Robinson, Althea Gibson, Larry Doby, Roy 12

Campanella and others struggled to secure *Black access* to the mainstream of American sports. From the late 1950s through the 1960s and into the 1970s, Jim Brown, Bill Russell, Curt Flood, Tommy Smith and John Carlos, Muhammad Ali and Arthur Ashe fought to secure *dignity and respect for Blacks* in sports. These were not knights in shining armor, but *pony express riders* carrying the burden of the Black struggle in sports over their particular stretches of historical terrain. And both the record books and the history books bear testament to the magnitude of the success of these great forerunners.

But as was stated at the outset, our circumstances in sports   13
are bound up with and deeply rooted in the broader Black experience in America. And so long as these circumstances—commensurate with developments in society at large—are dynamic and ever evolving, our struggle in sports also must be perpetual and *there can be no final victories.*

The challenges confronting Black people in the sports realm,   14
therefore, are but the latest. They will not be the last. The only question is will the next generation of Blacks in sports be able to move ahead and meet the challenges of their own historical era or will they have to first fight battles that we, both individually and collectively, should have fought—and won?

UNDERSTANDING DETAILS

1. What is the "triple tragedy in Black society" that Edwards refers to in this essay? In Edwards' estimation, what has caused the tragedy?
2. In the author's opinion, what is the relationship for African Americans between achievement in sports and in academics?
3. What main examples from the sports world does Edwards cite to support his theory of the "tragedies" caused by the single-minded involvement of African Americans in sports?

ANALYZING MEANING

1. In what ways are sports both a help and a hindrance to the African-American community? How do sports represent "the broader Black experience in America" (paragraph 2)?
2. What are the author's thoughts on the role of racism in athletics?
3. Which examples in this essay convince you most persuasively that "the single-minded pursuit of sports fame and fortune" (paragraph 1) among African-American youths today is threatening their advancement in society?

2. Paragraphs 4 through 7 present the situation many African-American youths now face. Paragraph 8 explains the depth of the dilemma and prepares the reader for a solution.

Paragraph 4: Over 95% of all athletes will not play their sport professionally.

— Only 5% of high school athletes go on to compete at the college level.
— Of those who go to college, 65 to 75% do not graduate.
— Many who do graduate (25 to 35%) do not have marketable skills.

Paragraph 5: "African Americans do not get top coaching and administrative jobs, despite academic and professional experience.

— Division I NCAA colleges have only 2 athletic directors, 3 football coaches, fewer than 30 basketball coaches, and no baseball coaches who are Black.
— Positions in coaching and management are still limited for Blacks.

Paragraph 6: Blacks have found few opportunities in sports broadcasting.

— "Of 664 beat writers . . . , only 28 are black."
— Most Black press representatives achieved their status through the fame they gained as sports figures rather than through college journalism.

Paragraph 7: A "plantation system" exists in sports.

— Whites have the power, and most Blacks are laborers.
— Blacks have moved from cotton fields to football fields.
— The social structure is the same.

Paragraph 8: The number of athletes who play professional sports is limited.

— Out of every 100 college athletes, only 2 will sign a professional contract.
— Most of these professional contracts last three and a half years or less.
— Athletes are frequently left with little money and few marketable skills.

3. Edwards' article, first published in *Ebony* (1988), is aimed primarily at an African-American audience. He is making a special appeal to young African-American athletes through his use of statistics that forcefully communicate the lack of opportunities in professional sports.

PREWRITING

In preparation for the writing assignments, the Preparing to Write questions ask students to focus on the connection between racism and success before they write an essay on a related topic. See pages 16–23 for suggestions on generating ideas in response to these questions.

ADDITIONAL DISCUSSION/WRITING TOPIC

Edwards recalls African-American athletes from the 1930s to the 1970s as legitimate heroes who "fought to secure dignity and respect for Blacks in sports" (para. 12). What role do you foresee for African-American athletes of the 1990s? Write an essay on today's rising professional African-American athletes. Are they products of their environment? Are they successes or failures in sharing the "responsibility for improving Black circumstances and outcomes in American sports"(para. 11)? What does the future hold for African-American superstars? Cite examples from today's college stars and professional athletes to support your conclusions.

REVISING STRATEGY

A keen sense of direction is crucial to any essay. In one of your example essays, write out your thesis and then underline all parts of your essay that help you achieve that goal. Notice where your intention could be clearer or better focused. Then revise your paper so that it communicates a clear, consistent purpose to your intended audience.

DISCOVERING RHETORICAL STRATEGIES

1. List the author's main points in this essay. Why does he choose to deal with these topics in this particular order?
2. What factual examples does Edwards use to support his main points in paragraphs 4, 5, 6, 7, and 8? Outline these five paragraphs to show how the examples work in his essay.
3. Describe Edwards' intended audience in as much detail as possible. Why do you think he has aimed his essay at this particular group?

IDEAS FOR DISCUSSION/WRITING

Preparing to Write

Write freely about the response of contemporary society to African Americans: In what areas of our society have African Americans advanced most dramatically? Where has their advancement been least dramatic? Why do you think African Americans have had more success in some areas than in others? How does racism in America prevent African Americans from making social and economic progress? Which aspects of American life are most blatantly racist? Which are least racist? How do you account for this difference?

Choosing a Topic

1. Using many examples to support his argument, Edwards claims in his essay that sports are both a help and a hindrance to African Americans. From your view of the world, write an example essay explaining to your friends one aspect of American life that is both a help and a hindrance to you.
2. As a college student, you see many events every day that could qualify as tragedies if they persisted. Write an essay for your school newspaper entitled "Triple Tragedy in _____." Fill in the blank, and then, through carefully chosen examples, explain to the college community the extent of the problem you have identified.
3. Comedian Dick Gregory has traveled the United States proclaiming that African Americans naively and unwisely use sports as an attempt to escape from reality; Edwards admits that sports offer some limited opportunities for African Americans, but he argues that American athletics are still ultimately racist in principle. What is your opinion? Should African Americans and other minorities pursue other interests and careers? Direct your comments to the general public, and use examples to support your opinion.

HAROLD KRENTS
(1944–1987)

■ ■ ■

Darkness at Noon

Raised in New York City, Harold Krents earned a B.A. and a law degree at Harvard, studied at Oxford University, worked as a partner in a Washington, D.C., law firm, was the subject of a long-running Broadway play, and wrote a popular television movie—all despite the fact that he was born blind. His "1-A" classification by a local draft board, which doubted the severity of his handicap, brought about the 1969 Broadway hit play *Butterflies Are Free* by Leonard Gershe. Krents once explained that he was merely the "prototype" for the central character: "I gave the story its inspiration—the play's plot is not my story; its spirit is." In 1972 Krents wrote *To Race the Wind*, which was made into a CBS-TV movie in 1980. During his career as a lawyer, Krents worked hard to expand legal protection for the handicapped and fought to secure their right to equal opportunity in the business world. He died in 1987 of a brain tumor.

Preparing to Read

In the following article, originally published in the *New York Times* (1978), the author gives examples of different kinds of discrimination he has suffered because of his blindness. As you prepare to read this essay, take a few minutes to think about disabilities or handicaps in general: Do you have a disability? If so, how are you treated by others? How do you feel others respond to your handicap? Do you know someone else who has a disability? How do you respond to that person? How do you think he or she wants to be treated? To what extent do you think disabilities should affect a person's job opportunities? What can be done to improve society's prejudices against the disabled?

QUOTATION ON THINKING

"When the process of concept formation is seen in all its complexity, it appears a movement of thoughts constantly alternating between two directions, from the particular to the general, and from the general to the particular."

Lev Vygotsky

PREREADING

The purpose of this Preparing to Read material is to encourage your students to identify with people who have disabilities of some sort. You might guide your students in a meditation exercise before they respond to the questions here, having them focus on either a real or an imagined handicap and consider the reactions they would get from other people. You might take your students through a relaxation technique first and then let their minds wander freely on various problems, solutions, and the reactions connected with specific disabilities. See pages 3–6 for other ways to generate thoughts on these questions.

Blind from birth, I have never had the opportunity to see myself and have been completely dependent on the image I create in the eye of the observer. To date it has not been narcissistic.   1

BACKGROUND INFORMATION

In his entertaining yet brutally honest "Darkness at Noon," Harold Krents provides several examples of thoughtless people viewing his blindness as a disability rather than an ability. The author ends his brief essay with the hope that employers in the United States will one day treat their handicapped and nonhandicapped employees in exactly the same fashion.

READABILITY LEVEL

9.4

RELATED READINGS

Prejudice

Lewis Sawaquat, "For My Indian Daughter"   96
Maya Angelou, "Graduation"   110
Harry Edwards, "Triple Tragedy in Black Society"   161
Alleen Pace Nilsen, "Sexism in English: A 1990s Update"   183
Shelby Steele, "Affirmative Action: The Price of Preference"   450

COLLABORATIVE LEARNING: CLASS ACTIVITY

(Bring blindfolds, earplugs, and wheelchairs to class.) Have each student in your class take on a physical disability before you begin a discussion of Krents' essay. (Have students with real handicaps take on a new disability.) Your students could choose to be blind, deaf, mute, or confined to a wheelchair. Then, begin a class discussion of the essay. You might use one or more of the questions after the essay as the focus of your discussion. Try to build in small group work or include the Small Group Activity described on page 169 of this AIE so that the "disabled students" are forced to maneuver around the room. Also, be aware of your use of the chalkboard and your related explanations in reference to the blind and deaf students. Your purpose here is to conduct a ten- to twenty-minute discussion, leaving the students feeling the frustration most handicapped people feel to some degree.

There are those who assume that since I can't see, I obviously also cannot hear. Very often people will converse with me at the top of their lungs, enunciating each word very carefully. Conversely, people will also often whisper, assuming that since my eyes don't work, my ears don't either. 2

For example, when I go to the airport and ask the ticket agent for assistance to the plane, he or she will invariably pick up the phone, call a ground hostess and whisper: "Hi, Jane, we've got a 76 here." I have concluded that the word "blind" is not used for one of two reasons: Either they fear that if the dread word is spoken, the ticket agent's retina will immediately detach, or they are reluctant to inform me of my condition of which I may not have been previously aware. 3

On the other hand, others know that of course I can hear, but believe that I can't talk. Often, therefore, when my wife and I go out to dinner, a waiter or waitress will ask Kit if *"he* would like a drink" to which I respond that "indeed *he* would." 4

This point was graphically driven home to me while we were in England. I had been given a year's leave of absence from my Washington law firm to study for a diploma in law degree at Oxford University. During the year I became ill and was hospitalized. Immediately after admission, I was wheeled down to the X-ray room. Just at the door sat an elderly woman—elderly I would judge from the sound of her voice. "What is his name?" the woman asked the orderly who had been wheeling me. 5

"What's your name?" the orderly repeated to me. 6
"Harold Krents," I replied. 7
"Harold Krents," he repeated. 8
"When was he born?" 9
"When were you born?" 10
"November 5, 1944," I responded. 11
"November 5, 1944," the orderly intoned. 12

This procedure continued for approximately five minutes at which point even my saint-like disposition deserted me. "Look," I finally blurted out, "this is absolutely ridiculous. Okay, granted I can't see, but it's got to have become pretty clear to both of you that I don't need an interpreter." 13

"He says he doesn't need an interpreter," the orderly reported to the woman. 14

The toughest misconception of all is the view that because I can't see, I can't work. I was turned down by over forty law firms because of my blindness, even though my qualifications included 15 a cum laude degree from Harvard College and a good ranking in my Harvard Law School class.

The attempt to find employment, the continuous frustration of being told that it was impossible for a blind person to practice law, the rejection letters, not based on my lack of ability but rather on my disability, will always remain one of the most disillusioning experiences of my life.

I therefore look forward to the day, with the expectation that it is certain to come, when employers will view their handicapped workers as a little child did me years ago when my family still lived in Scarsdale.

I was playing basketball with my father in our backyard according to procedures we had developed. My father would stand beneath the hoop, shout, and I would shoot over his head at the basket attached to our garage. Our next-door neighbor, aged five, wandered over into our yard with a playmate. "He's blind," our neighbor whispered to her friend in a voice that could be heard distinctly by Dad and me. Dad shot and missed; I did the same. Dad hit the rim; I missed entirely; Dad shot and missed the garage entirely. "Which one is blind?" whispered back the little friend.

I would hope that in the near future when a plant manager is touring the factory with the foreman and comes upon a handicapped and nonhandicapped person working together, his comment after watching them work will be, "Which one is disabled?"

UNDERSTANDING DETAILS

1. According to Krents, what are three common misconceptions about blind people?
2. In what ways was Krents frustrated in his search for employment? Was he qualified for the jobs he sought? Why or why not?
3. What attitude toward the handicapped does Krents look forward to in the future?

ANALYZING MEANING

1. What does Krents mean when he says that his image in the eyes of others "has not been narcissistic" (paragraph 1)? Why do you think this is the case?
2. How do you account for the reactions to his blindness that Krents tells us about in this essay? Are you aware of such behavior in yourself? In others?

COLLABORATIVE LEARNING: SMALL GROUP ACTIVITY

16 In groups based on the handicaps students chose for the Class Activity for this essay, have your students discuss their potential with these disabilities in the working world: What jobs could they handle with these disabilities? What jobs are unrealistic? If your students did not experience the Class Activity, have them choose disabili- 17 ties, break up into groups based on those handicaps, and then consider these questions about their personal and professional lives.

18 ### ANSWERS TO QUESTIONS: UNDERSTANDING DETAILS (p. 169)

1. Krents believes that sighted people commonly assume, perhaps subconsciously, that blind people can't hear, can't communicate, and can't hold difficult jobs.

2. Krents was well qualified for the positions he sought because of his cum laude degree from Harvard Law School. Despite his obvious qualifications, he was rejected 19 by over 40 law firms. Krents believes he was not turned down because of some flaw in his record or for lack of skill, but because of his blindness.

3. Krents hopes that all people will eventually be treated as equals regardless of any handicaps they may have. In fact, Krents looks forward to the day when employees will have difficulty determining which members of their staff are handicapped and which are not.

ANSWERS TO QUESTIONS: ANALYZING MEANING (p. 169)

1. As Krents describes the ways people have treated him, the reader understands that the image these sighted people have of him is really very different from the image he has of himself. That is not to say that Krents is conceited, but simply that he doesn't see himself as "inferior" in any way.

2. Responses to this question will vary.

3. Responses to this question will vary.

1. Krents organizes his ideas so the reader is first exposed to actions that nearly everyone would condemn, such as treating a blind person as if he or she is deaf. Krents follows these two ridiculous, yet altogether possible, reactions he received with the example of the responses he received when applying for work. Each example is set up equally so that if the readers think the first two examples are maddening, they have no alternative but to transfer this feeling to the last example, which represents equally outrageous behavior.

2. In addition to his examples, Krents uses narration in the essay to support his thesis that all people should be treated with equal respect and be given an equal opportunity to succeed. This is especially obvious in Krents' story about two children (para. 18) who have difficulty distinguishing whether he is blind or simply an incompetent basketball player. Krents uses this situation as an example of the way blind people should be treated and as an analogy that emphasizes Krents' conviction that employers need to be less aware of *disabilities* and more aware of *abilities*.

3. Short, choppy dialogue juxtaposed with a few long, flowing sentences and brief, to-the-point illustrations hasten Krents' prose along in a quick-moving essay that presents several ideas with an urgent, emotional rhythm. Thus Krents is not only trying to explain a problem to the reader, he is demonstrating the need for immediate action.

PREWRITING

In preparation for the writing assignments, the Preparing to Write questions ask students to consider before writing an essay on a related topic the biases they associate with certain disabilities. See pages 16–23 for suggestions on generating ideas in response to these questions.

3. Do you think we will ever arrive at the point in the working world that Krents describes in the last paragraph? How can we get there? What advantages or disadvantages might accompany such a change?

DISCOVERING RHETORICAL STRATEGIES

1. How does Krents organize the three main points in his essay? Why does he put them in this order? What is the benefit of discussing employment last?
2. Although the author's dominant rhetorical mode is example in this essay, what other strategies does he use to develop his ideas? Give examples of each of these strategies.
3. Krents establishes a fairly fast pace in this essay as he discusses several related ideas in a small amount of space. How does he create this sense of speed? What effect does this pace have on his essay as a whole?

IDEAS FOR DISCUSSION/WRITING

Preparing to Write

Write freely about disabilities: If you are disabled, what is your response to the world? Why do you respond the way you do? How does society respond to you? Are you pleased or not with your relationship to society in general? If you are not disabled, what do you think your attitude would be if you were disabled? How do you respond to disabled people? To what extent does your response depend upon the disability? Are you satisfied with your reaction to other people's disabilities? Are you prejudiced in any way against people with disabilities? Do you think our society as a whole demonstrates any prejudices toward the disabled? If so, how can we correct these biases?

Choosing a Topic

1. As a reporter for your campus newspaper, you have been assigned to study and write about the status of disabled services on your campus. Is your school equipped with handicapped parking? A sufficient number of ramps for wheelchairs? Transportation for the handicapped? Other special services for the handicapped? Interview some disabled students to get their views on these services. Write an example essay for the newspaper, explaining the situation.
2. With your eyes closed, take a walk through a place that you know well. How does it feel to be sightless? What senses begin to compensate for your loss of vision? Write an essay to your classmates detail-

ing your reactions. Use specific examples to communicate your feelings.

3. Do you have any phobias or irrational fears that handicap you in any way? Write a letter to a friend explaining one of these "handicaps" and your method of coping with it.

ADDITIONAL DISCUSSION/WRITING TOPIC

Imagine that you own a small business and you have advertised a clerical position in the local paper. After weeding through all the applications and resumes, you are left with two final candidates. Each one seems extremely well qualified. Your secretary sets up the interviews. As you walk into your office for your first interview, you see that the applicant is in a wheelchair. You also interview the other applicant. Both interviews go very well. Now you must choose whom you will hire. What role, if any, will your personal feelings about handicaps play in your selection process? Can you separate your personal and professional biases? Write an honest essay about your final decision. Was it affected by one applicant's disability? Would your decision have been the same if neither applicant were disabled?

REVISING STRATEGY

All good writers make certain the examples they use are closely related to the thesis statements of their essays. In one of your example essays, underline all the examples you use. Then put your thesis in the center of a page and draw a picture (or map) of the relationship of each of these examples to your thesis. Notice which examples need to be developed further and which need to be changed altogether. Then revise your paper so that all your examples are related to your central idea. Such revisions will give your essay unity and coherence.

JANE GOODALL
(1934–)

■ ■ ■

The Mind of the Chimpanzee

From the age of eight, Jane Goodall knew exactly what she wanted to be when she grew up: a specialist in primate behavior who lived with and studied wild animals in the jungles of Africa. Twenty-six years later, her dream became reality when world-famous anthropologist Dr. Louis Leakey rescued her from an obscure secretarial position at the National Museum of Natural History in Nairobi, Kenya, and selected her to research chimpanzee behavior at the Gombe Stream Research Center on the shore of Lake Tanganyika in Tanzania. Soon thereafter, Goodall earned her Ph.D. at Cambridge University, where she was one of only a handful of students ever awarded a doctorate without first completing a baccalaureate degree. A series of stunning discoveries at Gombe—evidence that chimpanzees eat meat, have an extremely sophisticated social hierarchy, and fashion tools out of grass and twigs—brought Goodall to public prominence and forced the scientific establishment to reevaluate the ever-narrowing boundaries between humans and animals. Goodall has written nine books, including *Primate Behavior* (1965), *In the Shadow of Man* (1971), *Chimps* (1989), and *Through a Window: My Thirty Years with the Chimpanzees of Gombe* (1990). She currently serves as scientific director of the Gombe Research Center in Tanzania. In her spare time she enjoys horseback riding, listening to classical music, and reading.

Preparing to Read

In the following excerpt from *Through a Window*, Goodall describes some of her discoveries in Tanzania as she studied the cognitive abilities of chimpanzees. As you prepare to read this essay, take a few minutes to think about the roles of research and learning in American society today: What value do you place on the process of learning? What are you being forced to learn? What do you want to learn more about? Have you ever studied something on your own? Were you pleased with your discoveries? Do your friends value learning? Do they value the process of education? How are education and learning related?

PREREADING

The purpose of this Preparing to Read material is to encourage students to think about the role of education and learning in their lives today. To help your students focus their attention before they respond to the questions here, have them investigate the meaning of "education" in one of the principal encyclopedias or in the *Oxford English Dictionary* and present to the class two interesting pieces of information about the word "education." See pages 3–6 for other ways to generate thoughts on these questions.

Often I have gazed into a chimpanzee's eyes and wondered what was going on behind them. I used to look into Flo's, she so old, so wise. What did she remember of her young days? David Greybeard had the most beautiful eyes of them all, large and lustrous, set wide apart. They somehow expressed his whole personality, his serene self-assurance, his inherent dignity—and, from time to time, his utter determination to get his way. For a long time I never liked to look a chimpanzee straight in the eye—I assumed that, as is the case with most primates, this would be interpreted as a threat or at least as a breach of good manners. Not so. As long as one looks with gentleness, without arrogance, a chimpanzee will understand, and may even return the look. And then—or such is my fantasy—it is as though the eyes are windows into the mind. Only the glass is opaque so that the mystery can never be fully revealed.

I shall never forget my meeting with Lucy, an eight-year-old home-raised chimpanzee. She came and sat beside me on the sofa and, with her face very close to mine, searched in my eyes—for what? Perhaps she was looking for signs of mistrust, dislike, or fear, since many people must have been somewhat disconcerted when, for the first time, they came face to face with a grown chimpanzee. Whatever Lucy read in my eyes clearly satisfied her for she suddenly put one arm round my neck and gave me a generous and very chimp-like kiss, her mouth wide open and laid over mine. I was accepted.

For a long time after that encounter I was profoundly disturbed. I had been at Gombe for about fifteen years then and I was quite familiar with chimpanzees in the wild. But Lucy, having grown up as a human child, was like a changeling, her essential chimpanzeeness overlaid by the various human behaviors she had acquired over the years. No longer purely chimp yet eons away from humanity, she was man-made, some other kind of being. I watched, amazed, as she opened the refrigerator and various cupboards, found bottles and a glass, then poured herself a gin and tonic. She took the drink to the TV, turned the set on, flipped from one channel to another then, as though in disgust, turned it off again. She selected a glossy magazine from the table and, still carrying her drink, settled in a comfortable chair. Occasionally, as she leafed through the magazine she identified something she saw, using the signs of ASL, the American Sign Language used by the deaf. I, of course, did not understand, but my hostess, Jane Temerlin (who was also Lucy's "mother"), translated: "That dog," Lucy commented, pausing at a photo of a

BACKGROUND INFORMATION

The principal thesis of this essay is that chimpanzees are more like people than previously acknowledged. Chimpanzees' skills in language use, tool-making, and social customs blur the line between "animal" and "human" abilities and place them closer to us in evolutionary terms. Based on her thirty years of observing chimpanzees in the wild, Goodall catalogs several interesting ways in which chimpanzees are similar to humans.

READABILITY LEVEL

7.4

RELATED READINGS

Environment

John McPhee, "The Pines"   56

DEFINITIONS

primates (para. 1): an order of mammals characterized by flexible hands and feet with five digits.
Gombe (para. 3): Gombe Stream Research Center in Tanzania.
changeling (para. 3): a child secretly substituted for another.
Jane Temerlin (para. 3): one of Lucy's trainers; wife of Maury Temerlin.
Maury Temerlin (para. 4): a former professor of psychology; author of *Lucy: Growing Up Human.*
Lucy: Growing Up Human (1975) (para. 4): a book by Maury Temerlin on how he raised a chimpanzee called Lucy as a human member of his family.
DNA (para. 4): deoxyribonucleic acid, the molecular basis of the genetic code and hereditary patterns in many organisms, including humans.
hepatitis B (para. 4): an acute viral inflammation of the liver, characterized by jaundice, fever, nausea, and vomiting.
AIDS (para. 4): acronym for Acquired Immune Deficiency Syndrome, a lack of cells that reject foreign tissue in the human immune system, resulting in infection, cancer, and nervous-system degeneration.

ethological (para. 5): relating to the scientific study of the characteristic behavior patterns of animals.

truculent (para. 8): rude, harsh.

Cambridge (para. 8): a prestigious university in Cambridge, England, that was founded in the early twelfth century.

Louis Leakey (1930–1972) (para. 8): a well-known British anthropologist.

Robert Hinde (1923–) (para. 8): a British psychologist; Goodall's supervisor during her Ph.D. work.

anthropomorphic (para. 9): attributing human shape or characteristics to an animal, a god, or an inanimate object.

gambols (para. 10): jumps or skips about playfully.

joie de vivre (para. 10): French. The joy of living.

Grub (para. 11): Goodall's nickname for her son.

Wolfgang Kohler (1887–1967) (para. 12): a German psychologist.

Robert Yerkes (1876–1956) (para. 12): an American psychologist.

The Mentality of Apes (1926) (para. 12): a book by Wolfgang Kohler describing his research on the behavior of apes.

Project Washoe (para. 15): a scientific study beginning in 1966 in which chimpanzees were taught American Sign Language.

Trixie and Allen Gardner (para. 15): Beatrix T. Gardner (1930–) and R. Allen Gardner (1930–) American psychologists.

Richard and Cathy Hayes (para. 15): a husband and wife who assisted in raising chimpanzees; Cathy Hayes wrote *The Ape in Our House* (1951).

Homo sapiens (para. 16): the scientific name for humans.

cross-modal transfer of information (para. 17): the imagining in one sense of an object perceived in another sense.

cognitive (para. 19): related to the process of knowing in the broadest sense, including perception, memory, and judgment.

small white poodle. She turned the page. "Blue," she declared, pointing then signing as she gazed at a picture of a lady advertising some kind of soap powder and wearing a brilliant blue dress. And finally, after some vague hand movements—perhaps signed mutterings—"This Lucy's, this mine," as she closed the magazine and laid it on her lap. She had just been taught, Jane told me, the use of the possessive pronouns during the thrice weekly ASL lessons she was receiving at the time.

The book written by Lucy's human "father," Maury Temerlin, was entitled *Lucy: Growing Up Human.* And in fact, the chimpanzee is more like us than is any other living creature. There is close resemblance in the physiology of our two species and genetically, in the structure of the DNA, chimpanzees and humans differ by only just over one per cent. This is why medical research uses chimpanzees as experimental animals when they need substitutes for humans in the testing of some drug or vaccine. Chimpanzees can be infected with just about all known human infectious diseases including those, such as hepatitis B and AIDS, to which other non-human animals (except gorillas, orangutans and gibbons) are immune. There are equally striking similarities between humans and chimpanzees in the anatomy and wiring of the brain and nervous system, and—although many scientists have been reluctant to admit to this—in social behavior, intellectual ability, and the emotions. The notion of an evolutionary continuity in physical structure from pre-human ape to modern man has long been morally acceptable to most scientists. That the same might hold good for mind was generally considered an absurd hypothesis—particularly by those who used, and often misused, animals in their laboratories. It is, after all, convenient to believe that the creature you are using, while it may react in disturbingly human-like ways, is, in fact, merely a mindless and, above all, unfeeling, "dumb" animal.

When I began my study at Gombe in 1960 it was not permissible—at least not in ethological circles—to talk about an animal's mind. Only humans had minds. Nor was it quite proper to talk about animal personality. Of course everyone knew that they *did* have their own unique characters—everyone who had ever owned a dog or other pet was aware of that. But ethologists, striving to make theirs a "hard" science, shied away from the task of trying to explain such things objectively. One respected ethologist, while acknowledging that there was "variability between individual animals," wrote that it was best that this fact be "swept under the carpet." At that time ethological carpets fairly bulged with all that was hidden beneath them.

How naive I was. As I had not had an undergraduate science education I didn't realize that animals were not supposed to have personalities, or to think, or to feel emotions or pain. I had no idea that it would have been more appropriate to assign each of the chimpanzees a number rather than a name when I got to know him or her. I didn't realize that it was not scientific to discuss behavior in terms of motivation or purpose. And no one had told me that terms such as *childhood* and *adolescence* were uniquely human phases of the life cycle, culturally determined, not to be used when referring to young chimpanzees. Not knowing, I freely made use of all those forbidden terms and concepts in my initial attempt to describe, to the best of my ability, the amazing things I had observed at Gombe. . . .

The editorial comments on the first paper I wrote for publication demanded that every *he* or *she* be replaced with *it*, and every *who* be replaced with *which*. Incensed, I, in my turn, crossed out the *its* and *whichs* and scrawled back the original pronouns. As I had no desire to carve a niche for myself in the world of science, but simply wanted to go on living among and learning about chimpanzees, the possible reaction of the editor of the learned journal did not trouble me. In fact I won that round: The paper when finally published did confer upon the chimpanzees the dignity of their appropriate genders and properly upgraded them from the status of mere "things" to essential Being-ness.

However, despite my somewhat truculent attitude, I did want to learn, and I was sensible of my incredible good fortune in being admitted to Cambridge. I wanted to get my Ph.D., if only for the sake of Louis Leakey and the other people who had written letters in support of my admission. And how lucky I was to have, as my supervisor, Robert Hinde. Not only because I thereby benefited from his brilliant mind and clear thinking, but also because I doubt that I could have found a teacher more suited to my particular needs and personality. Gradually he was able to cloak me with at least some of the trappings of a scientist. Thus although I continued to hold to most of my convictions—that animals had personalities; that they could feel happy or sad or fearful; that they could feel pain; that they could strive towards planned goals and achieve greater success if they were highly motivated—I soon realized that these personal convictions were, indeed, difficult to prove. It was best to be circumspect—at least until I had gained some credentials and credibility. And Robert gave me wonderful advice on how best to tie up some of my more rebellious ideas with scientific ribbon. "You can't *know* that

COLLABORATIVE LEARNING: CLASS ACTIVITY

6 In a full-class discussion, examine the inferences Goodall is making in paragraph 16. Lead your class toward the heart of the essay by discussing the social implications of Goodall's research. What associations do your students make with Goodall's findings? What do these findings suggest for the future of chimpanzees? For the future of animals in general? For the future of humans? What can we learn about ourselves from this research?

7

8

Divide your students into groups of 3 or 4, and have them discuss Goodall's natural inclination to name her subjects. What do these names add to her essay? How does the act of naming the chimps support her argument? Then, have one person from each group summarize the group's discussion for the rest of the class. To begin this group project, you might show one of the films the National Geographic Society has made of Goodall interacting with her subjects, so your students can get a real sense of the nature of her daily work. (To order videos, call 1-800-368-2728 or write the National Geographic Society, Educational Services, P.O. Box 98019, Washington, D.C., 20090.)

Fifi was jealous," he admonished on one occasion. We argued a little. And then: "Why don't you just say *If Fifi were a human child we would say she was jealous.*" I did.

It is not easy to study emotions even when the subjects are human. I know how I feel if I am sad or happy or angry, and if a friend tells me that he is feeling sad, happy or angry, I assume that his feelings are similar to mine. But of course I cannot know. As we try to come to grips with the emotions of beings progressively more different from ourselves the task, obviously, becomes increasingly difficult. If we ascribe human emotions to non-human animals we are accused of being anthropomorphic—a cardinal sin in ethology. But is it so terrible? If we test the effect of drugs on chimpanzees because they are biologically so similar to ourselves, if we accept that there are dramatic similarities in chimpanzee and human brain and nervous system, is it not logical to assume that there will be similarities also in at least the more basic feelings, emotions, moods of the two species? 9

In fact, all those who have worked long and closely with chimpanzees have no hesitation in asserting that chimps experience emotions similar to those which in ourselves we label pleasure, joy, sorrow, anger, boredom, and so on. Some of the emotional states of the chimpanzee are so obviously similar to ours that even an inexperienced observer can understand what is going on. An infant who hurls himself screaming to the ground, face contorted, hitting out with his arms at any nearby object, banging his head, is clearly having a tantrum. Another youngster, who gambols around his mother, turning somersaults, pirouetting and, every so often, rushing up to her and tumbling into her lap, patting her or pulling her hand towards him in a request for tickling, is obviously filled with *joie de vivre*. There are few observers who would not unhesitatingly ascribe his behavior to a happy, carefree state of well-being. And one cannot watch chimpanzee infants for long without realizing that they have the same emotional need for affection and reassurance as human children. An adult male, reclining in the shade after a good meal, reaching benignly to play with an infant or idly groom an adult female, is clearly in a good mood. When he sits with bristling hair, glaring at his subordinates and threatening them, with irritated gestures, if they come too close, he is clearly feeling cross and grumpy. We make these judgments because the similarity of so much of a chimpanzee's behavior to our own permits us to empathize. 10

It is hard to empathize with emotions we have not experienced. I can imagine, to some extent, the pleasure of a female 11 chimpanzee during the act of procreation. The feelings of her male partner are beyond my knowledge—as are those of the human male in the same context. I have spent countless hours watching mother chimpanzees interacting with their infants. But not until I had an infant of my own did I begin to understand the basic, powerful instinct of mother-love. If someone accidentally did something to frighten Grub, or threaten his well-being in any way, I felt a surge of quite irrational anger. How much more easily could I then understand the feelings of the chimpanzee mother who furiously waves her arm and barks in threat at an individual who approaches her infant too closely, or at a playmate who inadvertently hurts her child. And it was not until I knew the numbing grief that gripped me after the death of my second husband that I could even begin to appreciate the despair and sense of loss that can cause young chimps to pine away and die when they lose their mothers. . . .

When first I began to read about human evolution, I learned that one of the hallmarks of our own species was that we, and only we, were capable of making tools. *Man the Toolmaker* was an oft-cited definition—and this despite the careful and exhaustive research of Wolfgang Kohler and Robert Yerkes on the tool-using and tool-making abilities of chimpanzees. Those studies, carried out independently in the early twenties, were received with skepticism. Yet both Kohler and Yerkes were respected scientists, and both had a profound understanding of chimpanzee behavior. Indeed, Kohler's descriptions of the personalities and behavior of the various individuals in his colony, published in his book *The Mentality of Apes*, remain some of the most vivid and colorful ever written. And his experiments, showing how chimpanzees could stack boxes, then climb the unstable constructions to reach fruit suspended from the ceiling, or join two short sticks to make a pole long enough to rake in fruit otherwise out of reach, have become classic, appearing in almost all textbooks dealing with intelligent behavior in non-human animals. 12

By the time systematic observations of tool-using came from Gombe, those pioneering studies had been largely forgotten. Moreover, it was one thing to know that humanized chimpanzees in the lab could use implements: It was quite another to find that this was a naturally occurring skill in the wild. I well remember writing to Louis about my first observations, describing how David Greybeard not only used bits of straw to fish for termites but actually stripped leaves from a stem and thus *made* a tool. And I remember too receiving the now oft-quoted telegram he 13 sent in response to my letter: "Now we must redefine *tool*, redefine *Man*, or accept chimpanzees as humans."

There were, initially, a few scientists who attempted to write   14
off the termiting observations, even suggesting that I had taught the chimps! By and large, though, people were fascinated by the information and by the subsequent observations of the other contexts in which the Gombe chimpanzees used objects as tools. And there were only a few anthropologists who objected when I suggested that the chimpanzees probably passed their tool-using traditions from one generation to the next, through observations, imitation and practice, so that each population might be expected to have its own unique tool-using culture. Which, incidentally, turns out to be quite true. And when I described how one chimpanzee, Mike, spontaneously solved a new problem by using a tool (he broke off a stick to knock a banana to the ground when he was too nervous to actually take it from my hand), I don't believe there were any raised eyebrows in the scientific community. Certainly I was not attacked viciously, as were Kohler and Yerkes, for suggesting that humans were not the only beings capable of reasoning and insight.

The mid-sixties saw the start of a project that, along with   15
other similar research, was to teach us a great deal about the chimpanzee mind. This was Project Washoe, conceived by Trixie and Allen Gardner. They purchased an infant chimpanzee and began to teach her the signs of ASL, the American Sign Language used by the deaf. Twenty years earlier another husband and wife team, Richard and Cathy Hayes, had tried, with an almost total lack of success, to teach a young chimp, Vikki, to talk. The Hayes's undertaking taught us a lot about the chimpanzee mind, but Vikki, although she did well in IQ tests and was clearly an intelligent youngster, could not learn human speech. The Gardners, however, achieved spectacular success with their pupil, Washoe. Not only did she learn signs easily, but she quickly began to string them together in meaningful ways. It was clear that each sign evoked, in her mind, a mental image of the object it represented. If, for example, she was asked, in sign language, to fetch an apple, she would go and locate an apple that was out of sight in another room. . . .

When news of Washoe's accomplishments first hit the scien-   16
tific community it immediately provoked a storm of bitter protest. It implied that chimpanzees were capable of mastering a human language, and this, in turn, indicated mental powers of generalization, abstraction, and concept-formation as well as an

ability to understand and use abstract symbols. And these intellectual skills were surely the prerogatives of *Homo sapiens*. Although there were many who were fascinated and excited by the Gardners' findings, there were many more who denounced the whole project, holding that the data was suspect, the methodology sloppy, and the conclusions not only misleading, but quite preposterous. The controversy inspired all sorts of other language projects. And, whether the investigators were skeptical to start with and hoped to disprove the Gardners' work, or whether they were attempting to demonstrate the same thing in a new way, their research provided additional information about the chimpanzee's mind.

And so, with new incentive, psychologists began to test the 17 mental abilities of chimpanzees in a variety of different ways; again and again the results confirmed that their minds are uncannily like our own. It had long been held that only humans were capable of what is called "cross-modal transfer of information"— in other words, if you shut your eyes and someone allows you to feel a strangely shaped potato, you will subsequently be able to pick it out from other differently shaped potatoes simply by looking at them. And vice versa. It turned out that chimpanzees can "know" with their eyes what they "feel" with their fingers in just the same way. In fact, we now know that some other non-human primates can do the same thing. I expect all kinds of creatures have the same ability. . . .

The fact that chimpanzees have excellent memories surprised 18 no one. Everyone, after all, has been brought up to believe that "an elephant never forgets" so why should a chimpanzee be any different? The fact that Washoe spontaneously gave the name-sign of Beatrice Gardner, her surrogate mother, when she saw her after a separation of eleven years was no greater an accomplishment than the amazing memory shown by dogs who recognize their owners after separations of almost as long—and the chimpanzee has a much longer life span than a dog. Chimpanzees can plan ahead, too, at least as regards the immediate future. This, in fact, is well illustrated at Gombe, during the termiting season: often an individual prepares a tool for use on a termite mound that is several hundred yards away and absolutely out of sight.

This is not the place to describe in detail the other cognitive 19 abilities that have been studied in laboratory chimpanzees. Among other accomplishments chimpanzees possess pre-mathematical skills: They can, for example, readily differentiate between *more* and *less*. They can classify things into specific

1. According to Goodall, chimpanzees resemble humans in their physiological and genetic makeup, in their nervous systems, and (though many scholars disagree) in their "social behavior, intellectual ability, and . . . emotions" (para. 4). The only difference Goodall refers to between humans and chimpanzees is the human ability to use verbal speech.

2. Goodall discovered that individual chimpanzees display remarkable differences in personality. Many scientists were uncomfortable with attributing these differences to personality and with using "human" terms to describe chimpanzee behavior.

3. Project Washoe allowed the Gardners to display in an objective way what Goodall and many others had long suspected—that chimpanzees can acquire language and use it in ways similar to the ways humans communicate with each other. Beyond this point, responses will vary.

ANSWERS TO QUESTIONS:
ANALYZING MEANING (p. 181)

1. Goodall states, "It was one thing to know that humanized chimpanzees in the lab could use implements: It was quite another to find that this was a naturally occurring skill in the wild" (para. 13). The use of tools in the wild provides proof that chimpanzees have natural reasoning, insight, and problem-solving abilities and can pass these skills on to successive generations in a way that helps preserve their species. Because these higher-reasoning skills were previously thought to be limited to humans, this discovery required a redefinition of how we differ from other animals.

2. Goodall became interested in the chimpanzee's mind after she met domesticated, humanized chimpanzees and contrasted them with those she had observed in the wild. Though she found that wild chimpanzees possess many of the same skills as those in captivity, she was fascinated by the different ways captive and wild chimpanzees use their abilities. Goodall wanted to promote better understanding within the scientific community of the characteristics

categories according to a given criterion—thus they have no difficulty in separating a pile of food into *fruit* and *vegetables* on one occasion, and, on another, dividing the same pile of food into *large* versus *small* items, even though this requires putting some vegetables with some fruits. Chimpanzees who have been taught a language can combine signs creatively in order to describe objects for which they have no symbol. Washoe, for example, puzzled her caretakers by asking, repeatedly, for a *rock berry*. Eventually it transpired that she was referring to Brazil nuts, which she had encountered for the first time a while before. Another language-trained chimp described a cucumber as a *green banana*, and another referred to an Alka-Seltzer as a *listen drink*. They can even invent signs. Lucy, as she got older, had to be put on a leash for her outings. One day, eager to set off but having no sign for *leash*, she signalled her wishes by holding a crooked index finger to the ring on her collar. This sign became part of her vocabulary. Some chimpanzees love to draw, and especially to paint. Those who have learned sign language sometimes spontaneously label their works, "This [is] apple"—or bird, or sweetcorn, or whatever. The fact that the paintings often look, to our eyes, remarkably unlike the objects depicted by the artists either means that the chimpanzees are poor draftsmen or that we have much to learn regarding ape-style representational art!

People sometimes ask why chimpanzees have evolved such complex intellectual powers when their lives in the wild are so simple. The answer is, of course, that their lives in the wild are not so simple! They use—and need—all their mental skills during normal day-to-day life in their complex society. They are always having to make choices—where to go, or with whom to travel. They need highly developed social skills—particularly those males who are ambitious to attain high positions in the dominance hierarchy. Low-ranking chimpanzees must learn deception—to conceal their intentions or to do things in secret—if they are to get their way in the presence of their superiors. Indeed, the study of chimpanzees in the wild suggests that their intellectual abilities evolved, over the millennia, to help them cope with daily life. And now, the solid core of data concerning chimpanzee intellect collected so carefully in the lab setting provides a background against which to evaluate the many examples of intelligent, rational behavior that we see in the wild. . . .

20

UNDERSTANDING DETAILS

1. Based on Goodall's research, what are some of the main similarities between chimpanzees and humans? The differences?
2. What gave Goodall the idea that animals have unique personalities?
3. Explain Project Washoe in your own words.

ANALYZING MEANING

1. In what way was tool-making a focal point of Goodall's research?
2. Why did Goodall become interested in the chimpanzee's mind?
3. Why do you think Goodall's discoveries about the mind of the chimpanzee were so important to the scientific community? What do her findings imply about the distinctions between animals and humans?

DISCOVERING RHETORICAL STRATEGIES

1. Explain Goodall's reference in paragraph 1 to "windows" and "glass." How are chimpanzees' eyes like windows?
2. List the author's main points in the essay. Why do you think she chose to deal with these topics in this particular order?
3. Describe Goodall's intended audience in as much detail as possible. Why do you think she has aimed her essay at this particular group?

IDEAS FOR DISCUSSION/WRITING

Preparing to Write

Write freely about the role of learning in contemporary society: What are your main interests? Do you have a desire to learn about anything in particular? How do you pursue this desire? What topics are you especially curious about? How do your friends approach learning? How is learning valued in American society today? Do you feel this value is justified? How is learning related to the American education process?

Choosing a Topic

1. As a college student, you see many different people studying various subjects every day. Some people learn best in groups; others need to study alone. Some learn best by hearing the information, others by seeing it. Some vary their study techniques according to subject matter; others study each subject the same way. Write an essay for your

chimpanzees share with humans. She wanted to describe their emotional and social capabilities in human behavioral terms, but the use of these terms to define their behavior was not yet acceptable in the scientific community.

3. Goodall's discoveries about chimpanzee tool-making and personality are significant because they raise important questions about chimpanzee intelligence and its similarity to the human intellect. The chimpanzees that Goodall describes have exhibited the ability to live within social units, to be creative, to communicate through their own language, and to confront challenging situations with surprising, humanlike skills.

ANSWERS TO QUESTIONS:
DISCOVERING RHETORICAL
STRATEGIES (p. 181)

1. The chimpanzee's eyes reveal emotion and personality to Goodall, thereby providing a window into the chimpanzee's mind. However, the window is not completely transparent; some thoughts are obvious (e.g., the tantrum Goodall describes), whereas other emotions and ideas are obscure.

2. The following is a list of Goodall's main points:

—The scientific community has done little research on the mental and emotional states of chimpanzees.

—Goodall's doctoral work at Cambridge and her experience with chimpanzees in the wild convince her that chimpanzees are remarkably similar to humans in many important ways.

—The tools made by chimpanzees in the wild illustrate a human problem-solving ability.

—Language acquisition studies help prove that chimpanzees have the mental aptitude for abstract thinking and the need to communicate thoughts and language skills to younger chimpanzees.

—Chimpanzees have developed these advanced, "human" mental faculties because of the complex lives they lead in the wild.

3. Goodall explains the scientific procedures, observations, and discoveries in her essay for a general audience. She obviously has great affection for chimpanzees and expects that her readers will share her enthusiasm. Most of her readers enjoy her prose because of its lack of scientific and technical terms; they also share her natural curiosity about chimpanzees and other life forms. By aiming her essay at those who want to learn about animal behavior, she can influence others to see chimpanzees in the same favorable light, promoting both understanding and sympathy for the chimpanzees in the wild and in captivity.

PREWRITING

In preparation for the writing assignments, the Preparing to Write questions ask students to consider the current relationship between education and learning in American society. See pages 16–23 for suggestions on generating ideas in response to these questions.

ADDITIONAL DISCUSSION/WRITING TOPIC

Why are we so aware of animals and animal rights today? How have these sensitivities evolved? How does this subject fit into the larger issue of ecology? Where do you stand on these related issues? Write a coherent essay using specific examples to explain this contemporary awareness and suggest some reasons for this current trend.

REVISING STRATEGY

The order of your examples in an example essay should make your readers as interested in the topic as possible. Choose one of your example essays, and list all of your examples in the order they occur. Review this list, and decide which examples would be more effective in a different place in the essay. Then revise your paper, paying close attention to the flow of the examples from one point in the essay to another.

school newspaper explaining your observations about the different ways people learn. Use carefully chosen examples to illustrate your observations.

2. You have been asked to respond to a national survey on the role of education in our lives. The organization conducting the survey wants to know the extent to which education has helped or hindered you in achieving your goals. In a well-developed essay written for a general audience, explain the benefits and liabilities of education in your life at present. Use specific examples to develop your essay.

3. In her essay, Goodall outlines the many similarities between the cognitive abilities of chimpanzees and humans. She also implies that chimps should have the protection from exploitation and injury accorded to other intelligent creatures. How do you feel about animal rights? What basic rights should animals have? Does your opinion depend on the type of animal? Should chimpanzees, for example, have more rights than alligators or snails have? How do you feel about using animals in laboratory research to study disease? Direct your comments to the general public, and use several specific examples to support your opinion.

ALLEEN PACE NILSEN
(1936–)

■ ■ ■

Sexism in English:
A 1990s Update

QUOTATION ON WRITING

"All good writing is swimming under water and holding your breath."

F. Scott Fitzgerald

While researching books written for children, Alleen Pace Nilsen became interested in linguistic sexism. In 1973, she completed a doctoral dissertation at the University of Iowa entitled "The Effect of Grammatical Gender on the Equal Treatment of Males and Females in Children's Literature." With her husband, she has co-authored two books: *Pronunciation Contrasts in English* (1971) and *Semantic Theory: A Linguistic Perspective* (1975). She is also coeditor of *Sexism and Language* (1977), a book-length collection of essays published by the National Council of Teachers of English, and of a textbook entitled *Literature for Today's Adults* (1980). Nilsen, whose current scholarly interests include the uses of humor in literature and society, is assistant vice-president for academic affairs and professor of English at Arizona State University, where she can occasionally be found playing an energetic game of tennis. She advises students using *The Prose Reader to* "read their essays out loud to someone they admire and respect—perhaps even love. They can then use this human audience to help revise and improve their work."

Preparing to Read

"Sexism in English: A 1990s Update" is a 1989 revision of an essay on linguistic sexism originally published in *Female Studies VI: Closer to the Ground* (1972), one among a series of volumes sponsored by the Modern Language Association's Commission on the Status of Women. In this interesting and well-written article, Nilsen examines the extent to which the English language reveals and reinforces a cultural bias against women. Before reading this essay, think for a few moments about sexism in general: What evidence of sexual bias—against either women or men—can you cite from your own experience? How is this bias expressed in our language use? What examples of sexism in language can you think of? Why do you believe such sexual stereotyping exists in our culture today?

PREREADING

The purpose of this Preparing to Read material is to encourage students to consider the relationship between language and sexual bias (against either women or men). To help your students focus their attention before they respond to the questions here, have them consider some words or phrases that have recently been recast, such as "firefighter" (instead of "fireman"), "mail carrier" (instead of "mailman"), "humanity" (instead of "mankind"), "chair" or "head" (instead of "chairman"), and "salesperson" (instead of "salesman"), and discuss the changes that result from these linguistic adjustments. See pages 3–6 for other ways to generate thoughts on these questions.

Alleen Pace Nilsen's "Sexism in English: A 1990s Update" examines the intricate and revealing relationship between language and the treatment of women in America. Armed only with her dictionary and an inquisitive spirit, she has cataloged a great number of linguistic examples that portray women as sexy, passive, and negative, whereas men are depicted as successful, active, and positive. Her inescapable conclusion is that sexism is a major part of the fabric of everyday thought and language.

READABILITY LEVEL

9.1

RELATED READINGS

Prejudice

Sexism

Sexuality

Women's Roles

Twenty years ago I embarked on a study of the sexism inherent in American English. I had just returned to Ann Arbor, Michigan, after living for two years (1967–69) in Kabul, Afghanistan, where I had begun to look critically at the role society assigned to women. The Afghan version of the *chaderi* prescribed for Moslem women was particularly confining. Few women attended the American-built Kabul University where my husband was teaching linguistics because there were no women's dormitories, which meant that the only females who could attend were those whose families happened to live in the capital city. Afghan jokes and folklore were blatantly sexist, for example this proverb, "If you see an old man, sit down and take a lesson; if you see an old woman, throw a stone." 1

But it wasn't only the native culture that made me question women's roles; it was also the American community. Nearly six hundred Americans lived in Kabul, mostly supported by U.S. taxpayers. The single women were career secretaries, schoolteachers, or nurses. The three women who had jobs comparable to the American men's jobs were textbook editors with the assignment of developing reading books in Dari (Afghan Persian) for young children. They worked at the Ministry of Education, a large building in the center of the city. There were no women's restrooms, so during their two-year assignment whenever they needed to go to the bathroom they had to walk across the street and down the block to the Kabul Hotel. 2

The rest of the American women were like myself—wives and mothers whose husbands were either career diplomats, employees of USAID, or college professors who had been recruited to work on various contract teams including an education team from Teachers College, Columbia University, and an agricultural team from the University of Wyoming. These were the women who were most influential in changing my way of thinking. We were suddenly bereft of our traditional roles; some of us became alcoholics; others got very good at bridge, while others searched desperately for ways to contribute either to our families or to the Afghans. The local economy provided few jobs for women and certainly none for foreigners; we were isolated from former friends and the social goals we had grown up with. Most of us had three servants (they worked for $1.00 a day) because the cook refused to wash dishes and the dishwasher refused to water the lawn or sweep the sidewalks—it was their form of unionization. Occasionally, someone would try to get along without servants, but it was impossible because the houses were huge and we 3 didn't have the mechanical aids we had at home. Drinking water had to be brought from the deep well at the American Embassy, and kerosene and wood stoves had to be stocked and lit. The servants were all males, the highest-paid one being the cook, who could usually speak some English. Our days revolved around supervising these servants. One woman's husband got so tired of hearing her complain about such annoyances as the *bacha* (the housekeeper) stealing kerosene and needles and batteries, and about the cook putting chili powder instead of paprika on the deviled eggs, and about the gardener subcontracting his work and expecting her to pay all his friends, that he scheduled an hour a week for listening to complaints. The rest of the time he wanted to keep his mind clear to focus on his important work with his Afghan counterparts and with the president of the university and the Minister of Education. What he was doing in this country was going to make a difference! In the great eternal scheme of things, of what possible importance would be his wife's trivial troubles with the servants?

4   These were the thoughts in my mind when we finished our contract and returned in the fall of 1969 to the University of Michigan in Ann Arbor. I was surprised to find that many other women were also questioning the expectations that they had grown up with. In the spring of 1970, a women's conference was announced. I hired a babysitter and attended, but I returned home more troubled than ever. Now that I knew housework was worth only a dollar a day, I couldn't take it seriously, but I wasn't angry in the same way these women were. Their militancy frightened me. Since I wasn't ready for a revolution, I decided I would have my own feminist movement. I would study the English language and see what it could tell me about sexism. I started reading a desk dictionary and making notecards on every entry that seemed to tell something about male and female. I soon had a dog-eared dictionary, along with a collection of notecards filling two shoe boxes.

5   Ironically, I started reading the dictionary because I wanted to avoid getting involved in social issues, but what happened was that my notecards brought me right back to looking at society. Language and society are as intertwined as a chicken and an egg. The language that a culture uses is telltale evidence of the values and beliefs of that culture. And because there is a lag in how fast a language changes—new words can easily be introduced, but it takes a long time for old words and usages to disappear—a careful look at English will reveal the attitudes that our ancestors held

DEFINITIONS

chaderi (para. 1): a head-to-toe-length garment worn over regular clothing, designed to cover the wearer completely; worn by women in Afghanistan and other Moslem countries whenever they leave their houses.

arachnoid (para. 8): spiderlike.

Susan Glascoe (para. 21): a fictitious name.

Charlotte Brontë (1816–1855) (para. 21): a British novelist, best known for writing *Jane Eyre*.

Amelia Earhart (1898–1937) (para. 21): an American aviation pioneer.

Helen Hayes (1900–) (para. 21): an American stage and screen actress.

Jenny Lind (1820–1887) (para. 21): a Swedish soprano; known as the "Swedish Nightingale," she was internationally renowned in the mid-nineteenth century.

Cornelia Otis Skinner (1901–1979) (para. 21): an American actress and writer.

Harriet Beecher Stowe (1811–1896) (para. 21): an American writer, best known for *Uncle Tom's Cabin*.

Edith Sitwell (1887–1965) (para. 21): a British poet.

Divide the class in half and assign them a
point of view: either that culture shapes language or that language shapes culture.
Then, have the whole class argue this issue
only from the perspective they have been
assigned.

INTRO ↑

MAIN Body

and that we as a culture are therefore predisposed to hold. My
notecards revealed three main points. Friends have offered the
opinion that I didn't need to read the dictionary to learn such obvious facts. Nevertheless, it was interesting to have linguistic evidence of sociological observations.

Women Are Sexy; Men Are Successful

First, in American culture a woman is valued for the attrac- 6
tiveness and sexiness of her body, while a man is valued for his
physical strength and accomplishments. A woman is sexy. A man
is successful.

A persuasive piece of evidence supporting this view are the 7
eponyms—words that have come from someone's name—found
in English. I had a two-and-a-half-inch stack of cards taken from
men's names, but less than a half-inch stack from women's
names, and most of those came from Greek mythology. In the
words that came into American English since we separated from
Britain, there are many eponyms based on the names of famous
American men: *bartlett pear, boysenberry, diesel engine, franklin
stove, ferris wheel, gatling gun, mason jar, sideburns, sousaphone,
schick test,* and *winchester rifle.* The only common eponyms taken
from American women's names are *Alice blue* (after Alice
Roosevelt Longworth), *bloomers* (after Amelia Jenks Bloomer),
and *Mae West jacket* (after the buxom actress). Two out of the three
feminine eponyms relate closely to a woman's physical anatomy,
while the masculine eponyms (except for *sideburns,* after General
Burnside) have nothing to do with the namesake's body, but instead honor the man for an accomplishment of some kind.

Although in Greek mythology women played a bigger role 8
than they did in the biblical stories of the Judeo-Christian cultures
and so the names of goddesses are accepted parts of the language
in such place names as Pomona from the goddess of fruit and
Athens from Athena and in such common words as *cereal* from
Ceres, *psychology* from Psyche, and *arachnoid* from Arachne, the
same tendency to think of women in relation to sexuality is seen
in the eponyms *aphrodisiac* from Aphrodite, the Greek name for
the goddess of love and beauty, and *venereal disease,* from Venus,
the Roman name for Aphrodite.

Another interesting word from Greek mythology is *Amazon.* 9
According to Greek folk etymology, the *a* means "without" as in
atypical or *amoral,* while *mazon* comes from *mazos,* meaning *breast*
as still seen in *mastectomy.* In the Greek legend, Amazon women
cut off their right breasts so they could better shoot their bows.

Apparently, the storytellers had a feeling that for women to play the active, "masculine" role that the Amazons adopted for themselves, they had to trade in part of their femininity.

This preoccupation with women's breasts is not limited to ancient stories. As a volunteer for the University of Wisconsin's *Dictionary of American Regional English (DARE),* I read a western trapper's diary from the 1830s. I was to make notes of any unusual usages or language patterns. My most interesting finding was that he referred to a range of mountains as *The Teats,* a metaphor based on the similarity between the shapes of the mountains and women's breasts. Because today we use the French wording, *The Grand Tetons,* the metaphor isn't as obvious, but I wrote to mapmakers and found the following listings: *Nippletop* and *Little Nipple Top* near Mt. Marcy in the Adirondacks, *Nipple Mountain* in Archuleta County, Colorado, *Nipple Peak* in Coke County, Texas, *Nipple Butte* in Pennington, South Dakota, *Squaw Peak* in Placer County, California (and many other locations), *Maiden's Peak* and *Squaw Tit* (they're the same mountain) in the Cascade Range in Oregon, *Mary's Nipple,* near Salt Lake City, Utah, and *Jane Russell* Peaks near Stark, New Hampshire.

Except for the movie star Jane Russell, the women being referred to are anonymous—it's only a sexual part of their body that is mentioned. When topographical features are named after men, it's probably not going to be to draw attention to a sexual part of their bodies but instead to honor individuals for an accomplishment. For example, no one thinks of a part of the male body when hearing a reference to Pike's Peak, Colorado, or Jackson Hole, Wyoming.

Going back to what I learned from my dictionary cards, I was surprised to realize how many pairs of words we have in which the feminine word has acquired sexual connotations while the masculine word retains a serious businesslike aura. For example, a *callboy* is the person who calls actors when it is time for them to go on stage, but a *callgirl* is a prostitute. Compare *sir* and *madam.* *Sir* is a term of respect while *madam* has acquired the specialized meaning of a brothel manager. Something similar has happened to *master* and *mistress.* Would you rather have a painting by an *old master* or an *old mistress*?

It's because the word *woman* had sexual connotations, as in "She's his woman," that people began avoiding its use, hence such terminology as *ladies room, lady of the house,* and *girls' school* or *school for young ladies.* Feminists, who ask that people use the term *woman* rather than *girl* or *lady,* are rejecting the idea that

10

11

12

13

COLLABORATIVE LEARNING: SMALL GROUP ACTIVITY

Divide your students into groups of 3 or 4, and have them list 5 to 10 related words that communicate a certain bias our society holds. Have one person from each group present their ideas to the class.

woman is primarily a sexual term. They have been at lest partially successful in that today *woman* is commonly used to communicate gender without intending implications about sexuality.

I found two hundred pairs of words with masculine and feminine forms, e.g., *heir–heiress, hero–heroine, steward–stewardess, usher–usherette,* etc. In nearly all such pairs, the masculine word is considered the base, with some kind of a feminine suffix being added. The masculine form is the one from which compounds are made, e.g., from *king–queen* comes kingdom but not *queendom,* from *sportsman–sportslady* comes *sportsmanship* but not *sportsladyship.* There is one—and only one—semantic area in which the masculine word is not the base or more powerful word. This is in the area dealing with sex and marriage. When someone refers to a *virgin,* a listener will probably think of a female unless the speaker specifies *male* or uses a masculine pronoun. The same is true for *prostitute.*   14

In relation to marriage, there is much linguistic evidence showing that weddings are more important to women than to men. A woman cherishes the wedding and is considered a bride for a whole year, but a man is referred to as a groom only on the day of the wedding. The word *bride* appears in *bridal attendant, bridal gown, bridesmaid, bridal shower,* and even *bridegroom. Groom* comes from the Middle English *grom,* meaning "man," and in this sense is seldom used outside of a wedding. With most pairs of male/female words, people habitually put the masculine word first—*Mr. and Mrs., his and hers, boys and girls, men and women, kings and queens, brothers and sisters, guys and dolls,* and *host and hostess*—but it is the *bride and groom* who are talked about, not the *groom and bride.*   15

The importance of marriage to a woman is also shown by the fact that when a marriage ends in death, the woman gets the title of *widow.* A man gets the derived title of *widower.* This term is not used in other phases or contexts, but *widow* is seen in *widowhood, widow's peak,* and *widow's walk.* A *widow* in a card game is an extra hand of cards, while in typesetting it is an extra line of type.   16

How changing cultural ideas bring changes to language is clearly visible in this semantic area. The feminist movement has caused the differences between the sexes to be downplayed, and since I did my dictionary study two decades ago, the word *singles* has largely replaced such sex-specific and value-laden terms as *bachelor, old maid, spinster, divorcee, widow,* and *widower.* And in 1970 I wrote that when a man is called a *professional* he is thought to be a doctor or lawyer, but when people hear a woman referred   17 to as a *professional* they are likely to think of a prostitute. That's not as true today because so many women have become doctors and lawyers that it's no longer incongruous to think of women in those professional roles.

Another change that has taken place is in wedding announcements. They used to be sent out from the bride's parents and did not even give the name of the groom's parents. Today, most couples choose to list either all or none of the parents' names. Also it is now much more likely that both the bride and groom's picture will be in the newspaper, while a decade ago only the bride's picture was published on the "Women's" or the "Society" page. Even the traditional wording of the wedding ceremony is being changed. Many officials now pronounce the couple "husband and wife" instead of the old "man and wife," and they ask the bride if she promises "to love, honor, and cherish," instead of "to love, honor, and obey." 18

Women Are Passive; Men Are Active

The wording of the wedding ceremony also relates to the second point that my cards showed, which is that women are expected to play a passive or weak role while men play an active or strong role. In the traditional ceremony, the official asks, "Who gives the bride away?" and the father answers, "I do." Some fathers answer, "Her mother and I do," but that doesn't solve the problem inherent in the question. The idea that a bride is something to be handed over from one man to another bothers people because it goes back to the days when a man's servants, his children, and his wife were all considered to be his property. They were known by his name because they belonged to him and he was responsible for their actions and their debts. 19

The grammar used in talking or writing about weddings as well as other sexual relationships shows the expectation of men playing the active role. Men *wed* women while women *become* brides of men. A man *possesses* a woman; he *deflowers* her; he *performs*; he *scores*; he *takes away* her virginity. Although a woman can *seduce* a man, she cannot offer him her virginity. When talking about virginity, the only way to make the woman the actor in the sentence is to say that "She lost her virginity," but people lose things by accident rather than by purposeful actions, and so she's only the grammatical, not the real-life, actor. 20

The reason that women tried to bring the term *Ms.* into the language to replace *Miss* and *Mrs.* relates to this point. Married women resented being identified only under their husband's 21 names. For example, when Susan Glascoe did something news-worthy, she would be identified in the newspaper only as Mrs. John Glascoe. The dictionary cards showed what appeared to be an attitude on the part of editors that it was almost indecent to let a respectable woman's name march unaccompanied across the pages of a dictionary. Women were listed with male names whether or not the male contributed to the woman's reason for being in the dictionary or in his own right was as famous as the woman. For example, Charlotte Brontë was identified as Mrs. Arthur B. Nicholls, Amelia Earhart as Mrs. George Palmer Putnam, Helen Hayes as Mrs. Charles MacArthur, Jenny Lind as Mme. Otto Goldschmit, Cornelia Otis Skinner as the daughter of Otis Skinner, Harriet Beecher Stowe as the sister of Henry Ward Beecher, and Edith Sitwell as the sister of Osbert and Sacheverell. A very small number of women got into the dictionary without the benefit of a masculine escort. They were rebels and crusaders: temperance leaders Frances Elizabeth Caroline Willard and Carry Nation, women's rights leaders Carrie Chapman Catt and Elizabeth Cady Stanton, birth control educator Margaret Sanger, religious leader Mary Baker Eddy, and slaves Harriet Tubman and Phyllis Wheatley.

22   Etiquette books used to teach that if a woman had *Mrs.* in front of her name then the husband's name should follow because *Mrs.* is an abbreviated form of *Mistress* and a woman couldn't be a mistress of herself. As with many arguments about "correct" language usage, this isn't very logical because *Miss* is also an abbreviation of *Mistress.* Feminists hoped to simplify matters by introducing *Ms.* as an alternative to both *Mrs.* and *Miss,* but what happened is that *Ms.* largely replaced *Miss* to become a catch-all business title for women. Many married women still prefer the title *Mrs.,* and some resent being addressed with the term *Ms.* As one frustrated newspaper reporter complained, "Before I can write about a woman, I have to know not only her marital status but also her political philosophy." The result of such complications may contribute to the demise of titles, which are already being ignored by many computer programmers who find it more efficient to simply use names; for example, in a business letter: "Dear Joan Garcia," instead of "Dear Mrs. Joan Garcia," "Dear Ms. Garcia," or "Dear Mrs. Louis Garcia."

23   The titles given to royalty provide an example of how males can be disadvantaged by the assumption that they are always to play the more powerful role. In British royalty, when a male holds a title, his wife is automatically given the feminine equivalent.

But the reverse is not true. For example, a *count* is a high political officer, with a *countess* being his wife. The same is true for a *duke* and a *duchess* and a *king* and a *queen.* But when a female holds the royal title, the man she marries does not automatically acquire the matching title. For example, Queen Elizabeth's husband has the title of *prince* rather than *king*, but if Prince Charles should become king while he is still married to Lady or Princess Diana, she will be known as the queen. The reasoning appears to be that since masculine words are stronger, they are reserved for true heirs and withheld from males coming into the royal family by marriage. If Prince Philip were called *King Philip*, it would be much easier for British subjects to forget where the true power lies.

The names that people give their children show the hopes   24
and dreams they have for them, and when we look at the differences between male and female names in a culture we can see the cumulative expectations of that culture. In our culture girls often have names taken from small, aesthetically pleasing items, e.g., *Ruby, Jewel,* and *Pearl. Esther* and *Stella* mean "star," *Ada* means "ornament," and *Vanessa* means "butterfly." Boys are more likely to be given names with meanings of power and strength, e.g., *Neil* means "champion," *Martin* is from Mars, the god of war, *Raymond* means "wise protection," *Harold* means "chief of the army," *Ira* means "vigilant," *Rex* means "king," and *Richard* means "strong king."

We see similar differences in food metaphors. Food is a passive   25
substance just sitting there waiting to be eaten. Many people have recognized this and so no longer feel comfortable describing women as "delectable morsels." However, when I was a teenager, it was considered a compliment to refer to a girl (we didn't call anyone a *woman* until she was middle-aged) as a *cute tomato*, a *peach,* a *dish,* a *cookie, sugar,* or *sweetiepie.* When being affectionate, women will occasionally call a man *honey* or *sweetie,* but in general, food metaphors are used much less often with men than with women. If a man is called a *fruit,* his masculinity is being questioned. But it's perfectly acceptable to use a food metaphor if the food is heavier and more substantive than that used for women. For example, pin-up pictures of women have long been known as *cheesecake,* but when Burt Reynolds posed for a nude centerfold, the picture was immediately dubbed *beefcake,* c.f. *a hunk of meat.* That such sexual references to men have come into the general language is another reflection of how society is beginning to lessen the differences between their attitudes toward men and women.

Something similar to the *fruit* metaphor happens with refer- 26
ences to plants. We insult a man by calling him a *pansy,* but it
wasn't considered particularly insulting to talk about a girl being
a *wallflower,* a *clinging vine,* or a *shrinking violet,* or to give girls
such names as *Ivy, Rose, Lily, Iris, Daisy, Camellia, Heather,* and
Flora. A plant metaphor can be used with a man if the plant is big
and strong, for example Andrew Jackson's nickname of *Old
Hickory.* Also, the phrases *blooming idiots* and *budding geniuses* can
be used with either sex, but notice how they are based on the
most active thing a plant can do, which is to bloom or bud.

Animal metaphors also illustrate the different expectations 27
for males and females. Men are referred to as *studs, bucks,* and
wolves while women are referred to with such metaphors as *kitten,
bunny, beaver, bird, chick,* and *lamb.* In the 1950s we said that boys
went *tomcatting,* but today it's just *catting around* and both boys
and girls do it. When the term *foxy,* meaning that someone was
sexy, first became popular, it was used only for girls, but now
someone of either sex can be described as a *fox.* Some animal
metaphors that are used predominantly with men have negative
connotations based on the size and/or strength of the animals,
e.g., *beast, bullheaded, jackass, rat, loan shark,* and *vulture.* Negative
metaphors used with women are based on smaller animals, e.g.,
social butterfly, mousy, catty, and *vixen.* The feminine terms con-
note action, but not the same kind of large-scale action as with the
masculine terms.

Women Are Connected with Negative Connotations, Men with Positive Connotations

The final point that my notecards illustrated was how many 28
positive connotations are associated with the concept of masculine, while there are either trivial or negative connotations connected with the corresponding feminine concept. An example
from the animal metaphors makes a good illustration. The word
shrew, taken from the name of a small but especially vicious animal, was defined in my dictionary as "an ill-tempered scolding
woman," but the word *shrewd,* taken from the same root, was defined as "marked by clever, discerning awareness" and was illustrated with the phrase "a shrewd businessman."

Early in life, children are conditioned to the superiority of the 29
masculine role. As child psychologists point out, little girls have
much more freedom to experiment with sex roles than do little
boys. If a girl acts like a *tomboy,* most parents have mixed feelings,
being at least partially proud. But if their little boy acts like a *sissy*

(derived from *sister*), they call a psychologist. It's perfectly acceptable for a little girl to sleep in the crib that was purchased for her brother, to wear his hand-me-down jeans and shirts, and to ride the bicycle that he has outgrown. But few parents would put a boy baby in a white and gold crib decorated with frills and lace, and virtually no parents would have their little boy wear his sister's hand-me-down dresses, nor would they have their son ride a girl's pink bicycle with a flower-bedecked basket. The proper names given to girls and boys show this same attitude. Girls can have "boy" names—*Cris, Craig, Jo, Kelly, Shawn, Teri, Toni,* and *Sam*—but it doesn't work the other way around. A couple of generations ago, *Beverly, Frances, Hazel, Marion,* and *Shirley* were common boys' names. As parents gave these names to more and more girls, they fell into disuse for males, and some older men who have these names prefer to go by their initials or by such abbreviated forms as *Haze* or *Shirl.*

When a little girl is told to *be a lady,* she is being told to sit   30
with her knees together and to be quiet and dainty. But when a little boy is told to *be a man,* he is being told to be noble, strong, and virtuous—to have all the qualities that the speaker looks on as desirable. The concept of manliness has such positive connotations that it used to be a compliment to call someone a *he-man,* to say that he was doubly a man. Today many people are more ambivalent about this term and respond to it much as they do to the word *macho.* But calling someone a *manly man* or a *virile man* is nearly always meant as a compliment. *Virile* comes from the Indo-European *vir* meaning "man," which is also the basis of *virtuous.* Contrast the positive connotations of both *virile* and *virtuous* with the negative connotations of *hysterical.* The Greeks took this latter word from their name for *uterus* (as still seen in *hysterectomy*). They thought that women were the only ones who experienced uncontrolled emotional outbursts and so the condition must have something do to with a part of the body that only women have.

Differences between positive male and negative female con-   31
notations can be seen in several pairs of words which differ denotatively only in the matter of sex. *Bachelor* as compared to *spinster* or *old maid* has such positive connotations that women try to adopt them by using the term *bachelor-girl* or *bachelorette. Old maid* is so negative that it's the basis for metaphors: pretentious and fussy old men are called *old maids,* as are the leftover kernels of unpopped popcorn and the last card in a popular children's game.

1. Nilsen was inspired to research the relationship between language and sex roles by her experiences living for two years in Afghanistan and by the similar sexism she recognized in the United States upon her return. She became involved with the women's movement but found it a bit too revolutionary, so she decided to deal with her own frustration by conducting a private study of the language.

2. Nilsen uses the evidence from her dictionary to prove her three major points. Her first is that women are treated as sexual objects, whereas men are treated as successful people without regard for their attractiveness and sexuality. One example Nilsen cites is the great number of mountains named after women's breasts. She points out that men usually give their names to products rather than to landscapes or objects that resemble parts of their anatomy. Nilsen's second point is that women are portrayed as passive through the surname system and that men are depicted as active. The only exception to this, according to Nilsen, is in the wedding ceremony, which makes the woman active to a certain extent and the man passive. Probably the best example used by the author is her description of the British royalty system, which passively awards a wife the title that corresponds with her husband's but forces a man to "earn" his rank. The final point Nilsen makes is that negative connotations are often associated with women through language, whereas men are usually linked to the positive. Some effective examples of this phenomenon include word pairs such as tailor/seamstress, bachelor/old maid (or spinster), and chef/cook. Each of these titles essentially describes people who hold the same positions, yet the former terms add prestige and are usually used for men, whereas the latter terms carry with them less dignity or importance and are principally used for women.

3. Language is the only way the thoughts of a human being can be fully understood. The choices a writer or speaker makes indicate a great deal about the belief system to which he or she subscribes. Though some choices are made consciously and others

Patron and *matron* (Middle English for *father* and *mother*) have such different levels of prestige that women try to borrow the more positive masculine connotations with the word *patroness*, literally "female father." Such a peculiar term came about because of the high prestige attached to *patron* in such phrases as *a patron of the arts* or *a patron saint*. *Matron* is more apt to be used in talking about a woman in charge of a jail or a public restroom. 32

When men are doing jobs that women often do, we apparently try to pay the men extra by giving them fancy titles; for example, a male cook is more likely to be called a *chef*, while a male seamstress will get the title of *tailor*. The armed forces have a special problem in that they recruit under such slogans as "The Marine Corps Builds Men!" and "Join the Army! Become a Man." Once the recruits are enlisted, they find themselves doing much of the work that has been traditionally thought of as "women's work." The solution to getting the work done and not insulting anyone's masculinity was to change the titles as shown below: 33

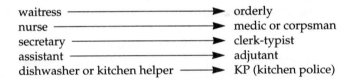

Compare *brave* and *squaw*. Early settlers in America truly admired Indian men and hence named them with a word that carried connotations of youth, vigor, and courage. But they used the Algonquin's name for "woman," and over the years it developed almost opposite connotations to those of *brave*. *Wizard* and *witch* contrast almost as much. The masculine *wizard* implies skill and wisdom combined with magic, while the feminine *witch* implies evil intentions combined with magic. Part of the unattractiveness of both *witch* and *squaw* is that they have been used so often to refer to old women, something with which our culture is particularly uncomfortable, just as the Afghans were. Imagine my surprise when I ran across the phrases *grandfatherly advice* and *old wives' tales* and realized that the underlying implication is the same as the Afghan proverb about old men being worth listening to while old women talk only foolishness. 34

Other terms which show how negatively we view old women as compared to young women are *old nag* as compared to *filly*, *old crow* or *old bat* as compared to *bird*, and being *catty* as compared to being *kittenish*. There is no matching set of metaphors for men. The chicken metaphor tells the whole story of a woman's life. In 35 her youth she is a *chick*. Then she marries and begins *feathering her nest*. Soon she begins feeling *cooped up*, so she goes to *hen parties* where she *cackles* with her friends. Then she has her *brood*, begins to *henpeck* her husband, and finally turns into *an old biddy*.

conclusion I embarked on my study of the dictionary not with the intention of prescribing language change but simply to see what the language would tell me about sexism. Nevertheless I have been both surprised and pleased as I've watched the changes that have occurred over the past two decades. I'm one of those linguists who believes that new language customs will cause a new generation of speakers to grow up with different expectations. This is why I'm happy about people's efforts to use inclusive language, to say *he or she* or *they* when speaking about individuals whose names they do not know. I'm glad that leading publishers have developed guidelines to help writers use language that is fair to both sexes, and I'm glad that most newspapers and magazines list women by their own names instead of only by their husbands' names and that educated and thoughtful people no longer begin their business letters with "Dear Sir" or "Gentlemen," but instead use a memo form or begin with such salutations as "Dear Colleagues," "Dear Reader," or "Dear Committee Members." I'm also glad that such words as *poetess, authoress, conductress,* and *aviatrix* now sound quaint and old-fashioned and that *chairman* is giving way to *chair* or *head, mailman* to *mail carrier, clergyman* to *clergy,* and *stewardess* to *flight attendant.* I was also pleased when the National Oceanic and Atmospheric Administration bowed to feminist complaints and in the late '70s began to alternate men's and women's names for hurricanes. However, I wasn't so pleased to discover that the change did not immediately erase sexist thoughts from everyone's mind as shown by a headline about Hurricane David in a 1979 New York tabloid, "David Rapes Virgin Islands." More recently a similar metaphor appeared in a headline in the *Arizona Republic* about Hurricane Charlie: "Charlie Quits Carolinas, Flirts with Virginia."

What these incidents show is that sexism is not something existing independently in American English or in the particular dictionary that I happened to read. Rather, it exists in people's minds. Language is like an x-ray in providing visible evidence of invisible thought. The best thing about people being interested in and discussing sexist language is that as they make conscious decisions about what pronouns they will use, what jokes they will tell or laugh at, how they will write their names, or how they will begin their letters, they are forced to think about the underlying

36

unconsciously, each choice reflects some part of the writer/speaker's inner world, a world that cannot be seen except through the use of language.

ANSWERS TO QUESTIONS
ANALYZING MEANING (p. 196)

1. Nilsen attempts to prove that masculinity is perceived as positive and femininity as negative by using animal metaphors, the original meanings of proper names, root words, and male–female word pairs. Beyond this point, student opinions and examples will vary.

2. Nilsen claims that words derived from people's names, otherwise called "eponyms," testify to her theory that in American culture women are seen primarily in terms of their sexuality and men are viewed in terms of their accomplishments. In her dictionary search, she found fewer names of women than of men, and all the women's names, most of which came from Greek mythology, were tied to the physical anatomy of a woman. As expected, the men's names were derived from their personal accomplishments, most of which had nothing at all to do with physical attributes. Nilsen uses male–female word pairs to illustrate this concept. In most cases, the words that begin denoting equal stations acquire a sexual connotation in the case of the female part of the pair and remain respectable in the case of the male counterpart (as seen in the terms "callgirl/callboy"). Beyond this point, student opinions will vary.

3. A revolution in language over the last two decades has occurred because of changes in society. As Nilsen states, "language is like an x-ray" (para. 37), and thus as the culture changes so too will the language. In fact, Nilsen acknowledges many such changes in the language, such as the ways in which women are addressed (Ms., Dear Chair, etc.), the titles given to female workers, the customs and rituals associated with marriage, and the publication of books that are stripped of bias. Beyond this point, student opinions and examples will vary.

37

1. Nilsen aims her essay primarily at feminists and those interested in the changes in language and its effects on society, yet her essay is clear enough for the general reader to find interesting. Her control over the topic enables her to include those who do not agree with her, as well as feminists anxious for further linguistic changes.

2. The examples Nilsen uses to illustrate each of her points are carefully selected and interpreted to give support to her essay. In presenting her case, however, she neglects to offer any examples of masculine place names with anatomical references (aside from two very unlikely interpretations) or uncomplimentary masculine images. Furthermore, she frequently presents her views of the perceptions of others with little solid evidence to back her contention.

3. Nilsen clearly believes that sexism is not a result of language but that language reflects the sexist beliefs in our society. Sexism is at the core of sexist language, a core that can be examined only by surveying the language itself as it is used in everyday settings. This is the task Nilsen undertook. What she found was that our society is more sexist than she had at first anticipated.

issue of sexism. This is good, because as a problem that begins in people's assumptions and expectations, it's a problem that will be solved only when a great many people have given it a great deal of thought.

UNDERSTANDING DETAILS

1. What inspired Nilsen's current interest in the relationship between language and sex roles?
2. What are Nilsen's three main points in this essay? Explain each in your own words, using Nilsen's examples or adding some of your own.
3. What does Nilsen mean at the end of the essay when she says "Language is like an x-ray" (paragraph 37)?

ANALYZING MEANING

1. Which principal examples does the author use to support her theory that the concept of masculinity is generally positive whereas femininity is generally negative? Do you agree with this conclusion? Can you think of any examples that argue the contrary position?
2. According to Nilsen, how does the English language describe women as sexy and men as successful? Do you agree with this view? Explain your answer.
3. Based on the author's research, what changes in the language have occurred over the last two decades? What additional linguistic changes can you think of? In what way do these changes reflect our society's view of sex roles?

DISCOVERING RHETORICAL STRATEGIES

1. Describe in as much detail as possible Nilsen's intended audience. Why do you think she aims her essay at this particular group?
2. How does Nilsen organize the examples she chooses to make each major point? Do you think she selected effective examples? Explain your answer.
3. Nilsen's conclusion clearly summarizes her view of the relationship between language and sexism. What are her thoughts on this subject? How does this ending affect you as the reader? What effect does it have on the essay as a whole?

IDEAS FOR DISCUSSION/WRITING

Preparing to Write

Write freely about the interdependence of language and culture: How do you think they affect one another? How is this relationship demonstrated in our society? In what ways can language and culture be separated? How sexist is our language? Our culture? How could these biases be controlled?

Choosing A Topic

1. Write an essay for a college-educated audience based on one of the following statements: "Culture shapes language" or "Language shapes culture." Use carefully selected examples to prove your point. Keep your audience in mind at all times as you organize and write your essay.
2. Listen to some everyday conversations between men and women. Is there any evidence of sexual bias in these discussions, either against women or against men? Write an example essay for the general public in which you support your observations.
3. Using the multivolume *Oxford English Dictionary,* study the etymology (history) of the following words: *woman, lady, madam, mistress, female, mother, honey, whore, bitch.* Based on your own observations and discussions with friends, do the modern connotations of these words differ significantly from their original dictionary definitions? If so, why? Write an essay explaining to your English class what these words have in common and how each might affect our perceptions of women.

PREWRITING

In preparation for the writing assignments, the Preparing to Write questions ask students to explore the relationship between language and culture before they write an essay on a related topic. See pages 16–23 for suggestions on generating ideas in response to these questions.

ADDITIONAL DISCUSSION/WRITING TOPIC

Our language is constantly changing as we add new words and discard old ones. What interesting linguistic changes have you noticed most recently? How do these changes represent new developments in our society? Write an essay explaining the intimate relationship between language and change as it is illustrated in the linguistic examples you have chosen.

REVISING STRATEGY

Transitions make writing smooth and understandable. In one of your example essays, underline all your transitions. Notice which transitions could do a better job of logically connecting information. Then revise your paper, concentrating on making these transitions as accurate and useful as possible.

CHAPTER 4

PROCESS ANALYSIS
■ ■ ■
Explaining Step by Step

Using Process Analysis

Human nature is characterized by the perpetual desire to understand and analyze the process of living well. The bestseller list is always crowded with books on how to know yourself better, how to be assertive, how to become famous, how to avoid a natural disaster, or how to be rich and happy—all explained in three easy lessons. Open almost any popular magazine, and you will find numerous articles on how to lose weight, how elections are run in this country, how to dress for success, how a political rally evolved, how to gain power, or how to hit a successful topspin backhand. People naturally gravitate toward material that tells them how something is done, how something happened, or how something works, especially if they think the information will help them improve their lives in a significant way.

Defining Process Analysis

A *process* is a procedure that follows a series of steps or stages; *analysis* involves taking a subject apart and explaining its components in order to better understand the whole. Process analysis, then, explains an action, a mechanism, or an event from beginning to end. It can concentrate on either a mental or a phys-

INTRODUCTORY NOTES

The key to a good process analysis essay is concentration on audience. If your students know to whom they are addressing their process analysis and why their readers want this particular information, the writing task will be much easier than it would be otherwise. As a result, all the writing assignments in this chapter designate a clear audience and purpose.

This chapter includes four directive essays and one informational essay. First, Alan Monroe, in "Characteristics of the Successful Speaker," outlines the essential traits of a good public speaker; the questions and writing assignments before and after the essay ask students to consider success and failure in a variety of different activities. Next, "Let's Get Vertical!," by Beth Wald, analyzes the process of rock climbing. The exercises and assignments accompanying this essay ask students to consider Wald's essay and then analyze some games and/or sports that they know well. The next essay, an excerpt called "Managing Your Time," from Edwin Bliss' *Getting Things Done: The ABC's of Time Management*, gives its readers strategies for using time efficiently; the exercises preceding and following the reading selection have the students consider, discuss, and write about various aspects of time management. Jessica Mitford's "Behind the Formaldehyde Curtain" is the only purely informative essay in this chapter; she explains the process of embalming, though she certainly does not expect the reader to replicate the process. The exercises accompanying this reading selection ask the students to think and write about various customs they have observed. In the last essay in this chapter, "How to Say Nothing in Five Hundred Words," Paul Roberts explains how to write an effective expository essay; the questions before and after range from having the students catalog their weaknesses and strengths in writing to devising a writing assignment of their own in order to analyze their writing according to Roberts' guidelines.

ical operation: how to solve a chemistry problem, how to tune up your car, how John F. Kennedy was shot, how the telephone system works. In fact, the explanation of the writing process beginning on page 16 of this book is a good case in point: It divides writing into three interrelated verbal activities and explains how they each work—separately and together.

A process analysis can take one of two main forms: (1) It can give directions, thereby explaining how to do something (directive), or (2) it can give information about how something happened (informative). The first type of analysis gives directions for a task the reader might wish to attempt in the future. Examples could include how to make jelly, how to lose weight, how to drive to Los Angeles, how to assemble stereo equipment, how to make money, how to use a microscope, how to knit, how to resuscitate a dying relationship, how to win friends, how to discipline your child, and how to backpack.

The second type of analysis furnishes information about what actually occurred in specific situations. Examples include how Hiroshima was bombed, how certain Hollywood stars live, how the tax system works, how *Batman* was filmed, how Willie Mays earned a place in the Baseball Hall of Fame, how gold was first discovered in California, how computers work, how a kibbutz functions, and how the Gulf War began. These subjects and others like them fulfill a certain fascination we all have with mastering some processes and understanding the intricate details of others. They all provide us with opportunities to raise our own standard of living, either by helping us directly apply certain processes to our own lives or by increasing our understanding of the ways our complex twentieth-century world functions.

The following student paragraph analyzes the process of constructing a garden compost pit. Written primarily for people who might wish to make such a pit, this piece is directive rather than informative. Notice in particular the amount of detail the student calls upon to explain each stage of the process and the clear transitions she uses to guide us through her analysis.

No garden is complete without a functioning compost pit. Here's a simple, inexpensive way to make your garbage work for you! To begin with, make a pen out of hog wire or chicken wire, four feet long by eight feet wide by four feet high, splitting it down the middle with another piece of wire so that you end up with a structure that looks like a capital "E" on its side. This is a compost duplex. In the first pen, place a layer of soda ash, just sprinkled on the surface of the dirt. Then, pile an inch or so of leaves, grass clippings, or sawdust on top of the soda ash. You're now ready for the exciting part. Start throwing in all the organic refuse from your kitchen (no meat, bones, or grease, please). After the food is a foot or so deep, throw in a shovelful of steer manure and cover the entire mess with a thin layer of dirt. Then water it down. Continue this layering process until the pile is about three to three-and-a-half feet high. Allow the pile to sit until it decomposes (from one month in warm climates to six months in colder weather). Next, take your pitchfork and start slinging the contents of pen one into pen two (which will land in reverse order, of course, with the top on the bottom and the bottom on the top). This assures that everything will decompose evenly. Water this down and begin making a new pile in pen one. That's all there is to it! You now have a ready supply of fertilizer for your garden.

Reading and Writing Process Analysis Essays

Your approach to a process analysis essay should be fairly straightforward. As a reader, you should be sure you understand the author's statement of purpose and then try to visualize each step as you go along. As a writer, you need to adapt the mechanics of the way you normally write to the demands of a process analysis paper, beginning with an interesting topic and a number of clearly explained ideas or stages. As usual, the intended audience determines the choice of words and the degree of detail.

HOW TO READ A PROCESS ANALYSIS ESSAY

Preparing to Read. Preparing to read a process analysis essay is as uncomplicated as the essay itself. The title of Edwin Bliss' essay in this chapter, "Managing Your Time," tells us exactly what we are going to learn about. Paul Roberts' essay teaches us "How to Say Nothing in Five Hundred Words." Scanning each selection to assess the author's audience will give you an even better idea of what to expect in these essays, while the synopsis of each in the Rhetorical Table of Contents will help focus your attention on its subject.

Also important as you prepare to read these essays are the qualifications of each author to write on this subject—has he or she performed the task, worked with the mechanism, or seen the event? Is the writer's experience firsthand? When Beth Wald tells us about rock climbing, is she writing from her personal experi-

TEACHING PROCESS ANALYSIS:
ONE INSTRUCTOR'S COMMENTS

When applied to patterns of reasoning, process analysis improves students' critical thinking ability. Instead of reading a "recipe type" article and assigning a "how-to type" essay, a problem–solution pattern is more productive. For example, a business major can write about the process banks use to determine their prime lending rate, a dance major can write about the selection of a body movement sequence to interpret a particular mood, or an education major can write about the stages for mainstreaming a learning-disabled child. In each instance, the student must perceive and explain the reasoning process involved in making selections or reaching conclusions from among several options. Thus, the actual process being analyzed is critical thinking.

Edwin Bliss' essay "Managing Your Time" provides a series of brief case studies as Bliss reasons through various experiences and arrives at viable suggestions for time management. It clearly demonstrates to the student reader that living and decision making are processes, just like baking a cake and learning to ride a bicycle.

Louis Emond
Dean Junior College
Franklin, Massachusetts

To stress the importance of process analysis, I challenge students to give me directions on changing a tire on their cars. They work in groups, preparing written instructions. I then attempt to change one tire per group. The students enjoy seeing me labor, though I have never had to complete the task because a crucial beginning step is always missing (i.e., put the key in the trunk). The results can be comical, but students remember the experience. They quickly grasp that while their daily lives may seem routine, almost everything they do consists of a complex series of learned patterns involving process analysis.

Bruce C. Swaffield
Roanoke College
Salem, Virginia

ence as a rock climber? What is Jessica Mitford's experience with mortuaries? How does she know what goes on "Behind the Formaldehyde Curtain"? The biography preceding each essay will help you uncover this information and find out other publication details that will encourage you to focus on the material you are about to read.

Finally, before you begin reading, answer the prereading questions and then do some brainstorming on the subject of the essay: What do you want to know about being a successful speaker (Alan Monroe)? How well do you manage your time, and what do you think you can learn about the subject from Bliss?

Reading. When you read the essays in this chapter for the first time, record your initial reactions to them. Consider the preliminary information you have been studying in order to create a context for each author's composition: Why did Monroe write "Characteristics of the Successful Speaker"? What circumstances prompted Mitford's "Behind the Formaldehyde Curtain"? Who do you think is Roberts' target audience in "How to Say Nothing in Five Hundred Words"? Also determine at this point whether the essay you are reading is directive (explaining how to do something) or informative (giving information about how something happened). This fundamental understanding of the author's intentions, along with a reading of the questions following the essay, will prepare you to approach the contents of each selection critically when you read it a second time.

Rereading. As you reread these process analysis essays, look for an overview of the process at the beginning of the essay so you know where each writer is headed. The body of each essay, then, is generally a discussion of the stages of the process.

This central portion of the essay is often organized *chronologically* (as in Wald's and Mitford's essays), with clear transitions so that readers can easily follow the writer's train of thought. Other methods of organization are *cyclical*, describing a process that has no clear beginning or end, and *simultaneous* (such as the essays by Monroe on giving a speech, by Bliss on organizing our time, and by Roberts on writing an essay), in which many activities occur at the same time with a clear beginning and end. Most of these essays discuss the process as a whole at some point. During this second reading, you will also benefit from discovering what rhetorical modes each writer uses to support his or her process analysis and why these rhetorical modes work effectively. Do the examples that Wald uses help explain the process of rock climbing? What does Bliss' cause/effect reasoning add to his essay on time management? And how do the descriptions in Mitford's essay on mortuaries heighten the horror of the American mortuary business? How do all the rhetorical modes in each essay help create a coherent whole? After reading each essay for a second time, answer the questions that follow the selection to see if you are understanding your reading material on the literal, interpretative, and analytical levels before you take on the discussion/writing assignments.

For an overview of the entire reading process, you might consult the checklists on pages 15–16 of the Introduction.

HOW TO WRITE A PROCESS ANALYSIS ESSAY

Prewriting. As you begin a process analysis assignment, you first need to become as familiar as you can with the action, mechanism, or event you are going to describe. If possible, try to go through the process yourself at least once or twice. Then try to read something about the process. After all this preparation (and careful consideration of your audience and purpose), you should be ready to brainstorm, freewrite, cluster, or use your favorite prewriting technique (see pages 16–23 of the Introduction) in response to the prewriting questions before you start composing your paper.

Writing. The essay should begin with an overview of the process or event to be analyzed. This initial section should introduce the subject, divide it into a number of recognizable steps, and describe the result once the process is complete. Your thesis in a process essay is usually a purpose statement that clearly and briefly explains your approach to the procedure you will discuss: "Building model airplanes can be divided into four basic steps" or "The American courts follow three stages in prosecuting a criminal case."

Next, the directive or informative essay should proceed through the various stages of the process in a logical fashion from beginning to end. The parts of a process usually fall nicely into chronological order, supported by such transitions as "at first," "in the beginning," "next," "then," "after that," and "finally." Some processes, however, are either simultaneous, forcing the writer to choose a more complex logical order for the essay (such as classification), or cyclical, requiring the writer to choose a starting point and then explain the cycle stage by stage. Playing the guitar, for example, involves two separate and simultaneous components that must work together: holding the strings against the frets with the fingers of one hand and strumming with the other hand. In analyzing this procedure, you would probably want to describe both parts of the process and then explain how the hands work together to produce music. An example of a cyclical process would be the changing of the seasons. To explain this concept to a reader, you would need to pick a starting point, such as spring, and describe the entire cycle stage by stage from that point onward.

In a process paper, you need to be especially sensitive to your intended audience or they will not be able to follow your explanation. The amount of information, the number of examples and illustrations, and the terms to be defined all depend on the prior knowledge and background of your readers. A writer explaining to a group of amateur cooks how to prepare a soufflé would take an entirely different approach to the subject than he or she would if the audience were a group of bona fide chiefs hoping to land jobs in elegant French restaurants. The professional chefs would need more sophisticated and precise explanations than their recreational counterparts, who would probably find such an approach tedious and complicated because of the extraneous details.

The last section of a process analysis paper should consider the process as a whole. If, for example, the writer is giving directions on how to build a model airplane, the essay might end with a good description or drawing of the plane. The informative essay on our legal system could offer a summary of the stages of judging and sentencing a criminal. And the essay on cooking a soufflé could finish with a photograph of the mouth-watering dish.

Rewriting.   In order to revise a process analysis essay, first make sure your main purpose is apparent throughout your paper: Have you written a directive or an informative essay? Is your purpose statement clear? Is your purpose consistent throughout? Next, you need to determine if your paper is aimed at the proper audience: Is your vocabulary, for example, appropriate for that audience? At the beginning of the essay, have you given your readers an overview of the process you are going to discuss? Do you go through the process you are explaining step by step, making sure each phase of the description is comprehensible to your intended audience? Finally, at the end of the essay, do you help your readers see the process as a complete entity?

The checklists on pages 27–28 will give you further guidelines for writing, revising, and proofreading.

Student Essay: Process Analysis at Work

The student essay that follows analyzes the process of using a "home permanent" kit. Notice that once the student gives an overview of the process, she discusses each step one at a time, being careful to follow a logical order (in this case, chronological) and to use clear transitions. Then, see how the end of the essay shows the process as a whole.

Follow the Simple Directions

Although fickle hairstylists in Paris and Hollywood decide what is currently "in," many romanticists disregard fashion and yearn for a mane of delicate tendrils. *Purpose statement for informative process analysis* Sharing this urge but resenting the cost, I opted for a "home perm" kit. Any literate person with normal dexterity could follow illustrated directions, I reasoned, and the eight easy *Overview* steps would energize my limp locks in less than two hours. "Before" and "after" photos of flawless models showed the metamorphosis one might *First step (chronological order)* achieve. Confidently, I assembled towels, rollers, hair clips, waving lotion, neutralizer, end papers, and a plastic cap. While shampooing, I chortled about my ingenuity and economy.

Transition After towel-drying my hair, I applied the *Second step* gooey, acidic waving lotion thoroughly. Then I *Third step* wrapped an end paper around a parted section and rolled the first curl ("securely but not too tightly"). Despite the reassuring click of the fastened rollers, as I sectioned each new curl the previous one developed its own volition and slowly unrolled itself. Resolutely, I reapplied waving lotion and rewound—and rewound—each curl. *Transition* Since my hair was already saturated, I regarded the next direction skeptically: "Apply waving lotion to each curl." *Fourth step* Faithfully, however, I complied with the instructions. *Transition* Ignoring the fragile state of the fastened rollers, I then feigned assurance and enclosed my *Fifth step* entire head in a plastic cap. In forty minutes, chemical magic would occur.

Restless with anticipation, I puttered about the house; while absorbed in small chores, I felt the first few drops of lotion escape from the plastic tent. Stuffing wads of cotton around the cap's edges did not help, and the small drops soon became rivulets that left red streaks on my neck and face and splattered on the floor. (Did I overdo the waving lotion?) Ammonia fumes so permeated each room that I was soon asked to leave. Retreating to the bathroom, I opened the window and dreamed of frivolous new hairstyles.

Transition Finally, the waving time had elapsed; neutral- **Sixth**
izing was next. I removed my plastic cap, carefully **step**
heeding the caution: "Do not disturb curlers as you rinse waving lotion from hair." With their usual impudence, however, all the curlers soon bobbed in the sink; undaunted, I continued. "This next step is critical," warned the instructions. Thinking halfhearted curls were better than no curls at all, I poured the entire bottle of neutralizer on my hair.

Transition After a drippy ten-minute wait, I read the next step:
Transition "Carefully remove rollers." As this advice was su- **Seventh**
perfluous, I moved anxiously to the finale: "Rinse **step**
all solution from your hair, and enjoy your curls." **Eighth**
step

Final Lifting my head from the sink and expecting vi-
product sions of Aphrodite, I saw instead Medusa's image in the mirror. Limp question-mark spirals fell over my eyes, and each "curl" ended in an explosion of steelwool frizz. Reflecting on my ineptitude, I knew why the direction page was illustrated only with drawings. After washing a large load of ammonia-scented **Conclud-**
towels, I took two aspirin and called my hairdresser. **ing re-**
Some repair services are cheap at any price. **mark**

Student Writer's Comments

Any person with normal dexterity probably *could* do it! Even though a process essay is excellent practice for detailing a sequence of ideas or steps, it can sometimes be a bit dull. The satirical approach I chose simultaneously relates the proper procedure while allowing me to poke fun at myself. The obvious hyperbole makes it clear that I was inept and/or failed to follow directions correctly. I'm still not sure I've gotten all the frizz out of my hair!

Some Final Thoughts on Process Analysis

In this chapter, a single process dictates the development and organization of each of the essays. Both directional and informational methods are represented here. Notice in particular the clear purpose statements that set the focus of the essays in each case, as well as the other rhetorical modes (such as narration, comparison/contrast, and definition) that are used to help support the writers' explanations.

ALAN MONROE
(1903–1975)

■ ■ ■

Characteristics of the Successful Speaker

A well-known author of books and articles about speech communications, Alan Monroe earned his B.S., M.A., and Ph.D. degrees from Northwestern University. From 1924 to 1966, he was a member of the speech department at Purdue University, where he wrote a number of important books on speech and related topics: *Projects in Speech* (1931), *Principles and Types of Speech* (1935), *Interview Problems* (1938), *Principles of Speech* (1943, a military edition), *Working for More Effective Speech* (1955), and *An Introduction to Graduate Study* (1961). *Principles and Types of Speech* is now in its tenth edition. A congenial and energetic man with high academic standards, Monroe was on the editorial boards of two important periodicals, *Quarterly Journal of Speech* and *Speech Monographs*, and served as a member of the editorial committee for the *Thorndike-Barnhart Dictionary* series (1960–1963).

Preparing to Read

The following essay, taken from *Principles of Speech*, describes the essential characteristics of an effective speaker. Although Monroe's advice first appeared in 1943, it is as valid today as it was then—perhaps more so in our age of television, which greatly magnifies a speaker's potential audience. As you prepare to read this essay, take a minute or two to think about your own experiences as a speaker: Have you been called upon to give many speeches or talks in the past? How large were your audiences? Were you very nervous? How successful were you in giving these speeches? How do you measure success in other activities that you enjoy? How do you know when you have failed? When you have succeeded?

QUOTATION ON THINKING

"Words answer the same purpose as pictures; they bring up to the mind subjects and thoughts which they are designed to represent."

John Henry Cardinal Newman

PREREADING

The purpose of this Preparing to Read material is to encourage students to consider the relative success and failure of their speaking experiences. To help your students focus their attention on these experiences before responding to the questions here, have them come up to the front of the classroom one by one and introduce themselves to the class, including such items as name, major, most successful writing assignment, least successful writing assignment, and favorite novel. Some of these announcements will cause the students varying degrees of anxiety, but that feeling will be important and necessary for answering the questions here and reading Alan Monroe's essay. See pages 3–6 for other ways to generate thoughts on these questions.

BACKGROUND INFORMATION

In "Characteristics of the Successful Speaker," Monroe offers several simple and valuable principles for improving one's public speaking skills. In this carefully constructed directive essay, he updates classic guidelines for effective oratory, demonstrating in the process the same relevance to modern society as Roman rhetoricians did for their own time some nineteen hundred years ago.

READABILITY LEVEL

10.0

DEFINITIONS

tonus (para. 10): a state of partial contraction characteristic of normal muscles.

PRESIDENT SPEAKS TO NATION 8:30 TONIGHT. This announcement heard over radio and television or read in the newspapers at a time of national crisis always arouses strong interest. Why does the President *speak* instead of issuing a written statement? Obviously he feels that by speaking he can make a more personal appeal for unified national support. Because of the great prestige of his office, the President's speech is front-page news. Not as newsworthy, perhaps, but equally significant is the fact that every day one hundred eighty-three million other citizens of this country speak, too. We order groceries, discuss the neighbor's new car, sell life insurance, teach school, address local groups, hold conferences and committee meetings, argue on street corners, or pay compliments to out sweethearts. All of these situations indicate that speech is a necessary part of our daily lives. 1

Because we use speech constantly, we tend to forget how important it is to us. But if we think for a minute, we will realize how difficult our lives would be if we could not talk. Furthermore, just talking is not in itself sufficient: We also need to talk *well*. Consider the ten or fifteen most influential men or women in your home community. Is it not true that most of them are able speakers? In a democratic society such as ours, the ability to express ideas is almost as essential as the capacity to have ideas. Even in your own circle of friends, the impression you make depends a great deal upon the ease and vigor with which you talk, the tact with which you advance and defend your convictions, and the attractiveness of your speaking manner. 2

Characteristics of a Good Speaker

In speaking, as in most human activities, success depends upon a combination of factors. A good speaker, according to most authorities both ancient and modern, must have integrity, knowledge, self-confidence, and skill. 3

INTEGRITY

Some nineteen hundred years ago the Roman teacher Quintilian insisted that a good speaker must first of all be a good man. Listeners, Quintilian maintained, cannot separate what is said from the person who says it: They are influenced by their impression of the speaker as well as by the arguments he presents. 4

If a person is habitually devious or unreliable, speech training may give him skills, but it cannot make him effective. His actions 5 will contradict his words: He cannot convincingly urge honesty in government if he himself cheats in school or business; his appeal for an open mind in others will go unheeded if he himself is bigoted. Even a speaker's choice of words and arguments betrays his character, for he may habitually appear to dodge issues rather than face them or to say what is popular rather than say what is true or just. A speaker of poor character may succeed for a time, but in the long run he will be found out and his appeals will be discounted.

KNOWLEDGE

Acquiring the knowledge necessary to become a good speaker is a lifelong and cumulative task. Through thoughtful reading, listening, and observing, you can gain increased intellectual depth and maturity. While the first speeches you deliver may be on relatively simple subjects and may be based in part on personal experiences, they should present worthwhile ideas and considered convictions. Soon you will want to reach out beyond immediate and familiar topics—to learn and to speak about subjects in new fields. The more you learn about many subjects, the more effective your speaking will become. Moreover, what you say on any particular topic will reflect the knowledge and understanding of the educated person.

CONFIDENCE

A self-confident speaker has an erect but comfortable posture; natural, easy gestures; direct eye contact with his audience; and earnestness and energy in his voice. Moreover, he adapts his information and arguments to the attitudes of his listeners.

Many factors help determine the amount of nervousness a speaker may feel—including the amount of sleep he had the night before his speech. But the experience of many generations of speakers has shown that, in addition to preparing carefully, you can do much to increase your poise and self-control by following three simple rules.

1. *Speak as often as you can.* The first time a person drives a car or flies an airplane alone, he is likely to be tense and unsure of himself, but with each additional experience his confidence grows. In the same way, each successful speech you make will strengthen your self-assurance. Welcome every opportunity to speak, both in your classes and to groups in the community. Select subjects that you know a good deal about and that you are deeply interested in. Prepare your talks carefully. You will find that after a time speaking becomes a pleasant rather than a painful experience.

6

7

8

9

COLLABORATIVE LEARNING: CLASS ACTIVITY

Have your students collectively confess the anxieties they feel when they are required to give a speech or oral presentation. You might also ask them if the suggestions Monroe offers for the "successful speaker" are reassuring and/or useful.

COLLABORATIVE LEARNING: SMALL GROUP ACTIVITY

Even though this essay is about 50 years old, its guidelines are relevant and current today in many areas of our personal and professional lives. To prove this, divide your class into four groups, having each focus on one of the four characteristics Monroe cites for "successful speakers": integrity, knowledge, confidence, and skill. Then, have each group consider how their guideline might also be a factor in succeeding in life in other ways (i.e., in their professional lives, their social lives, their love lives, and so on).

1. The principal attributes of a successful speaker are listed by Monroe as "integrity, knowledge, self-confidence, and skill" (para. 3). The author affirms the philosophy of the Roman teacher Quintilian, who maintained that "a good speaker must first of all be a good man. Listeners . . . cannot separate what is said from the person who says it" (para. 4). Thus, Quintilian and Monroe would both agree that the traits representing a good speaker must be characteristic of all that person's activities if he/she is to be considered a "good" person.

2. To develop self-confidence in speaking, Monroe suggests that the individual speak as often as possible, both in class and in public, from carefully prepared notes on familiar or well-researched topics, accepting nervous tension as a natural and energizing byproduct of the experience.

3. In order to develop a more effective speaking style, the author advocates that you "have something you want to say" (para. 19), suggesting careful research and preparation of your topic; "want someone else to understand or believe it" (para. 19), removing the focus from your personal performance to the requirements of the audience; and "say it as simply and directly as you can" (para. 19), thereby eliminating the theatrics and linguistic acrobatics that can detract from the subject being addressed.

2. *Remember that some nervous tension is both natural and good for you.* Even in the deepest sleep our muscles are never completely relaxed. When we are awake our "muscle tonus" is higher, and it increases still more when the mind or body is called upon for some unusual exertion. Naturally, then, when you stand up to talk to a group of people, the tonus of your muscles will rise. But this only means that you are more alert and alive. Much of the sparkle that we admire in good speakers comes from this physical verve and energy. If you are keyed up before you begin to speak, regard this as a good sign: It means that there is small chance of your making a dull or listless speech. 10

3. *Never allow yourself to give up.* Each time you meet a situation and master it, the more confident you will become; each time you acknowledge yourself beaten or evade an issue, the less confident you will be the next time. Avoid setting yourself too difficult a task in your first speeches—that is, avoid subjects that are detailed or complex—but once you have begun to work on a topic, go through with the job. Confidence, like muscles, develops by overcoming resistance. 11

SKILL

Fluency, poise, control of voice, and coordinated movements of the body mark the skillful speaker. Combined with the qualities of integrity, knowledge, and self-confidence, such skills heighten the speaker's effectiveness by enabling him to communicate his ideas clearly and attractively. 12

Skill in speaking is gained principally through practice. In practicing, however, take care not to develop artificiality. Good speaking is distinct and lively; it is forceful, but it is also natural and conversational; it commands attention because of the speaker's earnest desire to communicate. Note how speech becomes ineffective when these principles are violated. Doubtless you will recognize some of the following types of speakers: 13

The Elocutionist—one who talks for display rather than communication. He permits himself to be carried away by the sound of his voice and the graceful manipulation of his body, and forgets that his purpose is not to display his own speaking skills, but to get other people to understand or believe. 14

The Verbal Gymnast—one who makes a parade of language. He never uses a familiar word if he can find an esoteric one; he delights in complex sentences and mouth-filling phrases. Disraeli once described the verbal gymnast as a man "intoxicated with the exuberance of his own verbosity." 15

The Gibberer—one who emits a continuous stream of words with little or no thought behind them. He jumps from one point to another until his listeners are thoroughly confused. He usually concludes his speech with the abrupt remark, "Well, I guess that's all I have to say on the subject."

The Hermit—one who mumbles to himself. He may have a wealth of ideas, well-organized and developed, but he looks at the ceiling or floor, talks in a weak, monotonous voice, and makes no effort to be heard or understood.

The Culprit—one who seems ashamed of what he is saying. He shrinks from his hearers both in voice and manner. Sometimes he apologizes verbally; always he seems self-conscious and tentative. He is never forthright in his statements, and thus gives the impression that he does not believe them himself.

How can you develop the natural, energetic, conversational delivery which the Elocutionist and his follow "orators" lack? For the present it will help you speak in a lively, conversational way if you always
1. have something you want to say;
2. want someone else to understand or believe it; and
3. say it as simply and directly as you can.

UNDERSTANDING DETAILS

1. According to Monroe, what are the principal characteristics of a successful speaker?
2. What concrete suggestions does the author have for building self-confidence before speaking to an audience? Do you think these would work for you?
3. What three guidelines does the author offer at the end of his essay to help produce a successful speech? Explain each of them in your own words.

ANALYZING MEANING

1. Which of the two main types of process analysis does this essay represent? Why does it fall into that category? What is Monroe's statement of purpose in this essay?
2. In what ways do the characteristics of a good speaker mirror the guidelines for most other successful activities?

ANSWERS TO QUESTIONS:
ANALYZING MEANING (p. 211)

16   1. This essay is a directive process analysis that explains how to become a successful speaker. Its statement of purpose is reflected in the assertion that "the impression you make depends a great deal upon the ease and vigor with which you talk, the tact with which you advance and defend your convictions, and the attractiveness of your
17   speaking manner" (para. 2).

2. In order to succeed at any activity, the person participating must by knowledgeable, confident, and skillful. Though honesty may not be required for success in all activities, some are impossible to do without a sense of ethics. Using these principles, almost any goal would be easier to reach.

3. In his classification of speakers, Monroe describes "The Elocutionist" (para. 14), who focuses on a theatrical exhibition of his oratorical dexterity; "The Verbal Gymnast" (para. 15), who is obsessed with esoteric complexities of the English language; "The Gibberer" (para. 16), who emits a chaotic flood of dissociated ideas, leaving only confusion in his wake; "The Hermit" (para. 17), whose indistinct monotone disappears behind the podium; and "The Culprit" (para. 18), whose timid voice and downcast eyes suggest an abstract culpability for actions unknown. The common deficiency in all these speakers is a lack of camaraderie with the audience and an inordinate focus on self.

ANSWERS TO QUESTIONS:
DISCOVERING RHETORICAL
STRATEGIES (p. 212)

1. The subheadings increase the clarity of the essay, allowing the reader to focus upon each characteristic individually so that the information is received in short, easily comprehensible segments.

2. Whereas integrity is innate and knowledge may be absorbed, self-confidence can be developed in an individual only through discipline and purposeful action. The shift from explanatory statements to a list of commands gives the reader a mandate for action that may be lacking in the hesitant speaker.

3. In the list that closes the essay, the author very simply and effectively sums up the advice he offers in the body of the article.

PREWRITING

In preparation for the writing assignments, the Preparing to Write questions ask students to consider the criteria of success and failure in various activities they enjoy. See pages 16–23 for suggestions on generating ideas in response to these questions.

ADDITIONAL DISCUSSION/WRITING TOPIC

Following Monroe's guidelines for giving effective speeches, write an essay evaluating a speech given by one of your classmates. (If your classmates have not given any speeches in connection with this chapter, perhaps you could evaluate a student's speech in another class or a speech delivered in the community or through the media.) Include in this essay some clear suggestions of your own on how to present an effective speech.

REVISING STRATEGY

In the introduction to a process analysis paper, a clear overview of the process to be explained is a basic requirement. Reread the introduction to one of your process analysis essays, and look closely at your overview. It should introduce the process, divide it into steps, and describe the desired results. It should also contain a clear purpose statement. Notice where you need more information in your introduction. Then revise your paper, concentrating on presenting this overview as clearly as possible.

3. In Monroe's system of classifying speakers, what distinguishes one type from another? Explain all five of his categories by giving examples of people you know who fit each classification.

DISCOVERING RHETORICAL STRATEGIES

1. Do the subheadings help or hinder you in reading this essay? Explain your response.
2. The author shifts from explanatory statements to a list of commands when he discusses self-confidence. Why do you think he makes this shift? What effect does it create in the essay?
3. Why do you think Monroe ends his essay with a list? Is this an effective conclusion? Why or why not?

IDEAS FOR DISCUSSION/WRITING

Preparing to Write

Write freely about your favorite activities: List the hobbies you like. List other pastimes you enjoy. Is public speaking one of these? Why do you like these particular activities? What characteristics determine success in these activities? How do you know when someone is successful? How do you measure his or her success? How do you measure failure?

Choosing a Topic

1. Using Monroe's essay as a model, explain what characterizes success in one of the activities you enjoy. Direct your essay to someone who has tried the activity but is not yet very good at it.
2. You have just failed at one of your favorite pastimes. In order to get a laugh, explain to your peers in a well-organized essay how to fail at one of the activities you enjoy.
3. Following the guidelines Monroe offers in this essay, prepare for your English class a two- to three-minute talk on one of the following topics:

My Favorite Television Show
My Favorite Play
My Favorite Movie
My Favorite Sport
My Favorite Magazine
My Favorite Musical Group
My Favorite Book
My Favorite Concert
My Favorite Quality in My Mother/Father
My Favorite Quality in Myself

BETH WALD
(1960–)

■ ■ ■

Let's Get Vertical!

QUOTATION ON READING

"Reading is to the mind what exercise is to the body."

Richard Steele

An avid rock climber, sportswoman, and camera buff, Beth Wald has designed a "perfect career" for herself as a freelance writer and photographer specializing in photo-essays shot in exotic locations. Her work as a contributing editor to *Climbing* magazine and several European outdoor sports periodicals has taken her rock climbing all over the world—most recently to Central America, the former Soviet Union, and northern Mexico. Wald's skill as a climber enables her to reach inaccessible rock ledges and pinnacles, where she often snaps her pictures while dangling precariously from a few slender feet of nylon rope. Her current interest in the cultural and environmental survival of third-world nations has helped her focus her work (as well as her travel plans) during the past few years. Her advice to students using *The Prose Reader* is "Look hard at your writing. Be your own toughest critic. Don't let other people force you into a style of writing that isn't yours. Find your own innate style and develop it." Wald lives in Boulder, Colorado.

Preparing to Read

In the following essay, originally published in *Listen* magazine, Wald details the joy, excitement, and danger of rock climbing. Before reading this essay, think for a few minutes about your favorite sport or game. Why do you like this activity? Why should others try it? What are the basic rules of this sport or game? Could anyone learn it? Or does someone need special knowledge or abilities to be successful? What skills do you derive from this activity that you can use in other situations?

PREREADING

The purpose of this Preparing to Read material is to encourage students to think about their favorite sport or game. To help your students focus their attention on this activity before they respond to the questions here, ask them to name some of their favorite sports or games while you write them on a chalkboard or on a transparency. This list should generate other ideas for your students. Then, you might discuss their various reactions to these activities as they were in the process of learning them: How well did your students like these activities when first introduced to them? Do they like the activities more or less now? Did they ever contemplate giving up the activities? Why or why not? See pages 3–6 for other ways to generate thoughts on these questions.

Here I am, 400 feet up on the steep west face of Devil's Tower, a tiny figure in a sea of petrified rock. I can't find enough footholds and handholds to keep climbing. My climbing partner anxiously looks up at me from his narrow ledge. I can see the

1

BACKGROUND INFORMATION

In this essay, Beth Wald presents an exciting view of a sport most of us will never attempt—rock climbing. It is an excellent example of a process analysis essay that is also a sales pitch for the sport. She begins the essay with an exhilarating firsthand account of some dramatic moments in a climb, then discusses the "challenges and rewards" of the sport before she begins to focus on the process of climbing. Wald next explains the details of rock climbing in a section of the essay she calls "Anyone Can Climb." At the conclusion of her essay, many of her readers will be ready to sign up for a climbing class at their nearest mountain range.

READABILITY LEVEL

8.6

RELATED READINGS

Sports and Fitness

Joyce Carol Oates, "On Boxing"   331
Tom Wolfe, "The Right Stuff"   363
Robert Hughes, "The N.R.A. in a Hunter's
    Sights"   462

DEFINITIONS

Devil's Tower (para. 1): a columnar rock formation in northeast Wyoming rising 865 feet above its base.
belayer (para. 11): the person on a rock-climbing team who anchors the rope and gradually feeds it to the lead climber.

silver sparkle of the climbing devices I've jammed into the crack every eight feet or so.

I study the last device I've placed, a half-inch aluminum wedge 12 feet below me. If I slip, it'll catch me, but only after a 24-foot fall, a real "screamer." It's too difficult to go back; I have to find a way up before my fingers get too tired. I must act quickly. 2

Finding a tiny opening in the crack, I jam two fingertips in, crimp them, pull hard, and kick my right foot onto a sloping knob, hoping it won't skid off. At the same time, I slap my right hand up to what looks like a good hold. To my horror, it's round and slippery. 3

My fingers start to slide. Panic rivets me for a second, but then a surge of adrenalin snaps me back into action. I scramble my feet higher, lunge with my left hand, and catch a wider crack. I manage to get a better grip just as my right hand pops off its slick hold. My feet find edges, and I regain my balance. Whipping a chock (wedge) off my harness, I slip it into the crack and clip my rope through a carabiner (oblong metal snaplink). After catching my breath, I start moving again, and the rest of the climb flows upward like a vertical dance. 4

The Challenges and Rewards

I've tried many sports, but I haven't found any to match the excitement of rock climbing. It's a unique world, with its own language, communities, controversies, heroes, villains, and devoted followers. I've lived in vans, tepees, tents, and caves; worked three jobs to save money for expenses; driven 24 hours to spend a weekend at a good rock; and lived on beans and rice for months at a time—all of this to be able to climb. What is it about scrambling up rocks that inspires such a passion? The answer is, no other sport offers so many challenges and so many rewards. 5

The physical challenges are obvious. You need flexibility, balance, and strength. But climbing is also a psychological game of defeating your fear, and it demands creative thinking. It's a bit like improvising a gymnastic routine 200 feet in the air while playing a game of chess. 6

Climbers visit some of the most spectacular places on earth and see them from a unique perspective—the top! Because the sport is so intense, friendships between climbers tend to be strong and enduring. 7

Anyone Can Climb

Kids playing in trees or on monkey bars know that climbing 8 is a natural activity, but older people often have to relearn to trust their instincts. This isn't too hard, though. The ability to maintain self-control in difficult situations is the most important trait for a beginning climber to have. Panic is almost automatic when you run out of handholds 100 feet off the ground. The typical reaction is to freeze solid until you fall off. But with a little discipline, rational thinking, and/or distraction tactics such as babbling to yourself, humming, or even screaming, fear can change to elation as you climb out of a tough spot.

Contrary to popular belief, you don't have to be superhumanly strong to climb. Self-confidence, agility, a good sense of balance, and determination will get you farther up the rock than bulging biceps. Once you've learned the basics, climbing itself will gradually make you stronger, though many dedicated climbers speed up the process by training at home or in the gym.

Nonclimbers often ask, "How do the ropes get up there?" It's quite simple; the climbers bring them up as they climb. Most rock climbers today are "free climbers." In free climbing, the rope is used only for safety in case of a fall, *not* to help pull you up. (Climbing without a rope, called "free soloing," is a *very* dangerous activity practiced only by extremely experienced—and crazy—climbers.)

First, two climbers tie into opposite ends of a 150-foot-long nylon rope. Then one of them, the belayer, anchors himself or herself to a rock or tree. The other, the leader, starts to climb, occasionally stopping to jam a variety of aluminum wedges or other special gadgets, generically referred to as protection, into cracks in the rock. To each of these, he or she attaches a snaplink, called a carabiner, and clips the rope through. As the leader climbs, the belayer feeds out the rope, and it runs through the carabiners. If the leader falls, the belayer holds the rope, and the highest piece of protection catches the leader. The belayer uses special techniques and equipment to make it easy to stop falls.

When the leader reaches the end of a section of rock—called the pitch—and sets an anchor, he or she becomes the belayer. This person pulls up the slack of the rope as the other partner climbs and removes the protection. Once together again, they can either continue in the same manner or switch leaders. These worldwide techniques work on rock formations, cliffs, peaks, even buildings.

Rocks, Rocks Everywhere

Some of the best climbing cliffs in the country are in the Shawangunk Mountains, only two hours from New York City.

COLLABORATIVE LEARNING: CLASS ACTIVITY

Have the students in your class individually investigate the health advantages of their favorite sport. Next, have the class as a whole talk about the benefits of pursuing a sport, while you write these advantages on the chalkboard or on a transparency. Then, lead the class in a discussion of the relationship between sports and health: How are they related? Why are they related in this way? What other methods besides sports can students use to maintain their good health?

9

10

11

12

COLLABORATIVE LEARNING: SMALL GROUP ACTIVITY

Have each student write a brief description of a sport without actually naming the activity. Then, have the students swap descriptions, and have the reader record at the bottom of the description the name of the sport he or she thinks the writer is describing. The students should return the papers to their authors and find out if their guesses are correct.

13

1. In rock climbing, two climbers tie themselves together for protection with a 150-foot rope. The belayer, on one end of the rope, anchors himself or herself to a rock or tree. The leader, on the other end, starts to climb and pounds wedges into the rock along the way. The belayer feeds out rope while the leader keeps climbing. Once the leader reaches the top of a section of rock, he or she becomes the belayer, pulling up the slack from the partner climbing below.

2. According to Wald, the most important trait for a climber is the "ability to maintain self-control in difficult situations" (para. 8). Climbers also need strength, flexibility, balance, self-confidence, agility, and determination. She emphasizes both the need for these skills and the potential for improving these skills during climbing.

3. Because rock climbers focus on finding a pathway up a rock and controlling any urges to panic, they develop self-control and concentration, which allow them an escape from the trivial, as well as time to get to know their own inner strengths.

1. For Wald, rock climbing is a therapeutic as well as a physical activity. She specifically describes both the physical exertion of climbing and the mental rewards that result from the sport. She then provides essential information for the beginning rock climber.

2. Responses to this question will vary.

3. Almost every occupation or situation at home would be easier for a person who can control anxiety, plan effectively, and communicate well with others. Being successful requires all of these important skills.

1. Wald presents a typical climbing experience to illustrate the adrenalin surge and discipline that accompany each climb. The reader, from Wald's description, begins to understand her enthusiasm for rock climb-

Seneca Rocks in West Virginia draws climbers from Washington, D.C., and Pittsburgh, Pennsylvania. Chattanooga, Tennessee, has a fine cliff within the city limits. Most states in the U.S. and provinces in Canada offer at least one or two good climbing opportunities.

Even if there are no large cliffs or rock formations nearby, you can climb smaller rocks to practice techniques and get stronger. This is called bouldering. Many climbers who live in cities and towns have created climbing areas out of old stone walls and buildings. Ask someone at your local outdoor shop where you can go to start climbing. 14

Get a Helping Hand

There's no substitute for an expert teacher when it comes to learning basic techniques and safety procedures. One of the best (and least expensive) ways to learn climbing is to convince a veteran climber in your area to teach you. You can usually meet these types at the local crag or climbing shop. 15

As another option, many universities and colleges, some high schools, and some YMCAs have climbing clubs. Their main purpose is to introduce people to climbing and to teach the basics. Other clubs, such as the Appalachian Mountain Club in the eastern U.S. and the Mountaineers on the West Coast, also provide instruction. Ask at your outdoor shop for the names of clubs in your area. 16

If you live in a place completely lacking rocks and climbers, you can attend one of the fine climbing schools at the major climbing area closest to you. Magazines like *Climbing, Rock & Ice*, and *Outside* publish lists of these schools. Once you learn the basics, you're ready to get vertical. 17

In rock climbing, you can both lose yourself and find yourself. Life and all its troubles are reduced to figuring out the puzzle of the next section of cliff or forgotten in the challenge and delight of moving through vertical space. And learning how to control anxiety, how to piece together a difficult sequence of moves, and how to communicate with a partner are all skills that prove incredibly useful back on the ground! 18

UNDERSTANDING DETAILS

1. Explain in your own words the process of rock climbing.
2. According to Wald, what is the most important trait for a beginning

climber to have? Name some other necessary characteristics cited by the author.
3. What does Wald mean when she says, "In rock climbing, you can both lose yourself and find yourself" (paragraph 18)?

ANALYZING MEANING

1. What is the author's principal purpose in this essay? What is her purpose in rock climbing?
2. Are you convinced by Wald's essay that "anyone can climb"? What details are most persuasive to you?
3. How might "learning how to control anxiety, how to piece together a difficult sequence of moves, and how to communicate with a partner" be useful in everyday life "back on the ground" (paragraph 18)?

DISCOVERING RHETORICAL STRATEGIES

1. How does Wald's introduction prepare us for the information that follows? In your opinion, is this an effective beginning to her essay?
2. Wald explains the challenges and rewards of rock climbing before disclosing the process. Why do you think she introduces her various topics in this order? How effective is this order?
3. Is Wald's title for this essay well chosen? Explain your answer.

IDEAS FOR DISCUSSION/WRITING

Preparing to Write

Write freely about your favorite sport or game: Are you as excited about this activity as Wald is about rock climbing? What are its "challenges and rewards"? Who can learn this sport or game? What are its basic steps? Why do you enjoy this activity so much? What skills that you learned in this activity can you apply to other aspects of your life?

Choosing a Topic

1. A sports magazine has asked you to write a detailed essay explaining the rules of your favorite sport or game to a group of people who want to learn this activity. Write a process analysis essay on a topic of your choice for this magazine.
2. The editors of this sports magazine have asked you to revise your essay for a group of people looking for activities that suit their needs.

ing and the need for rigorous training before attempting the sport. When she later presents the sequence of steps in climbing, readers can more easily relate to the process because this early description has provided them with necessary background information.

2. Wald makes climbing appealing to her reader before she describes the actual process so that nonclimbers will be tempted to read this essay and perhaps give climbing a try. By presenting her description, then reasons for climbing, and finally the process itself, Wald effectively draws in the novice without boring the rock-climbing enthusiast.

3. Wald's title is catchy because rock climbers will understand it, nonclimbers will be curious about its meaning, and most readers will be titillated by the sexual innuendo.

PREWRITING

In preparation for the writing assignments, the Preparing to Write questions ask students to write spontaneously about their favorite sport or game before completing an essay on a related topic. See pages 16–23 for suggestions on generating ideas in response to these questions.

ADDITIONAL DISCUSSION/WRITING TOPIC

For the students in your composition class, write a process analysis paper on the steps one must take to stay healthy. Take into consideration what we now know about nutrition and cardiovascular conditioning. Make your explanations direct and straightforward, taking your readers through each step of the process. Be certain that your final draft contains all the features of a good process analysis essay, including an overview of the process in the introduction, an explanation of each stage of the process, and a final look at the entire process in the conclusion.

The purpose of a process analysis essay should be clear throughout your explanation of the process. In one of your process analysis essays, mark the places in your paper where your purpose is clear; read the essay again and put an X where your purpose is not so clear. Then revise your paper, making your purpose as precise as possible throughout your essay.

This time the editors want you to persuade their readers to try your favorite activity. In this case, present your process analysis essay as a sales pitch to the general public, explaining the benefits of this sport or game along with your detailed directions for learning it.

3. As Wald says in her last paragraph, rock climbing teaches climbers skills that can be applied to other real-life experiences. In fact, many extracurricular activities teach us specialized skills that help us lead better lives. For your English class, write an essay discussing the relationship between extracurricular activities and real life, citing as often as possible examples from your experience.

EDWIN BLISS
(1923–)

■ ■ ■

Managing Your Time

QUOTATION ON WRITING

"I write; therefore, I am."

Samuel Johnson

An internationally known consultant on time-management techniques, Edwin Bliss earned his B.S. and M.S. degrees at the University of Utah, worked as a reporter for the *Columbus Dispatch*, taught journalism at a variety of schools, and was a lobbyist for the National Industrial Council and the U.S. Chamber of Commerce. Not until he became a member of the Washington staff of Senator Wallace F. Bennett, however, did he begin to understand the importance of time management. Since then, Bliss has put his management techniques to work as a consultant for a number of businesses in American and abroad through public seminars sponsored by a company called CareerTrack. "Organizing your time properly is especially important for college students," he claims; "a knowledge of time-management skills can help you avoid writers' block so that you turn your papers in on time." His first book, *Getting Things Done: The ABC's of Time Management*, was published in 1976 (updated and reissued in 1991); his second, *Doing It Now: A Twelve-Step Program for Overcoming Procrastination*, came out in 1983. Bliss currently lives in central California, where he is writing a book on how to operate a small business.

Preparing to Read

In the following essay, which is excerpted from *Getting Things Done: The ABC's of Time Management*, Bliss offers a number of specific suggestions to help you organize your time more efficiently. Before reading his essay, take a few minutes to think about how you arrange each day: How carefully do you schedule your time? Do you make lists of things you want to do every day? Do you usually accomplish more or less than you wanted to in a typical day? How well do you concentrate on a single activity? Are you able to say "no" to events you don't want to participate in? How much do you procrastinate? Are all aspects of your life in a healthy balance (e.g., work, recreation, school, family)? If not, what could you do to create a more balanced life for yourself?

PREREADING

The purpose of this Preparing to Read material is to encourage students to think about how they manage their time on a daily basis. To help your students evaluate their use of time before they respond to the questions here, have them make out a typical week's schedule, including as many routine activities as they can think of. Then, have them break up into pairs and evaluate each other's time management techniques based on their own experience. See pages 3–6 for other ways to generate thoughts on these questions.

Business management consultant Edwin Bliss sets forth in this essay ten important tips that analyze the process of using time more effectively: (1) plan ahead, (2) concentrate, (3) take frequent small breaks, (4) avoid clutter, (5) don't be a perfectionist, (6) don't be afraid to say no, (7) don't procrastinate, (8) cut out time-wasting activities, (9) delegate authority, and (10) don't be a workaholic. Following these simple suggestions, he asserts, can make all of us more efficient time-managers.

READABILITY LEVEL

11.6

I first became interested in the effective use of time when I was an assistant to a U.S. Senator. Members of Congress are faced with urgent and conflicting demands on their time—for committee work, floor votes, speeches, interviews, briefings, correspondence, investigations, constituents' problems, and the need to be informed on a wide range of subjects. The more successful Congressmen develop techniques for getting maximum benefit from minimum investments of time. If they don't, they don't return.

Realizing that I was not one of those who use time effectively, I began to apply in my own life some of the techniques I had observed. Here are ten I have found most helpful.

Plan.   You need a game plan for your day. Otherwise, you'll allocate your time according to whatever happens to land on your desk. And you will find yourself making the fatal mistake of dealing primarily with problems rather than opportunities. Start each day by making a general schedule, with particular emphasis on the two or three major things you would like to accomplish—including things that will achieve long-term goals. Remember, studies prove what common sense tells us: The more time we spend planning a project, the less total time is required for it. Don't let today's busywork crowd planning-time out of your schedule.

Concentrate.   Of all the principles of time management, none is more basic than concentration. People who have serious time-management problems invariably are trying to do too many things at once. The amount of time spent on a project is not what counts: It's the amount of *uninterrupted* time. Few problems can resist an all-out attack; few can be solved piecemeal.

Take Breaks.   To work for long periods without taking a break is not an effective use of time. Energy decreases, boredom sets in, and physical stress and tension accumulate. Switching for a few minutes from a mental task to something physical—isometric exercises, walking around the office, even changing from a sitting position to a standing position for a while—can provide relief.

Merely resting, however, is often the best course, and you should not think of a "rest" break as poor use of time. Not only will being refreshed increase your efficiency, but relieving tension will benefit your health. Anything that contributes to health is good time management.

Avoid Clutter. Some people have a constant swirl of papers on their desks and assume that somehow the most important matters will float to the top. In most cases, however, clutter hinders concentration and can create tension and frustration—a feeling of being "snowed under."

Whenever you find your desk becoming chaotic, take time out to reorganize. Go through all your papers (making generous use of the wastebasket) and divide them into categories: (1) Immediate action, (2) Low priority, (3) Pending, (4) Reading material. Put the highest priority item from your first pile in the center of your desk, then put everything else out of sight. Remember, you can think of only one thing at a time, and you can work on only one task at a time, so focus all your attention on the most important one. A final point: Clearing the desk completely, or at least organizing it, each evening should be standard practice. It gets the next day off to a good start.

Don't Be a Perfectionist. There is a difference between striving for excellence and striving for perfection. The first is attainable, gratifying and healthy. The second is often unattainable, frustrating and neurotic. It's also a terrible waste of time. The stenographer who retypes a lengthy letter because of a trivial error, or the boss who demands such retyping, might profit from examining the Declaration of Independence. When the inscriber of that document made two errors of omission, he inserted the missing letters between the lines. If this is acceptable in the document that gave birth to American freedom, surely it would be acceptable in a letter that will be briefly glanced at en route to someone's file cabinet or wastebasket?

Don't Be Afraid to Say No. Of all the time-saving techniques ever developed, perhaps the most effective is frequent use of the word *no*. Learn to decline, tactfully but firmly, every request that does not contribute to your goals. If you point out that your motivation is not to get out of work but to save your time to do a better job on the really important things, you'll have a good chance of avoiding unproductive tasks. Remember, many people who worry about offending others wind up living according to other people's priorities.

Don't Procrastinate. Procrastination is usually a deeply rooted habit. But we can change our habits provided we use the right system. William James, the father of American psychology, discussed such a system in his famous *Principles of Psychology*, published in 1890. It works as follows:

COLLABORATIVE LEARNING: CLASS ACTIVITY

7 Have each student interview a professional whom the student views as exceptionally efficient. Ask the professional how he or she manages time so successfully. Have the students put their findings in the form of commands, like the guidelines in Bliss' essay.

8 Then, collect these lists from the students and print them up in a single handout to be distributed during the next class meeting. This exercise provides an excellent way for you to get your students talking with some good professionals and also gives them a functional list of time-management suggestions to apply to their own lives. If time allows, have the students list for their personal and professional use the guidelines from this collective list they intend to incorporate into their own lives.

9

10

COLLABORATIVE LEARNING: SMALL GROUP ACTIVITY

11 Break your class into groups of 4 or 5. Then have each group discuss how Bliss' ten guidelines could help them manage their time in settings other than the business world. Have your students refer to the schedules they prepared before they read the essay, if they completed that assignment.

1. Bliss learned the following ten techniques for time management.

—Planning includes organizing the goals for the day to avoid misusing time.

—Concentrating allows serious chunks of undivided attention to be given to projects, producing better work and a feeling of efficiency.

—Taking breaks enhances efficiency by alleviating energy shortages, boredom, tension, and feeling overworked.

—Avoiding clutter keeps frustration at a minimum level by creating a sense of organization and productivity.

—Striving for excellence can lead to greatness; however, trying to achieve perfection wastes time and leads to useless stress and fatigue.

—Saying "no" to unproductive tasks can save endless hours of wasted time that neither advance personal goals nor lead to the completion of important tasks.

—Refraining from procrastination means doing all current tasks according to a general schedule.

—Eliminating dissatisfying chores that take away from work, family life, and other pursuits can relieve frustration and stress by allowing time to accomplish more productive goals.

—Delegating authority and duties can alleviate everyday pressures and leave time for personal interests.

—Working to the exclusion of all other activities makes work seem overwhelming and miserable; a more agreeable way is to balance work with other activities that include family and friends.

2. A "workaholic" is someone who is "addicted to work" (para. 17). Workaholics place greater importance on work-related goals and activities than on other parts of their lives. Bliss believes that many other activities are more important than work and insinuates that workaholics lack prior-

1. Decide to start changing as soon as you finish reading this article, while you are motivated. Taking that first step promptly is important.
2. Don't try to do too much too quickly. Just force yourself right now to do one thing you have been putting off. Then, beginning tomorrow morning, start each day by doing the most unpleasant thing on your schedule. Often it will be a small matter: an overdue apology; a confrontation with a fellow worker; an annoying chore you know you should tackle. Whatever it is, do it before you begin your usual morning routine. This simple procedure can well set the tone for your day. You will get a feeling of exhilaration from knowing that although the day is only 15 minutes old, you have already accomplished the most unpleasant thing you have to do all day.

There is one caution: Do not permit any exceptions. William James compared it to rolling up a ball of string; a single slip can undo more than many turns can wind up. Be tough with yourself, for the first few minutes of each day, for the next two weeks, and I promise you a new habit of priceless value. 12

Apply Radical Surgery. Time-wasting activities are like cancers. They drain off vitality and have a tendency to grow. The only cure is radical surgery. If you are wasting your time in activities that bore you, divert you from your real goals and sap your energy, cut them out, once and for all. 13

The principle applies to personal habits, routines and activities as much as to ones associated with your work. Check your appointment calendar, your extracurricular activities, your reading list, your television viewing habits, and ax everything that doesn't give you a feeling of accomplishment or satisfaction. 14

Delegate. An early example of failure to delegate is found in the Bible. Moses, having led his people out of Egypt, was so impressed with his own knowledge and authority that he insisted on ruling personally on every controversy that arose in Israel. His wise father-in-law, Jethro, recognizing that this was poor use of a leader's time, recommended a two-phase approach: First, educate the people concerning the laws; second, select capable leaders and give them full authority over routine matters, freeing Moses to concentrate on major decisions. The advice is still sound. 15

You don't have to be a national leader or a corporate executive to delegate, either. Parents who don't delegate household chores are doing a disservice to themselves and their children. 16

Running a Boy Scout troop can be as time-consuming as running General Motors if you try to do everything yourself. One caution: Giving subordinates jobs that neither you nor anyone else wants to do isn't delegating, it's assigning. Learn to delegate the challenging and rewarding tasks, along with sufficient authority to make necessary decisions. It can help to free your time.

Don't Be a "Workaholic." Most successful executives I know work long hours, but they don't let work interfere with the really important things in life, such as friends, family and fly fishing. This differentiates them from the workaholic who becomes addicted to work just as people become addicted to alcohol. Symptoms of work addiction include refusal to take a vacation, inability to put the office out of your mind on weekends, a bulging briefcase, and a spouse, son or daughter who is practically a stranger.

Counseling can help people cope with such problems. But for starters, do a bit of self-counseling. Ask yourself whether the midnight oil you are burning is adversely affecting your health. Ask where your family comes in your list of priorities, whether you are giving enough of yourself to your children and spouse, and whether you are deceiving yourself by pretending that the sacrifices you are making are really for them.

Above all else, good time management involves an awareness that today is all we ever have to work with. The past is irretrievably gone, the future is only a concept. British art critic John Ruskin had the word "TODAY" carved into a small marble block that he kept on his desk as a constant reminder to "Do It Now." But my favorite quotation is by an anonymous philosopher:

> Yesterday is a canceled check.
> Tomorrow is a promissory note.
> Today is ready cash. Use It!

UNDERSTANDING DETAILS

1. What are the ten techniques for managing time that Bliss learned from observing successful members of Congress at work? Explain each in your own words.
2. What is a "workaholic" (paragraph 17)? What characteristics identify this type of person?
3. Explain Bliss' favorite quotation:

ity and balance in their schedules because they overemphasize work.

3. Regretting days gone by or relying on the future does nothing but waste time. Bliss' quotation emphasizes these two themes by providing an analogy that compares spending time to spending money.

ANSWERS TO QUESTIONS:
ANALYZING MEANING (p. 224)

17

1. Responses to this question will vary.

2. Bliss stresses that work is only one aspect of a successful person's life. In fact, he advises that many things are more important, such as family, friends, fun, and good health. This concept seems to conflict with other ideas he presents, except that a well-rounded individual will be happier and calmer and thus more able to concentrate, plan, and effectively use the other techniques Bliss lists.

18

3. The last three ideas for time management in this essay include hints to help us in our personal lives. He proposes that we (1) learn to eliminate "time-wasting activities" (para. 13), (2) delegate authority, and (3) balance work with other activities. Though these notions have some merit and are plausible for some readers, applying these techniques would be difficult or impossible for others. First of all, time-wasting activities often cannot be avoided either because of obligations to others or necessary inconveniences such as waiting in line or getting stuck in traffic. In addition, many jobs are not arranged to include delegation of tasks to others. An executive might be able to delegate, but employees of lesser status often have no way to carry out this suggestion. Last, Bliss' advice to balance work with other "really important" (para. 17) activities is refreshing but often difficult to carry out because of the endless demands of some jobs.

19

1. Present participles would suggest ideas for change rather than give commands for action. By using commands, Bliss makes a strong statement and motivates his readers to become more efficient.

2. Bliss organizes his ten points in a logical order so they begin with planning and proceed through working, organizing, and, finally, living. By following his advice about giving up trying to be perfect, learning how to say "no," avoiding clutter, and refusing to procrastinate, the reader can learn how to create a more organized work environment.

3. Bliss uses two other rhetorical modes to support his process analysis essay. He employs examples in two ways: First, he presents an example of a busy lifestyle (a congressman's) to demonstrate that effective planning is directly related to accomplishments and success; second, he gives examples in each section of his list of techniques for time management to show how each one works. He gives additional strength to his analysis of time management through his memorable analogy comparing time to money, both of which need to be properly managed.

PREWRITING

In preparation for the writing assignments, the Preparing to Write questions ask students to weigh their time-management skills and the effect of these skills on the quality of their lives. They should refer to their schedules if they have made them for the Group Activity on page 221. See pages 16–23 for other suggestions on generating ideas in response to these questions.

Yesterday is a canceled check.
Tomorrow is a promissory note.
Today is ready cash. Use It!

What does this saying have to do with time management?

ANALYZING MEANING

1. Which of Bliss' guidelines for managing time could you benefit from most? How could it help you? Why do you have trouble in this area?
2. Why does Bliss advise us not to be workaholics? Does this advice conflict with the other guidelines Bliss lists in this essay? Why or why not?
3. In what parts of the essay does Bliss refer to our personal lives? According to the author, how can we balance our personal and professional lives? How realistic are these ideas?

DISCOVERING RHETORICAL STRATEGIES

1. Bliss introduces each new suggestion for managing time as a command and then fully explains each command. How effective is this approach? What effect would headings beginning with present participles have on the essay (e.g., planning, taking breaks, avoiding clutter)?
2. How does Bliss organize his techniques for managing time? Is this order successful? Explain your answer.
3. What other rhetorical modes does Bliss use to support this process analysis essay? Give examples of each of these modes.

IDEAS FOR DISCUSSION/WRITING

Preparing to Write

Write freely about various aspects of time management: Do you manage time well from day to day? What benefits do you receive from managing your time better? Can you identify any disadvantages that result from managing your time better? How can you avoid these problems? Are you a workaholic, or do you strike a good balance between the various aspects of your life? What is the relationship between time management and quality of life?

Choosing a Topic

1. You have been asked by the editor of your campus newspaper to adapt Bliss' suggestions to the life of a student. Write a process analysis essay adjusting Bliss' ten guidelines to a college environment.

2. Interview someone in your class about his or her ability to use time wisely. Use Bliss' guidelines to establish whether or not the person manages time well. Then, direct a process analysis essay to this person, briefly evaluating his or her time-management skills and then offering suggestions for improvement.

3. At times, Bliss' approach to time management (do all you can in a day) seems to conflict with the fundamental tenets for leading a quality life (relax and enjoy yourself). Do you think these two aspects of life are incompatible, or are there ways to reconcile the two? Write an essay for your classmates detailing a solution to this dilemma.

ADDITIONAL DISCUSSION/WRITING TOPIC

Following Bliss' guidelines for efficient time management, write an essay advising your classmates how to manage time more effectively than you yourself currently do.

REVISING STRATEGY

A good process analysis essay proceeds through the stages of its process in a logical fashion from beginning to end. In one of your process analysis essays, list the steps of the process you are explaining and compare that list to your essay. Remember that your process can be chronological (like watching a concert), simultaneous (like playing a guitar), or cyclical (like the changing of the seasons). Notice any parts of your explanation that don't make sense because they are out of order. Then revise your paper, paying close attention to its logic and organization.

JESSICA MITFORD
(1917–)

■ ■ ■

Behind the Formaldehyde Curtain

Once called "Queen of the Muckrakers" in a *Time* magazine review, Jessica Mitford has written scathing exposés of the Famous Writers' School, American funeral directors, television executives, prisons, a "fat farm" for wealthy women, and many other venerable social institutions. She was born in England into the gentry, immigrated to the United States, and later became a naturalized American citizen. After working at a series of jobs, she achieved literary fame at age forty-six with the publication of *The American Way of Death* (1963), which relentlessly shatters the image of funeral directors as "compassionate, reverent family-friends-in-need." Her other major works include *Kind and Unusual Punishment: The Prison Business* (1973); *Poison Penmanship: The Gentle Art of Muckraking* (1979), an anthology of Mitford's articles in *The Atlantic, Harper's,* and other periodicals covering a twenty-two-year time span; two volumes of autobiography, *Daughters and Rebels* (1960) and *A Fine Old Madness* (1977); *Faces of Philip: A Memoir of Philip Toynbee* (1984); and *Grace Had an English Heart: The Story of Grace Darling, Heroine and Victorian Superstar* (1988). Superbly skilled in the techniques of investigative reporting, satire, and black humor, Mitford was described in a *Washington Post* article as "an older, more even-tempered, better-read Jane Fonda who has maintained her activism long past middle age."

Preparing to Read

The following essay, taken from *The American Way of Death*, clearly illustrates the ruthless manner in which Mitford exposes the greed and hypocrisy of the American mortuary business. As you prepare to read this article, think for a few minutes about funeral customs in our society: Have you attended a funeral service recently? Which rituals seemed particularly vivid to you? What purpose did these symbolic actions serve? What other interesting customs are you aware of in American society? What purpose do these customs serve? What public images do these customs have? Are these images accurate? Do you generally approve or disapprove of these customs?

The drama begins to unfold with the arrival of the corpse at the mortuary.

Alas, poor Yorick! How surprised he would be to see how his counterpart of today is whisked off to a funeral parlor and is in short order sprayed, sliced, pierced, pickled, trussed, trimmed, creamed, waxed, painted, rouged and neatly dressed—transformed from a common corpse into a Beautiful Memory Picture. This process is known in the trade as embalming and restorative art, and is so universally employed in the United States and Canada that the funeral director does it routinely, without consulting corpse or kin. He regards as eccentric those few who are hardy enough to suggest that it might be dispensed with. Yet no law requires embalming, no religious doctrine commends it, nor is it dictated by considerations of health, sanitation, or even of personal daintiness. In no part of the world but in Northern America is it widely used. The purpose of embalming is to make the corpse presentable for viewing in a suitably costly container; and here too the funeral director routinely, without first consulting the family, prepares the body for public display.

Is all this legal? The processes to which a dead body may be subjected are after all to some extent circumscribed by law. In most states, for instance, the signature of next of kin must be obtained before an autopsy may be performed, before the deceased may be cremated, before the body may be turned over to a medical school for research purposes; or such provision must be made in the decedent's will. In the case of embalming, no such permission is required nor is it ever sought. A textbook, *The Principles and Practices of Embalming*, comments on this: "There is some question regarding the legality of much that is done within the preparation room." The author points out that it would be most unusual for a responsible member of a bereaved family to instruct the mortician, in so many words, to *"embalm"* the body of a deceased relative. The very term "embalming" is so seldom used that the mortician must rely upon custom in the matter. The author concludes that unless the family specifies otherwise, the act of entrusting the body to the care of a funeral establishment carries with it an implied permission to go ahead and embalm.

Embalming is indeed a most extraordinary procedure, and one must wonder at the docility of Americans who each year pay hundreds of millions of dollars for its perpetuation, blissfully ignorant of what it is all about, what is done, how it is done. Not one in ten thousand has any idea of what actually takes place. Books on the subject are extremely hard to come by. They are not to be found in most libraries or bookshops.

BACKGROUND INFORMATION

In "Behind the Formaldehyde Curtain," Jessica Mitford presents a shattering exposé of the mortuary profession as a business that squeezes vast sums of money from countless bereaved families for services lacking in both rationale and dignity. With a graphic description of the grisly details of the embalming process, Mitford questions "the docility of Americans who each year pay hundreds of millions of dollars for its perpetuation" (para. 4).

READABILITY LEVEL

9.0

RELATED READINGS

Paradoxes and Irony

Judith Viorst, "The Truth about Lying" 283

Ellen Goodman, "Putting In a Good Word for Guilt" 444

DEFINITIONS

formaldehyde (title and para. 6): a colorless, pungent gas used chiefly as a disinfectant and preservative.
Alas, poor Yorick! (para. 2): Hamlet's exclamation in the gravediggers' scene (V. i) as he holds in his hand the skull of Yorick, his father's former court jester.
raison d'être (para. 6): French. Reason for being.
phenol (para. 12): a form of alcohol derived from benzene.
Bon Ami (para. 12): the brand name of a household scouring cleanser.
il faut souffrir pour être belle (para. 17): French. "One must suffer to be beautiful."

COLLABORATIVE LEARNING:
CLASS ACTIVITY

Have your students pool their knowledge about funerals by sharing insights and observations concerning funerals they have attended. What were the details of these funerals? What purpose do funerals serve in the lives of the relatives of the deceased? In the lives of his or her friends?

In an era when huge television audiences watch surgical operations in the comfort of their living rooms, when, thanks to the animated cartoon, the geography of the digestive system has become familiar territory even to the nursery school set, in a land where the satisfaction of curiosity about almost all matters is a national pastime, the secrecy surrounding embalming can, surely, hardly be attributed to the inherent gruesomeness of the subject. Custom in this regard has within this century suffered a complete reversal. In the early days of American embalming, when it was performed in the home of the deceased, it was almost mandatory for some relative to stay by the embalmer's side and witness the procedure. Today, family members who might wish to be in attendance would certainly be dissuaded by the funeral director. All others, except apprentices, are excluded by law from the preparation room.

A close look at what does actually take place may explain in large measure the undertaker's intractable reticence concerning a procedure that has become his major *raison d'être*. Is it possible he fears that public information about embalming might lead patrons to wonder if they really want this service? If the funeral men are loath to discuss the subject outside the trade, the reader may, understandably, be equally loath to go on reading at this point. For those who have the stomach for it, let us part the formaldehyde curtain. . . .

The body is first laid out in the undertaker's morgue—or rather, Mr. Jones is reposing in the preparation room—to be readied to bid the world farewell.

The preparation room in any of the better funeral establishments has the tiled and sterile look of a surgery, and indeed the embalmer-restorative artist who does his chores there is beginning to adopt the term "dermasurgeon" (appropriately corrupted by some mortician-writers as "demisurgeon") to describe his calling. His equipment, consisting of scalpels, scissors, augers, forceps, clamps, needles, pumps, tubes, bowls and basins, is crudely imitative of the surgeon's, as is his technique, acquired in a nine- or twelve-month post-high-school course in an embalming school. He is supplied by an advanced chemical industry with a bewildering array of fluids, sprays, pastes, oils, powders, creams, to fix or soften tissue, shrink or distend it as needed, dry it here, restore the moisture there. There are cosmetics, waxes and paints to fill and cover features, even plaster of Paris to replace entire limbs. There are ingenious aids to prop and stabilize the cadaver:

A Vari-Pose Head Rest, the Edwards Arm and Hand Positioner, the Repose Block (to support the shoulders during the embalming), and the Throop Foot Positioner, which resembles an old-fashioned stocks.

Mr. John H. Eckels, president of the Eckels College of Mortuary Science, thus describes the first part of the embalming procedure: "In the hands of a skilled practitioner, this work may be done in a comparatively short time and without mutilating the body other than by slight incision—so slight that it scarcely would cause serious inconvenience if made upon a living person. It is necessary to remove the blood, and doing this not only helps in the disinfecting, but removes the principal cause of disfigurements due to discoloration."

Another textbook discusses the all-important time element: "The earlier this is done, the better, for every hour that elapses between death and embalming will add to the problems and complications encountered. . . ." Just how soon should one get going on the embalming? The author tells us, "On the basis of such scanty information made available to this profession through its rudimentary and haphazard system of technical research, we must conclude that the best results are to be obtained if the subject is embalmed before life is completely extinct—that is, before cellular death has occurred. In the average case, this would mean within an hour after somatic death." For those who feel that there is something a little rudimentary, not to say haphazard, about this advice, a comforting thought is offered by another writer. Speaking of fears entertained in early days of premature burial, he points out, "One of the effects of embalming by chemical injection, however, has been to dispel fears of live burial." How true; once the blood is removed, chances of live burial are indeed remote.

To return to Mr. Jones, the blood is drained out through the veins and replaced by embalming fluid pumped in through the arteries. As noted in *The Principles and Practices of Embalming*, "every operator has a favorite injection and drainage point—a fact which becomes a handicap only if he fails or refuses to forsake his favorites when conditions demand it." Typical favorites are the carotid artery, femoral artery, jugular vein, subclavian vein. There are various choices of embalming fluid. If Flextone is used, it will produce a "mild, flexible rigidity. The skin retains a velvety softness, the tissues are rubbery and pliable. Ideal for women and children." It may be blended with B. and G. Products Company's Lyf-Lyk tint, which is guaranteed to reproduce "na-

9

10

11

COLLABORATIVE LEARNING: SMALL GROUP ACTIVITY

Divide your students into groups of 3 or 4, and have them discuss details in Mitford's essay that are most horrific to them; ask them to speculate on the reasons for their feelings. After a brief discussion, have each student write freely about one especially disturbing detail in the essay. Encourage each student to explore his or her reasons for these feelings.

ture's own skin texture . . . the velvety appearance of living tissue." Suntone comes in three separate tints: Suntan; Special Cosmetic Tint, a pink shade "especially indicated for young female subjects"; and Regular Cosmetic Tint, moderately pink.

About three to six gallons of a dyed and perfumed solution of formaldehyde, glycerin, borax, phenol, alcohol and water is soon circulating through Mr. Jones, whose mouth has been sewn together with a "needle directed upward between the upper lip and gum and brought out through the left nostril," with the corners raised slightly "for a more pleasant expression." If he should be bucktoothed, his teeth are cleaned with Bon Ami and coated with colorless nail polish. His eyes, meanwhile, are closed with flesh-tinted eye caps and eye cement.   12

The next step is to have at Mr. Jones with a thing called a trocar. This is a long, hollow needle attached to a tube. It is jabbed into the abdomen, poked around the entrails and chest cavity, the contents of which are pumped out and replaced with "cavity fluid." This done, and the hole in the abdomen sewn up, Mr. Jones's face is heavily creamed (to protect the skin from burns which may be caused by leakage of the chemicals), and he is covered with a sheet and left unmolested for a while. But not for long—there is more, much more, in store for him. He has been embalmed, but not yet restored, and the best time to start the restorative work is eight to ten hours after embalming, when the tissues have become firm and dry.   13

The object of all this attention to the corpse, it must be remembered, is to make it presentable for viewing in an attitude of healthy repose. "Our customs require the presentation of our dead in the semblance of normality . . . unmarred by the ravages of illness, disease or mutilation," says Mr. J. Sheridan Mayer in his *Restorative Art*. This is rather a large order since few people die in the full bloom of health, unravaged by illness and unmarked by some disfigurement. The funeral industry is equal to the challenge: "In some cases the gruesome appearance of a mutilated or disease-ridden subject may be quite discouraging. The task of restoration may seem impossible and shake the confidence of the embalmer. This is the time for intestinal fortitude and determination. Once the formative work is begun and affected tissues are cleaned or removed, all doubts of success vanish. It is surprising and gratifying to discover the results which may be obtained."   14

The embalmer, having allowed an appropriate interval to elapse, returns to the attack, but now he brings into play the skill   15 and equipment of sculptor and cosmetician. Is a hand missing? Casting one in plaster of Paris is a simple matter. "For replacement purposes, only a cast of the back of the hand is necessary; this is within the ability of the average operator and is quite adequate." If a lip or two, a nose or an ear should be missing, the embalmer has at hand a variety of restorative waxes with which to model replacements. Pores and skin texture are simulated by stippling with a little brush, and over this cosmetics are laid on. Head off? Decapitation cases are rather routinely handled. Ragged edges are trimmed, and head joined to torso with a series of splints, wires and sutures. It is a good idea to have a little something at the neck—a scarf or a high collar—when time for viewing comes. Swollen mouth: Cut out tissue as needed from inside the lips. If too much is removed, the surface contour can easily be restored by padding with cotton. Swollen necks and cheeks are reduced by removing tissue through vertical incisions made down each side of the neck. "When the deceased is casketed, the pillow will hide the suture incisions. . . . As an extra precaution against leakage, the suture may be painted with liquid sealer."

The opposite condition is more likely to present itself—that of emaciation. His hypodermic syringe now loaded with massage cream, the embalmer seeks out and fills the hollowed and sunken areas by injection. In this procedure the backs of the hands and fingers and the under-chin area should not be neglected.   16

Positioning the lips is a problem that recurrently challenges the ingenuity of the embalmer. Closed too tightly, they tend to give a stern, even disapproving expression. Ideally, embalmers feel, the lips should give the impression of being ever so slightly parted, the upper lip protruding slightly for a more youthful appearance. This takes some engineering, however, as the lips tend to drift apart. Lip drift can sometimes be remedied by pushing one or two straight pins through the inner margin of the lower lip and then inserting them between the two front upper teeth. If Mr. Jones happens to have no teeth, the pins can just as easily be anchored in his Armstrong Face Former and Denture Replacer. Another method to maintain lip closure is to dislocate the lower jaw, which is then held in its new position by a wire run through holes which have been drilled through the upper and lower jaws at the midline. As the French are fond of saying, *il faut souffrir pour être belle.*   17

If Mr. Jones had died of jaundice, the embalming fluid will very likely turn him green. Does this deter the embalmer? Not if he has intestinal fortitude. Masking pastes and cosmetics are   18 heavily laid on, burial garments and casket interiors are color-correlated with particular care, and Jones is displayed beneath rose-colored lights. Friends will say "How *well* he looks." Death by carbon monoxide, on the other hand, can be rather a good thing from the embalmer's viewpoint: "One advantage is the fact that this type of discoloration is an exaggerated form of a natural pink coloration." This is nice because the healthy glow is already present and needs but little attention.

The patching and filling completed, Mr. Jones is now shaved, washed and dressed. Cream-based cosmetic, available in pink, flesh, suntan, brunette and blond, is applied to his hands and face, his hair is shampooed and combed (and, in the case of Mrs. Jones, set), his hands manicured. For the horny-handed son of toil special care must be taken; cream should be applied to remove ingrained grime, and the nails cleaned. "If he were not in the habit of having them manicured in life, trimming and shaping is advised for appearance—never questioned by kin." 19

Jones is now ready for casketing (this is the present participle of the verb "to casket"). In this operation his right shoulder should be depressed slightly "to turn the body a bit to the right and soften the appearance of lying flat on the back." Positioning the hands is a matter of importance, and special rubber positioning blocks may be used. The hands should be cupped slightly for a more lifelike, relaxed appearance. Proper placement of the body requires a delicate sense of balance. It should lie as high as possible in the casket, yet not so high that the lid, when lowered, will hit the nose. On the other hand, we are cautioned, placing the body too low "creates the impression that the body is in a box." 20

Jones is next wheeled into the appointed slumber room where a few last touches may be added—his favorite pipe placed in his hand or, if he was a great reader, a book propped into position. (In the case of little Master Jones a Teddy bear may be clutched.) Here he will hold open house for a few days, visiting hours 10 A.M. to 9 P.M. 21

All now being in readiness, the funeral director calls a staff conference to make sure that each assistant knows his precise duties. Mr. Wilber Kriege writes "This makes your staff feel that they are a part of the team, with a definite assignment that must be properly carried out if the whole plan is to succeed. You never heard of a football coach who failed to talk to his entire team before they go on the field. They have drilled on the plays they are to execute for hours and days, and yet the successful coach knows the importance of making even the bench-warming third- 22 string substitute feel that he is important if the game is to be won." The winning of *this* game is predicated upon glass-smooth handling of the logistics. The funeral director has notified the pallbearers whose names were furnished by the family, has arranged for the presence of clergyman, organist, and soloist, has provided transportation for everybody, has organized and listed the flowers sent by friends. In *Psychology of Funeral Service*, Mr. Edward A. Martin points out: "He may not always do as much as the family thinks he is doing, but it is his helpful guidance that they appreciate in knowing they are proceeding as they should. . . . The important thing is how well his services can be used to make the family believe they are giving unlimited expression to their own sentiment."

The religious service may be held in a church or in the chapel of the funeral home; the funeral director vastly prefers the latter arrangement, for not only is it more convenient for him but it affords him the opportunity to show off his beautiful facilities to the gathered mourners. After the clergyman has had his say, the mourners queue up to file past the casket for a last look at the deceased. The family is *never* asked whether they want an open-casket ceremony; in the absence of their instruction to the contrary, this is taken for granted. Consequently, well over 90 percent of all American funerals feature the open casket—a custom unknown in other parts of the world. Foreigners are astonished by it. An English woman living in San Francisco described her reaction in a letter to the writer:

23

> I myself have attended only one funeral here—that of an elderly fellow worker of mine. After the service I could not understand why everyone was walking towards the coffin (sorry, I mean casket), but thought I had better follow the crowd. It shook me rigid to get there and find the casket open and poor old Oscar lying there in his brown tweed suit, wearing a suntan makeup and just the wrong shade of lipstick. If I had not been extremely fond of the old boy, I have a horrible feeling that I might have giggled. Then and there I decided that I could never face another American funeral—even dead.

The casket (which has been resting throughout the service on a Classic Beauty Ultra Metal Casket Bier) is now transferred by a hydraulically operated device called Porto-Lift to a balloon-tired, Glide Easy casket carriage which will wheel it to yet another conveyance, the Cadillac Funeral Coach. This may be lavender, cream, light green—anything but black. Interiors, of course, are

24

2. The title "Behind the Formaldehyde Curtain," drawn from the popular term for the Communist bloc, the "Iron Curtain," suggests weighty secrets and concealed activities. Also implied by the metaphor is a stage curtain that opens to reveal a dramatic presentation—the artificiality of embalming—and sets up the comparison of today's deceased with Hamlet's Yorick.

3. The grisly reality of the essay is introduced by the author in her warning that the reader may be "equally loath to go on reading at this point" (para. 6) and by the restriction of her invitation to "those who have the stomach for it" (para. 6) to take a look at what actually occurs in "the preparation room" (para. 7). The horror of the essay is achieved in the matter-of-fact detailing of gruesome particulars that encourages the reader to visualize each step of the embalming process.

ANSWERS TO QUESTIONS:
DISCOVERING RHETORICAL
STRATEGIES (p. 235)

1. The one-sentence paragraph opening the essay with the words "The drama begins to unfold" (para. 1) introduces the metaphor of the funeral as a dramatic production. This short paragraph parallels the abrupt raising of the stage curtain to reveal the set and the cast of characters. The image is supported in paragraph 27 with references to the "role" of the funeral director and his "well-oiled performance."

2. "Beautiful Memory Picture" (para. 2) is a pleasant phrase used to distract family members from the gruesome reality that they are looking at a lifeless corpse. This concentration on the beautification of the corpse is evident throughout the essay in Mitford's references to such aids as the tint "guaranteed to reproduce 'nature's own skin texture' " (para. 11); the "variety of restorative waxes with which to model replacements" (para. 15) for missing or disfigured limbs or features; "masking pastes and cosmetics" (para. 18); and "special rubber positioning blocks" (para. 20) to assist in arranging the hands. Euphemistic language appears throughout the essay in references such as the deceased "reposing in the preparation room" (para. 7); the funeral di-

color-correlated, "for the man who cannot stop short of perfection."

At graveside, the casket is lowered into the earth. This office, once the prerogative of friends of the deceased, is now performed by a patented mechanical lowering device. A "Life-time Green" artificial grass mat is at the ready to conceal the sere earth, and overhead, to conceal the sky, is a portable Steril Chapel Tent ("resists the intense heat and humidity of summer and the terrific storms of winter . . . available in Silver Grey, Rose or Evergreen"). Now is the time for the ritual scattering of earth over the coffin, as the solemn words "earth to earth, ashes to ashes, dust to dust" are pronounced by the officiating cleric. This can today be accomplished "with a mere flick of the wrist with the Gordon Leak-Proof Earth Dispenser. No grasping of a handful of dirt, no soiled fingers. Simple, dignified, beautiful, reverent! The modern way!" The Golden Earth Dispenser (at $5) is of nickel-plated brass construction. It is not only "attractive to the eye and long wearing"; it is also "one of the 'tools' for building better public relations" if presented as "an appropriate non-commercial gift" to the clergyman. It is shaped something like a saltshaker.

Untouched by human hand, the coffin and the earth are now united. 26

It is in the function of directing the participants through the maze of gadgetry that the funeral director has assigned to himself his relatively new role of "grief therapist." He has relieved the family of every detail, he has revamped the corpse to look like a living doll, he has arranged for it to nap for a few days in a slumber room, he has put on a well-oiled performance in which the concept of *death* has played no part whatsoever—unless it was inconsiderately mentioned by the clergyman who conducted the religious service. He has done everything in his power to make the funeral a real pleasure for everybody concerned. He and his team have given their all to score an upset victory over death. 27

UNDERSTANDING DETAILS

1. List the major steps of the embalming process that the author reveals in this essay.
2. Why, according to Mitford, do funeral directors not want to make public the details of embalming? To what extent do you think their desire for secrecy is warranted?
3. Why isn't the permission of a family member needed for embalming? What does this custom reveal about Americans?

ANALYZING MEANING

1. What is Mitford's primary purpose in this essay? Why do you think she has analyzed this particular process in such detail?
2. Explain the title of this essay.
3. Do you think the author knows how gruesome her essay is? How can you tell? What makes the essay so horrifying? How does such close attention to macabre detail help Mitford accomplish her purpose?

DISCOVERING RHETORICAL STRATEGIES

1. Why does Mitford begin her essay with a one-sentence paragraph? Is it effective? Why or why not?
2. A euphemism is the substitution of a deceptively pleasant term for a straightforward, less pleasant one. In what way is "Beautiful Memory Picture" (paragraph 2) a euphemism? How are we reminded of this phrase throughout the essay? What other euphemisms can you find in this selection?
3. What tone does Mitford establish in the essay? What is her reason for creating this particular tone? What is your reaction to it?

IDEAS FOR DISCUSSION/WRITING

Preparing to Write

Write freely about a particularly interesting custom in America or in another country: Why does this custom exist? What role does it play in the society? What value does it have? What are the details of this custom? In what way is this custom a part of your life? Your family's life? What purpose does it serve for you? Is it worth continuing? Why or why not?

Choosing a Topic

1. In a process analysis essay directed to your classmates, explain a custom you do not approve of. Decide on your tone and purpose before you begin.
2. In a process analysis essay directed to your classmates, explain a custom you approve of. Select a specific tone and purpose before you begin to write.
3. You have been asked to address a group of students at a college of mortuary science. In this role, you have an opportunity to influence the opinion of these students concerning the practice of embalming. Write a well-reasoned lecture to this group arguing either for or against the process of embalming.

rector as " 'grief therapist' " (para. 27); and an array of specialized products such as the "Lyf-Lyk tint" (para. 11), the "'Glide-Easy' casket carriage" (para. 24), and the "Gordon Leak-Proof Earth Dispenser" (para. 25).

3. Mitford uses a satirical tone to expose the funeral industry, juxtaposing sardonic humor with the gruesome particulars of embalming to accentuate the repulsiveness of the process. (Having students circle inflammatory words and phrases to demonstrate this tone is a very valuable classroom exercise.)

PREWRITING

In preparation for the writing assignments, the Preparing to Write questions ask students to analyze a custom that is an important part of their lives. See pages 16–23 for suggestions on generating ideas in response to these questions.

ADDITIONAL DISCUSSION/WRITING TOPIC

All of us have suffered losses in our lives—for example, the loss of a person, the loss of a pet, or the loss of a special possession. Write an essay explaining to your classmates how to grieve for a specific loss. Do different types of losses call for different forms of grief?

REVISING STRATEGY

Transitions make writing comprehensible and smooth. In one of your process analysis essays, underline all of your transitions. Notice which transitions do not logically connect information. Then revise your paper, concentrating on making these transitions as accurate and useful as possible.

PAUL ROBERTS
(1917–1967)

■ ■ ■

How to Say Nothing in Five Hundred Words

Paul Roberts was an English professor and specialist in structural linguistics who wrote a number of influential books and articles on language use. Born in San Luis Obispo, California, the author received his B.A. from San Jose States University and his M.A. and Ph.D. from the University of California at Berkeley. He taught English and linguistics for several years at San Jose State and at Cornell University, then became director of languages at the Center of American Studies in Rome, where he lived until his death in 1967. His principal books, familiar to a generation of college students, include *Understanding Grammar* (1954), *Patterns of English* (1956), *Understanding English* (1958), *English Sentences* (1962), and *English Syntax* (1964).

Preparing to Read

The following essay, excerpted from *Understanding English*, discusses ways to avoid several common problems faced by beginning college writers. As you prepare to read this article, pause for a moment to consider your own ability in writing: What are your strengths? What types of errors do you commonly make? What have you done in the past to remedy these flaws? Do you have any writing problems for which you have no solutions? What advice would you give to another student who wishes to improve his or her writing?

It's Friday afternoon, and you have almost survived another week of classes. You are just looking forward dreamily to the weekend when the English instructor says: "For Monday you will turn in a five-hundred-word composition on college football."

Well, that puts a good big hole in the weekend. You don't 2 have any strong views on college football one way or the other. You get rather excited during the season and go to all the home games and find it rather more fun than not. On the other hand, the class has been reading Robert Hutchins in the anthology and perhaps Shaw's "Eighty-Yard Run," and from the class discussion you have got the idea that the instructor thinks college football is for the birds. You are no fool. You can figure out what side to take.

After dinner you get out the portable typewriter that you got 3 for high school graduation. You might as well get it over with and enjoy Saturday and Sunday. Five hundred words is about two double-spaced pages with normal margins. You put in a sheet of paper, think up a title, and you're off:

Why College Football Should Be Abolished

College football should be abolished because it's bad for the school and also bad for the players. The players are so busy practicing that they don't have any time for their studies.

This, you feel, is a mighty good start. The only trouble is that 4 it's only thirty-two words. You still have four hundred and sixty-eight to go, and you've pretty well exhausted the subject. It comes to you that you do your best thinking in the morning, so you put away the typewriter and go to the movies. But the next morning you have to do your washing and some math problems, and in the afternoon you go to the game. The English instructor turns up too, and you wonder if you've taken the right side after all. Saturday night you have a date, and Sunday morning you have to go to church. (You can't let English assignments interfere with your religion.) What with one thing and another, it's ten o'clock Sunday night before you get out the typewriter again. You make a pot of coffee and start to fill out your views on college football. Put a little meat on the bones.

Why College Football Should Be Abolished

In my opinion, it seems to me that college football should be 5 abolished. The reason why I think this to be true is because I feel that football is bad for the colleges in nearly every aspect. As Robert Hutchins says in his article in our anthology in which he discusses college football, it would be better if the colleges had race horses and had races with one another, because then the horses would not have to attend classes. I firmly agree with Mr. Hutchins on this point, and

BACKGROUND INFORMATION

In "How to Say Nothing in Five Hundred Words," Paul Roberts gives a skillful analysis of the process of writing good essays through an intimate understanding of the thought processes of today's reluctant English composition student. Many people will identify with his portrait of the student mind at work on a writing project.

READABILITY LEVEL

8.3

RELATED READINGS

Writing

Russell Baker, "The Saturday Evening Post" 124

Annie Dillard, "When You Write" 544

Kurt Vonnegut, "How to Write with Style" 546

William Zinsser, "Writing with a Word Processor" 550

DEFINITIONS

Robert Hutchins (1899–1977) (para. 2): the American educator who wrote "Alumni, Athletics, and Academic Freedom" (printed in 1956 in his book entitled *Some Observations on American Education*), blasting the "big business" orientation of college sports.

Shaw's "Eighty-Yard Run" (para. 2): a short story by Irwin Shaw about a man recalling a feat performed during college football practice fifteen years earlier that set him up for a life of failure ever after.

confidence man (para. 11): a criminal, a con artist; one who swindles by fraud and false promises.

bromides (para. 12): commonplace or hackneyed statements.

vacuity of mind (para. 16): marked by a lack of intelligence or ideas.

Joseph Pattison has written a similar essay entitled "How to Write an F Paper." His guidelines are printed below.

Obscure the ideas:

1. Select a topic that is big enough to let you wander around the main ideas without ever being forced to state it precisely.

2. Pad! Pad! Pad!

3. Disorganize your discussion.

4. Begin a new paragraph every sentence or two.

Mangle the sentences:

5. Fill all the areas of your sentences with deadwood.

6. Using fragments and run-on or comma-spliced sentences.

7. Your sentence order invert for statement of the least important matters.

8. You, in the introduction, body, and conclusion of your paper, to show that you can contrive ornate, graceful sentences, should use involution.

Slovenize the diction:

9. Add the popular "-wise" and "-ize" endings to words.

10. Use vague words in place of precise ones.

11. Employ lengthy Latinate locutions whenever possible.

12. Inject humor into your writing by using the wrong word occasionally.

13. Find a "tried and true" phrase to use to clinch a point.

(Excerpted from *College English,* October 1963.)

Have your class discuss how these guidelines are similar to those recommended by Roberts.

I am sure that many other students would agree too.

One reason why it seems to me that college football is bad is that it has become too commercial. In the olden times when people played football just for the fun of it, maybe college football was all right, but they do not play football just for the fun of it now as they used to in the old days. Nowadays college football is what you might call a big business. Maybe this is not true at all schools, and I don't think it is especially true here at State, but certainly this is the case at most colleges and universities in America nowadays, as Mr. Hutchins points out in his very interesting article. Actually the coaches and alumni go around to the high schools and offer the high school stars large salaries to come to their colleges and play football for them. There was one case where a high school star was offered a convertible if he would play football for a certain college.   6

Another reason for abolishing college football is that it is bad for the players. They do not have time to get a college education, because they are so busy playing football. A football player has to practice every afternoon from three to six and then he is so tired that he can't concentrate on his studies. He just feels like dropping off to sleep after dinner, and then the next day he goes to his classes without having studied and maybe he fails the test.   7

(Good ripe stuff so far, but you're still a hundred and fifty-one words from home. One more push.)

Also I think college football is bad for the colleges and the universities because not very many students get to participate in it. Out of a college of ten thousand students only seventy-five or a hundred play football, if that many. Football is what you might call a spectator sport. That means that most people go to watch it but do not play it themselves.   8

(Four hundred and fifteen. Well, you still have the conclusion, and when you retype it, you can make the margins a little wider.)

These are the reasons why I agree with Mr. Hutchins that college football should be abolished in American colleges and universities.   9

On Monday you turn it in, moderately hopeful, and on Friday it comes back marked "weak in content" and sporting a big "D."   10

This essay is exaggerated a little, not much. The English instructor will recognize it as reasonably typical of what an assignment on college football will bring in. He knows that nearly half of the class will contrive in five hundred words to say that college   11 football is too commercial and bad for the players. Most of the other half will inform him that college football builds character and prepares one for life and brings prestige to the school. As he reads paper after paper all saying the same thing in almost the same words, all bloodless, five hundred words dripping out of nothing, he wonders how he allowed himself to get trapped into teaching English when he might have had a happy and interesting life as an electrician or a confidence man.

Well, you may ask, what can you do about it? The subject is one on which you have few convictions and little information. Can you be expected to make a dull subject interesting? As a matter of fact, this is precisely what you are expected to do. This is the writer's essential task. All subjects, except sex, are dull until somebody makes them interesting. The writer's job is to find the argument, the approach, the angle, the wording that will take the reader with him. This is seldom easy, and it is particularly hard in subjects that have been much discussed: College Football, Fraternities, Popular Music, Is Chivalry Dead?, and the like. You will feel that there is nothing you can do with such subjects except repeat the old bromides. But there are some things you can do which will make your papers, if not throbbingly alive, at least less insufferably tedious than they might otherwise be.

Avoid the Obvious Content

Say the assignment is college football. Say that you've decided to be against it. Begin by putting down the arguments that come to your mind: It is too commercial, it takes the students' minds off their studies, it is hard on the players, it makes the university a kind of circus instead of an intellectual center, for most schools it is financially ruinous. Can you think of any more arguments, just off hand? All right. Now when you write your paper, *make sure that you don't use any of the material on this list.* If these are the points that leap to your mind they will leap to everyone else's too, and whether you get a "C" or a "D" may depend on whether the instructor reads your paper early when he is fresh and tolerant or late, when the sentence "In my opinion, college football has become too commercial," inexorably repeated, has brought him to the brink of lunacy.

Be against college football for some reason or reasons of your own. If they are keen and perceptive ones, that's splendid. But even if they are trivial or foolish or indefensible, you are still ahead so long as they are not everybody else's reasons too. Be against it because the colleges don't spend enough money on it to

12

13

14

COLLABORATIVE LEARNING: SMALL GROUP ACTIVITY

Divide your students into groups of three, and have each group draft an F paper. Then, have one person from each group read the creation to the rest of the class.

make it worthwhile, because it is bad for the characters of the spectators, because the players are forced to attend classes, because the football stars hog all the beautiful women, because it competes with baseball and is therefore un-American and possibly Communist inspired. There are lots of more or less unused reasons for being against college football.

Sometimes it is a good idea to sum up and dispose of the trite   15
and conventional points before going on to your own. This has the advantage of indicating to the reader that you are going to be neither trite nor conventional. Something like this:

> We are often told that college football should be abolished because it has become too commercial or because it is bad for the players. These arguments are no doubt very cogent, but they don't go to the heart of the matter.

Then you go to the heart of the matter.

Take the Less Usual Side

One rather simple way of getting into your paper is to take   16
the side of the argument that most of the citizens will want to avoid. If the assignment is an essay on dogs, you can, if you choose, explain that dogs are faithful and lovable companions, intelligent, useful as guardians of the house and protectors of children, indispensable in police work—in short, when all is said and done, man's best friends. Or you can suggest that those big brown eyes conceal, more often than not, a vacuity of mind and an inconstancy of purpose; that the dogs you have known most intimately have been mangy, ill-tempered brutes, incapable of instruction; and that only our nobility of mind and fear of arrest prevent you from kicking the flea-ridden animals when you pass them on the street.

Naturally personal convictions will sometimes dictate your   17
approach. If the assigned subject is "Is Methodism Rewarding to the Individual?" and you are a pious Methodist, you have really no choice. But few assigned subjects, if any, will fall in this category. Most of them will lie in broad areas of discussion with much to be said on both sides. They are intellectual exercises, and it is legitimate to argue now one way and now another, as debaters do in similar circumstances. Always take the side that looks to you hardest, least defensible. It will almost always turn out to be easier to write interestingly on that side.

This general advice applies where you have a choice of sub-   18 jects. If you are to choose among "The Value of Fraternities" and "My Favorite High School Teacher" and "What I Think About Beetles," by all means plump for the beetles. By the time the instructor gets to your paper, he will be up to his ears in tedious tales about the French teacher at Bloombury High and assertions about how fraternities build character and prepare one for life. Your views on beetles, whatever they are, are bound to be a refreshing change.

Don't worry too much about figuring out what the instructor   19
thinks about the subject so that you can cuddle up with him. Chances are his views are no stronger than yours. If he does have convictions and you oppose him, his problem is to keep from grading you higher than you deserve in order to show he is not biased. This doesn't mean that you should always cantankerously dissent from what the instructor says; that gets tiresome too. And if the subject assigned is "My Pet Peeve," do not begin, "My pet peeve is the English instructor who assigns papers on 'my pet peeve.'" This was still funny during the War of 1812, but it has sort of lost its edge since then. It is in general good manners to avoid personalities.

Slip Out of Abstraction

If you will study the essay on college football [near the begin-   20
ning of this essay], you will perceive that one reason for its appalling dullness is that it never gets down to particulars. It is just a series of not very glittering generalities: "Football is bad for the colleges," "it has become too commercial," "football is a big business," "it is bad for the players," and so on. Such round phrases thudding against the reader's brain are unlikely to convince him, though they may well render him unconscious.

If you want the reader to believe that college football is bad   21
for the players, you have to do more than say so. You have to display the evil. Take your roommate, Alfred Simkins, the second-string center. Picture poor old Alfy coming home from football practice every evening, bruised and aching, agonizingly tired, scarcely able to shovel the mashed potatoes into his mouth. Let us see him staggering up to the room, getting out his econ textbook, peering desperately at it with his good eye, falling asleep and failing the test in the morning. Let us share his unbearable tension as Saturday draws near. Will he fail, be demoted, lose his monthly allowance, be forced to return to the coal mines? And if he succeeds, what will be his reward? Perhaps a slight ripple of applause when the third-string center replaces him, a moment of

elation in the locker room if the team wins, of despair if it loses. What will he look back on when he graduates from college? Toil and torn ligaments. And what will be his future? He is not good enough for pro football, and he is too obscure and weak in econ to succeed in stocks and bonds. College football is tearing the heart from Alfy Simpkins and, when it finishes with him, will callously toss aside the shattered hulk.

This is no doubt a weak enough argument for the abolition of college football, but it is a sight better than saying, in three or four variations, that college football (in your opinion) is bad for players.   22

Look at the work of any professional writer and notice how constantly he is moving from the generality, the abstract statement, to the concrete example, the facts and figures, the illustration. If he is writing on juvenile delinquency, he does not just tell you that juveniles are (it seems to him) delinquent and that (in his opinion) something should be done about it. He shows you juveniles begin delinquent, tearing up movie theatres in Buffalo, stabbing high school principals in Dallas, smoking marijuana in Palo Alto. And more than likely he is moving toward some specific remedy, not just a general wringing of the hands.   23

It is no doubt possible to be *too* concrete, too illustrative or anecdotal, but few inexperienced writers err this way. For most the soundest advice is to be seeking always for the picture, to be always turning general remarks into seeable examples. Don't say, "Sororities teach girls the social graces." Say, "Sorority life teaches a girl how to carry on a conversation while pouring tea, without sloshing the tea into the saucer." Don't say, "I like certain kinds of popular music very much." Say, "Whenever I hear Gerber Sprinklittle play 'Mississippi Man' on the trombone, my socks creep up my ankles."   24

Get Rid of Obvious Padding

The student toiling away at his weekly English theme is too often tormented by a figure: five hundred words. How, he asks himself, is he to achieve this staggering total? Obviously by never using one word when he can somehow work in ten.   25

He is therefore seldom content with a plain statement like "Fast driving is dangerous." This has only four words in it. He takes thought, and the sentence becomes: 26

In my opinion, fast driving is dangerous.

Better, but he can do better still:

> In my opinion, fast driving would seem to be rather dangerous.

If he is really adept, it may come out:

> In my humble opinion, though I do not claim to be an expert on this complicated subject, fast driving, in most circumstances, would seem to be rather dangerous in many aspects, or at least so it would seem to me.

Thus four words have been turned into forty, and not an iota of content has been added.

Now this is a way to go about reaching five hundred words, and if you are content with a "D" grade, it is as good a way as any. But if you aim higher, you must work differently. Instead of stuffing your sentences with straw, you must try steadily to get rid of the padding, to make your sentences lean and tough. If you are really working at it, your first draft will greatly exceed the required total, and then you will work it down, thus: 27

> It is thought in some quarters that fraternities do not contribute as much as might be expected to campus life.
>
> Some people think that fraternities contribute little to campus life.
>
> The average doctor who practices in small towns or in the country must toil night and day to heal the sick.
>
> Most country doctors work long hours.
>
> When I was a little girl, I suffered from shyness and embarrassment in the presence of others.
>
> I was a shy little girl.
>
> It is absolutely necessary for the person employed as a marine fireman to give the matter of steam pressure his undivided attention at all times.
>
> The fireman has to keep his eye on the steam gauge.

You may ask how you can arrive at five hundred words at this rate. Simple. You dig up more real content. Instead of taking a couple of obvious points off the surface of the topic and then circling warily around them for six paragraphs, you work in and explore, figure out the details. You illustrate. You say that fast driving is dangerous, and then you prove it. How long does it   28 take to stop a car at forty and at eighty? How far can you see at night? What happens when a tire blows? What happens in a head-on collision at fifty miles an hour? Pretty soon your paper will be full of broken glass and blood and headless torsos, and reaching five hundred words will not really be a problem.

Call a Fool a Fool

Some of the padding in freshman themes is to be blamed not on anxiety about the word minimum but on excessive timidity. The student writes, "In my opinion, the principal of my high school acted in ways that I believe every unbiased person would have to call foolish." This isn't exactly what he means. What he means is, "My high school principal was a fool." If he was a fool, call him a fool. Hedging the thing about with "in-my-opinion's" and "it-seems-to-me's" and "as-I-see-it's" and "at-least-from-my-point-of-view's" gains you nothing. Delete these phrases whenever they creep into your paper.   29

The student's tendency to hedge stems from a modesty that in other circumstances would be commendable. He is, he realizes, young and inexperienced, and he half suspects that he is dopey and fuzzy-minded beyond the average. Probably only too true. But it doesn't help to announce your incompetence six times in every paragraph. Decide what you want to say and say it as vigorously as possible, without apology and in plain words.   30

Linguistic diffidence can take various forms. One is what we call *euphemism*. This is the tendency to call a spade "a certain garden implement" or women's underwear "unmentionables." It is stronger in some eras than others and in some people than others but it always operates more or less in subjects that are touchy or taboo: death, sex, madness, and so on. Thus we shrink from saying "He died last night" but say instead "passed away," "left us," "joined his Maker," "went to his reward." Or we try to take off the tension with a lighter cliché: "kicked the bucket," "cashed in his chips," "handed in his dinner pail." We have found all sorts of ways to avoid saying *mad:* "mentally ill," "touched," "not quite right upstairs," "feeble-minded," "innocent," "simple," "off his trolley," "not in his right mind." Even such a now plain word as *insane* began as a euphemism with the meaning "not healthy."   31

Modern science, particularly psychology, contributes many polysyllables in which we can wrap our thoughts and blunt their force. To many writers there is no such thing as a bad schoolboy. Schoolboys are maladjusted or unoriented or misunderstood or in the need of guidance or lacking in continued success toward   32 satisfactory integration of the personality as a social unit, but they are never bad. Psychology no doubt makes us better men and women, more sympathetic and tolerant, but it doesn't make writing any easier. Had Shakespeare been confronted with psychology, "To be or not to be" might have come out, "To continue as a social unit or not to do so. That is the personality problem. Whether 'tis a better sign of integration at the conscious level to display a psychic tolerance toward the maladjustments and repressions induced by one's lack of orientation in one's environment or—" But Hamlet would never have finished the soliloquy.

Writing in the modern world, you cannot altogether avoid   33
modern jargon. Nor, in an effort to get away from euphemism, should you salt your paper with four-letter words. But you can do much if you will mount guard against those roundabout phrases, those echoing polysyllables that tend to slip into your writing to rob it of its crispness and force.

Beware of Pat Expressions

Other things being equal, avoid phrases like "other things   34
being equal." Those sentences that come to you whole, or in two or three doughy lumps, are sure to be bad sentences. They are no creation of yours but pieces of common thought floating in the community soup.

Pat expressions are hard, often impossible, to avoid, because   35
they come too easily to be noticed and seem too necessary to be dispensed with. No writer avoids them altogether, but good writers avoid them more often than poor writers.

By "pat expressions" we mean such tags as "to all practical   36
intents and purposes," "the pure and simple truth," "from where I sit," "the time of his life," "to the ends of the earth," "in the twinkling of an eye," "as sure as you're born," "over my dead body," "under cover of darkness," "took the easy way out," "when all is said and done," "told him time and time again," "parted the best of friends," "stand up and be counted," "gave him the best years of her life," "worked her fingers to the bone." Like other clichés, these expressions were once forceful. Now we should use them only when we can't possibly think of anything else.

Some pat expressions stand like a wall between the writer   37
and thought. Such a one is "the American way of life." Many student writers feel that when they have said that something accords with the American way of life or does not they have exhausted the subject. Actually, they have stopped at the highest level of ab-

straction. The American way of life is the complicated set of bonds between a hundred and eighty million ways. All of us know this when we think about it, but the tag phrase too often keeps us from thinking about it.

So with many another phrase dear to the politician: "this   38
great land of ours," "the man in the street," "our national heritage." These may prove our patriotism or give a clue to our political beliefs, but otherwise they add nothing to the paper except words.

Colorful Words

The writer builds with words, and no builder uses a raw ma-   39
terial more slippery and elusive and treacherous. A writer's work is a constant struggle to get the right word in the right place, to find that particular word that will convey his meaning exactly, that will persuade the reader or soothe him or startle or amuse him. He never succeeds altogether—sometimes he feels that he scarcely succeeds at all—but such successes as he has are what make the thing worth doing.

There is no book of rules for this game. One progresses   40
through everlasting experiment on the basis of ever-widening experience. There are few useful generalizations that one can make about words as words, but there are perhaps a few.

Some words are what we call "colorful." By this we mean   41
that they are calculated to produce a picture or induce an emotion. They are dressy instead of plain, specific instead of general, loud instead of soft. Thus, in place of "Her heart beat," we may write, "Her heart *pounded, throbbed, fluttered, danced.*" Instead of "He sat in his chair," we may say, "He *lounged, sprawled, coiled.*" Instead of "It was hot," we may say, "It was *blistering, sultry, muggy, suffocating, steamy, wilting.*"

However, it should not be supposed that the fancy word is al-   42
ways better. Often it is as well to write "Her heart beat" or "It was hot" if that is all it did or all it was. Ages differ in how they like their prose. The nineteenth century liked it rich and smoky. The twentieth has usually preferred it lean and cool. The twentieth century writer, like all writers, is forever seeking the exact word, but he is wary of sounding feverish. He tends to pitch it low, to understate it, to throw it away. He knows that if he gets too colorful, the audience is likely to giggle.

See how this strikes you: "As the rich, golden glow of the   43
sunset died away along the eternal western hills, Angela's limpid blue eyes looked softly and trustingly into Montague's flashing

brown ones, and her heart pounded like a drum in time with the joyous song surging in her soul." Some people like that sort of thing, but most modern readers would say, "Good grief," and turn on the television.

Colored Words

Some words we call not so much colorful as colored—that is, loaded with associations, good or bad. All words—except perhaps structure words—have associations of some sort. We have said that the meaning of a word is the sum of the contexts in which it occurs. When we hear a word, we hear with it an echo of all the situations in which we have heard it before. 44

In some words, these echoes are obvious and discussable. The word *mother*, for example, has for most people, agreeable associations. When you hear *mother* you probably think of home, safety, love, food, and various other pleasant things. If one writes, "She was like a mother to me," he gets an effect which he would not get in "She was like an aunt to me." The advertiser makes use of the associations of *mother* by working it in when he talks about his product. The politician works it in when he talks about himself. 45

So also with such words as *home, liberty, fireside, contentment, patriot, tenderness, sacrifice, childlike, manly, bluff, limpid*. All of these words are loaded with associations that would be rather hard to indicate in a straightforward definition. There is more than a literal difference between "They sat around the fireside" and "They sat around the stove." They might have been equally warm and happy around the stove, but *fireside* suggests leisure, grace, quiet tradition, congenial company, and *stove* does not. 46

Conversely, some words have bad associations. *Mother* suggests pleasant things, but *mother-in-law* does not. Many mothers-in-law are heroically lovable and some mothers drink gin all day and beat their children insensible, but these facts of life are beside the point. The point is that *mother* sounds good and *mother-in-law* does not. 47

Or consider the word *intellectual*. This would seem to be a complimentary term, but in point of fact it is not, for it has picked up associations of impracticality and ineffectuality and general dopiness. So also such words as *liberal, reactionary, Communist, socialist, capitalist, radical, schoolteacher, truck driver, undertaker, operator, salesman, huckster, speculator*. These convey meaning on the literal level, but beyond that—sometimes, in some places—they convey contempt on the part of the speaker. 48

bingly alive, at least less insufferably tedious than they might otherwise be" (para. 12). He accomplishes this purpose using humor and skill.

2. Responses to this question will vary.

3. Except for his choice of topic and the side he is obliged to take (by the nature and purpose of his essay), Roberts consistently follows his own suggestions. His writing comes alive with his conversational style, his humorous projections into the mind of the frustrated student, and such colorful descriptions as "round phrases thudding against the reader's brain" (para. 20) and "pieces of common thought floating in the community soup" (para. 34).

ANSWERS TO QUESTIONS:
DISCOVERING RHETORICAL
STRATEGIES (p. 249)

1. In his organization of this essay, Roberts first takes the reader into the mind of an unwilling student attempting to throw together five hundred acceptable words for an inconsiderate English instructor who has given an assignment to be completed over the weekend. He then offers suggestions for making the process more effective, presenting five segments regarding the content of a college composition, then four sections on the improvement of style. (See the response to question 1 in "Understanding Details.") This arrangement is logical, because content should be considered first in outlining a composition.

2. Drawn from an English textbook, this excerpt is obviously directed at college writers. Confirming this conclusion are Roberts' introductory sentences: "It's Friday afternoon, and you have almost survived another week of classes. You are just looking forward dreamily to the weekend when the English instructor says: 'For Monday you will turn in a five-hundred-word composition on college football' " (para. 1).

3. Throughout the essay, Roberts makes his points by poking gentle fun at student literary efforts—first at a slightly exaggerated version of an indifferent attempt at a writing assignment, then at many of the typical failings he describes. His ability to raise language awareness by making students laugh

The question of whether to use loaded words or not depends on what is being written. The scientist, the scholar, try to avoid them; for the poet, the advertising writer, the public speaker, they are standard equipment. But every writer should take care that they do not substitute for thought. If you write, "Anyone who thinks that is nothing but a Socialist (or Communist or capitalist)," you have said nothing except that you don't like people who think that, and such remarks are effective only with the most naive readers. It is always a bad mistake to think your readers more naive than they really are.   49

Colorless Words

But probably most student writers come to grief not with words that are colorful or those that are colored but with those that have no color at all. A pet example is *nice*, a word we would find it hard to dispense with in casual conversation but which is no longer capable of adding much to a description. Colorless words are those of such general meaning that in a particular sentence they mean nothing. Slang adjectives like *cool* ("That's real cool") tend to explode all over the language. They are applied to everything, lose their original force, and quickly die.   50

Beware also of nouns of very general meaning, like *circumstances, cases, instances, aspects, factors, relationships, attitudes, eventualities,* etc. In most circumstances you will find that those cases of writing which contain too many instances of words like these will in this and other aspects have factors leading to unsatisfactory relationships with the reader resulting in unfavorable attitudes on his part and perhaps other eventualities, like a grade of "D." Notice also what "etc." means. It means "I'd like to make this list longer, but I can't think of any more examples."   51

UNDERSTANDING DETAILS

1. List the nine guidelines Roberts suggests for good writing, and explain each briefly.
2. Can you give five examples of euphemisms now in current use (without repeating any of the ones Roberts uses)? Why is our society so dependent upon euphemisms? What social function do such words serve?
3. What are "colorful words," "colored words," and "colorless words," according to Roberts? Add five examples of your own to each of these lists in the essay.

ANALYZING MEANING

1. What is the principal purpose of this essay? Does it accomplish its purpose in your opinion? Explain your answer.
2. To what extent do you identify with the college student described by the author at the outset of this essay? In what important ways are you different?
3. Does Roberts follow his own suggestions for good writing in this essay? Why or why not? Give examples that illustrate how successfully the author follows his own advice.

DISCOVERING RHETORICAL STRATEGIES

1. How does Roberts organize the elements of his essay? Why does he choose this particular order? Is it effective for achieving his purpose? Why or why not?
2. Describe in some detail Roberts' intended audience. How did you come to this conclusion?
3. Analyze Roberts' use of humor throughout this essay (especially in his last paragraph). How does he raise our awareness regarding language as he makes us laugh at ourselves?

IDEAS FOR DISCUSSION/WRITING

Preparing to Write

Write freely about your own writing weaknesses: What problems do you have to watch out for in your own writing? Do these problems fluctuate with different kinds of assignments (essays, reports, research papers, business writing)? How do you try to improve upon these weak areas when you find them?

Choosing a Topic

1. One of your friends who is still in high school has asked you for information about college-level English courses. Write to this friend, using process analysis to explain how to survive freshman composition. Decide on a purpose and a point of view before you begin to write.
2. The student may not be the only one who needs improvement in this essay. The instructor's assignment of "a five-hundred-word composition on college football" does not promise to generate exciting prose. Devise a writing assignment on the topic of college sports that will get students more involved than the original assignment. Include purpose, audience, and writer's role in your directions. Then write a

at themselves is clearly demonstrated in the last paragraph of the essay, where he presents a list of "nouns of very general meaning" (para. 51) that should always be avoided, then uses the entire list in the sentence that follows this warning. The essay closes with a cautionary statement about the abbreviation "etc.," which he defines as, "I'd like to make this list longer, but I can't think of any more examples" (para. 51)—an appropriate ending to a cleverly written essay.

PREWRITING

In preparation for the writing assignments, the Preparing to Write questions ask students to study their writing weaknesses before they write an essay on a related topic. You might have your students consider these questions in reference to one or more of their previous papers. See pages 16–23 for other suggestions on generating ideas in response to these questions.

ADDITIONAL DISCUSSION/WRITING TOPIC

Write an essay to your English instructor explaining how he or she could encourage you to produce your best writing. Make your explanation as specific as possible. Be sure to follow the guidelines for a good process analysis essay.

An effective process analysis essay is acutely sensitive to its intended audience. Different groups of people need different information, examples, and definitions. In one of your process analysis essays, highlight all the basic information, illustrations, and definitions, and then reread your essay from your intended audience's perspective. Decide where you need to give more or less information. Then revise your paper, adjusting it as carefully as possible to your intended audience's needs.

process analysis essay explaining how to create a well-crafted writing assignment.

3. Using the guidelines Roberts suggests in his article, write an essay analyzing one of your recent papers.

CHAPTER 5

DIVISION/
CLASSIFICATION
■ ■ ■
Finding Categories

Using Division/Classification

Both division and classification play important roles in our everyday lives: Bureau drawers separate one type of clothing from another; kitchen cabinets organize food, dishes, and utensils into proper groups; grocery stores shelve similar items together so shoppers can easily locate what they want to buy; school notebooks with tabs help students divide up their academic lives; newspapers classify local and national events in order to organize a great deal of daily information for the general public; and our own personal classification systems assist us in separating what we like from what we don't so that we can have access to our favorite foods, our favorite cars, our favorite entertainment, our favorite people. The two processes of division and classification are so natural to us, in fact, that we sometimes aren't even aware we are using them.

Defining Division/Classification

Division and classification are actually mirror images of each other. Division is the basic feature of process analysis, which we studied in the last chapter: It moves from a general concept to subdivisions of that concept or from a single category to multiple

Division and classification are natural, everyday acts that often occur instinctively on the unconscious level. We introduce division and classification as mirror images of each other—the first moving from one to many, the second from many to one.

All essays in this chapter use division and/or classification as their main method of organization. Judy Brady's "Why I Want a Wife" uses this rhetorical technique to satirize men's view of a woman's traditional place in our society; the exercises and writing assignments before and after this selection ask students to study the various roles they play in life. Next, in "Second Chances for Children of Divorce," Judith Wallerstein and Sandra Blakeslee divide and classify children's responses to divorce in America; the apparatus before and after this selection has the students consider the role of divorce (whether directly or indirectly) in their own lives. Susan Allen Toth in "Cinematypes" uses division and classification to discuss dates and movies; the exercises for this essay revolve around various love relationships the students have had. In "School," an excerpt from Garrison Keillor's *Lake*

Wobegon Days, the author divides and classifies different activities from his grade-school days; the questions and essays for this selection require the students to reflect on their own school memories, dividing and classifying various people (and their actions) from the past. The last essay, "The Truth about Lying" by Judith Viorst, examines various lies we all experience; the accompanying assignments have students consider the role lying plays in their lives.

subcategories. Classification works in the opposite direction, moving from specifics to a group with common traits or from multiple subgroups to a single, larger, and more inclusive category. These techniques work together in many ways: A college, for example, is *divided* into departments (single to multiple), whereas courses are *classified* by department (multiple to single); the medical field is divided into specialties, whereas each doctor is *classified* by a single specialty; a cookbook is *divided* into chapters, whereas recipes are *classified* according to type; and athletics is *divided* into specific sports, whereas athletes are *classified* by the sport in which they participate. Division is the separation of an idea or item into its basic parts, such as a home into rooms, a course into assignments, or a job into various duties or responsibilities; classification is the organization of items with similar features into a group or groups, such as ordering furniture to decorate a dining room, dropping all carbohydrates from your diet, or preferring to date only tall, suntanned swimmers.

Classification is an organizational system for presenting a large amount of material to a reader or listener. This process helps us make sense of the complex world we live in by letting us work with smaller, more understandable units of that world. Classification must be governed by some clear, logical purpose (such as focusing on all lower-division course requirements), which will then dictate the system of categories to be used. The plan of organization that results should be as flexible as possible, and it should illustrate the specific relationship of items in a group to each other and of the groups themselves to one another.

As you already know, many different ways of classifying the same elements are possible. If you consider the examples at the outset of this chapter, you will realize that bureau drawers vary from house to house and even from person to person; that no one's kitchen is set up exactly the same way as someone else's; and that grocery stores have similar but not identical systems of food classification. (Think, for instance, of the many different schemes for organizing dairy products, meats, foreign foods, etc.) In addition, your friends probably use a method different from yours to organize their school notebooks; different newspapers vary their presentation of the news; and two professors will probably teach the same course material in divergent ways. We all have distinct and uniquely logical methods of classifying elements in our own lives.

The following student paragraph about friends illustrates both division and classification. As you read it, notice how the student writer moves back and forth smoothly from general to specific and from multiple to single.

> The word "friend" can refer to many different types of relationships. Close friends are "friends" at their very best: people for whom we feel respect, esteem, and, quite possibly, even love. We regard these people and their well-being with kindness, interest, and good will; we trust them and will go out of our way to help them. Needless to say, we could all use at least one close friend. Next come "casual friends," people with whom we share a particular interest or activity. The investment of a great amount of time and energy in developing this type of friendship is usually not required, though casual friends often become close friends with the passage of time. The last division of "friend" is most general and is composed of all those individuals whose acquaintance we have made and who feel no hostility toward us. When one is counting friends, this group should certainly be included, since such friendships often develop into "casual" or "close" relationships. Knowing people in all three groups is necessary, however, because all types of friends undoubtedly help us live healthier, happier lives.

Reading and Writing Division/Classification Essays

Writers of division/classification essays must first decide if they are going to break down a topic into many separate parts or group together similar items into one coherent category; a writer's purpose will, of course, guide him or her in this decision. Readers must likewise recognize and understand which of these two parallel operations an author is using to structure an essay. Another important identifying feature of division/classification essays is an explanation (explicit or implicit) of the significance of a particular system of organization.

HOW TO READ A DIVISION/CLASSIFICATION ESSAY

Preparing to Read. As you approach the selections in this chapter, you should study all the material that precedes each essay so you can prepare yourself for your reading. First of all, what hints does the title give you about what you are going to read? To what extent does Judy Brady reveal in her title her attitude toward women? Who do you think Judith Wallerstein and Sandra Blakeslee's audience is in "Second Chances for Children of Divorce"? Does Judith Viorst's title give us any indication about her point of view in "The Truth about Lying"? Then, see

TEACHING DIVISION/CLASSIFICATION: ONE INSTRUCTOR'S COMMENTS

I teach division/classification because it trains students to order and thereby comprehend the world around them. More than any other, this rhetorical mode is necessary to move student thinking from the concrete to the conceptual. Practice in the mode improves not only writing skills, but thinking and reading skills as well. I ask students to find examples of division and classification in magazines and newspapers, then in their textbooks. I use the example of a pie to clarify division, citing Freud's parts of the personality, the parts of the American governmental process, etc. I use the idea of plurality, of a "crowd" that needs ordering into categories, to illustrate classification. Writing assignments include extracting division/classification patterns from an excerpt or essay and summarizing the content of each pattern, creating the patterns in informal pieces, and finally using the patterns to construct more formal and abstract essays.

Mary Boyles
Pembroke State University
Pembroke, North Carolina

TEACHING DIVISION/CLASSIFICATION: ONE INSTRUCTOR'S COMMENTS

The way to teach any rhetorical strategy is to apply it to the way students think and to help them use it in other classes. For example, I approach division/classification very practically. I start out by dividing students into groups—traditional and nontraditional, according to concentration or major, by job or professional interests. These divisions always inspire class discussion. Then I have my students write about their particular category. I approach every rhetorical strategy in this practical way, which has worked for me for 20 years. I firmly believe that if rhetorical modes are the sole province of the English department, we are not doing our jobs.

Janet Eber
County College of Morris
Randolph, New Jersey7y

what you can learn from scanning each essay and reading its synopsis in the Rhetorical Table of Contents.

Also important as you prepare to read the essays in this chapter is your knowledge about each author and the conditions under which each essay was written: What does the biographical material tell you about Brady's "Why I Want a Wife"? About the excerpt from Garrison Keillor's *Lake Wobegon Days*? Knowing where these essays were first published will give you even more information about each author's purpose and audience.

Finally, before you begin to read, answer the "Preparing to Read" questions and then think freely for a few minutes about the general topic: What do you want to know about the different types of movies discussed in "Cinematypes" (Susan Allen Toth)? What are some of your own stories about schools you have attended (Keillor)?

Reading. As you read each essay for the first time, write down your initial reactions to the topic itself, to the preliminary material, to the mood the writer sets, or to a specific incident in the essay. Make associations between the essay and your own experiences. In addition, create a context for each essay by drawing on the preliminary material you just read about the essay: What are Wallerstein and Blakeslee implying about the relationship between emotional health and divorce, and why do they care about this relationship? What is significant about Keillor's point of view in "School"? According to Viorst, why are some lies permissible? Also, in this first reading, notice whether the writers divided (split up) or classified (gathered together) their material to make their point. Finally, read the questions after each essay and let them guide your second reading of the selection.

Rereading. When you read these division/classification essays a second time, notice how the authors carefully match their dominant rhetorical approach (in this case, division or classification) to their purpose in a clear thesis. What, for example, is Brady's dominant rhetorical approach to her subject? How does this approach further her purpose? What other rhetorical strategies support her thesis? Then see how these writers present their division or classification systems to their readers in a logical fashion, defining new categories as their essays progress. Finally, notice how each writer either implicitly or explicitly explains the significance or value of his or her division/classification system. How do Wallerstein and Blakeslee explain their system of organization? And how does Toth give her organizing principle significance? Now answer the questions after each essay to check your understanding and to help you analyze your reading in preparation for the discussion/writing topics that follow.

For a more complete survey of reading guidelines, you may want to consult the checklists on pages 15–16 of the Introduction.

HOW TO WRITE A DIVISION/CLASSIFICATION ESSAY

Preparing to Write.   You should approach a division/classification essay in the same way you have begun all your other writing assignments—with some kind of prewriting activity that will help you generate ideas, such as the Preparing to Write questions featured in this chapter. The prewriting techniques outlined in the Introduction can help you approach these questions imaginatively. Before you even consider selection and arrangement of details, you need to explore your subject, choose a topic, and decide on a specific purpose and audience.

Writing.   As you begin to write, certain guidelines will help you structure your ideas for a division/classification essay: (1) First declare an overall purpose for your classification; (2) then divide the item or concept you are dealing with into categories; (3) arrange these categories into a logical sequence; (4) define each category, explaining the difference between one category and another and demonstrating that difference through examples; and (5) explain the significance of your classification system (Why is it worth reading? What will your audience learn from it?). All discussion in such an essay should reinforce the purpose stated at the beginning of the theme. Other rhetorical modes—such as narration, example, and comparison/contrast—will naturally be used to supplement your classification. To make your classification as workable as possible, take special care that your categories do not overlap and that all topics fall into their proper places. If, for example, you were classifying all the jobs performed by students in your writing class, the categories of (1) indoor work and (2) outdoor work would probably be inadequate. Most delivery jobs, for example, fall into both categories. At a pizza parlor, a florist, or a gift shop, a delivery person's time would be split between indoor and outdoor work. So you would need to design a different classification system to avoid this problem. The categories of (1) indoor work, (2) outdoor work, and (3) a combination of indoor and outdoor work would be much more useful for this task. The last suggestion in particular will help make your classification essays more readable and more accurate.

Rewriting. As you rewrite your division/classification essays, consider carefully the probable reactions of your readers to the form and content of your paper: Does your thesis communicate your purpose clearly? Have you divided your topic into separate and understandable categories? Are your categories original and unique? Are these categories arranged logically? Are the distinctions between your categories as clear as possible? Will your audience appreciate the significance of your particular classification system?

More guidelines for writing and rewriting are available on pages 27–28 of the Introduction.

Student Essay: Division/Classification at Work

The following student essay divides skiers into interesting categories based on their physical abilities. As you read it, notice how the student writer weaves the significance of his study into his opening statement of purpose. Also, pay particular attention to his logical method of organization and clear explanation of categories as he moves with ease from multiple to single and back to multiple again throughout the essay.

People on the Slopes

When I first learned to ski, I was amazed by the shapes who whizzed by me and slipped down trails marked only by a black diamond signifying "most difficult," while others careened awkwardly down the "bunny slopes." These skiers, I discovered, could be divided into distinct categories—for my own entertainment and for the purpose of finding appropriate skiing partners.

First are the poetic skiers. They glide down the mountainside silently with what seems like no effort at all. They float from side to side on the intermediate slopes, their knees bent perfectly above parallel skis, while their sharp skills allow them to bypass slower skiers with safely executed turns at remarkable speeds.

The crazy skiers also get down the mountain quickly, but with a lot more noise attending their descent. At every hill, they yell a loud "Yahoo!" and slam their skis into the snow. These go-for-broke athletes always whiz by faster than everyone

Margin annotations: Subject · Thesis statement · First category · Supporting details · Second category · Supporting details (with humor)

else, and they especially seem to love the crowded runs where they can slide over the backs of other people's skis. I often find crazy skiers in mangled messes at the bottoms of steep hills, where they are yelling loudly, but not the famous "Yahoo!"

After being overwhelmed by the crazy skiers, I am always glad to find other skiers like myself: the *Third* average ones. We are polite on the slopes, concen- *category* trate on improving our technique with every run, and ski the beginner slopes only at the beginning of the day to warm up. We go over the moguls (small hills) much more cautiously than the crazy or po- etic skiers, but still seek adventure with a slight jump or two each day. We remain a silent majority on the mountain.

Supporting details (comparative)

Below us in talent, but much more evident on *Fourth* the mountainside, are what I call the eternal begin- *category* ners. These skiers stick to the same beginner slope almost every run of every day during their vaca- tion. Should they venture onto an intermediate slope, they quickly assume the snowplow position (a pigeon-toed stance) and never leave it. Eternal beginners weave from one side of the run to the other and hardly ever fall, because they proceed so slowly; however, they do yell quite a bit at the cra- zies who like to run over the backs of their skis.

Supporting details

Having always enjoyed people-watching, I have fun each time I am on the slopes observing the myriad of skiers around me. I use these observa- tions to pick out possible ski partners for myself and others. Since my mother is an eternal beginner, she has more fun skiing with someone who shares her interests than with my dad, who is a poetic skier with solitude on his mind. After taking care of Mom, I am free to find a partner I'll enjoy. My sister, the crazy skier of the family, just heads for the row- diest group she can find! As the years go by and my talents grow, I am trusting my perceptions of skier *Concluding* types to help me find the right partner for life on *remarks* and off the slopes. No doubt watching my fellow skiers will always remain an enjoyable pastime.

Significance of classification system

Student Writer's Comments

To begin this paper—the topic of which occurred to me as I flew over snow-capped mountains on a trip—I brainstormed. I jotted down the general groups I believed existed on the slopes, then noted characteristics as they came to me. The ideas flowed quite freely, and I enjoyed picturing the people I was describing. The difficult part came when I had to organize the groups. The order of presentation in my last draft is totally different from my initial draft. The greatest part of this paper was realizing that I had used these mental groupings before in pairing my family and friends with other skiers; I had just never organized or verbalized the categories. Writing this paper helped me do that and was a lot of fun.

Some Final Thoughts on Division/Classification

The following essays collected in this chapter use division and/or classification as their primary organizing principle. Most of these essays show both techniques at work, but a few demonstrate how division works by itself.

JUDY BRADY
(1937–   )

■ ■ ■

Why I Want a Wife

QUOTATION ON WRITING

"Everyone agrees that a writer's sense of purpose usefully directs choices about what to say and where and how to say it."

C. H. Knoblauch

Judy Brady is a freelance writer and political activist who was born in San Francisco. She earned a B.F.A. in painting from the University of Iowa, married, raised two daughters, and then returned to San Francisco, where she is now an "ex-wife" who works as a secretary: "I must spend my days working in the corporate world where image has become so much more important than reality. It's crazy-making. My relief comes from doing political work with other people who have found the courage to acknowledge what is really going on and then act accordingly." Strong commitment to the feminist movement has taken her to Cuba for several visits, which have prompted the publication of articles about such diverse topics as abortion, literacy, unions, and the role of women in society. The author now devotes much of her time to political activity surrounding the issue of U.S. involvement in Central America. Her most recent publication is *Women and Cancer* (1990), an anthology of poems, stories, and essays that "make accessible through personal testimony the facts of the cancer epidemic in this country."

Preparing to Read

The following essay first appeared under the author's married name, Judy Syfers. It was originally published in the preview issue of *Ms.* magazine (Spring 1972) and was later reprinted in the periodical's December 1979 issue. In it, Brady presents a wry, satirical view of woman's conventional social role as a docile servant to her husband. As you prepare to read this article, take a few moments to think about the various roles you play in your life: How many distinct roles do you play? Do you act differently as a student? A friend? A lover? A member of your family? An employee? How does each role make you feel? What different expectations are placed upon you in each of these roles? Who sets these expectations? How clearly are they stated? What happens when you do not fulfill each of these roles properly?

PREREADING

The purpose of this Preparing to Read material is to encourage students to think about the various roles they play in their lives. To help your students generate these roles before they respond to the questions here, you might ask them to write out a typical schedule for a week and write the roles they play next to each item on the schedule. See pages 3–6 for other ways to generate thoughts on these questions.

BACKGROUND INFORMATION

Feminist Judy Brady presents a witty satire classifying the myriad duties of a wife and mother in "Why I Want a Wife." This humorous essay leaves the reader with some thought-provoking questions regarding the role of married women in American society.

READABILITY LEVEL

6.5

RELATED READINGS

Sexism

Alleen Pace Nilsen, "Sexism in English: A 1990s Update"   183
Germaine Greer, "A Child Is Born"   308
Nancy Gibbs, "When Is It Rape?"   345

Sexuality

Alleen Pace Nilsen, "Sex in English: A 1990s Update"   183
Germaine Greer, "A Child Is Born"   308
Nancy Gibbs, "When Is It Rape?"   345
Susan Sontag, "On AIDS"   378

Women's Roles

Amy Tan, "The Joy Luck Club"   49
Alleen Pace Nilsen, "Sexism in English: A 1990s Update"   183
Germaine Greer, "A Child Is Born"   308

I belong to that classification of people known as wives. I am A Wife. And, not altogether incidentally, I am a mother.

Not too long ago a male friend of mine appeared on the scene fresh from a recent divorce. He had one child, who is, of course, with his ex-wife. He is looking for another wife. As I thought about him while I was ironing one evening, it suddenly occurred to me that I, too, would like to have a wife. Why do I want a wife?

I would like to go back to school so that I can become economically independent, support myself, and, if need be, support those dependent upon me. I want a wife who will work and send me to school. And while I am going to school I want a wife to take care of my children. I want a wife to keep track of the children's doctor and dentist appointments. And to keep track of mine, too. I want a wife to make sure my children eat properly and are kept clean. I want a wife who will wash the children's clothes and keep them mended. I want a wife who is a good nurturant attendant to my children, who arranges for their schooling, makes sure that they have an adequate social life with their peers, takes them to the park, the zoo, etc. I want a wife who takes care of the children when they are sick, a wife who arranges to be around when the children need special care, because, of course, I cannot miss classes at school. My wife must arrange to lose time at work and not lose the job. It may mean a small cut in my wife's income from time to time, but I guess I can tolerate that. Needless to say, my wife will arrange and pay for the care of the children while my wife is working.

I want a wife who will take care of *my* physical needs. I want a wife who will keep my house clean. A wife who will pick up after my children, a wife who will pick up after me. I want a wife who will keep my clothes clean, ironed, mended, replaced when need be, and who will see to it that my personal things are kept in their proper place so that I can find what I need the minute I need it. I want a wife who cooks the meals, a wife who is a *good* cook. I want a wife who will plan the menus, do the necessary grocery shopping, prepare the meals, serve them pleasantly, and then do the cleaning up while I do my studying. I want a wife who will care for me when I am sick and sympathize with my pain and loss of time from school. I want a wife to go along when our family takes a vacation so that someone can continue to care for me and my children when I need a rest and change of scene.

I want a wife who will not bother me with rambling complaints about a wife's duties. But I want a wife who will listen to me when I feel the need to explain a rather difficult point I have come across in my course of studies. And I want a wife who will type my papers for me when I have written them.

I want a wife who will take care of the details of my social life. When my wife and I are invited out by my friends, I want a wife who will take care of the babysitting arrangements. When I meet people at school that I like and want to entertain, I want a wife who will have the house clean, will prepare a special meal, serve it to me and my friends, and not interrupt when I talk about things that interest me and my friends. I want a wife who will have arranged that the children are fed and ready for bed before my guests arrive so that the children do not bother us. I want a wife who takes care of the needs of my guests so that they feel comfortable, who makes sure that they have an ashtray, that they are passed the hors d'oeuvres, that they are offered a second helping of the food, that their wine glasses are replenished when necessary, that their coffee is served to them as they like it. And I want a wife who knows that sometimes I need a night out by myself.

I want a wife who is sensitive to my sexual needs, a wife who makes love passionately and eagerly when I feel like it, a wife who makes sure that I am satisfied. And, of course, I want a wife who will not demand sexual attention when I am not in the mood for it. I want a wife who assumes the complete responsibility for birth control, because I do not want more children. I want a wife who will remain sexually faithful to me so that I do not have to clutter up my intellectual life with jealousies. And I want a wife who understands that *my* sexual needs may entail more than strict adherence to monogamy. I must, after all, be able to relate to people as fully as possible.

If, by chance, I find another person more suitable as a wife than the wife I already have, I want the liberty to replace my present wife with another one. Naturally, I will expect a fresh, new life; my wife will take the children and be solely responsible for them so that I am left free.

When I am through with school and have a job, I want my wife to quit working and remain at home so that my wife can more fully and completely take care of a wife's duties.

My God, who *wouldn't* want a wife?

UNDERSTANDING DETAILS

1. How many categories of wifely duties does Brady refer to in this essay? How are they related?

COLLABORATIVE LEARNING: CLASS ACTIVITY

Have the class members ask some women they know whether or not they want "a wife" to take care of the traditionally female chores. Your students might need to preface their questions with some explanation about Brady's essay. At the same time, have them ask their male friends if they want "a husband" to take care of traditionally male chores. When the class comes together, tally and discuss the responses.

COLLABORATIVE LEARNING: SMALL GROUP ACTIVITY

Divide the class into groups of 3 or 4, and have your students list chores traditionally completed by females in American society in one column and those completed by males in another. Then, have each group discuss the division of labor in a home and try to come up with a fair division of the chores on their two lists. Have each group present their suggestions to the class.

ANSWERS TO QUESTIONS: UNDERSTANDING DETAILS (p. 261)

1. Brady discusses six categories of wifely duties: financial and child care (which she combines into a single category), physical needs, intellectual responsivity, social needs, sexual needs, and expendability. All these duties entail the complete sublimation of self to the needs of another.

2. The author defines "wife" as one who is devoted to the gratification of the needs of someone else. In her opinion, the husband is usually the one whose needs and desires are being gratified. Although Brady's portrayal of a wife may be somewhat exaggerated and more typical of an earlier period in our social history, much truth is contained in the article.

3. The author wants a wife because she "would like to go back to school so that I can become economically independent, support myself, and, if need be, support those dependent upon me" (para. 3). While she is completing her education, her wife would "work and send me to school" (para. 3) and continue to accomplish all the incidental tasks the author is responsible for now.

1. The author's purpose in this essay is to classify the duties of a wife in an attempt to illustrate what she feels is an unfair distribution of labor within the modern family. This purpose is evident not only in the contradictory expectations described in the essay and the easy expendability expected of such a person, but also in the final line of the essay: "My God, who *wouldn't* want a wife?" (para. 10).

2. Brady asks for a servant in her essay, an attendant whose role in life is to fulfill all of Brady's wants and needs. The wife Brady requests has no goals other than the primary task of serving a family.

3. Responses to this question will vary.

ANSWERS TO QUESTIONS: DISCOVERING RHETORICAL STRATEGIES (p. 262)

1. The author examines the role of a wife and divides into categories the various expectations of this role. Likewise, she looks at each classification and divides it into tasks. In the opposite direction, she pulls together the tasks performed by a wife and classifies them into categories. Brady also uses description as she details a day in the life of someone who fulfills the role of wife. Persuasion is also at the core of her essay, which successfully argues that a wife who does all the jobs she lists is little better than a slave.

2. The following is another example of parallel structure:

"A wife who will pick up after my children,
a wife who will pick up after me"* (para. 4).

The parallel structures and repetitions throughout the essay reflect the constant litany of demands that some wives face on a daily basis.

3. "Why I Want a Wife" is written from the first-person point of view, with a satirical look at wifehood from the perspective of one who has intimate knowledge of the role. Brady uses wit to ridicule the unrealistic expectations of a wife in an attempt to call attention to the inequities inherent in this traditional role.

2. How does the author define the term "wife"? Is her portrayal of wives realistic? According to this essay, how do husbands differ from wives?
3. Why does the author want a wife? Explain your answer in some detail.

ANALYZING MEANING

1. What is the overall purpose of Brady's essay? How do you know? What clues make this purpose clear?
2. What type of wife does Brady ask for in this essay? What motivates this wife? Where are this person's loyalties? What are this wife's convictions?
3. Is this essay as pertinent today as it was 20 years ago? From your perspective, how have sexual roles changed since 1972? How are wives' roles today different from your mother's role as a wife?

DISCOVERING RHETORICAL STRATEGIES

1. Where in this essay does the author use division? Where does she use classification? Give specific examples. What other rhetorical modes does Brady use in her essay?
2. This essay works principally through parallel structure, in which similar grammatical elements are repeated in a series of phrases or clauses. Look, for example, at the following sentence:

I want *a wife who* is sensitive to my sexual needs,
    a wife who makes love passionately and eagerly when I feel
        like it,
    a wife who makes sure that I am satisfied (para. 7).

The repetitions in this example are italicized, whereas the parallel structures are lined up under each other. Find two other instances of this technique in the essay, and explain how each works. What effect does this rhetorical technique have on you as you read this essay?
3. What point of view does Brady take in her article? What tone results from this point of view? Look up the term "satire" in a literary dictionary, and explain what use Brady is making of this verbal technique.

IDEAS FOR DISCUSSION/WRITING

Preparing to Write

Write freely about your own various roles in life: What are some of the major roles you play (e.g., husband, wife, girlfriend, boyfriend, sister, brother, son, daughter, student, friend, employee)? What personal characteristics define the different roles you play? Which of these roles is most comfortable for you? Which is least comfortable? How does each of these roles make you feel about yourself?

Choosing a Topic

1. Use division to explain one of the roles you play in life. Break down the role into its basic parts and then discuss those parts in an essay to your English class. Make sure you decide on a purpose and point of view before you begin to write.
2. Do you feel that husbands are ever categorized or exploited in much the same way as Brady's "wife"? Write an essay entitled "Why I Want a Husband" that presents the other side of the story.
3. Using Brady's ironic method, write an essay for your classmates in which you claim to need something that you could never have.

PREWRITING

In preparation for the writing assignments, the Preparing to Write questions ask students to consider, before writing an essay on a related topic, the different roles they play in their lives and the way they feel about each of these roles. See pages 16–23 for suggestions on generating ideas in response to these questions.

ADDITIONAL DISCUSSION/WRITING TOPIC

Use division and/or classification to explain all the roles you currently play in your life. Classify these roles according to some reasonable scheme or method of organization. Then explain that classification in an essay addressed to your English class.

REVISING STRATEGY

A clear sense of purpose is an important key to any essay. In one of your division/classification essays, write out your purpose, and then underline all parts of your essay that help you achieve that goal. Notice where your essay could be clearer or better focused. Then revise your paper so it communicates to your intended audience a clear, consistent purpose.

JUDITH WALLERSTEIN
(1921–)
SANDRA BLAKESLEE
(1943–)

■ ■ ■

Second Chances for Children of Divorce

Judith Wallerstein grew up in New York City, earned her Ph.D. at Lund University in Sweden, and now lives and works in Marin County, California, where she serves as director of the Center for the Family in Transition. Since 1965 she has taught psychology at the University of California at Berkeley, where she specializes in divorce and its effect on family members. Her first book, *Surviving the Breakup* (coauthored by Joan Kelly, 1980), analyzes the impact of divorce on young children in the family. Her next, *Second Chances: Men, Women, and Children a Decade After Divorce* (1989), is a study of the long-term effects of divorce on teenagers and young adults. Now hard at work on a study of happy marriages, Wallerstein is very concerned about what is happening to the American family. "There's a lot of anger in relationships between men and women today," she explains. "It's always easier to express anger than love." An avid reader, she collects ideas "like other people collect recipes." She advises college students to read as much as possible: "The first prerequisite a writer must have is a love of reading." Her coauthor on *Second Chances*, Sandra Blakeslee, was born in Flushing, New York, and earned her B.S. degree at Berkeley, where her specialty was neurobiology. She is currently the West-Coast science and medicine correspondent for the *New York Times*. A former Peace Corps volunteer in Borneo, she advises students using *The Prose Reader* to travel as much as possible: "You need a wide range of experiences to be a good writer." Blakeslee goes mountain biking and runs in her spare time.

Preparing to Read

In the following essay from *Second Chances*, Wallerstein and Blakeslee classify the psychological tasks children who have suffered through the divorce of their parents need to complete in order

PREREADING

The purpose of this Preparing to Read material is to encourage students to think about the effects of divorce on themselves, on someone they know, or on society in general. If some of your students have no personal experience with divorce, they might want to talk informally with someone who has had such an experience, or they could go into the library and browse through some current magazines that deal with the traumas of divorce. See pages 3–6 for other ways to generate thoughts on these questions.

to free themselves from the past. As you prepare to read this article, take a few minutes to think about the effects of divorce on yourself or someone you know. How close have you been to a divorce experience? How were people directly associated with the experience affected? What differences did you notice in the way adults and children responded to the same situation? What feelings were most common among the adults? Among the children? Why do you think the divorce rate has been so high during the last fifty years? Do you think this trend will continue or will it taper off in the next few years?

■ ─────────────────────────────── ■

At each stage in the life cycle, children and adults face predictable and particular issues that represent the coming together of the demands of society and a biological and psychological timetable. Just as we physically learn to sit, crawl, walk, and run, we follow an equivalent progression in our psychological and social development. Each stage presents us with a sequence of tasks we must confront. We can succeed or fail in mastering them, to varying degrees, but everyone encounters the tasks. They begin at birth and end at death.

Children move upward along a common developmental ladder, although each goes it alone at his or her own pace. Gradually, as they pass through the various stages, children consolidate a sense of self. They develop coping skills, conscience, and the capacity to give and receive love.

Children take one step at a time, negotiating the rung they are on before they can move up to the next. They may—and often do—falter in this effort. The climb is not steady under the best of circumstances, and most children briefly stand still in their ascent. They may even at times move backward. Such regressions are not a cause for alarm; rather, they may represent an appropriate response to life's stresses. Children who fail one task are not stalled forever; they will go on to the next stage, although they may be weakened in their climb. Earlier failures will not necessarily imperil their capacity as adults to trust a relationship, make a commitment, hold an appropriate job, or be a parent—to make use of their second chances at each stage of development.

I propose that children who experience divorce face an additional set of tasks specific to divorce in addition to the normal developmental tasks of growing up. Growing up is inevitably harder for children of divorce because they must deal with psy-

BACKGROUND INFORMATION

This essay is a study of the psychological tasks children of divorce must perform in order to get on with their lives. The book in which it appears is a follow-up study of the California Children of Divorce Project, an interdisciplinary grant dedicated to examining the feelings and needs of the children of divorce. In this particular essay, the authors divide and classify the psychological tasks children must go through before, during, and after the divorce of their parents. The authors explain that "children who experience divorce face an additional set of tasks specific to divorce in addition to the normal developmental tasks of growing up" (para. 4). Wallerstein and Blakeslee further claim that these tasks must be dealt with to some degree by all children of divorce.

READABILITY LEVEL

14.1

RELATED READINGS

Raising Children

Lewis Sawaquat, "For My Indian Daughter" 96
Bill Cosby, "The Baffling Questions," 157
Germaine Greer, "A Child Is Born" 308
Michael Dorris, "The Broken Cord" 400
Betty Gittman, "Pregnant Teenagers: A Challenge" 516

Societal Problems

Kimberly Wozencraft, "Notes from the Country Club" 63
Nancy Gibbs, "When Is It Rape?" 345
Michael Dorris, "The Broken Cord" 400
Michael Fabricant and Michael Driscoll-Kelly, "The Problem of Homelessness Is Serious" 484
Martin Morse Wooster, "The Problem of Homelessness Is Exaggerated" 484
Betty Gittman, "Pregnant Teenagers: A Challenge" 516
John Langone, "Group Violence" 525

Have your students investigate options for dealing with stress. Then, let them choose one method to present to the class in the form of a sales pitch.

chological issues that children from well-functioning intact families do not have to face.

The psychological tasks of children begin as difficulties escalate between the parents during the marriage, and continue through the separation and divorce and throughout the postdivorce years.

TASK: Understanding the Divorce

The first and most basic task at the time of separation is for the children to understand realistically what the divorce means in their family and what its concrete consequences will be. Children, especially very young children, are thrown back on frightening and vivid fantasies of being abandoned, being placed in foster care, or never seeing a departed parent again, or macabre fantasies such as a mother being destroyed in an earthquake or a father being destroyed by a vengeful mother. All of these fantasies and the feelings that accompany them can be undone only as the children, with the parents' continuing help, begin to understand the reality and begin to adjust to the actual changes that the divorce brings.

The more mature task of understanding what led to the marital failure awaits the perspective of the adolescent and young adult. Early on, most children regard divorce as a serious error, but by adolescence most feel that their parents never should have married. The task of understanding occurs in two stages. The first involves accurately perceiving the immediate changes that divorce brings and differentiating fantasy fears from reality. The second occurs later, when children are able at greater distance and with more mature understanding to evaluate their parents' actions and can draw useful lessons for their own lives.

TASK: Strategic Withdrawal

Children and adolescents need to get on with their own lives as soon as possible after the divorce, to resume their normal activities at school and at play, to get back physically and emotionally to the normal tasks of growing up. Especially for adolescents who may have been beginning to spread their wings, the divorce pulls them back into the family orbit, where they may become consumed with care for siblings or a troubled parent. It also intrudes on their academic and social life, causing them to spend class time preoccupied with worry and to pass up social activities because of demands at home. This is not to say that children should ignore the divorce. Their task is to acknowledge their concern and to provide appropriate help to their parents and siblings, but they should strive to remove the divorce from the center of their own thoughts so that they can get back to their own interests, pleasures, problems, and peer relationships. To achieve this task, children need encouragement from their parents to *remain* children.

Divide the class into groups of 3 or 4, and have each group generate a list of the events or feelings that cause them the most stress in life. Through group consensus, have them settle on five items that one person from each group reads to the rest of the class.

TASK: Dealing with Loss

In the years following divorce, children experience two profound losses. One is the loss of the intact family together with the symbolic and real protection it has provided. The second is the loss of the presence of one parent, usually the father, from their daily lives.   9

In dealing with these losses, children fall back on many fantasies to mask their unhappiness. As we have seen, they may idealize the father as representative of all that is lacking in their current lives, thinking that if only he were present, everything would be better.   10

The task of absorbing loss is perhaps the single most difficult task imposed by divorce. At its core, the task requires children to overcome the profound sense of rejection, humiliation, unlovability, and powerlessness they feel with the departure of one parent. When the parent leaves, children of all ages blame themselves. They say, "He left me because I was not lovable. I was not worthy." They conclude that had they been more lovable, worthy, or different, the parent would have stayed. In this way, the loss of the parent and lowered self-esteem become intertwined.   11

To stave off these intensely painful feelings of rejection, children continually try to undo the divorce scenario, to bring their parents back together, or to somehow win back the affection of the absent parent. The explanation "Had he loved me, he would not have left the family" turns into a new concern. "If he loved me, he would visit more often. He would spend more time with me." With this in mind, the children not only are pained at the outset but remain vulnerable, sometimes increasingly, over the years. Many reach out during adolescence to increase contact with the parent who left, again to undo the sad scenario and to rebuild their self-esteem as well.   12

This task is easier if parents and children have a good relationship, within the framework of a good visiting or joint custody arrangement.   13

Some children are able to use a good, close relationship with the visiting parent to promote their growth within the divorced   14 family. Others are able to acknowledge and accept that the visiting parent could never become the kind of parent they need, and they are able to turn away from blaming themselves. Still others are able to reject, on their own, a rejecting parent or to reject a role model that they see as flawed. In so doing, these youngsters are able to effectively master the loss and get on with their lives.

TASK: Dealing with Anger

Divorce, unlike death, is always a voluntary decision for at least one of the partners in a marriage. Everyone involved knows this. The child understands that divorce is not a natural disaster like an earthquake or tornado; it is caused by the decision of one or both of the parents to separate. Its true cause lies in the parents' failure to maintain the marriage, and someone is culpable. 15

Given this knowledge, children face a terrible dilemma. They know that their unhappiness has been caused by the very people charged with their protection and care—their parents are the agents of their distress. Furthermore, the parents undertook this role voluntarily. This realization puts children in a dreadful bind because they know something that they dare not express—out of fear, out of anxiety, out of a wish to protect their parents. 16

Children get angry at their parents, experiencing divorce as indifference to their needs and perceiving parents sometimes realistically as self-centered and uncaring, as preaching a corrupt morality, and as weak and unable to deal with problems except by running away. 17

At the same time, children are aware of their parents' neediness, weaknesses, and anxiety about life's difficulties. Although children have little understanding of divorce, except when the fighting has been open and violent, they fully recognize how unhappy and disorganized their parents become, and this frightens them very much. Caught in a combination of anger and love, the children are frightened and guilty about their anger because they love their parents and perceive them as unhappy people who are trying to improve their lives in the face of severe obstacles. Their concern makes it difficult even to acknowledge their anger. 18

A major task, then, for children is to work through this anger, to recognize their parents as human beings capable of making mistakes, and to respect them for their real efforts and their real courage. 19

Cooling of anger and the task of forgiveness go hand in hand with children's growing emotional maturity and capacity to appreciate the various needs of the different family members. As 20 anger diminishes, young people are better able to put the divorce behind them and experience relief. As children forgive their parents, they forgive themselves for feeling anger and guilt and for failing to restore the marriage. In this way, children can free themselves from identification with the angry or violent parent or with the victim.

TASK: Working Out Guilt

Young children often feel responsible for divorce, thinking   21
that their misbehavior may have caused one parent to leave. Or, in a more complicated way, they may feel that their fantasy wish to drive a wedge between their mother and father has been magically granted. Many guilty feelings arise at the time of divorce but dissipate naturally as children mature. Others persist, usually with roots in a profound continuing sense of having caused the unthinkable—getting rid of one parent so as to be closer to the other.

Other feelings of guilt are rooted in children's realization that   22
they were indeed a cause of marital difficulty. Many divorces occur after the birth of a child, and the child correctly comprehends that he or she really did drive a wedge between the adults.

We see another kind of guilt in girls who, in identifying with   23
their troubled mothers, become afraid to surpass their mothers. These young women have trouble separating from their mothers, whom they love and feel sorry for, and establishing their own successful relationships with suitable young men. The children of divorce need to separate from guilty ties that bind them too closely to a troubled parent and to go on with their lives with compassion and love.

TASK: Accepting the Permanence of the Divorce

At first, children feel a strong and understandable need to   24
deny the divorce. Such early denial may be a first step in the coping process. Like a screen that is alternately lowered and raised, the denial helps children confront the full reality of the divorce, bit by bit. They cannot take it in all at once.

Nevertheless, we have learned that five and even ten years   25
after divorce, some children and adolescents refuse to accept the divorce as a permanent state of affairs. They continue to hope, consciously or unconsciously, that the marriage will be restored, finding omens of reconciliation even in a harmless handshake or a simple friendly nod.

1. The seven psychological challenges Wallerstein and Blakeslee identify are (1) "Understanding the Divorce," (2) "Strategic Withdrawal," (3) "Dealing with Loss," (4) "Dealing with Anger," (5) "Working Out Guilt," (6) "Accepting the Permanence of the Divorce," and (7) "Taking a Chance on Love." The authors assert that most of these tasks, though they can be dealt with in childhood, can linger through late adolescence and into early adulthood for many children who experience divorce.

2. Responses to this question will vary.

3. The participants in Wallerstein and Blakeslee's study "were in search of romantic love . . . [but] were entirely unable to take the kind of chances necessary for them to move emotionally into successful young adulthood" because of their overwhelming anxiety and fears of betrayal (para. 29).

ANSWERS TO QUESTIONS:
ANALYZING MEANING (p. 271)

1. Responses to this question will vary.

2. According to Wallerstein and Blakeslee, when a parent leaves, children often blame themselves and believe that their misbehavior has caused the parent to leave. This feeling of personal rejection often causes them to replay in their minds a reconciliation fantasy in which improvement of their behavior or relationship with the departed parent will bring the family back together.

3. Parents who understand the anxiety their children are likely to feel over a recent divorce (along with the manifestations of these fears) will more easily reassure their children and help them deal with their feeling about the divorce. However, many people who are themselves involved in divorce may not be able to separate themselves sufficiently from the emotions they feel to look at their children objectively. Giving parents a clear guide to their children's reactions can help them provide more stability and security to ease their children's fears and pain as well as their own.

In accepting permanence, the children of divorce face a more difficult task than children of bereavement. Death cannot be undone, but divorce happens between living people who can change their minds. A reconciliation fantasy taps deep into children's psyches. Children need to feel that their parents will still be happy together. They may not overcome this fantasy of reconciliation until they themselves finally separate from their parents and leave home. 26

TASK: *Taking a Chance on Love*

This is perhaps the most important task for growing children and for society. Despite what life has dealt them, despite lingering fears and anxieties, the children of divorce must grow, become open to the possibility of success or failure, and take a chance on love. They must hold on to a realistic vision that they can both love and be loved. 27

This is the central task for youngsters during adolescence and at entry into young adulthood. And as we have seen, it is the task on which so many children tragically flounder. Children who lose a parent through death must take a chance on loving with the knowledge that all people eventually die and that death can take away our loved ones at any time. Children who lose the intact family through divorce must also take a chance on love, knowing realistically that divorce is always possible but being willing nevertheless to remain open to love, commitment, marriage, and fidelity. 28

More than the ideology of hoping to fall in love and find commitment, this task involves being able to turn away from the model of parents who could not stay committed to each other. While all the young people in our study were in search of romantic love, a large number of them lived with such a high degree of anxiety over fears of betrayal or of not finding love that they were entirely unable to take the kind of chances necessary for them to move emotionally into successful young adulthood. 29

This last task, taking a chance on love, involves being able to venture, not just thinking about it, and not thinking one way and behaving another. It involves accepting a morality that truly guides behavior. This is the task that occupies children of divorce throughout their adolescence. It is what makes adolescence such a critical and difficult time for them. The resolution of life's tasks is a relative process that never ends, but this last task, which is built on successfully negotiating all the others, leads to psychological freedom from the past. This is the essence of second chances for children of divorce. 30

UNDERSTANDING DETAILS

1. Name the seven categories into which Wallerstein and Blakeslee divide the psychological growth of the children of divorce. How long will it take most children to perform these tasks?
2. Choose one of these tasks and explain it in your own words.
3. What did Wallerstein and Blakeslee find out about their subjects' ability to deal with love in their lives?

ANALYZING MEANING

1. In your opinion, which of the emotional tasks that Wallerstein and Blakeslee describe is likely to be most difficult in a child's life after a divorce? On what do you base your conclusion?
2. What is the relationship suggested in this essay between the parents' divorce and a child's sense of rejection?
3. How might an understanding of the seven tasks discussed in this essay help people deal more effectively with children affected by divorce?

DISCOVERING RHETORICAL STRATEGIES

1. How do Wallerstein and Blakeslee organize their categories in this essay? Why do they place these tasks in this particular order?
2. Describe the authors' intended audience. What makes you think they are directing their comments to this group?
3. What other rhetorical modes do Wallerstein and Blakeslee use in this essay besides division and classification? How do these other modes support the authors' division/classification system?

IDEAS FOR DISCUSSION/WRITING

Preparing to Write

Write freely about your thoughts on divorce and the effects of divorce on others: Do you know anyone who has gone through a divorce? How did the experience affect the couple getting divorced? How did it affect their friends, their relatives, their children? How do you think the high divorce rate is affecting Americans in general? Why is America's national divorce rate so high? What changes could we make to lower the divorce rate?

Use division and/or classification to explain the range of stressful activities you face in college. Classify these activities according to a scheme that you have developed. Then, explain that classification in an essay addressed to your English class.

REVISING STRATEGY

The success of a divison/classification essay depends to a great extent on the accuracy of the categories into which you divide your subject. In one of your division/classification essays, underline your subdivisions within your paper; next check that these categories do not overlap and that all topics fall into their proper places. Then revise your paper, paying close attention to the appropriateness of your subdivisions.

Choosing a Topic

1. Assume that you are an expert on the variety and scope of college relationships. In an essay written for your classmates, divide your observations on different types of relationships into categories that will show students the full range of these associations in a college setting.

2. Because you have been involved with divorce in some way, you have been asked to submit to your college newspaper an editorial classifying the various ways in which different types of people react to divorce (husbands, wives, children, friends, and so on). You have been told to pay particular attention to the reactions of college students whose parents are going through or have gone through a divorce.

3. In an essay written for the general public, speculate about the reasons for the high national divorce rate. Use your own experience, interview others, or consult sources in the library to investigate the reasons for this trend. Suggest how we could solve this problem in America.

SUSAN ALLEN TOTH
(1940–   )

■ ■ ■

Cinematypes

Susan Allen Toth is an English professor and writer-in-residence who earned her B.A. at Smith College, her M.A. at the University of California at Berkeley, and her Ph.D. at the University of Minnesota. She now teaches at Macalester College in St. Paul, where she specializes in contemporary American literature, the novel, and creative writing. Her many essays and short stories have been published in *Harper's, Redbook, Ms., Cosmopolitan,* and *McCall's.* Her first book, entitled *Blooming: A Small-Town Girlhood* (1981), is a chronicle of her experiences growing up in Ames, Iowa. This was soon followed by *Ivy Days: Making My Way Out East* (1984), which detailed the traumas of moving from the Midwest to an Ivy-League college; *How to Prepare for Your High School Reunion: And Other Midlife Musings* (1988), a collection of essays; *Reading Poems* (1991), an anthology celebrating public libraries, coauthored with John Coughlan; and *A House of One's Own: An Architect's Guide to Designing the House of Your Dreams* (1991), written with her architect husband, James Stageberg. Toth began her writing career relatively late in life, in her mid-thirties, and now proudly sees herself as an example to other aspiring authors: "One *can* start writing in the middle years in a small upstairs room in Minnesota." She advises students to develop a prose style that "sounds like themselves, not like anybody else" and confesses that the hardest thing about writing for her is "carving out the time to do it—especially while raising a family." Toth lives in Minneapolis, where she loves cooking, hiking, bicycling, and swimming.

Preparing to Read

"Cinematypes," subtitled "Going to the Movies," was originally published in *Harper's* magazine in 1980. The essay wryly classifies Toth's movie dates according to their various cinemagraphic preferences and movie-house behavior. The men who escort her to these films can be "typed" just as easily as the films they choose to see. Prior to reading this essay, think about some of the dates you have had in the past: Were any of the people you dated easy to classify? Did they behave in predictable ways? Did they always seek out the same kinds of entertainment? What preferences did you share with

PREREADING

The purpose of this Preparing to Read material is to encourage students to think about the types of dates they have had. To help your students turn their attention to this topic, ask them to list the dates they have had in the last year or so. In this way, your students will have some names to work with as they respond to the prereading questions. See pages 3–6 for other ways to generate thoughts on these questions.

BACKGROUND INFORMATION

"Cinematypes" by Susan Allen Toth is an amusing and believable essay in which the author classifies several of the men she has dated according to their movie preferences and theater behavior.

READABILITY LEVEL

6.6

RELATED READINGS

Media

Marie Winn, "Television Addiction"   370
Stephen King, "Why We Crave Horror Movies"   395

DEFINITIONS

The Devil's Eye (1960) (para. 1): a comic film in which Don Juan returns to earth from Hell and falls in love with a young virgin.

Belle de Jour (1967) (para. 3): a film satirizing the bourgeoisie in which a bored housewife turns prostitute.

The Sorrow and the Pity (1977) (para. 4): a documentary account of the Nazi occupation of France.

Coming Home (1978) (para. 4): a film about Vietnam veterans and their families.

The China Syndrome (1978) (para. 6): a film about an accident at a nuclear power plant.

California Suite (1978) (para. 7): a Neil Simon comedy starring Alan Alda.

The Seduction of Joe Tynan (1979) (para. 7): a political film written by and starring Alan Alda.

Howard Keel, Kathryn Grayson (para. 10): co-stars of *Showboat* and *Lovely to Look At*.

Bergman (para. 10): Ingmar Bergman, a Swedish director of art films; best known for *Persona* and *Fanny and Alexander*.

Hepburn and Tracy (para. 11): Katherine Hepburn and Spencer Tracy, co-stars of such films as *Adam's Rib* and *Woman of the Year*.

Grant (para. 11): Cary Grant, an actor best known for his roles in *To Catch a Thief* and *The Philadelphia Story*.

Gable (para. 11): Clark Gable, an actor who starred in *Gone With The Wind*, *It Happened One Night*, and *Boom Town*.

Claudette Colbert (para. 11): an actress who starred with Clark Gable in *It Happened One Night* and *Boom Town*.

James Stewart (para. 11): an actor best known for his roles in *It's a Wonderful Life*, *Mr. Smith Goes to Washington,* and *The Man Who Shot Liberty Valance.*

Stella Dallas (1937) (para. 11): a tear-jerker starring Barbara Stanwyck.

Intermezzo (1936) (para. 11): a serious drama starring Ingrid Bergman.

peccadillo (para. 11): a minor offense.

Thelma Ritter (para. 11): an actress who played Miss Pritchard in *Daddy Long Legs* and appeared in *Rear Window* and *All About Eve.*

Daddy Long Legs (1955) (para. 11): a musical comedy starring Fred Astaire and Leslie Caron.

Fred Clark (para. 11): an actor who played Griggs in *Daddy Long Legs* and starred in *Move Over Darling* (with Thelma Ritter), *White Heat*, and *How to Marry a Millionaire.*

each of these people? How were you different from each other? Do you think any of these people considered you a *type*? If so, what type of date were you?

■━━━━━━━━━━━━━━━━━━━━━━━━━━━━━━━━━━━■

$\mathbf{A}$aron takes me only to art films. That's what I call them, anyway: strange movies with vague poetic images I don't always understand, long dreamy movies about a distant Technicolor past, even longer black-and-white movies about the general meaninglessness of life. We do not go unless at least one reputable critic has found the cinematography superb. We went to *The Devil's Eye*, and Aaron turned to me in the middle and said, "My God, this is *funny.*" I do not think he was pleased.   1

When Aaron and I go to the movies, we drive our cars separately and meet at the box office. Inside the theater he sits tentatively in his seat, ready to move if he can't see well, poised to leave if the film is disappointing. He leans away from me, careful not to touch the bare flesh of his arm against the bare flesh of mine. Sometimes he leans so far I am afraid he may be touching the woman on his other side. If the movie is very good, he leans forward, too, peering between the heads of the couple in front of us. The light from the screen bounces off his glasses; he gleams with intensity, sitting there on the edge of his seat, watching the screen. Once I tapped him on the arm so I could whisper a comment in his ear. He jumped.   2

After *Belle de Jour* Aaron said he wanted to ask me if he could stay overnight. "But I can't," he shook his head mournfully before I had a chance to answer, "because I know I never sleep well in strange beds." Then he apologized for asking. "It's just that after a film like that," he said, "I feel the need to assert myself."   3

Pete takes me only to movies that he thinks have redeeming social value. He doesn't call them "films." They tend to be about poverty, war, injustice, political corruption, struggling unions in the 1930s, and the military-industrial complex. Pete doesn't like propaganda movies, though, and he doesn't like to be too depressed, either. We stayed away from *The Sorrow and the Pity;* it would be, he said, just too much. Besides, he assured me, things are never that hopeless. So most of the movies we see are made in Hollywood. Because they are always topical, these movies offer what Pete calls "food for thought." When we saw *Coming Home*, Pete's jaw set so firmly within the first half-hour that I knew we would end up at Poppin' Fresh Pies afterward.   4

When Pete and I go to the movies, we take turns driving so no 5
one owes anyone else anything. We leave the car far from the theater so we don't have to pay for a parking space. If it's raining or
snowing, Pete offers to let me off at the door, but I can tell he'll feel
better if I go with him while he finds a spot, so we share the walk
too. Inside the theater Pete will hold my hand when I get scared if
I ask him. He puts my hand firmly on his knee and covers it completely with his own hand. His knee never twitches. After a while,
when the scary part is past, he loosens his hand slightly and I
know that is a signal to take mine away. He sits companionably
close, letting his jacket just touch my sweater, but he does not infringe. He thinks I ought to know he is there if I need him.

One night, after *The China Syndrome*, I asked Pete if he 6
wouldn't like to stay for a second drink, even though it was past
midnight. He thought a while about that, considering my offer
from all possible angles, but finally he said no. Relationships
today, he said, have a tendency to move too quickly.

Sam likes movies that are entertaining. By that he means 7
movies that Will Jones in the *Minneapolis Tribune* loved and either
Time or *Newsweek* rather liked; also movies that do not have
sappy love stories, are not musicals, do not have subtitles, and
will not force him to think. He does not go to movies to think. He
liked *California Suite* and *The Seduction of Joe Tynan*, though the
plots, he said, could have been zippier. He saw it all coming too
far in advance, and that took the fun out. He doesn't like to know
what is going to happen. "I just want my brain to be tickled," he
says. It is very hard for me to pick out movies for Sam.

When Sam takes me to the movies, he pays for everything. He 8
thinks that's what a man ought to do. But I buy my own popcorn,
because he doesn't approve of it; the grease might smear his flannel slacks. Inside the theater, Sam makes himself comfortable. He
takes off his jacket, puts one arm around me, and all during the
movie he plays with my hand, stroking my palm, beating a small
tattoo on my wrist. Although he watches the movie intently, his
body operates on instinct. Once I inclined my head and kissed him
lightly just behind his ear. He beat a faster tattoo on my wrist,
quick and musical, but he didn't look away from the screen.

When Sam takes me home from the movies, he stands out- 9
side my door and kisses me long and hard. He would like to
come in, he says regretfully, but his steady girlfriend in Duluth
wouldn't like it. When the *Tribune* gives a movie four stars, he has
to save it to see with her. Otherwise her feelings might be hurt.

I go to some movies by myself. On rainy Sunday afternoons I 10

Have your students list the movies they
have seen in the last year. Then, have them
write freely about what these movie choices
say about them as people. Each student
should try to look at the list of movie
choices as an uninterested observer would
and draw some conclusions about himself
or herself based on these choices. You might
also discuss how these personal characteristics dictate the types of people each of these
students chooses to date.

Have the class break into two or more
groups composed of all males or all females. Then, have each group try to classify
the types of people that make up the opposite sex.

1. While the author is primarily classifying
the men she has dated, she is, at the same
time, classifying the movies she has seen according to the men they attract. In her experience, the art films, "strange movies with
vague poetic images I don't always understand" (para. 1), attract men who are cere-
bral, serious, and relatively shy; films with
"redeeming social value" interest men who
like to discuss "poverty, war, injustice, political corruption, struggling unions in the
1930s, and the military-industrial complex"
(para. 4); and the "entertaining" movies
that "do not have sappy love stories, are not
musicals, do not have subtitles, and will not
force him to think" (para. 7) draw men who
are companionable and friendly, though
sometimes self-absorbed.

2. The author finds the art films that Aaron
prefers difficult to understand (para. 1). The
socially redeeming films she sees with Pete
seem artificial, because "most of the movies
we see are made in Hollywood" (para. 4).
The entertaining movies of Sam's taste are
generally mindless, because he "does not go
to movies to think" (para. 7).

3. Based on the author's description of
Aaron's distant posture in the theater ("care-

ful not to touch the bare flesh of his arm against the bare flesh of mine" [para. 2]), and his dislike for "funny" movies (para. 1), Toth finds Aaron superior in intelligence but lacking social maturity and a sense of humor. Pete, who prefers films with "redeeming social value" (para. 4) but dislikes movies that make him "too depressed" (para. 4), is, in her opinion, a phony liberal fearful of making a commitment. Sam is totally egocentric, disapproving of buttered popcorn because "the grease might smear his flannel slacks" (para. 8) and refusing to take her to see one of the *Tribune*'s four-star movies because his girlfriend in Duluth might have her feelings hurt.

ANSWERS TO QUESTIONS:
ANALYZING MEANING (p. 276)

1. Toth's principal purpose in this essay is the classification of her dates according to the movies they select. She is able to discover characteristics about herself and others through this process.

2. When Toth is by herself, she enjoys slipping into "a revival house or a college auditorium for old Technicolor musicals" (para. 10) and films with happy endings where "the men and women always like each other" (para. 11). Her choices suggest that she is basically a congenial, accepting person who delights in romance.

3. People prefer a certain type of movie because it agrees in some way with their personality. A person who is very sophisticated is not likely to enjoy a movie that is simplistic; a person very interested in politics probably would not want to see a propaganda film that misrepresents issues; and a person who loves romance and the simpler pleasures in life is not likely to be mesmerized by a very impressionistic art film. Each movie, and the microcosmic world it presents, is bound to please some moviegoers very much and others not at all.

ANSWERS TO QUESTIONS:
DISCOVERING RHETORICAL
STRATEGIES (p. 277)

1. In this essay, Toth considers the many different types of movies she has seen in her lifetime and divides them into categories;

often sneak into a revival house or a college auditorium for old Technicolor musicals, *Kiss Me Kate, Seven Brides for Seven Brothers, Calamity Jane,* even, once, *The Sound of Music.* Wearing saggy jeans so I can prop my feet on the seat in front, I sit toward the rear where no one can see me. I eat large handfuls of popcorn with double butter. Once the movie starts, I feel completely at home. Howard Keel and I are old friends; I grin back at him on the screen. I know the sound tracks by heart. Sometimes when I get really carried away I hum along with Kathryn Grayson, remembering how I once thought I would fill out a formal like that. I am rather glad now I never did. Skirts whirl, feet tap, acrobatic young men perform impossible feats, and then the camera dissolves into a dream sequence I know I can comfortably follow. It is not, thank God, Bergman.

If I can't find an old musical, I settle for Hepburn and Tracy, vintage Grant or Gable, on adventurous days Claudette Colbert or James Stewart. Before I buy my ticket I make sure it will all end happily. If necessary, I ask the girl at the box office. I have never seen *Stella Dallas* or *Intermezzo.* Over the years I have developed other peccadilloes: I will, for example, see anything that is redeemed by Thelma Ritter. At the end of *Daddy Long Legs* I wait happily for the scene when Fred Clark, no longer angry, at last pours Thelma a convivial drink. They smile at each other, I smile at them, I feel they are smiling at me. In the movies I go to by myself, the men and women always like each other.

11

UNDERSTANDING DETAILS

1. What exactly is Toth classifying—movies, people, or both? Explain each segment of her classification system.
2. What does the author think of the types of movies each of her male companions likes? Explain her reaction to each type.
3. How does Toth feel about each of these men? On what specific information from the essay do you base your conclusions?

ANALYZING MEANING

1. What is Toth's overall purpose in this essay? To what extent does she accomplish this purpose?
2. What kind of movies does Toth prefer? Given this information, what kind of person do you think she is?
3. What do the types of movies people prefer say about their personalities? Explain your answer.

DISCOVERING RHETORICAL STRATEGIES

1. In what ways does Toth use division and classification in this essay? How does she give significance or value to her system of organization? What other rhetorical techniques does she use to accomplish her purpose?
2. How do the words "film" and "movie" differ in connotation? Ask friends for their opinions of these two words. When does Toth use each of these words? Why? Explain your answer in detail.
3. Through her style, Toth gives her readers the impression that she is detached from her subject matter (both movies and men) in the first nine paragraphs and more involved in her subject matter in the last two. Look closely at her sentence structure and word choice (especially her use of verbs, adjectives, and adverbs), and explain what characterizes her style in these two parts of her essay.

IDEAS FOR DISCUSSION/WRITING

Preparing to Write

Write freely about various types of dates you have had: What were their personal traits? What did they talk about? What did they like to read? What did they like to do? Do these dates fall into any logical categories?

Choosing a Topic

1. Your current love (husband, wife, boyfriend, girlfriend) has asked about your past. Classify for this person five or six dates you have had in the past. Remember that each date should fit into a category. Decide on a purpose and a point of view before you begin to write. (What changes would you make in this classification system if your parents asked the same question?)
2. Describe to a close friend one person you have dated by analyzing that date's behavior and preferences. Remember that analysis is based on the process of division: Divide this person's behavior and preferences into several logical parts; then study those parts so that you can better understand the whole person. Decide on a purpose and point of view before you begin to write.
3. If the movies we choose to see say something about our personalities, analyze yourself by writing an essay that classifies the different movies (or television shows) you have viewed in the last year. Discuss your choices as you proceed.

she then classifies the men she has dated according to their film preferences, using narrative and examples in addition to classification/division to accomplish her purpose. The significance or value of her system is clear when she focuses on her own preferences. Apparently, her movie dates seldom reflect her own needs: "In the mov-ies I go to by myself, the men and women always like each other" (para. 11).

2. The word "film" connotes a literary and educational experience, whereas "movie" suggests a commercial and entertaining enterprise. Interestingly enough, only Aaron's art films are referred to as "films."

3. A sense of detachment is created in the first nine pararaphs of the essay (three pararaphs for each date) through the use of short, choppy sentences; colorless verbs; and minimal adjectives or adverbs. This style changes abruptly in the last two pararaphs as the author's personal involvement in the movies she chooses is reflected in the longer, smoother sentences; lively verbs; and vivid imagery.

PREWRITING

The Preparing to Write questions ask students to consider the personal characteristics of their dates before they write an essay on a related topic. See pages 16–23 for suggestions on generating ideas in response to these questions.

ADDITIONAL DISCUSSION/WRITING TOPIC

Use division and/or classification to describe your family or friends. Classify your family or friends according to some scheme that you develop. Then explain that classification in an essay addressed to your English class.

REVISING STRATEGY

Choose one of your division/classification essays, and list all the categories in the order they occur. Review this list along with your paper, and decide which categories would be more effective in a different place in the essay. Then revise your paper, paying close attention to the flow of the topics from one point in the essay to another.

GARRISON KEILLOR
(1942–   )

■ ■ ■

School

Best known for his creation of the Peabody-Award–winning radio program "A Prairie Home Companion," Garrison Keillor, a native of Anoka, Minnesota, began his career as a radio announcer and producer during his student days at the University of Minnesota. His show, which was broadcast live for thirteen years before it left the air in 1987, featured an eclectic mix of traditional jazz and folk music supplemented by Keillor's rambling, nostalgic, and often hilarious anecdotes about the zany inhabitants of the fictitious small town of Lake Wobegon, Minnesota. Chief among its residents were Father Emil, the local priest who blessed small animals on the lawn of Our Lady of Perpetual Responsibility Church; Dorothy, the garrulous owner of the Chatterbox Cafe; and Dr. Nute, a retired dentist who coaxed trout toward his fishing lure by intoning, "Open wide . . . this may sting a bit." Keillor—a tall, soft-spoken man who often performed in a tuxedo, high-top sneakers, red socks, and red suspenders—even had a pseudo-sponsor for the show: Powdermilk Biscuits, "a whole-wheat treat that gives shy people the strength to do what has to be done." Thus far, Keillor's monologues have spawned a number of short stories published in *The New Yorker* and five books: *Happy to Be Here: Stories and Comic Pieces* (1982), *Lake Wobegon Days* (1985), *Leaving Home* (1987), *We Are Still Married* (1989), and *WLT: A Radio Romance* (1992). In 1989, he began a new radio variety show called "Garrison Keillor's The American Radio Company," which is currently carried on more than 230 public radio stations across America.

Preparing to Read

The following excerpt from *Lake Wobegon Days* chronicles two particularly memorable events from the narrator's childhood. As you prepare to read this account, think for a few moments about your own school days: What characterized the students who attended your grade school? Your high school? How well did you fit in? Who were your favorite teachers? Your least favorites? How did these teachers earn your respect or disdain? What events and attitudes made your

PREREADING

The purpose of this Preparing to Read material is to encourage students to think about various memories from their past school days. To help your students focus on these days before they respond to the questions here, have them close their eyes and picture a particular school they attended, including its buildings, classrooms, students, teachers, principal, and other details. Have your students place themselves in this scene and conjure up some of the specific memories they have of these school days. You might want to guide your students as a class through some of this visualization. See pages 3–6 for other ways to generate thoughts on these questions.

school days particularly memorable? How do you think your early schooling differed from that of other generations?

School gave us marks every nine weeks, three marks for each subject: work, effort, and conduct. Effort was the important one, according to my mother, because that mark showed if you had gumption and stick-to-itiveness, and effort was my poorest showing. I was high in conduct except when dared to do wrong by other boys, and then I was glad to show what I could do. Pee on the school during recess? You don't think I would? Open the library door, yell "Boogers!" and run? Well, I showed them. I was not the one who put a big gob on the classroom doorknob during lunch though, the one that Darla Ingqvist discovered by putting her hand on it. Of all the people you'd want to see touch a giant gob, Darla was No. 1. She yanked her hand back just as Brian said, "Snot on you!" but she already knew. She couldn't wipe if off on her dress because she wore such nice dresses so she burst into tears and tore off to the girls' lavatory. Mrs. Meiers blamed me because I laughed. Brian, who did it, said, "That was a mean thing to do, shame on you" and I sat down on the hall floor and laughed myself silly. It was so *right* for Darla to be the one who got a gob in her hand. She was a jumpy, chatty little girl who liked to bring money to school and show it to everyone. Once a five-dollar bill—we never had a five-dollar bill, so all the kids crowded around to see it. That was what she wanted. She made us stand in line. It was dumb. All those dumb girls took turns holding it and saying what they would do if they had one, and then Darla said she had $400 in her savings account. "Liar, liar, pants on fire," Brian said, but we all knew she probably did have $400. Later Brian said, "I wish I had her five dollars and she had a feather in her butt, and we'd both be tickled," which made me feel a little better, but putting the gob on the knob, knowing that Darla was monitor and had the privilege of opening the door, *that* was a stroke of genius. I almost didn't mind Mrs. Meiers making me sit in the cloakroom for an hour. I put white paste on slips of paper and put them in the pockets of Darla's coat, hoping she'd think it was more of the same. . . .

I liked Mrs. Meiers a lot, though. She was a plump lady with bags of fat on her arms that danced when she wrote on the board: We named them Hoppy and Bob. That gave her a good mark for

1 **BACKGROUND INFORMATION**

In this excerpt from *Lake Wobegon Days*, Garrison Keillor takes a fond look back at his school days and the escapades of the high-spirited boys who made his fourth-grade class exciting. Using a variety of rhetorical modes, Keillor focuses on the pranks he and his friends played on a number of deserving victims.

READABILITY LEVEL

6.3

RELATED READINGS

School

Have each student describe either in written or oral form that person's favorite teacher since the beginning of his or her school years. Included in the description should be the physical and emotional characteristics of the teacher, the grade and subject the teacher taught, and the reasons the student thinks that person was such a good teacher. If you want to build oral presentations into class, have your students read these brief statements to the class one by one. An equally profitable idea is having them exchange papers or oral stories and have the partner answer two questions about the statement: (1) What do you like about this statement, and (2) Where do you need more information? If you don't have time for either of these activities, you could collect the statements, make notations on them, and return them to the students.

COLLABORATIVE LEARNING:
SMALL GROUP ACTIVITY

Divide your students into groups of 4 or 5, and have them discuss and agree upon the characteristics they think are most important in college instructors. They should limit these characteristics to five and put them in list form. Then, collect the lists and record them for discussion on the chalkboard, on a transparency, or in a handout: Are some characteristics more important in some academic disciplines than others? Why are these characteristics important at the college level? Are they equally important in high school? In elementary school? See if you can get the class to agree on the five most important characteristics for college instructors in all disciplines.

ANSWERS TO QUESTIONS:
UNDERSTANDING DETAILS (p. 281)

1. In his classification of types of misconduct that brought him continual pleasure, the author lists doing pranks on a dare, giggling at the misbehaviors of others, tormenting the arrogant teacher's pet, and attempting to startle Miss Conway into a nervous breakdown. These activities distract from the academic atmosphere and in

friendliness in my book, whereas Miss Conway of fourth grade struck me as suspiciously thin. What was her problem? Nerves, I suppose. She bit her lips and squinted and snaked her skinny hand into her dress to shore up a strap, and she was easily startled by loud noises. Two or three times a day, Paul or Jim or Lance would let go with a book, dropping it flat for maximum whack, and yell, "Sorry, Miss Conway!" as the poor woman jerked like a fish on the line. It could be done by slamming a door or dropping the window, too, or even scraping a chair, and once a loud slam made *her* drop a stack of books, which gave us a double jerk. It worked better if we were very quiet before the noise. Often, the class would be so quiet, our little heads bent over our work, that she would look up and congratulate us on our excellent behavior, and when she looked back down at her book, *wham!* and she did the best jerk we had ever seen. There were five classes of spasms: The Jerk, The Jump, The High Jump, The Pants Jump, and The Loopdeloop, and we knew when she was prime for the big one. It was after we had put her through a hard morning workout, including several good jumps, and a noisy lunch period, and she had lectured us in her thin weepy voice, then we knew she was all wound up for the Loopdeloop. All it required was an extra effort: *throwing* a dictionary flat at the floor or dropping the globe, which sounded like a car crash.

We thought about possibly driving Miss Conway to a nervous breakdown, an event we were curious about because our mothers spoke of it often. "You're driving me to a nervous breakdown!" they'd yell, but then, to prevent one, they'd grab us and shake us silly. Miss Conway seemed a better candidate. We speculated about what a breakdown might include—some good jumps for sure, maybe a couple hundred, and talking gibberish with spit running down her chin.

Miss Conway's nervous breakdown was prevented by Mrs. Meiers, who got wind of it from one of the girls—Darla, I think. Mrs. Meiers sat us boys down after lunch period and said that if she heard any more loud noises from Room 4, she would keep us after school for a half hour. "Why not the girls?" Lance asked. "Because I know that you boys can accept responsibility." Mrs. Meiers said. And that was the end of the jumps, except for one accidental jump when a leg gave way under the table that held Mr. Bugs the rabbit in his big cage. Miss Conway screamed and left the room, Mrs. Meiers stalked in, and we boys sat in Room 3 from 3:00 to 3:45 with our hands folded on our desks, and remembered that last Loopdeloop, how satisfying it was, and also how sad it was, being the last. Miss Conway had made some great jumps.

UNDERSTANDING DETAILS

1. What different types of conduct does Keillor discuss? How many types of spasms does he cite?
2. How did Miss Conway avoid a nervous breakdown?
3. What caused students to dislike Darla Ingqvist?

ANALYZING MEANING

1. What is Keillor's overall purpose in this excerpt? To what extent does he accomplish this purpose?
2. In your opinion, what were the advantages of the grading system in his school? The disadvantages?
3. Why did the boys delight so in aggravating Miss Conway but respond so well to Mrs. Meiers? What are the main differences between these two teachers?

DISCOVERING RHETORICAL STRATEGIES

1. Where does the author use division in this excerpt? Where does he use example? Cite at least one instance of each. What other rhetorical modes does Keillor use in this essay?
2. Who do you think is Keillor's intended audience? Describe it in detail.
3. Keillor occasionally uses figures of speech to make his prose more vivid and interesting. One example of a metaphor is, "She was a plump lady with bags of fat on her arms that danced when she wrote on the board" (paragraph 2). Find at least one other example of figurative language in this excerpt. What effect does it create?

IDEAS FOR DISCUSSION/WRITING

Preparing to Write

Write freely about the people you remember most clearly from your days in gradeschool and highschool: Who played important roles in your life then? How did these people affect your life? What did you have in common with your classmates? What traits characterized your closest friends? Your entire class? Your generation of students? How were you typical of this generation? In what important ways were you different?

terfere with the educational process. Miss Conway was known for five types of spasms. The boys in the class preferred watching "The Loopdeloop" (para. 2).

2. Miss Conway was saved from a nervous breakdown by Mrs. Meiers, who "sat us boys down after lunch period and said that if she heard any more loud noises from Room 4, she would keep us after school for a half hour" (para. 4). Unlike Miss Con-way, Mrs. Meiers was not intimidated by the boys.

3. Keillor presents Darla Ingqvist as a "chatty little girl who liked to bring money to school" (para. 1). She is manipulative and enjoys showing off things she has that others do not have.

ANSWERS TO QUESTIONS:
ANALYZING MEANING (p. 281)

1. Keillor's principal purpose in this excerpt is to characterize Miss Conway, which he accomplishes by classifying her physical reactions to various practical jokes the students play on her.

2. The advantages of the three-part system were many, including the opportunity to make good grades in the areas of effort and conduct even if one's academic achievements were weak. Conversely, the opportunities to make poor grades were equally numerous.

3. Miss Conway's students delighted in her jumps and spasms because she was not only nervous and fearful, but "suspiciously thin. . . . She bit her lips and squinted and snaked her skinny hand into her dress to shore up a strap, and she was easily startled by loud noises" (para. 2). Mrs. Meiers is presented as a more mature, responsible person who is strong and independent, whereas Miss Conway is meek and jumpy.

ANSWERS TO QUESTIONS:
DISCOVERING RHETORICAL
STRATEGIES (p. 281)

1. Division is used in the separation of Miss Conway's spasms into five classes: "The Jerk, The Jump, The High Jump, The Pants Jump, and the Loopdeloop" (para. 2). An example of one such spasm is illustrated by "The poor woman jerked like a fish on the line" (para. 2). In addition to division/classification, Keillor uses description, in his depiction of two very different teachers; narration, in the various stories from his youth; and example, in his lists of many different types of misconduct.

2. With a clear, unsophisticated style and with language that reflects the spirited innocence of the young narrator, Keillor aims this excerpt at the general population—anyone who might enjoy a nostalgic look into the simplicity and humor of the past.

3. The simile "The poor woman jerked like a fish on the line" (para. 2) creates a picture of a scrawny, timorous spinster abrupt-ly jolted by the crash of a dropped book.

PREWRITING

In preparation for the writing assignments, the Preparing to Write questions ask students to characterize themselves in relation to their classmates before they write an essay on a related topic. See pages 16–23 for suggestions on generating ideas in response to these questions.

ADDITIONAL DISCUSSION/WRITING TOPIC

Using division and/or classification, describe your writing course. Divide your course content into categories according to some scheme that you develop. Then, explain your division in an essay addressed to another English class.

REVISING STRATEGY

Clear definitions of your categories can make division/classification essays engaging and accessible to your intended audience. In one of your division/classification essays, underline all the categories that you define (along with their definitions). With your intended audience in mind, notice which categories need fuller explanations. Then revise your paper, making your categories consistently clear and accessible to your intended audience.

Choosing a Topic

1. Your high school graduating class has decided to put together a special publication commemorating your senior year. You have been asked to write a profile of one person of your choice for this publication. By dividing this person's behavior or personality into revealing categories, characterize him or her for your classmates. Make your essay as vivid as possible.

2. Pretend that your college newspaper is running a special issue distinguishing between different generations of students. In a coherent essay written for the readers of this newspaper, classify the people of your generation in some logical, interesting fashion. Remember that classification is a rhetorical movement from "many" to "one." Group the members of your generation by some meaningful guidelines or general characteristics that you establish. Be sure to decide on a purpose and a point of view before you begin to write.

3. You have had many different types of teachers over the years. Discuss one type of teacher by dividing into logical categories the classroom behavior of that type. Discuss each part of your division, giving examples as frequently as possible. Decide on a purpose and point of view before you begin to write.

QUOTATION ON THINKING
"Words are the copies of our ideas."

Hugh Blair

JUDITH VIORST
(1931–   )

■ ■ ■

The Truth About Lying

A poet, journalist, writer of children's books, and contributing editor of *Redbook* magazine, Judith Viorst reached the top of the *New York Times* bestseller list with *Necessary Losses* (1986), a detailed examination of "the loves, illusions, dependencies, and impossible expectations that all of us have to give up in order to grow." She earned her B.A. at Rutgers University in 1952 and began writing poetry. These early efforts, she claims, were "terrible poems about dead dogs, mostly . . . the meaning of life, death, pain, lust, and suicide." Her first complete book of poetry, however, entitled *The Village Square* (1965), was quite successful, as were such subsequent volumes as *People and Other Aggravations* (1971), *How Did I Get to Be Forty and Other Atrocities* (1976), *Love and Guilt and the Meaning of Life* (1984), and *Forever Fifty and Other Negotiations* (1989). Additional publications include *The Washington, D.C. Underground Gourmet* (1970), *Yes, Married: A Saga of Love and Complaint* (1972), *Love and Guilt and the Meaning of Life, Etc.* (1979), and several books for children. The author lives in Washington with her husband, Milton Viorst (a syndicated political columnist), and their three sons.

Preparing to Read

"The Truth about Lying," originally published in the March 1981 issue of *Redbook* magazine, classifies and describes the different categories of lies we all experience at some point in our lives. As you prepare to read this essay, take a few moments to consider various lies you have told: Under what conditions are you tempted to lie? When have you actually lied? Why did you do so? Can you generalize about the types of lies you habitually tell? Are you irritated when people lie to you? Why or why not? In what circumstances might lying be acceptable? Why?

PREREADING

The purpose of this Preparing to Read material is to encourage students to consider various lies they have experienced in their lives. To help your students focus their attention on these lies before responding to the questions here, have them list several falsehoods they have told or heard and then consider the effect of these lies upon their lives. See pages 3–6 for other ways to generate thoughts on these questions.

I've been wanting to write on a subject that intrigues and   1
challenges me: the subject of lying. I've found it very difficult to

BACKGROUND INFORMATION

In this essay, Judith Viorst divides and classifies four different types of lies that may play a part in our dealings with other people: social, peace-keeping, protective, and trust-keeping. All these lies carry consequences, claims the author, that affect our honesty, integrity, and social interaction with others.

READABILITY LEVEL

8.2

RELATED READINGS

Paradoxes and Irony

Jessica Mitford, "Behind the Formaldehyde Curtain"   226
Ellen Goodman, "Putting In a Good Word for Guilt"   444

do. Everyone I've talked to has a quite intense and personal but often rather intolerant point of view about what we can—and can never *never*—tell lies about. I've finally reached the conclusion that I can't present any ultimate conclusions, for too many people would promptly disagree. Instead, I'd like to present a series of moral puzzles, all concerned with lying. I'll tell you what I think about them. Do you agree?

Social Lies

Most of the people I've talked with say that they find social lying acceptable and necessary. They think it's the civilized way for folks to behave. Without these little white lies, they say, our relationships would be short and brutish and nasty. It's arrogant, they say, to insist on being so incorruptible and so brave that you cause other people unnecessary embarrassment or pain by compulsively assailing them with your honesty. I basically agree. What about you? 2

Will you say to people, when it simply isn't true, "I like your new hairdo," "You're looking much better," "It's so nice to see you," "I had a wonderful time"? 3

Will you praise hideous presents and homely kids? 4

Will you decline invitations with "We're busy that night—so sorry we can't come," when the truth is you'd rather stay home than dine with the So-and-sos? 5

And even though, as I do, you may prefer the polite evasion of "You really cooked up a storm" instead of "The soup"—which tastes like warmed-over coffee—"is wonderful," will you, if you must, proclaim it wonderful? 6

There's one man I know who absolutely refuses to tell social lies. "I can't play that game," he says; "I'm simply not made that way." And his answer to the argument that saying nice things to someone doesn't cost anything is, "Yes, it does—it destroys your credibility." Now, he won't, unsolicited, offer his views on the painting you just bought, but you don't ask his frank opinion unless you want *frank*, and his silence at those moments when the rest of us liars are muttering, "Isn't it lovely?" is, for the most part, eloquent enough. My friend does not indulge in what he calls "flattery, false praise and mellifluous comments." When others tell fibs he will not go along. He says that social lying is lying, that little white lies are still lies. And he feels that telling lies is morally wrong. What about you? 7

Peace-Keeping Lies

Many people tell peace-keeping lies; lies designed to avoid irritation or argument; lies designed to shelter the liar from possible blame or pain; lies (or so it is rationalized) designed to keep trouble at bay without hurting anyone.

I tell these lies at times, and yet I always feel they're wrong. I understand why we tell them, but still they feel wrong. And whenever I lie so that someone won't disapprove of me or think less of me or holler at me, I feel I'm a bit of a coward, I feel I'm dodging responsibility, I feel . . . guilty. What about you?

Do you, when you're late for a date because you overslept, say that you're late because you got caught in a traffic jam?

Do you, when you forget to call a friend, say that you called several times but the line was busy?

Do you, when you didn't remember that it was your father's birthday, say that his present must be delayed in the mail?

And when you're planning a weekend in New York City and you're not in the mood to visit your mother, who lives there, do you conceal—with a lie, if you must—the fact that you'll be in New York? Or do you have the courage—or is it the cruelty?—to say, "I'll be in New York, but sorry—I don't plan on seeing you"?

(Dave and his wife Elaine have two quite different points of view on this very subject. He calls her a coward. She says she's being wise. He says she must assert her right to visit New York sometimes and not see her mother. To which she always patiently replies: "Why should we have useless fights? My mother's too old to change. We get along much better when I lie to her.")

Finally, do you keep the peace by telling your husband lies on the subject of money? Do you reduce what you really paid for your shoes? And in general do you find yourself ready, willing and able to lie to him when you make absurd mistakes or lose or break things?

"I used to have a romantic idea that part of intimacy was confessing every dumb thing that you did to your husband. But after a couple of years of that," says Laura, "have I changed my mind!"

And having changed her mind, she finds herself telling peace-keeping lies. And yes, I tell them too. What about you?

Protective Lies

Protective lies are lies folks tell—often quite serious lies—because they're convinced that the truth would be too damaging. They lie because they feel there are certain human values that su-

COLLABORATIVE LEARNING: CLASS ACTIVITY

Viorst's essay is about lies. Although lying usually has negative connotations, it can also bring positive results. Initiate a class discussion about the various types of lies that might benefit rather than hurt those involved, and see how many categories the class can come up with. List the categories on the chalkboard or on a transparency. Then have your students organize the categories in some way (e.g., most to least important or least to most painful).

Have the students divide themselves into four groups, one for each subdivision in Viorst's essay. For this particular exercise, let the students choose which group they join. The groups can have varying numbers of students. Then, have them interview friends and classmates and other people on campus to discover whether or not Viorst's statements in their group's particular section of the essay are accurate. If you don't have time to allow the students to interview people outside of class, they could limit their interviews to classmates only. Have someone from each group summarize the findings for the class.

persede the wrong of having lied. They lie, not for personal gain, but because they believe it's for the good of the person they're lying to. They lie to those they love, to those who trust them most of all, on the grounds that breaking this trust is justified.

They may lie to their children on money or marital matters. 19

They may lie to the dying about the state of their health. 20

They may lie about adultery, and not—or so they insist—to 21
save their own hide, but to save the heart and the pride of the men they are married to.

They may lie to their closest friend because the truth about 22
her talents or son or psyche would be—or so they insist—utterly devastating.

I sometimes tell such lies, but I'm aware that it's quite pre- 23
sumptuous to claim I know what's best for others to know. That's called playing God. That's called manipulation and control. And we never can be sure, once we start to juggle lies, just where they'll land, exactly where they'll roll.

And furthermore, we may find ourselves lying in order to 24
back up the lies that are backing up the lie we initially told.

And furthermore—let's be honest—if conditions were re- 25
versed, we certainly wouldn't want anyone lying to us.

Yet, having said all that, I still believe that there are times 26
when protective lies must nonetheless be told. What about you?

If your Dad had a very bad heart and you had to tell him 27
some bad family news, which would you choose: to tell him the truth or lie?

If your former husband failed to send his monthly child-sup- 28
port check and in other ways behaved like a total rat, would you allow your children—who believed he was simply wonderful—to continue to believe that he was wonderful?

If your dearly beloved brother selected a wife whom you 29
deeply disliked, would you reveal your feelings or would you fake it?

And if you were asked, after making love, "And how was 30
that for you?" would you reply, if it wasn't too good, "Not too good"?

Now, some would call a sex lie unimportant, little more than 31
social lying, a simple act of courtesy that makes all human intercourse run smoothly. And some would say all sex lies are bad news and unacceptably protective. Because, says Ruth, "a man with an ego that fragile doesn't need your lies—he needs a psychiatrist." Still others feel that sex lies are indeed protective lies, more serious than simple social lying, and yet at times they tell

them on the grounds that when it comes to matters sexual, everybody's ego is somewhat fragile.

"If most of the time things go well in sex," says Sue, "I think 32 you're allowed to dissemble when they don't. I can't believe it's good to say, 'Last night was four stars, darling, but tonight's performance rates only a half.'"

I'm inclined to agree with Sue. What about you? 33

Trust-Keeping Lies

Another group of lies are trust-keeping lies, lies that involve 34 triangulation, with *A* (that's you) telling lies to *B* on behalf of *C* (whose trust you'd promised to keep). Most people concede that once you've agreed not to betray a friend's confidence, you can't betray it, even if you must lie. But I've talked with people who don't want you telling them anything that they might be called on to lie about.

"I don't tell lies for myself," says Fran, "and I don't want to 35 have to tell them for other people." Which means, she agrees, that if her best friend is having an affair, she absolutely doesn't want to know about it.

"Are you saying," her best friend asks, "that if I went off with 36 a lover and I asked you to tell my husband I'd been with you, that you wouldn't lie for me, that you'd betray me?"

Fran is very pained but very adamant. "I wouldn't want to 37 betray you, so . . . don't ask me."

Fran's best friend is shocked. What about you? 38

Do you believe you can have close friends if you're not pre- 39 pared to receive their deepest secrets?

Do you believe you must always lie for your friends? 40

Do you believe, if your friend tells a secret that turns out to be 41 quite immoral or illegal, that once you've promised to keep it, you must keep it?

And what if your friend were your boss—if you were per- 42 haps one of the President's men—would you betray or lie for him over, say, Watergate?

As you can see, these issues get terribly sticky. 43

It's my belief that once we've promised to keep a trust, we 44 must tell lies to keep it. I also believe that we can't tell Watergate lies. And if these two statements strike you as quite contradictory, you're right—they're quite contradictory. But for now they're the best I can do. What about you?

Some say that truth will out and thus you might as well tell 45

1. Social lies, which are the least damaging, involve small fibs that save us from being unkind to our friends; these might include telling an acquaintance that her hideous new hat is "charming" or politely declining a dinner invitation from boorish neighbors. Peace-keeping lies help us avoid arguments by sidestepping the truth when we have forgotten to return a phone call or we are late for an appointment. Protective lies shield our friends and relatives when telling them the truth would be painful or embarrassing; examples might include lying to a sick parent about her chances for survival or complimenting a spouse after an evening of mediocre sex. We tell trust-keeping lies when we have promised to keep a friend's secret and must lie in order to do so.

2. Viorst believes protective lies are the most serious because they often distort the truth severely and may have unexpected repercussions. By "serious," the author means that their potential for destruction is generally underestimated by the person telling the lie.

3. Although lying often makes Viorst feel guilty, the advantages sometimes outweigh the disadvantages. The real peril is that although other people may accept the lies she tells, the author does not.

**ANSWERS TO QUESTIONS:
ANALYZING MEANING (p. 289)**

1. According to Viorst, the temptation to lie presents us with moral dilemmas or "puzzles" (para. 1). The solutions to these puzzles depend upon the exact circumstances involved and the potential benefits that can accrue from telling the lie.

2. People's moral, ethical, and religious backgrounds will affect their degree of tolerance for dealing with lies.

3. Responses to this question will vary.

**ANSWERS TO QUESTIONS:
DISCOVERING RHETORICAL
STRATEGIES (p. 289)**

1. Viorst's main categories and supporting details are listed below.

the truth. Some say you can't regain the trust that lies lose. Some say that even though the truth may never be revealed, our lies pervert and damage our relationships. Some say . . . well, here's what some of them have to say.

"I'm a coward," says Grace, "about telling close people important, difficult truths. I find that I'm unable to carry it off. And so if something is bothering me, it keeps building up inside till I end up just not seeing them any more." 46

"I lie to my husband on sexual things, but I'm furious," says Joyce, "that he's too insensitive to know I'm lying." 47

"I suffer most from the misconception that children can't take the truth," says Emily. "But I'm starting to see that what's harder and more damaging for them is being told lies, is *not* being told the truth." 48

"I'm afraid," says Joan, "that we often wind up feeling a bit of contempt for the people we lie to." 49

And then there are those who have no talent for lying. 50

"Over the years, I tried to lie," a friend of mine explained, "but I always got found out and I always got punished. I guess I gave myself away because I feel guilty about any kind of lying. It looks as if I'm stuck with telling the truth." 51

For those of us, however, who are good at telling lies, for those of us who lie and don't get caught, the question of whether or not to lie can be a hard and serious moral problem. I liked the remark of a friend of mine who said, "I'm willing to lie. But just as a last resort—the truth's always better." 52

"Because," he explained, "though others may completely accept the lie I'm telling, I don't." 53

I tend to feel that way too. 54

What about you? 55

UNDERSTANDING DETAILS

1. Viorst discusses four types of lies in this essay. Explain each in your own words.
2. What types of lies are most serious? What does the author mean by "serious"?
3. According to Viorst, what is the relationship between lying and her self-image?

ANALYZING MEANING

1. In what ways is lying a moral problem?
2. Why do people respond in so many different ways to the issue of lying?
3. How do you feel about lying? Does your opinion vary according to the type of lie you tell? Why? Explain your answer in detail.

DISCOVERING RHETORICAL STRATEGIES

1. In this essay, Viorst works with both division and classification as she arranges lies into several distinct categories. Write down the main subdivisions of her classification system; then list under each category the examples she cites. How has the author organized these categories? Do all her examples support the appropriate classification? How does Viorst give significance or value to this system of classification?
2. What other rhetorical modes besides division/classification does Viorst use to make her point in the essay? Give specific examples to support your answer.
3. Notice that the author repeats the question "What about you?" several times. What effect does this repetition have on your response to the essay?

IDEAS FOR DISCUSSION/WRITING

Preparing to Write

Write freely about various lies you have told in the past: When did you lie? When did you consider lying, but told the truth? In what types of situations do you most often resort to lying? Why do you lie in these circumstances? How does lying make you feel? How does telling the truth make you feel? Do you have a general philosophy about lying that you try to follow? If so, what is it?

Choosing a Topic

1. At some time in our lives, we all tell or receive lies as Viorst defines them. Choose a particularly memorable lie (either one you told or received), and classify all your feelings connected with the experience. What did you learn from the situation?
2. You have decided that your future roommate/spouse deserves an honest profile of your personality before you begin living together. Analyze for him or her some fundamental truths about your character

Social Lies:

—offering trite and insincere praise, such as "I like your new hairdo" and "It's so nice to see you"
—admiring hideous presents
—complimenting homely kids
—declining unwanted dinner invitations
—commending someone's uninspired cooking

Peace-Keeping Lies:

—lying about being late
—lying about forgetting to call a friend
—lying about why your father's birthday present is late
—concealing the fact that you are visiting your mother's city
—lying about money

Protective Lies:

—lying to your children about money and marital matters
—lying to sick people about the state of their health
—lying about adultery
—lying to friends
—lying to your sick father to protect him from bad family news
—lying to your children about the behavior of their father
—lying to your brother about his choice of a wife
—lying about sexual satisfaction

Trust-Keeping Lies:

—lying to protect a confidence a friend has shared with you

All these examples are placed into and support the proper category. The author organizes the first three categories from least to most serious; the fourth includes lies that are compounded by the inclusion of two or more people. Viorst gives significance to her system of classification by questioning the connection between lies and morality.

2. Viorst defines each of her categories; she uses examples in her specific illustrations of the different types of lies; she narrates conversations with her friends to support her main points; and she speculates about the causes and potential effects of various lies.

3. The repetition of "What about you?" lends continuity to the essay and elicits a tacit response from the reader. Beyond this point, responses will vary.

PREWRITING

In preparation for the writing assignments, the Preparing to Write questions ask students to consider, before writing an essay on a related topic, specific lies they have encountered in their lives and their responses to those lies. See pages 16–23 for suggestions on generating ideas in response to these questions.

ADDITIONAL DISCUSSION/WRITING TOPIC

Sometimes lies can be beneficial. Use division and/or classification to explain to your classmates one lie that had positive results. Classify all your preparations for and reactions to that lie. What did you learn from the experience?

REVISING STRATEGY

A good division/classification essay conveys the significance or value of its classification system at some prominent point in the essay. Locate this portion in one of your division/classification papers: Is it clear? Is it placed in an effective location in reference to the purpose you are trying to accomplish and the audience you are attempting to reach? Identify the weakest parts of this statement. Then revise your paper, concentrating on communicating the significance of your division or classification system as effectively as possible.

by classifying your reactions to the information in one of the categories in Viorst's essay.

3. Being in school presents a number of potential opportunities for lying. Answers to such questions as "Why is your homework late?," "Why can't you go out this weekend?," and "Why did you miss class yesterday?" can get people *into* or *out of* all sorts of trouble. For a friend of yours still in high school, write an essay offering advice on handling situations such as these. Devise a useful classification system for these school-related dilemmas; then explain what your experiences have taught you in each case about lying.

CHAPTER 6

COMPARISON/ CONTRAST

■ ■ ■

Discovering Similarities and Differences

Using Comparison/Contrast

The ability to make comparisons is such a natural and necessary part of our everyday lives that we often do so without conscious effort. When we were children, we compared our toys with those of our friends, we contrasted our height and physical development to other children's, and we constantly evaluated our relative happiness in comparison with that evidenced by our parents and childhood companions. As we grew older, we habitually compared our dates, teachers, parents, friends, cars, and physical attributes. In college, we learn about anthropology by writing essays on the similarities and differences between two African tribes, about political science by contrasting the Republican and Democratic platforms, about business by comparing annual production rates, and about literature by comparing Shakespeare with Marlowe or Browning with Tennyson. Comparing and contrasting various elements in our lives helps us make decisions, such as which course to take or which house to buy, and it justifies preferences that we already hold, such as liking one city more than another or loving one person more than the next. In these ways and in many others, the skillful use of comparison and contrast is clearly essential to our social and professional lives.

INTRODUCTORY NOTES

The ability to make comparisons and contrasts helps us form most of our opinions—what food we like best, what clothes we want to wear, how our hair should look, whom we want to befriend, and what we want to do in our spare time. A comparison/contrast essay should not be a tedious recitation of similarities and differences but should have a clear purpose and be aimed at a specific audience.

This chapter opens with Bruce Catton's "Grant and Lee: A Study in Contrasts," a classic comparison of Generals Grant and Lee at the close of the Civil War; the pre-reading, prewriting, and writing questions ask the students to compare and contrast various other historical figures and events. In "A Child Is Born," Germaine Greer compares and contrasts the role of children born to families in the East and the role of those born to families in the West; the questions and writing assignments encourage students to think and write about the role of the family in Western society. "Japanese and American Workers: Two Casts of Mind" by

William Ouchi examines the work ethics in Japan and in America; the exercises accompanying this selection ask students to consider individual (American) and collective (Japanese) approaches to various activities. In "Growing Up in the U.S.: A First Generation Look," Elena Asturias presents her view of the similarities and differences between two cultures; the assignments before and after this essay focus on student opinions concerning cultural diversity. Joyce Carol Oates' "On Boxing" draws an analogy between a boxing match and a short story; the essay's exercises require students to consider various sports and forms of exercise.

Defining Comparison/Contrast

Both comparison and contrast are ways of understanding one subject by putting it next to another. Comparing involves discovering likenesses or similarities, whereas contrasting is based on finding differences. Like division and classification, both comparison and contrast are generally considered part of the same process, because we usually have no reason for comparing unless some contrast is also involved. Each technique implies the existence of the other. For this reason, the word "compare" is often used to mean both techniques.

Comparison and contrast are most profitably applied to two items that have something in common, such as cats and dogs or cars and motorcycles. A discussion of cats and motorcycles, for example, would probably not be very rewarding or stimulating, because they do not have much in common. If more than two items are compared in an essay, they are still most profitably discussed in pairs: for instance, motorcycles and cars, cars and bicycles, or bicycles and motorcycles.

An analogy is an extended, sustained comparison. Often used to explain unfamiliar, abstract, or complicated thoughts, this rhetorical technique can add energy and vividness to a wide variety of college-level writing. The process of analogy differs slightly from comparison/contrast in three important ways: Comparison/contrast begins with subjects from the same class and then places equal weight on both of them. In addition, it addresses both the similarities and the differences of these subjects. Analogy, conversely, seldom explores subjects from the same class and focuses principally on one familiar subject in an attempt to explain another, more complex one. Furthermore, it deals only with similarities, not with contrasts. A comparison/contrast essay, for example, might study two veterans' ways of coping with the trauma of the Gulf War by pointing out the differences between their methods as well as the similarities. An analogy essay might use the familiar notion of a fireworks display to reveal the chilling horror of the lonely hours after dark during this war: "Nights in the Persian Gulf were similar to a loud, unending fireworks display. We had no idea when the next blast was coming, how loud it would be, or how close. We cringed in terror after dark, hoping the next surprise would not be our own death." In this example, rather than simply hearing about an event, we participate in it through this highly refined form of comparison.

The following student paragraph compares and contrasts married and single life. As you read it, notice how the author compares similar social states and, in the process, justifies her current lifestyle.

Recently I saw a bumper sticker that read, "It used to be wine, women, and song, and now it's beer, the old lady, and TV." Much truth may be found in this comparison of single and married lifestyles. When my husband and I used to date, for example, we'd go out for dinner and drinks and then maybe see a play or concert. Our discussions were intelligent, often ranging over global politics, science, literature, and other lofty topics. He would open doors for me, buy me flowers, and make sure I was comfortable and happy. Now, three years later, after marriage and a child, the baby bottle has replaced the wine bottle, the smell of diapers wipes out the scent of roses, and our nights on the town are infrequent, cherished events. But that's okay. A little bit of the excitement and mystery may be gone, but these intangible qualities have given way to a sturdy, dependable trust in each other and a quiet confidence about our future together.

Reading and Writing Comparison/Contrast Essays

Many established guidelines regulate the development of a comparison/contrast essay and should be taken into account from both the reading and writing perspectives. All good comparative studies serve a specific purpose. They attempt either to examine their subjects separately or to demonstrate the superiority of one over the other. In evaluating two different types of cars, for example, a writer might point out the amazing gas mileage of one model and the smooth handling qualities of the other or the superiority of one car's gas mileage over the other. Whatever the intent, comparison/contrast essays need to be clear and logical with a precise purpose.

HOW TO READ A COMPARISON/CONTRAST ESSAY

Preparing to Read. As you begin reading this chapter, pull together as much preliminary material as possible for each essay so you can focus your attention and have the benefit of prior knowledge before you start to read. In particular, you are trying to discover what is being compared or contrasted and why. From the title of his essay, can you tell what Bruce Catton is comparing in "Grant and Lee: A Study in Contrasts"? Or what does William

---

TEACHING COMPARISON/CONTRAST: ONE INSTRUCTOR'S COMMENTS

When I assign comparison/contrast essays, I am reminded that this organizing pattern truly mimics the thinking skills used every time we make a decision. To let the students practice the form and organizational patterns, I assign some journal entries requiring decisions: which of two CD players or televisions should they buy, which TV show from the night's lineup should they watch, which pet at the pet store should they bring home, etc. Such practice will allow the students to master the organizing principles inherent in comparison/contrast essays before struggling with more thoughtful, analytical topics.

When my students are working on both the reading and writing of comparison/contrast essays, I provide some extra practice with sentence combining. The decisions the students need to make when choosing whether to coordinate or subordinate information within a revised sentence mirror the thinking process students use when comparing and contrasting elements within their essays. Working with similes and metaphors at this time is also a good idea. For example, the differences and similarities evident in Shakespeare's "My Mistress' Eyes Are Nothing Like the Sun" involve the same distinctions students should be making in their own writing. The stark imagery of haiku also demonstrates the power of comparison/contrast since it is so frequently centered on innate similarities or harsh juxtapositions.

The organizing principles students practice when writing comparison/contrast essays can provide a strong bridge from expository essays to analysis, synthesis, and research. After the class has studied the form of comparison/contrast writing, I assign some readings from the Interdisciplinary Table of Contents. (The essays listed under the headings "Art and Media," Aging," and "Women's Studies" work well for this activity.) The students first summarize each essay they read. Group presentations or in-class debates can check student mastery of this first step. Then, using a comparison/contrast format, I have my students discuss the various ideas found in the assigned readings, focusing on thesis, antithesis, and synthesis. Such a pseudo-research paper models the thinking, reading, and writing skills inherent in a larger research project.

Patricia Ross
Moorpark College
Moorpark, California

Ouchi's title ("Japanese and American Workers: Two Casts of Mind") suggest to you? From glancing at the essay itself and reading the synopsis in the Rhetorical Table of Contents, what does Joyce Carol Oates' essay try to accomplish?

Also, before you begin to read these essays, try to discover information about the author and about the conditions under which each essay was written. Why is Ouchi qualified to write about Japanese and American workers? Does he reveal his background in his essay? What is Elena Asturias' stand on cultural assimilation? To what extent do you expect her opinion on this issue to color her comparison of the American and Hispanic cultures?

Finally, just before you begin to read, answer the Preparing to Read questions and then make some free associations with the general topic of each essay: For example, what do you think are some of the similarities and differences in childbirth customs between Third World countries and the Western world (Germaine Greer)? What is your general view on cultural assimilation (Asturias)?

Reading. As you read each comparison/contrast essay for the first time, be sure to record your own feelings and opinions. Some of the issues presented in this chapter are highly controversial. You will often have strong reactions to them, which you should try to write down as soon as possible. In addition, you might want to comment on the relationship between the preliminary essay material, the author's stance in the essay, and the content of the essay itself. For example, what motivated Asturias to write "Growing Up in the U.S."? Who was her primary audience? What is Oates' tone in "On Boxing," and how does it further her purpose? Answers to questions such as these will provide you with a context for your first reading of these essays and will assist you in preparing to analyze the essays in more depth on your second reading. At this point in the chapter, you should make certain you understand each author's thesis and then take a close look at his or her principal method of organization: Is the essay arranged (1) point by point, (2) subject by subject, (3) as a combination of these two, or (4) as separate discussions of similarities and differences between two subjects? (See the chart on page 297 for an illustration of these options.) Last, preview the questions that follow the essay before you read it again.

Rereading. When you read these essays a second time, you should look at the comparison or contrast much more closely than you have up until now. First, look in detail at the writer's method of organization (see chart on page 297). How effective is it in advancing the writer's thesis? Next, you should consider whether or not each essay is fully developed and balanced: Does Catton compare similar items? Does Greer discuss the same qualities for her subjects? Does Ouchi deal with all aspects of the comparison between Japanese and American workers? Is Asturias' treatment of her two subjects well balanced? And does Oates give her audience enough specific details to clarify the extent of her comparison? Do all the writers in this chapter use well-chosen transitions so you can move smoothly from one point to the next? Also, what other rhetorical modes support each comparison/contrast in this chapter? Finally, the answers to the questions after each selection will let you evaluate your understanding of the essay and help you analyze its contents in preparation for the discussion/writing topics that follow.

For a more thorough inventory of the reading process, you should turn to pages 15–16 in the Introduction.

HOW TO WRITE A COMPARISON/CONTRAST ESSAY

Preparing to Write. As you consider various topics for a comparison/contrast essay, you should answer the Preparing to Write questions that precede the assignments and then use the prewriting techniques explained in the Introduction to generate even more ideas on these topics. As you focus your attention on a particular topic, keep the following suggestions in mind:

1. Always compare/contrast items in the same category (e.g., compare two professors, but not a professor and a swimming pool).
2. Have a specific purpose or reason for writing your essay.
3. Discuss the same qualities for each subject (if you evaluate teaching techniques for one professor, do so for the other professor as well).
4. Use as many pertinent details as possible to expand your comparison/contrast and accomplish your stated purpose.
5. Deal with all aspects of the comparison that are relevant to the purpose.
6. Balance the treatment of the different subjects of your comparison (i.e., don't spend more time on one than on another).
7. Determine your audience's background and knowledge so you will know how much of your comparison should be explained in detail and how much can be skimmed over.

TEACHING COMPARISON/CONTRAST: ONE INSTRUCTOR'S COMMENTS

To teach comparison/contrast, I break the ice by walking into the classroom and asking the students some personal questions: I saw you eating the veggie entree in the cafeteria at lunch; what did you have against the meat loaf? Why did you choose to come to college here? Having agreed that seeing how things are alike and different is fundamental to the way we perceive the world, students acknowledge the importance of writing in this mode.

In comparison/contrast essays, I find it more interesting when a paper shows one thing superior to another, instead of the mechanical listing of likenesses and differences. This structure, in particular, reveals a student's view of the world.

Perhaps more than any other assignments, the comparison/contrast essay provides the instructor with rhetorical situations for which he or she can show the efficacy of an outline, the utility of balanced sentences, and the power of metaphorical and analogous language. It's a short step from formally describing items that have a logical basis for comparison to imaginatively finding relationships between things that are essentially different: the job of most figurative language. I've had success in requiring students to include attempts at figures of speech in their comparison/contrast papers. I provide examples: "My mistress' eyes are nothing like the sun"; "Shall I compare thee to a summer's day?" Football games are filled with "bombs" and "blitzes." Basketball players "dunk" balls during "Show Time." Of course, neither my students nor I want to be compared to Shakespeare or even to sports commentators, but we can enjoy looking for inventive ways to illuminate the shades of difference in the world around us.

Anthony McCrann
Peru State College
Peru, Nebraska

Next, in preparation for a comparison/contrast project, you might list all the elements of both subjects that you want to compare. This list can then help give your essay structure as well as substance. At this stage in the writing process, the task may seem similar to pure description, but a discussion of two subjects in relation to one another rapidly changes the assignment from description to comparison.

Writing.   The introduction of a comparison/contrast essay should (1) clearly identify your subjects, (2) explain the basis of your comparison/contrast, and (3) state your purpose and the overall limits of your particular study. Identifying your subject is, of course, a necessary and important task in any essay. Similarly, justifying the elements you will be comparing and contrasting creates reader interest and gives your audience some specifics to look for in the essay. Finally, your statement of purpose or thesis (for example, to prove that one professor is superior to another) should include the boundaries of your discussion. You cannot cover all the reasons for your preference in one short essay, so you must limit your consideration to three or four basic categories (perhaps teaching techniques, clarity of assignments given, classroom attitude, and grading standards). The introduction is the place to make all these limits known.

The body of your paper can be organized in one of four ways: (1) a point-by-point or alternating comparison, (2) a subject-by-subject or divided comparison, (3) a combination of these two methods, or (4) a division between the similarities and differences. (See the chart on page 297.)

The point-by-point comparison evaluates both subjects in terms of each category. If the issue, for example, is which of two cars to buy, you might discuss both models' gasoline mileage first, then their horsepower, next their ease in handling, and finally their standard equipment. Following the second method of organization, subject by subject, you would discuss the gasoline mileage, horsepower, ease in handling, and standard equipment of car A first, then follow the same format for car B. The third option would allow you to introduce, say, the interior design of each car point by point (or car by car) and then explain the mechanical features of the automobiles (MPG, horsepower, gear ratio, and braking system) subject by subject. To use the last method of organization, you might discuss the similarities between the two models first and the differences second (or vice versa). If the cars you are comparing have similar MPG ratings but completely different horsepower, steering systems, and optional equipment, you could discuss the gasoline mileage first and then emphasize the differences by mentioning them later in the essay. If, instead, you are trying to emphasize the fact that the MPG of these models remains consistent despite their differences, then reverse the order of your essay.

Methods of Organization

Point by Point	**Subject by Subject**
MPG, car A MPG, car B horsepower, car A horsepower, car B handling, car A handling, car B equipment, car A equipment, car B	MPG, car A horsepower, car A handling, car A equipment, car A MPG, car B horsepower, car B handling, car B equipment, car B

Combination	**Similarities/Differences**

interior, car A
interior, car B
 	
———
 	
MPG, car A
horsepower, car A
 	
MPG, car B
horsepower, car B
	similarities:
	   MPG, cars A & B
	
	differences:
	   horsepower, cars A & B
	   handling, cars A & B
	   equipment, cars A & B

When confronted with the task of choosing a method of organization for a comparison/contrast essay, you need to find the pattern that best suits your purpose. If you want single items to stand out in a discussion, for instance, the best choice will be the point-by-point system; it is especially appropriate for long essays but has a tendency to turn into an exercise in listing if you don't pay careful attention to your transitions. If, however, the subjects themselves (rather than the itemized points) are the most interesting feature of your essay, you should use the subject-by-subject comparison; this system is particularly good for short essays in which the readers can retain what was said about one subject while they read about a second subject. Through this second system of organization, both subjects become unified wholes, which is generally a positive feature of an essay unless the theme becomes awkwardly divided into two separate parts. You must also remember, if you choose this second method of organization, that the second (or last) subject is in the most emphatic position, because that is what your readers will have seen most recently. The final two options for organizing a comparison/contrast essay give you some built-in flexibility so you can create emphasis and attempt to manipulate reader opinion simply by the structure of your essay.

Using logical transitions in your comparison/contrast essays will establish clear relationships between the items in your comparisons and will also move your readers smoothly from one topic to the next. If you wish to indicate comparisons, use such words as "like," "as," "also," "in like manner," "similarly," and "in addition"; to signal contrasts, try "but," "in contrast to," "unlike," "whereas," and "on the one hand/on the other hand."

The conclusion of a comparison/contrast essay summarizes the main points and states the deductions drawn from those points. As you choose your method of organization, remember not to get locked into a formulaic approach to your subjects, which will adversely affect the readability of your essay. To avoid making your reader feel like a spectator at a verbal ping-pong match, be straightforward, honest, and patient as you discover and recount the details of your comparison.

Rewriting.   When you review the draft of your comparison/contrast essay, you need once again to make sure that you communicate your purpose as effectively as possible to your intended audience. Three guidelines previously mentioned should help you accomplish this goal: Do you identify your subjects clearly? Do you explain the basis of your comparison/contrast? Does your thesis clearly state the purpose and overall limits of your particular study?

You will also need to pay close attention to the development of your essay: Are you attempting to compare/contrast items from the same general category? Do you discuss the same qualities for each subject? Do you use as many pertinent details as possible to expand your essay? Do you deal with all aspects of the topic that are relevant to your purpose? Do you balance the treatment of the different subjects of your essay? Did you organize your topic as effectively as possible?

For further information on writing and revising your comparison/contrast essays, consult the checklists on pages 27–28 of the Introduction.

Student Essay: Comparison/Contrast at Work

The following student essay compares the advantages and disadvantages of macaroni and cheese versus tacos in the life of a harried college freshman. As you read it, notice how the writer states his intention in the first paragraph and then expands his discussion with appropriate details to produce a balanced essay. Also, try to determine what effect he creates by using two methods of organization: first subject by subject, then point by point.

Dormitory Chef

Background   To this day, I will not eat either macaroni and cheese or tacos. No, it's not because of any allergy; it's because during my freshman year at college, I prepared one or the other of these scrumptious dishes more times than I care to remember. However, my choice of which culinary delight to **Thesis** cook on any given night was not as simple a decision as one might imagine. **statement**

Paragraph on Subject A: Macaroni and cheese   Macaroni and cheese has numerous advantages for the dormitory chef. First of all, it is inexpensive. No matter how poor one may be, there's probably enough change under the couch cushion to buy a box at the market. All that starch for only 89¢. What a bargain! Second, it can be prepared in just one pan. This is especially important given the meager resources of the average dorm kitchen. **Point 1 (Price)** **Point 2 (Preparation)**

Point 3 (Odor) Third, and perhaps most important, macaroni and cheese is odorless. By odorless, I mean that no one else can smell it. It is a well-known fact that dorm residents hate to cook and that they love nothing better than to wander dejectedly around the kitchen with big, sad eyes after someone else has been cooking. But with macaroni and cheese, no enticing aromas are going to find their way into the nose of any would-be mooch.

Paragraph   Tacos, on the other hand, are a different matter **Transition**

on Subject altogether. For the dorm cook, <u>the most significant</u>   Point 1
B: Tacos <u>difference is obviously the price.</u> To enjoy tacos for   (Price)
dinner, the adventurous dorm gourmet must pur-
chase no fewer than five ingredients from the market: corn tortillas, beef, lettuce, tomatoes, and
cheese. Needless to say, this is a major expenditure.   Point 2
Second, the chef must adroitly shuffle these ingre-   (Prepara-
<u>dients back and forth among his very limited sup-</u>   tion)
<u>ply of pans and bowls.</u> <u>And finally, tacos smell</u>   Point 3
<u>great.</u> That wouldn't be a problem if the tacos   (Odor)
didn't also smell great to about twenty of the cook's
newest—if not closest—friends, who appear with
those same pathetic, starving eyes mentioned earlier. When this happens, the cook will be lucky to
get more than two of his own creations.

Transition   <u>Tacos</u>, <u>then</u>, wouldn't stand much of a chance   Subject B
if they didn't outdo <u>macaroni and cheese</u> in one   Subject A
area—taste. Taste is almost—but not quite—an op-
Paragraph tional requirement in the opinion of a frugal dormi-
on Point tory hash-slinger. Taste is just important enough so
4: Taste that tacos are occasionally prepared, despite their
disadvantages.

Transition   <u>But</u> <u>tacos</u> have other advantages besides their   Subject B
taste. With their enticing, colorful ingredients, they
Paragraph even look good. The only thing that can be said
on Point about the color of <u>macaroni and cheese</u> is that it's a   Subject A
5: Color color not found in nature.

Transition   <u>On the other hand,</u> <u>macaroni and cheese</u> is   Subject A
quick. It can be prepared in about ten minutes,
Paragraph while <u>tacos</u> take more than twice as long. And there   Subject B
on Point 6: are occasions—such as final exam week—when
Time time is a scarce and precious resource.

Transition   <u>As you can see,</u> quite a bit of thinking went
into my choice of food in my younger years. These
two dishes essentially got me through my freshman
year and indirectly taught me how to make impor-
tant decisions (like what to eat). <u>But I still feel a cer-</u>   Concluding
<u>tain revulsion when I hear their names today.</u>   statement

Student Writer's Comments

I compare and contrast so many times during ordinary
thoughts that I took this rhetorical technique for granted; I overlooked it. Just be sure that there are enough parallel points in the
subjects you want to compare, and then apply the same logic you
use every day. The most difficult part of writing this essay was finding two appropriate topics to compare. Ideally, they should be

united by a similarity. For example, macaroni and cheese and tacos are two very different kinds of food. Proving this fact is easy and doesn't provide for an interesting essay. But their similar property of being popular dorm foods unites the two despite their differences. This similarity supplies the basic structure for the entire essay. It is the common theme against which I compared these two different topics.

Some Final Thoughts on Comparison/Contrast

The articles in this section demonstrate various methods of organization as well as a number of distinct stylistic approaches to writing a comparison/contrast essay. As you read these selections, pay particular attention to the clear, well-focused introductions; the different logical methods of organization; and the smooth transitions between sentences and paragraphs.

BRUCE CATTON
(1899–1978)

■ ■ ■

Grant and Lee: A Study in Contrasts

Bruce Catton was a much-loved and respected historian of the Civil War whose many books and articles have brought an "eyewitness" vividness to this crucial period in American development. Believing that history "ought to be a good yarn," Catton saw himself as more of a reporter than a historian, stripping away the romantic glamor of war to reveal with vigor and clarity the reality of this important historical era. A native of Benzonia, Michigan, the author was fascinated during his childhood with stories told by the many Civil War veterans who returned to his small town. Catton attended Oberlin College, worked for a time as a newspaper reporter, and then turned his attention principally to researching and writing about the Civil War. His most popular and influential book was *A Stillness at Appomattox* (1953), the third part of his *Army of the Potomac* trilogy, which won both the Pulitzer Prize and the National Book Award for history in 1954. Among his many other books are *This Hallowed Ground* (1956), *The Coming Fury* (1961), *Terrible Swift Sword* (1963), *Grant Takes Command* (1969), and *Michigan: A Bicentennial History* (1976). For the last twenty-four years of his life, Catton was also editor of *American Heritage* magazine.

Preparing to Read

The following essay was taken from *The American Story* (1956), a collection of essays by distinguished historians; it examines the similarities and differences between Generals Grant and Lee at the conclusion of the Civil War. As you prepare to read this article, take a few moments to consider heroes and heroines in your life: What special qualities turn people into heroic figures? Why do you think some heroes/heroines are admired more than others? What historical events bring forth heroes/heroines? How does American society act in general toward these people? Why do most of us seem to need heroic figures in our lives?

PREREADING

The purpose of this Preparing to Read material is to encourage students to think about heroes and heroines in their lives. To help them focus their attention before they respond to the questions here, have them individually list the names of people they consider their heroes and heroines. After each student generates such a list, you might conduct a brief discussion of the qualities heroic figures must possess and the reasons only certain people become our heroes and heroines. See pages 3–6 for other ways to generate thoughts on these questions.

<big>W</big>hen Ulysses S. Grant and Robert E. Lee met in the parlor of a modest house at Appomattox Court House, Virginia, on April 9, 1865, to work out the terms for the surrender of Lee's Army of Northern Virginia, a great chapter in American life came to a close, and a great new chapter began.

These men were bringing the Civil War to its virtual finish. To be sure, other armies had yet to surrender, and for a few days the fugitive Confederate government would struggle desperately and vainly, trying to find some way to go on living now that its chief support was gone. But in effect it was all over when Grant and Lee signed the papers. And the little room where they wrote out the terms was the scene of one of the poignant, dramatic contrasts in American history.

They were two strong men, these oddly different generals, and they represented the strengths of two conflicting currents that, through them, had come into final collision.

Back of Robert E. Lee was the notion that the old aristocratic concept might somehow survive and be dominant in American life.

Lee was tidewater Virginia, and in his background were family, culture, and tradition . . . the age of chivalry transplanted to a New World which was making its own legends and its own myths. He embodied a way of life that had come down through the age of knighthood and the English country squire. America was a land that was beginning all over again, dedicated to nothing much more complicated than the rather hazy belief that all men had equal rights and should have an equal chance in the world. In such a land Lee stood for the feeling that it was somehow of advantage to human society to have a pronounced inequality in the social structure. There should be a leisure class, backed by ownership of land; in turn, society itself should be keyed to the land as the chief source of wealth and influence. It would bring forth (according to this ideal) a class of men with a strong sense of obligation to the community; men who lived not to gain advantage for themselves, but to meet the solemn obligations which had been laid on them by the very fact that they were privileged. From them the country would get its leadership; to them it could look for the higher values—of thought, of conduct, of personal deportment—to give it strength and virtue.

Lee embodied the noblest elements of this aristocratic ideal. Through him, the landed nobility justified itself. For four years, the Southern states had fought a desperate war to uphold the

BACKGROUND INFORMATION

In "Grant and Lee: A Study in Contrasts," historian Bruce Catton takes a personal look at the two most important military figures of the Civil War, Ulysses S. Grant and Robert E. Lee. Although a substantial portion of the essay is devoted to the differences between the two men, Catton finds great significance in their similarities, particularly in their ability to accept the inevitable and "help the two sections to become one nation again" (para. 16).

READABILITY LEVEL

11.2

DEFINITIONS

tidewater Virginia (para. 5): an area of the South known for the social prominence of its inhabitants.

obeisance (para. 7): a bow made out of respect or submission.

1

2

3

4

5

6

ideals for which Lee stood. In the end, it almost seemed as if the Confederacy fought for Lee; as if he himself was the Confederacy . . . the best thing that the way of life for which the Confederacy stood could ever have to offer. He had passed into legend before Appomattox. Thousands of tired, underfed, poorly clothed Confederate soldiers, long since past the simple enthusiasm of the early days of the struggle, somehow considered Lee the symbol of everything for which they had been willing to die. But they could not quite put this feeling into words. If the Lost Cause, sanctified by so much heroism and so many deaths, had a living justification, its justification was General Lee.

Grant, the son of a tanner on the Western frontier, was everything Lee was not. He had come up the hard way and embodied nothing in particular except the eternal toughness and sinewy fiber of the men who grew up beyond the mountains. He was one of a body of men who owed reverence and obeisance to no one, who were self-reliant to a fault, who cared hardly anything for the past but who had a sharp eye for the future. 7

These frontier men were the precise opposites of the tidewater aristocrats. Back of them, in the great surge that had taken people over the Alleghenies and into the opening Western country, there was a deep, implicit dissatisfaction with a past that had settled into grooves. They stood for democracy, not from any reasoned conclusion about the proper ordering of human society, but simply because they had grown up in the middle of democracy and knew how it worked. Their society might have privileges, but they would be privileges each man had won for himself. Forms and patterns meant nothing. No man was born to anything, except perhaps to a chance to show how far he could rise. Life was competition. 8

Yet along with this feeling had come a deep sense of belonging to a national community. The Westerner who developed a farm, opened a shop, or set up in business as a trader could hope to prosper only as his own community prospered—and his community ran from the Atlantic to the Pacific and from Canada down to Mexico. If the land was settled, with towns and highways and accessible markets, he could better himself. He saw his fate in terms of the nation's own destiny. As its horizons expanded, so did his. He had, in other words, an acute dollars-and-cents stake in the continued growth and development of his country. 9

And that, perhaps, is where the contrast between Grant and Lee becomes most striking. The Virginia aristocrat, inevitably, 10 saw himself in relation to his own region. He lived in a static society which could endure almost anything except change. Instinctively, his first loyalty would go to the locality in which that society existed. He would fight to the limit of endurance to defend it, because in defending it he was defending everything that gave his own life its deepest meaning.

The Westerner, on the other hand, would fight with an equal tenacity for the broader concept of society. He fought so because everything he lived by was tied to growth, expansion, and a constantly widening horizon. What he lived by would survive or fall with the nation itself. He could not possibly stand by unmoved in the face of an attempt to destroy the Union. He would combat it with everything he had, because he could only see it as an effort to cut the ground out from under his feet.

So Grant and Lee were in complete contrast, representing two diametrically opposed elements in American life. Grant was the modern man emerging; beyond him, ready to come on the stage, was the great age of steel and machinery, of crowded cities and a restless burgeoning vitality. Lee might have ridden down from the old age of chivalry, lance in hand, silken banner fluttering over his head. Each man was the perfect champion of his cause, drawing both his strengths and his weaknesses from the people he led.

Yet it was not all contrast, after all. Different as they were—in background, in personality, in underlying aspiration—these two great soldiers had much in common. Under everything else, they were marvelous fighters. Furthermore, their fighting qualities were really very much alike.

Each man had, to begin with, the great virtue of utter tenacity and fidelity. Grant fought his way down the Mississippi Valley in spite of acute personal discouragement and profound military handicaps. Lee hung on in the trenches at Petersburg after hope itself had died. In each man there was an indomitable quality . . . the born fighter's refusal to give up as long as he can still remain on his feet and lift his two fists.

Daring and resourcefulness they had, too; the ability to think faster and move faster than the enemy. These were the qualities which gave Lee the dazzling campaigns of Second Manassas and Chancellorsville and won Vicksburg for Grant.

Lastly, and perhaps greatest of all, there was the ability, at the end, to turn quickly from war to peace once the fighting was over. Out of the way these two men behaved at Appomattox came the possibility of a peace of reconciliation. It was a possibility not

ANSWERS TO QUESTIONS: UNDERSTANDING DETAILS (p. 306)

1. For Catton, Lee symbolizes "the old aristocratic concept" (para. 4), based on "family, culture, and tradition" (para. 5). In contrast, Grant stands for democracy, community, competition, and "a deep, implicit dissatisfaction with a past that had settled into grooves" (para. 8).

2. In order to achieve his purpose, Catton contrasts the views of the two men, their backgrounds, and their loyalties. He then compares their fighting ability, their "utter tenacity and fidelity" (para. 14), their "daring and resourcefulness" (para. 15), and "the ability, at the end, to turn quickly from war to peace once the fighting was over" (para. 16).

3. More than their courage and military skill, Catton finds most commendable the dignity and grace with which they entered the meeting at Appomattox Court House for the surrender of Lee's armies. Through the respect that these two generals, beloved by their troops, accorded each other at this emotional meeting came "the possibility of a peace of reconciliation" (para. 16).

ANSWERS TO QUESTIONS: ANALYZING MEANING (p. 306)

1. Catton's principal purpose in this essay is to examine the differences and similarities between Generals Robert E. Lee and Ulysses S. Grant, the leaders of the opposing armies in the Civil War. According to the historian, these men "represented the strengths of two conflicting currents that, through them, had come into final collision" (para. 3). Although Catton devotes a substantial portion of the essay to their differences, he also illustrates the nobility that enabled these leaders to put their differences aside at Appomattox and work together toward the reunification of America.

2. Lee was representative of the aristocracy of the past, "a way of life that had come down through the age of knighthood and the English country squire" (para. 5). In contrast, Grant embodied a new form of government, democracy, and a society that "might have privileges, but they would be privileges each man had won for himself" (para. 8).

3. Catton explains that if Lee and Grant had let the bitterness between them continue and had not encouraged both sides to reunite, the United States would never have been the same. In many ways, we can still see in American life today Grant's expansionism, his belief in equality, and his rugged individualism and Lee's resistance to change, his struggle to maintain a leisure class, and his natural nobility.

ANSWERS TO QUESTIONS:
DISCOVERING RHETORICAL
STRATEGIES (p. 306)

1. In the organization of his essay, Catton focuses first on differences, then on similarities to achieve his purpose, devoting nine pararaphs to the contrasts between the two generals, then closing with four pararaphs discussing their similarities. This imbalance reflects the extent of the differences in the personality, background, and philosophy of the two men, yet Catton stresses the significance of the similarities that do exist when he attributes to these men the eventual healing of an injured nation.

2. Catton moves easily from one section to another with smooth transitions. In pararaph 7, he transfers his focus from Lee to Grant with the words, "Grant . . . was everything Lee was not." In pararaph 11, Catton moves from Lee to Grant with "The Westerner, on the other hand." Likewise, Catton shifts easily from contrast to comparison with the phrase, "Yet it was not all contrast, after all" (para. 13). This skillful transition between clearly defined segments gives the essay a smooth flow and a sense of unity.

3. Catton opens the essay with an introductory pararaph describing the meeting at Appomattox as a day when "a great chapter in American life came to a close, and a great new chapter began" (para. 1). In the last sentence, he repeats this sentiment, writing that "their encounter at Appomattox was one of the great moments of American history" (para. 16). This echoing technique not only contributes to the balance and the completeness of the article, but it emphasizes the positive aspects of the nation and of the two generals who had the most influence on this important period in American history.

wholly realized, in the years to come, but which did, in the end, help the two sections to become one nation again . . . after a war whose bitterness might have seemed to make such a reunion wholly impossible. No part of either man's life became him more than the part he played in this brief meeting in the McLean house at Appomattox. Their behavior there put all succeeding generations of Americans in their debt. Two great Americans, Grant and Lee—very different, yet under everything very much alike. Their encounter at Appomattox was one of the great moments of American history.

UNDERSTANDING DETAILS

1. What two conflicting views of American life does the author believe these two generals represent?
2. What special qualities of Grant and Lee does Catton contrast to achieve his purpose? What qualities does he compare?
3. What does Catton imply about the behavior of these two generals at Appomattox Court House? According to this essay, why was the encounter of Grant and Lee at Appomattox "one of the great moments of American history" (paragraph 16)?

ANALYZING MEANING

1. What is Catton's purpose in this essay? What truths, according to the author, needed to be made clear about these two great Civil War generals? Why did Catton study similarities as well as differences in these two men?
2. In what ways were Lee and Grant emblems of the past and future, respectively?
3. About the actions of these men at Appomattox, Catton says, "Their behavior there put all succeeding generations of Americans in their debt" (paragraph 16). What does he mean by this statement? What influences of these two men can we still see in our culture today?

DISCOVERING RHETORICAL STRATEGIES

1. Which of the four main methods of organizing a comparison/contrast essay does Catton use? How many paragraphs does the author spend on each part of his comparison? Why do you think he spends this amount of time on each?
2. What transitional words or phrases does the author use to move from

one part of this essay to the next? Give at least three specific examples. Do these devices hold the essay together effectively? Explain your answer.

3. In what ways does the last paragraph of this essay echo the first paragraph? Why is this echoing technique an effective way to end the essay?

IDEAS FOR DISCUSSION/WRITING

Preparing to Write

Write freely about heroes and heroines in American society: Name some public figures you respect. Why do you admire them? What qualifies someone as a heroic figure in your opinion? What do most of the heroes and heroines you admire have in common? How are they different? How are history and heroic figures related in your mind?

Choosing a Topic

1. In an essay written for your classmates, compare and/or contrast two famous people in history. As Catton did, try to explain what forces in society these figures represent. Decide on a clear focus and point of view before you begin.
2. Choose two people who have had a significant influence on your life. Then, compare and/or contrast the ways they affected you.
3. America has had many new beginnings throughout its history. The time at the end of the Civil War, discussed in this essay, was one of them. Explain to your classmates another new beginning for America. What were the details of this new start? Who were the heroes and heroines? Where, when, how, and why did it take place?

PREWRITING

In preparation for the writing assignments, the Preparing to Write questions ask students to consider characteristics people must maintain to become heroes. See pages 16–23 for suggestions on generating ideas in response to these questions.

ADDITIONAL DISCUSSION/WRITING TOPIC

Choose two events that have had a significant impact on your life. Then, write an essay for your classmates comparing and/or contrasting either the events or the ways these events affected you.

REVISING STRATEGY

A clear sense of purpose is an important key to any essay. In one of your comparison/contrast essays, write out your purpose, and then underline all parts of your essay that help you achieve that goal. Notice where your intention could be clearer or better focused. Then revise your paper so that it communicates a clear, consistent purpose to your intended audience.

GERMAINE GREER
(1939–   )

■ ■ ■

A Child Is Born

Germaine Greer is one of the world's best-known and most controversial feminist authors. Australian by birth, she earned degrees at the universities of Melbourne and Sydney, then won a scholarship to Cambridge University in England, where she received a doctorate in Shakespeare. Early jobs as a teacher and television actress gave way to a career as a writer and political activist. Her first book, *The Female Eunuch* (1970), is a sharply written indictment of women for allowing themselves to be passively stereotyped, subjugated, and symbolically castrated by society. *The Obstacle Race* (1979) followed, a survey of the trials and triumphs of women painters throughout history. *Sex and Destiny: The Politics of Human Fertility* (1984) is a well-researched, thorough investigation into the global politics of human reproduction. More recent publications include *Shakespeare* (1985), *The Madwoman's Underclothes* (1986), *Kissing the Rod: An Anthology of Seventeenth-Century Women's Verse* (1988), and *Daddy, We Hardly Knew You* (1989). Through her books, numerous articles, and television appearances, Greer continues to project a spirited, stimulating, and intelligent defense of women's rights. She lectures occasionally at the University of Warwick near her home in Coventry, England, and describes herself as an "anarchist," an "atheist," and a "supergroupie" with great affection for jazz and rock music.

Preparing to Read

In the following essay, excerpted from *Sex and Destiny*, Greer compares the role of children in traditional, agricultural societies with that of children in Western, industrialized countries. As you prepare to read this essay, take a few moments to think about your own family structure and that of other people you know: What has happened to the Western family unit over the last fifty to a hundred years? Does it play a more important or less important role in our society? What are the advantages of our society's concept of the "family"? The disadvantages? How do you think our family life differs from that of Eastern cultures? What are the advantages and disadvantages of these two approaches to the family unit? What do you think will be the future role of the family in the Western world?

In many societies women still go forth from their mother's house at marriage to live with a mother-in-law and the wives of their husband's brothers. It is a truism of anthropology that such women do not become members of their new family until they have borne a child. If we consider that in such societies the marriage was quite likely to have been arranged, it is understandable that the bride, too, longs for the child who will stand in the same intimate relationship to her as she with her own mother. The Western interpretation of such mores is that they are backward, cruel and wrong; it is assumed that the sexual relations between the spouses are perfunctory and exploitative and that all mothers-in-law are unjust and vindictive. At a conference to mark International Women's Day at the U.N. Secretariat in Vienna in 1981, two members of an organization called Amnesty for Women provided the assembled women with a description of typical Muslim marriage which was no more than a coarse ethnocentric libel. The one Muslim woman on the panel, who may have been virtually the only Muslim present, looked up in astonishment to hear the domestic life of her people described in terms of the utmost squalor, but, less willing to divide the consensus than were the speakers, she decided to hold her tongue. One of the greatest difficulties in the way of feminists who are not chauvinistic and want to learn from women who still live within a female society is the tendency of those women to withdraw into silent opposition when participating in international forums conducted in languages which they cannot speak with fluency; women officials of the Sudanese government told me that they had given up going to international conferences, even though the trips were a tremendous treat, because they were tired of being told about their own lives instead of being consulted.

Thus in the West we would regard it as outrageous that a woman could lose her own name and become known as the mother of her firstborn, once she has borne it—although of course most of us do not protest against the sinking of the woman's lineage under her husband's name at marriage. In many traditional societies the relationship between mother and child is more important than the relationship between husband and wife: In some, indeed, the child's relationship with the rest of his family is as important as or even more important than either. Among the fierce Rajputs, a bridegroom leaving to collect his bride "sucks his mother's breast to signify that the highest duty of a Rajput is to uphold the dignity of his mother's milk."

The woman who satisfies the longings of her peers by pro-

BACKGROUND INFORMATION

"A Child Is Born" by Germaine Greer takes a rare look at the private lives of women in traditional Muslim societies, particularly at how these women fulfill the role of mother. Ironically, this feminist author does not bewail the poverty and oppression of the women of these underdeveloped countries but suggests that "a successful matriarch might well pity Western feminists for having been duped into futile competition with men in exchange for the companionship and love of children and other women" (para. 12).

READABILITY LEVEL

10.4

DEFINITIONS

chauvinistic (para. 1): unreasonably
devoted to a particular group, place, or
viewpoint.
Rajput (para. 2): a tribe of northern India.
Sylheti (para. 3): a person from the Sylhet
district of the Surma Valley in East
Pakistan.
turmeric (para. 3): an East Indian perennial
herb of the ginger family.
pan (para. 3): Hindi. A betel leaf.
Amrit Wilson (1941–) (para. 4): a British
activist and writer; author of *Finding a
Voice: Asian Women in Britain* (1978).
impedimenta (para. 7): encumbrances,
baggage.
perambulator (para. 7): stroller.
cacophony (para. 8): harsh sounds.
ethos (para. 8): the distinguishing
character, moral nature, or guiding beliefs
of a person or group.
fissioning (para. 9): splitting, breaking up
into parts.
panegyric (para. 12): a laudatory discourse
or elaborate eulogy.
exiguous (para. 12): scanty; inadequate.

ducing the child they are all anxious to see finds her achievement
celebrated in ways that dramatize her success. Among the few
first-person accounts of how this works in practice is this one
from a young Sylheti woman:

> If a girl is lucky, and her parents are alive, she goes to her mother's
> house for the last few months of her pregnancy and about the first
> three months of the baby's life. There she gets a lot of love and care.
> She is asked, "What would you like to eat? What do you fancy?" All
> the time she is looked after. The whole matter of pregnancy is one of
> celebration. When the baby is born it is an occasion of joy for the
> whole family. The naming ceremony is lovely. It is held when the
> baby is seven days old. A new dress is bought for it and a new sari
> for the mother. There is feasting and singing until late at night. The
> women and girls gather and sing songs. Garlands of tumeric and
> garlic are worn to ward off evil spirits. That's when the name is cho-
> sen. . . . The ceremony is held for the birth of a boy or a girl. Of
> course it is considered better to have a boy, but the birth of a girl is
> celebrated with the same joy by the women in the family. We sit to-
> gether eating *pan* and singing. Some of us might be young unmar-
> ried girls, others aged ladies of forty or fifty. There are so many
> jokes, so much laughter. People look so funny eating *pan* and
> singing. The men don't take much part. They may come and have a
> look at the baby, but the singing, the gathering together at night—it
> is all women. The songs are simple songs which are rarely written
> down. They are about the lives of women in Bengal.

Among the rewards of pregnancy in this case, as in many oth-   4
ers, is that the woman gets to go home to visit her mother and sisters; the nostalgic tone of the description, which is clearly tinged
with rose, may be the product of the contrast that this young
woman finds in England. Another of the Asian women who
found a voice in Amrit Wilson's book gives a similarly rosy picture of rearing a child in Bangladesh:

> In Bangladesh children under the age of five or six are looked after
> by the whole family. All the children of the joint family are looked
> after together. They are taken to the pond for a bath perhaps by one
> daughter-in-law, and she bathes them all. Then they all come in and
> sit down to eat. Perhaps the youngest daughter-in-law has cooked
> the meal. Another woman feeds them. As for playing, the children
> play out of doors with natural objects. Here people say that Asian
> children don't play with toys. In Bangladesh they don't need toys.
> They make their own simple things. . . . In the afternoon they love to
> hear Rupthoka [fairy tales]. Maybe there is a favorite aunt; she tells
> them these stories. But at night when they get sleepy they always go

to their mother and sleep in her embrace. But other women do help a lot; in fact they have such strong relationships with the child that it is not uncommon for them to be called Big Mother or Small Mother.

The system does not always work as well as it does in this account by Hashmat Ara Begum, but it is the ideal that lies behind the common sight of children carrying children in the subcontinent. In the tone of her explanation of the fact that Asian children do not have toys, the strain of confrontation with the industrialized lifestyle can be sensed; deprived of the real Bangladeshi world, Asian children have yet to develop a taste for the expensive surrogate objects with which we placate our children for their lack of human contact. The Asian lifestyle seems austere to consumerist society; to the immigrants, the British lifestyle seems inhuman. Transplanted from their villages to the decaying inner suburbs of dull industrial towns, these women suffer greatly, despite the fact that they have a better chance of bearing healthy children than they had at home. Their misery is not simply explained by their ignorance of the language or the thinly disguised racist hostility that they encounter. Their entire support system has vanished; from never being alone they have moved into a situation of utter solitude, for which their relative affluence cannot compensate. The crisis of childbirth, faced, as it is for all women in the West, without psychological support and involving severe outrage to Muslim modesty, frequently precipitates them into depressed states. (The attitude of medical personnel to these women, based as it is on utter incomprehension of their terror and despair, is a contributory factor.) Amrit Wilson went to visit one such woman, forced into emotional dependence upon a husband who was working long hours to give the family the good life they had come to England to find. "Late, late at night my husband comes home. He loves the babies. He is a good husband, but what can he do? And what can I do? How can I live, sister, how can I live?"

Children in the West, then, are a far greater burden than they are in the countries that these women came from; not only are women more likely to be dealing with the children alone, but the children themselves are more demanding than they are in a non-consumer society. In the Egyptian village, for example, "there are invariably at least two grown-up women attending to the rearing of the child. As the newborn baby, or even any child, has no special cradle, cot or bed, it always sleeps by its mother or sits on her lap."

The Egyptian baby is not trained in consumer behavior any

5

6

7

COLLABORATIVE LEARNING: CLASS ACTIVITY

Greer's *Sex and Destiny* compares several aspects of reproduction in the East and the West and then poses some profound and disturbing questions about the nuclear family in our culture. Her most provocative insights focus on the way in which one's gender determines one's destiny. Ask your class to discuss what role they think sexual identity plays in our destiny—either personal or professional. What does this identity have to do with our self-image? With our concept of "family"? With our role in the larger society?

Divide the class in half, assigning them to represent either Western or Eastern culture. Then, in debate fashion, have them argue with one another over why their birthing methods are more effective than the other side's. Again, remind the students to represent the thoughts of the culture they have been assigned. These may or may not coincide with their own thoughts on this issue.

more than the Bangladeshi baby. In the last hundred years the consumerism of Western babies has gone ahead by leaps and bounds. The baby carriage, a relatively modern invention, is the most expensive item, and, significantly, the one that is paraded before the public; to it are added the baby's layette, crib, cot, diapers, and the like, all clearly designed for baby's use and therefore instantly obsolescent. Some of the impedimenta, such as bootees and talcum powder, are completely useless, but most are designed to keep baby dry, tidy and out of contact, hemmed in from the real world by bassinet walls or perambulator covers or, most bizarre of all, the bars of the playpen. The child who has no pram, no crib, and certainly no room of its own cannot be escaped, especially if it cannot be put down on the floor, either because precious water cannot be spared to wash it very often or because it is made of dirt. Children who are constantly attached to adults obviously cannot be segregated; they must come into the work place and into the sleeping place and the patterns of both must be modified to receive them. Often drudgery separates adults from children, if they are working on road gangs or construction sites, for example, but the separation is seen as another of the trials of poverty.

The child's socialization will be carried out in the midst of his   8
kin group; it is not easy to drive the wedge of professional care into traditional families. There is no need of a play group, because the play group is right there, nor for that matter of the nursery school. The noise of children is a constant accompaniment to daily life, and probably a good deal less fraying to the nerves than the cacophony of consumer society. Mothers are not so vulnerable to infantile ill temper because they do not have to take sole responsibility for it. Reward and punishment are doled out according to family practice; mothers don't have to rush to Dr. Spock to find out how to deal with some particularly antisocial manifestation. The family ethos prevails as it has prevailed for generations, without anxious soul-searching, which is not to say that it is always humane or just, but simply that it is not a cause of internalized tension. The extended family is in many ways a boring and oppressive environment, but it does offer a sense and a context to mothering which two-bedroom ranch houses in the suburbs do not. The children may be grubby, they may be less well-nourished than Western children, but they have a clear sense of the group they belong to, and their own role within it. They will not be found screaming for all the goods displayed in the supermarket (and to make them so scream is the point of the dis-

play), until their frantic mothers lose control and bash them, and then compound the injury by poking sweets into their mouths.

The closeness of adults and children in traditional societies is partly a result of the exclusion of women from the public sphere and their generally low levels of literacy, but these disabilities are in part compensated for by the centrality of the household in daily life. There is little in the way of public or commercial amusement; entertainments and celebrations take place in the household and children are included. Men may go to the coffeehouse or the mud-hif for their entertainment, but their freedom to do so is not re-garded with envy, for women and children are capable of having riotous good fun on their own. Perhaps the most important differ-ence between mothering in traditional societies and mothering in our own is that the traditional mother's role increases in complex-ity and importance as she grows older. If she is skillful and fortu-nate enough to keep her sons and her sons' wives as members of her household, she will enjoy their service and companionship as she grows older. She will have time to play with her grandchildren; her flagging pace will match their unsteady steps. As she sinks into feebleness, her sons' wives will assume her responsibilities and care for her until the last. The ideal situation is not inevitable—dis-possessed old women can be found begging and dying on the streets of India—but success is possible. The role of matriarch is a positive one which can be worked towards by an intelligent and determined woman. Mistreating daughters-in-law is unlikely to further her aims, because discontented wives are a principal cause of the fissioning of the extended family. Because the household is an essential unit in the production of goods and services, her role as manager of it is a challenging one, beside which the role of the Western housewife seems downright impoverished. Even her ab-sent daughters, whose departure for their husbands' dwelling places caused her such grief, keep close to her in feeling. One of the most remarkable aspects of Elizabeth Warnock Fernea's life as the veiled wife of an American anthropologist is an Iraqi village was the utter certainty of the Iraqi women that she must have been as attached to her mother as they were:

9

> "Where is your mother?" Kulthum asked. I told her she was in America far away. . . . The women clucked in sympathy.
> "Poor girl," they said, "poor child. . . ."
> "When you have children, you will not feel so alone without your mother," prophesied Kulthum.

1. In traditional societies, childbirth is an event to be celebrated in the company of the women of the family; in the West, the event is treated as a disease that thrusts the mother into sterile isolation with no one by her bed but medical personnel. The result of this attitude is that "children in the West . . . are a far greater burden than they are in the countries that these women came from" (para. 6). Likewise, mothers play a different role in traditional societies than in the West. The Muslim mother is honored with the birth of her child, often identified as "the mother of her firstborn" (para. 2), sharing the responsibility and the joy of rearing her child with the other women in the family. As she grows older, her role increases in prestige and respect: "The role of matriarch is a positive one which can be worked towards by an intelligent and determined woman" (para. 9).

2. A child born into a consumer society is accompanied by a baby carriage, crib, diapers, toys, and a plethora of implements "designed to keep baby dry, tidy and out of contact, hemmed in from the real world by bassinet walls or perambulator covers or, most bizarre of all, the bars of the playpen" (para. 2). This indulgence and isolation result in under-socialized, ill-mannered children who can be found "screaming for all the goods displayed in the supermarket . . . until their frantic mothers lose control and bash them, and then compound the injury by poking sweets into their mouths" (para. 8).

3. Unlike the nuclear family of the West, the household of the traditional extended family represents "an essential unit in the production of goods and services" (para. 9). Thus, for a woman who strives for influence within such a family, "her role as a manager of it is a challenging one, beside which the role of the Western housewife seems downright impoverished" (para. 9).

ANSWERS TO QUESTIONS:
ANALYZING MEANING (p. 315)

1. Responses to this question will vary.

2. Responses to this question will vary.

When she announced her impending return to America, the women saw only one reason for their going: 10

> "Ask Mr. Bob to bring your mother, and then you'll never have to leave us and go back to America."

Mrs. Fernea did not volunteer to reveal the truth about the status of mothers in Western society. Eventually the Iraqi women confronted her with it: 11

> "And is it true," asked Basima, "that in America they put all the old women in houses by themselves, away from their families?"
> I admitted that this was sometimes true and tried to explain, but my words were drowned in the general murmur of disapproval.
> "What a terrible place that must be!"
> "How awful!"
> "And their children let them go?"
> . . . . It had never occurred to me before, but the idea of old people's homes must have been particularly reprehensible to these women whose world lay within the family unit and whose lives of toil and childbearing were rewarded in old age, when they enjoyed repose and respect as members of their children's households.

This discussion of the difference in the role of mothers in highly industrialized bureaucratic communities and in traditional agricultural communities is not meant as a panegyric of the disappearing world, but simply to indicate something of the context in which the birthrate in the developed world has fallen. There is little point in feeling sorry for Western mothers, who are most often as anxious to be freed of their children as their children are to be freed of them. The inhabitants of old people's homes and retirement villages do not sit sobbing and railing against destiny, although they do compete with each other in displaying the rather exiguous proofs of their children's affection. As the recession bites deeper and unemployment rises, more and more adult children are having to remain dependent on their parents, who are lamenting loudly and wondering more vociferously than usual why they let themselves in for such a thankless task as parenting. The point of the contrast is simply to caution the people of the highly industrialized countries which wield such massive economic and cultural sway over the developing world against assuming that one of the things they must rescue the rest of the world from is parenting. Because motherhood is virtually meaningless in our society is no ground for supposing 12 that the fact that women are still defined by their mothering function in other societies is simply an index of their oppression. We have at least to consider the possibility that a successful matriarch might well pity Western feminists for having been duped into futile competition with men in exchange for the companionship and love of children and other women.

UNDERSTANDING DETAILS

1. How do traditional and Western childbearing methods vary? How does Greer account for these differences? What are the main differences and similarities between the roles of mothers in these two societies?
2. What is the relationship between consumerism and childrearing in Greer's comparison? What behavior results from this relationship?
3. According to the author, what is the precise difference between the extended family and the nuclear family?

ANALYZING MEANING

1. Of all the examples the author cites in her essay, which one convinces you most effectively that raising children in traditional countries is a more meaningful activity than it is in Western society? Why?
2. Why do you think the extended family has become relatively obsolete in the Western world? In your opinion, what is its future fate in Western society? Explain your reasoning.
3. This essay ends on a fairly negative note. Explain in your own words Greer's last sentence (paragraph 12), and discuss its implications about Western society. Why is this an effective ending?

DISCOVERING RHETORICAL STRATEGIES

1. Why do you think Greer has chosen comparison/contrast to prove her point in this essay? How effective is this technique? What other rhetorical modes does the author use to state her case?
2. How does the author organize her comparison? Which of the four main types of organization best describes Greer's essay? Is this format a good choice for accomplishing her purpose? Why or why not?
3. Does the author omit or downplay any of the distinctions between Western and traditional child care that might be detrimental to her argument? If so, what are these distinctions?

3. Greer chastises Western society for assuming that parenting in our hemisphere is somehow more dignified and humane than it is in the East. Her last sentence implies that Western women have made a tragic trade to achieve success in the workplace. This implication is the central point of her comparison/contrast, which explains that Asian childrearing and cultural upbringing are at least as legitimate as their counterparts in the West.

ANSWERS TO QUESTIONS:
DISCOVERING RHETORICAL
STRATEGIES (p. 315)

1. Greer notes in the beginning of her essay that "the Western interpretation of such mores [of traditional societies] is that they are backward, cruel and wrong" (para. 1). Facing the potential of such a strong opinion among her readers, Greer wisely chooses the rhetorical technique of comparison/contrast to organize the evidence she uses to counter these stereotypical images. In addition, description and example support her statements about the differences between childrearing practices in Eastern and Western societies.

2. The author uses alternating comparison/contrast techniques to organize her essay, first contrasting childbirth in the two cultures, then child care during the early years, and, finally, the role of the mother in later years. This arrangement allows the reader to focus on each aspect of the author's argument individually, absorbing only small amounts of this new information at one time.

3. The author tends to downplay the relationship between the Muslim woman and her spouse, commenting only on "the exclusion of women from the public sphere" (para. 9) and her compensation for this isolation through "the centrality of the household in daily life" (para. 9). She also avoids discussing in any depth those "dispossessed old women [who] can be found begging and dying on the streets of India" (para. 9), leaving the reader with questions regarding the identities of those women and why they are not among the respected matriarchs of Indian households.

In preparation for the writing assignments, the Preparing to Write questions ask students to think specifically about the family unit in our society before they write an essay on a related topic. See pages 16–23 for suggestions on generating ideas in response to these questions.

ADDITIONAL DISCUSSION/WRITING TOPIC

All families are characterized by habits, rituals, and values that make them unique. In an essay for your classmates, compare and/or contrast one or two unique aspects of your family with those of another family.

REVISING STRATEGY

A good comparison/contrast essay will fulfill the guidelines mentioned on pages 298–299. Look at this checklist and underline the parts of one of your essays that fulfill these criteria. Notice where your essay needs work. Then revise your paper according to these guidelines.

IDEAS FOR DISCUSSION/WRITING

Preparing to Write

Write freely about the Western family: What generally constitutes a "family" in the Western Hemisphere? How has its makeup changed over the years? Is the family unit a significant part of our society, or is the individual more important? What facts and observations support your opinion? In what ways do you think the American family will change in the next fifty to a hundred years? In your opinion, will these be positive or negative changes?

Choosing a Topic

1. For your college sociology class, compare the extended family with the nuclear family by discussing the principal advantages and disadvantages of each.
2. As objectively as possible, describe to a friend some of your family's cherished traditions. When possible, compare and/or contrast your family's traditions with those of your friend's family. Give someone you like more insight into yourself by helping the person understand which traditions your family values.
3. You have been asked to make a prediction about the future of the American family for *The Sociological Quarterly*. The readers of this journal are especially interested in whether the family as a group or the family as individuals will become more prominent after the year 2000. Offer your prediction and explain your reasoning in a comparison/contrast essay to be published in this periodical.

WILLIAM OUCHI
(1943–)

■ ■ ■

Japanese and American Workers: Two Casts of Mind

QUOTATION ON THINKING

"Writing and meditating are naturally allied activities. Both are important for their own sake, and through each people can practice the other."

James Moffett

Born in Honolulu, Hawaii, William Ouchi is an internationally known expert on business management—particularly on the relationship between American and Japanese corporations. Ouchi was educated at Williams College, Stanford University, and the University of Chicago; since then he has taught in business programs at several major American universities, most recently at the Graduate School of Management at UCLA. The author has also served as associate study director for the National Opinion Research Center and as a business consultant for many of America's most successful companies. He has written three books on organization and management: *Theory Z: How American Business Can Meet the Japanese Challenge* (1981) is a thorough analysis of the differences between American and Japanese industrial productivity; *The M-Form Society: How American Teamwork Can Recapture the Competitive Edge* (1984) is the result of a three-year study by a team of sixteen researchers led by Ouchi; and *Organizational Economics* (1986) is a textbook coedited with Jay Barney. Ouchi advises students using *The Prose Reader* to spend plenty of time revising their material. "No one writes a good first draft," he explains. "You must continue to revise your work till you understand exactly what you want to say and you have constructed a group of sentences that say it clearly." Ouchi lives in Santa Monica, California.

Preparing to Read

The following essay, excerpted from *Theory Z*, compares and contrasts Japan's collective work ethic with the American spirit of individualism. As you prepare to read this essay, think about your own work ethic: When you study, for example, do you prefer working alone or with a group of people? What kinds of jobs have you held during your life? Did they stress individual or collective behavior? Were you often rewarded for individual achievement, or did you work mostly within a homogeneous group? In what sort of work environment are you most productive? Most satisfied?

PREREADING

The purpose of this Preparing to Read material is to encourage students to think about their work ethic. To help your students focus their attention on this topic, discuss the definition of "work ethic": "the philosophy that equates hard work with success in life." Then, have your class generate a list of activities they consider duties and those they think of as pleasure. Next ask your students to discuss these two abstractions—work and pleasure. What do your students associate with these words? Are these associations positive or negative for them? See pages 3–6 for other ways to generate thoughts on these questions.

BACKGROUND INFORMATION

William Ouchi's "Japanese and American Workers: Two Casts of Mind" contrasts the value systems of two major industrial cultures in an attempt to help American business executives understand the thought processes of Japanese employees so that international working relationships can be made easier. In assessing the two systems, Ouchi concludes that, with the transformation of the West from an agricultural to an industrial society, "our technological advance seems to no longer fit our social structure: In a sense, the Japanese can better cope with modern industrialism" (para. 15).

READABILITY LEVEL

13.0

RELATED READINGS

Cultural Diversity

Amy Tan, "The Joy Luck Club"   49
Lewis Sawaquat, "For My Indian
    Daughter"   96
Mark Mathabane, "Passport to
    Knowledge"   133
Elena Asturias, "Growing Up in the U.S."
    325
Robert Ramirez, "The Barrio"   357
Richard Rodriguez, "The Fear of Losing a
    Culture"   406

DEFINITIONS

Meiji restoration (1868) (para. 11): a major turning point in Japanese history that restored the young emperor Meiji to power and eventually enabled Japan to modernize.
Plato (427?–347 B.C.) (para. 13): the Greek philosopher best known for *The Republic*, which attempts to construct an ideal state.
Hobbes (para. 13): Thomas Hobbes (1558–1679), the British philosopher who wrote about man as a "self-interested unit."
B. F. Skinner (1904–1990) (para. 13): a psychologist who developed the theory of behaviorism, the idea that humans can be conditioned to behave in a morally responsible manner.

Perhaps the most difficult aspect of the Japanese for Westerners to comprehend is the strong orientation to collective values, particularly a collective sense of responsibility. Let me illustrate with an anecdote about a visit to a new factory in Japan owned and operated by an American electronics company. The American company, a particularly creative firm, frequently attracts attention within the business community for its novel approaches to planning, organizational design, and management systems. As a consequence of this corporate style, the parent company determined to make a thorough study of Japanese workers and to design a plant that would combine the best of East and West. In their study they discovered that Japanese firms almost never make use of individual work incentives, such as piecework or even individual performance appraisal tied to salary increases. They concluded that rewarding individual achievement and individual ability is always a good thing. 1

In the final assembly area of their new plant long lines of young Japanese women wired together electronic products on a piece-rate system: The more you wired, the more you got paid. About two months after opening, the head foreladies approached the plant manager. "Honorable plant manager," they said humbly as they bowed, "we are embarrassed to be so forward, but we must speak to you because all of the girls have threatened to quit work this Friday." (To have this happen, of course, would be a great disaster for all concerned.) "Why," they wanted to know, "can't our plant have the same compensation system as other Japanese companies? When you hire a new girl, her starting wage should be fixed by her age. An eighteen-year-old should be paid more than a sixteen-year-old. Every year on her birthday, she should receive an automatic increase in pay. The idea that any one of us can be more productive than another must be wrong, because none of us in final assembly could make a thing unless all of the other people in the plant had done their jobs right first. To single one person out as being more productive is wrong and is also personally humiliating to us." The company changed its compensation system to the Japanese model. 2

Another American company in Japan had installed a suggestion system much as we have in the United States. Individual workers were encouraged to place suggestions to improve productivity into special boxes. For an accepted idea the individual received a bonus amounting to some fraction of the productivity savings realized from his or her suggestion. After a period of six months, not a single suggestion had been submitted. The 3

American managers were puzzled. They had heard many stories of the inventiveness, the commitment, and the loyalty of Japanese workers, yet not one suggestion to improve productivity had appeared.

The managers approached some of the workers and asked why the suggestion system had not been used. The answer: "No one can come up with a work improvement idea alone. We work together, and any ideas that one of us may have are actually developed by watching others and talking to others. If one of us was singled out for being responsible for such an idea, it would embarrass all of us." The company changed to a group suggestion system, in which workers collectively submitted suggestions. Bonuses were paid to groups which would save bonus money until the end of the year for a party at a restaurant or, if there was enough money, for family vacations together. The suggestions and productivity improvements rained down on the plant.

One can interpret these examples in two quite different ways. Perhaps the Japanese commitment to collective values is an anachronism that does not fit with modern industrialism but brings economic success despite that collectivism. Collectivism seems to be inimical to the kind of maverick creativity exemplified in Benjamin Franklin, Thomas Edison, and John D. Rockefeller. Collectivism does not seem to provide the individual incentive to excel which has made a great success of American enterprise. Entirely apart from its economic effects, collectivism implies a loss of individuality, a loss of the freedom to be different, to hold fundamentally different values from others.

The second interpretation of the examples is that the Japanese collectivism is economically efficient. It causes people to work well together and to encourage one another to better efforts. Industrial life requires interdependence of one person on another. But a less obvious but far-reaching implication of the Japanese collectivism for economic performance has to do with accountability.

In the Japanese mind, collectivism is neither a corporate or individual goal to strive for nor a slogan to pursue. Rather, the nature of things operates so that nothing of consequence occurs as a result of individual effort. Everything important in life happens as a result of teamwork or collective effort. Therefore, to attempt to assign individual credit or blame to results is unfounded. A Japanese professor of accounting, a brilliant scholar trained at Carnegie-Mellon University who teaches now in Tokyo, remarked that the status of accounting systems in Japanese indus-

COLLABORATIVE LEARNING:
CLASS ACTIVITY

Have the class as a whole cite the three main categories of Ouchi's comparison of Japanese and American workers (para. 5–9). Then, based on some testimonials from actual jobs represented in the classroom, discuss whether or not the Japanese workers' techniques could be successful in any jobs or working environments in the United States.

Divide the class in half, assigning them to represent either Western business ideas or Eastern business ideas. Then, have them debate why their business methods are more effective than the other side's. Again, remind the students to represent the work ethic of the culture they have been assigned. These assertions may or may not coincide with their own thoughts on the issue.

try is primitive compared to those in the United States. Profit centers, transfer prices, and computerized information systems are barely known even in the largest Japanese companies, whereas they are a commonplace in even small United States organizations. Though not at all surprised at the difference in accounting systems, I was not at all sure that the Japanese were primitive. In fact, I thought their system a good deal more efficient than ours.

Most American companies have basically two accounting systems. One system summarizes the overall financial state to inform stockholders, bankers, and other outsiders. That system is not of interest here. The other system, called the managerial or cost accounting system, exists for an entirely different reason. It measures in detail all of the particulars of transactions between departments, divisions, and key individuals in the organization, for the purpose of untangling the interdependencies between people. When, for example, two departments share one truck for deliveries, the cost accounting system charges each department for part of the cost of maintaining the truck and driver, so that at the end of the year, the performance of each department can be individually assessed, and the better department's manager can receive a larger raise. Of course, all of this information processing costs money, and furthermore may lead to arguments between the departments over whether the costs charged to each are fair. 8

In a Japanese company a short-run assessment of individual performance is not wanted, so the company can save the considerable expense of collecting and processing all of that information. Companies still keep track of which department uses a truck how often and for what purposes, but like-minded people can interpret some simple numbers for themselves and adjust their behavior accordingly. Those insisting upon clear and precise measurement for the purpose of advancing individual interests must have an elaborate information system. Industrial life, however, is essentially integrated and interdependent. No one builds an automobile alone, no one carries through a banking transaction alone. In a sense the Japanese value of collectivism fits naturally into an industrial setting, whereas the Western individualism provides constant conflicts. The image that comes to mind is of Chaplin's silent film "Modern Times" in which the apparently insignificant hero played by Chaplin successfully fights against the unfeeling machinery of industry. Modern industrial life can be aggravating, even hostile, or natural: All depends on the fit between our culture and our technology. 9

The *shinkansen* or "bullet train" speeds across the rural areas 10 of Japan giving a quick view of cluster after cluster of farmhouses surrounded by rice paddies. This particular pattern did not develop purely by chance, but as a consequence of the technology peculiar to the growing of rice, the staple of the Japanese diet. The growing of rice requires construction and maintenance of an irrigation system, something that takes many hands to build. More importantly, the planting and the harvesting of rice can only be done efficiently with the cooperation of twenty or more people. The "bottom line" is that a single family working alone cannot produce enough rice to survive, but a dozen families working together can produce a surplus. Thus the Japanese have had to develop the capacity to work together in harmony, no matter what the forces of disagreement or social disintegration, in order to survive.

Japan is a nation built entirely on the tips of giant, suboceanic volcanoes. Little of the land is flat and suitable for agriculture. Terraced hillsides make use of every available square foot of arable land. Small homes built very close together further conserve the land. Japan also suffers from natural disasters such as earthquakes and hurricanes. Traditionally homes are made of light construction materials, so a house falling down during a disaster will not crush its occupants and also could be quickly an inexpensively rebuilt. During the feudal period until the Meiji restoration of 1868, each feudal lord sought to restrain his subjects from moving from one village to the next for fear that a neighboring lord might amass enough peasants with which to produce a large agricultural surplus, hire an army and pose a threat. Apparently bridges were not commonly built across rivers and streams until the late nineteenth century, since bridges increased mobility between villages.

Taken all together, this characteristic style of living paints the picture of a nation of people who are homogeneous with respect to race, history, language, religion, and culture. For centuries and generations these people have lived in the same village next door to the same neighbors. Living in close proximity and in dwellings which gave very little privacy, the Japanese survived through their capacity to work together in harmony. In this situation, it was inevitable that the one most central social value which emerged, the one value without which the society could not continue, was that an individual does not matter.

To the Western soul this is a chilling picture of society. Subordinating individual tastes to the harmony of the group and knowing that individual needs can never take precedence over

11

12

13

ANSWERS TO QUESTIONS: UNDERSTANDING DETAILS (p. 323)

1. Ouchi describes the Japanese philosophy as one in which "everything important in life happens as a result of teamwork or collective effort" (para. 7). In contrast, in American society, the needs of the individual "take precedence over the interests of all" (para. 13). Through this comparison, the author attempts to demonstrate the advantages of the Japanese value system over the American system in our modern industrial society.

2. The most difficult aspect of the Japanese business ethic for Westerners to understand is "the strong orientation to collective values, particularly a collective sense of responsibility"(para. 1).

3. Ouchi feels that the cultural values of a people can be comprehended through an understanding of the background of their nation. He sees the Japanese tendency toward "collectivism" as being rooted in a long history of "living in close proximity and in dwellings which gave very little privacy" (para. 12). Even the rice farming that has sustained them for centuries is accomplished on tiny plots of land and "can only be done efficiently with the cooperation of twenty or more people" (para. 10). These terraced hillsides of Japan contrast strongly with the vast fields of the United States that give rise to families living in relative isolation, dependent on the qualities of "self-reliance and independence" (para. 14) to survive.

1. Ouchi obviously believes in the superior capability of the Japanese value system over the American to meet the needs of the industrial age. This opinion is only foreshadowed, however, in his introductory anecdotes. His first real statement of opinion regarding the business ethics of the Japanese is in the last pararaph: "Our technological advance seems to no longer fit our social structure: In a sense, the Japanese can better cope with modern industrialism" (para. 15).

2. The author introduces the origins of American and Japanese living conditions to stress the significance of the background of a people in forming the cultural basis of their value system.

3. Responses to this question will vary.

the interests of all is repellent to the Western citizen. But a frequent theme of Western philosophers and sociologists is that individual freedom exists only when people willingly subordinate their self-interests to the social interest. A society composed entirely of self-interested individuals is a society in which each person is at war with the other, a society which has no freedom. This issue, constantly at the heart of understanding society, comes up in every century, and in every society, whether the writer be Plato, Hobbes, or B. F. Skinner. The question of understanding which contemporary institutions lie at the heart of the conflict between automatism and totalitarianism remains. In some ages, the kinship group, the central social institution, mediated between these opposing forces to preserve the balance in which freedom was realized; in other times the church or the government was most critical. Perhaps our present age puts the work organization as the central institution.

In order to complete the comparison of Japanese and American living situations, consider a flight over the United States. Looking out of the window high over the state of Kansas, we see a pattern of a single farmhouse surrounded by fields, followed by another single homestead surrounded by fields. In the early 1800s in the state of Kansas there were no automobiles. Your nearest neighbor was perhaps two miles distant; the winters were long, and the snow was deep. Inevitably, the central social values were self-reliance and independence. Those were the realities of that place and age that children had to learn to value.   14

The key to the industrial revolution was discovering that non-human forms of energy substituted for human forms could increase the wealth of a nation beyond anyone's wildest dreams. But there was a catch. To realize this great wealth, non-human energy needed huge complexes called factories with hundreds, even thousands of workers collected into one factory. Moreover, several factories in one central place made the generation of energy more efficient. Almost overnight, the Western world was transformed from a rural and agricultural country to an urban and industrial state. Our technological advance seems to no longer fit our social structure: In a sense, the Japanese can better cope with modern industrialism. While Americans still busily protect our rather extreme form of individualism, the Japanese hold their individualism in check and emphasize cooperation.   15

UNDERSTANDING DETAILS

1. Describe in your own words the two different philosophies Ouchi is comparing in this essay. What is his main point in the essay?
2. According to the author, what is the most difficult aspect of the Japanese business ethic for Westerners to understand?
3. Why does "collectivism" work better for the Japanese than for the Americans? What is its history in Japan? How is it different from Western "individualism"?

ANALYZING MEANING

1. What is Ouchi's personal opinion about the two value systems he is comparing? At what points does he reveal his preference?
2. Why does the author introduce the origins of American and Japanese living conditions?
3. Which set of business values do you prefer after reading Ouchi's comparison? Explain the reasons for your preference.

DISCOVERING RHETORICAL STRATEGIES

1. How does Ouchi organize this essay? Outline the main points he covers for each subject.
2. Why do you think the author introduces the two anecdotes at the outset of this essay? How do these stories help Ouchi achieve his purpose?
3. Who do you think is the author's intended audience? How much knowledge about these two subjects does he assume they have? What evidence can you give to support your answer?

IDEAS FOR DISCUSSION/WRITING

Preparing to Write

Write freely about the work ethic that characterizes your immediate environment—at school, at home, or on the job: How do the people in each of these environments feel about one another? How do you feel about them? When are you most productive in these environments? What are the circumstances? Do you work better individually or collectively? Why?

ANSWERS TO QUESTIONS: DISCOVERING RHETORICAL STRATEGIES (p. 323)

1. Ouchi uses a combination of the alternating and divided methods of comparison/contrast. He opens with two anecdotes illustrating the failure of American motivational techniques in Japanese factories due to the collective values of the Japanese. He then judges collectivism from first an American, then a Japanese perspective and discusses the accounting systems of the two countries as a reflection of their basic values. He finally focuses on the backgrounds that generated the divergent sets of values and the compatibility of the Japanese model with modern industrial needs. The author does not offer a balanced treatment of the two systems but uses the deficiencies of the American methods to confirm the superiority of the Japanese system.

2. The author introduces the two anecdotes at the beginning of the essay to capture his audience's attention and to set up a strong foundation to support his later generalizations. These tangible examples of the value systems at work clearly illustrate the dissimilarities of the two conflicting cultures.

3. The author's intended audience is probably the educated American business executive with corporate connections in Japan who is having a difficult time comprehending the Japanese work ethic. This deduction is supported by the fact that the author describes successful American motivational techniques that were ineffective in Japan; offers several explanations of Japanese customs and traditions with only brief references to their Western counterparts; and uses Western philosophers such as "Plato, Hobbes, or B. F. Skinner" (para. 13) to analyze the unique value system of the Japanese.

PREWRITING

In preparation for the writing assignments, the Preparing to Write questions ask students to characterize their behavior when they work at school, at home, or on the job. See pages 16–23 for suggestions on generating ideas in response to these questions.

You have probably written essays both individually (with no help) and collaboratively (with help from someone else—a tutor, a roommate, a group of people, etc.). Compare and/or contrast the type of written work you produce in both of these situations. What implications do your observations have for your writing?

REVISING STRATEGY

The introduction of a comparison/contrast essay should (1) clearly identify your subjects, (2) explain the basis of your comparison/contrast, and (3) state your purpose and the limits of your comparison. Reread one of your comparison/contrast papers, checking for these elements in your introduction. Take note of what is missing or weak. Then revise your paper, based on a fully developed introduction.

Choosing a Topic

1. Would you prefer to live your social life individually or collectively (as Ouchi defines the two methods)? Explain your preference to a friend, comparing the advantages and disadvantages of both situations. What implications does your preference have? Be sure to make your purpose as clear as possible.

2. Would you rather work in a factory that follows the Japanese or the American method of organization outlined by Ouchi? Explain your preference to your best friend or your immediate supervisor at work. Compare the advantages and disadvantages of both situations. What implications does your preference have? Be sure to make your purpose as clear as possible.

3. *Leisure* magazine has asked you to compare work and leisure from a college student's point of view. Consider the advantages and disadvantages of each. Be sure to decide on a purpose before you begin to write your comparison.

ELENA ASTURIAS
(1963–   )

■ ■ ■

Growing Up in the U.S.: A First Generation Look

Lawyer and political activist Elena Asturias was born in San Francisco and raised in both Guatemala and the United States. Following her undergraduate education at the University of San Francisco, she earned a law degree at the University of the Pacific's McGeorge Law School and a Masters of Law at Georgetown University. Her current legal specialty is comparative and international law, with an emphasis on Latin American issues. She is also vice-president of the Latino Lawyers of San Francisco, an organization devoted to promoting a greater understanding of legal and policy issues affecting the Latin-American community in the United States. She has found success in life, she explains, by believing that "the only limits I have are those I place on myself." She advises students using *The Prose Reader* not to let "anyone else define or put artificial limits on what you can do. Set your own goals, and then work hard enough to achieve them." Students can become better writers, she suggests, by "reading a great deal so that you can internalize the words and use them as mirrors for what you want to say in your own writing." Asturias' skill as a writer may in part be attributed to genetics: Her famous Guatemalan cousin Miguel Angel Asturias won the Nobel Prize for Literature in 1967. Asturias now lives and works in San Francisco, where she enjoys playing classical guitar and participating in folkloric dancing in her free time.

Preparing to Read

In the following article, Asturias explains the special benefits available to those people who open their lives to cultural diversity. As you prepare to read this essay, which originally appeared in the bilingual magazine *Intercambios*, examine for a few minutes your own thoughts about the assimilation of various cultures: What are your fondest childhood memories? How many different sets of values and traditions do you represent? Have you successfully assimilated all the various aspects of your heritage? If so, what were the difficulties? The positive points? Do you think the assimilation of di-

QUOTATION ON READING

"Studying their own writing puts students in a position to see themselves as language users, rather than as victims of a language that uses them."
David Bartholomae

PREREADING

The purpose of this Preparing to Read material is to encourage students to set up their own framework for comparing or contrasting different cultures. To encourage your students to focus on this task, have them list in five different columns as many characteristics as they can of their original culture: social, educational, political, economic, and religious. Your students should complete this exercise before they respond to the questions here. If time allows, have them discuss these traits. See pages 3–6 for other ways to generate thoughts on these questions.

BACKGROUND INFORMATION

In this essay, Asturias discusses her upbringing in the United States and the virtues of assimilating into a foreign culture. Part Guatemalan and part Puerto Rican, Asturias was taught to merge her South American heritage with the North American customs within which she was raised. She found it a challenging task. As she says, however, "Assimilating an awareness of two cultures adds breadth to one's perspective" (para. 2).

READABILITY LEVEL

12.5

RELATED READINGS

Cultural Diversity

DEFINITIONS

Hispana (para. 2): a female of Latin-American or Spanish descent.
Quezaltenango (para. 3): a city in southern Guatemala.
Fajardo (para. 3): a town in northeast Puerto Rico once known for its excellent fishing and a sugar-cane refinery that supported the region economically.
La Perla del Caribe (para. 4): Spanish. "The Pearl of the Caribbean," synonymous here with Puerto Rico.
Don Quixote (para. 6): the first modern novel in Spanish; written between 1605 and 1615 by Don Miguel de Cervantes y Saavedra (1547–1616).
CriCri (para. 6): a Mexican singer and composer who came up with his stage name while listening to the sound of crickets; in this context, a character who is a cricket, much like the cartoon character Jiminy Cricket.
Three Kings Day (para. 13): January 6, a day of celebration in the Spanish tradition, when children receive gifts from the Three Kings, or Three Wise Men.
tamales (para. 13): shredded meat, spices, and vegetables rolled in cornmeal, wrapped in a corn husk or plantain leaf, and steamed.
paches (para. 13): Spanish. A Guatemalan version of tamales, but rolled in mashed potatoes and cornmeal.
pasteles (para. 13): Spanish. The Puerto Rican equivalent of tamales.
Las Mañanitas (para. 13): a song sung in Spain and Latin America on birthdays.

verse cultures into one dominant national culture is a positive or negative goal? From your perspective, what role does assimilation currently play in most people's lives in the United States? In your opinion, what role *should* it play?

When I was three, the name I learned to print was Elena María del Pilar Asturias Texidor. It would be shortened in school to Elena Asturias and, on occasion, altered by monolingual nuns to Helen. 1

Growing up in the United States as a first generation Hispana has had its advantages and disadvantages. Assimilating an awareness of two cultures adds breadth to one's perspective. Among the most utilitarian benefits for society at large is the ability to share different traditions, cultures, and perspectives with others. The constant arrival of new immigrants nourishes this diversity, recharging society and inspiring those already here. 2

However, I do not consider myself a typical Hispana, but rather just one example of a Latin American raised in the U.S. My parents are both educators. My father, a retired university professor, is from Quezaltenango, Guatemala, and my mother, a community college administrator, was born in Fajardo, Puerto Rico. Although both cultures share common themes, there are tremendous differences in their respective traditions and attitudes. In our family, we often joked that theirs was an "inter-racial marriage." 3

Summers were spent in Guatemala, and we occasionally vacationed on La Perla del Caribe, renting a home on the beach. The time spent visiting our parents' homelands bound us to their cultures and nurtured an appreciation for the roots they had sown in us. 4

My sister and I were educated in the American school system and the Latin American social system. We learned to behave properly at home, which included sitting and conversing with adults rather than entrenching ourselves in a world all our own. Our parents instilled in us the importance of caring for elderly and ill family members with constancy and patience. The traditional strength of the Latin family helped us as we developed a bicultural existence in the United States. 5

Preserving the language of their homelands was also of great importance to my parents. We spoke only Spanish at home, though both my parents speak flawless English. Help with school 6 work was the only exception to this rule; it was generously given in English. We read *Don Quixote* as well as *Cinderella*. Our childrens' songs were those of CriCri, not the U.S. equivalent. Raised to respect our families, along with a healthy dose of fear lest we bring shame upon those we loved, we were motivated to study, learn and serve our community.

Our parents' firm commitment to community service is perhaps the most unique heirloom handed down to us as children. They took us on peace marches in the 60s and 70s even before we were able to walk. I vividly recall the view perched atop my father's shoulders of a massive swell of humanity marching for peace.

My parents also taught us about our family history: how our grandfather was jailed and had to flee Guatemala because of his involvement in land reform; how he received the Orden del Quetzal, the highest medal given to a civilian, for his work in vaccinating an entire region of Guatemala. These and other similar stories gave us a special sense of pride in our heritage and obligation to our community.

As teenagers, my mother enlisted our help in the political campaigns she supported. We distributed leaflets, made phone calls, canvassed to get the vote out and were accustomed to attending and helping organize fundraisers and other political events. This involvement in the U.S. political process helped us see that individuals can make a difference and that opportunities to do so are there for achievement.

What we learned and lived at home set us up for very real confrontations with the world outside our four walls. The early curfews, the chaperons, the conservative manner we dressed—all contributed to the feeling that we were different. Our parents explained that these differences would add something extra to our characters. We were special, not different, and therefore more was expected of us. What made these "extra" requirements feasible was our parents' ability to balance our strict upbringing with the love and attention we needed.

Although some advantages of growing up in the U.S. are harder to measure, I gained a type of personal strength, self-reliance and independence I may not have found if I'd been raised in the more sheltered home life of the traditional Latin American household. However, there are trade-offs—the security and stability, the sense of belonging, of knowing one's roots fostered in a strong Latin home are often sacrificed to the risktaking needed to maximize one's potential in the U.S.

Jose Martí (1853–1895) (para. 15): a Cuban writer and leader in the Cuban war for independence who became known as the "Apostle of the Revolution"; his poems were collected in 1983 in *The Simple Verses of Jose Martí: An English Analysis*.

COLLABORATIVE LEARNING: CLASS ACTIVITY

7 Choose three students to come to the front of the classroom and answer questions from the class as Asturias, her mother, and her father would. Let the other students ask any questions that are on their minds. The important feature of this exercise is for the three students playing roles to stay in character.

8 You can repeat this activity as many times as you want with different students playing these roles.

COLLABORATIVE LEARNING: SMALL GROUP ACTIVITY

Asturias is clearly a proponent of assimilation. But many people believe assimilation has negative consequences as well. Divide

9 the class into two groups. Assign one group to speak on behalf of assimilation and the other against it. Within these groups, let the students decide who will do the basic research and who will present the material. Then stage a debate in class on the two sides of this issue. Have your students pre-

10 sent their material according to the following plan. (Any number of students can speak at each point on the schedule.)

Opening statement, affirmative	5 min.
Cross-examination, negative	2 min.
Opening statement, negative	5 min.
Cross-examination, affirmative	2 min.
Second statement, affirmative	4 min.
Cross-examination, negative	1 min.
Second statement, negative	4 min.
Cross-examination, affirmative	1 min.
Negative rebuttal	2 min.
Affirmative rebuttal	2 min.
Negative rebuttal	2 min.
Affirmative rebuttal	2 min.

11

Remind your students that the most important feature of a debate is the credibility and quality of the evidence. At the end of the debate, have the rest of the class vote on the winning team, based on the validity of the evidence presented.

1. Asturias is comparing the advantages and disadvantages of growing up as a first-generation Hispana in the United States.

2. Asturias learned to behave well at home; to care for family members "with constancy and patience" (para. 5); to speak, read, and write both Spanish and English; to study; to serve the community; and to become active in important political causes. In addition, Asturias learned to respect the traditions and ideas from both her parents' cultures as well as from American culture. The lessons she learned prepared her to assimilate, while still preserving her own identity.

3. Asturias believes her experience is different from that of other Hispanic immigrants because her parents are from two distinct Hispanic cultures. Also unusual is the fact that her parents are both educators who are bilingual, politically active, and traditionally Hispanic. As immigrants, her family is well adjusted to the United States.

ANSWERS TO QUESTIONS:
ANALYZING MEANING (p. 329)

1. Responses to this question will vary.

2. Asturias developed political awareness, a sense of family support and security, and a strong set of values in her early years. Her home life gave her high moral, social, and economic aspirations. Her effort and her parents' efforts on her behalf made her self-confident, assertive, and secure.

3. The advantages and disadvantages Asturias writes about are as follows:

Advantages

—The arrival of new immigrants creates national diversity and revitalizes society.

—The children of immigrants develop an appreciation for the traditions of their parents.

—The children are simultaneously motivated to learn about the culture of the country in which they live and the culture(s) of their parents.

—Individualism is balanced with traditional, societal, and family values.

The more I visited my Latin American cousins and relatives, the more I began to notice a growing distance in our attitudes over politics, social issues and familial questions. Our educations were shaping us into citizens of our respective countries with correspondent attitudes and concerns. Although we retained similar cultural values and traditions, the older we got the less we agreed on the international scale. 12

We celebrated Christmas on December 24th as well as the Three Kings Day, preparing for the arrival of the giftbearers with cereal for the camels and wine for the weary travelers. Mornings of January 6th meant awakening early and rushing downstairs to check shoes left by the door for our unwrapped gifts and the remains of the goodies we'd left. Special occasions were celebrated with tamales, *paches* (Guatemala) and *pasteles* (Puerto Rico) and *Las Mañanitas* was recited on our birthdays. The outward manifestations of Latin-American culture were not only for our enjoyment, but for the enjoyment of our non-Latin friends who were always included in these celebrations. 13

Perhaps the most poignant loss on a personal level is the inability to express myself as well in Spanish as in English. It's difficult when you're educated in one language to theorize in another or to write on topics as fluidly. My hope lies in the adage "practice makes perfect!" 14

If our upbringing taught us anything it is that as Hispanas transplanted as such in the U.S., we have a responsibility to educate society in the depth and beauty of our Latin American heritage and the immense contribution we can make to this country. By helping new arrivals and those less fortunate, we ensure the survival of our identity and the reinforcement of our values. To reiterate an appropriate verse of Jose Martí, recently quoted in Los Angeles at the National Network of Hispanic Women's Roundtable, ". . . *No hay caminos, los caminos se forman al hacer—no para nosotros pero para los por venir*" ("There are no established roads; roads are built by doing, not for ourselves, but for those to come"). 15

UNDERSTANDING DETAILS

1. What is Asturias comparing in this essay?
2. What values and traditions did Asturias' parents teach her as part of her upbringing? What role did these play in her growth as a child?
3. Why doesn't Asturias consider herself "a typical Hispana" (para-

graph 3)? In what ways is she different from other Hispanic immigrants?

ANALYZING MEANING

1. Asturias says, "Assimilating an awareness of two cultures adds breadth to one's perspective" (paragraph 2). To what extent do you agree with this statement? Explain your answer.
2. How did Asturias' early home life prepare her "for very real confrontations with the world outside our four walls" (paragraph 10)?
3. Merging two cultures is a difficult prospect that has advantages and disadvantages. What are the principal advantages and disadvantages, and which, in your opinion, are most important to a child's development?

DISCOVERING RHETORICAL STRATEGIES

1. How does Asturias organize her comparison in this essay? Which of the four main types of organization (mentioned in the chapter introduction) does she use?
2. What rhetorical strategies does the author use to support her comparison/contrast? Give examples of each.
3. Throughout this essay, Asturias chooses her words carefully to create a positive impression of the process of assimilation. She talks about diverse cultures adding breadth to one's life (paragraph 2); she discusses the importance of nourishing this diversity (paragraph 2); and she explains the "personal strength, self-reliance and independence" (paragraph 11) she gained from this process. Choose another topic Asturias discusses in this essay and show how she attempts to control the reader's attitude toward this topic with her word choice.

IDEAS FOR DISCUSSION/WRITING

Preparing to Write

Write freely about assimilation in American society: Knowing that the American people are a combination of various values and traditions, how important do you think assimilation is to the survival of the individual in our society? How important is cultural assimilation to the survival of our country? What are the advantages of assimilation? The disadvantages? What aspects of your ethnic or cultural background are you most reluctant to change? Do you believe everyone should share your opinions about assimilation?

—Personal strength increases because of the adjustments immigrants must make to live in a new country.

Disadvantages

—Preserving one's native language and learning a second language at the same time can be very difficult.

—Many sacrifices must be made so that assimilation can take place. Asturias has lost some of the stability and security she would have maintained in her parents' native countries.

—Communication may be difficult between family members from the native country and the new immigrants, because many parts of their everyday lives will change, causing their perspectives to be different.

Responses to the second part of this question will vary.

ANSWERS TO QUESTIONS: DISCOVERING RHETORICAL STRATEGIES (p. 329)

1. Asturias uses method 4, discussing the advantages and disadvantages of assimilation separately in her essay. She begins by providing her readers with her cultural background and an explanation of the way it has enriched her life. The transition "however, there are trade-offs" (para. 11) signals a rhetorical shift from the advantages to the disadvantages.

2. Narrative, example, cause/effect, and argumentation all play important roles in Austurias' essay. She uses example when she writes about the holidays her family celebrated, the vacations they took, and the food they ate. She uses narrative when she tells stories about her assimilation, such as how she was educated. Cause/effect is integral to this essay because its primary focus is on the way Asturias' parents raised her and how this affected her assimilation and other areas of her life. Asturias also uses persuasion as she argues that assimilation is a positive blending of people. She is very careful to maintain the balance of her argument while discussing such an emotional and provocative topic.

3. Responses to this question will vary.

In preparation for the writing assignments, the Preparing to Write questions ask students to begin to analyze the advantages and disadvantages of assimilation before they write an essay on a related topic. See pages 16–23 for suggestions on generating ideas in response to these questions.

ADDITIONAL DISCUSSION/WRITING TOPIC

Find out the career goals of all the students in your writing class. (Perhaps your instructor could have each student name aloud his or her chosen profession.) Record in one column the goals of the students born in the United States and in another of those born outside the United States. In an essay written for your classmates, compare and/or contrast the professional goals of these two groups. At the end of your essay, draw some conclusions from your comparison.

REVISING STRATEGY

The order you choose to present the details of your comparison/contrast essay is important to its success. Take a look at the overall organization of one of your comparison/contrast essays: Do you present your subject (1) in a point-by-point comparison, (2) in a subject-by-subject comparison, (3) in a combination of these two methods, or (4) in a division between similarities and differences? Is this the most effective order for achieving your purpose and reaching your audience? Revise your paper after reevaluating its overall organization.

Choosing a Topic

1. Compare two different approaches to the process of assimilation. Develop your own guidelines for making the comparison; then, write an essay for your fellow students about the similarities and differences you have observed between these two different approaches. Be sure to decide on a purpose and point of view before you begin to write.

2. Interview your mother and father about their separate family backgrounds. If you have grandparents or step-parents, interview them as well. Then compare and contrast these various influences in your life. Which of these are alike? Which are different? How have you personally dealt with these similarities and differences? Be sure to decide on a purpose and point of view before you begin to write.

3. In her essay, Asturias says in a variety of ways that sharing cultures and traditions is beneficial both to individuals and to society. Where do you stand on this issue? Write an essay to be published in your hometown newspaper weighing the pros and cons of this issue but defending only one side or the other.

JOYCE CAROL OATES
(1938–   )

■ ■ ■

On Boxing

A prolific author of short stories, novels, and critical essays, Joyce Carol Oates was born in Lockport, New York. After earning a B.A. from Syracuse University and an M.A. in English from the University of Wisconsin, she taught English and creative writing at the University of Detroit and the University of Windsor (Ontario, Canada) before becoming a professor of English and writer-in-residence at Princeton University. At age twenty-five, she published her first collection of short stories, *By the North Gate* (1963), which prompted praise from reviewers and comparisons with the work of William Faulkner, because both authors wrote about southern pride, rural violence, and fictitious communities "cradled in tradition." Subsequent publications have included *A Garden of Earthly Delights* (1967), *Marriage and Infidelities* (1972), *Crossing the Border* (1976), *Unholy Loves* (1979), *Angel of Light* (1981), *Solstice* (1985), *Wild Nights* (1985), *You Must Remember This* (1987), *On Boxing* (1987), *American Appetites* (1989), and *Because It Is Bitter, and Because It Is My Heart* (1990). Her most prominent books of literary criticism are *The Edge of Impossibility* (1971), *The Poetry of D. H. Lawrence* (1973), and *New Heaven, New Earth* (1974). Describing herself as an author "who writes in flurries," she nevertheless is "strongly in favor of intelligent, even fastidious revision, which is, or certainly should be, an art in itself. There are pages in recent novels that I've rewritten as many as seventeen times." Oates now lives near Princeton University, where she enjoys playing tennis and practicing the piano.

Preparing to Read

The following essay, taken from *On Boxing*, gives us insight into the sport of boxing by comparing it to a story—a "unique and highly condensed drama without words." Because the comparison is sustained for the entire essay, it is an analogy. As you prepare to read this extended comparison, take a few minutes to think about your favorite sport: Why do you like this sport? Do you usually watch it or participate in it? If you do both, what are the major differences between these two roles? Who are your heroes or heroines in this activ-

PREREADING

The purpose of this Preparing to Read material is to encourage students to think about their favorite sports. To help your students focus their attention on these sports before they respond to the questions here, you might have your class divide into groups of 3 or 4 and describe their favorite sport to the group (without using any direct references to each sport) until someone guesses it. See pages 3–6 for other ways to generate thoughts on these questions.

BACKGROUND INFORMATION

In this brief essay, Joyce Carol Oates depicts a boxing match as "a story . . . without words" (para. 1), a narrative event in which the language is "a dialogue between the boxers of the most refined sort" (para. 6).

READABILITY LEVEL

13.8

RELATED READINGS

Sports and Fitness

DEFINITIONS

Nietzsche (para. 4): Friedrich Nietzsche
(1844–1900), a German philosopher.
Hellenic (para. 4): pertaining to the ancient
Greeks.
Muhammad Ali (1942–) (para. 5): a
former professional boxer.
Joe Louis (1914–1981) (para. 7): a
professional boxer.
Billy Conn (1917–) (para. 7): a former
professional boxer.
Joe Frazier (1944–) (para. 7): a former
professional boxer.
Marvin Hagler (1954–) (para. 7): a former
professional boxer.
Thomas Hearns (1959–) (para. 7): a former
professional boxer.
Well-Tempered Clavier (para. 7): Johann
Sebastian Bach's collection of 48 preludes
and fugues.

COLLABORATIVE LEARNING:
CLASS ACTIVITY

Have your students think of analogies for
the following sports: soccer, volleyball,
swimming, tennis, basketball, and football.
Have them generate several analogies for
each sport. Then, have the whole class discuss the virtues of each analogy and decide
which one would work best for each sport.

COLLABORATIVE LEARNING:
SMALL GROUP ACTIVITY

Divide your students into groups of 4 or 5,
and have them choose another activity that
is like a story. Then, have each group act out
the activity for the class until the other students guess what it is. Encourage all students in each group to participate (even the
shy ones).

ity? Why are they your heroes or heroines? Do they serve as role
models for you in any other way?

■─────────────────────────────────■

Each boxing match is a story—a unique and highly con- 1
densed drama without words. Even when nothing sensational
happens: Then the drama is "merely" psychological. Boxers are
there to establish an absolute experience, a public accounting of
the outermost limits of their beings; they will know, as few of us
can know of ourselves, what physical and psychic power they
possess—of how much, or how little, they are capable. To enter
the ring near-naked and to risk one's life is to make of one's audience voyeurs of a kind: Boxing is so intimate. It is to ease out of
sanity's consciousness and into another, difficult to name. It is to
risk, and sometimes to realize, the agony of which *agon* (Greek,
"contest") is the root.

In the boxing ring there are two principal players, overseen 2
by a shadowy third. The ceremonial ringing of the bell is a summoning to full wakefulness for both boxers and spectators. It sets
into motion, too, the authority of Time.

The boxers will bring to the fight everything that is them- 3
selves, and everything will be exposed—including secrets about
themselves they cannot fully realize. The physical self, the maleness, one might say, underlying the "self." There are boxers possessed of such remarkable intuition, such uncanny prescience,
one would think they were somehow recalling their fights, not
fighting them as we watch. There are boxers who perform skillfully, but mechanically, who cannot improvise in response to another's alteration of strategy; there are boxers performing at the
peak of their talent who come to realize, mid-fight, that it will not
be enough; there are boxers—including great champions—whose
careers end abruptly, and irrevocably, as we watch. There has
been at least one boxer possessed of an extraordinary and disqui-
eting awareness not only of his opponent's every move and anticipated move but of the audience's keenest shifts in mood as well,
for which he seems to have felt personally responsible—Cassius
Clay/Muhammad Ali, of course. "The Sweet Science of Bruising"
celebrates the physicality of men even as it dramatizes the limitations, sometimes tragic, more often poignant, of the physical.
Though male spectators identify with boxers, no boxer behaves
like a "normal" man when he is in the ring and no combination of

blows is "natural." All is style.

Every talent must unfold itself in fighting. So Nietzche speaks of the Hellenic past, the history of the "contest"—athletic, and otherwise—by which Greek youths were educated into Greek citizenry. Without the ferocity of competition, without, even "envy, jealousy, and ambition" in the contest, the Hellenic city, like the Hellenic man, degenerated. If death is a risk, death is also the prize—for the winning athlete. . . .

If a boxing match is a story it is an always wayward story, one in which anything can happen. And in a matter of seconds. Split seconds! (Muhammad Ali boasted that he could throw a punch faster than the eye could follow, and he may have been right.) In no other sport can so much take place in so brief a period of time, and so irrevocably.

Because a boxing match is a story without words, this doesn't mean that it has no text or no language, that it is somehow "brute," "primitive," "inarticulate," only that the text is improvised in action; the language a dialogue between the boxers of the most refined sort (one might say, as much neurological as psychological: a dialogue of split-second reflexes) in a joint response to the mysterious will of the audience, which is always that the fight be a worthy one so that the crude paraphernalia of the setting— ring, lights, ropes, stained canvas, the staring onlookers themselves—be erased, forgotten. (As in the theater or the church, settings are erased by way, ideally, of transcendent action.) Ringside announcers give to the wordless spectacle a narrative unity, yet boxing as performance is more clearly akin to dance or music than narrative.

To turn from an ordinary preliminary match to a "Fight of the Century" like those between Joe Louis and Billy Conn, Joe Frazier and Muhammad Ali, Marvin Hagler and Thomas Hearns is to turn from listening or half-listening to a guitar being idly plucked to hearing Bach's *Well-Tempered Clavier* perfectly executed, and that too is part of the story's mystery: so much happens so swiftly and with such heart-stopping subtlety you cannot absorb it except to know that something profound is happening and it is happening in a place beyond words.

ANSWERS TO QUESTIONS: UNDERSTANDING DETAILS (p. 334)

1. Oates believes that the excitement of boxing comes from the fact that the struggle between fighters is a drama in which each boxer must anticipate what will happen next and, at the same time, respond in an original and skillful way. Thus, in boxing, the fighters must be as creative as possible in their battle against each other.

2. The language of boxing consists of physical and psychological reflexes and responses between the boxers, the audience, and the clock. Though it cannot be heard, the language of boxing reveals "that something profound is happening and [that] it is happening in a place beyond words" (para. 7).

3. Mystery evolves from boxing because the audience hopes to become lost in the match so that the "crude paraphernalia" (para. 6) disappears and only the fight, the competition, is apparent. Each action creates a reaction until the fight in its unpredictability is over and a winner is named.

ANSWERS TO QUESTIONS: ANALYZING MEANING (p. 334)

1. One of the ways boxing is like a story is that as the match proceeds it builds to a climax, the point in a fight when the audience waits for the knockout, for one fighter to fall and the other to be declared the victor. Spectators serve as part of the fundamental script in boxing, as the fighters respond to each other and to their audience.

Here is a list of equations Oates makes:

"Each boxing match is a story—a unique and highly condensed drama without words" (para. 1).

"When nothing sensational happens: Then the drama is 'merely' psychological" (para. 1).

The participants in this drama are the boxers, the audience, and the clock; these combined produce a drama that comes to life with a ring of the bell (para. 2).

Each boxer uses style in the ring (para. 3).

"If a boxing match is a story it is an always wayward story, one in which anything can happen" (para. 5).

The dialogue of the boxers is both "neurological" and "psychological" (para. 6).

Boxing is more closely related to "dance or music than narrative" (para. 6).

2. Responses to this question will vary.

3. Boxing is similar to dance and music because it is physically and emotionally expressive; the audience watches the visual images of an irrevocable struggle between two men.

ANSWERS TO QUESTIONS: DISCOVERING RHETORICAL STRATEGIES (p. 334)

1. Oates employs definition, division/classification, and example in her analogy essay. She uses definition to extend her analogy of boxing, division/classification to divide boxers into categories of performance, and example to cite the names and records of famous boxers. These rhetorical strategies are effective choices for rounding out Oates' analogy and making her comparison memorable.

2. Oates is writing to people who already appreciate boxing, though they may not know exactly why. She talks about identifying with the boxers and refers to famous boxers by name. After reading this essay, many people are likely to develop a new appreciation of the sport.

3. The sentence fragments Oates uses arouse in the reader the thrill Oates feels while watching boxers in action. Beyond this point, student responses will vary.

PREWRITING

In preparation for the writing assignments, the Preparing to Write questions ask students to try to explain their interest in a particular sport before they write an essay on a related topic. See pages 16–23 for suggestions on generating ideas in response to these questions.

ADDITIONAL DISCUSSION/WRITING TOPIC

Develop an analogy between a sport and your writing process. Then expand this analogy into a coherent essay.

UNDERSTANDING DETAILS

1. What does Oates mean when she says, "Every talent must unfold itself in fighting" (paragraph 4)? What specifically is she referring to?
2. If boxing is like a story, then what is the "language" of boxing?
3. What is so mysterious about boxing? How does this mystery make boxing profound?

ANALYZING MEANING

1. Exactly how does boxing resemble a story? List the equations that Oates makes throughout the essay. What role do the spectators play in this analogy?
2. Oates says, "In no other sport can so much take place in so brief a period of time, and so irrevocably" (paragraph 5). Do you agree with this statement about boxing? Can you think of an example to disprove this contention? What other sports could be described in this same way?
3. In what ways is boxing "akin to dance or music" (paragraph 6)?

DISCOVERING RHETORICAL STRATEGIES

1. What rhetorical modes does Oates use to support her analogy? How effective are these choices for her purpose?
2. Who do you think is Oates' intended audience? On what evidence do you base your answer?
3. Oates uses sentence fragments sporadically throughout this essay (e.g., "The physical self, the maleness, one might say, underlying the 'self'" [paragraph 3]). What effect do these fragmented thoughts have on you as the reader? What effect do they create within the essay as a whole?

IDEAS FOR DISCUSSION/WRITING

Preparing to Write

Write freely about your favorite sport or form of exercise: What other familiar activity does this sport remind you of? What are the parallels between the sport and the activity? Do these parallels help you understand the sport better in any way? Explain your new understanding of the sport. Why do you like this sport more than other sports? How do you feel when you are watching or participating in this sport?

Choosing a Topic

1. For people unfamiliar with the sport you like, compare it to something they know well. Explain as many parallels between the two as you can so the sport becomes more clearly defined as your essay progresses.
2. Write an analogy essay explaining your attraction to your favorite sport. Why do you like it? How does seeing it or doing it make you feel? Why do you think it affects you this way? What does your commitment to this sport say about you?
3. In an essay written for your peers, explain why you admire one of your sports heroes or heroines. Exactly what do you like about this person's performance? In what way is he or she a role model for you? How does this person help you enjoy the sport more?

REVISING STRATEGY

A good analogy will fulfill the guidelines mentioned on page 292. Look at this definition, and underline in one of your analogy essays the parts of your analogy that fulfill these criteria. Notice where your analogy needs work. Then revise your paper according to these guidelines.

CHAPTER 7

DEFINITION

■ ■ ■

Limiting the Frame of Reference

Using Definition

Definitions help us function smoothly in a complex world. All effective communication, in fact, is continuously dependent on our unique human ability to understand and employ accurate definitions of a wide range of words, phrases, and abstract ideas. If we did not work from a set of shared definitions, we would not be able to carry on coherent conversations, write comprehensible letters, or respond to even the simplest radio and television programs. Definitions help us understand basic concrete terms (such as automobiles, laser beams, and the gross national product), discuss various events in our lives (such as snow skiing, legal proceedings, and a Cinco de Mayo celebration), and grasp difficult abstract ideas (such as the concepts of democracy, ambition, and resentment). The ability to comprehend definitions and use them effectively helps us keep our oral and written level of communication accurate and accessible to a wide variety of people.

Defining Definition

Definition is the process of explaining a word, object, or idea in such a way that the reader (or listener) knows as precisely as possible what we mean. A good definition sets up intellectual

INTRODUCTORY NOTES

As the full title of this chapter suggests, definition limits our frame of reference, thus making communication as precise and efficient as possible. The process of creating clear definitions is usually supported by several diverse rhetorical modes. For example, to define "ballet" a writer might call on cause/effect to explain the reason for its existence as an art, on division/classification to discuss the exact type of art it represents, and on process analysis to reveal its mechanical details. In like manner, definition frequently supports other rhetorical approaches in the development of an essay.

All the essays in this chapter use other rhetorical modes to create good models of extended definition. In "When Is It Rape?," Nancy Gibbs uses examples and cause/effect to define acquaintance and date rape; the exercises and writing assignments before and after this selection ask students to consider both rape and crime in general. Robert Ramirez, in "The Barrio," primarily uses description to support his definition of the barrio; the exercises accompanying this essay suggest topics for thought and writing related to people and places that are special to your students. Tom Wolfe's "The Right Stuff" calls on description, narration, division/classification, and process analysis to define success in naval flight training; the prereading, prewriting, and writing assignments require students to consider and explain various facets of success and failure in other areas of life. "Television Addiction," by Marie Winn, defines this affliction mainly through comparison/contrast; the assignments before and after this essay ask students to consider the role of television in their own lives and then to discuss and write about that topic and related subjects. Susan Sontag's "On AIDS" uses numerous metaphors to define this frightening disease; the accompanying questions and writing assignments ask students to consider, discuss, and write about AIDS, our reactions to AIDS, and the metaphors used in defining various other diseases.

boundaries by focusing on the special qualities of a word or phrase that set it apart from other similar words or phrases. Clear definitions always give the writer and reader a mutual starting point on the sometimes bumpy road to successful communication.

Definitions vary from short, dictionary-length summaries to longer, "extended" accounts that determine the form of an entire essay. Words or ideas that require expanded definitions are usually abstract, complex, or unavoidably controversial; they generally bear many related meanings or many shades of meaning. Definitions can be *objective* (technically precise and generally dry) or *subjective* (colored with personal opinion), and they can be used to instruct, entertain, or accomplish a combination of these two fundamental rhetorical goals.

In the following excerpt, a student defines "childhood" by putting it into perspective with other important stages of life. Though mostly entertaining, the paragraph is also instructive as the student objectively captures the essence of this phase of human development.

> Childhood is a stage of growth somewhere between infancy and adolescence. Just as each developmental period in our lives brings new changes and concerns, childhood serves as the threshold to puberty—the time we learn to discriminate between good and bad, right and wrong, love and lust. Childhood is neither a time of irresponsible infancy nor responsible adulthood. Rather, it is marked by duties that we don't really want, challenges that excite us, feelings that puzzle and frighten us, and limitless opportunities that help us explore the world around us. Childhood is a time when we solidify our personalities in spite of pressures to be someone else.

Reading and Writing Definition Essays

Extended definitions, which usually range from two or three paragraphs to an entire essay, seldom follow a set pattern of development or organization. Instead, as you will see from the examples in this chapter, they draw on a number of different techniques to help explain a word, object, term, concept, or phenomenon.

HOW TO READ A DEFINITION ESSAY

Preparing to Read.   As you begin to read each of the definition essays in this chapter, take some time to consider the author's title and the synopsis of the essay in the Rhetorical Table of Contents: How much can you learn about Nancy Gibbs' topic from her title "When Is It Rape?" What is Marie Winn's attitude toward television in "Television Addiction"? What do you sense is the general mood of Susan Sontag's "On AIDS"?

Equally important as you prepare to read is scanning an essay and finding information from its preliminary material about the author and the circumstances surrounding the composition of the essay. What do you think is Robert Ramirez's purpose in his definition of the barrio? And what can you learn about Tom Wolfe and his qualifications for writing *The Right Stuff*?

Last, as you prepare to read these essays, answer the prereading questions before each essay and then spend a few minutes thinking freely about the general subject of the essay at hand: What do you want to know from Wolfe about astronaut training in the 1960s? What role does TV play in your life (Winn)? What information do you need about AIDS (Sontag)?

Reading. As you read a definition essay, as with all essays, be sure to record your initial reactions to your reading material. What are some of your thoughts or associations in relation to each essay? As you get more involved in the essay, reconsider the preliminary material so you can create a context within which to analyze what the writer is saying: What is Gibbs' purpose for writing "When Is It Rape?" Does her tone effectively supplement that purpose? Who do you think is Ramirez's primary audience? Do you think his essay will effectively reach that group of people? In what ways is Winn qualified to write about television addiction? Also, determine at this point whether the author's treatment of his or her subject is predominantly objective or subjective. Then, make sure you are understanding the main points of the essay on the literal, interpretive, and analytical levels by reading the questions that follow.

Rereading. When you read these definition essays for a second time, check to see how each writer actually sets forth his or her definition: Does the writer put each item in a specific category with clear boundaries? Do you understand how the item being defined is different from other items in the same category? Did the author name the various components of the item, explain its etymology (linguistic origin and history), discuss what it is not, or perform a combination of these tasks? To evaluate the effec-

TEACHING DEFINITION: ONE INSTRUCTOR'S COMMENTS

I teach definition because writers have an obligation to define those words/terms that may be unfamiliar to the reader. Definition plays a large part in adjusting material to a certain audience and enhancing the readability of an essay. A knowledge of the techniques used to define can also help students in reading their textbooks in other courses, particularly those with technical terms.

Definition works for me either as an introduction to several of the modes (classification/division, comparison/contrast, example, etc.) or as a "wrap-up" to show their use in defining.

I like to open a class session on definition by asking students, "What do you know about a tiger?" This question quickly generates enough information to write a formal definition (the class to which a tiger belongs and the characteristics that distinguish it from other members of that class). Then, "What do you know about a lion?" can lead to comparison and contrast.

Mary Lou Conlin
Cuyahoga Community College
Cleveland, Ohio

To illustrate that the clear definition of terms is essential for good communication and a useful tool in general, I ask each student to choose what George Orwell ("Politics and the English Language") calls a "meaningless" term"—a term with too much meaning that requires further clarification, such as *truth, tyranny, love, beauty*. Their final papers extend the definitions of this term, using whatever aids to definition they need. This assignment forces them to think clearly and precisely and is their most difficult (and usually best) paper.

Joanne H. McCarthy
Tacoma Community College
Tacoma, Washington

tiveness of a definition essay, you need to reconsider the essay's primary purpose and audience. If Wolfe is trying to get the general reader to understand the rigors of military flight training, how effective is he in doing so? In like manner, is Winn successful in communicating the nature and seriousness of TV addiction? Especially applicable is the question of what other rhetorical strategies help the author communicate this purpose. What other modes does Ramirez use to help him define the barrio? Through what other modes does Sontag define AIDS?

For an inventory of the reading process, you can review the guidelines on pages 15–16 of the Introduction.

HOW TO WRITE A DEFINITION ESSAY

Preparing to Write. As with other essays, you should begin the task of writing a definition essay by answering the prewriting questions featured in this text and then by exploring your subject and generating other ideas. (See the explanation of various prewriting techniques in the Introduction.) Be sure you know what you are going to define and how you will approach your definition. You should then focus on a specific audience and purpose as you approach the writing assignment.

Writing. The next step toward developing a definition essay is usually to describe the general category to which the word belongs and then to contrast the word with all other words in that group. To define "exposition," for example, you might say that it is a type of writing. Then, to differentiate it from other types of writing, you could go on to say that its main purpose is to "expose" or present information, as opposed to rhetorical modes such as description or narration, which have different purposes. In addition, you might want to cite some expository methods—such as example, process analysis, division/classification, or comparison/contrast.

Yet another way to begin a definition essay is to provide a term's etymology. Tracing a word's origin often illuminates its current meaning and usage as well. "Exposition," for example, comes from the Latin *exponere*, meaning "to put forth, set forth, display, declare, or publish" (*ex* = out; *ponere* = to put or place). This information can generally be found in any good dictionary or in a good encyclopedia.

Another approach to defining a term is to explain what it does *not* mean. "Exposition" is not description or narration; nor is it poetry of any kind. By limiting the readers' frame of reference in these various ways, you are helping to establish a working definition for the term under consideration.

Finally rhetorical methods that we have already studied, such as description, narration, example, process analysis, division/classification, and comparison/contrast, are particularly useful to writers in expanding their definitions. To clarify the term "exposition," you might **describe** the details of an expository theme, **narrate** a story about the wide use of the term in today's classroom, or **give examples** of assignments that would produce good expository writing. In other situations, you could **analyze** various writing assignments and discuss the **process** of producing an expository essay, **classify** exposition apart from creative writing and then **divide** it into categories similar to the headings of this book, or **compare** and **contrast** it with creative writing. Writers also use definition quite often to support other rhetorical modes.

Rewriting.   Reviewing and revising a definition essay is a relatively straightforward task: Have you chosen an effective beginning for your paper? Have you used appropriate rhetorical strategies for developing your ideas? Will your explanation be clear to your intended audience? Do you achieve your overall purpose as effectively as possible?

Other guidelines to direct your writing and revising appear on pages 27–28 of the Introduction.

Student Essay: Definition at Work

In the following essay, a student defines "the perfect yuppie." Notice how the writer puts this term in a category, then explains the limits of that category and the uniqueness of this term within the category. To further inform her audience about the features of "yuppiedom," the student calls upon the word's etymology, its dictionary definition, an itemization of the term's basic characteristics, a number of examples that explain those characteristics, and, finally, a general discussion of cause/effect.

The Perfect Yuppie

Etymology/dictionary definition

Many people already know that the letters "Y.U.P." stand for "young urban professional." "Young" in this context is understood to mean thirtyish; "urban" often means suburban; and "professional" means most definitely college-educated.

General category of word being defined

Double the "P" and add an "I" and an "E" at the

Subject end, and you get yuppie—that 1980s bourgeois, the
marketers' darling, and the sixties' inheritance. But

Limitations set let's not generalize. Not every 30-year-old suburban college graduate qualifies as a yuppie. Nor is
Why the dictionary definition is inadequate
every yuppie in his or her thirties. True yuppiness
involves much more than the words that make up

Writer establishes credibility the acronym. Being the little sister of a couple of
yups, I am in an especially good position to define
the perfect yuppie. I watched two develop.

The essence of yuppiness is generally new
General characteristic
money. In the yuppie's defense, I will admit that
most yuppies have worked hard for their money
and social status. Moreover, the baby boom of
which they are a part has caused a glut of manpower in their age bracket, forcing them to be competitive if they want all the nice things retailers
have designed for them. But with new money

General characteristic comes an interesting combination of wealth,
naivete, and pretentiousness.

For example, most yuppies worthy of the title
Specific example have long ago traded in their fringed suede jackets
for fancy fur coats. Although they were animal
rights activists in the sixties, they will not notice the
irony of this change. In fact, they may be shameless
enough to parade in their fur coats—fashion-show
Specific example
style—for friends and family. Because of their "innocence," yuppies generally will not see the vul-
garity of their actions.

Because they are often quite wealthy, yuppies
General characteristic tend to have a lot of "things." They are simply
overwhelmed with the responsibility of spending
all that money. For example, one yup I know has 14
Specific example
pairs of sunglasses and 7 watches. She, her husband, and their three children own at least twenty
collections of everything from comic books to Civil
Specific example
War memorabilia. Most yuppies have so much
money that I often wonder why the word "yuppie"
does not have a $ in it somewhere.

Perhaps in an effort to rid themselves of this fi-
General characteristic nancial burden, all good yuppies go to Europe as
soon as possible. Not Germany or France or Portu-
gal, mind you, but Europe. They do not know what
they are doing there, and thus generally spend
much more money than they need to—but, after
all, no yuppie ever claimed to be frugal. Most im-

General characteristic · portant, they <u>bring home slides of Europe and show them</u> to everyone they know. A really good yuppie will forget and show you his or her slides more than once. Incidentally, when everyone has seen the slides of Europe twice, the yuppie's next stop is Australia.

General characteristic · A favorite pastime of yuppies is having <u>wine-tasting parties</u> for their yuppie friends. At these parties, they must <u>make a great to-do about tasting the wine</u>, · Specific example · cupping their faces over the glass with their palms (as if they were having a facial), and even sniffing the cork, for goodness sake. I once knew a yuppie who <u>did not understand that a bottle of wine could not be rejected simply because he found he "did not like that kind."</u> · Specific example · Another enjoyed · Specific example · <u>making a show of having his wife choose and taste the wine occasionally, which they both thought was adorable.</u>

What it is not · Some yuppie wanna-be's drive red or black <u>BMWs</u>; but don't let them fool you. A genuine, hard-core yuppie will usually <u>own a gold or silver Volvo station wagon</u>. · General characteristic · In this <u>yuppie-mobile</u>, the yuppie wife will chauffeur her young yupettes to and from their <u>modeling classes, track meets, ballet, the manicurist, and boy scouts</u>, · Specific examples · for the young yuppie is generally as competitive and socially active as his or her parents. On the same topic, one particularly annoying trait of yuppie parents is bragging about their yupettes. You will know yuppies by the fact that they <u>have the smartest, most talented children in the world</u>. · General characteristic · They <u>will show you their kids' report cards, making sure you notice any improvements from last quarter.</u> · Specific example

Perhaps I have been harsh in my portrayal of the perfect yuppie, and, certainly, I will be accused by some of stereotyping. But consider this: I never classify people as yuppies who do not so classify themselves. The ultimate criterion for being yuppies is that <u>they will always proudly label themselves as such.</u> · General characteristic and concluding statement

Student Writer's Comments

For me, the most difficult part about writing a definition essay was choosing a topic. I knew it had to be a word or phrase with different shades of meaning; but it also had to be either something I know more about than the average person or something I have an unusual perspective on. I figured "yuppie" was a good word, not only because it has different meanings for different people, but also because it is an acronym, and acronyms tend to be greater than the sum of their parts. I started by looking the word up in the dictionary and using the etymology for my opening sentence. After explaining why the dictionary definition was inadequate, I gave some general characteristics of yuppies, working with humorous examples from my personal experience. I suppose you could say I also used a little argument and persuasion, because I was trying to make a point about how some yuppies have lost the 1960s values they once had.

Some Final Thoughts on Definition

The following selections feature extended definitions whose main purpose is to explain a specific term or idea to their readers. Each essay in its own way helps the audience identify with various parts of its definitions, and each successfully communicates the unique qualities of the term or idea in question. Notice what approaches to definition each writer takes and how these approaches limit the readers' frame of reference in the process of effective communication.

NANCY GIBBS
(1960–   )

■ ■ ■

When Is It Rape?

Nancy Gibbs, a New York City native, graduated *summa cum laude* from Yale with a degree in history; she also attended Oxford University, where she studied politics and philosophy while on a prestigious Marshall Scholarship. She began working for *Time* magazine in 1985, where she was originally assigned to the international section. Two years later she transferred to business and the economy just in time to help cover the stock market crash of 1987. The following year she became a feature writer, covering such topics as child labor laws, racism on campus, the elderly in America, emergency care, the right to die, homelessness, and the changing doctor–patient relationship. She currently writes on national affairs and domestic policy issues for *Time*'s Nation section. Her book *Children of Light* (1985) details the history of Quaker education in the state of New York. A frequent guest on radio and television talk shows, Gibbs is also an active member of the Fifth Avenue Presbyterian Church, where she serves as head of the Board of Deacons. In her spare time she enjoys sailing and dancing. Her advice to students using *The Prose Reader* is to "keep writing." "The more you do it," she explains, "the better you get." She also urges student writers to seek out criticism from someone they respect: "Find a writing mentor, and pay attention to what that person tells you."

Preparing to Read

The following essay, originally published in *Time* (June 3, 1991), examines the social, legal, and moral aspects of rape—particularly "date rape"—and its effects upon the men and women involved. As you prepare to read Gibbs' definition of date rape, pause a few moments to think about any associations you make with the word "rape": What is your definition of "rape"? Why might different people have developed different definitions for this word? Why has this topic been so hotly debated on college campuses recently? What biases do people have in connection with rape? Why do so few rape victims ever report the crime? How successful has our legal system been in dealing with this problem in the past?

QUOTATION ON THINKING

"Language is often seen as a window which keeps us from enjoying an immediate vision. The pedagogical corollary is that the best we can do is to teach window washing, trying to keep the view of what's 'really there' unobstructed by keeping the prose clean and clear."

Ann E. Berthoff

PREREADING

The purpose of this Preparing to Read material is to encourage students to think about their personal associations with the word "rape." To help your students focus their attention on this crime before responding to the questions here, you might have the class members privately list for three minutes any associations they have with the word "rape." A time limit is necessary so that students, at this point, can concentrate on their most immediate connotations. A discussion of these items is not advisable now, because it might become too emotional or heated before all students are able to discover their personal opinions on this highly charged subject. See pages 3–6 for other ways to generate thoughts on these questions.

BACKGROUND INFORMATION

This essay deals with a subject that is sensitive for both males and females. Rape has long been a crime in American society, but only recently has the public's attention been turned to the occurrence of rape on college campuses. The terms "acquaintance rape" and "date rape" now encompass approximately 80 percent of the rapes that take place in our country. Gibbs does a good job of defining this new extension of an old crime and posing some important questions in a new light.

READABILITY LEVEL

9.5

RELATED READINGS

Crime

Sexism

Sexuality

Societal Problems

1 Be careful of strangers and hurry home, says a mother to her daughter, knowing that the world is a frightful place but not wishing to swaddle a child in fear. Girls grow up scarred by caution and enter adulthood eager to shake free of their parents' worst nightmares. They still know to be wary of strangers. What they don't know is whether they have more to fear from their friends.

2 Most women who get raped are raped by people they already know—like the boy in biology class, or the guy in the office down the hall, or their friend's brother. The familiarity is enough to make them let down their guard, sometimes even enough to make them wonder afterward whether they were "really raped." What people think of as "real rape"—the assault by a monstrous stranger lurking in the shadows—accounts for only 1 out of 5 attacks.

3 So the phrase "acquaintance rape" was coined to describe the rest, all the cases of forced sex between people who already knew each other, however casually. But that was too clinical for headline writers, and so the popular term is the narrower "date rape," which suggests an ugly ending to a raucous night on the town.

4 These are not idle distinctions. Behind the search for labels is the central mythology about rape: that rapists are always strangers, and victims are women who ask for it. The mythology is hard to dispel because the crime is so rarely exposed. The experts guess—that's all they can do under the circumstances—that while 1 in 4 women will be raped in her lifetime, less than 10% will report the assault, and less than 5% of the rapists will go to jail.

5 When a story of the crime lodges in the headlines, the myths have a way of cluttering the search for the truth. The tale of Good Friday in Palm Beach landed in the news because it involved a Kennedy, but it may end up as a watershed case, because all the mysteries and passions surrounding date rape are here to be dissected. William Kennedy Smith met a woman at a bar, invited her back home late at night and apparently had sex with her on the lawn. She says it was rape, and the police believed her story enough to charge him with the crime. Perhaps it was the bruises on her leg; or the instincts of the investigators who found her, panicked and shaking, curled up in the fetal position on a couch; or the lie-detector tests she passed.

6 On the other side, Smith has adamantly protested that he is a man falsely accused. His friends and family testify to his gentle nature and moral fiber and insist that he could not possibly have

committed such a crime. Maybe the truth will come out in court—but regardless of its finale, the case has shoved the debate over date rape into the minds of average men and women. Plant the topic in a conversation, and chances are it will ripen into a bitter argument or a jittery sequence of pale jokes.

Women charge that date rape is the hidden crime; men complain it is hard to prevent a crime they can't define. Women say it isn't taken seriously; men say it is a concept invented by women who like to tease but not take the consequences. Women say the date-rape debate is the first time the nation has talked frankly about sex; men say it is women's unconscious reaction to the excesses of the sexual revolution. Meanwhile, men and women argue among themselves about the "gray area" that surrounds the whole murky arena of sexual relations, and there is no consensus in sight.

In court, on campus, in conversation, the issue turns on the elasticity of the word *rape*, one of the few words in the language with the power to summon a shared image of a horrible crime.

At one extreme are those who argue that for the word to retain its impact, it must be strictly defined as forced sexual intercourse: a gang of thugs jumping a jogger in Central Park, a psychopath preying on old women in a housing complex, a man with an ice pick in a side street. To stretch the definition of the word risks stripping away its power. In this view, if it happened on a date, it wasn't rape. A romantic encounter is a context in which sex *could* occur, and so what omniscient judge will decide whether there was genuine mutual consent?

Others are willing to concede that date rape sometimes occurs, that sometimes a man goes too far on a date without a woman's consent. But this infraction, they say, is not as ghastly a crime as street rape, and it should not be taken as seriously. The *New York Post,* alarmed by the Willy Smith case, wrote in a recent editorial, "If the sexual encounter, *forced or not,* has been preceded by a series of consensual activities—drinking, a trip to the man's home, a walk on a deserted beach at 3 in the morning—the charge that's leveled against the alleged offender should, it seems to us, be different than the one filed against, say, the youths who raped and beat the jogger."

This attitude sparks rage among women who carry scars received at the hands of men they knew. It makes no difference if the victim shared a drink or a moonlit walk or even a passionate kiss, they protest, if the encounter ended with her being thrown to the ground and forcibly violated. Date rape is not about a mis-

---

DEFINITIONS:

William Kennedy Smith (1960–   ) (para. 5): a medical student acquitted by a Palm Beach, Florida, jury on December 11, 1991, of the charge of rape; nephew of Senator Edward Kennedy.

William the Conqueror (1027–1087) (para. 23): the Duke of Normandy who invaded England in 1066 and won the throne; king of England from 1066 to 1087.

onus (para. 37): burden of proof.

celluloid (para. 38): films, movies.

Gone With the Wind (1939) (para. 39): the Academy Award-winning movie about the decline of the South during the Civil War, based on a book by Margaret Mitchell that won a Pulitzer Prize in 1937.

Errol Flynn (1909–1959) (para. 39): an American actor best known for his roles as a swashbuckling hero.

A Streetcar Named Desire (1947) (para. 39): a play by Tennessee Williams that won a Pulitzer Prize in 1947.

Homer (para. 39): the Greek epic poet who wrote the *Iliad* and *Odyssey* (850 B.C.).

Jane Austen (1775–1817) (para. 39): an English author; wrote *Pride and Prejudice* and other novels.

Don Giovanni (para. 39): an opera composed by Mozart in 1787.

Rigoletto (para. 39): an opera composed by Giuseppi Verdi in 1851.

The Accused (1988) (para. 41): a movie starring Jodie Foster about a woman gang-raped in a bar who presses charges against her rapists and those cheering them on even though she is encouraged by her lawyer not to do so.

Prized Possessions (1990) (para. 41) a book about an upper-class Manhattan girl who is raped by an acquaintance at her private college's freshman orientation; written by Avery Corman, best known for his book *Kramer Versus Kramer*.

Have the entire class discuss Gibbs' summary in paragraph 7 of the different views men and women have on the issue of date rape. To what extent are both of these stands reasonable? What makes them both reasonable? Which seems more truthful to you? What is the "gray area" that Gibbs refers to? Why does Gibbs say there is no consensus in sight? Do you agree?

understanding, they say. It is not a communications problem. It is not about a woman's having regrets in the morning for a decision she made the night before. It is not about a "decision" at all. Rape is rape, and any form of forced sex—even between neighbors, co-workers, classmates and casual friends—is a crime.

A more extreme form of that view comes from activists who see rape as a metaphor, its definition swelling to cover any kind of oppression of women. Rape, seen in this light, can occur not only on a date but also in a marriage, not only by violent assault but also by psychological pressure. A Swarthmore College training pamphlet once explained that acquaintance rape "spans a spectrum of incidents and behaviors, ranging from crimes legally defined as rape to verbal harassment and inappropriate innuendo." 12

No wonder, then, that the battles become so heated. When innuendo qualifies as rape, the definitions have become so slippery that the entire subject sinks into a political swamp. The only way to capture the hard reality is to tell the story. 13

A 32-year-old woman was on business in Tampa last year for the Florida supreme court. Stranded at the courthouse, she accepted a lift from a lawyer involved in her project. As they chatted on the ride home, she recalls, "he was saying all the right things, so I started to trust him." She agreed to have dinner, and afterward, at her hotel door, he convinced her to let him come in to talk. "I went through the whole thing about being old-fashioned," she says. "I was a virgin until I was 21. So I told him talk was all we were going to do." 14

But as they sat on the couch, she found herself falling asleep. "By now, I'm comfortable with him, and I put my head on his shoulder. He's not tried anything all evening, after all." Which is when the rape came. "I woke up to find him on top of me, forcing himself on me. I didn't scream or run. All I could think about was my business contacts and what if they saw me run out of my room screaming rape. 15

"I thought it was my fault. I felt so filthy, I washed myself over and over in hot water. Did he rape me?, I kept asking myself. I didn't consent. But who's gonna believe me? I had a man in my hotel room after midnight." More than a year later, she still can't tell the story without a visible struggle to maintain her composure. Police referred the case to the state attorney's office in Tampa, but without more evidence it decided not to prosecute. Although her attacker has admitted that he heard her say no, maintains the woman, "he says he didn't know that I meant no. 16

He didn't feel he'd raped me, and he even wanted to see me again."

Her story is typical in many ways. The victim herself may not be sure right away that she has been raped, that she had said no and been physically forced into having sex anyway. And the rapist commonly hears but does not heed the protest. "A date rapist will follow through no matter what the woman wants because his agenda is to get laid," says Claire Walsh, a Florida-based consultant on sexual assaults. "First comes the dinner, then a dance, then a drink, then the coercion begins." Gentle persuasion gives way to physical intimidation, with alcohol as the ubiquitous lubricant. "When that fails, force is used," she says. "Real men don't take no for an answer."

The Palm Beach case serves to remind women that if they go ahead and press charges, they can expect to go on trial along with their attacker, if not in a courtroom then in the court of public opinion. The *New York Times* caused an uproar on its own staff not only for publishing the victim's name but also for laying out in detail her background, her high school grades, her driving record, along with an unattributed quote from a school official about her "little wild streak." A freshman at Carleton College in Minnesota, who says she was repeatedly raped for four hours by a fellow student, claims that she was asked at an administrative hearing if she performed oral sex on dates. In 1989 a man charged with raping at knife-point a woman he knew was acquitted in Florida because his victim had been wearing lace shorts and no underwear.

From a purely legal point of view, if she wants to put her attacker in jail, the survivor had better be beaten as well as raped, since bruises become a badge of credibility. She had better have reported the crime right away, before taking the hours-long shower that she craves, before burning her clothes, before curling up with the blinds down. And she would do well to be a woman of shining character. Otherwise the strict constructionist definitions of rape will prevail in court. "Juries don't have a great deal of sympathy for the victim if she's a willing participant up to the nonconsensual sexual intercourse," says Norman Kinne, a prosecutor in Dallas. "They feel that many times the victim has placed herself in the situation."Absent eyewitnesses or broken bones, a case comes down to her word against his, and the mythology of rape rarely lends her the benefit of the doubt.

She should also hope for an all-male jury, preferably composed of fathers with daughters. Prosecutors have found that

17

18

19

20

COLLABORATIVE LEARNING:
SMALL GROUP ACTIVITY

Divide your students into groups of 4 or 5, and have each group design a plan for raising the students' consciousness about rape on your campus. What specific groups of people need to be informed of the dangers and consequences of this crime? What policies need to be changed on your campus? What publicity should highlight these policies? What punishments should be established? How should these punishments be enforced? Then, have one person from each group read their complete plan to the rest of the class.

women tend to be harsh judges of one another—perhaps because to find a defendant guilty is to entertain two grim realities: that anyone might be a rapist, and that every women could find herself a victim. It may be easier to believe, the experts muse, that at some level the victim asked for it. "But just because a woman makes a bad judgment, does that give the guy a moral right to rape her?" asks Dean Kilpatrick, director of the Crime Victim Research and Treatment Center at the Medical University of South Carolina. "The bottom line is, Why does a woman's having a drink give a man the right to rape her?"

Last week the Supreme Court waded into the debate with a   21
7-to-2 ruling that protects victims from being harassed on the witness stand with questions about their sexual history. The Justices, in their first decision on "rape shield laws," said an accused rapist could not present evidence about a previous sexual relationship with the victim unless he notified the court ahead of time. In her decision, Justice Sandra Day O'Connor wrote that "rape victims deserve heightened protection against surprise, harassment and unnecessary invasions of privacy."

That was welcome news to prosecutors who understand the   22
reluctance of victims to come forward. But there are other impediments to justice as well. An internal investigation of the Oakland police department found that officers ignored a quarter of all reports of sexual assaults or attempts, though 90% actually warranted investigation. Departments are getting better at educating officers in handling rape cases, but the courts remain behind. A New York City task force on women in the courts charged that judges and lawyers were routinely less inclined to believe a woman's testimony than a man's.

The present debate over degrees of rape is nothing new: All   23
through history, rapes have been divided between those that mattered and those that did not. For the first few thousand years, the only rape that was punished was the defiling of a virgin, and that was viewed as a property crime. A girl's virtue was a marketable asset, and so a rapist was often ordered to pay the victim's father the equivalent of her price on the marriage market. In early Babylonian and Hebrew societies, a married woman who was raped suffered the same fate as an adulteress—death by stoning or drowning. Under William the Conqueror, the penalty for raping a virgin was castration and loss of both eyes—unless the violated woman agreed to marry her attacker, as she was often pressured to do. "Stealing an heiress" became a perfectly conventional means of taking—literally—a wife.

It may be easier to prove a rape case now, but not much. Until the 1960s it was virtually impossible without an eyewitness; judges were often required to instruct jurors that "rape is a charge easily made and hard to defend against; so examine the testimony of this witness with caution." But sometimes a rape was taken very seriously, particularly if it involved a black man attacking a white woman—a crime for which black men were often executed or lynched.   24

Susan Estrich, author of *Real Rape,* considers herself a lucky victim. This is not just because she survived an attack 17 years ago by a stranger with an ice pick, one day before her graduation from Wellesley. It's because police, and her friends, believed her. "The first thing the Boston police asked was whether it was a black guy," recalls Estrich, now a University of Southern California law professor. When she said yes and gave the details of the attack, their reaction was, "So, you were really raped." It was an instructive lesson, she says, in understanding how racism and sexism are factored into perceptions of the crime.   25

A new twist in society's perception came in 1975, when Susan Brownmiller published her book *Against Our Will: Men, Women and Rape.* In it she attacked the concept that rape was a sex crime, arguing instead that is was a crime of violence and power over women. Throughout history, she wrote, rape has played a critical function. "It is nothing more or less than a conscious process of intimidation, by which *all men* keep *all women* in a state of fear."   26

Out of this contention was born a set of arguments that have become politically correct wisdom on campus and in academic circles. This view holds that rape is a symbol of women's vulnerability to male institutions and attitudes. "It's sociopolitical," insists Gina Rayfield, a New Jersey psychologist. "In our culture men hold the power, politically, economically. They're socialized not to see women as equals."   27

This line of reasoning has led some women, especially radicalized victims, to justify flinging around the term rape as a political weapon, referring to everything from violent sexual assaults to inappropriate innuendos. Ginny, a college senior who was really raped when she was 16, suggests that false accusations of rape can serve a useful purpose. "Penetration is not the only form of violation," she explains. In her view, rape is a subjective term, one that women must use to draw attention to other, nonviolent, even nonsexual forms of oppression. "If a woman did falsely accuse a man of rape, she may have had reasons to," Ginny says, "Maybe she wasn't raped, but he clearly violated her in some way."   28

Catherine Comins, assistant dean of student life at Vassar,   29
also sees some value in this loose use of "rape." She says angry
victims of various forms of sexual intimidation cry rape to regain
their sense of power. "To use the word carefully would be to be
careful for the sake of the violator, and the survivors don't care a
hoot about him." Comins argues that men who are unjustly accused can sometimes gain from the experience. "They have a lot
of pain, but it is not a pain that I would necessarily have spared
them. I think it ideally initiates a process of self-exploration.
'How do I see women?' 'If I didn't violate her, could I have?' 'Do I
have the potential to do to her what they say I did?' Those are
good questions."

Taken to extremes, there is an ugly element of vengeance at   30
work here. Rape is an abuse of power. But so are false accusations
of rape, and to suggest that men whose reputations are destroyed
might benefit because it will make them more sensitive is an attitude that is sure to backfire on women who are seeking justice for
all victims. On campuses where the issue is most inflamed, male
students are outraged that their names can be scrawled on a bath-
room-wall list of rapists and they have no chance to tell their side
of the story.

"Rape is what you read about in the *New York Post* about 17   31
little boys raping a jogger in Central Park," says a male freshman
at a liberal-arts college, who learned that he had been branded a
rapist after a one-night stand with a friend. He acknowledges that
they were both very drunk when she started kissing him at a
party and ended up back in his room. Even through his haze, he
had some qualms about sleeping with her: "I'm fighting against
my hormonal instincts, and my moral instincts are saying, 'This is
my friend and if I were sober, I wouldn't be doing this,'" But he
went ahead anyway. "When you're drunk, and there are all sorts
of ambiguity, and the woman says 'Please, please' and then she
says no sometime later, even in the middle of the act, there still
may very well be some kind of violation, but it's not the same
thing. It's not rape. If you don't hear her say no, if she doesn't say
it, if she's playing around with you—oh, I could get squashed for
saying it—there is an element of say no, mean yes."

The morning after their encounter, he recalls, both students   32
woke up hung over and eager to put the memory behind them.
Only months later did he learn that she had told a friend that he
had torn her clothing and raped her. At this point in the story, the
accused man starts using the language of rape. "I felt violated,"
he says. "I felt like she was taking advantage of me when she was

very drunk. I never heard her say 'No!,' 'Stop!,' anything." He is angry and hurt at the charges, worried that they will get around, shatter his reputation and force him to leave the small campus.

So here, of course, is the heart of the debate. If rape is sex without consent, how exactly should consent be defined and communicated, when and by whom? Those who view rape through a political lens tend to place all responsibility on men to make sure that their partners are consenting at every point of a sexual encounter. At the extreme, sexual relations come to resemble major surgery, requiring a signed consent form. Clinical psychologist Mary P. Koss of the University of Arizona in Tucson, who is a leading scholar on the issue, puts it rather bluntly: "It's the man's penis that is doing the raping, and ultimately he's responsible for where he puts it."

Historically, of course, this has never been the case, and there are some who argue that it shouldn't be—that women too must take responsibility for their behavior, and that the whole realm of intimate encounters defies regulation from on high. Anthropologist Lionel Tiger has little patience for trendy sexual politics that make no reference to biology. Since the dawn of time, he argues, men and women have always gone to bed with different goals. In the effort to keep one's genes in the gene pool, "it is to the male advantage to fertilize as many females as possible, as quickly as possible and as efficiently as possible." For the female, however, who looks at the large investment she will have to make in the offspring, the opposite is true. Her concern is to "select" who "will provide the best set up for their offspring." So, in general, "the pressure is on the male to be aggressive and on the female to be coy."

No one defends the use of physical force, but when the coercion involved is purely psychological, it becomes hard to assign blame after the fact. Journalist Stephanie Gutmann is an ardent foe of what she calls the date-rape dogmatists. "How can you make sex completely politically correct and completely safe?" she asks. "What a horribly bland, unerotic thing that would be! Sex is, by nature, a risky endeavor, emotionally. And desire is a violent emotion. These people in the date-rape movement have erected so many rules and regulations that I don't know how people can have erotic or desire-driven sex."

Nonsense, retorts Cornell professor Andrea Parrot, co-author of *Acquaintance Rape: The Hidden Crime.* Seduction should not be about lies, manipulation, game playing or coercion of any kind, she says. "Too bad that people think that the only way you can have passion and excitement and sex is if there are miscommunications, and one person is forced to do something he or she doesn't want to do." The very pleasures of sexual encounters should lie in the fact of mutual comfort and consent: "You can hang from the ceiling, you can use fruit, you can go crazy and have really wonderful sensual erotic sex, if both parties are consenting."

It would be easy to accuse feminists of being too quick to   37
classify sex as rape, but feminists are to be found on all sides of the debate, and many protest the idea that all the onus is on the man. It demeans women to suggest that they are so vulnerable to coercion or emotional manipulation that they must always be escorted by the strong arm of the law. "You can't solve society's ills by making everything a crime," says Albuquerque attorney Nancy Hollander. "That comes out of the sense of overprotection of women, and in the long run that is going to be harmful to us."

What is lost in the ideological debate over date rape is the fact   38
that men and women, especially when they are young, and drunk, and aroused, are not very good at communicating. "In many cases," says Estrich, "the man thought it was sex, and the woman thought it was rape, and they are both telling the truth." The man may envision a celluloid seduction, in which he is being commanding, she is being coy. A woman may experience the same event as a degrading violation of her will. That some men do not believe a woman's protests is scarcely surprising in a society so drenched with messages that women have rape fantasies and a desire to be overpowered.

By the time they reach college, men and women are loaded   39
with cultural baggage, drawn from movies, television, music videos and "bodice ripper" romance novels. Over the years they have watched Rhett sweep Scarlett up the stairs in *Gone With the Wind*; or Errol Flynn, who was charged twice with statutory rape, overpower a protesting heroine who then melts in his arms; or Stanley rape his sister-in-law Blanche du Bois while his wife is in the hospital giving birth to a child in *A Streetcar Named Desire*. Higher up the cultural food chain, young people can read of date rape in Homer or Jane Austen, watch it in *Don Giovanni* or *Rigoletto*.

The messages come early and often, and nothing in the femi-   40
nist revolution has been able to counter them. A recent survey of sixth- to ninth-graders in Rhode Island found that a fourth of the boys and a sixth of the girls said it was acceptable for a man to force a woman to kiss him or have sex if he has spent money on

her. A third of the children said it would not be wrong for a man to rape a woman who had had previous sexual experiences.

Certainly cases like Palm Beach, movies like *The Accused* and novels like Avery Corman's *Prized Possessions* may force young people to re-examine assumptions they have inherited. The use of new terms, like acquaintance rape and date rape, while controversial, has given men and women the vocabulary they need to express their experiences with both force and precision. This dialogue would be useful if it helps strip away some of the dogmas, old and new, surrounding the issue. Those who hope to raise society's sensitivity to the problem of date rape would do well to concede that it is not precisely the same sort of crime as street rape, that there may be very murky issues of intent and degree involved.

On the other hand, those who downplay the problem should come to realize that date rape is a crime of uniquely intimate cruelty. While the body is violated, the spirit is maimed. How long will it take, once the wounds have healed, before it is possible to share a walk on a beach, a drive home from work, or an evening's conversation without always listening for a quiet alarm to start ringing deep in the back of the memory of a terrible crime?

UNDERSTANDING DETAILS

1. Define the term "date rape" in your own words.
2. What are the main differences of opinion between men and women on the issue of date rape?
3. According to most women, when does sex become a crime?

ANALYZING MEANING

1. Explain three of the many ambiguous issues associated with the word "rape."
2. Why is Gibbs not surprised that some men don't believe women's protests? What lessons have these men learned from the media as they were growing up?
3. Exactly what is Gibbs asking when she says, "How long will it take, once the wounds have healed, before it is possible to share a walk on a beach, a drive home from work, or an evening's conversation without always listening for a quiet alarm to start ringing deep in the back of the memory of a terrible crime?" (paragraph 42)?

ANSWERS TO QUESTIONS:
UNDERSTANDING DETAILS (p. 355)

1. Responses to this question will vary.

2. Women, according to Gibbs, generally view date rape as (1) a violation of their will and their bodies, (2) a violent crime, (3) a crime that brings shame upon them, and (4) a crime that isn't reported or tried without great personal sacrifice on their part. But men most often characterize date rape as (1) a problem in communication, (2) a vaguely defined, almost subjective crime, (3) an exaggerated complaint that may result from postcoital remorse, or (4) a justifiable consequence of feminine flirtatious behavior.

3. Gibbs asserts that most women would agree that sex becomes a crime when it is physically forced on a man or woman and that psychological coercion can also play a role in this crime.

ANSWERS TO QUESTIONS:
ANALYZING MEANING (p. 355)

1. Responses to this question will vary.

2. Gibbs aptly points out the effect romantic movies and novels have had in promoting the idea that "no" often means "yes" when it comes from a woman. A man may believe that a woman is "being coy" (para. 38) when in reality she is simply rejecting his advances.

3. Gibbs' final question highlights a problem that is often overlooked or ignored: Women who have been raped, especially by someone they know and trust, will often have difficulty overcoming the scar of this breach of faith. A violation of trust is the very reason many will have trouble ever trusting another man again.

1. In this essay, Gibbs very carefully sets date rape apart from other types of rape. Because her topic is controversial, she must remain fairly objective throughout her essay. She maintains her objectivity by telling many sides of the story in her definition of date rape. Gibbs' personal point of view is apparent, however. She obviously believes that date rape is a frequently committed and deeply reprehensible crime.

2. Responses to this question will vary.

3. Responses to this question will vary.

PREWRITING

In preparation for the writing assignments, the Preparing to Write questions ask students to think about crime in general before they write an essay on a related topic. See pages 16–23 for suggestions on generating ideas in response to these questions.

ADDITIONAL DISCUSSION/WRITING TOPIC

In a coherent essay written for your classmates, define the term "relationship." Refer to the chapter introduction for guidelines to follow in developing a definition essay (pages 337–344).

REVISING STRATEGY

A clear sense of purpose and audience is an important key to any essay. In one of your definition papers, write out your purpose and describe your intended audience. Then underline all parts of your essay that help you achieve those goals. Notice where your intention could be clearer or more focused. Then revise this paper so that it communicates a clear, consistent purpose to your intended audience.

DISCOVERING RHETORICAL STRATEGIES

1. What rhetorical techniques explained at the beginning of this chapter does Gibbs use in her definition?
2. Choose from this essay a difference of opinion between men and women, and explain the reasoning at work on each side.
3. Gibbs has to choose her words very carefully in an essay on a subject charged with so many emotional and political ramifications. Choose one paragraph from this essay, and explain how different words would send different messages and associations. Would these changes be for the better or worse, considering Gibbs' intended audience?

IDEAS FOR DISCUSSION/WRITING

Preparing to Write

Write freely about your reactions to crimes in general: What makes an action a crime? What are the most common crimes in America today? Has your definition of rape changed since you read this article? Is there a distinction in your mind between "street rape" and "date or acquaintance rape"? If so, what is the difference? Why do you think rape has become such a frequently committed crime? Why is the issue of rape receiving so much attention on college campuses? What other crimes are common occurrences on college campuses?

Choosing a Topic

1. In a coherent essay written for your classmates, define a serious injustice or crime (other than rape) that frequently takes place on college campuses. Who typically commits these injustices or crimes? Why do they do so? Why are such activities "unjust" or "criminal"? Before you begin to write, decide on a purpose and point of view.
2. Do you think rape is a sex crime or a "crime of violence and power over women" (paragraph 26), as Susan Brownmiller argues in her book? Discuss this issue in a well-developed essay, and draw your own conclusions from your discussion.
3. Choose one of the definitional techniques explained in the introduction to this chapter, and define the word "crime" in a well-developed, logically organized essay written for the general public. Introduce your main topic at the beginning of your essay; then explain and illustrate it clearly as your essay progresses. You may use other definition techniques in addition to the controlling one.

ROBERT RAMIREZ
(1949–   )

■ ■ ■

The Barrio

QUOTATION ON READING

"But the images of men's wits and knowledges remain in books, exempted from the wrong of time, and capable of perpetual renovation."

Francis Bacon

Robert Ramirez was born and raised in Edinburg, a southern Texas town near the Mexican border in an area that has been home to his family for almost two hundred years. After graduating from the University of Texas–Pan American, he taught freshman composition and worked for a while as a photographer. For the next several years he was a salesman, reporter, and announcer/anchor for the CBS affiliate station KGBT-TV in Harlingen, Texas. His current job has brought him full-circle, back to the University of Texas–Pan American, where he serves as a development officer responsible for alumni fundraising. He loves baseball and once considered a professional career, but now contents himself with playing on local amateur teams, bike riding, and swimming. A conversion to the Baha'i faith in the 1970s has brought him much spiritual happiness. When asked to give advice to students using *The Prose Reader*, Ramirez responded, "The best writing, like anything else of value, requires a great deal of effort. Rewriting is 90 percent of the process. Sometimes, if you are fortunate, your work can take on a life of its own, and you end up writing something important that astounds and humbles you. This is what happened with 'The Barrio,' which is much better than the essay I originally intended. There's an element of the divine in it, as there is in all good writing."

Preparing to Read

First titled "The Woolen Sarape," Ramirez's essay was written while he was a student at the University of Texas–Pan American. His professor, Edward Simmens, published it in an anthology entitled *Pain and Promise: The Chicano Today* (1972). In it, the author defines the exciting, colorful, and close-knit atmosphere typical of many Hispanic barrios or communities. As you prepare to read this essay, take a few moments to think about a place that is very special to you: What are its physical characteristics? What memories are connected to this place for you? What kinds of people live there? What is the relationship of these people to each other? To people in other places? Why is this place so special to you? Is it special to anyone else?

PREREADING

The purpose of this Preparing to Read material is to encourage students to think about a place that is special to them. To help your students focus their attention on this place before they respond to the questions here, you might guide them on a mental journey with their eyes closed asking them to relax and then letting them drift off in their minds to a special place. See pages 3–6 for other ways to generate thoughts on these questions.

In this essay, Robert Ramirez defines "The Barrio" as a vivid series of unique sights, smells, noises, tastes, and textures that distinguish Chicano communities from "the coldness of the Anglo world" (para. 4) that surrounds them.

READABILITY LEVEL

8.0

RELATED READINGS

Cultural Diversity:

Hispanic Issues

Neighborhoods

DEFINITIONS

barrio (title): a Spanish-speaking segment of an urban area inhabited primarily by Hispanics.
Nahuatl (para. 2): a Native-American language; dominant language of Mexico and Central America at the time of the Spanish Conquest.
pariah (para. 4): a person rejected or despised by others; an outcast.
sarape (para. 5): variation of *serape*, a brightly colored woolen blanket often worn as an outer garment by men of Spanish-speaking countries.

The train, its metal wheels squealing as they spin along the silvery tracks, rolls slower now. Through the gaps between the cars blinks a streetlamp, and this pulsing light on a barrio streetcorner beats slower, like a weary heartbeat, until the train shudders to a halt, the light goes out, and the barrio is deep asleep. 1

Throughout Aztlán (the Nahuatl term meaning "land to the north"), trains grumble along the edges of a sleeping people. From Lower California, through the blistering Southwest, down the Rio Grande to the muddy Gulf, the darkness and mystery of dreams engulf communities fenced off by railroads, canals, and expressways. Paradoxical communities, isolated from the rest of the town by concrete columned monuments of progress, and yet stranded in the past. They are surrounded by change. It eludes their reach, in their own backyards, and the people, unable and unwilling to see the future, or even touch the present, perpetuate the past. 2

Leaning from the expressway or jolting across the tracks, one enters a different physical world permeated by a different attitude. The physical dimensions are impressive. It is a large section of town which extends for fifteen blocks north and south along the tracks, and then advances eastward, thinning into nothingness beyond the city limits. Within the invisible (yet sensible) walls of the barrio, are many, many people living in too few houses. The homes, however, are much more numerous than on the outside. 3

Members of the barrio describe the entire area as their home. It is a home, but it is more than this. The barrio is a refuge from the harshness and the coldness of the Anglo world. It is a forced refuge. The leprous people are isolated from the rest of the community and contained in their section of town. The stoical pariahs of the barrio accept their fate, and from the angry seeds of rejection grow the flowers of closeness between outcasts, not the thorns of bitterness and the mad desire to flee. There is no want to escape, for the feeling of the barrio is known only to its inhabitants, and the material needs of life can also be found here. 4

The *tortillería* fires up its machinery three times a day, producing steaming, round, flat slices of barrio bread. In the winter, the warmth of the tortilla factory is a wool sarape in the chilly morning hours, but in the summer, it unbearably toasts every noontime customer. 5

The *panadería* sends its sweet messenger aroma down the dimly lit street, announcing the arrival of fresh, hot, sugary *pan dulce*. 6

The small corner grocery serves the meal-to-meal needs of customers, and the owner, a part of the neighborhood, willingly gives credit to people unable to pay cash for foodstuffs.

The barbershop is a living room with hydraulic chairs, radio, and television, where old friends meet and speak of life as their salted hair falls aimlessly about them.

The pool hall is a junior level country club where *'chucos*, strangers in their own land, get together to shoot pool and rap, while veterans, unaware of the cracking, popping balls on the green felt, complacently play dominoes beneath rudely hung *Playboy* foldouts.

The *cantina* is the night spot of the barrio. It is the country club and the den where the rites of puberty are enacted. Here the young become men. It is in the taverns that a young dude shows his *machismo* through the quantity of beer he can hold, the stories of *rucas* he has had, and his willingness and ability to defend his image against hardened and scarred old lions.

No, there is no frantic wish to flee. It would be absurd to leave the familiar and nervously step into the strange and cold Anglo community when the needs of the Chicano can be met in the barrio.

The barrio is closeness. From the family living unit, familial relationships stretch out to immediate neighbors, down the block, around the corner, and to all parts of the barrio. The feeling of family, a rare and treasurable sentiment, pervades and accounts for the inability of the people to leave. The barrio is this attitude manifested on the countenances of the people; on the faces of their homes, and in the gaiety of their gardens.

The color-splashed homes arrest your eyes, arouse your curiosity, and make you wonder what life scenes are being played out in them. The flimsy, brightly colored, wood-frame houses ignore no neon-brilliant color. Houses trimmed in orange, chartreuse, lime green, yellow, and mixtures of these and other hues beckon the beholder to reflect on the peculiarity of each home. Passing through this land is refreshing like Brubeck, not narcoticizing like revolting rows of similar houses, which neither offend nor please.

In the evenings, the porches and front yards are occupied with men calmly talking over the noise of children playing baseball in the unpaved extension of the living room, while the women cook supper or gossip with female neighbors as they water the *jardines*. The gardens mutely echo the expressive verses of the colorful houses. The denseness of multicolored plants and

panadería (para. 6): Spanish. Bakery.
pan dulce (para. 6): Spanish. Sweet bread.
7 *'chucos* (para. 9): Spanish slang. Young Chicano men, often members of gangs.
cantina (para. 10): Spanish. A bar or saloon.
machismo (para. 10): Spanish. Toughness,
8 manhood.
rucas (para. 10): Spanish. Fights.
Brubeck (para. 13): Dave Brubeck (1920–), an American jazz pianist and
9 composer.
jardines (para. 14): Spanish. Gardens.

COLLABORATIVE LEARNING: CLASS ACTIVITY

10 Have your students individually record the associations they make with the word "neighborhood." Then, on the chalkboard or on a transparency, list all the associations your students made with this word. Note how many times each association was mentioned. Next, after your students discuss
11 these associations, list separately the associations that appear three or more times. Last, organize the words on this list from most to least common.

12

13

14 **COLLABORATIVE LEARNING: SMALL GROUP ACTIVITY**

Have your students list the characteristics of their neighborhoods, read the lists to the class, and then gather in groups according to neighborhoods. Next, have the groups devise labels for their neighborhoods.

1. The barrio is a community of people who live with all the comforts and characteristics of a big family. Financial difficulties keep people in the barrio and create an atmosphere in which people feel the need to help one another. This interdependence creates a "family" that stretches outside one's immediate family and includes responsibility to neighbors and other community members.

2. The fences in the Anglo world are insurmountable barriers, whereas the fences in the barrio decorate and show ownership without being exclusive. These fences neither prevent nor discourage barrio residents from crossing property lines.

3. Economic needs in the barrio necessitate "interdependence and closeness" within both the family and the community. Using communal family and community structures, people in the barrio combine their wages and resources to make a better life for everyone.

ANSWERS TO QUESTIONS: ANALYZING MEANING (p. 361)

1. Ramirez refers to barrio residents as "leprous" because they are forced to stay in "their section of town" (para. 4) and must become closer through a determination to live well despite rejection by the outside world. These people become so dependent upon their way of life and the closeness it brings they are unable to leave the barrio.

2. Ramirez refers to the barrio as "closeness" because it provides the closeness and interdependence inhabitants need to survive. Without this type of relationship, people in the barrio would be only distantly linked and would soon lose this sense of community responsibility. Beyond this point, responses will vary.

3. Outsiders might envy the barrio life because of the closeness, trust, and pride it embodies, but its financial problems make it less attractive. Those who inhabit the barrio cannot leave because they are financially and emotionally dependent on the barrio system, just as that system is dependent

trees gives the house the appearance of an oasis or a tropical island hideaway, sheltered from the rest of the world.

Fences are common in the barrio, but they are fences and not the walls of the Anglo community. On the western side of town, the high wooden fences between houses are thick, impenetrable walls, built to keep the neighbors at bay. In the barrio, the fences may be rusty, wire contraptions or thick green shrubs. In either case you can see through them and feel no sense of intrusion when you cross them. 15

Many lower-income families of the barrio manage to maintain a comfortable standard of living through the communal action of family members who contribute their wages to the head of the family. Economic need creates interdependence and closeness. Small barefooted boys sell papers on cool, dark Sunday mornings, deny themselves pleasantries, and give their earnings to *mamá*. The older the child, the greater the responsibility to help the head of the household provide for the rest of the family. 16

There are those, too, who for a number of reasons have not achieved a relative sense of financial security. Perhaps it results from too many children too soon, but it is the homes of these people and their situation that numbs rather than charms. Their houses, aged and bent, oozing children, are fissures in the horn of plenty. Their wooden homes may have brick-pattern asbestos tile on the outer walls, but the tile is not convincing. 17

Unable to pay city taxes or incapable of influencing the city to live up to its duty to serve all the citizens, the poorer barrio families remain trapped in the nineteenth century and survive as best they can. The backyards have well-worn paths to the outhouses, which sit near the alley. Running water is considered a luxury in some parts of the barrio. Decent drainage is usually unknown, and when it rains, the water stands for days, an incubator of health hazards and an avoidable nuisance. Streets, costly to pave, remain rough, rocky trails. Tires do not last long, and the constant rattling and shaking grind away a car's life and spread dust through screen windows. 18

The houses and their *jardines*, the jollity of the people in an adverse world, the brightly feathered alarm clock pecking away at supper and cautiously eyeing the children playing nearby, produce a mystifying sensation at finding the noble savage alive in the twentieth century. It is easy to look at the positive qualities of life in the barrio, and look at them with a distantly envious feeling. One wishes to experience the feelings of the barrio and not the hardships. Remembering the illness, the hunger, the feeling of 19 time running out on you, the walls, both real and imagined, reflecting on living in the past, one finds his envy becoming more elusive, until it has vanished altogether.

Back now beyond the tracks, the train creaks and groans, the cars jostle each other down the track, and as the light begins its pulsing, the barrio, with all its meanings, greets a new dawn with yawns and restless stretchings.

UNDERSTANDING DETAILS

1. Define the barrio in your own words.
2. What is the difference between fences in the barrio and in the Anglo community?
3. In Ramirez's view, what creates "interdependence and closeness" (paragraph 16)? How does this phenomenon work in the barrio?

ANALYZING MEANING

1. Why does Rarmirez call the people in the barrio "leprous" (paragraph 4)?
2. What does the author mean when he says that "the barrio is closeness" (paragraph 12)? How does this statement compare with the way you feel about your neighborhood? Why can't people leave the barrio?
3. Why might people look at the barrio with "a distantly envious feeling" (paragraph 19)? What other feelings may alter or even erase this sense of envy?

DISCOVERING RHETORICAL STRATEGIES

1. How does Ramirez use the train to help him define the barrio? In what ways would the essay be different without the references to the train?
2. Ramirez uses metaphors masterfully throughout this essay to help us understand the internal workings of the barrio. He relies on this technique especially in paragraphs 4 through 10. For example, a metaphor that explains how relationships develop in the barrio is, "The stoical pariahs of the barrio accept their fate, and from the angry seeds of rejection grow the flowers of closeness between outcasts, not the thorns of bitterness and the mad desire to flee" (paragraph 4). In this garden metaphor, "rejection" is likened to "angry seeds," "closeness between outcasts" to "flowers," and "bitterness" to "thorns." Find four other

upon them. In some cases, student examples may vary.

**ANSWERS TO QUESTIONS:
DISCOVERING RHETORICAL
STRATEGIES (p. 361)**

20

1. Ramirez uses the train to symbolize the lack of modernization within the barrio and to show the slow movement of change there. In the first paragraph, the train slows down as it comes to the barrio, which is asleep. The essay is framed by this description of the train, which in paragraph 20 takes on even more symbolism when it introduces a barrio that must greet "a new dawn with yawns and restless stretchings." This ending foreshadows the changes Ramirez sees coming. The people in the barrio are happy with the system Ramirez describes, but the yawns and the stretches lead the reader to believe that change will eventually alter this interdependent society.

2. Ramirez refers to the barrio as a refuge and to its people as "leprous" to set the stage for his view of the barrio as a "refuge from the harshness and the coldness of the Anglo world" (para. 4). This passage describes the discrimination and problems of the Anglo world as troubles from which the people of the barrio must find shelter just as a person escapes from bad weather. Though Ramirez never overtly points out that change is coming, he implies that something is sick or problematic within this seemingly serene and benevolent community. He describes the barrio further by giving the reader a tour of the *tortilleria*, which serves as a "wool sarape" (para. 5), and "the *panadería*," which becomes a "sweet messenger" (para. 6) for the community. In paragraph 10, Ramirez uses two metaphors that describe the *cantina* as a lion's den where "hardened and scarred old lions" challenge "the young" in their pursuit of manhood. Each of these metaphors ties together scenes from the barrio, a feeling that can be known only by "inhabitants" (para. 4). Because his audience includes people who have not lived in the barrio and may not understand the Spanish names he uses, these metaphors provide universal images through which the reader can understand the unfamiliar images and customs of this unique place.

3. Ramirez is critical of the barrio's resistance to change but is at the same time reverent and understanding. This paradoxical focus creates a serious but affectionate tone. The author's tender descriptions of barrio life and interdependence make obvious his fondness for the barrio and its people, yet the use of the train as an example of progress suggests that change is inevitable and necessary.

PREWRITING

In preparation for the writing assignments, the Preparing to Write questions ask students to consider a special place of theirs from two different perspectives before writing an essay on a related topic. See pages 16–23 for suggestions on generating ideas in response to these questions.

ADDITIONAL DISCUSSION/WRITING TOPIC

Define the word "neighborhood" for your classmates. Your definition should include both the denotations and the connotations connected with this word and should allow for a variety of interpretations.

REVISING STRATEGY

Your tone or attitude toward your subject is an important feature of successful writing. In one of your definition essays, underline all words or phrases that help you create a specific mood. Next, reread what you have underlined, and label the tone these words or phrases communicate. Is your tone consistent throughout? Is this the most effective tone for achieving your purpose and reaching your audience? Then revise your paper, making your tone as consistent and effective as possible throughout the essay.

metaphors in these paragraphs, and explain how the comparisons work. What are the familiar and less familiar items in each comparison?

3. What tone does Ramirez establish in this essay? How does he create this tone?

IDEAS FOR DISCUSSION/WRITING

Preparing to Write

Write freely about a place that is special to you: Describe this place from your perspective. Is this place special to anyone else? Describe this place from someone else's perspective. How do these descriptions differ? What characteristics differentiate this place from other places? What makes this place special for you? Use some metaphors to relay to your readers your feelings about certain features of this place. Do you think this place will always be special to you? Why or why not?

Choosing a Topic

1. Ramirez's definition of the barrio demonstrates a difference between an insider's view and an outsider's view of the same location. In an essay for your classmates, define your special place from both the inside and the outside. Then, discuss the similarities and differences between these two points of view.

2. In essay form, define the relationships among the people who are your extended family. These could be people from your neighborhood, your school, your job, or a combination of places. How did these relationships come about? Why are you close to these people? Why are these people close to you? To each other?

3. What primary cultural or social traditions have made you what you are today? In an essay written to a close friend, define the two or three most important traditions you practiced as a child, and explain what effects they had on you.

TOM WOLFE
(1931–   )

■ ■ ■

The Right Stuff

QUOTATION ON WRITING

"That is why I started to write. To save myself."

Eldridge Cleaver

Writer, journalist, artist, and social commentator Tom Wolfe was born in Richmond, Virginia, and began his literary career with a Ph.D. in American Studies from Yale University. He is best known for his contribution to a prose style called "the new journalism," which features factual writing enlivened by such fiction techniques as in-depth character analysis, expanded dialogue, and detailed descriptions of setting, clothing, and other physical features. Early articles in *Esquire* and *The New York Herald Tribune* led to his first book, *The Kandy-Kolored Tangerine-Flake Streamline Baby* (1965), a collection of twenty-two of his best essays that examine and satirize several 1960s American trends and pop-culture heroes. Wolfe followed soon after with *The Electric Kool-Aid Acid Test* (1968), which tells the story of West Coast novelist Ken Kesey and his group of "Merry Pranksters," and *Radical Chic and Mau Mauing the Flak Catchers* (1970), which in one of its two long essays describes how composer Leonard Bernstein hosted a fund-raising party for the Black Panthers. *The Painted Word* (1975) is an exposé of modern art, whereas *From Bauhaus to Our House* (1981) offers a similar treatment of modern architecture. Wolfe's finest book, according to many critics, is *The Right Stuff* (1979), a brilliantly written study of the early years of the U.S. space program (later made into a movie of the same title). In 1987, he published his first novel, *The Bonfire of the Vanities* (also made into a movie). Wolfe now lives in New York City, where he plays tennis in long white pants and works out daily using the Royal Canadian Air Force exercises. He advises student writers to be patient and persistent in their work. "Sometimes," he explains, "marvelous rushes of words will just fall into place. Other times you just have to put your head in a vise and make them come out."

Preparing to Read

The following excerpt from *The Right Stuff* attempts to define what it took to succeed in the rigorous naval flight training required of such Mercury astronauts as Scott Carpenter, John Glenn, and Gus Grissom. As you prepare to read this essay, take a few moments to think about success and failure in general: What marks success in different

PREREADING

The purpose of this Preparing to Read material is to encourage students to think about the qualities of both success and failure. To help your students focus their attention on these characteristics before responding to the questions here, provide them with dictionary definitions of these two words:

Success—satisfactory completion of a particular task.

Failure—an inability to perform a task adequately.

Then ask them each to write down all the random associations they have with these two words. Have them record their associations in two columns, one for each word. See pages 3–6 for other ways to generate thoughts on these questions.

areas of life for you—at work, at school, at home? What marks failure? How do you feel when you have succeeded at something? When you have failed? Have you ever thought you had succeeded at a task, then realized you were only part way there? What were the circumstances? How did this realization make you feel?

BACKGROUND INFORMATION

In this excerpt from *The Right Stuff*, Tom Wolfe looks at the rigors of naval flight training to define the quality separating those who qualify as naval aviators from those who do not. Particularly effective is his portrayal of the fear and anxiety prompted by a young trainee's first experience landing on an aircraft carrier.

READABILITY LEVEL

8.0

RELATED READINGS

Sports and Fitness

Beth Wald, "Let's Get Vertical" 213
Joyce Carol Oates, "On Boxing"   331
Robert Hughes, "The N.R.A. in a Hunter's
　Sights"   462

DEFINITIONS

moxie (para. 2): energy; determination; know-how.
élan (para. 5): French. Spirited self-assurance.
vestibular system (para. 6): the system of cavities or spaces leading to other cavities or spaces in the body.
Gideon's warriors (para. 7): an army of 300 specially selected men who helped the ancient Jewish leader Gideon defeat the Midianites.
primordial (para. 8): created or developed first in time; primitive.

A young man might go into military flight training believing that he was entering some sort of technical school in which he was simply going to acquire a certain set of skills. Instead, he found himself all at once enclosed in a fraternity. And in this fraternity, even though it was military, men were not rated by their outward rank as ensigns, lieutenants, commanders, or whatever. No, herein the world was divided into those who had it and those who did not. This quality, this *it*, was never named, however, nor was it talked about in any way. 1

As to just what this ineffable quality was . . . well, it obviously involved bravery. But it was not bravery in the simple sense of being willing to risk your life. The idea seemed to be that any fool could do that, if that was all that was required, just as any fool could throw away his life in the process. No, the idea here (in the all-enclosing fraternity) seemed to be that a man should have the ability to go up in a hurtling piece of machinery and put his hide on the line and then have the moxie, the reflexes, the experience, the coolness, to pull it back in the last yawning moment—and then go up again *the next day*, and the next day, and every next day, even if the series should prove infinite—and, ultimately, in its best expression, do so in a cause that means something to thousands, to a people, a nation, to humanity, to God. Nor was there *a test* to show whether or not a pilot had this righteous quality. There was, instead, a seemingly infinite series of tests. A career in flying was like climbing one of those ancient Babylonian pyramids made up of a dizzy progression of steps and ledges, a ziggurat, a pyramid extraordinarily high and steep; and the idea was to prove at every foot of the way up that pyramid that you were one of the elected and anointed ones who had *the right stuff* and could move higher and higher and even—ultimately, God willing, one day—that you might be able to join that special few at the very top, that elite who had the capacity to bring tears to men's eyes, the very Brotherhood of the Right Stuff itself. 2

None of this was to be mentioned, and yet it was acted out in 3 a way that a young man could not fail to understand. When a new flight (i.e., a class) of trainees arrived at Pensacola, they were brought into an auditorium for a little lecture. An officer would tell them: "Take a look at the man on either side of you." Quite a few actually swiveled their heads this way and that in the interest of appearing diligent. Then the officer would say: "One of the three of you is not going to make it!"—meaning, not get his wings. That was the opening theme, the *motif* of primary training. We already know that one-third of you do not have the right stuff—it only remains to find out who.

Furthermore, that was the way it turned out. At every level in one's progress up that staggeringly high pyramid, the world was once more divided into those men who had the right stuff to continue the climb and those who had to be *left behind* in the most obvious way. Some were eliminated in the course of the opening classroom work, as either not smart enough or not hardworking enough, and were left behind. then came the basic flight instruction, in single-engine, propeller-driven trainers, and a few more—even though the military tried to make this stage easy—were washed out and left behind. Then came more demanding levels, one after the other, formation flying, instrument flying, jet training, all-weather flying, gunnery, and at each level more were washed out and left behind. By this point easily a third of the original candidates had been, indeed, eliminated . . . from the ranks of those who might prove to have the right stuff.

In the Navy, in addition to the stages that Air Force trainees went through, the neophyte always had waiting for him, out in the ocean, a certain grim gray slab; namely, the deck of an aircraft carrier; and with it perhaps the most difficult routine in military flying, carrier landings. He was shown films about it, he heard lectures about it, and he knew that carrier landings were hazardous. He first practiced touching down on the shape of a flight deck painted on an airfield. He was instructed to touch down and gun right off. This was safe enough—the shape didn't move, at least—but it could do terrible things to, let us say, the gyroscope of the soul. *That shape!—It's so damned small!* And more candidates were washed out and left behind. Then came the day, without warning, when those who remained were sent out over the ocean for the first of many days of reckoning with the slab. The first day was always a clear day with little wind and a calm sea. The carrier was so steady that it seemed, from up there in the air, to be resting on pilings, and the candidate usually made his first carrier landing successfully, with relief and even *élan*. Many young can-

4

5

Have your students define "success" and "failure" as the terms relate to your composition class. Have each student read his or her definition to the class. Then, guide your students in a discussion of these two terms, working toward definitions that everyone can agree on.

didates looked like terrific aviators up to that very point—and it was not until they were actually standing on the carrier deck that they first began to wonder if they had the proper stuff, after all. In the training film the flight deck was a grand piece of gray geometry, perilous, to be sure, but an amazing abstract shape as one looks down upon it on the screen. And yet once the newcomer's two feet were on it . . . *Geometry*—my God, man, this is a . . . skillet! It *heaved*, it moved up and down underneath his feet, it pitched up, it pitched down, it rolled to port (this great beast *rolled!*) and it rolled to starboard, as the ship moved into the wind and, therefore, into the waves, and the wind kept sweeping across, sixty feet up in the air out in the open sea, and there were no railings whatsoever. This was a *skillet!*—a frying pan!—a short-order grill!—not gray but black, smeared with skid marks from one end to the other and glistening with pools of hydraulic fluid and the occasional jet-fuel slick, all of it still hot, sticky, greasy, runny, virulent from God knows what traumas—still ablaze!—consumed in detonations, explosions, flames, combustion, roars, shrieks, whines, blasts, horrible shudders, fracturing impacts, as little men in screaming red and yellow and purple and green shirts with black Mickey Mouse helmets over their ears skittered about on the surface as if for their very lives (you've said it now!), hooking fighter planes onto the catapult shuttles so that they can explode their afterburners and be slung off the deck in a red-mad fury with a *kaboom!* that pounds through the entire deck—a procedure that seems absolutely controlled, orderly, sublime, however, compared to what he is about to watch as aircraft return to the ship for what is known in the engineering stoicisms of the military as "recovery and arrest." To say that an F-4 was coming back onto this heaving barbecue from out of the sky at a speed of 135 knots . . . that might have been the truth in the training lecture, but it did not begin to get across the idea of what the newcomer saw from the deck itself, because it created the notion that perhaps the plane was gliding in. On the deck one knew differently! As the aircraft came closer and the carrier heaved on into the waves and the plane's speed did not diminish and the deck did not grow steady—indeed, it pitched up and down five or ten feet per greasy heave—one experienced a neural alarm that no lecture could have prepared him for: This is not an *airplane* coming toward me, it is a brick with some poor sonofabitch riding it (*someone much like myself!*), and it is not *gliding*, it is *falling*, a thirty-thousand-pound brick, headed not for a stripe on the deck but for *me*—and with a horrible *smash!* it hits the skillet, and with a blur of momentum as big as a freight train's it hurtles toward the far end of the deck—another blinding storm!—another roar as the pilot pushes the throttle up to full military power and another smear of rubber screams out over the skillet—and this is nominal!—quite okay!—for a wire stretched across the deck has grabbed the hook on the end of the plane as it hit the deck tail down, and the smash was the rest of the fifteen-ton brute slamming onto the deck, as it tripped up, so that it is now straining against the wire at full throttle, in case it hadn't held and the plane had "boltered" off the end of the deck and had to struggle up into the air again. And already the Mickey Mouse helmets are running toward the fiery monster. . . .

And the candidate, looking on, begins to *feel* that great heaving sun-blazing deathboard of a deck wallowing in his own vestibular system—and suddenly he finds himself backed up against his own limits. He ends up going to the flight surgeon with so-called conversion symptoms. Overnight he develops blurred vision or numbness in his hands and feet or sinusitis so severe that he cannot tolerate changes in altitude. On one level the symptom is real. He really cannot see too well or use his fingers or stand the pain. But somewhere in his subconscious he knows it is a plea and a beg-off; he shows not the slightest concern (the flight surgeon notes) that the condition might be permanent and affect him in whatever life awaits him outside the arena of the right stuff.

Those who remained, those who qualified for carrier duty— and even more so those who later on qualified for *night* carrier duty—began to feel a bit like Gideon's warriors. *So many have been left behind!* The young warriors were now treated to a deathly sweet and quite unmentionable sight. They could gaze at length upon the crushed and wilted pariahs who had washed out. They could inspect those who did not have that righteous stuff.

The military did not have very merciful instincts. Rather than packing up these poor souls and sending them home, the Navy, like the Air Force and the Marines, would try to make use of them in some other role such as flight controller. So the washout has to keep taking classes with the rest of his group, even though he can no longer touch an airplane. He sits there in the classes staring at sheets of paper with cataracts of sheer human mortification over his eyes while the rest steal looks at him . . . this man reduced to an ant, this untouchable, this poor sonofabitch. And in what test had he been found wanting? Why, it seemed to be nothing less than *manhood* itself. Naturally, this was never mentioned, either. Yet there it was. *Manliness, manhood, manly courage* . . . there was

ANSWERS TO QUESTIONS: UNDERSTANDING DETAILS (p. 368)

1. According to the author, "the right stuff" is manifested in "the ability to go up in a hurling piece of machinery and put his hide on the line and then have the moxie, the reflexes, the experience, the coolness, to pull it back in the last yawning moment—and then to go up again *the next day*, and the next day, and every next day, even if the series should prove infinite" (para. 2). The climax comes with one's nomination to the company of that special few at the very top: the elite who had "the capacity to bring tears to men's eyes, the very Brotherhood of the Right Stuff itself" (para. 2).

2. Gideon's warriors were a small force of three hundred men chosen by the Old Testament Hebrew leader Gideon to rout the huge Midianite army from their camp, armed with ram's horn trumpets, torches in clay jars, and the special blessing of Jehovah. Those who qualified for carrier duty are, like Gideon's warriors, among the few chosen to accomplish a special, heroic task.

3. "Primordial" describes the existence of something from the beginning. Thus, Wolfe sees *"manliness, manhood, manly courage"* (para. 8) as traits that cannot be taught or developed but are inherent from birth in men with "the right stuff."

ANSWERS TO QUESTIONS: ANALYZING MEANING (p. 368)

1. The aspect of naval flight training that Wolfe equates with being "enclosed in a fraternity" (para. 1) is the presence of an elusive quality in those who are chosen to be admitted, the quality that divides the group into "those who had it and those who did not" (para. 1). He also compares flight training with "climbing one of those ancient Babylonian pyramids" (para. 2), being a member of "Gideon's warriors" (para. 7), and searching for *"manhood* itself" (para. 8). (You might refer your students to the definition of "allusion" in the glossary in response to this question.)

2. Responses to the first part of this question will vary. "The right stuff," as defined by Wolfe, appears to reflect an attitude of optimism, determination, and confidence— traits that generate success in all areas of

1. A partial response might include the following:

> Fear—"grim gray slab," "skillet" (para. 5)
>
> Failure—"reduced to an ant," "cataracts of sheer human mortification" (para. 8)

In his attempt to make his abstractions "concrete," Wolfe uses either examples of the behaviors that characterize such traits or metaphors reflecting the concepts being discussed.

2. The central metaphor of "climbing one of those ancient Babylonian pyramids" (para. 2) parallels the concept of continual testing, reaching higher to prove oneself at each level of the program, attempting to remain part of the ever-shrinking group until finding the rarefied air at the top, "the Brotherhood of the Right Stuff itself" (para. 2).

3. Paragraph 5, the climax of Wolfe's definition, is exceptionally long and is composed, in the first third, of sentences short to moderate in length that illustrate the theoretical concept of carrier landings. As the actual landings begin, the sentences become longer and more complex, reflecting the manic push of activity and the slowing down of time. Words and phrases within these sentences are frequently punctuated with exclamation points; pauses are marked by dashes and parentheses; and sentences too frightening to complete end abruptly with ellipses. Words reflecting the shock and wonder of the experience are written in italics, while vivid imagery illustrates heat, noise, and frenzied activity. The effect of the word choice, the repetition, the pauses, and the shifts of thought following the incomplete sentences mirror the pitch and roll of the carrier and the retardation of time caused by fear and anxiety.

something ancient, primordial, irresistible about the challenge of this stuff, no matter what a sophisticated and rational age one might think he lived in.

UNDERSTANDING DETAILS

1. According to Wolfe, how do people prove they have "the right stuff"? What is the climax of this proof?
2. Who were Gideon's warriors? Why might those who qualified for carrier duty "feel a bit like Gideon's warriors" (paragraph 7)?
3. What does "primordial" mean? What is primordial about *manliness, manhood, manly courage* (paragraph 8)?

ANALYZING MEANING

1. Why does Wolfe equate military training with being "enclosed in a fraternity" in paragraph 1? With what else does he compare military training? Give at least three specific examples.
2. Is the necessity of having "the right stuff" limited to men? To pilots? To military training? In what other areas of life is "the right stuff" desirable?
3. To make this essay meaningful, Wolfe relies in part on the reader's identification with the details involved in the astronauts' military training program. To what extent can women identify with this essay? In what ways did you yourself identify with the experiences Wolfe relates? On the basis of your answers to these questions, explain how successfully Wolfe defines "the right stuff" within your frame of reference.

DISCOVERING RHETORICAL STRATEGIES

1. Throughout this essay, Wolfe is attempting to define an abstract subject ("the right stuff") in concrete terms. Divide a piece of paper into two columns. In the first column, list all the various abstractions the author presents; in the other column, list the concrete examples of these qualities that Wolfe discusses. Then, explain the relationships he draws between these two columns and the effects of those relationships on his readers.
2. Wolfe equates a career in flying with climbing an ancient Babylonian pyramid (a ziggurat) "made up of a dizzy progression of steps and ledges" (paragraph 2). In what way does this metaphor bring order and coherence to his essay?

3. Wolfe reaches a climax in his definition of "the right stuff" in paragraph 5 when he describes the details of the carrier landings. How does Wolfe's use of sentence structure (including word choice and length of sentences) and punctuation tell us that this is the climax of the essay?

IDEAS FOR DISCUSSION/WRITING

Preparing to Write

Write freely about the qualities that constitute success and failure in your immediate environment as a student: How do you know when you succeed? When you fail? How do you feel in each of these different situations? Has success ever turned into failure for you? Has the reverse ever occurred? How important are success and failure in your life as a student? In the lives of your friends? What roles do success and failure play in academia in general? To what extent do these roles prepare us for the "real world"?

Choosing a Topic

1. Write an essay for your classmates defining "the right stuff" for social success in college.
2. Choose an area other than military training and school. Then use examples to define "the wrong stuff" in that area to members of your composition class.
3. The relationship between college and the "real world" has changed since your parents were in school. Explain to them the current relationship between academic success (or failure) and the job market. What do you think the connections are between doing well in college and having a successful career?

PREWRITING

In preparation for the writing assignments, the Preparing to Write questions ask students to explore the relationships between success, failure, and the "real world" before they write an essay on a related topic. See pages 16–23 for suggestions on generating ideas in response to these questions.

ADDITIONAL DISCUSSION/WRITING TOPIC

In a coherent essay written for your classmates, define the word "success" or "failure." Include in your definition both the denotations and the connotations connected with the word you choose.

REVISING STRATEGY

After you describe the general category in which the word you are defining belongs and contrast it with other words in that same group, you have several options for completing the introduction to your definition essays: (1) name the components or features of the term, (2) discuss its etymology, or (3) explain what it does *not* mean. Check to see that the introduction of one of your definition essays follows one or more of these suggestions. Note any weaknesses or inconsistencies. Then revise your paper, paying close attention to the introduction.

MARIE WINN
(1936–   )

■ ■ ■

Television Addiction

Born in Prague, Czechoslovakia, Marie Winn attended New York City public schools, Radcliffe College, and then Columbia University, from which she graduated in 1959. An expert on culture and education, Winn is best known for *The Plug-In Drug: Television, Children, and the Family* (1977, revised 1985), an indictment of America's addiction to TV that has subsequently been translated into French, German, Italian, Spanish, Japanese, and Swedish. Other publications include *The Playgroup Book* (1967), *The Baby Reader* (1973), *The Sick Book* (1976), *Children without Childhood* (1983), and *Unplugging the Plug-In Drug* (1987), plus translations of a novel, *Summer in Prague* (1973), and of two plays by Vaclav Havel produced at the Public Theatre in New York: *Largo Desolato* (1987) and *Temptation* (1989). Frequent television appearances have confirmed Winn's reputation as an influential commentator on a wide range of interrelated topics concerning American society. One of Winn's most passionate hobbies is "bird observing," which she does in New York City and at her lakeside cabin in Putnam County, New York. Her advice for students using *The Prose Reader* is to "read a lot of excellent writers in order to absorb the cadences of good writing into their blood. Writing is simply communicating. Don't get caught up in thoughts that are too complicated or words that are too big. Say what you have to say in clear, simple prose."

PREREADING

The purpose of this Preparing to Read material is to encourage students to think about their own TV viewing habits. To help your students focus on these habits before they respond to the questions here, have them construct a log of all the television shows they watched this week. If time allows, you might have them swap logs with another student so they have some grounds for judging their own TV watching. See pages 3–6 for other ways to generate thoughts on these questions.

Preparing to Read

The following chapter from *The Plug-In Drug* argues that television is just as addictive as drugs or alcohol. As you prepare to read this essay, take a few moments to think about the role of television in your life: How much TV do you watch each day? How much did you watch five years ago? Ten years ago? Do you think you watch too much TV now, or would you like to have time to watch more? What sorts of programs do you see most frequently? What would you do with your time if you didn't watch TV as often? Why do you enjoy watching television?

The word "addiction" is often used loosely and wryly in conversation. People will refer to themselves as "mystery book addicts" or "cookie addicts." E. B. White wrote of his annual surge of interest in gardening: "We are hooked and are making an attempt to kick the habit." Yet nobody really believes that reading mysteries or ordering seeds by catalogue is serious enough to be compared with addictions to heroin or alcohol. The word "addiction" is here used jokingly to denote a tendency to overindulge in some pleasurable activity.

People often refer to being "hooked on TV." Does this, too, fall into the lighthearted category of cookie eating and other pleasures that people pursue with unusual intensity, or is there a kind of television viewing that falls into the more serious category of destructive addiction?

When we think about addiction to drugs or alcohol we frequently focus on negative aspects, ignoring the pleasures that accompany drinking or drug-taking. And yet the essence of any serious addiction is a pursuit of pleasure, a search for a "high" that normal life does not supply. It is only the inability to function without the addictive substance that is dismaying, the dependence of the organism upon a certain experience and an increasing inability to function normally without it. Thus people will take two or three drinks at the end of the day not merely for the pleasure drinking provides, but also because they "don't feel normal" without them.

Real addicts do not merely pursue a pleasurable experience one time in order to function normally. They need to *repeat* it again and again. Something about that particular experience makes life without it less than complete. Other potentially pleasurable experiences are no longer possible, for under the spell of the addictive experience, their lives are peculiarly distorted. The addict craves an experience and yet is never really satisfied. The organism may be temporarily sated, but soon it begins to crave again.

Finally, a serious addiction is distinguished from a harmless pursuit of pleasure by its distinctly destructive elements. Heroin addicts, for instance, lead a damaged life: Their increasing need for heroin in increasing doses prevents them from working, from maintaining relationships, from developing in human ways. Similarly alcoholics' lives are narrowed and dehumanized by their dependence on alcohol.

Let us consider television viewing in the light of the conditions that define serious addictions.

BACKGROUND INFORMATION

Marie Winn warns us of the dangers of being "hooked on TV" (para. 2) in this sobering essay entitled "Television Addiction." Likening an obsession with television to drug or alcohol addiction, Winn describes the addict as "living in a holding pattern, as it were, passing up the activities that lead to growth or development or a sense of accomplishment" (para. 9), exchanging reality for a distorted imitation of life emanating from the small screen.

READABILITY LEVEL

13.9

RELATED READINGS

Addiction

Michael Dorris, "The Broken Cord"   400
Alice Walker, "My Daughter Smokes"   419
Courtland Milloy and Jesse Philips, "Drug Testing Does Not Violate Workers' Rights"   472
The New Republic, "Drug Testing Violates Workers' Rights"   472

Media

Susan Allen Toth, "Cinematypes"   273
Stephen King, "Why We Crave Horror Movies"   375

DEFINITIONS

Cow Palace (para. 19): one of San Francisco's major exhibition and indoor sports facilities.

Duplicate a section of TV Guide for the
class, and have your students classify the
TV programs by some method that the class
as a whole devises. Then, get them to draw
some conclusions about the range and interest level of these shows.

Not unlike drugs or alcohol, the television experience allows   7
the participant to blot out the real world and enter into a pleasurable and passive mental state. The worries and anxieties of reality
are as effectively deferred by becoming absorbed in a television
program as by going on a "trip" induced by drugs or alcohol.
And just as alcoholics are only vaguely aware of their addiction,
feeling that they control their drinking more than they really do
("I can cut it out any time I want—I just like to have three or four
drinks before dinner"), people similarly overestimate their control over television watching. Even as they put off other activities
to spend hour after hour watching television, they feel they could
easily resume living in a different, less passive style. But somehow or other, while the television set is present in their homes,
the click doesn't sound. With television pleasures available, those
other experiences seem less attractive, more difficult somehow.

A heavy viewer (a college English instructor) observes: 8

> I find television almost irresistible. When the set is on, I cannot
> ignore it. I can't turn it off. I feel sapped, will-less, enervated. As I
> reach out to turn off the set, the strength goes out of my arms. So I sit
> there for hours and hours.

Self-confessed television addicts often feel they "ought" to do   9
other things—but the fact that they don't read and don't plant
their garden or sew or crochet or play games or have conversations means that those activities are no longer as desirable as television viewing. In a way the lives of heavy viewers are as
imbalanced by their television "habit" as a drug addict's or an alcoholic's. They are living in a holding pattern, as it were, passing
up the activities that lead to growth or development or a sense of
accomplishment. This is one reason people talk about their television viewing so ruefully, so apologetically. They are aware that it
is an unproductive experience, that almost any other endeavor is
more worthwhile by any human measure.

Finally it is the adverse effect of television viewing on the   10
lives of so many people that defines it as a serious addiction. The
television habit distorts the sense of time. It renders other experiences vague and curiously unreal while taking on a greater reality for itself. It weakens relationships by reducing and sometimes
eliminating normal opportunities for talking, for communicating.

And yet television does not satisfy, else why would the   11
viewer continue to watch hour after hour, day after day? "The
measure of health," writes Lawrence Kubie, "is flexibility . . . and

especially the freedom to cease when sated." But heavy television viewers can never be sated with their television experiences— these do not provide the true nourishment that satiation requires—and thus they find that they cannot stop watching.

A former heavy watcher (filmmaker) describes such a syndrome:

12

> I remember when we first got the set I'd watch for hours and hours, whenever I could, and I remember that feeling of tiredness and anxiety that always followed those orgies, a sense of time terribly wasted. It was like eating cotton candy; television promised so much richness, I couldn't wait for it, and then it just evaporated into air. I remember feeling terribly drained after watching for a long time.

Similarly, a nursery school teacher remembers her own childhood television experience:

13

> I remember bingeing on television when I was a child and having that vapid feeling after watching hours of TV. I'd look forward to watching whenever I could, but it just didn't give back a real feeling of pleasure. It was like no orgasm, no catharsis, very frustrating. Television just wasn't giving me the promised satisfaction, and yet I kept on watching. It filled some sort of need or had to do with an inability to get something started.

The testimonies of ex-television addicts often have the evangelistic overtones of stories heard at Alcoholics Anonymous meetings.

14

A handbag repair shop owner says:

15

> I'd get on the subway home from work with the newspaper and immediately turn to the TV page to plan out my evening's watching. I'd come home, wash, change my clothes, and tell my wife to start the machine so it would be warmed up. (We had an old-fashioned set that took a few seconds before an image appeared.) And then we'd watch TV for the rest of the evening. We'd eat our dinner in the living room while watching, and we'd only talk every once in a while, during the ads, if at all. I'd watch anything, good, bad, or indifferent.
>
> All the while we were watching I'd feel terribly angry at myself for wasting all that time watching junk. I could never go to sleep until at least the eleven o'clock news, and then sometimes I'd still stay up for the late-night talk show. I had a feeling that I *had* to watch the news programs, that I *had* to know what was happening,

even though most of the time nothing much was happening and I could easily find out what was by reading the paper the next morning. Usually my wife would fall asleep on the couch while I was watching. I'd get angry at her for doing that. Actually, I was angry at myself. I had a collection of three years of back issues of different magazines that I planned to read sometime, but I never got around to reading them. I never got around to sorting or labeling my collection of slides I had made when traveling. I only had time for television. We'd take the telephone off the hook while watching so we wouldn't be interrupted! We like classical music, but we never listened to any, never!

Then one day the set broke. I said to my wife, 'Let's not fix it. Let's just see what happens.' Well, that was the smartest thing we ever did. We haven't had a TV in the house since then.

Now I look back and I can hardly believe we could have lived like that. I feel that my mind was completely mummified for all those years. I was glued to that machine and couldn't get loose, somehow. It really frightens me to think of it. Yes, I'm frightened of TV now. I don't think I could control it if we had a set in the house again. I think it would take over no matter what I did.

A further sign of addiction is that "an exclusive craving for something is accompanied by a loss of discrimination towards the object which satisfies the craving. . . . The alcoholic is not interested in the taste of liquor that is available; likewise the compulsive eater is not particular about what he eats when there is food around," write the authors of a book about the nature of addiction. And just so, for many viewers the process of *watching* television is far more important than the actual contents of the programs being watched. The knowledge that the act of watching is more important than *what* is being watched lies behind the practice of "roadblocking," invented by television advertisers and adopted by political candidates who purchase the same half-hour on all three channels in order to force-feed their message to the public. As one prominent candidate put it, "People will watch television no matter what is on, and if you allow them no other choice they will watch your show."   16

The comparison between television addiction and drug addictions is often made by addicts themselves. A lawyer says: 17

I watch TV the way an alcoholic drinks. If I come home and sit in front of the TV, I'll watch any program at all, even if there's nothing on that especially appeals to me. Then the next thing I know it's eleven o'clock and I'm watching the Johnny Carson show, and I'll realize I've spent the whole evening watching TV. What's more, I can't stand Johnny Carson! But I'll still sit there watching him. I'm addicted to TV, when it's there, and I'm not happy about the addiction. I'll sit there getting madder and madder at myself for watching, but still I'll sit there. I can't turn it off.

Nor is the television addict always blind to the dysfunctional aspects of his addiction. A housewife says: 18

> Sometimes a friend will come over while I'm watching TV. I'll say, 'Wait a second. Just let me finish watching this,' and then I'll feel bad about that, letting the machine take precedence over people. And I'll do that for the stupidest programs, just because I *have* to watch, somehow.

In spite of the potentially destructive nature of television addiction, it is rarely taken seriously in American society. Critics mockingly refer to television as a "cultural barbiturate" and joke about "mainlining the tube." Indeed, a spectacle called a "Media Burn," which took place in San Francisco in 1975 and which involved the piling of 44 old television sets on top of each other in the parking lot of the old Cow Palace, soaking them with kerosene, and applying a torch, perfectly illustrates the feeling of good fun that surrounds the issue of television addiction. According to the programs distributed before the event, everybody was supposed to experience "a cathartic explosion" and "be free at last from the addiction to television." 19

The issue of television addiction takes on a more serious air when the addicts are our own children. A mother reports: 20

> My ten-year-old is as hooked on TV as an alcoholic is hooked on drink. He tries to strike desperate bargains: 'If you let me watch just ten more minutes, I won't watch at all tomorrow,' he says. It's pathetic. It scares me.

Another mother tells about her six-year-old son: 21

> We were in Israel last summer where the TV stations sign off for the night at about ten. Well, my son would turn on the set and watch the Arabic stations that were still on, even though he couldn't understand a word, just because he had to watch *something*.

Other signs of serious addiction come out in parents' descriptions of their children's viewing behavior: 22

1. An "addiction," in the words of Winn, is "a pursuit of pleasure, a search for a 'high' that normal life does not supply" (para. 3); it involves the inability to control a behavior that may be injurious to one's mental and emotional health. Student definitions will vary.

2. The author sees the only real difference between alcohol or drug addiction and television addiction as the frivolous disregard connected with the latter as opposed to the acknowledged gravity of the more "serious" addictions.

3. According to Winn, people watch television to seek pleasure, to satisfy a craving, to "blot out the real world" (para. 7), or merely to fulfill a habit.

ANSWERS TO QUESTIONS:
ANALYZING MEANING (p. 376)

1. The author asserts that the potentially destructive effects of a serious addiction to television include the following: "The television habit distorts the sense of time. It renders other experiences vague and curiously unreal while taking on a greater reality for itself. It weakens relationships by reducing and sometimes eliminating normal opportunities for talking, for communicating" (para. 10).

2. Responses to this question will vary.

3. Responses to this question will vary.

ANSWERS TO QUESTIONS:
DISCOVERING RHETORICAL
STRATEGIES (p. 377)

1. The author places the term "television addiction" into the general category of "addiction," then immediately differentiates it from other forms of addiction. She further narrows the frame of reference by listing various components of television addiction. Finally, she expands her definition through the use of classification, narration, and example.

2. Winn's first paragraph is very general, not citing television addiction at all, but focusing on the word "addiction" as it refers to overindulgence in any enjoyable activity.

We used to have very bad reception before we got on Cable TV. I'd come into the room and see my eight-year-old watching this terrible, blurry picture and I'd say, 'Heavens, how can you see? Let me try to fix it,' and he'd get frantic and scream, 'Don't touch it!' It really worried me, that he wanted to watch so badly that he was even willing to watch a completely blurred image.

Another mother tells of her eight-year-old son's behavior when deprived of television: 23

There was a time when both TV sets were out for about two weeks, and Jerry reached a point where I felt that if he didn't watch something, he was really going to start climbing the walls. He was fidgety and nervous. He'd crawl all over the furniture. He just didn't know what to do with himself, and it seemed to get worse every day. I said to my husband, 'He's having withdrawal symptoms,' and I really think that's what it was. Finally I asked one of my friends if he could go and watch the Saturday cartoons at their house.

UNDERSTANDING DETAILS

1. According to Winn, what is an "addiction"? Define the term in your own words.
2. What is the difference, according to the author, between alcohol or drug addiction and TV addiction? Do you agree with this distinction? Why or why not?
3. Based upon Winn's observations, what are some of the reasons people watch TV?

ANALYZING MEANING

1. Why does TV have the potential to be so destructive?
2. The author cites many personal testimonies to prove that people of all ages can be addicted to television. In your opinion, which of these stories is most convincing? Why do you find some testimonies more convincing than others?
3. How much TV do you watch? What kinds of programs? Do you feel you are "addicted" to television? Why or why not?

DISCOVERING RHETORICAL STRATEGIES

1. What techniques explained at the beginning of this chapter does Winn use to define television addiction? What other rhetorical modes does the author use to support her definition?
2. Note that Winn's article moves from general to specific as it attempts to define TV addiction. Explain this movement by discussing the details Winn uses in at least one paragraph.
3. Who do you think is the author's intended audience in this essay? Why? Describe them in detail.

IDEAS FOR DISCUSSION/WRITING

Preparing to Write

Write freely about your television viewing habits: How much TV do you watch daily? Weekly? Monthly? Why do you watch TV? Is it a satisfying experience for you? Does it ever conflict with other activities in your life? What are your favorite programs? Why do you like these shows so much?

Choosing a Topic

1. You have been asked to speak at freshman orientation at your college. Your assigned topic is "The Role of Television in a College Student's Life." Using Winn's article as a resource, define "television addiction" from a student's perspective. (Remember to cite your source whenever necessary.) Supplement your definition with examples of television addiction from your own experience and observation.
2. For a group of people your own age, define "entertainment." In your definition, consider what activities you find entertaining. Why are they enjoyable? Before you write your essay, limit your subject and settle on a main point of view. Make your purpose clear throughout the essay.
3. Write a letter to the manager of one of your local television stations either complimenting or criticizing the general selection of programs offered by the station.

Television addiction is introduced in paragraph 2 with the question of whether it should be classified in the category of overindulgence or serious addiction. Paragraphs 3 to 5 discuss the components of serious addiction. Beginning with paragraph 6, Winn changes her focus to the specific signs of this type of addiction and the related adverse effects of inordinate television viewing, offering a variety of personal testimonies and closing with two alarming accounts of the bizarre behavior of child addicts deprived of their favorite pastime.

3. Considering American society's fixation on the latest Nielsen ratings and this year's Emmy nominees, the author seems to be admonishing this huge population of televiewers, with the hope that at least a few of her readers may recognize themselves in the experiences of others and take steps to confront their addiction.

PREWRITING

In preparation for the writing assignments, the Preparing to Write questions ask students to scrutinize their daily, weekly, and monthly TV viewing habits before writing an essay on a related topic. See pages 16–23 for suggestions on generating ideas in response to these questions.

ADDITIONAL DISCUSSION/WRITING TOPIC

In a coherent essay written for your classmates, define the word "addiction." Refer in your definition to as many types of addiction as you want. Supplement your definition with examples from your own experience and observation.

REVISING STRATEGY

The order in which you present material in an essay determines a large part of its overall effect. Choose one of your definition essays, and list all the details in the order they occur. Review this list along with your paper, and decide which details would be more effective in a different place in the essay. Then revise your paper, paying close attention to the flow of the details from one point in the essay to another.

SUSAN SONTAG
(1933–   )

■ ■ ■

On AIDS

Susan Sontag is a novelist, essayist, screenwriter, and film and theater director who is one of America's foremost social commentators. Born in New York City and raised in Arizona and California, she studied at the University of California at Berkeley and the University of Chicago, earning her degree at the age of eighteen from the latter. After doing graduate work in philosophy at Harvard, she held a succession of jobs as a teacher and writer-in-residence at several universities. Her first important publication was *Against Interpretation, and Other Essays* (1966), which established Sontag as an influential critic and cultural analyst. The autobiographical *Trip to Hanoi* (1968) followed, then *Styles of Radical Will* (1969). Her prose fiction includes two novels, *The Benefactor* (1963) and *Death Kit* (1967), and a collection of short stories entitled *I, etcetera* (1978). She has also written and directed four films: *Duet for Cannibals* (1969) and *Brother Carl* (1971), both made in Sweden; *Promised Lands* (1974), a documentary about Israel; and *Unguided Tour* (1975), based on an earlier short story. One of Sontag's best-known books is *On Photography* (1977), a systematic inquiry into the source and meaning of visual imagery. In this seminal text, the author uses already established critical tools of literary analysis, linguistics, and philosophy to help describe the effect of modern art and photography on its viewers. Other recent books include *Illness as Metaphor* (1977), *Under the Sign of Saturn* (1980), and *AIDS and Its Metaphors* (1988). Sontag lives and works in New York City.

Preparing to Read

The following chapter from Sontag's most recent book, *AIDS and Its Metaphors*, examines the figurative language commonly used to describe and define this terrifying disease: The virus "invades" and "pollutes" our bodies, while in military fashion our immune systems "mobilize" and "defend" against the "attack of alien cells." As you begin to read this essay, take a few minutes to consider what you know about AIDS: What facts do you have about the disease? Do you know anyone who has AIDS? Anyone who has died from AIDS? How do different people respond to those suffering from the

PREREADING

The purpose of this Preparing to Read material is to encourage students to think about what they actually know (and don't know) about the AIDS virus. To help your students focus their attention on AIDS before they respond to the questions here, make sure they understand the acronym, which stands for Acquired Immune Deficiency Syndrome. You might also provide them with any material your college health center has on the subject. See pages 3–6 for other ways to generate thoughts on these questions.

virus? Are you afraid of being infected? Have you altered your behavior in any way because of the threat of contagion? Do you think our government is doing enough to help prevent the spread of this disease? When do you think a cure will be found?

■————————————————————————————————■

Just as one might predict for a disease that is not yet fully understood as well as extremely recalcitrant to treatment, the advent of this terrifying new disease, new at least in its epidemic form, has provided a large-scale occasion for the metaphorizing of illness.

Strictly speaking, AIDS—acquired immune deficiency syndrome—is not the name of an illness at all. It is the name of a medical condition, whose consequences are a spectrum of illnesses. In contrast to syphilis and cancer, which provide prototypes for most of the images and metaphors attached to AIDS, the very definition of AIDS requires the presence of other illnesses, so-called opportunistic infections and malignancies. But though not in *that* sense a single disease, AIDS lends itself to being regarded as one—in part because, unlike cancer and like syphilis, it is thought to have a single cause.

AIDS has a dual metaphoric genealogy. As a microprocess, it is described as cancer is: an invasion. When the focus is transmission of the disease, an older metaphor, reminiscent of syphilis, is invoked: pollution. (One gets it from the blood or sexual fluids of infected people or from contaminated blood products.) But the military metaphors used to describe AIDS have a somewhat different focus from those used in describing cancer. With cancer, the metaphor scants the issue of causality (still a murky topic in cancer research) and picks up at the point at which rogue cells inside the body mutate, eventually moving out from an original site or organ to overrun other organs or systems—a domestic subversion. In the description of AIDS the enemy is what causes the disease, an infectious agent that comes from the outside:

> The invader is tiny, about one sixteen-thousandth the size of the head of a pin. . . . Scouts of the body's immune system, large cells called macrophages, sense the presence of the diminutive foreigner and promptly alert the immune system. It begins to mobilize an array of cells that, among other things, produce antibodies to deal with the threat. Single-mindedly, the AIDS virus ignores many of

1 **BACKGROUND INFORMATION**

In this essay, Susan Sontag examines the various ways in which definitions of AIDS rely upon the use of metaphor to help describe this deadly disease. Like cancer, AIDS is often defined as a warlike "invasion" of the immune system; like syphilis, it "pollutes" our bodies. Some descriptions, adopting science-fiction jargon, depict the illness as an "alien" attack that "takes over" the body's healthy cells. Sontag then discusses the extent to which each of these metaphors shapes and distorts our image of the disease and its treatment.

READABILITY LEVEL

15.8

RELATED READINGS

Sexuality

Alleen Pace Nilsen, "Sexism in English: A 1990s Update"   183
Judy Brady, "Why I Want a Wife"   259
Germaine Greer, "A Child Is Born"   308
Nancy Gibbs, "When Is It Rape?"   345

DEFINITIONS

T cell (para. 3): a type of cell that rejects foreign tissue and regulates cellular immunity.
RNA (para. 3): ribonucleic acid, a component of cells that is associated with the control of cellular activities.
DNA (para. 3): deoxyribonucleic acid, the molecular basis of the genetic code and heredity patterns in many organisms, including humans.

the blood cells in its path, evades the rapidly advancing defenders and homes in on the master coordinator of the immune system, a helper T cell. . . .

This is the language of political paranoia, with its characteristic distrust of a pluralistic world. A defense system consisting of cells "that, among other things, produce antibodies to deal with the threat" is, predictably, no match for an invader who advances "single-mindedly." And the science-fiction flavor, already present in cancer talk, is even more pungent in accounts of AIDS—this one comes from *Time* magazine in late 1986—with infection described like the high-tech warfare for which we are being prepared (and inured) by the fantasies of our leaders and by video entertainments. In the era of Star Wars and Space Invaders, AIDS has proved an ideally comprehensible illness:

> On the surface of that cell, it finds a receptor into which one of its envelope proteins fits perfectly, like a key into a lock. Docking with the cell, the virus penetrates the cell membrane and is stripped of its protective shell in the process. . . .

Next the invader takes up permanent residence, by a form of alien takeover familiar in science-fiction narratives. The body's own cells *become* the invader. With the help of an enzyme the virus carries with it,

> the naked AIDS virus converts its RNA into . . . DNA, the master molecule of life. The molecule then penetrates the cell nucleus, inserts itself into a chromosome and takes over part of the cellular machinery, directing it to produce more AIDS viruses. Eventually, overcome by its alien product, the cell swells and dies, releasing a flood of new viruses to attack other cells. . . .

As viruses attack other cells, runs the metaphor, so "a host of opportunistic diseases, normally warded off by a healthy immune system, attacks the body," whose integrity and vigor have been sapped by the sheer replication of "alien product" that follows the collapse of its immunological defenses. "Gradually weakened by the onslaught, the AIDS victim dies, sometimes in months, but almost always within a few years of the first symptoms." Those who have not already succumbed are described as "under assault, showing the telltale symptoms of the disease," while millions of others "harbor the virus, vulnerable at any time to a final, all-out attack."

Cancer makes cells proliferate; in AIDS, cells die. Even as this original model of AIDS (the mirror image of leukemia) has been altered, descriptions of how the virus does its work continue to echo the way the illness is perceived as infiltrating the society. "AIDS Virus Found to Hide in Cells, Eluding Detection by Normal Tests" was the headline of a recent front-page story in the *New York Times* announcing the discovery that the virus can "lurk" for years in the macrophages—disrupting their disease-fighting function without killing them, "even when the macrophages are filled almost to bursting with virus," and without producing antibodies, the chemicals the body makes in response to "invading agents" and whose presence has been regarded as an infallible marker of the syndrome. That the virus isn't lethal for *all* the cells where it takes up residence, as is now thought, only increases the illness-foe's reputation for wiliness and invincibility.

What makes the viral assault so terrifying is that contamination, and therefore vulnerability, is understood as permanent. Even if someone infected were never to develop any symptoms— that is, the infection remained, or could by medical intervention be rendered, inactive—the viral enemy would be forever within. In fact, so it is believed, it is just a matter of time before something awakens ("triggers") it, before the appearance of "the telltale symptoms." Like syphilis, known to generations of doctors as "the great masquerader," AIDS is a clinical construction, an inference. It takes its identity from the presence of *some* among a long, and lengthening, roster of symptoms (no one has everything that AIDS could be), symptoms which "mean" that what the patient has is this illness. The construction of the illness rests on the invention not only of AIDS as a clinical entity but of a kind of junior AIDS, called AIDS-related complex (ARC), to which people are assigned if they show "early" and often intermittent symptoms of immunological deficit such as fevers, weight loss, fungal infections, and swollen lymph glands. AIDS is progressive, a disease of time. Once a certain density of symptoms is attained, the course of the illness can be swift, and brings atrocious suffering. Besides the commonest "presenting" illnesses (some hitherto unusual, at least in a fatal form, such as a rare skin cancer and a rare form of pneumonia), a plethora of disabling, disfiguring, and humiliating symptoms make the AIDS patient steadily more infirm, helpless, and unable to control or take care of basic functions and needs.

The sense in which AIDS is a slow disease makes it more like

4

5

6

1. The term "invasion" describes the process of AIDS taking over an infected person's body, whereas "pollution" refers to the spread of AIDS to other people rather than within one infected person.

2. AIDS metaphors are different from those used for cancer in that, unlike cancer, the descriptions of AIDS focus on the enemy, the cause of AIDS, whereas cancer is described in terms of a group of cells within the body that begins to mutate. Because far too little is known about what causes this mutation, the metaphors describing cancer do not focus on causality the way that those of AIDS do. Syphilis, usually viewed as having stages, is closely linked with AIDS in that AIDS progresses in well-defined increments; however, the stages of AIDS progress much more quickly than those of syphilis. Syphilis may lie dormant for years or even decades, but AIDS is usually fatal within a few years.

3. Sontag uses this headline to demonstrate her theory that the military metaphors used to describe AIDS are indicative of the belief that AIDS is infiltrating or threatening society in much the same way it threatens individuals.

1. The permanent nature of AIDS is the aspect that Sontag believes makes it so terrifying. Even if a cure were found, the virus would still remain in the infected person's body.

2. Sontag uses the militant metaphor of invasion to reveal the war fought within the infected person's body. The body is invaded by a type of virus that then causes the body to weaken its defenses and allow other foreign invaders (or diseases) to enter and destroy it. The concept of pollution helps define AIDS through comparisons with other diseases such as cancer, which mutates but does not kill the cells it invades. The rapidity of the spread of AIDS, both within the individual and within society, makes it seem very similar to pollution, which destroys the atmosphere and makes the world unfit for human life. Beyond this point, student responses will vary.

3. Responses to this question will vary.

ANSWERS TO QUESTIONS:
DISCOVERING RHETORICAL
STRATEGIES (p. 383)

1. Sontag uses the language of science fiction to produce a graphic account of the way aids viruses take over the body's cells. The language of science fiction provides a euphemism through which Sontag can define the process of infection without terrifying her readers, who, more often than not, would prefer to ignore the disease rather than understand it.

2. Sontag's quotations clearly illustrate themetaphors people use in an effort to define and understand AIDS. Without her quote from *Time,* for example, the reader would have difficulty believing that language they hear in *Star Wars* is also used to describe AIDS. In addition, these quotes show subtle fears, such as the feeling that AIDS is invading and polluting society as well as the cells of individuals.

3. Responses to this question will vary.

syphilis, which is characterized in terms of "stages," than like cancer. Thinking in terms of "stages" is essential to discourse about AIDS. Syphilis in its most dreaded form is "tertiary syphilis," syphilis in its third stage. What is called AIDS is generally understood as the last of three stages—the first of which is infection with a human immunodeficiency virus (HIV) and early evidence of inroads on the immune system—with a long latency period between infection and the onset of the "telltale" symptoms. (Apparently not as long as syphilis, in which the latency period between secondary and tertiary illness might be decades. But it is worth noting that when syphilis first appeared in epidemic form in Europe at the end of the fifteenth century, it was a rapid disease, of an unexplained virulence that is unknown today, in which death often occurred in the second stage, sometimes within months or a few years.) Cancer *grows* slowly: It is not thought to be, for a long time, latent. (A convincing account of a process in terms of "stages" seems invariably to include the notion of a normative delay or halt in the process, such as is supplied by the notion of latency.) True, a cancer is "staged." This is a principal tool of diagnosis, which means classifying it according to its gravity, determining how "advanced" it is. But it is mostly a spatial notion: that the cancer advances through the body, traveling or migrating along predictable routes. Cancer is first of all a disease of the body's geography, in contrast to syphilis and AIDS, whose definition depends on constructing a temporal sequence of stages.

UNDERSTANDING DETAILS

1. In what ways do the words "invasion" and "pollution" (paragraph 3) help define AIDS? What two points of view of the disease do these words represent?
2. How is the language of AIDS different from that of cancer? From that of syphilis?
3. Explain the headline Sontag cites in paragraph 4: "AIDS Virus Found to Hide in Cells, Eluding Detection by Normal Tests."

ANALYZING MEANING

1. According to Sontag, what makes the attack of AIDS so "terrifying" (paragraph 5)?

2. Explain all aspects of the two main metaphors Sontag uses to define AIDS (invasion and pollution). How does Sontag's examination of these metaphors help you understand the AIDS virus more specifically?
3. Devise a new metaphor to explain the progress of this disease.

DISCOVERING RHETORICAL STRATEGIES

1. How does Sontag use the language of science fiction to define AIDS?
2. What effect does Sontag's use of quotations have on the essay?
3. Sontag uses both comparison/contrast and analogy to define AIDS in this essay. Find an example of each of these rhetorical modes, and explain how it works.

IDEAS FOR DISCUSSION/WRITING

Preparing to Write

Write freely about your current reactions to the AIDS virus: How do you feel about the disease? What should we be doing to control the spread of AIDS? What should we be doing to protect the rights of AIDS victims? To protect the rights of people who do not have AIDS? What do you think the future of the virus in America will be?

Choosing a Topic

1. Choose an ailment other than AIDS (for example, something serious, such as a stroke or heart trouble, or something less threatening, such as the flu or a cold), and write an essay in which you define this illness through an extended comparison.
2. For a medical report prepared by your college or university, define "health" as it relates to college students today. Determine an audience and focus before you begin to write.
3. The central feud in connection with the AIDS epidemic in the United States revolves around the civil rights of the AIDS victims versus the rights of people not infected with the virus. Many states are taking actions that require physicians to report AIDS victims to a central agency. Write an editorial for your local newspaper explaining where you stand on this issue and why.

PREWRITING

In preparation for the writing assignments, the Preparing to Write questions ask students to consider both their emotional and intellectual reactions to AIDS and its victims before writing an essay on a related topic. See pages 16–23 for suggestions on generating ideas in response to these questions.

ADDITIONAL DISCUSSION/WRITING TOPIC

In a coherent essay written for your classmates, define the word "epidemic." Does the AIDS virus fall into this category? Refer to both the denotations and connotations of this term in your essay.

REVISING STRATEGY

Although one rhetorical mode may be dominant, a combination of modes plays a part in all essays. In one of your definition essays, identify the rhetorical modes you use to support your main definition. Decide whether other rhetorical modes should replace or be used in addition to the strategies you have already incorporated into your essay. Then revise your paper, concentrating on the effectiveness of your rhetorical modes in helping you achieve your purpose with a specific audience.

CHAPTER 8

CAUSE/EFFECT

■ ■ ■

Tracing Reasons and Results

Using Cause/Effect

Wanting to know why things happen is one of our earliest, most basic instincts: Why can't I go out, Mommy? Why are you laughing? Why won't the dog stop barking? Why can't I swim faster than my big brother? These questions, and many more like them, reflect the innately inquisitive nature that dwells within each of us. Closely related to this desire to understand *why* is our corresponding interest in *what* will happen in the future as a result of some particular action: What will I feel like tomorrow if I stay up late tonight? How will I perform in the track meet Saturday if I practice all week? What will be the result if I mix together these two potent chemicals? What will happen if I turn in my next English assignment two days early?

A daily awareness of this intimate relationship between causes and effects allows us to begin to understand the complex and interrelated series of events that make up our lives and the lives of others. For example, trying to understand the various causes of the conflict in the Persian Gulf can teach us about international relations; knowing our biological reactions to certain foods will help us make decisions about what to eat; understanding the interrelated reasons for the outbreak of World War II offers us insight into historical trends and human nature; knowing the effects of sunshine on various parts of our bodies can help us

Cause/effect reasoning is one of the most common forms of thinking in our daily lives, but often it is also the most misused. We generally turn to cause/effect for one of three purposes: (1) to prove a specific point, (2) to argue against a widely accepted belief, or (3) to speculate on a theory. The problem arises, however, in the way this technique is used. Many people will look no further than the immediate causes or effects of an event (a malfunction in a nuclear plant that caused an explosion), when only uncovering the ultimate or real causes or effects (the poor engineering that caused the malfunction in the first place) will begin to solve the problem or puzzle at hand.

The apparatus in this chapter—including prereading and prewriting suggestions, questions on comprehension and rhetorical strategies, and writing assignments—all work to help students trace the relationships between fundamental causes, real effects, and the events to which they are connected. The questions accompanying the first essay, "Why We Crave Horror Movies," by Stephen King, for example, ask students to consider the causes and effects of our natural desire to see horror movies and respond to other social evils. The apparatus accompanying Michael Dorris' essay "The Broken Cord" has students contemplate the problems of growing up with a drug or alcohol addiction, along with the causes and effects of those problems, whereas the questions and assignments accompanying "The Fear of Losing a Culture," by Richard Rodriguez, encourage students to speculate on various cultural and racial issues in America. The questions and exercises accompanying "Rx for Mathophobia" by Mitchell Lazarus suggest that students consider various phobias, their causes, and their effects. Finally, Alice Walker's essay, entitled "My Daughter Smokes," prompts students to think and write about various addictive behaviors.

make decisions about how much ultraviolet exposure we can tolerate and what suntan lotion to use; and understanding the causes of America's most recent recession will help us respond appropriately to the next economic crisis we encounter. More than anything else, tracing causes and effects teaches us how to think clearly and react intelligently to our multifaceted environment.

In college you will often be asked to use this natural interest in causes and effects to analyze particular situations and discern general principles. For example, you might be asked some of the following questions on essay exams in different courses:

Anthropology: Why did the Mayan culture disintegrate?
Psychology: Why do humans respond to fear in different ways?
Biology: How do lab rats react to caffeine?
History: What were the positive effects of the Spanish-American War?
Business: Why did so many computer manufacturing companies go bankrupt in the early 1980s?

Your ability to answer such questions will depend in large part on your skill at writing a cause/effect essay.

Defining Cause/Effect

Cause/effect analysis requires the ability to look for connections between different elements and to analyze the reasons for those connections. As the name implies, this rhetorical mode has two separate components: cause and effect. A particular essay might concentrate on cause (Why do you live in a dorm?), on effect (What are the resulting advantages and disadvantages of living in a dorm?), or on some combination of the two. In working with causes, we are searching for any circumstances from the past that might have caused a single event; in looking for effects, we seek occurrences that took place after a particular event and resulted from that event. Like process analysis, cause/effect makes use of our intellectual ability to analyze. Process analysis addresses *how* something happens, whereas causal analysis discusses *why* it happened and *what* the result was. A process analysis paper, for example, might explain how to advertise more effectively to increase sales, whereas a cause/effect study would discover that three specific reasons contributed to the increase in sales: effective advertising, personal service, and selective discounts. The study of causes and effects, therefore, provides many different and helpful ways for humans to clarify their views of the world.

Looking for causes and effects requires an advanced form of thinking. It is more complex than most rhetorical strategies we have studied, because it can exist on a number of different and progressively more difficult levels. The most accurate and effective causal analysis accrues from digging for the real or ultimate causes or effects, as opposed to those that are merely superficial or immediate. Actress Angela Lansbury would have been out of work on an episode of the television show "Murder, She Wrote," for example, if her character had stopped her investigation at the immediate cause of death (slipping in the bath tub) rather than searching diligently for the real reason (an overdose of cocaine administered by an angry companion, thereby causing the slip in the tub). Similarly, voters would be easy to manipulate if they considered only the immediate effects of a tax increase (a slightly higher tax bill) rather than the ultimate benefits that would result (the many years of improved education our children would receive because of the specialized programs created by such an increase). Only the discovery of the actual reasons behind an event or an idea will lead to a logical and accurate analysis of causes and effects.

Faulty reasoning assigns causes to a sequence of actions without adequate justification. One such logical fallacy is called *post hoc, ergo propter hoc* ("after this, therefore because of this"): The fact that someone lost a job after walking under a ladder does not mean that the two events are causally related; by the same token, if we get up every morning at 5:30 A.M., just before the sun rises, we cannot therefore conclude that the sun rises *because* we get up (no matter how self-centered we are). Faulty reasoning can also occur when we oversimplify a particular situation. Most events are connected to a multitude of causes and effects. Sometimes one effect can have many causes: A student might fail a history exam because she's been working two part-time jobs, she was sick, she didn't study hard enough, and she found the instructor very boring. One cause can also have many effects. If a house burns down, the people who lived in it will be out of a home. If we look at such a tragic scene more closely, however, we might also note that the fire traumatized a child who lived there, helped the family learn what good friends they had, encouraged the family to double their future fire insurance, and provided the happy stimulus they needed to make a long-dreamed-of move to another city. One

TEACHING CAUSE/EFFECT: ONE INSTRUCTOR'S COMMENTS

I teach cause/effect to develop analytical skills. I ask students to begin with a characteristic about themselves or a situation they find themselves in and ask WHY? For example, "Why Do I Love Chocolate?" elicits a list of causes like "The caffeine in it gives me a high"; "I can eat it on ice cream, in candy bars, and smothered on cakes and cookies"; "I love the sweet/bitter taste"; "I associate it with holidays and other special occasions."

Asking WHAT WILL HAPPEN about a real or imagined situation or event helps students analyze effects. For example, "What will happen if I win the lottery?" results in an imaginary description of a life of luxury and fulfilled dreams.

Once the students move out of the personal realm, they can apply the same strategy to analyzing larger issues: Why am I a Democrat/Republican? What will happen if we proceed with the war against drugs? Why did I take up smoking? What will happen if I give up the habit? I usually ask students to focus on either causes or effects in a beginning composition course. Advanced students can combine cause and effect analysis in one essay—for example, "Why did I take up smoking, and what benefits have I received because I broke the habit?"

Ellen Dugan-Barrette
Brescia College
Owensboro, Kentucky

Elizabeth Wahlquist
Brigham Young University
Provo, Utah

I teach cause/effect indirectly, meaning I have students first write a cause/effect essay without calling it that and then read a model essay demonstrating the mode. I believe that the material, purpose, audience, etc., have to determine the form of an essay. So I have my students struggle with Cummings' "since feeling is first" and try to determine whether or not feeling is first for them or if syntax, form, structure, and mode are first in their experience; I then ask them whether or not these elements are causally related or if they happen without one causing the other. After my students have struggled with these variables and written an essay in this mode, we analyze some professional models. Then I have them revise what they have already written.

event has thus resulted in many interrelated effects. The act of building an argument on insecure foundations or oversimplifying the causes or effects connected with an event will seriously hinder the construction of a rational essay. No matter what the nature of the cause/effect analysis, it must always be based on clear observation, accurate facts, and rigorous logic.

In the following paragraph, a student writer analyzes some of the causes and effects connected with the controversial issue of euthanasia. Notice how he makes connections and then analyzes those connections as he consistently explores the immediate and ultimate effects of being able to stretch life beyond its normal limits through new medical technology.

> Along with the many recent startling advancements in medical technology have come a number of complex moral, ethical, and spiritual questions which beg to be answered. We now have the ability to prolong the life of the human body for a very long time. But what rights do patients and their families have to curtail cruel and unusual medical treatment that stretches life beyond its normal limits? This dilemma has produced a ripple effect in society. Is the extension of life an unquestionable goal in itself, regardless of the quality of that life? Modern scientific technology has forced doctors to reevaluate the exact meaning and purpose of their profession. For example, many medical schools and undergraduate university programs now routinely offer classes on medical ethics—an esoteric and infrequently taught subject only a few years ago. Doctors and scholars alike are realizing that medical personnel alone cannot be expected to determine the exact parameters of life. In like manner, the judicial process must now evaluate the legal complexities of mercy killings and the rights of patients to die with dignity and without unnecessary medical intervention. The insurance business, too, wrestles with the catastrophic effects new technology has had on the costs of today's hospital care. In short, medical progress entails more than microscopes, chemicals, and high-tech instruments. If we are to develop as a thoughtful, just, and merciful society, we must consider not only the physical well-being of our nation's patients, but their emotional, spiritual, and financial status as well.

Reading and Writing Cause/Effect Essays

Causal analysis will usually be employed for one of three main purposes: (1) to prove a specific point (such as the necessity for stricter gun control), in which case the writer will generally deal totally with facts and with conclusions drawn from those facts; (2) to argue against a widely accepted belief (for example, the assertion that cocaine is addictive), in which case the writer will rely principally on facts, with perhaps some pertinent opinions; or (3) to speculate on a theory (for instance, why the crime rate is higher in most major cities than it is in rural areas), in which case the writer will probably present hypotheses and opinions along with facts.

HOW TO READ A CAUSE/EFFECT ESSAY

Preparing to Read. As you set out to read the essays in this chapter, begin by focusing your attention on the title and the synopsis of the essay you are about to read and by scanning the essay itself: What do you think Stephen King is going to talk about in "Why We Crave Horror Movies"? What does the synopsis tell you about Michael Dorris' "The Broken Cord" or about Richard Rodriguez's "The Fear of Losing a Culture"?

Also, at this stage in the reading process, you should try to learn as much as you can about the author of an essay and the reasons he or she wrote it. Ask yourself questions like the following: What is King's intention in "Why We Crave Horror Movies"? Who is Mitchell Lazarus' intended audience in "Rx for Mathophobia"? And what is Alice Walker's point of view in "My Daughter Smokes"?

Finally, before you begin to read, answer the prereading questions for each essay and then consider the proposed essay topic from a variety of perspectives: For example, concerning Rodriguez's topic, how important to you is your ethnic or national background? Which segments of American society are most aware of cultural differences? Which the least? Do you have a fear of math? What do you want to know from Lazarus about curing or controlling that fear?

Reading. As you read each essay in this chapter for the first time, record your spontaneous reactions to it, drawing as often as possible on the preliminary material you already know: What do you think of horror movies (King)? Why did Lazarus choose the title he did? What is Dorris suggesting about fetal alcohol babies? Have you experienced an addiction of any kind? Whenever you can, try to create a context for your reading: What is the tone of Rodriguez's comments about culture? How does this tone help him communicate with his audience? What do you think Walker's purpose is in her essay on smoking? How clearly does she get this purpose across to you? Also, during this reading, note the essay's thesis and check to see if the writer thoroughly explores all possibilities before settling on the primary causes and/or effects of a particular situation; in addition, determine whether the writer clearly states the assertions that naturally evolve from a discussion of the topic. Finally, read the questions following each essay to get a sense of the main issues and strategies in the selection.

Rereading.   When you reread these essays, you should focus mainly on the writer's craft. Notice how the authors narrow and focus their material, how they make clear and logical connections between ideas in their essays, how they support their conclusions with concrete examples, how they use other rhetorical modes to accomplish their cause/effect analysis, and how they employ logical transitions to move us smoothly from one point to another. Most important, however, ask yourself if the writer actually discusses the real causes and/or effects of a particular circumstance: What does King say are the primary reasons people crave horror movies? What does Lazarus consider to be the main causes of mathophobia? What solutions does he offer? What are the primary causes and effects of Walker's daughter's smoking?

For a thorough outline of the reading process, consult the checklist on pages 15–16 of the Introduction.

HOW TO WRITE A CAUSE/EFFECT ESSAY

Preparing to Write.   Beginning a cause/effect essay requires—as does any other essay—exploring and limiting your subject, specifying a purpose, and identifying an audience. The Preparing to Write questions before the essay assignments, coupled with the prewriting techniques outlined in the Introduction, encourage you to consider specific issues related to your reading. The assignments themselves will then help you limit your topic and determine a particular purpose and audience for your message. For cause/effect essays, determining a purpose is even more important than usual, because your readers can get hopelessly lost without a clear focus for your analysis.

Writing.   For all its conceptual complexity, a cause/effect essay can be organized quite simply. The introduction generally presents the subject(s) and states the purpose of the analysis in a clear thesis. The body of the paper then explores all relevant causes and/or effects, typically progressing either from least to most influential or from most to least influential. Finally, the concluding section summarizes the various cause-and-effect relationships established in the body of the paper and clearly states the conclusions that can be drawn from those relationships.

The following additional guidelines should assist you in producing an effective cause/effect essay in all academic disciplines:

1. Narrow and focus your material as much as possible.
2. Consider all possibilities before assigning real or ultimate causes or effects.
3. Show connections between ideas by using transitions and key words—such as "because," "reasons," "results," "effects," and "consequences"—to guide your readers smoothly through your essay.
4. Support all inferences with concrete evidence.
5. Be as objective as possible in your analysis so you don't distort logic with personal biases.
6. Understand your audience's opinions and convictions, so that you know what to emphasize in your essay.
7. Qualify your assertions to avoid overstatement and oversimplification.

These suggestions apply to both cause/effect essay assignments and exam questions.

Rewriting. As you revise your cause/effect essays, ask yourself the following important questions: Is your thesis stated clearly at the outset of your paper? Do you accomplish your purpose as effectively as possible for your particular audience? Do you use logical reasoning throughout the essay? Do you carefully explore all relevant causes and/or effects, searching for the real (as opposed to the immediate) reasons in each case? Do you state clearly the conclusions that can be drawn from the various cause/effect relationships discussed in your paper?

More specific guidelines for writing and revising your essays appear on pages 27–28 of the Introduction.

Student Essay: Cause/Effect at Work

In the following essay, the student writer analyzes the effects of contemporary TV soap operas on young people: Notice how she states her subject and purpose at the beginning of the essay and then presents a combination of facts and opinions in her exploration of the topic. Notice also that, in her analysis, the writer is careful to draw clear connections between her perceptions of the issue and various objective details in an attempt to trace the effects of this medium in our society today. At the end of her essay, look at her summary of the logical relationships she establishes in the body of the essay and her statements about the conclusions she draws from these relationships.

Distortions of Reality

Background   Television's contributions to society, positive and negative, have been debated continually since this piece of technology invaded the average American household in the 1950s. Television has brought an unlimited influx of new information, ideas, and cultures into our homes. However, based on my observations of my thirteen-year-old cousin, Katie, and her friends, I think we need to take a closer look at the effects of soap operas on adolescents today. The distortions of reality portrayed on these programs are frightenly misleading and, in my opinion, can be very confusing to young people.   Thesis statement

Transition   During the late 1980s, the lifestyle of the typical soap opera "family" has been radically transformed from comfortable pretentiousness to blatant and unrealistic decadence. The characters neither live nor dress like the majority of their viewers, who are generally middle-class Americans. These television families live in large, majestic homes that are flawlessly decorated. The actors are   First distortion of reality

Concrete examples   often adorned in beautiful designer clothing, fur coats, and expensive jewelry, but this opulent lifestyle is sustained by people with no visible means of income. Very few of the characters seem to "work" for a living. When they do, upward mobility—without the benefit of the proper education or suitable training—and a well-planned marriage come quickly.

Transition   From this constant barrage of conspicuous consumption, my cousin and her friends seem to have a distorted view of everyday economic realities. I see Katie and her group becoming obsessed with the appearance of their clothes and possessions.   First effect

Concrete examples   I frequently hear them berate their parents' jobs and modest homes. With noticeable arrogance, these young adolescents seem to view their parents' lives as "failures" when compared to the effortless, luxurious lifestyles portrayed in the soaps.

Transition   One of the alluring features of this genre is its masterful use of deception. Conflicts between char-

Concrete examples — acters in soap operas are based on secrecy and misinformation. Failure to tell the truth and to perform honorable deeds further complicates the entangled lives and love affairs of the participants. But when the truth finally comes out and all mistakes and misdeeds become public, the culprits and offenders hardly ever suffer for their actions. In fact, they appear to leave the scene of the crime guilt-free.

Second distortion of reality

Transition — Regrettably, Katie and her friends consistently express alarming indifference in response to this lack of moral integrity. In their daily viewing, they

Concrete examples — shrug off underhanded scenes of scheming and conniving, and they marvel at how the characters manipulate each other into positions of powerlessness or grapple in distasteful love scenes. I can only conclude that continued exposure to this amoral behavior is eroding the fundamental values of truth and fidelity in these kids.

Second effect

Transition — Also in the soaps, the powers-that-be conveniently disregard any sense of responsibility for wrongdoing. Characters serve jail terms quickly

Concrete examples — and in relative comfort. Drug or alcohol abuse does not mar anyone's physical appearance or behavior, and poverty is virtually nonexistent. Usually, the wrongdoer's position, wealth, and prestige are quickly restored—with little pain and suffering.

Third distortion of reality

Adolescents are clearly learning that people can act without regard for the harmful effects of their actions on themselves and others when they see this type of behavior go unpunished. Again, I notice the result of this delusion in my cousin. Re-

Third effect

Concrete examples — cently, when a businessman in our community was convicted of embezzling large sums of money from his clients, Katie was outraged because he was sentenced to five years in prison, unlike her daytime T.V. "heartthrob" who was given a suspended sentence for a similar crime. With righteous indignation, Katie claimed the victims, many of whom had lost their entire savings, should have realized that any business investment involves risk and the threat of loss. Logic and common sense evaded Katie's reasoning as she insisted on comparing television justice with real-life scruples.

The writers and producers of soap operas argue that the shows are designed to entertain viewers and are not meant to be reflections of reality. Theoretically, this may be true, but I can actually see how these soap operas are affecting my cousin and her crowd. Although my personal observations are limited, I cannot believe they are unique or unusual. Too many young people think that they can amass wealth and material possessions without an education, hard work, or careful financial planning; that material goods are the sole measure of a person's success in life; and that honesty and integrity are not necessarily admirable qualities.

Ultimate effect

Soap operas should demonstrate a realistic lifestyle and a responsible sense of behavior. The many hours adolescents spend in front of the television can obviously influence their view of the world. As a society, we cannot afford the consequences resulting from the distortions of reality portrayed every day in these shows.

Proposed solution

Student Writer's Comments

Writing this essay was not as easy as I had anticipated in my prewriting phase. Although I was interested in and familiar with my topic, the challenge was in selecting specific examples to support my thesis statement and then in narrowing my focus to a few main points. Although all writing requires support and focus, a cause/effect essay demands special attention to the relationship between specific examples and their ultimate causes and/or effects.

Some Final Thoughts on Cause/Effect

The essays in this chapter deal with both causes and effects in a variety of ways. As you read each essay, try to discover its primary purpose and the ultimate causes and/or effects of the issue under discussion. Note also the clear causal relationships each author sets forth on solid foundations supported by logical reasoning. Although the subjects of these essays vary dramatically, each essay exhibits the basic elements of effective causal analysis.

STEPHEN KING
(1947–   )

■ ■ ■

Why We Crave Horror Movies

"People's appetites for terror seem insatiable," Stephen King once remarked, which may help justify his phenomenal success as a writer of horror fiction over the past two decades. His twenty-one books have sold over one hundred million copies, and the movies made from them have generated more income than the gross national product of several small countries. After early jobs as a janitor, laundry worker, and high school English teacher in Portland, Maine, King turned to writing full time following the spectacular sales of his first novel, *Carrie* (1974), which focuses on a shy, socially ostracized young girl who takes revenge on her cruel classmates through newly developed telekinetic powers. King's subsequent books have included *Salem's Lot* (1975), *The Shining* (1976), *Firestarter* (1980), *Cujo* (1981), *The Dark Tower* (1982), *Christine* (1983), *Pet Sematary* (1983), *Misery* (1987), and *The Stand* (1990). Asked to explain why readers and moviegoers are so attracted to his tales of horror, King told a *Chicago Tribune* interviewer that most people's lives "are full of fears—that their marriage isn't working, that they aren't going to make it on the job, that society is crumbling all around them. But we're really not supposed to talk about things like that, and so they don't have any outlets for all those scary feelings. But the horror writer can give them a place to put their fears, and it's OK to be afraid then, because nothing is real, and you can blow it all away when it's over." A cheerful though somewhat superstitious person, King, who now lives in Bangor, Maine, admits to doing most of his best writing during the morning hours. "You think I want to write this stuff at night?" he once asked a reviewer.

Preparing to Read

As you prepare to read this article, consider your thoughts on America's emotional condition: How emotionally healthy are Americans? Were they more emotionally healthy twenty years ago? A century ago? What makes a society emotionally healthy? Emotionally unhealthy? How can a society maintain good health? What is the relationship between emotional health and a civilized society?

PREREADING

The purpose of this Preparing to Read material is to encourage students to speculate on America's emotional condition. To help your students focus their attention on the nation's collective psychological state before they respond to the questions here, you might provide them with definitions of two words that are pivotal in Stephen King's essay:

civilization—A condition of human society marked by an advanced stage of development in the arts and sciences and by corresponding social, political, and cultural complexity.
anticivilization—A condition of human society marked by a decline in the development of the arts and sciences and by corresponding social, political, and cultural simplicity.

Then, conduct a brief discussion concerning each of these conditions within our society. See pages 3–6 for other ways to generate thoughts on these questions.

BACKGROUND INFORMATION

In this essay, King deals lightheartedly with "morbidity unchained, our most base instincts let free, our nastiest fantasies realized" (para. 12). He implies that we need to have an acceptable outlet for these emotions so we can remain a civilized society.

READABILITY LEVEL

9.2

RELATED READINGS

Media

Susan Allen Toth, "Cinematypes"   273
Marie Winn, "Television Addiction"   370

DEFINITIONS

Freda Jackson (1909–   ) (para. 4): a melodramatic character actress of stage and film.

Die, Monster, Die! (1965) (para. 4): a British horror movie starring Boris Karloff and Freda Jackson.

Robert Redford (1937–   ) (para. 4): an American actor and director; star of such movies as *Butch Cassidy and the Sundance Kid* and *The Candidate*.

Diana Ross (1944–   ) (para. 4): a singer and performer whose vocal group, The Supremes, was one of the early Motown successes of the 1960s.

Jack the Ripper (para. 8): an unknown murderer who killed and mutilated five prostitutes in London between August 31 and November 9, 1888.

Cleveland Torso Murderer (para. 8): an unknown murderer who left five headless corpses in different locations in Cleveland from 1934 to 1938.

Leonard Nimoy (para. 9): an American actor and poet, best known for his role as "Mr. Spock" in *Star Trek*.

Dawn of the Dead (1979) (para. 12): a sequel to *Night of the Living Dead* (1968) in which the dead return to life and eat the living.

Lennon and McCartney (para. 13): John Lennon and Paul McCartney, members of The Beatles and co-writers of many of the group's songs.

I think that we're all mentally ill; those of us outside the asylums only hide it a little better—and maybe not all that much better, after all. We've all known people who talk to themselves, people who sometimes squinch their faces into horrible grimaces when they believe no one is watching, people who have some hysterical fear—of snakes, the dark, the tight place, the long drop . . . and, of course, those final worms and grubs that are waiting so patiently underground. 1

When we pay our four or five bucks and seat ourselves at tenth-row center in a theater showing a horror movie, we are daring the nightmare. 2

Why? Some of the reasons are simple and obvious. To show that we can, that we are not afraid, that we can ride this roller coaster. Which is not to say that a really good horror movie may not surprise a scream out of us at some point, the way we may scream when the roller coaster twists through a complete 360 or plows through a lake at the bottom of the drop. And horror movies, like roller coasters, have always been the special province of the young; by the time one turns 40 or 50, one's appetite for double twists or 360-degree loops may be considerably depleted. 3

We also go to reestablish our feelings of essential normality; the horror movie is innately conservative, even reactionary. Freda Jackson as the horrible melting woman in *Die, Monster, Die!* confirms for us that no matter how far we may be removed from the beauty of a Robert Redford or a Diana Ross, we are still light-years from true ugliness. 4

And we go to have fun. 5

Ah, but this is where the ground starts to slope away, isn't it? Because this is a very peculiar sort of fun, indeed. The fun comes from seeing others menaced—sometimes killed. One critic has suggested that if pro football has become the voyeur's version of combat, then the horror film has become the modern version of the public lynching. 6

It is true that the mythic, "fairy-tale" horror film intends to take away the shades of gray. . . . It urges us to put away our more civilized and adult penchant for analysis and to become children again, seeing things in pure blacks and whites. It may be that horror movies provide psychic relief on this level because this invitation to lapse into simplicity, irrationality, and even outright madness is extended so rarely. We are told we may allow our emotions a free rein . . . or no rein at all. 7

If we are all insane, then sanity becomes a matter of degree. If your insanity leads you to carve up women, like Jack the Ripper 8 or the Cleveland Torso Murderer, we clap you away in the funny farm (but neither of those two amateur-night surgeons was ever caught, heh-heh-heh); if, on the other hand, your insanity leads you only to talk to yourself when you're under stress or to pick your nose on your morning bus, then you are left alone to go about your business . . . though it is doubtful that you will ever be invited to the best parties.

The potential lyncher is in almost all of us (excluding saints, past and present; but then, most saints have been crazy in their own ways), and every now and then, he has to be let loose to scream and roll around in the grass. Our emotions and our fears form their own body, and we recognize that it demands its own exercise to maintain proper muscle tone. Certain of these emotional muscles are accepted—even exalted—in civilized society; they are, of course, the emotions that tend to maintain the status quo of civilization itself. Love, friendship, loyalty, kindness— these are all the emotions that we applaud, emotions that have been immortalized in the couplets of Hallmark cards and in the verses (I don't dare call it poetry) of Leonard Nimoy.

When we exhibit these emotions, society showers us with positive reinforcement; we learn this even before we get out of diapers. When, as children, we hug our rotten little puke of a sister and give her a kiss, all the aunts and uncles smile and twit and cry, "Isn't he the sweetest little thing?" Such coveted treats as chocolate-covered graham crackers often follow. But if we deliberately slam the rotten little puke of a sister's fingers in the door, sanctions follow—angry remonstrance from parents, aunts and uncles; instead of a chocolate-covered graham cracker, a spanking.

But anticivilization emotions don't go away, and they demand periodic exercise. We have such "sick" jokes as, "What's the difference between a truckload of bowling balls and a truckload of dead babies?" (You can't unload a truckload of bowling balls with a pitchfork . . . a joke, by the way, that I heard originally from a ten-year-old.) Such a joke may surprise a laugh or a grin out of us even as we recoil, a possibility that confirms the thesis: If we share a brotherhood of man, then we also share an insanity of man. None of which is intended as a defense of either the sick joke or insanity but merely as an explanation of why the best horror films, like the best fairy tales, manage to be reactionary, anarchistic, and revolutionary all at the same time.

The mythic horror movie, like the sick joke, has a dirty job to do. It deliberately appeals to all that is worst in us. It is morbidity unchained, our most base instincts let free, our nastiest fantasies

11

12

1. According to King, "anticivilization emotions don't go away, and they demand periodic exercise" (para. 11). As a result, he believes that horror films provide a temporary outlet to exercise these socially unacceptable feelings, thus making us "normal" again.

2. Horror films and fairy tales are reactionary, anarchistic, and revolutionary because they pose basic questions of human behavior while reaffirming no specific law or system as a norm. Both the horror film and the fairy tale reduce us to a child's perspective while requiring us to examine serious and adult subjects.

3. King asserts that venting anticivilized emotions by watching horror movies allows us to keep our basic animalism in check. We "feed our gators" by exercising these negative emotions in a relatively harmless manner.

ANSWERS TO QUESTIONS:
DISCOVERING RHETORICAL
STRATEGIES (p. 398)

1. Horror movies, as King views them, "provide psychic relief . . . because this invitation to lapse into simplicity, irrationality, and even outright madness is extended so rarely. We are told we may allow our emotions a free rein . . . " (para. 7). Horror movies maintain our sanity because we can vicariously live out the worst of our fears and fantasies with impunity and thereby gain balance and stability from this release from terror.

2. Shock value and emotional denial motivate King to use a phrase such as this. Knowing that many will not agree with his viewpoint, he must show them that they are hiding something, that they have a secret "gator" within, before he can convince them to exercise it.

3. King's audience is adult, though probably younger than "40 or 50, [when] one's appetite for double twists or 360-degree loops may be considerably depleted" (para. 3). His use of the pronoun "we" and his casual references to several popular horror films imply that he is addressing a large audience familiar with the genre.

realized . . . , and it all happens, fittingly enough, in the dark. For those reasons, good liberals often shy away from horror films. For myself, I like to see the most aggressive of them—*Dawn of the Dead*, for instance—as lifting a trap door in the civilized forebrain and throwing a basket of raw meat to the hungry alligators swimming around in that subterranean river beneath.

Why bother? Because it keeps them from getting out, man. It 13 keeps them down there and me up here. It was Lennon and McCartney who said that all you need is love, and I would agree with that.

As long as you keep the gators fed. 14

UNDERSTANDING DETAILS

1. Why, in King's opinion, do civilized people enjoy horror movies?
2. According to King, how are horror films like public lynchings?
3. What is the difference between "emotions that tend to maintain the status quo of civilization" (paragraph 9) and "anticivilization emotions" (paragraph 11)?

ANALYZING MEANING

1. How can horror movies "reestablish our feelings of essential normality" (paragraph 4)?
2. What is "reactionary, anarchistic, and revolutionary" (paragraph 11) about fairy tales? About horror films?
3. Explain the last line of King's essay: "As long as you keep the gators fed" (paragraph 14).

DISCOVERING RHETORICAL STRATEGIES

1. What is the cause/effect relationship King notes in society between horror movies and sanity?
2. Why does King begin his essay with such a dramatic statement as "I think that we're all mentally ill" (paragraph 1)?
3. Who do you think is the author's intended audience for this essay? Describe them in detail. How did you come to this conclusion?

IDEAS FOR DISCUSSION/WRITING

Preparing to Write

Write freely about how most people maintain a healthy emotional attitude: How would you define emotional well-being? When are people most emotionally healthy? Most emotionally unhealthy? What do your friends and relatives do to maintain a healthy emotional life? What do you do to maintain emotional health? What is the connection between our individual emotional health and the extent to which our society is civilized?

Choosing a Topic

1. Think of a release other than horror films for our most violent emotions. Is it an acceptable release? Write an essay for the general public explaining the relationship between this particular release and our "civilized" society.
2. If you accept King's analysis of horror movies, what role in society do you think other types of movies play (e.g., love stories, science-fiction movies, comedies)? Choose one type, and explain its role to your college composition class.
3. Your psychology instructor has asked you to explain your opinions on the degree of sanity or insanity in America at present. In what ways are we sane? In what ways are we insane? Write an essay for your psychology instructor explaining in detail your observations along these lines.

PREWRITING

In preparation for the writing assignments, the Preparing to Write questions ask students to think about the psychological well-being of one or two specific people they know before writing an essay on a related topic. See pages 16–23 for suggestions on generating ideas in response to these questions.

ADDITIONAL DISCUSSION/WRITING TOPIC

Choose a movie, book, or music video, and explain someone's reactions to it. You could analyze your own reactions or those of someone else or a group of people. Discuss both the causes and effects of these reactions. Be sure your discussion considers both the immediate and ultimate causes and effects.

REVISING STRATEGY

A clear sense of purpose is an important key to any essay. A cause/effect essay should fulfill one of the following purposes: (1) to prove a specific point, (2) to argue against a widely accepted belief, or (3) to speculate on a theory. This purpose should be stated clearly in the introduction of a cause/effect essay. In one of your cause/effect essays, check that your purpose is explained in your introduction, and then underline all parts of your essay that help you achieve that goal. Notice where your intention could be clearer or more focused. Then revise this paper so that it communicates a clear, consistent purpose to your intended audience.

PREREADING

The purpose of this Preparing to Read material is to encourage students to think about their own physical and mental development. To help your students turn their attention to this topic before they respond to the questions here, have them brainstorm about their various physical and intellectual potentials and then discuss their individual schemes for fulfilling those potentials. See pages 3–6 for other ways to generate thoughts on these questions.

BACKGROUND INFORMATION

The book from which this essay was taken is an emotionally charged account of Michael Dorris' joys and sorrows as an adoptive father of a baby with fetal alcohol syndrome. Dorris learned early in his child's life that his son would never reach the full potential of other people his age. In this essay, the author talks through his feelings and coping strategies as he comes to terms with this hidden tragedy: "A drowning man is not separated from the lust for air by a bridge of thought—he is one with it—and my son, conceived and grown in an ethanol bath, lives each day in the act of drowning. For him there is no shore" (para. 19). Dorris offers a compelling description of his fears and awarenesses through analogy and poignant figurative language, so all readers can identify with the author's heartbreaking story.

READABILITY LEVEL

11.9

MICHAEL DORRIS
(1945–   )

■ ■ ■

The Broken Cord

Michael Dorris, a descendant of Modoc American Indians and Irish and French settlers, grew up in Kentucky and Montana. He earned his B.A. at Georgetown University and his Master of Philosophy at Yale and was for many years a professor of anthropology and Native-American Studies at Dartmouth, where he was also head of the Native-American Studies program. His training has been quite eclectic: "I came to cultural anthropology," he has explained, "by way of an undergraduate program in English and classics and a master's degree in history of the theater." He has been a Guggenheim Fellow (1978), a Rockefeller Fellow (1985), a member of the Smithsonian Institution Council, a National Endowment for the Humanities consultant, a National Public Radio commentator, and a member of the editorial board of *The American Indian Culture and Research Journal* during his distinguished academic career. His many publications have included *Native Americans: Five Hundred Years After* (1975); a bestselling novel, *A Yellow Raft in Blue Water* (1987); and *The Broken Cord* (1989), a work of nonfiction that won the Heartland Prize, the Christopher Medal, and the National Book Critics Circle Award. Dorris has also coauthored several books with his wife, Louise Erdrich, including *Route Two and Back* (1991), a collection of travel essays. He currently lives and works in Cornish Flat, New Hampshire.

Preparing to Read

The following excerpt from *The Broken Cord* details some of Dorris' frustrations in raising his adopted son, Adam, who suffered from fetal alcohol syndrome until his death in 1991. As you prepare to read this article, take a few moments to think about your own physical and mental growth: What do you know about your birth? How did you develop as a child? Are you reaching your physical and mental potential? How do you know? Are there any barriers between you and this potential? What are they? How can you surmount them? How will you maintain your potential?

Adam's birthdays are, I think, the hardest anniversaries, even though as an adoptive father I was not present to hear Adam's first cry, to feel the aspirated warmth of his body meeting air for the first time. I was not present to count his fingers, to exclaim at the surprise of gender, to be comforted by the hope at the heart of his new existence.

From what I've learned, from the sum of gathered profiles divided by the tragedy of each case, the delivery of my premature son was unlikely to have been a joyous occasion. Most fetal alcohol babies emerge not in a tide, the facsimile of saline, primordial, life-granting sea, but instead enter this world tainted with stale wine. Their amniotic fluid literally reeks of Thunderbird or Ripple, and the whole operating theater stinks like the scene of a three-day party. Delivery room staff who have been witness time and again tell of undernourished babies thrown into delirium tremens when the cord that brought sustenance and poison is severed. Nurses close their eyes at the memory. An infant with the shakes, as cold turkey as a raving derelict deprived of the next fix, is hard to forget.

Compared to the ideal, Adam started far in the hole, differently from the child who began a march through the years without the scars of fetters on his ankles, with eyes and ears that worked, with nothing to carry except what he or she collected along the path.

Adam's birthdays are reminders for me. For each celebration commemorating that he was born, there is the pang, the rage, that he was not born whole. I grieve for what he might have, what he should have been. I magnify and sustain those looks of understanding or compassion or curiosity that fleet across his face, fast as a breeze, unexpected as the voice of God—the time he said to me in the car, the words arising from no context I could see, "Kansas is between Oklahoma and Texas." But when I turned in amazement, agreeing loudly, still ready after all these years to discover a buried talent or passion for geography, for anything, that possible person had disappeared.

"What made you say that?" I asked.

"Say what?" he answered. "I didn't say anything."

The sixteenth birthday, the eighteenth. The milestones. The driver's license, voting, the adult boundary-marker birthdays. The days I envisioned while watching the mails for the response to my first adoption application, the days that set forth like distant skyscrapers as I projected ahead through my years of fatherhood. I had given little specific consideration to what might come

fetal alcohol babies (para. 2): babies born to alcoholic mothers; victims of fetal alcohol syndrome, a pattern of irreversible abnormalities including mental retardation, growth deficiencies, and joint defects.
primordial (para. 2): created or developed first in time; primitive.
amniotic fluid (para. 2): the fluid around the embryo in a pregnant woman's womb.
Thunderbird or Ripple (para. 2): cheap, sweet wines.
delirium tremens (para. 2): a state of confusion accompanied by trembling and hallucinations arising in chronic alcoholics after withdrawal or abstinence.
fetters (para. 3): restraints or shackles.
Franconia (para. 7): a small town in northwestern New Hampshire.
Hanover (para. 9): a town in western New Hampshire; home of Dartmouth College.
Ken Kramberg (para. 10): the director of a White River Junction, Vermont, high-school vocational program for the handicapped.
Cornish (para. 10): a small town near Hanover in western New Hampshire.

COLLABORATIVE LEARNING: CLASS ACTIVITY

Have the class discuss other types of dependencies that affect a person's life as completely and devastatingly as a mother's alcoholism affects the birth and health of her child. Have your students analyze the problems that lie behind addictions and try to get at the reasons for such behavior.

COLLABORATIVE LEARNING: SMALL GROUP ACTIVITY

Divide your students into groups of 4 or 5, and have them plan their own solution to one of the addictive problems that plagues our society today (alcohol, smoking, drugs, compulsive eating, anorexia, sexual obsessions, and others). Make sure the groups discuss both the causes and the effects of the addictive problem they are working with in order to arrive at a viable solution. Have one person from each group explain their solution to the rest of the class.

between, but of those outstanding days I had been sure. They were the pillars I followed, the oases of certainty. Alone in the cabin in Alaska or in the basement apartment near Franconia while I waited for the definition of the rest of my life to commence, I planned the elaborate cake decorations for those big birthdays, the significant presents I would save to buy. Odd as it may seem, the anticipation of the acts of letting Adam go began before I even knew his name. I looked forward to the proud days on which the world would recognize my son as progressively more his own man. Those were among the strongest hooks that bonded me to him in my imagination.

8   As each of these anniversaries finally came and went, nothing like I expected them to be, I doubly mourned. First, selfishly, for me, and second for Adam, because he didn't know what he was missing, what he had already missed, what he would miss. I wanted to burst through those birthdays like a speeding train blasts a weak gate, to get past them and back into the anonymous years for which I had made no models, where there were no obvious measurements, no cakes with candles that would never be lit.

9   It was a coincidence that Adam turned twenty-one as this book neared completion, but it seemed appropriate. On the morning of his birthday, I rose early and baked him a lemon cake, his favorite, and left the layers to cool while I drove to Hanover to pick him up. His gifts were wrapped and on the kitchen table— an electric shaver, clothes, a Garfield calendar. For his special dinner he had requested tacos, and as always I had reserved a magic candle—the kind that keeps reigniting no matter how often it is blown out—for the center of his cake.

10   I was greeted at Adam's house by the news that he had just had a seizure, a small one this time, but it had left him groggy. I helped him on with his coat, bent to tie his shoelace, all the while talking about the fun we would have during the day. He looked out the window. Only the week before he had been laid off from his dishwashing job. December had been a bad month for seizures, some due to his body's adjustment to a change in dosage and some occurring because Adam had skipped taking medicine altogether. The bowling alley's insurance carrier was concerned and that, combined with an after-Christmas slump in business, decided the issue. Now he was back at Hartford for a few weeks while Ken Krambert and his associates sought a new work placement. I thought perhaps Adam was depressed about this turn of events, so I tried to cheer him up as we drove south on the familiar road to Cornish.

"So, Adam," I said, making conversation, summoning the conventional words, "do you feel any older? What's good about being twenty-one?"

He turned to me and grinned. There *was* something good.

"Well," he answered, "now the guys at work say I'm old enough to drink."

His unexpected words kicked me in the stomach. They crowded every thought from my brain.

"Adam, you can't," I protested. "I've told you about your birth-mother, about your other father. Do you remember what happened to them?" I knew he did. I had told him the story several times, and we had gone over it together as he read, or I read to him, parts of this book.

Adam thought for a moment. "They were sick?" he offered finally. "That's why I have seizures?"

"No, they weren't sick. They died, Adam. They died from drinking. If you drank, it could happen to you." My memory played back all the statistics about sons of alcoholic fathers and their particular susceptibility to substance abuse. "It would not mix well with your medicine."

Adam sniffed, turned away, but not before I recognized the amused disbelief in his expression. He did not take death seriously, never had. It was an abstract concept out of his reach and therefore of no interest to him. Death was less real than Santa Claus—after all, Adam had in his album a photograph of himself seated on Santa Claus's lap. Death was no threat, no good reason to refuse his first drink.

My son will forever travel through a moonless night with only the roar of wind for company. Don't talk to him of mountains, of tropical beaches. Don't ask him to swoon at sunrises or marvel at the filter of light through leaves. He's never had time for such things, and he does not believe in them. He may pass by them close enough to touch on either side, but his hands are stretched forward, grasping for balance instead of pleasure. He doesn't wonder where he came from, where he's going. He doesn't ask who he is, or why. Questions are a luxury, the province of those at a distance from the periodic shock of rain. Gravity presses Adam so hard against reality that he doesn't feel the points at which he touches it. A drowning man is not separated from the lust for air by a bridge of thought—he is one with it—and my son, conceived and grown in an ethanol bath, lives each day in the act of drowning. For him there is no shore.

1. The causes and effects Dorris explains in his essay are as follows:

Causes (of Adam's behavior)

—"fetal alcohol babies emerge not in a . . . life-granting sea, but instead enter this world tainted with stale wine. Their amniotic fluid literally reeks of Thunderbird or Ripple . . ." (para. 2).

—"Undernourished babies [are] thrown into delirium tremens when the cord that brought sustenance and poison is severed" (para. 2).

—"Adam started far in the hole . . . [with] fetters on his ankles" (para. 3).

—"Some [seizures were] due to his body's adjustment to a change in dosage and some . . . because Adam had skipped taking medicine altogether" (para. 10).

—"I've told you about your birthmother, about your other father . . . " 'They were sick?' he offered finally. 'That's why I have seizures?'" (para. 15 and 16).

—"My memory played back all the statistics about sons of alcoholic fathers and their particular susceptibility to substance abuse" (para. 17).

—"My son, conceived and grown in an ethanol bath, lives each day in the act of drowning" (para. 19).

Effects (of Adam's behavior)

—"For each celebration commemorating that he was born, there is the pang, the rage, that he was not born whole". (para. 4).

—"I doubly mourned. First, selfishly, for me, and second for Adam, because he didn't know what he was missing, what he had already missed, what he would miss" (para. 8).

—"I was greeted at Adam's house by the news that he had just had a seizure . . ." (para. 10).

—"He had been laid off from his dishwashing job" (para. 10).

—"December had been a bad month for seizures" (para. 10).

[*Editors' Note:* Michael Dorris' son Adam died on September 22, 1991, after being struck by a car as he walked home from work. He was described in his obituary as "a brave, forgiving, and trusting person, gentle of heart and quick to laugh."]

UNDERSTANDING DETAILS

1. Why are Adam's birthdays difficult for Dorris?
2. What are some of the problems Adam was born with?
3. Why will Adam never reach his full potential?

ANALYZING MEANING

1. Why does Dorris "doubly" mourn (paragraph 8) his son's birthdays? Explain your answer.
2. In what way is "the definition of the rest of [Dorris'] life" (paragraph 7) connected with his son's birthdays?
3. What does Dorris mean when he says "Questions are a luxury" for his son (paragraph 19)?

DISCOVERING RHETORICAL STRATEGIES

1. At what points in this essay does Dorris either directly or indirectly analyze the causes of Adam's behavior? When does he study its effects (on either himself or his son)? Divide a piece of paper in half. List the causes on one side and the effects on the other. Record the paragraph references in each case. Then, discuss the pattern that emerges from your two lists. Does Dorris give more attention to the causes or effects of Adam's behavior? Why do you think the author develops his essay around this particular emphasis?
2. Dorris uses several comparisons to help his readers understand what raising a fetal alcohol child is like. Look, for example, at paragraph 19, in which he compares Adam's life to "a moonless night" and to "the act of drowning." Find two other vivid comparisons in this essay. What do all these comparisons add to the essay? What effect do they have on the essay as a whole?
3. What tone does Dorris establish in his essay? Describe it in three or four well-chosen words. How does he create this tone? What effect does this particular tone have on you as a reader?

IDEAS FOR DISCUSSION/WRITING

Preparing to Write

Write freely about the process of growing up and reaching your potential: What special problems did you experience while growing up? How did you deal with these problems? How did your parents deal with these problems? Do you feel you are heading toward your full potential, or have you already reached it? How do you plan to reach or maintain your potential? What experiences or people have disappointed you mainly because they were not what you expected? What were their shortcomings? Can these shortcomings be remedied? What effects do such shortcomings have on society as a whole?

Choosing a Topic

1. In a conversation with your mother, father, or another close relative, explain what problems you found most difficult as you were growing up, and speculate about the causes of those problems. In dialogue form, record the conversation as accurately as possible. Add an introduction, a conclusion, and an explanation of your discussion in order to mold the conversation into an essay.
2. In the last paragraph of his essay, Dorris implies that his son is slowly drowning in his birth-parents' alcohol abuse. This essay is Dorris' process of grieving about "what [his son] was missing, what he had already missed, what he would miss" (paragraph 8). In an essay of your own, explain something (a process, a person, an event, a relationship, or an activity) that disappointed you mainly because your expectations weren't met. What were the principal reasons for your disappointment? What were the effects of your disappointment? What could have changed the situation?
3. Many forms of addiction and abuse plague our society at present. In an essay written for your composition class, choose one of these problems and speculate on its primary causes and effects in society today. As often as possible, give specific examples to support your observations.

—"He did not take death seriously, never had" (para. 18).

—"He may pass by them close enough to touch on either side, but his hands are stretched forward, grasping for balance instead of pleasure. . . . Questions are a luxury" (para. 19).

Dorris gives more emphasis to the effects of fetal alcohol syndrome, but he makes the causes and irresponsibility of this affliction obvious. He presents the conditions of Adam's birth at the beginning and end of his essay and details the effects of Adam's biological parents' poor judgment. Dorris concentrates on the effects to prevent others from conceiving children like Adam and to show what Adam has been denied.

2. Responses to this question will vary.

3. Dorris is somber, pensive, sad, and surprisingly candid in his description. He creates this tone by juxtaposing his hopes and dreams for Adam with the reality of Adam's mental and physical condition.

PREWRITING

In preparation for the writing assignments, the Preparing to Write questions ask students to consider their process of growing up and reaching their potential. See pages 16–23 for suggestions on generating ideas in response to these questions.

ADDITIONAL DISCUSSION/WRITING TOPIC

Are you addicted to anything? What would happen if you tried to eliminate this addiction from your life? Write an essay explaining the principal causes of this addiction and its effects on your life. What will your life be like in twenty years if you are unable to break free from this addictive behavior?

REVISING STRATEGY

A good cause/effect essay explores all real or ultimate causes or effects rather than just immediate causes or effects. In one of your cause/effect essays, determine whether or not your discussion gets to the ultimate causes or effects. Notice where weaknesses or inconsistencies occur. Then revise your paper, carrying each discussion of a cause or an effect to its ultimate conclusion.

PREREADING

The purpose of this Preparing to Read material is to encourage students to think about their culture. To help them focus their attention before they respond to the questions here, have each student bring an item to class that represents his or her culture and put it in the center of a circle made up of students. Next, have your students choose an item and write about it. See pages 3–6 for other ways to generate thoughts on these questions.

BACKGROUND INFORMATION

In this compact and highly allusive essay, Richard Rodriguez discusses the reasons many Hispanic-Americans have seemed to resist assimilation into the American culture. After explaining these causes, he describes the effects we can expect when the two cultures eventually merge. America will be stronger, he reasons, through the infusion of Latin passions and generosity of spirit.

READABILITY LEVEL

11.6

RELATED READINGS

Cultural Diversity

RICHARD RODRIGUEZ (1944–   )

■ ■ ■

The Fear of Losing a Culture

Richard Rodriguez was raised in Sacramento, California, the son of industrious working-class Mexican immigrant parents. He attended parochial schools there and later continued his education at Stanford, Columbia, London's Warburg Institute, and, finally, the University of California at Berkeley, where he earned a Ph.D. in English Renaissance literature. A writer and journalist, he is now associate editor of the Pacific News Service in San Francisco. In 1982 he received wide critical acclaim for the publication of his autobiography, *Hunger of Memory: The Education of Richard Rodriguez,* which detailed his struggle to succeed in a totally alien culture. A regular contributor to the *Los Angeles Times,* he has also published essays in *The New Republic, Time, Harper's, The American Scholar, The Columbia Forum,* and *College English.* His most recent book is *Mexico's Children* (1991), a study of Mexican immigrants in America. Asked to provide advice for students using *The Prose Reader.* Rodriguez explained that "there is no 'secret' to becoming a writer. Writing takes time—and patience, more than anything else. If you are willing to rewrite and rewrite and rewrite, you will become a good writer."

Preparing to Read

The following essay, originally published in *Time* magazine (July 11, 1988), discusses the causes and effects of cultural pride. As you prepare to read this essay, take a few moments to think about culture and assimilation: How would you describe America's culture? Does it have a central core of its own? What are the main features of this American culture? To what extent are Americans threatened by the intrusion of other cultures? What can be gained in assimilation between cultures? What can be lost?

What is culture, after all? The immigrant shrugs. Latin 1 Americans initially come to the U.S. with only the things they need in mind—not abstractions like culture. They need dollars. They need food. Maybe they need to get out of the way of bullets. Most of us who concern ourselves with Hispanic-American culture, as painters, musicians, writers—or as sons and daughters— are the children of immigrants. We have grown up on this side of the border, in the land of Elvis Presley and Thomas Edison. Our lives are prescribed by the mall, by the 7-Eleven, by the Internal Revenue Service. Our imaginations vacillate between an Edenic Latin America, which nevertheless betrayed our parents, and the repellent plate-glass doors of a real American city, which has been good to us.

Hispanic-American culture stands where the past meets the future. The cultural meeting represents not just a Hispanic milestone, not simply a celebration at the crossroads. America transforms into pleasure what it cannot avoid. Hispanic-American culture of the sort that is now in evidence (the teen movie, the rock song) may exist in an hourglass, may in fact be irrelevant. The U.S. Border Patrol works through the night to arrest the flow of illegal immigrants over the border, even as Americans stand patiently in line for *La Bamba*. While Americans vote to declare, once and for all, that English shall be the official language of the U.S., Madonna starts recording in Spanish.

Before a national TV audience, Rita Moreno tells Geraldo Rivera that her dream as an actress is to play a character rather like herself: "I speak English perfectly well. . . . I'm not dying from poverty. . . . I want to play *that* kind of Hispanic woman, which is to say, an American citizen." This is an actress talking; these are show-biz pieties. But Moreno expresses as well a general Hispanic-American predicament. Hispanics want to belong to America without betraying the past. Yet we fear losing ground in any negotiation with America. Our fear, most of all, is of losing our culture.

We come from an expansive, an intimate, culture that has long been judged second-rate by the U.S. Out of pride as much as affection, we are reluctant to give up our past. Our notoriety in the U.S. has been our resistance to assimilation. The guarded symbol of Hispanic-American culture has been the tongue of flame: Spanish. But the remarkable legacy Hispanics carry from Latin America is not language—an inflatable skin—but breath itself, capacity of soul, an inclination to live. The genius of Latin America is the habit of synthesis. We assimilate.

What Latin America knows is that people create one another when they meet. In the music of Latin America you will hear the

DEFINITIONS

Elvis Presley (1935–1977) (para. 1): an extremely popular singer whose musical style had a strong influence on rock and roll.
Thomas Edison (1847–1931) (para. 1): an inventor of electrical and communication devices, such as the phonograph and the light bulb.
La Bamba (1988) (para. 2): a film biography of the Hispanic rock-and-roll star Richie Valens (Ricardo Valenzuela)
Madonna (1958–) (para. 2): an American pop singer.
Rita Moreno (1931–) (para. 3): an American movie actress of Hispanic descent.
Geraldo Rivera (1943–) (para. 3): an American television news reporter and talk show host of Hispanic descent.
minaret (para. 5): a high, slender tower attached to a mosque from which a crier calls Muslims to prayer.
mestizo (para. 6): a person of mixed parentage, usually Hispanic or Portuguese and Native American.
miscegenation (para. 8): marriage or cohabitation between members of different races.

COLLABORATIVE LEARNING: CLASS ACTIVITY

Have a few international students share some of their attempts to assimilate into our culture. Do they feel that blending their culture with ours is beneficial, harmful, necessary, etc.? Allow the class to ask questions. (If you don't have any international students in class or you can't get any to come to class, have your students interview people from different cultures about their views on assimilation and bring their ideas back to the class for discussion.)

Set up a panel discussion in your class with 6 to 8 students arguing for cultural diversity and 6 to 8 students arguing for cultural unity as a way to gain strength and understanding. Let the speakers alternate, each presenting a 2- to 3-minute statement with close attention to the quality of the evidence brought to bear on his or her side of the issue. The audience can ask questions after all the speakers have made their statements. An important feature of this exercise is to make sure equal time is given to the speakers on both sides of the issue.

ANSWERS TO QUESTIONS:
UNDERSTANDING DETAILS (p. 409)

1. Rodriguez sees the meeting of Hispanic and American cultures as a combining of tradition and old-world values with the modern American way. Rodriguez views this merger as a mutual assimilation in which both sides are afraid of losing their culture and are faced with difficult choices about whether or not to go through the assimilation process.

2. Asian and Latin-American cultures are "communal" in their approach to the family and to the past. Each community views the family in terms of generations, and traditions have been passed down through time. Americans, conversely, tend to think of the family as mother, father, and children. Traditions, in Rodriguez's view, have been replaced in the American system by the newest fad. He believes change is at the basis of the American system.

3. Rodriguez believes that some Americans have been hostile toward Hispanics because of the Hispanic resistance to assimilation and their attempt to protect their culture from change.

ANSWERS TO QUESTIONS:
ANALYZING MEANING (p. 409)

1. Responses to this question will vary.
2. Latin America and North America have different religious structures (predominantly Catholic and predominantly Prot-

litany of bloodlines: the African drum, the German accordion, the cry from the minaret. The U.S. stands as the opposing New World experiment. In North America the Indian and the European stood separate. Whereas Latin America was formed by a Catholic dream of one world, of meltdown conversion, the U.S. was shaped by Protestant individualism. America has believed its national strength derives from separateness, from diversity. The glamour of the U.S. is the Easter promise: You can be born again in your lifetime. You can separate yourself from your past. You can get a divorce, lose weight, touch up your roots.

Immigrants still come for that promise, but the U.S. has wavered in its faith. America is no longer sure that economic strength derives from individualism. And America is no longer sure that there is space enough, sky enough, to sustain the cabin on the prairie. Now, as we near the end of the American Century, two alternative cultures beckon the American imagination: the Asian and the Latin American. Both are highly communal cultures, in contrast to the literalness of American culture. Americans devour what they might otherwise fear to become. Sushi will make them lean, subtle corporate warriors. Combination Plate No. 3, smothered in mestizo gravy, will burn a hole in their hearts. 6

Latin America offers passion. Latin America has a life—big clouds, unambiguous themes, tragedy, epic—that the U.S., for all its quality of life, yearns to have. Latin America offers an undistressed leisure, a crowded kitchen table, even a full sorrow. Such is the urgency of America's need that it reaches right past a fledgling, homegrown Hispanic-American culture for the darker bottle of Mexican beer, for the denser novel of a Latin American master. 7

For a long time, Hispanics in the U.S. felt hostility. Perhaps because we were preoccupied by nostalgia, we withheld our Latin American gift. We denied the value of assimilation. But as our presence is judged less foreign in America, we will produce a more generous art, less timid, less parochial. Hispanic Americans do not have a pure Latin American art to offer. Expect bastard themes. Expect winking ironies, comic conclusions. For Hispanics live on this side of the border, where Kraft manufactures Mexican-style Velveeta, and where Jack in the Box serves Fajita Pita. Expect marriage. We will change America even as we will be changed. We will disappear with you into a new miscegenation. 8

Along and across the border there remain real conflicts, real fears. But the ancient tear separating Europe from itself—the Catholic Mediterranean from the Protestant north—may yet heal 9 itself in the New World. For generations, Latin America has been the place, the bed, of a confluence of so many races and cultures that Protestant North America shuddered to imagine it.

The time has come to imagine it.

UNDERSTANDING DETAILS

1. What does Rodriguez mean when he says "Hispanic-American culture stands where the past meets the future" (paragraph 2)?
2. In what ways are Asian-American and Latin-American cultures "communal" whereas America's is "literal" (paragraph 6)?
3. What does Rodriguez claim is the source of the hostility Hispanics have traditionally felt from other Americans?

ANALYZING MEANING

1. To what extent do you think Hispanics can belong to America "without betraying the past" (paragraph 3)? How might they accomplish this?
2. What is the main difference in philosophy between North America and Latin America? Why is assimilation so difficult under these circumstances?
3. What do North America and Latin America have to offer each other? What can they learn from each other? What does Rodriguez mean in the last sentence of this essay?

DISCOVERING RHETORICAL STRATEGIES

1. According to Rodriguez, the fact that Hispanics often don't easily assimilate into American culture causes some consequences and is the result of others. List the causes of this action in one column and the effects in another. In what way does the question of assimilation become a focal point for the essay?
2. Why does Rodriguez introduce the Asian culture into this essay? How does this reference help further his argument?
3. Rodriguez ends his essay with a one-sentence paragraph. What effect does this ending have on you? Explain your answer.

estant, respectively) and have a basic fear of losing part or all of their cultural underpinnings. Assimilation is difficult because these close neighbors speak different languages and have different basic family structures. When these groups are in their 10 own country, they can admire and respect each other, but when people from either group cross the border, both sides feel strained because of their fear of losing the right to speak their language, practice the religion of their choice, and continue their cultural development uninterrupted.

3. Latin and North Americans can offer each other the richness of both of their cultures. Rodriguez emphasizes traditional Latin-American values but fails to mention their counterparts in North America. Each of these cultures is valuable and can enrich the other. What Latin- and North-American cultures can learn most from each other is the way to accept people who are different. As Rodriguez implies, change will come; North Americans and Latin Americans will learn to live together and adopt parts of each other's heritage until eventually, much as the groups of early Americans changed the shape of America, a relationship without the loss of culture will exist.

ANSWERS TO QUESTIONS: DISCOVERING RHETORICAL STRATEGIES (p. 409)

1. | *Para.* | *Causes* |
   |---|---|
   | 3 | Hispanics don't want to betray the past. |
   | 3 | Hispanics are afraid of losing their culture. |
   | 5 | "The U.S. stands as the opposing New World experiment." |
   | 5 | "The U.S. was shaped by Protestant individualism." |
   | 5 | America believes "its national strength derives from separateness, from diversity." |

Para.	*Effects*
8	Hispanics felt hostility.
8	Hispanics "denied the value of assimilation."

The question of assimilation becomes a focal point for the essay because it is the source of the Hispanics' fear of losing their culture. This issue has also become a source of hostility for many Americans. In essence, it is a pivotal point between American and Hispanic cultures.

2. Rodriguez refers to Asian culture in passing to show that America has different values than other cultures and tends to make use of what it needs while ignoring other important characteristics of immigrants. This reference helps to justify his position that Latin Americans have the right to fear that their cultural attributes will be altered, if not destroyed, by Americans.

3. Responses to this question will vary.

PREWRITING

In preparation for the writing assignments, the Preparing to Write questions ask students to consider the process of assimilation among cultures before writing an essay on a related topic. You might first discuss the meaning of "assimilation," defined in *Webster's Collegiate Dictionary* as "the act of absorbing into a cultural tradition; or becoming similar": When is assimilation desirable in our society? When is it undesirable? See pages 16–23 for other suggestions on generating ideas in response to these questions.

ADDITIONAL DISCUSSION/WRITING TOPIC

Cultural heritage is important to some people and not as important to others. Talk to a few people about the role their cultural heritage plays in their lives. Then, in a coherent essay, discuss the causes or effects of your findings.

REVISING STRATEGY

A good cause/effect essay will fulfill the guidelines mentioned on page 391. Look at this checklist, and underline the parts of one of your essays that fulfill these criteria. Notice where your essay needs work. Then revise your paper according to these guidelines.

IDEAS FOR DISCUSSION/WRITING

Preparing to Write

Write freely about culture and assimilation: What makes up a culture? In what ways do merging cultures threaten one another? What does assimilation consist of? Why is assimilation between cultures such an emotional issue? What are the ground rules in the process of assimilation? What major cultural changes is our country experiencing at present? In what way are these changes affecting you personally?

Choosing a Topic

1. We all confront assimilation on a daily basis in different situations. We might choose to assimilate into a club we want to join but refuse to make the necessary changes to fit into a fast-moving party scene. For an article in your campus newspaper demonstrating the constant role of assimilation in our lives, explain the causes and/or effects of one time you chose or refused to assimilate. What were the circumstances leading up to your decision? What were the consequences of your decision?

2. America is currently undergoing some dramatic cultural changes. We are rapidly becoming a multiracial, multicultural society. In an essay written for your local newspaper, analyze the causes and effects of some of these changes, and explain how they are affecting you personally.

3. As a foreign-exchange student, you have just arrived in another country to attend college for one year. Naturally, you realize that you must adapt to many new customs and attitudes; however, you will still cling to many of your country's ways. In an essay, explain which of your national traditions you would find most difficult to give up and why. Do you think assimilating into a new culture and still holding on to your beliefs and customs is possible? Explain your reasoning.

MITCHELL LAZARUS
(1942–   )

■ ■ ■

Rx for Mathophobia

QUOTATION ON WRITING

"A writer's style, we believe, is the characteristic route he takes through all the choices presented in both the prewriting and writing stages. It is the manifestation of his conception of his topic, modified by his audience, situation, and intention—what we might call his 'universe of discourse'."

Richard E. Young
and Alton L. Becker

Lawyer and author Mitchell Lazarus is the product of a varied educational background. Canadian by birth, he has a bachelor's degree in electrical engineering from McGill University, an M.S. in the same field from Massachusetts Institute of Technology, a Ph.D. in psychology from M.I.T., and a law degree from Georgetown University. "Some people think it's odd having so many degrees," he says, "but I thoroughly enjoyed getting them. Besides, knowledge is never wasted. Back in engineering school, I never dreamed of becoming a lawyer, but now I use the engineering skills every day in my legal practice. And the scientific outlook I picked up doing doctoral research in psychology (on visual perception) gave me a deeper view of the world and enriched my life immeasurably. Sure, it's important to specialize—but it doesn't have to be forever. You can specialize for the time being." This unique educational philosophy has led Lazarus to a number of interesting jobs. He has worked in computer design; taught electrical engineering, mathematics, and psychology at M.I.T.; and worked at the Education Development Center in Newton, Massachusetts, where he helped produce "Infinity Factory," a PBS television series on mathematics. He currently practices law in Washington, D.C., specializing in computers and communication. During the last twenty years, Lazarus has published over sixty articles and reviews, mostly on education or law, and five books, including *Educating the Handicapped* (1980) and *Goodbye to Excellence: A Critical Look at Minimum Competency Testing* (1981). He lives in Takoma Park, Maryland, where he relaxes with the *London Sunday Times* crossword puzzles and struggles to master ever-more-complicated yo-yo tricks.

Preparing to Read

The following article on "mathophobia," originally published in the *Saturday Review* (June 28, 1975), explains why the fear of mathematics haunts so many Americans. Before you read this essay, think for a moment about some of the fears that affect your life: What are you most afraid of? How and when did this fear start? What effect does it have on your daily life? What other fears do you have? How do

PREREADING

The purpose of this Preparing to Read material is to encourage students to examine their individual fears in life. To help your students focus their attention on their fears before responding to the questions here, have them talk as openly as possible about some of their most serious worries. See pages 3–6 for other ways to generate thoughts on these questions.

411

you cope with these fears? Do you have any anxieties related to suc-ceeding in school? What are you doing to overcome them?

_____

BACKGROUND INFORMATION

In "Rx for Mathophobia," Mitchell Lazarus takes a close look at a common disorder, the fear of mathematics. He not only examines the causes and effects of this problem in people from all professions, but he also pre-scribes a treatment designed to "put ele-mentary mathematics into a form that will make sense to children" (para. 27).

READABILITY LEVEL

14.9

DEFINITIONS

Rx (title): an abbreviation for "prescription".
etiology (para. 4): all the causes of a disease or abnormal condition.
ken (para. 13): knowledge or realm of understanding.

Most people dislike—or fear—mathematics. Somehow, a   1
vast majority of the population has come to believe that mathe-matics must be difficult, unpleasant, and mysterious. Even peo-ple who are good at mathematics and use it every day are comfortable only to a point. I hold a graduate degree in engineer-ing, and my own mathematics is pretty good, but I still feel un-easy listening to arguments based on mathematics more advanced than I can understand. Yet, I can converse among histo-rians, musicians, philosophers, and others, understanding just as little but feeling much less uncomfortable about it.

Now, my work involves designing new approaches to the   2
teaching of elementary mathematics. And whenever I talk about this work, about sensible ways of handling mathematics educa-tion that will appeal to children, the reaction is nearly always the same: "I wish there had been something like that when I was a kid. I always hated math in school!"

Jerrold Zacharias, noted physicist and educator, calls the   3
problem *mathophobia:* a fear of mathematics. Most people will in-deed try to avoid mathematical problems, sometimes with the ve-hemence of an acrophobe avoiding a high place. Both the acrophobe and the mathophobe deny themselves fascinating views and vistas, unnecessarily narrowing their horizons.

Curiously, there has been virtually no formal research con-   4
cerning this very widespread—nearly universal—problem. In the absence of organized data, my colleagues and I have had to fall back on anecdotal evidence. Over the past few years we have dis-cussed mathematics experiences with people in all walks of life. These were not formal interviews; we have no coded data. In-stead, they were casual conversations with friends, acquain-tances, and people met in passing. With their help we have tried to construct an etiology of mathophobia and to indicate strategies for its prevention.

For example, many adults say that they liked mathematics   5
"until we did so-and-so in school"—until they were exposed to some topic that seemed particularly difficult. But did the enjoy-ment of mathematics ever return after the hard topic was past? Almost never. The dislike is usually irreversible.

If one looks at the curricula in use at most schools, this aversion is not surprising. The mathematics taught in each grade depends strongly on most of the work done in preceding years: Trouble in any year, for any reason, is nearly certain to spell trouble in all the years to come.

A second factor in the curriculum is the frequent lack of any meaningful connection between school mathematics and the rest of the student's life. Thus the mathematics people *do* learn in school is quickly forgotten; most of us have little use for it after graduation.

Perhaps another element is mathophobia's social acceptability. Even those who are otherwise proud of their education tend to speak up freely about their mathematical ignorance. They can say, "I'm terrible at math," almost with a hint of pride, as if being poor at mathematics somehow is a mark of good taste in failure.

This attitude affects our treatment of children in school. Parents often seem unconcerned about a child's failure in mathematics, as if to say, "Well, I was never good at math in school; so I shouldn't be too upset if Johnny isn't, either." Unfortunately, Johnny is likely to sense this attitude and react accordingly.

Moreover, many teachers are themselves affected by mathophobia, sometimes admitting that they feel uncomfortable when they teach mathematics. If the teacher is tense and ill at ease with mathematics, such feelings infect the class with the idea that mathematics is hard or unpleasant.

When people withdraw from mathematics, exactly what are they avoiding?

From conversations with many mathophobes, two distinct impressions emerge of what mathematics is like. One view equates mathematics with the tedious, boring, exacting routines of school arithmetic. Yet, if total exposure to music over several years were limited to just scales and mechanical exercises, music would be unpleasant, too.

The other popular view of mathematics sees it as the arcane province of a select few geniuses. Someone who feels that mathematics must forever be beyond his or her ken will quite naturally shy away from it and need not hesitate to admit—or even boast of—a distaste for the subject.

In reality arithmetic is always a means to an end, never an end in itself—except in school. Indeed, very few activities call for actual skill in arithmetic nowadays. With computers, elaborate cash registers, and now the small electronic calculators, the mechanics of arithmetic take second place, in practice, to choosing

Through class discussion, try to discover why "most people dislike—or fear—mathematics" (para. 1). Do your students have similar fears connected with writing?

Have your class break into pairs and share stories about their math and/or writing anxieties. Then, have each student respond to his or her partner's anxieties by suggesting some well-thought-out remedies.

the necessary calculations and the right numbers to work with. Thus, we ask children to spend several years learning difficult, tedious skills that are rapidly coming to be of limited value. In doing so, we inadvertently teach that mathematics is not only hard but also not very useful. Rote arithmetic is a difficult and tedious branch of mathematics—a poor starting point for most students.

The "new math" tried to help by showing why arithmetic results come out the way they do, starting from "basic principles" that typically included set theory and number base. But for a great many students (and their parents), these special topics were at least as confusing as the arithmetic had been. 15

Parts of the "new math" tried to deemphasize pure arithmetic or at least to set arithmetic in a wider mathematical context. But the "new math" context is that of the professional mathematician: abstract, definitional, axiomatic, and supposedly rigorous. The result is to pull mathematics even farther from its actual uses. 16

Mathematics does not belong to the professional mathematician alone. It cuts across many other fields of endeavor and touches upon many people's lives. This perspective—mathematics that is useful to people—should be the starting point for a new approach to mathematics education. This alternative builds upon usefulness as a basic ingredient of elementary mathematics. Choice of topics and ways of teaching should center on mathematics as a helpful force in day-to-day life and should take into account the fact that the technology has made longhand arithmetic all but obsolete. Such a program has a twofold aim: to provide the mathematical tools and skills children will find useful and enlightening now and in later life and to make them comfortable with, and appreciative of, mathematical subject matter. The two aims are very closely related. 17

The new approach will find its place in the vast middle ground between rote arithmetic and the work of the professional mathematician. It includes, for example, the mathematics of cooking, carpentry, engineering, wallpaper hanging, dressmaking, magazine editing, bartending, storekeeping, and a vast array of other occupations and pastimes. It is the kind of mathematics that grows from real problems and returns in real solutions. It adapts recipes to serve more than the prescribed number of guests, fits bookshelves neatly into alcoves, purchases the right amount of shelf paper, carries the driver from one gasoline pump to the next, and in general helps people through a multitude of ordinary tasks. It also develops the kind of understanding that 18 children will find most useful in their ongoing activities—the kind that will apply to many of their current interests.

The topics stressed should be those with the most direct link between mathematics and the real world—the topics most helpful to people who use mathematics for practical reasons. These include, for example, measurement and estimation, making rough maps and sketching simple graphs, and the performance of quick, approximate arithmetic in our heads—skills that will not get rusty because they will be used constantly by people of all ages.   19

One important development not covered by conventional curricula would be an appreciation of inexact answers. "Mathematics is an exact science," many teachers say, "and there is only one right answer." Often that statement is worse than wrong. It is constraining and intimidating. Estimations, approximation, rough calculation—all part of mathematics—are often very useful, need not be exact, and can have many "right answers," if a right answer is one to meet our needs. Most of us tried to learn in school how to find that 49×319 works out to be 15,631. Few of us learned to see the problem quickly and roughly as 50×300, which mentally becomes 15,000—close enough for most practical purposes.   20

A widescale approach to mathematics that stems from realistic situations which children find interesting and which gives them new power to cope with situations outside of school would go a long way toward preventing mathophobia. Mathematics can be a part of everyday life; it need not be special and apart. Most people can read street maps, for example, which involves a lot of mathematics that ordinarily we do not recognize. We understand how an "average family" can have 1.9 children, even though we may joke about it. The concept of odds in betting is clear to most of us, although it is based on quite sophisticated concepts. People who cook know that it is safe to triple recipes for soup, but not for cake.   21

As an educational issue, reading street maps, for example, is unimportant in itself. But maps involve a number of mathematical ideas that *are* important and general: ratio, proportion, scaling, measuring and estimating length and distance, estimating time, and some geometry. In most curricula nowadays these ideas appear in the abstract if they appear at all. A proportion problem, for example, might appear as: $20/5 = ?/2$. The new approach would stay with the street map—or even better, a student-made map of the classroom—and ask: According to the map, how far is   22

1. Lazarus suggests that most people fear mathematics because they perceive the discipline as tedious, boring, and so difficult that it "must forever be beyond" their abilities (para. 13). The author lists three immediate causes of this fear: a classroom aversion to a particularly difficult aspect of the subject, resulting in a weak foundation upon which to build the next level of study; the lack of an obvious relationship between school mathematics and life itself; and the "social acceptability" (para. 8) of mathophobia. The ultimate cause is the apparent lack of relevance between mathematics and the rest of our lives.

2. The "new math" was developed to make math seem more usable and adaptable; what it did instead was to create a more "abstract, definitional, axiomatic, and supposedly rigorous" (para. 16) math that led students away from practical uses while making the subject seem even more esoteric than before.

3. Lazarus begins dealing with solutions in paragraph 17, after discussing the problems faced by those who fear math and "new math." To overcome mathophobia, the author proposes that educators adapt their curriculum to focus on the utility of mathematics, "to provide the mathematical tools and skills children will find useful and enlightening now and in later life and to make them comfortable with, and appreciative of, mathematical subject matter" (para. 17).

ANSWERS TO QUESTIONS:
ANALYZING MEANING (p. 417)

1. The title "Rx for Mathophobia" introduces the essay's central metaphor: the fear of mathematics as a disorder, or phobia, that can be cured. In this context, "Rx" represents the medical abbreviation for the prescribed treatment of this specific disease.

2. Lazarus believes that students are frequently forced to repeat countless tiresome arithmetic exercises with no hint of any potential usefulness in this chore.

it from the door to the chalkboard? The mathematical issue of proportion is the same, but the map puts the idea in a much more concrete and realistic context. Thus the student can better understand the idea of proportion and how it applies in real situations. Moreover, the "hands-on" experience of making the measurements, sketching the map, and checking the results is a valuable aid in acquiring the concept and contributes to a good "feel" for what proportion is about.

Symbols and abstraction for their own sakes, now very common in mathematics curricula, often strike students as pointless and confusing. As far as possible, all of the concepts presented to students should appear in realistic, familiar contexts. Symbols and abstraction are still important—indeed, are the essence of mathematics—but should serve ends that students can understand. Presentations ought to begin and end with reality in order that students can make sense of the mathematics in between. 23

Applications have always been a part of mathematics education, but until now they have played a very minor role. The applications in most textbooks were contrived—transparent excuses for more calculation. Use of applications of primary function, so that calculation serves as the means (rather than the other way around), will impart to school mathematics the pertinence, meaning, and impact that it presently lacks. Children will understand why mathematics is important and worth knowing. 24

Some students do very well in the "new math," and some even seem to enjoy rote calculation. Students with a knack and a flair for mathematics will find as much in this approach that captures their interest as there was in earlier curricula, for here there is a great deal of room for exploring theoretical relationships and plenty of opportunity for calculation. The topics are rich and the pedagogy open-ended. Just as important, however, is the fact that many students who have *not* liked mathematics until now—and these are a majority—will begin to see a place for mathematics in their own lives and will start feeling comfortable with mathematical ideas. 25

Eventually, a curriculum reform on the scale of the "new math" will probably be necessary. The "new math" is not working out well, and there is a strong national trend away from it. Most educators seem disinclined to go back to the "old math," seeing that the arguments against it are still valid. In contrast, the approach outlined here will appeal directly to students' interests and needs and will provide a strong foundation for more advanced work. 26

The key to preventing mathophobia is letting mathematics 27

take root in the student's daily life. Reality-based teaching will go a long way toward solving the national mathematics problem because it will put elementary mathematics into a form that will make sense to children.

UNDERSTANDING DETAILS

1. According to Lazarus, why are most people afraid of math? What are the immediate causes of this fear? The ultimate causes?
2. Explain the "new math," giving examples with your explanation.
3. At what point in the essay does the author begin discussing solutions to mathophobia? What solutions does the author propose?

ANALYZING MEANING

1. Explain the title of this essay. How effective is it in your opinion? Can you suggest an alternate title?
2. What does Lazarus mean when he comments on "the frequent lack of any meaningful connection between school mathematics and the rest of the student's life" (paragraph 7)? Do you think math in grade school and high school should be more relevant to everyday life? What other subjects should be made more relevant? At what academic levels?
3. According to Lazarus, why would the appreciation of "inexact answers" (paragraph 20) be an important development in mathematics? Do you agree with the author's reasoning on this issue? Why or why not?

DISCOVERING RHETORICAL STRATEGIES

1. At what points in the article does the author explore causes? When does he consider effects? Is this balance between causes and effects appropriate to the essay's purpose? Why or why not?
2. How has Lazarus organized the characteristics of mathophobia? Why does he discuss the characteristics in this manner?
3. Who do you think is Lazarus' intended audience? Describe them in detail. How did you come to this conclusion?

3. Lazarus claims that mathematics as "an exact science" is "constraining and intimidating. Estimation, approximation, rough calculation—all part of mathematics—are often very useful, need not be exact, and can have many 'right answers,' if a right answer is one to meet our needs" (para. 20).

ANSWERS TO QUESTIONS: DISCOVERING RHETORICAL STRATEGIES (p. 417)

1. The author's attention to causes begins in paragraph 5, with the public's aversion to a particularly difficult aspect of mathematics, and continues through paragraph 9, which discusses the public's negative attitude toward math. He considers the effects of mathophobia in paragraphs 11 to 13, describing the boredom instilled in many students by the mechanical exercises and the fear that math is "the arcane province of a select few geniuses" (para. 13). The somewhat symmetrical treatment of causes and effects suggests that no particular cause or effect has more significance than any other.

2. Lazarus organizes his discussion of mathophobia by devoting the first half of the essay to an introduction of the problem, its causes and effects, and the unsuccessful attempt to relieve the tedium of arithmetic with the introduction of "new math." The second half of the essay concentrates on a new approach to mathematics, a "reality-based" method that will "go a long way toward solving the national mathematics problem because it will put elementary mathematics into a form that will make sense to children" (para. 27). By ending his essay with a cure for this disorder, the author places more emphasis on the solution to the problem than on the problem itself.

3. Based on the wide variety of examples he provides and the level of verbal complexity, Lazarus appears to be writing for a diverse and well-educated audience.

In preparation for the writing assignments, the Preparing to Write questions ask students to study their own fears before writing an essay on a related topic. See pages 16–23 for suggestions on generating ideas in response to these questions.

ADDITIONAL DISCUSSION/WRITING TOPIC

You are sitting in your math class about to begin a final exam. As the test is distributed, you feel your heart rate increase and your anxiety level rise. Write a dialogue between your mind and your body. Try to talk your body out of being nervous. How does your body respond?

REVISING STRATEGY

The order of your details and examples in a cause/effect essay should be based as much as possible on logical reasoning. Outline one of your cause/effect essays to ensure that each point you make follows logically from the previous statement. Notice gaps and weaknesses in your logic as you review your outline. Then revise your paper to reflect clear logic and straightforward reasoning.

IDEAS FOR DISCUSSION/WRITING

Preparing to Write

Write freely about any fears that you have: Does any particular type of schoolwork frighten you? Any people? Any activities? Any specific situations? Why do you think these various fears haunt you? How do you cope with these problems? Are you content with your solutions?

Choosing a Topic

1. A college counselor has asked all students at your college to explain what frightens them most. What is your response to this question? Write an essay for the counselor explaining in detail your greatest fear. Cover both the causes and the effects of your fear. (This fear does not have to be related to school matters.)
2. Your college mathematics instructor wants to know if you are afraid of math. In a detailed essay written for this instructor, explain why you are or are not frightened by this subject. What events/attitudes/ teachers have played a part in developing your feelings toward mathematics? Has your attitude toward math become more positive or negative over the past five years?
3. Is mathophobia the only academic anxiety that strikes today's students? What about "writer's phobia"? How do you feel about writing essays and papers? What events/attitudes/teachers have shaped this feeling? What effects does this attitude have on your performance as a writer? Address those questions in an essay designed for your composition instructor. (Now don't panic. Take a deep breath. . . .)

ALICE WALKER
(1944–   )

■ ■ ■

My Daughter Smokes

Born in Eatonton, Georgia, and educated at Spelman College and Sarah Lawrence University, Alice Walker is best known for her Pulitzer-Prize-winning novel *The Color Purple* (1983), which was later made into an immensely popular movie of the same title. The book details a young African-American woman's search for self-identity within a world contaminated by racial prejudice and family crisis. Although many critics have argued that the work "transcends culture and gender," Walker's focus on the racial and ethnic climate of the deep South is crucial to the novel's success and importance. The author has explained that "the Black woman is one of America's greatest heroes," though she has been denied credit for her accomplishments and "oppressed beyond recognition." Most of Walker's other novels and collections of short stories echo the same theme, and most share the "sense of affirmation" featured in *The Color Purple* that overcomes the anger and social indignity suffered by so many of her characters. The author's many other publications include *In Love and Trouble: Stories of Black Women* (1973), *Meridian* (1976), *You Can't Keep a Good Woman Down* (1981), *In Search of Our Mothers' Gardens* (1983), *Living By the Word* (1988), *To Hell With Dying* (1988), and *The Temple of My Familiar* (1989). Walker has been a professor and writer-in-residence at Wellesley College, the University of Massachusetts, the University of California at Berkeley, and Brandeis University. She is also a member of the Board of Trustees of Sarah Lawrence University. Walker currently lives in San Francisco.

Preparing to Read

In the following essay from *Living By the Word*, the author laments her daughter's addiction to tobacco, which is a painful reminder of her own father's slow and agonizing death from cigarettes. As you begin to read this essay, take a few minutes to consider the role of addiction in our lives: Are you addicted to anything? Are any of your friends or relatives? What are your concerns about these addictions? Do you believe these addictions should be controlled? How do you think they could be controlled? How do addictions take control of people? How many people that you know are suffering from

DEFINITIONS

Queen Victoria (1819–1901) (para. 2): the queen of England from 1837 until her death in 1901; granddaughter of King George III.
Prince Albert (para. 2): the husband of Queen Victoria.
frock coat (para. 2): a double-breasted dress coat with a full skirt reaching the knees, popularized by Prince Albert.
bronchitis (para. 13): an inflammation of the airways that connect the windpipe to the lungs, resulting in a persistent cough.
emphysema (para. 13): a disease in which the tiny air sacs in the lungs become damaged, resulting in shortness of breath and in some cases respiratory or heart failure.
mono-cropping (para. 17): growing only one crop on a piece of land without ever using the land for other purposes.

COLLABORATIVE LEARNING: CLASS ACTIVITY

Have your students discuss the relationship between addiction and abuse. What do these two behaviors have in common? How are they different? How does society suffer from these behaviors?

some kind of addiction? What do these various addictions say about our society?

▬▬▬▬▬▬▬▬▬▬▬▬▬▬▬▬▬▬▬▬▬▬▬▬▬▬▬▬▬▬

My daughter smokes. While she is doing her homework, her feet on the bench in front of her and her calculator clicking out answers to her algebra problems, I am looking at the half-empty package of Camels tossed carelessly close at hand. Camels. I pick them up, take them into the kitchen, where the light is better, and study them—they're filtered, for which I am grateful. My heart feels terrible. I want to weep. In fact, I do weep a little, standing there by the stove holding one of the instruments, so white, so precisely rolled, that could cause my daughter's death. When she smoked Marlboros and Players I hardened myself against feeling so bad; nobody I knew ever smoked these brands. 1

She doesn't know this, but it was Camels that my father, her grandfather, smoked. But before he smoked "ready-mades"—when he was very young and very poor, with eyes like lanterns—he smoked Prince Albert tobacco in cigarettes he rolled himself. I remember the bright-red tobacco tin, with a picture of Queen Victoria's consort, Prince Albert, dressed in a black frock coat and carrying a cane. 2

The tobacco was dark brown, pungent, slightly bitter. I tasted it more than once as a child, and the discarded tins could be used for a number of things: to keep buttons and shoelaces in, to store seeds, and best of all, to hold worms for the rare times my father took us fishing. 3

By the late forties and early fifties no one rolled his own anymore (and few women smoked) in my hometown, Eatonton, Georgia. The tobacco industry, coupled with Hollywood movies in which both hero and heroine smoked like chimneys, won over completely people like my father, who were hopelessly addicted to cigarettes. He never looked as dapper as Prince Albert, though; he continued to look like a poor, overweight, overworked colored man with too large a family; black, with a very white cigarette stuck in his mouth. 4

I do not remember when he started to cough. Perhaps it was unnoticeable at first. A little hacking in the morning as he lit his first cigarette upon getting out of bed. By the time I was my daughter's age, his breath was a wheeze, embarrassing to hear; he could not climb stairs without resting every third or fourth 5 step. It was not unusual for him to cough for an hour.

It is hard to believe there was a time when people did not understand that cigarette smoking is an addiction. I wondered aloud once to my sister—who is perennially trying to quit—whether our father realized this. I wondered how she, a smoker since high school, viewed her own habit.

It was our father who gave her her first cigarette, one day when she had taken water to him in the fields.

"I always wondered why he did that," she said, puzzled, and with some bitterness.

"What did he say?" I asked.

"That he didn't want me to go to anyone else for them," she said, "which never really crossed my mind."

So he was aware it was addictive, I thought, though as annoyed as she that he assumed she would be interested.

I began smoking in eleventh grade, also the year I drank numerous bottles of terrible sweet, very cheap wine. My friends and I, all boys for this venture, bought our supplies from a man who ran a segregated bar and liquor store on the outskirts of town. Over the entrance there was a large sign that said COLORED. We were not permitted to drink there, only to buy. I smoked Kools, because my sister did. By then I thought her toxic darkened lips and gums glamorous. However, my body simply would not tolerate smoke. After six months I had a chronic sore throat. I gave up smoking, gladly. Because it was a ritual with my buddies—Murl, Leon, and "Dog" Farley—I continued to drink wine.

My father died from "the poor man's friend," pneumonia, one hard winter when his bronchitis and emphysema had left him low. I doubt he had much lung left at all, after coughing for so many years. He had so little breath that, during his last years, he was always leaning on something. I remember once, at a family reunion, when my daughter was two, that my father picked her up for a minute—long enough for me to photograph them—but the effort was obvious. Near the very end of his life, and largely because he had no more lungs, he quit smoking. He gained a couple of pounds, but by then he was so emaciated no one noticed.

When I travel to Third World countries I see many people like my father and daughter. There are large billboards directed at them both: the tough, "take-charge," or dapper older man, the glamorous, "worldly" young woman, both puffing away. In these poor countries, as in American ghettos and on reservations, money that should be spent for food goes instead to the tobacco companies; over time, people starve themselves of both food and

COLLABORATIVE LEARNING: SMALL GROUP ACTIVITY

Divide your students into groups of 3 or 4, and have them research one form of addiction by talking to people and reading relevant articles in *Time* and *Newsweek*. Let the groups discuss their findings and choose one interesting item from each person to report to the rest of the class. Then, have one student present these items to the class.

ANSWERS TO QUESTIONS: UNDERSTANDING DETAILS (p. 423)

1. Walker is expressing her contempt both for the effect smoking has on her daughter and the effect it has had on her family and her life. Obviously, she is also encouraging people to stop smoking.

2. Ironically, Walker's sister was given her first cigarette by the man who helped bring her into this world. She is bitter because her father should have tried to keep her away from cigarettes, rather than having encouraged her to smoke them.

3. Walker smoked for about six months when she was in the eleventh grade. She quit after developing a persistent sore throat.

ANSWERS TO QUESTIONS: ANALYZING MEANING (p. 423)

1. The tobacco companies, through advertising, work hard to create cigarette addiction in poor American neighborhoods and Third World countries. They represent smoking as an activity that "'take-charge,'" "glamorous" people engage in (para. 14). However, as Walker points out, people who smoke "starve themselves of both food and air" (para. 14) to continue their habit.

2. According to Walker, the tobacco companies (represented in her essay by "rich white men" [para. 20]) have enslaved tobacco to make others slaves (addicts). She uses the plant metaphorically to show how African Americans, many of whose ancestors were once slaves on tobacco plantations, are still being enslaved by tobacco companies that advertise in their neighborhoods to develop a new form of slavery: addiction.

3. Because known health risks are associated with smoking, people who smoke are abusing their bodies and ignoring their health needs to further their addiction.

ANSWERS TO QUESTIONS:
DISCOVERING RHETORICAL
STRATEGIES (p. 423)

1. Walker's daughter provides the most personal and persuasive reason Walker is against smoking. The anecdote about her daughter contrasts Walker's concern for her daughter's health with her daughter's carefree attitude toward smoking. It sets a serious tone for the essay because Walker has lost her father to smoking and doesn't want to lose her daughter, her sister, or her community. Her daughter represents a microcosm of smoking behavior, but Walker is also concerned with the effects smoking might have on the world at large.

2. The first part of Walker's essay describes her family members who smoke. The major focus of this first part is ignorance. Walker's father, her sister, her daughter, and even Walker herself began smoking without considering the health problems that might result from this addictive behavior.

The second part of this essay presents advertising's role in addiction and shows how addiction affects not only the immediate family, but entire communities and countries. At the end of this section, Walker poses a question about why people worry about family members who are willing to throw away their own good health for the sake of an addiction.

The third section of the essay makes an analogy between addiction and slavery, thereby suggesting that people who smoke are slaves to tobacco.

The fourth and last division depicts smoking as a type of murder. When Walker advocates peace, she is also saying that smoking is a violent form of self-battery and family abuse. She cites the tobacco companies' control over money and people as the major reason people still smoke.

Walker's essay progresses from showing the effects of smoking, to describing the causes of a smoking addiction, and finally to examining reasons other than better health for quitting a smoking habit.

air, effectively weakening and addicting their children, eventually eradicating themselves. I read in the newspaper and in my gardening magazine that cigarette butts are so toxic that if a baby swallows one, it is likely to die, and that the boiled water from a bunch of them makes an effective insecticide.

My daughter would like to quit, she says. We both know the statistics are against her; most people who try to quit smoking do not succeed.* 15

There is a deep hurt that I feel as a mother. Some days it is a feeling of futility. I remember how carefully I ate when I was pregnant, how patiently I taught my daughter how to cross a street safely. For what, I sometimes wonder; so that she can wheeze through most of her life feeling half her strength, and then die of self-poisoning, as her grandfather did? 16

But, finally, one must feel empathy for the tobacco plant itself. For thousands of years, it has been venerated by Native Americans as a sacred medicine. They have used it extensively— its juice, its leaves, its roots, its (holy) smoke—to heal wounds and cure diseases and in ceremonies of prayer and peace. And though the plant as most of us know it has been poisoned by chemicals and denatured by intensive mono-cropping and is therefore hardly the plant it was, still, to some modern Indians it remains a plant of positive power. I learned this when my Native American friends, Bill Wahpepah and his family, visited with me for a few days and the first thing he did was sow a few tobacco seeds in my garden. 17

Perhaps we can liberate tobacco from those who have captured and abused it, enslaving the plant on large plantations, keeping it from freedom and its kin, and forcing it to enslave the world. Its true nature suppressed, no wonder it has become deadly. Maybe by sowing a few seeds of tobacco in our gardens and treating the plant with the reverence it deserves, we can redeem tobacco's soul and restore its self-respect. 18

Besides, how grim, if one is a smoker, to realize one is smoking a slave. 19

There is a slogan from a battered women's shelter that I especially like: "Peace on earth begins at home." I believe everything does. I think of a slogan for people trying to stop smoking: "Every home a smoke-free zone." Smoking is a form of self-battering that also batters those who must sit by, occasionally cajole or complain, and helplessly watch. I realize now that as a child I 20

*Three months after reading this essay, my daughter stopped smoking.

sat by, through the years, and literally watched my father kill himself: Surely one such victory in my family, for the rich white men who own the tobacco companies, is enough.

UNDERSTANDING DETAILS

1. What is Walker's main purpose in this essay?
2. Why did Walker's sister remember her first cigarette "with some bitterness" (paragraph 8)?
3. When did Walker herself smoke?

ANALYZING MEANING

1. What connection does the author make between Third World countries and her daughter's smoking?
2. Whom is Walker referring to when she talks about "those who have captured and abused [tobacco]" (paragraph 18)? How have they "enslav[ed] the plant on large plantations, keeping it from freedom and its kin, and forcing it to enslave the world" (paragraph 18)?
3. In what way is smoking "a form of self-battering" (paragraph 20)?

DISCOVERING RHETORICAL STRATEGIES

1. Why does Walker begin her essay with a personal story about her daughter? What effect does this anecdote have on the essay as a whole?
2. Walker divides her essay into four parts. What is the theme of each part? Why did she place these themes in this particular order?
3. Divide a piece of paper in half. On one side, list the causes Walker gives for people's addiction to cigarettes; on the other, list the effects of this addiction. Record the paragraph references in each case. Then, discuss how the writer's attitude emerges from the pattern you have outlined.

IDEAS FOR DISCUSSION/WRITING

Preparing to Write

Write freely about addiction and its role in your generation: What qualifies as an addiction? Why do you think addiction plays such a major role in the current generation? What role has it played in previous generations? Why has it become such a significant social issue?

3. *Causes of addiction:*
   —"The tobacco industry, coupled with Hollywood movies in which both hero and heroine smoked like chimneys, won over completely people like my father, who were hopelessly addicted to cigarettes" (para. 4).
   —"It was our father who gave her her first cigarette . . ." (para. 7).
   —"I smoked Kools, because my sister did" (para. 12).
   —"There are large billboards . . . [showing] the tough, 'take-charge,' or dapper older man, the glamorous, 'worldly' young woman, both puffing away" (para. 14).
   —"The plant as most of us know it has been poisoned by chemicals and denatured by intensive mono-cropping. . . ." (para. 17).

Effects of addiction:
   —"I do not remember, when he started to cough. . . . His breath was a wheeze . . . ; he could not climb stairs without resting . . ." (para. 5).
   —"My body simply would not tolerate smoke. After six months I had a chronic sore throat" (para. 12).
   —"My father died from 'the poor man's friend,' pneumonia, one hard winter when his bronchitis and emphysema had left him low" (para. 13).
   —"I doubt he had much lung left at all. . . . He was always leaning on something" (para. 13).
   —"He was so emaciated" (para. 13).
   —"People starve themselves of both food and air, effectively weakening and addicting their children, eventually eradicating themselves" (para. 14).
   —"Most people who try to quit smoking do not succeed" (para. 15).
   —"She will die of self-poisoning" (para. 16).
   —"How grim, if one is a smoker, to realize one is smoking a slave" (para. 19).
   —"Smoking is a form of self-battering that also batters those who must sit by . . . " (para. 20).

Walker's attitude about smoking emerges through her descriptions of how she and others have been hurt by it. She is careful not only to bring out the personal weaknesses that lead to this habit but the power structure that allows the promotion and sale of a harmful, addictive substance.

PREWRITING

In preparation for the writing assignments, the Preparing to Write questions ask students to write about addiction and its effect on their generation before they write an essay on a related topic. See pages 16–23 for suggestions on generating ideas in response to these questions.

ADDITIONAL DISCUSSION/WRITING TOPIC

The head of the English department on your campus has requested a description of the students in your composition class. Characterize for him or her the members of your class as a group. As you develop your description, introduce certain collective features of the group and then discuss their causes and effects.

REVISING STRATEGY

The conclusion of a cause/effect essay should contain a summary of the cause/effect relationships in the paper and an explanation of the deductions that can be drawn from those relationships. Reread one of your cause/effect essays, paying close attention to its conclusion: Does it present a summary of its main points and explain the deductions drawn from those points? Note any weaknesses in this format. Then revise your paper, strengthening those weaknesses and bringing closure to your concluding statement.

What impact does it have on society? How can we control this problem? What other features characterize your generation, your parents' generation, the current generation? Which features that characterize the current generation do you think are most constructive in American society? Which are most destructive? Do you think society in general is moving in a positive or negative direction?

Choosing a Topic

1. Although addiction and substance abuse afflict many members of the current college generation, this group of students has many redeeming qualities as well. Think of one important positive feature of this generation, and explain its causes and effects in an essay written for the general public.

2. Your campus newspaper is printing a special issue highlighting different generations of college students. Interview some people who represent a generation other than your own. Then, characterize an earlier generation of students for the newspaper. In essay form, introduce the features you have discovered, and then discuss their causes and effects.

3. Some medical professionals say addictions are forms of disease; others say that addictions are the result of weak willpower. What do you think? *Time* magazine is soliciting student reactions on this issue and has asked for your opinion. Where do you stand on this question? The editors of *Time* are especially interested in discovering the causes and effects of this problem. Give specific examples that support your opinion. Respond in essay form.

CHAPTER 9

ARGUMENT AND PERSUASION

■ ■ ■

Inciting People to Thought or Action

Using Argument and Persuasion

Almost everything we do or say is an attempt to persuade. Whether we dress up to impress a potential employer or argue openly with a friend about an upcoming election, we are trying to convince various people to see the world our way. Some aspects of life are particularly dependent upon persuasion. Think, for example, of all the television, magazine, and billboard ads we see urging us to buy certain products or of the many impassioned appeals we read and hear on such controversial issues as school prayer, abortion, gun control, and nuclear energy. Religious leaders devote their professional lives to convincing people to live a certain way and believe in certain religious truths, whereas scientists and mathematicians use rigorous logic and natural law to convince us of various hypotheses. Politicians make their living persuading voters to elect them and then support them throughout their terms of office. In fact, anyone who wants something from another person or agency, ranging from federal money for a research project to a new bicycle for Christmas, must use some form of persuasion to get what he or she desires. The success or failure of this type of communication is easily determined: If the people being addressed change their actions or attitudes in favor of the writer or speaker, the attempt at persuasion has been successful.

INTRODUCTORY NOTES

If all writing is persuasive to some degree, argument is the highest, most refined form of persuasion. In the introduction to this chapter, we discuss all three traditional methods of appeal: logical, emotional, and ethical. In our opinion, your most efficient approach to this particular mode is to help your students understand the importance of adjusting these appeals to their specific purpose and audience in each writing assignment. Our primary focus throughout this chapter, however, is on logic, because it plays such a vital role in all college writing. An important lesson students should learn in this chapter is that supporting their opinions with facts and examples is absolutely essential in a successful argument. Finally, you should make certain your students know that good argument and persuasion essays habitually rely upon other rhetorical modes. All the authors represented in this chapter let their purpose and audience dictate the amount of emphasis placed on each rhetorical strategy, the support necessary for their main points, and the other rhetorical modes that will best help develop their arguments. The essays in this chapter are persuasive because all of these characteristics are integrated effectively.

The apparatus before and after each essay attempts to highlight its best features and help the students see how this particular persuasive essay works. For example, the questions accompanying Donald Drakeman's "Religion's Place in Public Schools" ask students to think, read, and write about the role of religion in public schools as well as to discover what features of this highly logical essay work most effectively. Next, the questions accompanying "Putting In a Good Word for Guilt," by Ellen Goodman, ask students to analyze how guilt affects their lives either directly or indirectly. Next, the questions accompanying Shelby Steele's "Affirmative Action: The Price of Preference" ask students to contemplate the relationship between the job market and affirmative action as they learn to appreciate Steele's adept combination of all three appeals. Robert Hughes' essay, entitled "The N.R.A. in a Hunter's Sights," is supported by questions on guns and people's rights to bear arms. And the apparatus surrounding Barbara Ehrenreich's essay, "The Warrior Culture," asks students to take a close look at America's strategies for achieving world peace.

The next four essays show argument and persuasion at work in two sets of opposing viewpoints. With these essays, your students will have the opportunity to see a debate in action as the writers present differing points of view on two controversial issues—drug testing and homelessness. We purposely chose two sets of essays that were written to be published together so that students could see a logical "battle" between two conflicting viewpoints. The resultant clash of opinions will help your students see the basic components of a well-reasoned argument and should lead them quite naturally to more complex arguments such as those provided by the documented essays in Chapter 10. These pro/con essays also furnish students with a bridge to the next chapter by introducing secondary sources into their discussions. Although these selections work well in generating class debates and research projects, they are equally valuable for in-class discussion and general writing assignments.

Defining Argument and Persuasion

The terms argument and persuasion are often used interchangeably, but one is actually a subdivision of the other. Persuasion names a purpose for writing. To persuade your readers is to convince them to think, act, or feel a certain way. Much of the writing you have been doing in this book has persuasion as one of its goals: A description of an African tribe has a "dominant impression" you want your readers to accept; in an essay comparing various ways of celebrating Thanksgiving, you are trying to convince your readers to believe that these similarities and differences actually exist; and in writing an essay exam on the causes of the Vietnam War, you are trying to convince your instructor that your reasoning is clear and your conclusions sound. In a sense, some degree of persuasion propels all writing.

More specifically, however, the process of persuasion involves appealing to one or more of the following: to reason, to emotion, or to a sense of ethics. An *argument* is an appeal predominantly to your readers' reason and intellect. You are working in the realm of argument when you deal with complex issues that are debatable; opposing views (either explicit or implicit) are a basic requirement of argumentation. But argument and persuasion are taught together because good writers are constantly blending these three appeals and adjusting them to the purpose and audience of a particular writing task. Although reason and logic are the focus of this chapter, you need to learn to use all three methods of persuasion as skillfully as possible to write effective essays.

An appeal to reason relies upon logic and intellect and is usually most effective when you are expecting your readers to disagree with you in any way. This type of appeal can help you change your readers' opinions or influence their future actions through the sheer strength of logical validity. If you wanted to argue, for example, that pregnant women should refrain from smoking cigarettes, you could cite abundant statistical evidence that babies born to mothers who smoke have lower birth weights, more respiratory problems, and a higher incidence of sudden infant death syndrome than the children of nonsmoking mothers. Because smoking clearly endangers the health of the unborn child, reason dictates that mothers who wish to give birth to the healthiest possible babies should avoid smoking during pregnancy.

Emotional appeals, however, attempt to arouse your readers'

feelings, instincts, senses, and biases. Used most profitably when your readers already agree with you, this type of essay generally validates, reinforces, and/or incites in an effort to get your readers to share your feelings or ideas. In an attempt to urge our lawmakers to impose stricter jail sentences for alcohol abuse, you might describe a recent tragic accident involving a local twelve-year-old girl who was killed by a drunk driver as she rode her bicycle to school one morning. By focusing on such poignant visual details as the condition of her mangled bike, the bright blood stains on her white dress, and the anguish on the faces of parents and friends, you could build a powerfully persuasive essay that would be much more effective than a dull recitation of impersonal facts and nationwide statistics.

An appeal to ethics, the third technique writers often use to encourage readers to agree with them, involves cultivating a sincere, honest tone that will establish your reputation as a reliable, qualified, experienced, well-informed, and knowledgeable person whose opinions on the topic under discussion are believable because they are ethically sound. Such an approach is often used in conjunction with logical or emotional appeals to foster a verbal environment that will result in minimal resistance from its readers. Ed McMahon, Johnny Carson's congenial announcer on the "Tonight Show" for many years and the host of "Star Search," is an absolute master at creating this ethical, trustworthy persona as he coaxes his television viewers to purchase everything from dog food to beer. In fact, the old gag question "Would you buy a used car from this man?" is our instinctive response to all forms of attempted persuasion, whether the salesperson is trying to sell us Puppy Chow or gun control, hair spray or school prayer. The more believable we are as human beings, the better chance we will have of convincing our audience.

The following student paragraph is directed primarily toward the audience's logical faculties. Notice how the writer states her assertion and then gives reasons to convince her readers to change their ways. The student writer also brings both emotion and ethics into the argument by choosing her words and examples with great precision.

> Have you ever watched a pair of chunky thighs, a jiggling posterior, and an extra-large sweatshirt straining to cover a beer belly and thought, "Thank God I don't look like that! I'm in pretty good shape . . . for someone my age." Well, before you become too smug and self-righteous, consider what kind of shape you're really in. Just be-

In responding to these essays that represent opposing viewpoints, your students will be required to read, comprehend, and then synthesize material. Each argument is accompanied by a "Further Reading" list in the AIE, so you can use the essays in several different pedagogical contexts. The writing assignments following these essays include both argument/persuasion tasks and questions that require library work.

428   *Chapter 9 ▪ Argument and Persuasion*

Persuasion is the communication of a particular message to a targeted audience for a specific occasion to affect a change in the reader(s). Making students aware of message and occasion, while tricky, is straightforward enough; sensitizing them to audience, purpose, and the range of choices and techniques available to them has been far more difficult for me. Once I teach the strategies of exposition, which are frequently determined or suggested by a writer's material, I seem naturally to advance to argument in my pedagogical progression. But argument presumes an antagonistic occasion; similarly, persuasion implies an ethical compromise that tends to repel beginning students. Thus, I emphasize a melding of the two forms, concentrating on writing for an audience that is largely disinterested, but one that includes the writer's opposition. Little else I do so emphasizes the centrality of considering audience in my students' writing strategies, and little else has proven as successful and effective in making my students aware of the degree of control they have over their ability to communicate, simultaneously alerting them to the importance of objective self-awareness and analysis in their subjective writing processes.

Rodney Simard
California State University
San Bernardino, California

cause you don't look like Shamu the Whale doesn't mean you're in good condition. What's missing, you ask? Exercise. You can diet all day, wear the latest slim-cut designer jeans, and still be in worse shape than someone twice your age if you don't get a strong physical workout at least three times a week. Exercise is not only good for you, but it can also be fun—especially if you find a sport that makes you happy while you sweat. Your activity need not be expensive: Jogging, walking, basketball, tennis, and handball are not costly, unless you're seduced by the glossy sheen of the latest sporting fashions and accessories. Most of all, however, regular exercise is important for your health. You can just as easily drop dead from a sudden heart attack in the middle of a restaurant when you're slim and trim as when you're a slob. Your heart and lungs need regular workouts to stay healthy. So do yourself a favor and add some form of exercise to your schedule. You'll feel better and live longer, and your looks will improve, too!

Reading and Writing Persuasive Essays

Although persuasive writing can be approached essentially in three different ways—logically, emotionally, and/or ethically—our stress in this chapter is on logic and reason, because it is at the heart of most college writing. As a reader, you will see how various forms of reasoning and different methods of organization affect your reaction to an essay. Your stand on a particular issue will control the way you process information in an argument/persuasion essay. As you read these essays, you will also learn to recognize emotional and ethical appeals and the different effects they create. In your role as writer, you need to be fully aware of the options available to you as you compose. Although the basis of your writing will be logical argument, you can learn to control your readers' responses to your essays by choosing your evidence carefully, organizing it wisely, and seasoning it with the right amount of emotion and ethics—depending on your purpose and audience.

HOW TO READ PERSUASIVE ESSAYS

Preparing to Read.   As you prepare to read the essays in this chapter, spend a few minutes browsing through the preliminary material for each selection: What does Donald Drakeman's title, "Religion's Place in Public Schools," prepare you for? What can you learn from scanning Ellen Goodman's essay, "Putting In a Good Word for Guilt," and reading its synopsis in the Rhetorical Contents?

Also, you should bring to your reading as much information as you can from the authors' biographies: Why do you think Shelby Steele writes about affirmative action? Does he have the proper qualifications to teach us about "The Price of Preference"? What is the source of Barbara Ehrenreich's interest in "The Warrior Culture"? For the essays in this chapter that present two sides of an argument, what biographical details prepare us for each writer's stand on the issue? Who were the original audiences for these pro and con arguments?

Last, before you read these essays, try to generate some ideas on each topic so that you can take the role of an active reader. In this text, the Preparing to Read questions will prepare you for this task. Then, you should speculate further on the general subject of the essay: How do you think affirmative action is working nationally? What would you change about America's approach to this controversial topic? What would you continue? What do you want to know from Robert Hughes about gun control? Which side of this issue are you on? On what do you base your current opinion?

Reading. Be sure to record your spontaneous reactions to the persuasive essays in this chapter as you read them for the first time: What are your opinions on each subject? Why do you hold these opinions? Be especially aware of your responses to the essays representing opposing viewpoints at the end of the chapter; know where you stand in relation to each side of the issues here. Use the preliminary material before an essay to help you create a framework for your responses to it: Who was Drakeman's primary audience when his essay was first published? In what ways is the tone of his essay appropriate for that audience? Why is Steele so interested in affirmative action? What motivated Hughes to publish his arguments on gun control? Which argument do you find most convincing? Your main job at this stage of reading is to determine each author's primary assertion or proposition (thesis statement) and create an inquisitive environment for thinking critically about the essay's ideas. In addition, take a look at the questions after each selection to make sure you are picking up the major points of the essay.

Rereading. As you reread these persuasive essays, notice how the writers integrate their appeals to logic, to emotion, and to ethics. Also, pay attention to the emphasis the writers place on one or more appeals at certain strategic points in the essays: How does Goodman integrate these three appeals in "Putting In a

---

TEACHING ARGUMENT AND PERSUASION: ONE INSTRUCTOR'S COMMENTS

I think that teaching argument and persuasion is important because it combines instruction in rhetoric, logic, critical thinking, and the writing process. In class, we work with various issues and emphasize brainstorming on both sides of an issue before identifying the most critical elements of a problem. We read prose models of argumentation and persuasion and analyze the rhetorical strategies at work in those examples. We also read advocacy documents related to each issue we address. Teaching argumentation and persuasive writing requires attention to all aspects of the writing process while focusing on the construction of logical arguments. As a result, I think that understanding techniques and strategies of argument and persuasion is useful in approaching almost any mode of writing. A particular teaching technique I emphasize is anticipating and countering opposing views (the proleptical argument) in the fine art of persuasion.

John White
California State University
Fullerton, California

Good Word for Guilt"? Which of these appeals does she rely on to help bring her essay to a close? How persuasive is her final appeal? What combination of appeals does Ehrenreich use in "The Warrior Culture"? In what way does the tone of her writing support what she is saying? How does she establish the tone? Also, determine what other rhetorical strategies help these writers make their primary points. How do these strategies enable each writer to establish a unified essay with a beginning, a middle, and an end? Then, answer the questions after each reading selection to make certain you understand the essay on the literal, interpretive, and analytical levels in preparation for the discussion/writing assignments that follow.

For a list of guidelines for the entire reading process, see the checklists on pages 15–16 of the Introduction.

HOW TO WRITE PERSUASIVE ESSAYS

Preparing to Write.   The first stage of writing an essay of this sort involves, as usual, exploring and then limiting your topic. As you prepare to write your persuasive paper, first try to generate as many ideas as possible—regardless of whether they appeal to logic, emotion, or ethics. To do this, review the prewriting techniques in the Introduction and answer the Preparing to Write questions,. Then, choose a topic. Next, focus on a purpose and specific audience before you begin to write.

Writing.   Most persuasive essays should begin with an assertion or proposition stating what you believe about a certain issue. This thesis should generally be phrased as a debatable statement, such as, "If individual states reinstituted the death penalty, Americans would notice an immediate drop in violent crimes." At this point in your essay, you should also justify the significance of the issue you will be discussing: "Such a decline in the crime rate would affect all our lives and make this country a safer place in which to live."

The essay should then support your thesis in a variety of ways. This support might take the form of facts, figures, examples, opinions by recognized authorities, case histories, narratives/anecdotes, comparisons, contrasts, or cause/effect studies. This evidence is most effectively organized from least to most important when you are confronted with a hostile audience (so that you can lead your readers through the reasoning step by step) and from most to least important when you are facing a supportive audience (so that you can build on their loyalty and enthusiasm as you advance your thesis). In fact, you will be able to engineer your best support if you know your audience's opinions, feelings, and background before you write your essay so that your intended "target" is as clear as possible. The body of your essay will undoubtedly consist of a combination of logical, emotional, and ethical appeals—all leading to some final summation or recommendation.

The concluding paragraph of a persuasive essay should restate your main assertion (in slightly different terms than your original statement) and offer some constructive recommendations about the problem you have been discussing (if you haven't already done so). This section of your paper should clearly bring your argument to a close in one final attempt to move your audience to accept or act upon the viewpoint you present. Let's look more closely now at each of the three types of appeals used in such essays: logical, emotional, and ethical.

To construct a *logical* argument, you have two principal patterns available to you: inductive reasoning or deductive reasoning. The first encourages an audience to make what is called an "inductive leap" from several particular examples to a single, useful generalization. In the case of the death penalty, you might cite a number of examples, figures, facts, and case studies illustrating the effectiveness of capital punishment in various states, thereby leading up to your firm belief that the death penalty should be reinstituted. Used most often by detectives, scientists, and lawyers, the process of inductive reasoning addresses the audience's ability to think logically by moving them systematically from an assortment of selected evidence to a rational and ordered conclusion.

In contrast, deductive reasoning moves its audience from a broad, general statement to particular examples supporting that statement. In writing such an essay, you would present your thesis statement about capital punishment first and then offer clear, orderly evidence to support that belief. Although the mental process we go through in creating a deductive argument is quite sophisticated, it is based upon a three-step form of reasoning called the "syllogism," which most logicians believe is the foundation of logical thinking. The traditional syllogism has

a major premise:	All humans fear death.
a minor premise:	Criminals are humans.
and a conclusion:	Therefore, criminals fear death.

As you might suspect, this type of reasoning is only as accurate as its original premises, so you need to be careful with the truth of the premises as well as with the logical validity of your argument.

In constructing a logical argument, you should take great care to avoid the two types of fallacies in reasoning found most frequently in lower-division college papers: giving too few examples to support an assertion, or citing examples that do not represent the assertion fairly. If you build your argument on true statements and abundant, accurate evidence, your essay will be effective.

Persuading through *emotion* necessitates controlling your readers' instinctive reactions to what you are saying. You can accomplish this goal in two different ways: (1) by choosing your words with even greater care than usual and (2) by using figurative language whenever appropriate. In the first case, you must be especially conscious of using words that have the same general denotative (or dictionary) meaning but bear decidedly favorable or unfavorable connotative (or implicit) meanings: For example, notice the difference between "slender" and "scrawny," "patriotic" and "chauvinistic," or "compliment" and "flattery." Your careful attention to the choice of such words can help readers form visual images with certain positive or negative associations that subtly encourage them to follow your argument and adopt your opinions. Second, the effective use of figurative language—especially similes and metaphors—makes your writing more vivid, thus triggering your readers' senses and encouraging them to accept your views. Both of these techniques will help you manipulate your readers into the position of agreeing with your ideas.

Ethical appeals, which establish you as a reliable, well-informed person, are accomplished through (1) the tone of your essay and (2) the number and type of examples you cite. Tone is created through deliberate word choice: Careful attention to the mood implied in the words you use can convince your readers that you are serious, friendly, authoritative, jovial, or methodical—depending on your intended purpose. In like manner, the examples you supply to support your assertions can encourage readers to see you as experienced, insightful, relaxed, or intense. In both of these cases, winning favor for yourself will usually also gain approval for your opinions.

Rewriting.   To rework your persuasive essays, you should play the role of your readers and impartially evaluate the different appeals you have used to accomplish your purpose: Is your thesis statement clear? Is the main thrust of your essay argumentative (an appeal to reason)? Which of your supporting details appeal to emotion? To ethics? Will the balance of these appeals effectively accomplish your purpose with your intended audience? You should also look closely at the way your appeals work together in your essay: When you use logic, is that section of your paper arranged through either inductive or deductive reasoning? Is that the most effective order to achieve your purpose? In appealing to the emotions, have you chosen your words with proper attention to their denotative and connotative effects? Have you used figurative language whenever appropriate? And in your ethical appeals, have you created the right tone for your essay? Is it suitable for your purpose and your audience? Have you chosen examples carefully to support your thesis statement?

Any additional guidance you may need as you write and revise your persuasive essays is furnished on pages 27–28 of the Introduction.

Student Essay: Argument and Persuasion at Work

The following student essay uses all three appeals to make its point about the power of language in shaping our view of the world. First, the writer sets forth her character references (ethical appeal) in the first paragraph, after which she presents her thesis and its significance in paragraph 2. The support for her thesis is a combination of logical and emotional appeals, heavy on the logical, as the writer moves her paragraphs from general to particular in an effort to convince her readers to adopt her point of view and adjust their language use accordingly.

The Language of Equal Rights

Ethical appeal   Up front, I admit it. I'm a women's libber, a card-carrying feminist since junior high school. I want to see an Equal Rights Amendment to the U.S. Constitution, equal pay for equal—and comparable—work, and I go dutch on dates. Furthermore, I am quite prickly on the subject of language. I'm one of those women who bristles at terms   Emotional like "lady doctor" (you know they don't mean a   appeal gynecologist), "female policeman" (a paradox), and "mankind" instead of humanity (are they really talking about me?).

Many people ask "How important are mere words, anyway? You know what we really mean." A question like this ignores the symbolic and psychological importance of language. **What words "mean" can go beyond what a speaker or writer consciously intends, reflecting personal and cultural biases that run so deep that most of the time we aren't even aware they exist.** "Mere words" are incredibly important—they are our framework for seeing and understanding the world.

Assertion or thesis statement

Significance of assertion

Logical appeal

"Man," we are told, means woman as well as man, just as "mankind" supposedly stands for all of humanity. In the introduction of a sociology textbook I recently read, the author was anxious to demonstrate his awareness of the controversy over sexist language and to assure his female readers that, despite his use of noninclusive terms, he was not forgetting the existence or importance of women in society. He was making a conscious decision to continue to use "man" and "mankind" instead of "people," "humanity," etc., because of ease of expression and esthetic reasons. "Man" simply sounds better, he explained. I flipped through the table of contents and found "Man and Society," "Man and Nature," "Man and Technology," and, near the end, "Man and Woman." At what point did "Man" quit meaning people and start meaning men again? The writer was obviously unaware of the answer to this question, because it is one he would never think to ask. Having consciously addressed the issue only to dismiss it, he reverted to form.

Examples organized deductively

Emotional appeal

Logical appeal

The very ambiguity of "man" as the generic word for our species ought to be enough to combat any arguments that we keep it because we all "know what it means" or because it is both traditional and sounds better. And does it really sound all that better, or are we just more used to it, more comfortable? Our own national history proves that we can be comfortable with a host of words and attitudes that strike us as unjust and ugly today. A lot of White folks probably thought that Negroes were getting pretty stuffy and picky when they began to insist on being called Blacks. After all, weren't there more important things to worry about, like civil rights? But Black activists recognized the emotional and symbolic significance of having a name that

Examples organized deductively

Emotional appeal

was parallel to the name the dominant race used for itself—a name equal in dignity, lacking that vaguely alien, anthropological sound. After all, Whites were called Caucasians only in police reports, textbooks, and autopsies. "Negro" may have sounded better to people in the bad old days of blatant racial bigotry, but we've adjusted to the word "Black," and more and more people of each race are adjusting to the wider implications and demands of practical, as well as verbal, equality.

Logical appeal

In a world where "man" and "human" are offered as synonymous terms, I don't think it is a coincidence that women are still vastly underrepresented in positions of money, power, and respect. Children grow up learning a language that makes maleness the norm for anything that isn't explicitly designated as female, giving little girls a very limited corner of the universe to picture themselves in. Indeed, the language that nonfeminists today claim to be inclusive was never intended to cover women in the first place. "One man, one vote" and "All men are created equal" meant just that. Women had to fight for decades to be included even as an afterthought; it took constitutional amendments to convince the government and the courts that women are human, too.

Examples organized deductively

Conclusion/ restatement

The message is clear. We have to start speaking about people, not men, if we are going to start thinking in terms of both women and men. A "female man" will never be the equal of her brother.

Student Writer's Comments

The hardest task for me on this essay was trying to come up with a topic! The second hardest task was trying to be effective without getting preachy, strident, or wordy. I wanted to persuade an audience that would no doubt include the bored, the hostile, and the indifferent, and I was worried about losing their attention. Although my main approach to the topic is argumentative, I strategically introduce emotional and ethical appeals in the essay. I appeal to ethics to establish my credibility, and I appeal to emotion to vary my pace and help my argument gain a little momentum. After many revisions, I think the balance of appeals finally works.

Some Final Thoughts on Argument and Persuasion

As you can tell from the selections that follow, the three different types of persuasive appeals usually complement each other in practice. Most good persuasive essays use a combination of these methods to achieve their purposes. Good persuasive essays also rely upon various rhetorical modes we have already studied—such as example, process analysis, division/classification, comparison/contrast, definition, and cause/effect—to advance their arguments. In the following essays, you will see a combination of appeals at work and a number of different rhetorical modes furthering the arguments.

Religion's Place
in Public Schools

Donald Drakeman describes himself as a business executive and corporate lawyer with a "therapeutic" interest in church–state affairs. He was born in Camden, New Jersey, and proceeded to earn a B.A. degree in religion from Dartmouth College, a Ph.D. in religion from Princeton University, and a law degree from Columbia University. In addition to working as an attorney, he is president of a company using biotechnology to treat cancer and other diseases. Drakeman has published a number of articles on religion in public schools, religious cults, and First Amendment rights. His two books are titled *Church and State in American History: The Burden of Religious Pluralism* (coedited with John F. Wilson, 1988) and *Church–State Constitutional Issues: Making Sense of the Establishment Clause* (1991). Drakeman lives in Princeton, New Jersey, where he enjoys teaching part-time at Princeton University, playing squash, practicing the trumpet, and spending time with his family. When asked for permission to publish the following essay in *The Prose Reader*, the author replied: "If you are including my article as an example of good writing, I am honored. If my piece is representative of poor writing, please send me a copy of your book so that I may improve."

Preparing to Read

In the following essay, originally published in *The Christian Century* magazine in May 1984, Drakeman logically and carefully presents his opinions concerning the appropriate role of religion in the public schools. As you prepare to read his suggestions on this controversial topic, take a few moments to focus your own thoughts on the subject: What do you think the proper relationship should be between religion and education? Does your opinion depend upon whether the schools in question are public or private? Grade schools, high schools, or colleges? What is the role of education in American life? Of religion? Why do you think these topics are so controversial in America today?

PREREADING

The purpose of this Preparing to Read material is to encourage students to think about the relationship between religion and public education. To help your students focus their thoughts, you might stage a formal debate on the subject: The affirmative side would be that religion should be part of the public-school curriculum; the negative side, that it should not. The format of a one-on-one debate follows:

Opening statement, affirmative	3 min.
Cross-examination, negative	1 min.
Opening statement, negative	4 min.
Cross-examination, affirmative	1 min.
Affirmative rebuttal	2 min.
Negative rebuttal	3 min.
Affirmative rebuttal	1 min.

Adapt this schedule to your purposes. Then, have the class vote on the winning side based on the credibility and quality of the evidence provided. See pages 3–6 for other ways to generate thoughts on these questions.

BACKGROUND INFORMATION

In "Religion's Place in Public Schools," attorney Donald Drakeman uses the "moment-of-silence" legislation (requiring public schools to have a moment of silence for "quiet and private contemplation and introspection")* as a springboard to discuss various issues surrounding the separation of church and state. Originally published in *The Christian Century*, this essay demonstrates that denying students "the opportunity to meet for religious purposes is to say that religion cannot stand as an equal with football, debating, cheerleading, and the classics club" (para. 15).

*This legislation became law in New Jersey in 1982 but was then struck down by Federal district and appellate courts throughout the United States and finally by the U.S. Supreme Court in 1987.

READABILITY LEVEL

9.4

DEFINITIONS

"friend of the court" (para. 2): from Latin *amicus curiae*, a person or group, not involved in the case, who volunteers or is invited by the court to give advice upon some matter before the court.
pluralistic (para. 4): referring to a society in which diverse racial, ethnic, religious, or social groups maintain their traditional cultures within a common civilization.
How the Grinch Stole Christmas (para. 6): a popular Dr. Suess children's story.
imprimatur (para. 12): sanction; approval.

Recently I represented the New Jersey Council of Churches in a federal lawsuit challenging New Jersey's "moment-of-silence" legislation—a law requiring public-school teachers to provide a minute of silence at the beginning of the school day for students to engage in "contemplation or introspection." 1

The American Civil Liberties Union immediately sued to have the law declared unconstitutional on the grounds that it was designed to bring back prayer into the public schools—something the U.S. Supreme Court had outlawed 20 years ago. There was a great deal of evidence showing that the New Jersey legislators wanted to return prayer to the classroom, but had left the word out of the bill in hopes of avoiding the court's pronouncements. To the surprise of many, the New Jersey Council of Churches, an interdenominational Christian body, intervened in the case as a "friend of the court" to oppose the law. 2

At the same time, religious and civil liberties groups have been in a quandary over what to do about cases involving students who want to meet for religious purposes during noninstructional times at the public schools. Two federal appellate courts have declared such practices unconstitutional, saying that they are not qualitatively different from the school-sponsored prayers held unconstitutional in the 1960s. The issue remains open, however, and it is not clear—at least to me—that a mandatory moment of silence (or prayer) is the same thing as permitting students to elect a religious activity in place of the chess club or debating team. 3

Once again in American history, the public schools are at the intersection of church and state (or, perhaps more accurately, religion and government). This issue of when and where students may pray at school not only raises thorny questions of constitutional interpretation, but also asks us how we should relate our Christian faith to a world that has been called secular, amoral, modern, postmodern and even anti-Christian. Or, as ethicist Paul Ramsey has eloquently put it, "How shall we sing the Lord's song in a pluralistic land?" 4

To try to come to terms with this problem, we will need to look briefly at its legal dimensions, since the Constitution has set the parameters within which we must act, and then to relate the constitutional issues to the role of the Christian in our society. 5

The language of the Constitution is deceptively simple: The federal government and the states may not make laws "respecting an establishment of religion or prohibiting the free exercise thereof." In two famous cases in the early '60s, the United States 6

Supreme Court declared that school-sponsored prayer and Bible reading in the public schools violate the Constitution's establishment clause. These decisions brought a shower of public wrath upon the court. Many religious leaders feared that a godless, atheistic empire would soon take the place of the Christian republic that has been built on a foundation of faith and Scripture. The governors of every state but New York called for a constitutional amendment reversing the court's decisions, and the justices soon became the Grinches that stole Christmas from our children's school pageants.

Subsequently, the Supreme Court struck down a Kentucky law requiring that the Ten Commandments be posted in public-school classrooms, and other federal courts have outlawed school-sponsored grace before meals, student-led classroom prayer, and mandatory moments of silence. In each case, the courts have tried to follow the Supreme Court's conclusion that religious activities supported and sponsored by the schools are contrary t.o the Constitution even if the activities are "nondenominational" and voluntary.

Thus, the primary constitutional issues are: (1) Is the activity *religious*, and (2) Is it supported and sponsored by the school? Or, as the Supreme Court has expressed it: Does the state's action have a clearly secular purpose? Does it have a primary effect that neither advances nor inhibits religion? And does it avoid excessive government entanglement with religion? Each of these tests must be met for an action of the government to be constitutional.

Three federal courts have already decided that the moment-of-silence laws are unconstitutional. The evidence for these findings is compelling, despite legislative efforts to use neutral language such as "introspection," "contemplation" or "meditation" to avoid having the bill appear to be clearly religious. In every case, the moment-of-silence bills have evolved within the context of returning prayer to the classroom. Not only is the moment of silence directly within the long tradition of commencing the school day with a prayer (a practice still found in many schools despite Supreme Court pronouncements), but it is also legislatively designed to be a religious activity. In every state that has recently enacted a moment-of-silence law, the floor debate has been almost exclusively devoted to the topic of putting prayer, and religion generally, back into the minds and hearts of our public-school students. Only then, posit our lawmakers, will America return to its former days of glory.

Faced with this evidence of the legislators' religious intent

7

8

9

10

COLLABORATIVE LEARNING: CLASS ACTIVITY

Have your students discuss the advantages and disadvantages of combining religion and traditional schoolwork. Help them see during the discussion that there might be a continuum relevant to this topic ranging from a great deal of involvement of religion in the public schools to no involvement at all. Help them place Drakeman's ideas on this continuum.

COLLABORATIVE LEARNING: SMALL GROUP ACTIVITY

Divide your students into groups of 3 or 4, and have them take on the role of the Board of Education at a particular public school that has received Drakeman's proposal. After the students discuss the plan and reach a consensus, have each group draft a letter to Drakeman explaining their reactions to his suggestions.

1. Drakeman's statement alludes to the most recent battle in a series of conflicts between the authority of the state and the influence of the church in the public schools.

2. The pluralism described by Paul Ramsey reflects the multitude of religious beliefs represented in the United States at the present time. Because the majority of proponents of prayer in the public schools have a Christian background, the introduction of the prayers of these many "exotic" faiths would surely cause confusion among those who advocate a return to the "foundation of faith and Scripture" (para. 6).

3. Drakeman believes that mandatory prayer has no place in the public schools because of the diversity of faiths in the United States and the possibility that we might therefore be giving the state "the authority to regulate the exercise of our religion by excluding, limiting, or defining the kinds of prayer in which we, or our children, may engage " (para. 12). But he does feel that students should be permitted to meet for religious activities during noninstructional periods.

(which is enough, under Supreme Court precedents, to invalidate the moment-of-silence laws), lawyers defending the laws have created a variety of after-the-fact secular rationales for commencing the school day with a quiet moment. These arguments simply do not work; legislative history cannot so easily be rewritten. But, more important, the public cannot help but see the moment of silence as morning prayer. In many schools, most of the parents and teachers alike must have begun their own school days by saying prayers or reading the Bible. The moment-of-silence laws cannot be evaluated without taking into account this cultural fact that will unavoidably give a religious coloring to an ostensibly neutral law.

Although the moment-of-silence laws run afoul of the establishment clause, does it necessarily follow that we, as Christians, should oppose religion in the schools? After all, many religious groups are calling for a constitutional amendment that would permit teachers and students to lead prayers in public-school classrooms.   11

The crux of this issue is whether we think the state should have the power to favor one religion (or type of religion) over another. By having a time set aside for prayer during the part of the school day when teachers have virtually total control over their students, the schools are putting their imprimatur on those religions that believe in prayer. Moreover, if we admit that the state, through its schools, may regulate religion by encouraging prayer, we are tacitly giving it the authority to regulate the exercise of our religion by excluding, limiting, or defining the kinds of prayer in which we, or our children, may engage.   12

As our nation becomes increasingly diverse and secular, the likelihood that school-supported religious activities will correspond with the students' particular beliefs will diminish. Most of those who support school prayer hope for a return to the "Judeo-Christian" prayers of our educational past. But what if in some schools prayers are addressed instead to Shiva, the Ayatollah Khomeini, or Sun Myung Moon? For all of us, believers and nonbelievers alike, the safest course is to keep the schools out of the religion business.   13

Now that I have taken prayer out of the schools, I would like to put it back in under different auspices. Many public schools, particularly at the junior and senior high school levels, have noninstructional periods during which students are free to choose from among a variety of activities—sports, service clubs, language societies, and the like. In a number of communities, volun-   14 tary student religious groups have sought to meet during these activity periods. As I noted earlier, several federal courts have made no distinction between these requests and legislative attempts to bring back school-sponsored prayer. I think they are wrong.

During the instructional portion of the school day, teachers have almost complete control over the students' activities. Inserting prayer during those parts of the day clearly runs contrary to the mandates of the Constitution. But when students are asked to select from a wide variety of extracurricular activities, the school's role changes dramatically. No longer the domineering ruler of the students' every move, it becomes the host for a great number of (theoretically) socially enriching activities. To deny students the opportunity to meet for religious purposes is to say that religion cannot stand as an equal with football, debating, cheerleading, and the classics club. It is to single out religion as the one activity always inappropriate within the schools.

Even if we agree that voluntary, student-initiated religious groups may meet during noninstructional periods, will our present Constitution countenance it, or must we join those calling for a constitutional amendment? Fortunately, the Constitution provides ample support for allowing such student groups. While our government may not "establish" religion, it may not prohibit the free exercise of religion or restrict the free speech of its citizens (including students). When the school prescribes prayer, it is establishing religion; when it proscribes prayer, it is prohibiting students from freely exercising their religions.

Although there is some element of religious establishment when a school allows students to meet for religious purposes, the state support of religion is minimal. If the meetings are truly voluntary, the school must only exercise the basic supervision necessary to ensure that the students do not damage themselves or public property. On balance, this degree of "establishment" is insignificant compared to the detrimental impact on religious exercise and speech if students are told that they may elect any activity but prayer and discuss any subject but God.

There is no question that the public schools are important purveyors of our culture and its fundamental values. Teachers have control over our children for a vast portion of their formative and impressionable years. Precisely for this reason we must be particularly concerned about the schools' interaction with our faith and the faith of others. We must urge the schools to let religion compete on an equal footing with secular extracurricular ac-

15

16

17

18

ANSWERS TO QUESTIONS: ANALYZING MEANING (p. 442)

1. The "establishment clause" (para. 6) of the U.S. Constitution proscribes the "establishment of religion or prohibiting the free exercise thereof" (para. 6) by the U.S. government.

2. The issue of religion's role in the public schools gained prominence in the 1960s with the Supreme Court's declaration that school-sponsored prayer and Bible reading are unconstitutional. A general appeal for a constitutional amendment reversing these decisions failed while subsequent decisions struck down religiously oriented Christmas pageants in schools as well as the display of religious maxims, such as the Ten Commandments. The pivotal issue is the constitutionality of a mandatory moment of silence at the beginning of the school day to permit the students "'contemplation or introspection'" (para. 1).

3. This issue is crucial because "the public schools are important purveyors of our culture and its fundamental values. Teachers have control over our children for a vast portion of their formative and impressionable years" (para. 18). As a result, we must "be wary of any attempt to make the schools transmitters of religious beliefs and practices" (para. 18).

ANSWERS TO QUESTIONS: DISCOVERING RHETORICAL STRATEGIES (p. 442)

1. Drakeman's appeal to logic and reason implies that he is expecting some of his readers to disagree with him. In contrast, his presentation of arguments from the strongest to the weakest reflects anticipation of support. This contradiction, plus the publication of the article in a religious periodical, suggests an audience that generally supports the author's religious leanings, though it also allows for possible dissension regarding specific aspects of his conclusions.

2. The author's deductive reasoning begins with a question at the start of section 2: "Although the moment-of-silence laws run afoul of the establishment clause, does it necessarily follow that we, as Christians, should oppose religion in the schools?" (para. 11). This inquiry is followed with supporting arguments, appealing mainly to logic, because the subject is already full of emotion and because each side claims a strong ethical position.

3. Although the essay primarily represents logical argument, the author appeals occasionally to the readers' emotions as well as to their sense of ethics. Examples of emotional appeals may be found in Drakeman's reference to the justices who became "the Grinches that stole Christmas from our children's school pageants" (para. 6) and in the following question: "But what if in some schools prayers are addressed to Shiva, the Ayatollah Khomeini, or Sun Myung Moon?" (para. 13). Drakeman creates a strong sense of ethics when he establishes his own credentials as having "represented the New Jersey Council of Churches in a federal lawsuit challenging New Jersey's 'moment-of-silence' legislation" (para. 1), when he includes himself among the Christians ("we, as Christians," para. 11), and when he knowledgeably presents the judicial history of the issue of religion in the schools. In combination with logical and ethical appeals, Drakeman uses definition and cause/effect to reinforce his opinion that school-supported prayer should not be instituted: Drakeman uses definition to explain what "the intersection of church and state" (para. 4) actually means; and he relies on cause/effect (with special emphasis on effect) to show the possible unwanted consequences that could occur as a result of "'moment-of-silence' legislation" (para. 1).

tivities. But at the same time, we must be wary of any attempt to make the schools transmitters of religious beliefs and practices. It is the place of churches and families to guide us in the ways of faith. The schools must not be given the power to tell our children when, where, or how to pray.

UNDERSTANDING DETAILS

1. What does Drakeman mean when he says, "Once again in American history, the public schools are at the intersection of church and state" (paragraph 4)?
2. Why does Paul Ramsey call America "a pluralistic land" (paragraph 4)? What effect might this feature of American life have on the role of prayer in the public schools?
3. What does the author feel the appropriate role of religion in the public schools should be?

ANALYZING MEANING

1. What does the author mean when he refers to the "establishment clause" (paragraph 6) of the Constitution? What connotations does this phrase bear for you?
2. In your own words, explain the constitutional background of this issue. Do you think Drakeman's summary of this topic is accurate? Why or why not?
3. Why is religion's place in public schools such an important, controversial issue?

DISCOVERING RHETORICAL STRATEGIES

1. This essay appeared in a periodical called *The Christian Century*. With this in mind, who do you think is Drakeman's intended audience? Describe them in detail. How might this audience have affected the author's choice of evidence in this particular argument?
2. Is the author's reasoning primarily inductive or deductive? Give one example from the essay to support your answer. Why do you think Drakeman relies so heavily upon an appeal to logic in this essay?
3. The author occasionally uses emotional and ethical appeals to support his logic. When does he invoke our emotions in this essay? Our sense of ethics? What other rhetorical modes does he use to further his argument?

IDEAS FOR DISCUSSION/WRITING

Preparing to Write

Write freely about your view on the role of religion in the public schools: What role should religion play in our lives? How, when, and where should religion be taught? What role should school play in our lives? What subjects should American high schools be allowed to teach? What subjects should they exclude? Should education and religion merge at any one point? Under what conditions? What are the advantages of combining the two? The disadvantages? What are the advantages of separating the two? The disadvantages?

Choosing a Topic

1. In a letter addressed to the U.S. Supreme Court, answer one or more of the questions Drakeman poses in paragraph 8 of his essay as they relate to school prayer. Keep in mind that the judges, after reading your response, will be clarifying once again their interpretation of the establishment clause of the Constitution.
2. In a letter to your representative in Congress, argue for or against Drakeman's plan to allow religious groups to meet during noninstructional periods of the school day.
3. Your old high school has asked you to present to the current senior class your views on whether or not organized prayer should be included as part of the public school day. Explain your stand as thoroughly as possible using the background Drakeman furnishes in his essay.

PREWRITING

In preparation for the writing assignments, the Preparing to Write questions ask students form an opinion on the role of religion in the public schools before writing an essay on a related topic. See pages 16–23 for suggestions on generating ideas in response to these questions.

ADDITIONAL DISCUSSION/WRITING TOPIC

The Board of Education for your school district is thinking about offering ethics classes in the public schools. What might be taught in an ethics class? How is ethics different from religion? At what age should children receive instruction in ethics? If the schools teach ethics, are they reaching into an area of parental responsibility? You have been granted an audience with the Board of Education; argue for or against offering a course in ethics in your district's public-school curriculum.

REVISING STRATEGY

Getting an argument off to a good start is an important part of the persuasive process. Most readers instinctively look for a thesis statement early in an essay so that they can focus on a controlling idea. In one of your persuasive essays, underline your thesis: Is your thesis an assertion or proposition that states what you believe about a certain issue? Is your thesis phrased as a debatable question? Is your stand on this question clear? Have you also justified the significance of the issue you are discussing? Does the rest of your essay support your thesis statement? Mark any problems you notice in your introduction along these lines. Then revise your paper, paying special attention to your thesis and to the way the rest of your essay supports that thesis.

ELLEN GOODMAN
(1941–   )

■   ■   ■

Putting In a Good Word for Guilt

Ellen Goodman is a nationally syndicated columnist and associate editor for the *Boston Globe*. Once referred to as a "serious writer about soft subjects," she frequently pens newspaper columns on such topics as feminism, childrearing, divorce, alternative lifestyles, and gardening. Although Goodman once appealed principally to women, her essays now interest readers of both sexes who are, in the words of *New York Times* critic John Leonard, "full of gratitude for having been introduced to a witty and civilized human being in a vulgar and self-pitying decade." Born in Newton, Massachusetts, and educated at Radcliffe College, Goodman began her career in journalism as a researcher and reporter at *Newsweek* magazine, then moved to the *Detroit Free Press* as a feature writer. In 1967, she was hired as a feature writer and "At Large" columnist by the *Boston Globe*. Her first book was *Turning Points* (1979), which examines how men and women have reacted to the changes brought on by the feminist movement. More recent publications include four collections of her best newspaper columns: *Close to Home* (1979), *At Large* (1981), *Keeping in Touch* (1985), and *Making Sense* (1989). In 1980, Goodman's reputation as a first-rate journalist was confirmed when she was awarded the Pulitzer Prize for distinguished commentary. Syndicated now in more than 300 newspapers throughout the country, Goodman lives in Brookline, Massachusetts.

Preparing to Read

The following essay, originally written for *Redbook* magazine (June 1982), suggests that we all need a certain amount of therapeutic guilt in our lives. Before you read this essay, take a few moments to think about your own perceptions of guilt: Are there different types of guilt? How often do you feel guilty? What are the usual reasons? What general feelings do you associate with the word "guilt"? Are these associations generally positive or negative? What value might guilt have in our lives? What problems might it cause? Do you consider yourself guilt-free, overly guilty, or somewhere in the middle?

What brings you to this conclusion about yourself? Are you content with this feature of your personality? Why or why not?

∎——————————————————————————————————∎

Feeling guilty is nothing to feel guilty about. Yes, guilt can be the excess baggage that keeps us paralyzed unless we dump it. But it can also be the engine that fuels us. Yes, it can be a self-punishing activity, but it can also be the conscience that keeps us civilized.

Not too long ago I wrote a story about that amusing couple Guilt and the Working Mother. I'll tell you more about that later. Through the mail someone sent me a gift coffee mug carrying the message "I gave up guilt for Lent."

My first reaction was to giggle. But then it occurred to me that this particular Lent has been too lengthy. For the past decade or more, the pop psychologists who use book jackets rather than couches all were busy telling us that I am okay, you are okay, and whatever we do is okay.

In most of their books, guilt was given a bad name—or rather, an assortment of bad names. It was a (1) Puritan (2) Jewish (3) Catholic hangover from our (1) parents (2) culture (3) religion. To be truly liberated was to be free of guilt about being rich, powerful, number one, bad to your mother, thoughtless, late, a smoker or about cheating on your spouse.

There was a popular notion, in fact, that self-love began by slaying one's guilt. People all around us spent a great portion of the last decade trying to tune out guilt instead of decoding its message and learning what it was trying to tell us.

With that sort of success, guilt was ripe for revival. Somewhere along the I'm-okay-you're-okay way, many of us realized that, in fact, I am not always okay and neither are you. Furthermore, we did not want to join the legions who conquered their guilt en route to new depths of narcissistic rottenness.

At the deepest, most devastating level, guilt is the criminal in us that longs to be caught. It is the horrible, pit-of-the-stomach sense of having done wrong. It is, as Lady Macbeth obsessively knew, the spot that no one else may see . . . and we can't see around.

To be without guilt is to be without a conscience. Guilt-free people don't feel bad when they cause pain to others, and so they go on guilt-freely causing more pain. The last thing we need more of is less conscience.

Freud once said, "As regards conscience, God has done an

1 **BACKGROUND INFORMATION**

Ellen Goodman's "Putting In a Good Word for Guilt" takes a light look at a serious subject—popular psychological theory maintaining that all guilt is self-destructive.
2 Using humor and an intimate tone, Goodman insists that guilt is not a constraining emotion from which all human beings must be liberated, but "the conscience that keeps
3 us civilized" (para. 1).

READABILITY LEVEL

7.3

4 **RELATED READINGS**

Paradoxes and Irony

Jessica Mitford, "Behind the Formaldehyde Curtain"   226
Judith Viorst, "The Truth About Lying"   283

5 **DEFINITIONS**

Freud (para. 9): Sigmund Freud (1856–1939), an Austrian psychiatrist;
6 founder of psychoanalysis.
puritanism (para. 11): a movement in the sixteenth and seventeenth centuries to "purify" the Church of England of its excesses; based on self-reliance, frugality, and industry.
7 **hedonism** (para. 11): the doctrine that pleasure is the highest good
Karl Menninger (1893–1990) (para. 14): an American psychiatrist.

8

9

uneven and careless piece of work, for a large majority of men have brought along with them only a modest amount of it, or scarcely enough to be worth mentioning."

Now, I am not suggesting that we all sign up for a new guilt   10
trip. But there has to be some line between the accusation that we all should feel guilty for, say, poverty or racism and the assertion that the oppressed have "chosen" their lot in life.

There has to be something between puritanism and hedo-   11
nism. There has to be something between the parents who guilt-trip their children across every stage of life and those who offer no guidance, no—gulp—moral or ethical point of view.

At quite regular intervals, for example, my daughter looks up   12
at me in the midst of a discussion (she would call it a lecture) and says: "You're making me feel guilty." For a long time this made me, in turn, feel guilty. But now I realize that I am doing precisely what I am supposed to be doing: instilling in her a sense of right and wrong so that she will feel uncomfortable if she behaves in hurtful ways.

This is, of course, a very tricky business. Guilt is ultimately   13
the way we judge ourselves. It is the part of us that says, "I deserve to be punished." But we all know people who feel guilty just for being alive. We know people who are paralyzed by irrational guilt. And we certainly don't want to be among them, or to shepherd our children into their flock.

But it seems to me that the trick isn't to become flaccidly non-   14
judgmental, but to figure out whether we are being fair judges of ourselves. Karl Menninger once wrote that one aim of psychiatric treatment isn't to get rid of guilt but "to get people's guilt feelings attached to the 'right' things."

In his book Feelings, Willard Gaylin quotes a Reverend Tillot-   15
son's definition of guilt as "nothing else but trouble arising in our mind from our consciousness of having done contrary to what we are verily perswaded [sic] was our Duty."

We may, however, have widely different senses of duty. I had   16
lunch with two friends a month ago when they both started talking about feeling guilty for neglecting their mothers. One, it turned out, worried that she didn't call "home" every day; the other hadn't even chatted with her mother since Christmas.

We are also particularly vulnerable to feelings of duty in a   17
time of change. Today an older and ingrained sense of what we should do may conflict with a new one. In the gaps that open between what we once were taught and what we now believe grows a rich crop of guilt.

Mothers now often tell me that they feel guilty if they are working and guilty if they aren't. One set of older expectations, to be a perfect milk-and-cookies supermom, conflicts with another, to be an independent woman or an economic helpmate.

But duty has its uses. It sets us down at the typewriter, hustles us to the job on a morning when everything has gone wrong, pushes us toward the crying baby at 3 a.m.

If guilt is a struggle between our acceptance of shoulds and should nots, it is a powerful and intensely human one. Gaylin writes, "Guilt represents the noblest and most painful of struggles. It is between us and ourselves." It is better to struggle with ourselves than give up on ourselves.

This worst emotion, in a sense, helps bring out the best in us. The desire to avoid feeling guilty makes us avoid the worst sort of behavior. The early guilt of a child who has hurt a younger sister or brother, even when no one else knows, is a message. The adult who has inflicted pain on an innocent, who has cheated, lied, stolen, to get ahead of another—each of us has a list—wakes up in the middle of the night and remembers it.

In that sense guilt is the great civilizer, the internal commandment that helps us choose to be kind to each other rather than to join in a stampede of me-firsts. "If guilt is coming back," said Harvard Professor David Riesman, who wrote The Lonely Crowd, "one reason is that a tremendous surge of young people overpowered the adults in the sixties. You might say the barbarians took Rome. Now there are more adults around who are trying to restore some stability."

Guilt is the adult in each of us, the parent, the one who upholds the standards. It is the internal guide against which we argue in vain that "everybody else is doing it."

We even wrestle with ethical dilemmas and conflicts of conscience so that we can live with ourselves more comfortably. I know two people who were faced with a crisis about their infidelities. One woman resolved the triangle she was in by ending her marriage. The other ended her affair. In both cases, it was the pain that had motivated them to change.

It is not easy to attach our guilt to the right things. It is never easy to separate right from wrong, rational guilt from neurotic guilt. We may resolve one by changing our view of it and another by changing our behavior.

In my own life as a working mother, I have done both half a dozen times. When my daughter was small and I was working, I worried that I was not following the pattern of the good mother,

1. Goodman explains that people feel very different "senses of duty" (para. 16). Whereas one person may feel guilty about not calling parents every day, another may feel no remorse after not calling for months. Thus, simply saying that we need to connect guilt with the proper causes does not deal with the lack of guilt or an overworked sense of duty. By becoming "fair judges of ourselves" (para. 14), we feel a sense of duty, yet we avoid feeling an overabundance of guilt.

2. The author points out that people are particularly vulnerable to unproductive guilt during periods of social change. She uses the example of mothers today who "feel guilty if they are working and guilty if they aren't" (para. 18), which reflects the conflicting expectations of being a mother and a career woman at the same time.

3. Guilt as "the great civilizer" (para. 22) is described by the author as "the internal commandment that helps us choose to be kind to each other rather than to join in a stampede of me-firsts" (para. 22).

ANSWERS TO QUESTIONS: DISCOVERING RHETORICAL STRATEGIES (p. 449)

1. Although Goodman's essay is primarily an appeal to logic, she incorporates both emotional and ethical appeals into the argument. She evokes emotion with an example of two friends "feeling guilty for neglecting their mothers" (para. 16) and with a reminder of the conflicting expectations of being "a perfect milk-and-cookies supermom" at the same time as being "an independent woman or an economic helpmate" (para. 18). An ethical appeal is established in her quotes from such figures as Freud (para. 9), Karl Menninger (para. 14), Willard Gaylin (paras. 15 and 20), and David Riesman (para. 22).

2. The author's intended audience is the educated, successful woman with an awareness of the directions taken in popular psychology. This is determined from the author's intimate tone and her assumption that my mother. Only through time and perspective and reality did I change that view; I realized that my daughter clearly did not feel neglected and I clearly was not uncaring. Good child care, love, luck and support helped me to resolve my early guilt feelings.

Then again, last winter I found myself out of town more than 27 I was comfortable with. This time I changed my schedule instead of my mind.

For all of us, in the dozens of daily decisions we make, guilt is 28 one of the many proper motivations. I am not saying our lives are ruled by guilt. Hardly. But guilt is inherent in the underlying question: "If I do that, can I live with myself?"

People who don't ask themselves that question, people who 29 never get no for an answer, may seem lucky. They can, we think, be self-centered without self-punishment, hedonistic without qualms. They can worry about me-first and forget about the others.

It is easy to be jealous of those who go through life without a 30 moment of wrenching guilt. But envying the guiltless is like envying a house pet. Striving to follow their lead is like accepting a catatonic as your role model. They are not the free but the antisocial. In a world in which guilt is one of the few emotions experienced only by human beings, they are, even, unhuman.

Guilt is one of the most human of dilemmas. It is the claim of 31 others on the self, the recognition both of our flaws and of our desire to be the people we want to be.

UNDERSTANDING DETAILS

1. Which two sides of the argument about guilt does Goodman present in the first paragraph of her essay? Which side does she end up favoring? How can we predict from the first paragraph that she is going to take that side?
2. What does the author mean when she states, "guilt was given a bad name" (paragraph 4)?
3. According to Goodman, how are guilt and conscience related?

ANALYZING MEANING

1. Goodman quotes Karl Menninger as saying that one aim of psychiatric treatment isn't to get rid of guilt but "'to get people's guilt feelings attached to the "right" things'" (paragraph 14). What explanations of this statement does the author offer? What examples does she cite to help us understand it? What does this statement have to do with being "fair judges of ourselves" (paragraph 14)?

2. Why does the author mention working mothers in connection with guilt?
3. In what ways can guilt serve as "the great civilizer" (paragraph 22)?

DISCOVERING RHETORICAL STRATEGIES

1. To what extent does the author convince you that guilt can play a valuable role in our lives? What types of appeals does she use to accomplish this purpose? Where does she use these appeals? Be as specific as possible in answering this question.
2. Characterize Goodman's original audience for this essay. Can you make any assumptions about its sexual, ethnic, and economic demographics? Support your answer with specific references to the essay.
3. How would you describe Goodman's tone in this essay? What particular words and phrases help her establish that tone? What effect does this tone have on you as a reader?

IDEAS FOR DISCUSSION/WRITING

Preparing to Write

Write freely about the advantages and disadvantages of guilt: From your experience, what is the principal value of guilt? Has guilt ever helped you accomplish something important or worthwhile? Has it ever hindered you from accomplishing something? Has the feeling of guilt ever been extremely uncomfortable for you? How often do you feel guilty? Why do you think you developed this particular ethical stance? Are you content with your "guilt quotient"?

Choosing a Topic

1. Do you agree or disagree with Goodman's main assertion that guilt can be "the conscience that keeps us civilized" (paragraph 1)? Write an argumentative essay to the same *Redbook* audience Goodman addressed supporting or refuting this proposition.
2. What stages do you go through to complete a writing assignment? Does guilt play any part in your composing process? If so, does it help or hinder your work? Write an essay for your classmates arguing for or against the value of guilt in reference to writing. Use concrete examples to support your argument.
3. Should children be forced to say "I'm sorry"? Does this practice help them develop a conscience? What is the best way to develop an appropriate guilt quotient in children? *Parents* magazine wants to know your opinion on this issue. Write an article for the readers of this magazine focusing on the difference between inducing necessary guilt and emotionally abusing children.

that her readers are familiar with various figures in psychology and with certain popular psychological trends.

3. The tone of Goodman's essay is light, personal, and intimate. The light tone is maintained not only by the humorous title, but by phrases such as "My first reaction was to giggle" (para. 3), "parents who guilt-trip their children across every stage of life" (para. 11), and "envying the guiltless is like envying a house pet" (para. 30). The personal approach and the mood of intimacy are established by the first-person point of view and by phrases such as "I am not always okay and neither are you" (para. 6), "the way we judge ourselves" (para. 13), and "for all of us" (para. 28).

PREWRITING

In preparation for the writing assignments, the Preparing to Write questions ask students to consider both the advantages and disadvantages of guilt before writing an essay on a related topic. See pages 16–23 for suggestions on generating ideas in response to these questions.

ADDITIONAL DISCUSSION/WRITING TOPIC

Since the Vietnam War, many Vietnam veterans have suffered from overwhelming feelings of guilt. In a report to the U.S. Department of Defense, argue for or against the need for the U.S. government to help Vietnam veterans cope with the guilt brought on by that war.

REVISING STRATEGY

The types of appeals you use to persuade your audience make a great deal of difference in the overall effect of your essay. In one of your persuasive essays, underline all of your appeals to logic: Is this material arranged inductively or deductively? Is this order the most effective for your purpose and audience? Notice any weaknesses or inconsistencies in these particular appeals. Then revise your paper, correcting the problems you have identified.

SHELBY STEELE
(1946–   )

■ ■ ■

Affirmative Action: The Price of Preference

Born in Chicago, Shelby Steele earned his B.A. at Coe College in Iowa, his M.A. at Southern Illinois University, and his Ph.D. at the University of Utah. An early succession of articles in *Harper's, The American Scholar,* the *Washington Post, The New Republic,* and the *New York Times Book Review* earned him a National Magazine Award in 1989. One of his essays on race relations was selected for inclusion in *The Best American Essays of 1989.* His most well-known publication, however, is *The Content of Our Character: A New Vision of Race in America,* a controversial bestseller that won the National Book Critics Circle Award in 1991. In it, the author examines his own life as a middle-class African American in a world where both Blacks and Whites have become trapped into seeing "color before character." He argues that social policies designed to lessen racial differences have instead made these diversities much greater and that the posture of "victimization" adopted by many members of his own race has detracted from rather than enhanced the movement toward cultural equality. His advice to students using *The Prose Reader* is concise and helpful: "Use simple, concrete, Anglo-Saxon words; avoid jargon, colloquialisms, and the passive voice. Try to give clarity and immediacy to your work by writing about emotions and events you know from your own experience." For many years a professor of English at San Jose State University in California, Steele is now working on his next book. In his infrequent spare time, he enjoys swimming, jogging, and reading.

Preparing to Read

In the following chapter from *The Content of Our Character,* Steele argues that affirmative action programs, however well intentioned and fairly administered, demoralize and stigmatize Blacks as "inferior" to their White counterparts in society. The net result is a culture of "victimization" that seeks to exploit rather than overcome past racial injustices. As you prepare to read this essay, take a few moments to think about your own views on affirmative action: Ex-

PREREADING

The purpose of this Preparing to Read material is to encourage students to think about their personal views on affirmative action. To help your students focus on their opinions before they respond to the questions here, have them brainstorm aloud about examples of affirmative action familiar to them. Write these examples on the chalkboard or on a transparency as the students discuss them. Then, have them briefly discuss the reasons for our current affirmative action practices. See pages 3–6 for other ways to generate thoughts on these questions.

actly how does this concept work? How effective is it in your community? In your job? In your school? In what ways has affirmative action affected you directly? From your perspective, what are the principal advantages of affirmative action? The disadvantages? How much longer do you think it will be necessary in America?

In a few short years, when my two children will be applying to college, the affirmative action policies by which most universities offer black students some form of preferential treatment will present me with a dilemma. I am a middle-class black, a college professor, far from wealthy, but also well-removed from the kind of deprivation that would qualify my children for the label "disadvantaged." Both of them have endured racial insensitivity from whites. They have been called names, have suffered slights, and have experienced firsthand the peculiar malevolence that racism brings out in people. Yet, they have never experienced racial discrimination, have never been stopped by their race on any path they have chosen to follow. Still, their society now tells them that if they will only designate themselves as black on their college applications, they will likely do better in the college lottery than if they conceal this fact. I think there is something of a Faustian bargain in this.

Of course, many blacks and a considerable number of whites would say that I was sanctimoniously making affirmative action into a test of character. They would say that this small preference is the meagerest recompense for centuries of unrelieved oppression. And to these arguments other very obvious facts must be added. In America, many marginally competent or flatly incompetent whites are hired every day—some because their white skin suits the conscious or unconscious racial preference of their employer. The white children of alumni are often grandfathered into elite universities in what can only be seen as a residual benefit of historic white privilege. Worse, white incompetence is always an individual matter, while for blacks it is often confirmation of ugly stereotypes. The Peter Principle was not conceived with only blacks in mind. Given that unfairness cuts both ways, doesn't it only balance the scales of history that my children now receive a slight preference over whites? Doesn't this repay, in a small way, the systematic denial under which their grandfather lived out his days?

1 **BACKGROUND INFORMATION**

In this essay, Shelby Steele argues that the advantages of affirmative action bring overwhelming disadvantages. Although federal law mandates that minority candidates now get preference in hiring over White applicants with equal qualifications, Steele believes that this preferential treatment "mark[s] whites with an exaggerated superiority just as [it] mark[s] blacks with an exaggerated inferiority" (para. 20). According to Steele, this "implied inferiority" (para. 12) prompts "personal self-doubt" (para. 12) in the Black community and in the long run keeps Blacks out of the competition for high-level executive positions. Steele claims that what we need instead of affirmative action are social policies that provide for the "educational and economic 2 development of disadvantaged people" (para. 27). Steele submits that our current affirmative action program has mistakenly focused on its end result rather than on the means for achieving its goals.

READABILITY LEVEL

16.3

RELATED READINGS

Black Issues

DEFINITIONS

Faustian (para. 1): derived from Dr. Johann Faust, a magician of German legend who enters into a contract with the Devil.
Peter Principle (para. 2): from *The Peter Principle* by L. J. Peter and R. Hull (1986), suggesting that employees in an organization tend to be promoted until they reach their level of incompetence.
pluralism (para. 5): diverse racial, ethnic, religious, or social groups maintaining their traditional cultures within a common civilization.
crucible (para. 6): a container for melting metal ores; in this context, a harsh test or trial.
EEOC (para. 7): the Equal Employment Opportunity Commission.
atavistic (para. 13): relating to atavism, the appearance in an individual of a characteristic found in a remote ancestor but not in nearer ancestors.
prima facie (para. 24): Latin. At face value.
jerry-building (para. 25): creating a flimsy, short-term remedy.

So, in theory, affirmative action certainly has all the moral symmetry that fairness requires—the injustice of historical and even contemporary white advantage is offset with black advantage; preference replaces prejudice, inclusion answers exclusion. It is reformist and corrective, even repentant and redemptive. And I would never sneer at these good intentions. Born in the late forties in Chicago, I started my education (a charitable term in this case) in a segregated school and suffered all the indignities that come to blacks in a segregated society. My father, born in the South, only made it to the third grade before the white man's fields took permanent priority over his formal education. And though he educated himself into an advanced reader with an almost professorial authority, he could only drive a truck for a living and never earned more than ninety dollars a week in his entire life. So yes, it is crucial to my sense of citizenship, to my ability to identify with the spirit and the interests of America, to know that this country, however imperfectly, recognizes its past sins and wishes to correct them. 3

Yet good intentions, because of the opportunity for innocence they offer us, are very seductive and can blind us to the effects they generate when implemented. In our society, affirmative action is, among other things, a testament to white goodwill and to black power, and in the midst of these heavy investments, its effects can be hard to see. But after twenty years of implementation, I think affirmative action has shown itself to be more bad than good and that blacks—whom I will focus on in this essay—now stand to lose more from it than they gain. 4

In talking with affirmative action administrators and with blacks and whites in general, it is clear that supporters of affirmative action focus on its good intentions while detractors emphasize its negative effects. Proponents talk about "diversity" and "pluralism"; opponents speak of "reverse discrimination," the unfairness of quotas and set-asides. It was virtually impossible to find people outside either camp. The closest I came was a white male manager at a large computer company who said, "I think it amounts to reverse discrimination, but I'll put up with a little of that for a little more diversity." I'll live with a little of the effect to gain a little of the intention, he seemed to be saying. But this only makes him a halfhearted supporter of affirmative action. I think many people who don't really like affirmative action support it to one degree or another anyway. 5

I believe they do this because of what happened to white and black Americans in the crucible of the sixties when whites were 6 confronted with their racial guilt and blacks tasted their first real power. In this stormy time white absolution and black power coalesced into virtual mandates for society. Affirmative action became a meeting ground for these mandates in the law, and in the late sixties and early seventies it underwent a remarkable escalation of its mission from simple antidiscrimination enforcement to social engineering by means of quotas, goals, timetables, set-asides, and other forms of preferential treatment.

Legally, this was achieved through a series of executive orders and EEOC guidelines that allowed racial imbalances in the workplace to stand as proof of racial discrimination. Once it could be assumed that discrimination explained racial imbalances, it became easy to justify group remedies to presumed discrimination, rather than the normal case-by-case redress for proven discrimination. Preferential treatment through quotas, goals, and so on is designed to correct imbalances based on the assumption that they always indicate discrimination. This expansion of what constitutes discrimination allowed affirmative action to escalate into the business of social engineering in the name of anti-discrimination, to push society toward statistically proportionate racial representation, without any obligation of proving actual discrimination.

7

What accounted for this shift, I believe, was the white mandate to achieve a new racial innocence and the black mandate to gain power. Even though blacks had made great advances during the sixties without quotas, these mandates, which came to a head in the very late sixties, could no longer be satisfied by anything less than racial preferences. I don't think these mandates in themselves were wrong, since whites clearly needed to do better by blacks and blacks needed more real power in society. But, as they came together in affirmative action, their effect was to distort our understanding of racial discrimination in a way that allowed us to offer the remediation of preference on the basis of mere color rather than actual injury. By making black the color of preference, these mandates have reburdened society with the very marriage of color and preference (in reverse) that we set out to eradicate. The old sin is reaffirmed in a new guise.

8

But the essential problem with this form of affirmative action is the way it leaps over the hard business of developing a formerly oppressed people to the point where they can achieve proportionate representation on their own (given equal opportunity) and goes straight for the proportionate representation. This may satisfy some whites of their innocence and

9

Divide your students into groups of 4 or 5, and have them discuss alternatives to affirmative action. Have them focus on how employers can control the difficult hiring dilemmas affirmative action can create. What are the applicants' rights in these situations? Then, have one person from each group present the group's ideas to the entire class.

some blacks of their power, but it does very little to truly uplift blacks.

A white female affirmative action officer at an Ivy League university told me what many supporters of affirmative action now say: "We're after diversity. We ideally want a student body where racial and ethnic groups are represented according to their proportion in society." When affirmative action escalated into social engineering, diversity became a golden word. It grants whites an egalitarian fairness (innocence) and blacks an entitlement to proportionate representation (power). *Diversity* is a term that applies democratic principles to races and cultures rather than to citizens, despite the fact that there is nothing to indicate that real diversity is the same thing as proportionate representation. Too often the result of this on campuses (for example) has been a democracy of colors rather than of people, an artificial diversity that gives the appearance of an educational parity between black and white students that has not yet been achieved in reality. Here again, racial preferences allow society to leapfrog over the difficult problem of developing blacks to parity with whites and into a cosmetic diversity that covers the blemish of disparity—a full six years after admission, only about 26 percent of black students graduate from college. 10

Racial representation is not the same thing as racial development, yet affirmative action fosters a confusion of these very different needs. Representation can be manufactured; development is always hard-earned. However, it is the music of innocence and power that we hear in affirmative action that causes us to cling to it and to its distracting emphasis on representation. The fact is that after twenty years of racial preferences, the gap between white and black median income is greater than it was in the seventies. None of this is to say that blacks don't need policies that ensure our right to equal opportunity, but what we need more is the development that will let us take advantage of society's efforts to include us. 11

I think that one of the most troubling effects of racial preferences for blacks is a kind of demoralization, or put another way, an enlargement of self-doubt. Under affirmative action the quality that earns us preferential treatment is an implied inferiority. However this inferiority is explained—and it is easily enough explained by the myriad deprivations that grew out of our oppression—it is still inferiority. There are explanations, and then there is the fact. And the fact must be borne by the individual as a condition apart from the explanation, apart even from the fact that 12 others like himself also bear this condition. In integrated situations where blacks must compete with whites who may be better prepared, these explanations may quickly wear thin and expose the individual to racial as well as personal self-doubt.

All of this is compounded by the cultural myth of black inferiority that blacks have always lived with. What this means in practical terms is that when blacks deliver themselves into integrated situations, they encounter a nasty little reflex in whites, a mindless, atavistic reflex that responds to the color black with alarm. Attributions may follow this alarm if the white cares to indulge them, and if they do, they will most likely be negative—one such attribution is intellectual ineptness. I think this reflex and the attributions that may follow it embarrass most whites today; therefore, it is usually quickly repressed. Nevertheless, on an equally atavistic level, the black will be aware of the reflex his color triggers and will feel a stab of horror at seeing himself reflected in this way. He, too, will do a quick repression, but a lifetime of such stabbings is what constitutes his inner realm of racial doubt. 13

The effects of this may be a subject for another essay. The point here is that the implication of inferiority that racial preferences engender in both the white and black mind expands rather than contracts this doubt. Even when the black sees no implication of inferiority in racial preferences, he knows that whites do, so that—consciously or unconsciously—the result is virtually the same. The effect of preferential treatment—the lowering of normal standards to increase black representation—puts blacks at war with an expanded realm of debilitating doubt, so that the doubt itself becomes an unrecognized preoccupation that undermines their ability to perform, especially in integrated situations. On largely white campuses, blacks are five times more likely to drop out than whites. Preferential treatment, no matter how it is justified in the light of day, subjects blacks to a midnight of self-doubt, and so often transforms their advantage into a revolving door. 14

Another liability of affirmative action comes from the fact that it indirectly encourages blacks to exploit their own past victimization as a source of power and privilege. Victimization, like implied inferiority, is what justifies preference, so that to receive the benefits of preferential treatment one must, to some extent, become invested in the view of one's self as a victim. In this way, affirmative action nurtures a victim-focused identity in blacks. The obvious irony here is that we become inadvertently invested in the very condition we are trying to overcome. Racial prefer- 15 ences send us the message that there is more power in our past suffering than our present achievements—none of which could bring us a *preference* over others.

When power itself grows out of suffering, then blacks are en-   16
couraged to expand the boundaries of what qualifies as racial op-pression, a situation that can lead us to paint our victimization in vivid colors, even as we receive the benefits of preference. The same corporations and institutions that give us preference are also seen as our oppressors. At Stanford University minority stu-dents—some of whom enjoy as much as $15,000 a year in finan-cial aid—recently took over the president's office demanding, among other things, more financial aid. The power to be found in victimization, like any power, is intoxicating and can lend itself to the creation of a new class of super-victims who can feel the pea of victimization under twenty mattresses. Preferential treatment rewards us for being underdogs rather than for moving beyond that status—a misplacement of incentives that, along with its deepening of our doubt, is more a yoke than a spur.

But, I think, one of the worst prices that blacks pay for prefer-   17
ence has to do with an illusion. I saw this illusion at work recently in the mother of a middle-class black student who was going off to his first semester of college. "They owe us this, so don't think for a minute that you don't belong there." This is the logic by which many blacks, and some whites, justify affirmative action—it is something "owed," a form of reparation. But this logic over-looks a much harder and less digestible reality, that it is impossible to repay blacks living today for the historic suffering of the race. If all blacks were given a million dollars tomorrow morning it would not amount to a dime on the dollar of three cen-turies of oppression, nor would it obviate the residues of that op-pression that we still carry today. The concept of historic reparation grows out of man's need to impose a degree of justice on the world that simply does not exist. Suffering can be endured and overcome; it cannot be repaid. Blacks cannot be repaid for the injustice done to the race, but we can be corrupted by society's guilty gestures of repayment.

Affirmative action is such a gesture. It tells us that racial pref-   18
erences can do for us what we cannot do for ourselves. The cor-ruption here is in the hidden incentive *not* to do what we believe preferences will do. This is an incentive to be reliant on others just as we are struggling for self-reliance. And it keeps alive the illu-sion that we can find some deliverance in repayment. The hardest thing for any sufferer to accept is that his suffering excuses him

from very little and never has enough currency to restore him. To think otherwise is to prolong the suffering.

Several blacks I spoke with said they were still in favor of af- 19 firmative action because of the "subtle" discrimination blacks were subject to once on the job. One photojournalist said, "They have ways of ignoring you." A black female television producer said, "You can't file a lawsuit when your boss doesn't invite you to the insider meetings without ruining your career. So we still need affirmative action." Others mentioned the infamous "glass ceiling" through which blacks can see the top positions of authority but never reach them. But I don't think racial preferences are a protection against this subtle discrimination; I think they contribute to it.

In any workplace, racial preferences will always create two- 20 tiered populations composed of preferreds and unpreferreds. This division makes automatic a perception of enhanced competence for the unpreferreds and of questionable competence for the preferreds—the former earned his way, even though others were given preference, while the latter made it by color as much as by competence. Racial preferences implicitly mark whites with an exaggerated superiority just as they mark blacks with an exaggerated inferiority. They not only reinforce America's oldest racial myth but, for blacks, they have the effect of stigmatizing the already stigmatized.

I think that much of the "subtle" discrimination that blacks 21 talk about is often (not always) discrimination against the stigma of questionable competence that affirmative action delivers to blacks. In this sense, preferences scapegoat the very people they seek to help. And it may be that at a certain level employers impose a glass ceiling, but this may not be against the race so much as against the race's reputation for having advanced by color as much as by competence. Affirmative action makes a glass ceiling virtually necessary as a protection against the corruptions of preferential treatment. This ceiling is the point at which corporations shift the emphasis from color to competency and stop playing the affirmative action game. Here preference backfires for blacks and becomes a taint that holds them back. Of course, one could argue that this taint, which is, after all, in the minds of whites, becomes nothing more than an excuse to discriminate against blacks. And certainly the result is the same in either case—blacks don't get past the glass ceiling. But this argument does not get around the fact that racial preferences now taint this color with a new theme of suspicion that makes it even more vulnerable to the impulse in

ANSWERS TO QUESTIONS:
UNDERSTANDING DETAILS (p. 460)

1. Steele describes himself as a "middle-class black, a college professor, far from wealthy, but also well-removed from the kind of deprivation that would qualify my children for the label 'disadvantaged'" (para. 1). Steele's children face a "Faustian bargain" (para. 1) over whether they should specify their race on college application forms (and thereby gain an advantage over other applicants) or omit this information at the risk of not being accepted at the school of their choice.

2. Affirmative action, according to Steele, has "all the moral symmetry that fairness requires" (para. 3), "is reformist and corrective" (para. 3), and "is crucial to my sense of citizenship, to my ability to identify with the spirit and the interests of America, to know that this country, however imperfectly, recognizes its past sins and wishes to correct them" (para. 3). Affirmative action is "a testament to white goodwill and to black power . . ." (para. 4).

3. Steele believes the effects of affirmative action are "hard to see" (para. 4). Because "a full six years after admission, only about 26 percent of black students graduate from college" (para. 10), "the gap between white and black median income is greater than it was in the seventies" (para. 11), "racial preferences will always create two-tiered populations composed of preferreds and unpreferreds" (para. 20), and "preferential treatment does not teach skills, or educate, or instill motivation" (para. 23). Steele maintains that affirmative action defeats its purpose and is therefore counterproductive in helping African Americans achieve racial equality.

others to discriminate. In this crucial yet gray area of perceived competence, preferences make whites look better than they are and blacks worse, while doing nothing whatever to stop the very real discrimination that blacks may encounter. I don't wish to justify the glass ceiling here, but only to suggest the very subtle ways that affirmative action revives rather than extinguishes the old rationalizations for racial discrimination.

In education, a revolving door; in employment, a glass ceiling.   22

I believe affirmative action is problematic in our society   23 because it tries to function like a social program. Rather than ask it to ensure equal opportunity we have demanded that it create parity between the races. But preferential treatment does not teach skills, or educate, or instill motivation. It only passes out entitlement by color, a situation that in my profession has created an unrealistically high demand for black professors. The social engineer's assumption is that this high demand will inspire more blacks to earn Ph.D.'s and join the profession. In fact, the number of blacks earning Ph.D.'s has declined in recent years. A Ph.D. must be developed from preschool on. He requires family and community support. He must acquire an entire system of values that enables him to work hard while delaying gratification. There are social programs, I believe, that can (and should) help blacks *develop* in all these areas, but entitlement by color is not a social program; it is a dubious reward for being black.

It now seems clear that the Supreme Court, in a series of recent   24 decisions, is moving away from racial preferences. It has disallowed preferences except in instances of "identified discrimination," eroded the precedent that statistical racial imbalances are *prima facie* evidence of discrimination, and in effect granted white males the right to challenge consent decrees that use preference to achieve racial balances in the workplace. One civil rights leader said, "Night has fallen on civil rights." But I am not so sure. The effect of these decisions is to protect the constitutional rights of everyone rather than take rights away from blacks. What they do take away from blacks is the special entitlement to more rights than others that preferences always grant. Night has fallen on racial preferences, not on the fundamental rights of black Americans. The reason for this shift, I believe, is that the white mandate for absolution from past racial sins has weakened considerably during the eighties. Whites are now less willing to endure unfairness to themselves in order to grant special entitlements to blacks, even when these entitlements are justified in the name of past suffering. Yet the black mandate for more power in society has remained unchanged. And I think part of the anxiety that many blacks feel over these decisions has to do with the loss of black power they may signal. We had won a certain specialness and now we are losing it.

But the power we've lost by these decisions is really only the power that grows out of our victimization—the power to claim special entitlements under the law because of past oppression. This is not a very substantial or reliable power, and it is important that we know this so we can focus more exclusively on the kind of development that will bring enduring power. There is talk now that Congress will pass new legislation to compensate for these new limits on affirmative action. If this happens, I hope that their focus will be on development and anti-discrimination rather than entitlement, on achieving racial parity rather than jerry-building racial diversity.

I would also like to see affirmative action go back to its original purpose of enforcing equal opportunity—a purpose that in itself disallows racial preferences. We cannot be sure that the discriminatory impulse in America has yet been shamed into extinction, and I believe affirmative action can make its greatest contribution by providing a rigorous vigilance in this area. It can guard constitutional rather than racial rights and help institutions evolve standards of merit and selection that are appropriate to the institution's needs yet as free of racial bias as possible (again, with the understanding that racial imbalances are not always an indication of racial bias). One of the most important things affirmative action can do is to define exactly what racial discrimination is and how it might manifest itself within a specific institution. The impulse to discriminate *is* subtle and cannot be ferreted out unless its many guises are made clear to people. Along with this there should be monitoring of institutions and heavy sanctions brought to bear when actual discrimination is found. This is the sort of affirmative action that America owes to blacks and to itself. It goes after the evil of discrimination itself, while preferences only sidestep the evil and grant entitlement to its *presumed* victims.

But if not preferences, then what? I think we need social policies that are committed to two goals: the educational and economic development of disadvantaged people, regardless of race, and the eradication from our society—through close monitoring and severe sanctions—of racial, ethnic, or gender discrimination. Preferences will not deliver us to either of these goals, since they

ANSWERS TO QUESTIONS: ANALYZING MEANING (p. 460)

1. Steele suggests that "diversity" is a political term used by businesses and campuses to describe the representation of racial and ethnic groups in the total population. However, the goal of diversity is not proportional representation, but instead an emphasis on "a democracy of colors" (para. 10). For example, in a business, the office personnel may look like a racially diverse group, but the diversity may be reflected only at lower levels of the company. On a campus, some groups of students may be overrepresented in some areas of study but forgotten in other areas.

2. "Racial representation" (para. 11) occurs when racial groups are equally and adequately represented on the job and in schools; however, this term does not guarantee that a race of people will develop the skills they need to share equal opportunities both at home and at work. Affirmative action fills quotas, but it does not provide the learning, family life, and personal enrichment that allow people to take full advantage of their opportunities in life. Preferences, in fact, send out the erroneous signal that skin color and ethnicity are more important to success than education and hard work.

3. Affirmative action provides for the preferential treatment of African Americans and assumes that, given equal education and qualifications, racial preference is still necessary for Blacks to obtain their goals. This makes Whites look as if they are superior and capable of providing preferential treatment, while it causes Blacks to doubt their own abilities and think they cannot achieve equality without special help. If people know they can reach a goal based principally on their preferred racial status, they may not work as hard and build the self-confidence necessary to compete with other employees.

1. Preferential treatment may bring African Americans into entry-level jobs, but because they are not being hired strictly on their merits, they may find themselves looking through a "glass ceiling" (para. 22) at employees hired solely on merit, who have ascended to more prestigious, higher-paying positions in the same firm. Students who are given collegiate admission based principally on preferred racial status may experience similar difficulties, because preferential treatment cannot guarantee their success in college. These two dilemmas effectively demonstrate the way preferential treatment can provide false and misleading opportunities and in the long run hinder its recipients.

2. Steele uses a predominantly logical appeal to his readers by presenting a well-reasoned argument using several examples and additional evidence to support his conclusions. He bolsters this with an ethical appeal by discussing his personal concerns for his children and for the African-American community as a whole. Beyond this point, student opinions will vary.

3. Steele is writing primarily to a middle-class African-American audience who probably share the same concerns he has, although they may view affirmative action in a more positive light. His readers undoubtedly include educated, professional men and women who are directly or indirectly influenced by affirmative action.

tend to benefit those who are not disadvantaged—middle-class white women and middle-class blacks—and attack one form of discrimination with another. Preferences are inexpensive and carry the glamour of good intentions—change the numbers and the good deed is done. To be against them is to be unkind. But I think the unkindest cut is to bestow on children like my own an undeserved advantage while neglecting the development of those disadvantaged children on the East Side of my city who will likely never be in a position to benefit from a preference. Give my children fairness; give disadvantaged children a better shot at development—better elementary and secondary schools, job training, safer neighborhoods, better financial assistance for college, and so on. Fewer blacks go to college today than ten years ago; more black males of college age are in prison or under the control of the criminal justice system than in college. This despite racial preferences.

The mandates of black power and white absolution out of which preferences emerged were not wrong in themselves. What was wrong was that both races focused more on the goals of these mandates than on the means to the goals. Blacks can have no real power without taking responsibility for their own educational and economic development. Whites can have no racial innocence without earning it by eradicating discrimination and helping the disadvantaged to develop. Because we ignored the means, the goals have not been reached, and the real work remains to be done.

28

UNDERSTANDING DETAILS

1. Why does specifying his children's race on their college applications present a problem for Steele?
2. According to Steele, what is fair about affirmative action?
3. Why does Steele think affirmative action is "more bad than good" (paragraph 4)?

ANALYZING MEANING

1. What does Steele mean when he says "*diversity* is a term that applies democratic principles to races and cultures rather than to citizens" (paragraph 10)?
2. In Steele's opinion, what is the difference between "racial representation" (paragraph 11) and "racial development" (paragraph 11)? Why is affirmative action not closing this gap?

3. How do racial preferences "mark whites with an exaggerated superiority just as they mark blacks with an exaggerated inferiority" (paragraph 20)? What is the relationship in Steele's mind between the "implied inferiority" of affirmative action (paragraph 12) and "personal self-doubt" (paragraph 12) in the African-American community?

DISCOVERING RHETORICAL STRATEGIES

1. In paragraph 22, Steele uses the metaphors of "a revolving door" and "a glass ceiling" to help illustrate the problems of preferential treatment. Explain these two images in as much detail as you can. How effective are they in making Steele's points?
2. What is the dominant type of appeal (see pages 431–432 of the chapter introduction) that Steele uses in this essay? What parts of Steele's argument are most persuasive to you? Why do you think they are persuasive?
3. Who do you think is Steele's intended audience? Describe them in detail.

IDEAS FOR DISCUSSION/WRITING

Preparing to Write

Write freely about your thoughts on affirmative action: In what areas does affirmative action work most effectively? In what areas does it work less well? What are the main social consequences of affirmative action? Are you directly affected by affirmative action in any way? Have you witnessed or experienced any discrimination in hiring? What solutions do you propose to solve the problem of discrimination in the job market? How might these solutions be implemented?

Choosing a Topic

1. In paragraph 16 of this essay, Steele claims that "Preferential treatment rewards us for being underdogs rather than for moving beyond that status." Direct an essay to your classmates in which you agree or disagree with this statement. Be sure to explain your reasoning carefully.
2. In your opinion, how serious is racial or sexual discrimination at your school or at your job? How is it manifested? Who suffers most from this discrimination? In a coherent essay, persuade your friends that discrimination is or is not a serious social evil at your school or your workplace.
3. In an essay written for a group of employers, present a proposal other than affirmative action for controlling discrimination in the workplace. Explain the details of its implementation and its projected long-term effects.

PREWRITING

In preparation for the writing assignments, the Preparing to Write questions ask students to think about the way affirmative action functions in the United States. See pages 16–23 for suggestions on generating ideas in response to these questions.

ADDITIONAL DISCUSSION/WRITING TOPIC

In a coherent argumentative essay, persuade your classmates that affirmative action usually does or does not result in reverse discrimination.

REVISING STRATEGY

The types of appeals you choose in seeking to persuade your audience make a great deal of difference in the overall effect of your essay. In one of your persuasive essays, underline all of your emotional appeals: Have you taken into account both the connotations (associations) and denotations (dictionary definitions) of the words you use in these appeals? Do you use figurative language when appropriate to carry out these appeals? Notice any weaknesses or inconsistencies in these particular appeals. Then revise your paper, correcting the problems you have identified.

PREREADING

The purpose of this Preparing to Read material is to encourage students to solidify their own opinions on the volatile issue of gun control. To help your students focus their thoughts, you might direct an open discussion on the advantages and disadvantages of gun control. Help them see during the discussion that opinions on this topic range from advocating a great deal of government control to wanting a minimum of control. Help them locate Hughes' proposal on this continuum.

BACKGROUND INFORMATION

Hughes' essay presents a compromise position on firearms control that might satisfy both gun owners and gun-control advocates. He works hard to set up a strong ethical appeal, establishing his personal history of gun use and his stand on the National Rifle Association; this background helps to support his logical argument. After presenting his reasons carefully, Hughes recommends that "all fireable guns should be licensed; delays and stringent checks should be built into their purchase, right across the board; and some types, including machine guns and semiautomatic assault weapons, should not be available to the civilian public at all" (para. 10).

READABILITY LEVEL

12.7

RELATED READINGS

Sports and Fitness

Violence

ROBERT HUGHES
(1938–   )

■ ■ ■

The N.R.A. in a Hunter's Sights

Born and educated in Sydney, Australia, Robert Hughes refers to himself as "a journalist who has had the good luck never to be bored by his subject." He has been *Time* magazine's art critic for over twenty years, and he has published such books as *Recent Australian Paintings* (1961), *The Art of Australia* (1966), *The New Generation* (1966), and *Heaven and Hell in Western Art* (1968). His best-known book, *The Shock of the New* (1980), was adapted from his eight-hour PBS television series of the same title. In his preface, he explains that "Art no longer acts on us in the same way that it did on our grandparents. I want to see why." The resulting examination of modern art and its effects on its audience has won much praise from art scholars, who variously described it as "brilliant," "provocative." "brash," "electric," and "elegant." According to *Saturday Review* critic John Canaday, it is "the best book to date on twentieth-century art." In 1987 Hughes published *The Fatal Shore,* a long and fascinating history of the dramatic origins of his native country. This international bestseller, which won several prestigious literary awards for nonfiction, is being made into a movie. Hughes has also written more than twenty television documentaries for Australian television and the BBC, including two 75-minute programs on the artists Caravaggio and Rubens.

Preparing to Read

The following essay, which first appeared in *Time* (April 3, 1989), examines America's constitutional "right" to bear arms and argues strenuously for the licensing of firearms. As you prepare to read Hughes' thoughts on this controversial topic, focus your attention on the subject: Where do you stand on the issue of gun control? Do you favor minimal government control, total control, or a compromise between these positions? How did you arrive at this opinion? What arguments best support your views? Do you own a gun? Does anyone in your family? To what extent does this ownership (or lack thereof) affect your views? Has your opinion on gun control changed over the years? In what ways? What caused the change?

Like George Bush and thousands of other people, I am a
Small White Hunter. Which means that, two or three times a year,
one scrambles into one's brush pants and jacket, pulls on a pair of
snake boots and goes ambling off on a sedate horse with friends
and dogs in pursuit of quail in a pine forest in southern Georgia.
Or spends cold predawn hours in a punt on Long Island Sound,
or a damp blind on a California marsh, waiting for the gray light
to spread and the ducks to come arrowing in.

I have done this at intervals most of my life, ever since I was
eleven years old in Australia and my father first issued me a sin-
gle-shot .22 and two bullets and told me to bring back one rabbit.
I hope to keep doing it as long as I can walk and see.

I don't shoot deer anymore; the idea of large-game trophy
hunting repels me. But I have never thought there was anything
wrong with killing as much small game in one day as I and a few
friends could eat in the evening—no more than that and always
within the limits. On a good day I can break 24 targets out of 25 at
trapshooting, and 22 or so at skeet, which is O.K. for an art critic.

In short, I am supposed—if you believe the advertisements of
the National Rifle Association—to be exactly the kind of person
whose rights the N.R.A. claims to want to protect. Why, then,
have I never joined the N.R.A.? And why do I think of this once
omnipotent though now embattled lobby as the sportsman's embarrassment and not his ally?

The answer, in part, goes back to the famous Second Amendment of the American Constitution, which the N.R.A. keeps bran-
dishing like Holy Writ. "A well-regulated militia, being necessary
to the security of a free State," it reads, "the right of the people to
keep and bear arms shall not be infringed."

The part the N.R.A. quotes is always the second half. The first
half is less convenient because it undermines the lobby's propaganda for universal weaponry.

The Founding Fathers, in their wisdom—and more pointedly,
their experience—distrusted standing armies. They associated
British ones with tyranny and lacked the money and manpower
to create their own. Without a citizens' militia, the Revolution
would have failed. Does the Constitution let you have the second
half of the Second Amendment, the right to keep and bear arms,
without the first part, the intended use of those arms in the exercises and, when necessary, the campaigns of a citizens' militia to
which the gun owner belongs—as in Switzerland today? That is
still very much a subject for legal debate.

The constitutional framers no more had in mind the socially

DEFINITIONS

punt (para. 1): a long, narrow, flat-
bottomed boat with square ends.
blind (para. 1): a concealed place used by
hunters.
Holy Writ (para. 5): a document having
unquestionable religious authority.
Founding Fathers (para. 7): members of the
American Constitutional Convention of
1787, where the original draft of the U.S.
Constitution was written.
MAC-10 (para. 8): a small machine gun.
Saturday Night special (para. 8): any kind
of small, cheap handgun.
AK-47 (para. 8): an automatic assault rifle
whose private use is prohibited in the
United States.
Kalashnikov (para. 9): the manufacturer of
the AK-47 (an automatic assault rifle).
Winchester pump (para. 9): a pump-action
shotgun.
Kevlar (para. 9): a tough, light, synthetic
fiber used to make bulletproof vests.
Uzi (para. 9): a hand-held automatic
weapon whose private use is prohibited in
the United States.

COLLABORATIVE LEARNING:
CLASS ACTIVITY

Have your students discuss the advantages
and disadvantages of gun control by participating in a formal debate on the subject:
The affirmative side would be in favor of
gun control; the negative side, opposed.
The format of a one-on-one debate follows:

Opening statement, affirmative	3 min.
Cross-examination, negative	1 min.
Opening statement, negative	4 min.
Cross-examination, affirmative	1 min.
Affirmative rebuttal	2 min.
Negative rebuttal	3 min.
Affirmative rebuttal	1 min.

Adapt this schedule to your purposes.
Then, have the class vote on the winning
side based on the credibility and quality of
the evidence presented.

Divide your students into groups of 3 or 4, and have them take on the role of your local representative to Congress who has received Hughes' idea in the form of a proposal. After the students discuss the plan and reach a consensus, have each group draft a letter to Hughes explaining their reactions to his suggestions.

ANSWERS TO QUESTIONS:
UNDERSTANDING DETAILS (p. 465)

1. Responses to this question will vary.

2. Hughes is embarrassed by the N.R.A. because it misrepresents the Constitution, because its "rigid ideological belief" system (para. 9) supports the ownership of any type of firearm or weaponry, and because it refuses to see the obvious and catastrophic problems guns are creating in American society. He is especially angered by its use of these principles to "protect" the rights of hunters.

3. Hughes recommends that "all fireable guns should be licensed; delays and stringent checks should be built into their purchase . . . ; and some types . . . should not be available to the civilian public at all" (para. 10).

ANSWERS TO QUESTIONS:
ANALYZING MEANING (p. 465)

1. Hughes calls the N.R.A. paranoid because he believes its fear that the government will try to take away the right to own all types of guns is extreme and unfounded. Beyond this point, student opinions will vary.

2. The N.R.A. serves those who manufacture and import guns by trying to keep any restrictions against the manufacture, sale, and private ownership of guns from being enacted. Because the manufacturers are primarily interested in selling as many guns as possible, the N.R.A.'s support of these rights keeps their businesses successful.

psychotic prospect of every Tom, Dick, and Harriet with a barnful of MAC-10s, Saturday night specials, and AK-47s than, in writing the First Amendment, they had in mind the protection of child-porn video, which did not exist in the 18th century either. Nowhere does the Constitution say the right to bear arms means the right to bear any or all arms. *Which* arms is the real issue. At present, firepower has outstripped the law's power to contain it within rational limits.

Where the N.R.A. has always revealed its nature as a para- 9 noid lobby, a political anachronism, is in its rigid ideological belief that *any* restriction on the private ownership of *any* kind of hand-held gun leads inexorably to *total* abolition of *all* gun ownership—that, if today the U.S. Government takes the Kalashnikov from the hands of the maniac on the school playground, it will be coming for my Winchester pump tomorrow. There is no evidence for this absurd belief, but it remains an article of faith. And it does so because the faith is bad faith: the stand the N.R.A. takes is only nominally on behalf of recreational hunters. The people it really serves are gun manufacturers and gun importers, whose sole interest is to sell as many deadly weapons of as many kinds to as many Americans as possible. The N.R.A. never saw a weapon it didn't love. When American police officers raised their voices against the sale of "cop-killer" bullets—Teflon-coated projectiles whose sole purpose is to penetrate body armor—the N.R.A. mounted a campaign to make people believe this ban would infringe on the rights of deer hunters, as though the woods of America were full of whitetails in Kevlar vests. Now that the pressure is on to restrict public ownership of semiautomatic assault weapons, we hear the same threadbare rhetoric about the rights of hunters. No serious hunter goes after deer with an Uzi or an AK-47; those weapons are not made for picking off an animal in the woods but for blowing people to chopped meat at close-to-medium range, and anyone who needs a banana clip with 30 shells in it to hit a buck should not be hunting at all. These guns have only two uses: you can take them down to the local range and spend a lot of money blasting off 500 rounds an afternoon at silhouette targets of the Ayatollah, or you can use them to off your rivals and create lots of police widows. It depends on what kind of guy you are. But the N.R.A. doesn't care—underneath its dumb incantatory slogans ("Guns don't kill people; people kill people"), it is defending both guys. It helps ensure that cops are outgunned right across America. It preaches hunters' rights in order to defend the distribution of weapons in what is, in effect, a drug-based civil war.

But we who love hunting have much more to fear from the backlash of public opinion caused by the N.R.A.'s pigheadedness than we do from the Government. Sensible hunters see the need to follow the example of other civilized countries. All fireable guns should be licensed; delays and stringent checks should be built into their purchase, right across the board; and some types, including machine guns and semiautomatic assault weapons, should not be available to the civilian public at all. It is time, in this respect, that America enter the 20th century, since it is only a few years away from the 21st.

UNDERSTANDING DETAILS

1. Characterize in your own words the author's attitude toward the use of firearms.
2. Why does Hughes find the N.R.A. an embarrassment to gun enthusiasts?
3. What is Hughes' recommended compromise concerning gun legislation?

ANALYZING MEANING

1. Why does Hughes call the N.R.A. "paranoid" (paragraph 9)? Do you agree or disagree with him?
2. In what ways does the N.R.A. serve the interests of gun manufacturers and importers?
3. According to the author, how does the N.R.A. misuse the Second Amendment of the U.S. Constitution? Do you agree with Hughes' analysis of this section of the Constitution?

DISCOVERING RHETORICAL STRATEGIES

1. Explain the title of this essay. What exactly is the author referring to?
2. Is the author's reasoning primarily inductive or deductive? Give one example from the essay to support your answer. Why do you think Hughes relies so heavily on an appeal to logic in this essay?
3. The author occasionally uses emotional and ethical appeals to support his logical argument. When does he invoke our emotions in this essay? Our sense of ethics? What other rhetorical modes does he use to further his argument?

3. The N.R.A. abuses the Second Amendment because it quotes only the section of the amendment that supports its view. The phrase "'A well-regulated militia, being necessary to the security of a free State'" (para. 5) does not fit the argument or needs of the N.R.A. and hence is ignored by the organization. Responses to the second part of this question will vary.

**ANSWERS TO QUESTIONS:
DISCOVERING RHETORICAL
STRATEGIES (p. 465)**

1. Hughes is a hunter, and, in this essay, his prey is the N.R.A. He systematically "shoots down" all of its arguments while presenting an alternative view on behalf of other hunters.
2. Hughes asks if the N.R.A. is helping or hindering the hunter. He answers this question by inductively presenting reasons and examples that could only lead his readers to conclude that the N.R.A. is indeed a hindrance to the hunter. Responses to the second part of this question will vary.
3. Hughes involves the reader emotionally when he refers to widows, barns full of guns, child pornography, deer in bullet-proof vests, and the "drug-based civil war" (para. 9). He uses an ethical appeal when he compares his love of hunting to that of George Bush, when he quotes the Constitution, and when he states "I don't shoot deer anymore; the idea of large-game trophy hunting repels me" (para. 3).

Besides argument/persuasion, Hughes uses narration, especially in his boyhood hunting story; example in his discussion of the Founding Fathers; division/classification in his description of the two types of uses for some N.R.A.-approved guns; and definition in his discussion interpreting the N.R.A.'s position.

In preparation for the writing assignments, the Preparing to Write questions ask students to firm up their opinions on gun control before writing an essay on a related topic. See pages 16–23 for suggestions on generating ideas in response to these questions.

ADDITIONAL DISCUSSION/WRITING TOPIC

What other goods and services in America should the government regulate? Alcohol? Tobacco? Drugs? Prostitution? Noise pollution? Junk food? Pick one American product (other than firearms), and write an essay arguing that the government should have either more or less control over its sale and use than it currently has.

REVISING STRATEGY

The types of appeals you choose in trying to persuade your audience make a great deal of difference in the overall effect of your essay. In one of your persuasive essays, underline all your ethical appeals: Have you created the appropriate tone with these appeals? Is it suitable for achieving your purpose and reaching your particular audience? Have you chosen relevant, effective examples to support your principal assertion? Notice any weaknesses or inconsistencies in these particular appeals. Then revise your paper, correcting the problems you have identified.

IDEAS FOR DISCUSSION/WRITING

Preparing to Write

Write freely about your views on gun control: What are the main issues involved in the question of gun control? Where do you stand on these issues? What role does the Constitution play in your reasoning? Do you think different rules should apply to different types of guns, such as handguns, machine guns, and semiautomatic weapons? Do you own a gun? Should everyone be allowed to own and carry a gun for self-defense? Do you know people who own guns? What are their opinions on gun control? Should there be any limits on gun ownership?

Choosing a Topic

1. Your local newspaper is soliciting community opinions on gun control. The editors of the paper want to know your stand on the issue and the reasons behind your position. In a well-organized essay, explain your thoughts on this controversial issue.
2. In a letter to the editor of your local newspaper, play the opposing side, and take issue with one of the points you made in your response to topic #1.
3. In the last paragraph of his essay, Hughes proposes a compromise plan on the issue of gun control. What do you think of this solution? Respond to Hughes' ideas in an essay written for the readers of *Time* magazine. Be sure to address all three parts of Hughes' proposal.

BARBARA EHRENREICH
(1941–   )

■ ■ ■

The Warrior Culture

QUOTATION ON WRITING

"It is only by working, by writing, by practicing the art long and regularly that a writer develops his ear, i.e., that sense which eventually enables a writer to hear where the power of the word lies and, ultimately, his own voice."

John Fairfax and John Moat

Barbara Ehrenreich is a respected author, lecturer, and social commentator with opinions on a wide range of topics. After earning a B.A. from Reed College in chemistry and physics and a Ph.D. from Rockefeller University in cell biology, she turned almost immediately to freelance writing, producing a succession of books and pamphlets on a dazzling array of subjects. Early publications examined student uprisings, health care in America, nurses and midwives, poverty, welfare, economic justice for women, and the sexual politics of disease. Her most recent books include *The Hearts of Men*: *American Dreams and the Flight from Commitment* (1983), *Fear of Falling: The Inner Life of the Middle Class* (1989), and *The Worst Years of Our Lives: Irreverent Notes from a Decade of Greed* (1990)—an indictment of the 1980s that has been described by the *New York Times* as "elegant, trenchant, savagely angry, morally outraged, and outrageously funny." Ehrenreich is also well known as a frequent guest on television and radio programs, including "The Today Show," "Good Morning America," "Nightline," "Crossfire," and "The Phil Donahue Show." Her many articles and reviews have appeared in the *New York Times Magazine, Esquire,* the *Atlantic Monthly, The New Republic, Vogue, Harper's,* and the *Wall Street Journal.* She has been an essayist for *Time* since 1990. Ehrenreich, whose favorite hobby is "voracious reading," lives in Syosset, New York.

Preparing to Read

The following essay, which was first published in *Time* (October 15, 1990), examines the extent to which American culture defines itself through the ritual of war. Before you read the essay, think about your perceptions of war: What associations do you have with war? What is the source of these associations? Do you see any warrior characteristics in American society? How does a nation respond to peace? To war? What accounts for any differences you perceive in these responses? How have different presidents and their administrations affected America's sense of war and peace? To what extent do the media influence your opinions about war and peace?

PREREADING

The purpose of this Preparing to Read material is to encourage students to think about the role of war and peace in America's history and culture. To help your students focus on this topic, have them discuss specific symbols of war and peace in America. Which are most predominant? Which have associations that are most exciting? Most appealing? See pages 3–6 for other ways to generate thoughts on these questions.

BACKGROUND INFORMATION

In this essay, Barbara Ehrenreich suggests that the United States acts "like a primitive warrior culture" (para. 4). She goes on to argue that this type of behavior has a tendency to be anachronistic in "a world that pines for peace" (para. 10). Her purpose here is simply to get us to see these qualities in American society and to consider their impact in relation to the rest of the world.

READABILITY LEVEL

13.9

RELATED READINGS

Violence

Masai (para. 1): a southeast African tribe located principally in Kenya and Tanzania.

Solomon Islands (para. 1): a group of islands in the southwest Pacific, east of New Guinea.

Aztec (para. 1): a Mexican people known for their advanced civilization and cities before their conquest by Hernando Cortés in 1519.

Daniel Patrick Moynihan (1927–   ) (para. 4): a member of the U.S. Senate from New York since 1977.

invasion of Panama (para. 5): an invasion by the United States in 1989 to suppress a coup by Communist guerrillas.

Dianne Feinstein (1933–   ) (para. 6): the Democratic mayor of San Francisco from 1979–1988; defeated by Republican Pete Wilson in the 1990 California gubernatorial election.

Berlin Wall (para. 7): a wall that divided East and West Berlin; torn down in December 1989.

bandolier (para. 8): a belt designed to carry bullets; worn over the shoulder and across the chest.

Operation Desert Shield (para. 10): the name given to the presence of the Allied military in Saudi Arabia and the Persian Gulf during the Middle East crisis; changed to Operation Desert Storm after the United States and its allies invaded Iraq.

imperialism (para. 11): an empire or a system of government having control over other countries or governments.

internationalism (para. 11): the principle of international cooperation for the good of all nations involved.

COLLABORATIVE LEARNING: CLASS ACTIVITY

Have your entire class do a group cluster for the word "war." As they call out free associations, put their ideas in a cluster on the chalkboard or on a transparency. (See pp. 19 and 20 for more information on clustering.) This activity should last about 3 to 5 minutes.

In what we like to think of as "primitive" warrior cultures, the passage to manhood requires the blooding of a spear, the taking of a scalp or head. Among the Masai of eastern Africa, the North American Plains Indians, and dozens of other pretechnological peoples, a man could not marry until he had demonstrated his capacity to kill in battle. Leadership too in a warrior culture is typically contingent on military prowess and wrapped in the mystique of death. In the Solomon Islands a chief's importance could be reckoned by the number of skulls posted around his door, and it was the duty of the Aztec kings to nourish the gods with the hearts of human captives.

All warrior peoples have fought for the same high-sounding reasons: honor, glory, or revenge. The nature of their real and perhaps not conscious motivations is a subject of much debate. Some anthropologists postulate a murderous instinct, almost unique among living species, in human males. Others discern a materialistic motive behind every fray: a need for slaves, grazing land, or even human flesh to eat. Still others point to the similarities between war and other male pastimes—the hunt and outdoor sports—and suggest that it is boredom, ultimately, that stirs men to fight.

But in a warrior culture it hardly matters which motive is most basic. Aggressive behavior is rewarded whether or not it is innate to the human psyche. Shortages of resources are habitually taken as occasions for armed offensives, rather than for hard thought and innovation. And war, to a warrior people, is of course the highest adventure, the surest antidote to malaise, the endlessly repeated theme of legend, song, religious myth and personal quest for meaning. It is how men die and what they find to live for.

"You must understand that Americans are a warrior nation," Senator Daniel Patrick Moynihan told a group of Arab leaders in early September, one month into the Middle East crisis. He said this proudly, and he may, without thinking through the ugly implications, have told the truth. In many ways, in outlook and behavior, the U.S. has begun to act like a primitive warrior culture.

We seem to believe that leadership is expressed, in no small part, by a willingness to cause the deaths of others. After the U.S. invasion of Panama, President Bush exulted that no one could call him "timid"; he was at last a "macho man." The press, in even more primal language, hailed him for succeeding in an "initiation rite" by demonstrating his "willingness to shed blood."

For lesser offices too we apply the standards of a warrior culture. Female candidates are routinely advised to overcome the handicap of their gender by talking "tough." Thus, for example, Dianne Feinstein has embraced capital punishment, while Colorado senatorial candidate Josie Heath has found it necessary to announce that although she is the mother of an 18-year-old son, she is prepared to vote for war. Male candidates in some of the fall contests are finding their military records under scrutiny. No one expects them, as elected officials in a civilian government, to pick up a spear or a sling and fight. But they must state, at least, their willingness to have another human killed.

More tellingly, we are unnerved by peace and seem to find it 7 boring. When the cold war ended, we found no reason to celebrate. Instead we heated up the "war on drugs." What should have been a public-health campaign, focused on the persistent shame of poverty, became a new occasion for martial rhetoric and muscle flexing. Months later, when the Berlin Wall fell and communism collapsed throughout Europe, we Americans did not dance in the streets. What we did, according to the networks, was change the channel to avoid the news. Nonviolent revolutions do not uplift us, and the loss of mortal enemies only seems to leave us empty and bereft.

Our collective fantasies center on mayhem, cruelty, and vio- 8 lent death. Loving images of the human body—especially of bodies seeking pleasure or expressing love—inspire us with the urge to censor. Our preference is for warrior themes: the lone fighting man, bandoliers across his naked chest, mowing down lesser men in gusts of automatic-weapon fire. Only a real war seems to revive our interest in real events. With the Iraqi crisis, the networks report, ratings for news shows rose again—even higher than they were for Panama.

And as in any primitive warrior culture, our warrior élite 9 takes pride of place. Social crises multiply numbingly—homelessness, illiteracy, epidemic disease—and our leaders tell us solemnly that nothing can be done. There is no money. We are poor, not rich, a debtor nation. Meanwhile, nearly a third of the federal budget flows, even in moments of peace, to the warriors and their weaponmakers. When those priorities are questioned, some new "crisis" dutifully arises to serve as another occasion for armed and often unilateral intervention.

Now, with Operation Desert Shield, our leaders are reduced 10 to begging foreign powers for the means to support our warrior class. It does not seem to occur to us that the other great northern powers—Japan, Germany, the Soviet Union—might not have

3. In a time when many countries are solving political, social, and economic conflicts that date back to at least World War I, America should be encouraging world peace rather than becoming a force preventing it. America's warrior culture is ineffective both financially and politically and will eventually cause many more problems than it solves.

ANSWERS TO QUESTIONS:
DISCOVERING RHETORICAL
STRATEGIES (p. 470)

1. Ehrenreich obviously does not support the emphasis on military prowess in America. She questions money spent on the military (para. 9), criticizes the censorship of love but not of violence (para. 8), and cites the ironic case of the mother who would vote for war despite her eighteen-year-old son's eligibility for the draft. In addition, the very words she uses to describe America's warrior culture are negative and help express "the ugly implications" promoted by this part of America's culture (para. 4).

2. Ehrenreich uses example in her discussion of the warrior culture when she presents the tribal manhood rituals of the Masai, North American Plains Indians, and chiefs of the Solomon Islands (para. 1) and when she discusses the many political figures who have benefited from America's pro-military point of view (para. 6). She uses cause/effect when she examines the causes that stir "men to fight" (para. 2). She uses comparison/contrast when she reflects on the differences in Americans' reactions to peace versus war and to violence versus love in what they view and read (paras. 7, 8). Finally, in order to persuade her audience that Americans live in a "warrior culture," she defines this term throughout her essay to support her argument.

3. Ehrenreich is writing to a middle- to upper-class, politically conscious, educated audience. She includes many facts that would challenge the beliefs of a pro-military reader, while explaining her own point of view. The "we" in her essay invites the general American public to explore "our" culture for its fascination with war.

found the stakes so high or the crisis quite so threatening. It has not penetrated our imagination that in a world where the powerful, industrialized nation-states are at last at peace, there might be other ways to face down a pint-size Third World warrior state than with massive force of arms. Nor have we begun to see what an anachronism we are in danger of becoming: a warrior nation in a world that pines for peace, a high-tech state with the values of a warrior band.

A leftist might blame "imperialism"; a right-winger would call our problem "internationalism." But an anthropologist, taking the long view, might say this is just what warriors do. Intoxicated by their own drumbeats and war songs, fascinated by the glint of steel and the prospect of blood, they will go forth, time and again, to war.   11

UNDERSTANDING DETAILS

1. According to Ehrenreich, what are the main reasons people fight with each other?
2. What evidence does the author cite to prove that America is a warrior culture?
3. How is aggressive behavior rewarded in American culture?

ANALYZING MEANING

1. Do you think America is "'a warrior nation'" (paragraph 4), as Senator Moynihan remarked?
2. To what extent do you think America is "unnerved by peace" (paragraph 7) and revived by war (paragraph 8)? Explain your answer.
3. In what ways might America's warrior society become "an anachronism" (paragraph 10)?

DISCOVERING RHETORICAL STRATEGIES

1. Ehrenreich's opinions on her topic seep through her prose at a number of different points. What is her own attitude toward war? Toward America as a warrior nation? What specific passages betray her personal opinions toward the topic?
2. Which rhetorical modes does Ehrenreich principally use to support her argument? How effective are these modes? Give examples of each in your answer.
3. Who do you think is Ehrenreich's intended audience? Describe them in detail.

IDEAS FOR DISCUSSION/WRITING

Preparing to Write

Write freely about your feelings toward war and peace: Why do you think Americans were more fascinated with the Iraqi crisis on TV than with the fall of the Berlin Wall? What is so intriguing about war? Is peace as interesting? Why or why not? What features characterize America as a warrior nation? As a peaceful nation? How important to America's self-concept is its military power? How would this affect the national psyche?

Choosing a Topic

1. As a movie reviewer for a national magazine, you have been commissioned to evaluate the main character in a "warrior" movie of your choice. What warrior characteristics does this person embody? In what ways does he or she represent the larger character of American society?
2. In an essay written for *Time* magazine, you have been asked to respond directly to Ehrenreich's article. Do you think America is fundamentally a warrior culture or not? Give specific examples to support your argument.
3. Research and describe a primitive culture by focusing on its views of war. Explain how these views are expressed in its heroes, heroines, myths, dress, rituals, entertainment, and other social customs. Give as many examples as possible to support your interpretation of this culture.

PREWRITING

In preparation for the writing assignments, the Preparing to Write questions ask students to identify and confront their feelings on war and peace before writing an essay on a related topic. See pages 16–23 for suggestions on generating ideas in response to these questions.

ADDITIONAL DISCUSSION/WRITING TOPIC

The Persian Gulf War brought out many interesting traits of American culture and America's fundamental nature as a country. Write an essay for your classmates describing these basic traits and arguing for or against the country's decision to go to war in the Gulf.

REVISING STRATEGY

The final thoughts you leave your reader with are as important as those at the beginning of your essay. In your concluding paragraph, your reader should know you are closing your argument. In one of your persuasive essays, put a square around your concluding paragraph: Does this paragraph restate your original assertion in slightly different terms? Does your conclusion offer some constructive recommendations about the problem you have been discussing? Does this section of your paper make one final attempt to move your audience to accept or act upon the viewpoint you present? Finally, does it clearly bring your argument to a close? Mark any problems that you notice in your conclusion. Then revise it so that it brings your essay to an effective close.

OPPOSING VIEWPOINTS
Drug Testing

The following two essays argue respectively for and against drug testing on the job. The first is a compilation of two articles written by Courtland Milloy and Jesse Philips. Milloy is a popular and respected columnist on the metropolitan news staff of the *Washington Post.* After graduating from Southern Illinois University in 1973, he worked for the *Miami Herald,* covering courts and police in Miami and Fort Lauderdale. In 1975 he joined the staff of the *Post* to report on crime and the courts; in 1983 he began his twice-weekly column, which covers a wide range of issues relating to life in Washington, D.C. Philips is founder and chair emeritus of Philips Industries (recently renamed Tomkins Industries), a Fortune 500 company. He earned his B.A. from Oberlin College and his M.B.A. from Harvard University's Graduate School of Business Administration. A pioneer in the development of a national model antidrug program for industry, Philips is a member of the White House Conference for a Drug Free America. Still active in skiing and sailing, he recently donated his yacht *Charisma* to the Naval Academy.

The essay arguing against drug testing was written by the editorial staff of *The New Republic,* a liberal magazine headquartered in Washington, D.C., with a circulation of approximately 100,000 readers. Founded in 1914, the journal gives special attention to politics and public policy, but also features such topics as economics, law, foreign policy, media, films, music, and books. In 1987, senior editor Charles Krauthammer was awarded a Pulitzer Prize for distinguished commentary.

Preparing to Read

Milloy's article in favor of drug testing was originally published in the *Washington Post* (January 6, 1987); Philips' article appeared first in the *Wall Street Journal* (November 17, 1986). *The New Republic* editorial against drug testing was printed as "The Yellow Peril" in its March 31, 1986, issue. Before you begin to read these essays, think about drug testing and its consequences in American society: How widespread do you think drug use is in the workplace? How can employers monitor the use of drugs by their employees? Under what conditions, if any, do you think drug testing is justified? Do you believe drug testing is constitutional? How could testing help the business world? How might it help or hurt society as a whole?

PREREADING

The purpose of this Preparing to Read material is to encourage students to think about drug testing and its consequences in American society. To help your students focus their attention on drug testing before they respond to the questions here, provide them with some statistics on drug traffic in the United States: In the Midwest, for example, authorities estimate that small-time lab operations will produce 25 tons of crack cocaine in the next year. Twelve kilos (approximately twenty-six pounds) of powdered crack sells for $1 million on the street. Typical users are evenly distributed across cultures, ages, and social status; they spend up to $150 for a 1/8-ounce "bag" at a time, which provides several long-term "highs." The statistics on cocaine-related deaths in the United States follow:

1984—470 deaths

1986—930 deaths

1988—1,582 deaths

1990—2,483 deaths.

Discuss this information openly as a class. See pages 3–6 for other ways to generate thoughts on this subject.

COURTLAND MILLOY
(1952–   )
JESSE PHILIPS
(1914–   )

■ ■ ■

Drug Testing Does Not Violate Workers' Rights

I

A person I know said he had smoked marijuana for more than 10 years when he heard that his employer, the Air Force Reserves, was about to start a drug testing program. Until then, he thought he was hooked on the stuff, but the prospects of losing his job made him stop—cold turkey. This is the kind of testimonial we'll probably be hearing a lot about as the controversy over drug testing in the workplace comes to a head in courts across the country. Already, there is a dramatic reduction in drug use among college athletes who are subject to testing, and the same appears to be true among military personnel.

Why, then, are so many people opposed to drug testing?

In a case involving the U.S. Customs Service, employees contend that testing is a violation of their civil rights. A federal court has ruled in their favor, saying that probable cause for suspicion of drug use must be shown before a person can be ordered to submit to a test.

Under ordinary circumstances, if drugs were not undermining the fabric of this country, corrupting law enforcement and politicians alike, this would be an acceptable excuse. But for U.S. Customs Service employees, of all people, to refuse such tests does little to instill confidence in a group that is critical to our effort to stop the flow of drugs into this country.

Our Last Defense

I am obviously no lawyer, and my civil liberties card will no doubt be revoked, but all one needs to do is walk the streets of this

BACKGROUND INFORMATION

The first of these two pro/con essays on drug testing, by Courtland Milloy and Jesse Philips, argues that drastic and immediate action must be taken to halt the epidemic of drug abuse in America. As one step in the process, the authors assert that an antidrug policy consisting of pre-hiring tests, selective on-the-job testing, and rehabilitation programs should be implemented by all American businesses.

READABILITY LEVEL

10.3

RELATED READINGS

Addiction

Marie Winn, "Television Addiction"   370
Michael Dorris, "The Broken Cord"   400
Alice Walker, "My Daughter Smokes"   419
The New Republic, "Drug Testing Violates
   Workers' Rights"   472

DEFINITIONS

PCP (para. 11): phencyclidine hydrochloride; a powerful psychedelic drug that can cause mental disorders or death.
ACLU (para. 13): the American Civil Liberties Union.

Have your class discuss the advantages and disadvantages of drug testing in general. Help them focus their attention on the employers who are trying to run their businesses as efficiently and effectively as possible.

country—from Wall Street to the back streets—to know that drastic action is called for in the war on drugs, and that drug testing may well be our last line of defense.

6   Although we hear about the availability of drugs in our community, I believe people would be outraged if they knew how many school-aged children were starting out on what may well become a lifelong dependency on drugs. There is only one way to reach them. It is not telling them to "say no to drugs." It is to test them, and the deterrent effect alone would be worth the fuss.

7   Before this day is over, more than 1,000 people will dial a toll-free cocaine hot line. Most of them will be relatively well-off people, half of them women. When people pick up a phone in an effort to save their own life, you know they have a serious problem. But the greater problem is that more than 20 million people use illegal drugs regularly, and instead of calling for help they are driving cars, flying airplanes, sailing boats and operating all manner of hazardous equipment.

8   There is obviously only one way to reach them, and testing—for all its faults and imprecision—is the only way. Indeed the necessary technical improvements and testing methods can be made.

9   What must be faced here is that we are dealing with a spoiled baby boom generation that is having serious problems coping with the pain of growing up. There is no other explanation for America to be in the midst of a drug epidemic unlike anywhere else in the world. These people need help, even though they don't know how to ask for it—in fact, would not ask for it anymore than they would have asked for a dose of castor oil as children.

10   Despite the ravaging effects of drug use today, the situation will likely get worse in the near future.

11   The case of the naval laboratory chemist who was caught mixing up a batch of synthetic heroin 1,000 times more potent than pure China white is a harbinger of what is being cooked up in the drug world's next assault on our sensibilities. There is now synthetic cocaine more powerful than anything that has been on the market to date, and more PCP than ever with recipes so simple that kids can cook it up at home.

12   There are already too many addicts in our society, with thousands—perhaps millions—more in the making. As robbers, burglars, murderers and generally just sick people on the loose, they are much more likely to infringe on our constitutional rights than drug testing.

II

Attorney General Edwin Meese III spoke out on the responsibility of management to curb drug abuse in the workplace. His message was obscured by an outcry against what ACLU Director Ira Glasser referred to as "a totalitarian kind of response which will injure tens of millions of innocent people in an attempt to find the few who are using drugs and alcohol."

While the theorists contemplate the ethics and legality of management efforts in this regard, real managers must cope with a problem that, according to Mr. Meese's figures, costs employers $7,000 for each drug-abusing employee. Responsible managers recognize that a relatively drug-free, dignified workplace is not the responsibility of government; the buck stops at management's desk. Nor is the bottom line of drug-abuse prevention a question of morals or social responsibility or increased productivity or reduced absenteeism. It's merely a question of good old-fashioned business management.

Concern About Drug Abuse

And as I found out after writing a letter of inquiry to each of our workers at their home address, managers are not the only ones concerned with drug abuse in the workplace. American workers may gripe or be indifferent to corporate goals, but they are generally loyal, honest, caring, hard-working individuals. They very much resent having workers around them who are using drugs, who are unreliable and who are not carrying their own load.

To quote some workers' letters: "I believe it is unfair that a person using drugs which destroy mind and body should receive the same rewards in pay and benefits I do." Another wrote, "As a single parent I have enough to worry about just putting food on my table and clothes on our backs, without worrying about drugs and alcohol." And, "With all the glass, metal and machinery in here, everyone needs to be alert and careful at all times to keep from getting hurt themselves or hurting someone else. I'll be glad to support the drug program anyway I can."

I believe almost every company, large and small, has a drug-abuse problem. Philips Industries has 7,500 employees located in over 40 plants in 23 states. These are mostly small plants in rural or outlying communities. The manager of one plant wrote me that since he had a mature work force located in a rural area, he did not have a drug problem. But the workers in that same plant

13

14

15

16

17

COLLABORATIVE LEARNING: SMALL GROUP ACTIVITY

Divide your class into groups of 4 or 5, and have them discuss alternatives to or variations on drug testing. Have them focus on how employers can control the debilitating effects that drugs cause in the workplace. What are the workers' rights in these situations? Then, have one person from each group present the group's ideas to the entire class.

wrote quite the contrary: They had an acute problem.

An Acute Problem

Yet I am not ready to fault the plant manager. How was he to   18
know? He had no experience with people using or selling drugs.
He could readily spot drunken behavior. Drugs, however, are a
different story. The physical effects of drug abuse are not usually
as readily manifest or observable. That's why they are so insidi-
ous. In many cases we are not aware of drug use until something
untoward happens.

Thus, we have begun a crash program for our managers,   19
alerting them to warning signals indicating drug abuse—a
marked increase in errors or accidents by the worker, excessive
absenteeism, excessive confrontations with other workers, etc.
And we are alerting our managers that once they spot these
warning signals, they must avoid rash firings. This is not a witch
hunt. We are trying to help our workers and our company by
helping people to become productive again.

Nor can we expect Personnel to take the full load of responsi-   20
bility. It is powerless to act unless it has a clearly defined policy
and program. One personnel manager in a plant close to the Mexican border reported that in view of his turnover, he was not able
to find drug-free, qualified personnel or to be as selective as he
would like. And this problem is not limited to areas normally associated with drug use. In one of our plants in the Farm Belt, 71%
of those applying for a second shift failed a drug-screening test.

The Importance of Testing

The point is that we will probably never completely eliminate   21
drugs from the workplace. However, once the word gets around a
community that your company insists on drug testing for new
applicants, drug abusers are likely to think twice before applying.
For those who haven't heard, we have posted large notices in our
application areas alerting job-seekers that we are committed to
ending drug abuse and that drug testing will be part of the application procedure. Just this small effort will turn away a number
of drug abusers who could have ended up costing us too much
money.

A well-defined anti-drug-abuse policy might encompass the   22
following three points: (1) pre-hiring tests; (2) selective testing,
where abnormal or erratic behavior suggests it's necessary; (3) a
rehabilitative program. The program should be devised to protect

the rights of privacy and the dignity of the vast majority of our law-abiding workers. I find nothing wrong with properly administered urine tests. Our top 27 executives, including myself, have been tested. But again, the point is not to fire everyone with a trace of drugs in his body. The idea is to help in spotting drug abusers and offering them help before they destroy themselves and hurt the company.

The solution to our drug problem calls for a hands-on approach. It cannot be approached as a line budget item with cost-benefit analysis. When we began to consider our options, a division president pointed out to me that pre-hiring tests were not in his budget. Based on his turnover, it would probably cost $60,000 and he did not see how he could offset that expense. But the intangible human costs cannot be equated in dollars.   23

Getting the Job Done

Business and industry do not need money to clean up our work environment—we have the funds. What we do need to get the job done is leadership. Unfortunately, all too many executives are sitting on their hands waiting for the signal to get started. True, a goodly number of companies have started pre-hiring tests—probably a good first step. Yet, the vast majority are waiting for guidelines as to what is expected and how far they should go.   24

Here is where we need President Reagan. We need the president to use his great leadership talents to form an alliance of business and industry to clean up the workplace. Given the proper leadership support by the president, the private sector can clean up its own house—probably without any government funding.   25

THE NEW REPUBLIC

■ ■ ■

Drug Testing Violates Workers' Rights

BACKGROUND INFORMATION

In the second essay on drug testing, the editors of *The New Republic* magazine argue that such testing constitutes a gross invasion of privacy and probably also violates the "unreasonable searches and seizures" clause of the Fourth Amendment to the U.S. Constitution. What will corporate bureaucrats think of next? they ask. "Strip searches for weapons? Polygraphs for potential office thieves? Blood tests for AIDS?" (para. 14). Such attempts at social control, they say, are abhorrent in a democratic society.

READABILITY LEVEL

14.8

RELATED READINGS

Addiction

The President's Commission on Organized Crime spent 32 months and nearly five million dollars preparing its report on drug abuse and trafficking. There's something for everyone in the panel's 1,000-page study, but here's the gist of its recommendation: Since law-enforcement techniques have failed to curtail the supply of illegal narcotics, we should try to diminish the demand. In pursuit of that goal, the commission argues, the president should direct all federal agencies to implement "suitable drug testing programs." State and local governments and the private sector should follow suit, and federal contracts should be denied to firms that don't test for drugs. In other words, practically everyone should have his or her urine tested. Laboratory owners and manufacturers of small plastic cups should be delighted with the scheme. 1

Several members of the panel have dissented publicly, saying that the controversial suggestion was added without their knowledge. U.S. Court of Appeals Judge Irving R. Kaufman, who chairs the commission and supports the idea, has refused to answer their objections. But the report has been greeted with signs of approbation as well. Attorney General Edwin Meese III caused some confusion in the press when he stopped short of endorsing the plan (saying it might be too expensive), yet argued that drug testing doesn't violate anyone's constitutional rights. Representative Clay Shaw of Florida embraced the idea unreservedly. He volunteered himself and his staff for urine tests as soon as they can be arranged. 2

Too Close for Comfort

In fact, we are already much closer to universal urine testing than most people realize. One-quarter of all Fortune 500 companies, including IBM and General Motors, now administer urinalysis tests to applicants or current employees. Another 20 percent 3 are planning to institute programs. . . . According to a *USA Today* survey cited in the Kaufman Commission report, two-thirds of those firms won't hire anyone who fails a test. Of those testing current employees, 25 percent fire those who fail, while 64 percent require treatment, strongly recommend it, or take disciplinary action. Since a urine sample is usually taken as part of a medical examination, applicants and employees often don't know that they are being checked for drug use.

The tests are probably justified for air traffic controllers and Drug Enforcement Administration agents who now undergo them regularly. There's even a case to be made for testing professional athletes, part of whose job is to serve as role models to children. But need the same standards be applied to the entire work force? The *Los Angeles Times*, the *Chicago Tribune*, and the *New York Times*, for example, screen all new employees for drug use. Although the *New York Times* doesn't tell applicants that their urine will be tested for narcotics, a spokesman says the company's policy is to not hire anyone whose medical examination indicates use of illegal drugs, including marijuana. Once you are hired, there are no further tests.

And urinalysis is only one of the more intrusive new ways to search people for drugs. Many bus drivers and amusement-park ride operators are required to produce saliva samples, which are tested for the presence of marijuana. . . . It is now possible to test hair samples for drugs. Some companies have searched lockers and cars, frisked workers on their way into the factory, and set up hidden video cameras. G.M. hired undercover agents to pose as assembly-line workers in order to catch drug dealers. Capital Cities/ABC and the *Kansas City Times and Star* called off the drug-sniffing dogs after reporters ridiculed their plans for canine searches in the newsroom.

There is already a body of case law on the Fourth Amendment questions raised by the various drug tests. If a warrant is required to search someone's home, you need a probable cause to impound some of his urine. The Kaufman report notes that the Supreme Court ruled in favor of the Federal Railroad Administration's right to employ a range of tests for drugs and alcohol. But the commission ignores the fact that the railroad regulations delineate the need for "reasonable suspicion" that employees are under the influence on the job—not that they've used drugs away from work in previous weeks.

COLLABORATIVE LEARNING: CLASS ACTIVITY

Have your class discuss American society's conflicting needs for order and security versus freedom. How do these paradoxical needs apply to the drug testing debate? Which need is more important? Why? Does the pervasiveness of corruption, gangs, and crime change this balance?

4

5

COLLABORATIVE LEARNING: SMALL GROUP ACTIVITY

Set up a panel discussion in your class with 6 to 8 students arguing for drug testing and 6 to 8 arguing against. Let the speakers alternate, each presenting a 2- to 3-minute statement with close attention to the credibility and quality of the evidence brought to bear on his or her side of this issue. The rest of the students (the audience) can ask questions after all the speakers have made their statements. An important feature of this exercise is to make sure equal time is given to the speakers on both sides of the issue.

6

1. Milloy and Philips believe drug abuse is serious for the following reasons: Many U.S. Customs employees resist drug testing; most people who have a drug dependency will not ask for help; drug testing is very similar to selective service requirements; and letters they have received from individuals indicate a major drug problem in businesses. *The New Republic* editors agree that testing might be justified for air traffic controllers, Drug Enforcement Administration agents, and professional athletes, but do not agree with testing for all employees of all companies.

2. According to Milloy and Philips, the problem of violating civil liberties is not nearly as great as the drug problem that plagues America.

3. *The New Republic* editors believe that drug testing violates the Fourth Amendment, which they quote in their argument. In addition, they fear violations that may result from the decision to apply drug testing to every company and every job.

ANSWERS TO QUESTIONS:
ANALYZING MEANING (p. 482)

1. According to Milloy and Philips, drug testing is the only way to help the people using drugs. The authors see drug abuse as a pervasive problem with far-reaching implications. To stop drug abuse, Milloy and Philips believe that curbing the demand for drugs is the "last line of defense" (para. 5) against an overwhelming supply of drugs.

2. Drug testing appeals to businesses because it allows them to have a drug-free work force. Many employers are against testing, though, because of the costs involved.

3. Responses to this question will vary.

Invasion of Privacy

Beyond the constitutional questions, most would agree that asking people to produce a urine specimen if they want to apply for a job, or to keep the one they've got, is an unwarranted invasion of their privacy. To assure an honest sample, a supervisor must witness its production. The Coast Guard has someone follow each of its 38,000 employees into the bathroom. "We don't want them to bring in baby's urine," one Coast Guard officer told the *Washington Post.* 7

Why are these officers and supervisors, who administer the tests, always assumed to be clean? Programs for widespread testing almost always reflect class bias. Regulations are usually written for equipment operators or assembly-line workers without reference to supervisors or management. Isn't it just as important that they be drug-free? If we test train conductors, shouldn't we also analyze the urine of the railroad bosses? As the Kaufman Commission report indicates, heroin has been climbing up the socioeconomic ladder as cocaine has been descending. Yet lawyers, stock brokers, and senators are rarely included in drug-testing programs, perhaps because they are better able to fight the imposition of such indignities. 8

Besides running roughshod over personal privacy, the tests are impractical and imprecise. Urinalysis can't tell you whether someone is high on the job—only whether she has traces of narcotics in her system. Cocaine, heroin, and PCP—the drugs employers claim to be most worried about—vanish from the bloodstream in less than 48 hours. If the tests are scheduled, as most are, an employee can avoid detection by staying clean for a couple of days. 9

But THC, the active chemical in marijuana, remains in the blood months after it is ingested. That's why the vast majority of those who fail drug tests register positive for pot. What do we do with them? Nearly 40 million citizens smoke marijuana at least once a year. Half that number use the drug regularly. Should all of them be fired? If passing a drug test ought to be a condition of all kinds of employment, should a large segment of the population be unemployable? Eleven states have eliminated criminal penalties for possession of marijuana, and Alaskans can grow it legally in their backyards. Rather than weeding 20 million weed-smokers from the work force, employers ought to discipline, treat, or fire those who perform poorly at work, whether or not they use drugs. Axing workers who test positive but demonstrate no other problems doesn't make sense. 10

Like those who advocate widespread use of polygraph tests, the Kaufman panel puts boundless faith in far-from-perfect scientific techniques. Although the tests have been widely used for only a few years, they've ruined lives and fingered thousands of innocent people. The Pentagon, which administers six million urinalysis tests a year, provides plenty of examples. Urinalysis tests said time and again that a Navy doctor named Dale Mitchell was using morphine. When he failed a polygraph test, he began sending out job applications. Then someone at the Navy lab figured out that Mitchell was testing positive for poppy seed bagels. In 1982 and 1983 a group of 9,100 employees the Army said were using illegal drugs weren't so lucky. They had already gotten their dishonorable discharges when the Pentagon tried to track them down to apologize for convicting them on faulty evidence including mixed-up samples.

Most drug-testing laboratories acknowledge a margin of error of two or three percent. Even by that conservative estimate, four million innocents would lose their jobs if we tested the entire work force. But the conclusions of a secret study of the labs by the National Centers for Disease Control are far less optimistic. According to an article in the *Journal of the American Medical Association*, the worst laboratories indicated false positive results as much as 66 percent of the time. Only one lab was credited with acceptable performance in testing for cocaine. The CDC study didn't include any marijuana samples, which pose similar, if not more sever, lab problems. Herbal tea and prescription drugs can trigger false positive results, as can being in a room with people smoking marijuana. Those terminated unfairly may waste years and fortunes proving their innocence, if they are able to do so at all.

Little Plastic Cups

Despite the abundant hype, the use of legal and illegal drugs has decreased markedly over the past several years. Fewer people are taking heroin, PCP, marijuana, alcohol, and tobacco than they were ten years ago. LSD and Quaaludes have all but vanished. Cocaine use has increased slightly, but may well decline when its dangers become better known—which is what happened with heroin and PCP.

The failure of our policy of interdiction has combined with the hysteria to send the law-enforcement establishment on a search for sweeping solutions. [Attorney General Edwin] Meese suggested stepping up efforts to prosecute consumers of illegal

ANSWERS TO QUESTIONS: DISCOVERING RHETORICAL STRATEGIES (p. 482)

11 **1.** The story Milloy and Philips use at the beginning of their essay implies a question: How will people know that they can quit using drugs, if they don't have the incentive to do so? This question is a central focus of their justification for drug testing, and, in fact, the idea of legislating what others *should* do is necessary to their drug testing argument.

2. The statistics *The New Republic* editors cite are effective, because they show the results drug testing programs have had so far and the mistakes that have ruined people's lives. Not only has testing resulted in several thousand people being fired, but also the fact that the "Coast Guard has someone follow each of its 38,000 employees into the

12 bathroom" (para. 7) to get a urine sample suggests that widespread testing, though many think it will be effective, needs better guidelines before it is actually instituted. These statistics help the editors show the problems associated with testing and the lack of clear guidelines for such testing. Rather than give up rights that have lasted two hundred years, the editors want to keep the rights guaranteed them by the U.S. Constitution.

3. The headings help organize these two arguments by showing how each new set of evidence is related to the preceding material and by presenting new information that extends their point of view while supporting it. Beyond this point, responses to this question will vary.

13

14

In preparation for the writing assignments, the Preparing to Write questions ask students to consider various ways of controlling the use of drugs in America before they write an essay on a related topic. See pages 16–23 for suggestions on generating ideas in response to these questions.

ADDITIONAL DISCUSSION/WRITING TOPIC

In a well-organized essay, explain the rights of society with regard to drugs. Are there any parallels between drug and alcohol problems in this country? What can we learn from these parallels? Do newborns of addictive mothers have any rights? What role should drug testing play in America?

REVISING STRATEGY

To accomplish its purpose, a persuasive essay must argue its assertions in a clear, straightforward manner. Reread one of your persuasive essays from the point of view of your intended audience. Mark any inconsistencies, lapses in logic, or general weaknesses. Then revise your paper, correcting the problems you have noted.

drugs. What sort of indiscriminate check will catch the corporate imagination next? Strip searches for weapons? Polygraphs for potential office thieves? Blood tests for AIDS? All hold forth a similar promise of purity in the workplace, which is why they appeal so strongly to those who run businesses and governments. But such forms of social control, which force people to prove their innocence of crimes they haven't even been charged with, are abhorrent. What starts with little plastic cups ends in the urinalysis state.

UNDERSTANDING DETAILS

1. What examples do Milloy and Philips ("Drug Testing Does Not Violate Workers' Rights") cite to show that drug abuse is serious enough to justify testing? Under what circumstances might drug testing be warranted according to *The New Republic* editors ("Drug Testing Violates Workers' Rights")?
2. According to Milloy and Philips, what does drug testing have to do with civil liberties?
3. In what ways are drug tests unconstitutional, according to *The New Republic* editors?

ANALYZING MEANING

1. Why do Milloy and Philips say that "drug testing may well be our last line of defense" (paragraph 5)? Our last line of defense against *what?*
2. According to *The New Republic* editors, why do drug tests appeal to employers? Why are many employers against them?
3. Which side of this argument is most convincing to you? Which examples or statistics persuade you most effectively? Explain your reaction to these two positions on the issue of drug testing.

DISCOVERING RHETORICAL STRATEGIES

1. Is the story at the beginning of the Milloy and Philips essay an effective way to start the selection? Explain your answer.
2. Are the statistics *The New Republic* editors give to show the widespread use of drug testing effective? How does the editorial use this information to set up its argument?
3. Do the headings in these essays help you read and understand the information? If so, in what ways?

IDEAS FOR DISCUSSION/WRITING

Preparing to Write

Write freely about your views on drug testing: Do you think America should take an active role in controlling the use of drugs in the workplace? What do you think should be done? On what level (federal, state, local, individual business)? How might this action decrease the use of drugs on the job? What is your view of drug testing? What role should it play in the prevention of drug use in the workplace? In what ways might drug testing improve the situation? In what ways might it make the situation worse?

Choosing a Topic

1. Because teachers at all levels of education are such important role models for young people, drug testing has become an issue in your public schools. You have been asked to serve on a committee to recommend whether or not drug testing should be required when new teachers are hired. Present your argument on this issue in a coherent essay intended to be read by your fellow committee members.

2. How far should employers be allowed to delve into the personal lives of their employees? Should they, for example, be able to require weekly lie detector tests to see if their workers have stolen any supplies or made any private phone calls? Should they be allowed to use two-way mirrors to spy on their employees? In an essay written for your peers, argue for or against certain limits on professional scrutiny. How far should employers be able to go to protect themselves against dishonest, lazy, and/or drug-addicted employees? What rights do employees have in this regard?

3. In an essay written for a group of employees, present an alternate proposal (besides drug testing) for monitoring drugs in the workplace. Explain the details of its implementation and its likely effects.

Davis, Robert V., Kenneth H. Hawks, and Richard L. Blanke. "Assessment in Laboratory Quality in Urine Drug Testing: A Proficiency Testing Pilot Study." *The Journal of the American Medical Association* 260 (S 23/30 1988): 1749–1754.

Glantz, Leonard H. "A Nation of Suspects: Drug Testing and the Fourth Amendment." *American Journal of Public Health* 79 (October 1989): 1427–1431.

Harvey, Andrew J. "Drug Abuse and Testing in Law Enforcement: No Easy Answers." *FBI Law Enforcement Bulletin* 60 (June 1991): 12–15.

Linn, Lawrence S., Joel Yager, and Barbara Leake. "Professional vs. Personal Factors Related to Physicians' Attitudes Toward Drug Testing." *Journal of Drug Education* 20 (1990): 95–109.

Murphy, Kevin R., George C. Thornton, and Krintin Prue. "Influence of Job Characteristics on the Acceptability of Employee Drug Testing." *Journal of Applied Psychology* 76 (June 1991): 447–453.

Wells, Michael, Victoria E. Halperin, and William Thun. "The Estimated Predictive Value of Screening for Illicit Drugs in the Workplace." *American Journal of Public Health* 78 (July 1988): 817–819.

"A sentence should read as if its author, had he held a plow instead of a pen, could have drawn a furrow deep and straight to the end."

Henry David Thoreau

OPPOSING VIEWPOINTS
Homelessness

The coauthors of the first essay in this section, Michael Fabricant and Michael Driscoll-Kelly, are powerful and compelling advocates for the homeless in America. Fabricant, who earned his B.A. at the University of Pittsburgh and his Ph.D. at Brandeis University, is currently a professor in the School of Social Work at Hunter College (CUNY) in New York City, where his areas of specialization include juvenile delinquency and the family court system. The most recent of his four books is *The Welfare State Crisis and the Transformation of Social Service Work* (coauthored by Steve Burghardt, 1992), which examines the response of governmental service agencies to such persistent social problems as poverty and homelessness in America. He is also the founder of the Elizabeth Coalition to House the Homeless in his hometown of Elizabeth, New Jersey. A lover of baseball, Fabricant admits to being a "rabid Pittsburgh Pirates fan" and coaches a Little League team in Elizabeth. He thinks the most difficult transition for college-level writers to make is "from oral to written English." Michael Driscoll-Kelly earned his B.A. from Fordham University and his Masters in Social Work at Hunter College, where he was one of Fabricant's students. He and his wife, Joan Driscoll-Kelly, work together at the Center for Hope Hospice and the Transitional Housing Unit, both located in Elizabeth.

The author of the second essay, Martin Morse Wooster, is the Washington editor of *Reason* magazine, for which he covers political events, trends, and controversies that originate in the nation's capital. He earned his B.A. at Beloit University in Wisconsin, then worked as a staff writer for the Network News Syndicate. Editorial positions at *Harper's* and *The Wilson Quarterly* soon led to his current job at *Reason*, where he writes a monthly column touching on such diverse topics as space policy, immigration, computers, young children, public broadcasting, multinational corporations, arts policy, broadcasting, homelessness, education, and other social and political issues. "I try hard," he has explained, "not to pigeonhole myself as a writer on specific topics." His hobbies include reading, conversation, and "engaging in good arguments." He advises college students to learn how to use the library. "Thorough research," he says, "makes a good article better." As he prepares to write his monthly columns, he reads everything he can find concerning each particular subject. "Good writing is hard work," he laments, "but it's also more fun than most people admit."

Preparing to Read

The essay by Fabricant and Driscoll-Kelly, which stresses the severity of homelessness in America, was originally published in *Radical America* (March 1986). Wooster's response, which argues that the problem has been vastly overstated by governmental agencies and the media, appeared first in *Reason* (July 1987). As you prepare to read these two essays, take a few moments to think about your own views on homelessness in America: Do you think homelessness is a major social problem today? What is its source? What do you know about the homeless situation in your community? In America as a whole? What types of people do you think generally make up the homeless population? Does this problem affect you in any way? Does it affect any members of your family? How does it affect your immediate community? Can you envision any solutions to this problem—at the local, state, or national level? What would be the consequences of these solutions?

PREREADING

The purpose of this Preparing to Read material is to encourage students to articulate their views on the problem of homelessness in America. To help your students focus their attention on this critical issue before they respond to the questions here, have them discuss the extent of homelessness in your community. Ask class members who have some special knowledge about this problem to share detailed stories with the other students so everyone approaches this reading task with the same general information about homelessness in their immediate area. Then, have them briefly discuss the reasons they think this problem has occurred. See pages 3–6 for other ways to generate thoughts on these questions.

MICHAEL FABRICANT
(1948–)
MICHAEL DRISCOLL-KELLY
(1953–)

■ ■ ■

The Problem of Homelessness Is Serious

BACKGROUND INFORMATION

Arguing in favor of the seriousness of the homeless problem in America, Michael Fabricant and Michael Driscoll-Kelly claim that in the last 40 years "the homeless population has changed dramatically in appearance as well as quantity" (para. 7). They then argue for economic entitlement for the homeless—more specifically, "the economic right of citizens to housing and a job at a livable wage" (para. 21).

READABILITY LEVEL

17.3

Mitch Snyder, activist for the homeless and member of the Community for Creative Non-Violence in Washington, D.C., once spent the winter months living on the street. During the nights he slept on a heat grating. From this vantage point he observed:

> The streets became the province of the vast army of the homeless. Scores of street dwellers would file past our corner every night . . . we could watch the bent and the broken—mostly elderly—people wandering, marching to and from nowhere. They trembled in the cold, surrounded by heated, lighted, guarded and empty government buildings.

Snyder's observations reflect a growing national recognition of the homelessness problem, which now affects an expanding number of citizens. . . .

The Problem of Homelessness

Up to 3 million people now live without a home in the United States, mostly in our cities. In cities like New York, it is difficult to comprehend the scope of the homeless problem, with its more than 60,000 homeless riding the subways or seeking refuge in the train and bus stations at night. The cold restroom floor in Penn Station becomes a bed for some 50 women. Others stay in phone booths or blend into the dark recesses of the stations. Many catch a few hours of sleep in the waiting room until rousted by the rap of a policeman's nightstick against their chair. Some of the more ingenious homeless New Yorkers get needed rest and pass the night safely by camouflaging themselves on city streets where large amounts of garbage have been placed for disposal: They crawl into cardboard boxes or cover themselves with plastic trashcan liners.

In 1981, a Chicago newspaper reported that 50 homeless people had been buried in the city's Potter's Field in January, after silently freezing to death. A year later, the Chicago Coalition for the Homeless estimated 25,000 homeless wandered the city. Charles Ford, the Director of Emergency Services, said: "We have the feeling that the numbers are increasing. . . . We are finding more and more people who live on the street involuntarily—young people, who in ordinary times would be able to find jobs, and more women and children." By December 1982 every shelter in Chicago was filled to capacity and turning away 30–50 people per night.

Other cities of America's "heartland" have shared this experience. Detroit, with its massive unemployment, had over 27,000 homeless people in November 1984—a 300 percent increase from 1982. The U.S. Conference of Mayors reported that up to 1,000 people were living in cars, trailers, tents, or campgrounds in Tulsa while another 200–300 people lived under city bridges. In 1981–1982, 1,000 people in Milwaukee lost their homes.

In recent years, the prospering and temperate "Sunbelt" cities have been inundated with unemployed workers from the Northeast. Yet in Dallas, Phoenix, and Los Angeles, for example, they have found an extremely tight job market, high rents and a much lower level of entitlement than in their old homes.

The Union Rescue Mission of Los Angeles, the world's largest private mission, recently (for the first time in over 90 years) turned people away because all the 350 beds and 350 chairs were filled. Elsewhere, during the winter of 1983, Seattle turned away 4,000 families (roughly 16,000 people) who applied for shelter. And in Flagstaff, Arizona, many homeless families have been camping out in the National Forest which borders the city.

The homeless population has changed dramatically in appearance as well as quantity. Between 1945 and 1970 urban hobos, mostly older, alcoholic men, were the major skid row inhabitants. Since then, small but growing numbers of women have appeared. By the mid-1970s, many younger black and Hispanic men, unemployed and lacking job skills, began using urban shelters and flophouses. Many had drug or alcohol problems. In New York City, up to one third of them were veterans, mostly of the Vietnam War.

DEFINITIONS

Mitch Snyder (1944–1990) (para. 1): a national figure in the 1980s in support of the homeless.

flophouses (para. 7): cheap hotels often used by homeless people.

psychopharmacology (para. 8): the study of drugs and their effect on our mental and emotional states.

phenothiazines (para. 8): a group of drugs widely used to treat psychosis.

AFDC (para. 12): Aid for Families with Dependent Children, a welfare program designed to help poor families with children meet their basic needs.

tax abatement (para. 18): a reduction in taxes awarded to individuals who participate in a government program to convert low-income housing into luxury apartments.

At the same time, discharged mental patients became more prominent on the streets following deinstitutionalization. Those supporting this policy claimed that recent advances in psychopharmacology and treatment had now made community living feasible for institutionalized mental patients. New "wonder drugs," especially phenothiazines, were to supplant incarceration. Community-based treatment models became the new road towards "recovery" and social reintegration. . . . 8

The price paid in human misery has been monumental. Vital services, community supports, and follow-up treatments were not adequately developed. Many of the 400,000 people discharged from mental hospitals between 1950 and 1980 were forced to fend for themselves. Temporarily, some maintained a marginal existence in low-income housing, but by the mid-1970s this too disappeared. Other than the street, the only alternatives left were adult homes or shelters. In these newly emerging "deviant ghettos," one is likely to find neither compassion nor therapeutic treatments, but usually at best, some form of repressive tolerance on the outer fringes of society. . . . 9

Economic Victims

The high rates of inflation and unemployment during the recession of 1980–1982 produced yet another wave of homeless people. Massive layoffs and plant closings in 1983 produced situations in cities like Detroit, where in 1982 close to 20,000 workers per month lost their unemployment benefits. In 1983 Illinois had a 13.9 percent unemployment rate, or 759,000 unemployed citizens, and also had the nation's highest rate of home foreclosures (1.6 percent). Shelters in Chicago, Detroit and elsewhere cited "the loss of a job" as a primary reason for homelessness. 10

The inability of younger blacks or Hispanics to enter the labor market has also contributed to the homelessness explosion. Their unemployment rate (over 50 percent) is the highest in the nation. Unable to find jobs or affordable housing, many young black and Hispanic men are crowded out of their family's apartment. In 1980, virtually no people under the age of twenty-one stayed in New York City municipal shelters. By 1985, they comprised 7 percent of the total shelter population. Recent estimates showed approximately 22,000 homeless youth in New York City, the single largest subgroup of homeless. 11

Finally, homeless families are the newest and, perhaps, most frightening wave of homelessness. Headed mostly by women, living on AFDC, they represent the fastest growing group of homeless. 12

Government Responses

To this grievous problem, the government response has sometimes been nightmarish. In Fort Lauderdale, a city councilman urged the spraying of trash with poison to cut off the "vermin's" food supply. In Phoenix, and President Reagan's home city of Santa Barbara, anti-homeless ordinances prohibit sitting, sleeping, or lying down in public areas such as parks and consider trash-bin refuse as public property. Hence, foraging for food is a criminal act. At the Federal level, a Department of Housing and Urban Development Survey concluded that there were but 200,000–300,000 homeless nationwide. Despite its numerous methodological flaws, which considerably underestimate the problem, this survey has nonetheless been used to minimize government action. For example, HUD's recommendation against new, temporary shelters has seriously inhibited efforts for more significant change.

Obviously, the need for safe, decent shelter greatly outstrips the number of slots available. Recent estimates show only 330 shelter beds in Detroit, for a homeless population of 27,000. Chicago has approximately 1,000 beds for 20,000–25,000. In Connecticut, the second richest state, the less than 950 shelter beds far underserve its 10,000 homeless men, women, and children. One shelter in Hartford turned away more than 3,500 applicants in a recent 12-month period.

Shelters also fail to meet the differing needs of homeless people. Alcoholics, the unemployed, the elderly and former mental patients are all lumped into one space. Sanitary conditions are often poor. Bathroom and shower facilities are woefully inadequate given the crowded conditions. Some municipal shelters, like the one in Washington, D.C., feature myriad abuses, including random beatings of homeless people by vicious security guards. Given these conditions, many homeless people have apparently "preferred the rats and the cold to contending with the degradation of the public shelters." . . .

Welfare and Housing Cuts

Recent reports by journalists, academics, advocates, and the government underscore the dramatic reduction of entitlement benefits and services. Between 1980 and 1981 an intense drive emerged to make across-the-board cuts in all social welfare pro-

13

14

15

16

COLLABORATIVE LEARNING: SMALL GROUP ACTIVITY

Divide your students into groups of 4 or 5, and have them discuss solutions to the homeless problem in your community. Review the major issues related to this problem before the groups begin work. Then, have one person from each group present the group's ideas to the entire class.

grams. Overall, cash welfare benefits declined by 17 percent. One million people were eliminated from Food Stamp coverage. Ninety percent of the working, AFDC families had their benefits reduced or eliminated. Finally, the value of general assistance payments has declined substantially. While these trends did not begin during Reagan's presidency, they have been dramatically intensified by this administration.

As cash benefits have eroded, both private and public sector housing investment decisions have also changed. The Federal government effectively withdrew from the public housing market. In 1979 over 40,000 units of conventional public housing were completed; by 1982 the number had dropped to 25,000 units. In 1979 there were 23,860 new starts for the elderly and handicapped; in 1983 only 14,112 units were funded. During fiscal year 1985 the Reagan administration arranged to fund only 12,500 new units of subsidized housing, 10,000 for the elderly and handicapped, 2,500 for Native Americans.   17

The central city renovations characterizing many U.S. cities have made matters worse. In New York, tax abatements gave incentives to convert low-income housing to luxury apartment buildings. Between 1975 and 1981 approximately 35,000 units of low-income housing were lost. New York City offers the most dramatic example of these market forces. Cities such as Cleveland, Phoenix, Newark, San Francisco, Denver, and Chicago also report substantial losses in their low-income housing stock to downtown renovation or luxury housing development. These trends partly respond to the changing economic structure which has allowed some elite professionals and entrepreneurs to benefit from a polarized job market which has hurt most workers. The increased demand for urban housing from relatively affluent people has pushed many low-income individuals and families out of the formal housing market.   18

Consequences

The consequent increase in urban rents leaves poor people particularly vulnerable. Increasingly, general assistance and AFDC payments are simply insufficient to meet the new urban rent levels throughout the country. As has been noted, "the amount of public assistance a recipient was allotted for rent—whether as a separate shelter allowance or as part of a flat grant—ranged from 20 percent to 60 percent of local fair market rent."   19

When basic rent allowances are insufficient to meet prevailing rents, then grants have more symbolic than real value. Entitle-   20 ments that increasingly fail to meet basic survival needs (such as permanent housing) most dramatically indicate the growing inadequacy of today's "social wage." . . .

The homeless crisis reflects the unraveling of many of the advances of the last fifty years. Shelters and soup lines do not offer those presently homeless, or those who risk falling through the "safety net" to the streets, a basis for recreating their lives. At best, these services only temporarily halt the physical, emotional, and intellectual deterioration of the homeless person. If the needs of the homeless, chronically unemployed, or temporarily unemployed are to be met, then economic entitlement must be expanded or advanced, not diminished. This expansion or redefinition must begin with the economic right of citizens to housing and a job at a livable wage.

MARTIN MORSE WOOSTER
(1957–   )

■ ■ ■

The Problem of Homelessness Is Exaggerated

BACKGROUND INFORMATION

Martin Wooster claims that "the problem of homelessness is exaggerated." His main argument is that the two most prominent advocates for the homeless—Robert Hayes, a New York City lawyer, and Mitch Snyder, a Washington, D.C., advertising executive—have ulterior motives. As a result, Wooster goes on to argue, the numbers we have to work with in identifying the extent of this problem are grossly inflated and misleading. At the end of his essay, he leaves us with a series of questions to consider as we continue to deal with this problem in America.

READABILITY LEVEL

15.1

RELATED READINGS

Societal Problems

DEFINITIONS

the Bowery (para. 4): a district in lower Manhattan known for its extreme poverty.
flophouse (para. 13): cheap hotels often used by homeless people.

Homelessness is the issue by which the champions of the welfare state hope to regain lost ground. Bills pending in Congress will, if passed, use the homeless issue to increase federal welfare spending by up to $4 billion—the largest one-year increase since the Carter administration.

Yet advocates of massive federal spending for the homeless have failed to show the need for increases. Nor have they demonstrated whether spending more tax dollars on public housing—a favorite plea—will reduce the homeless population. If the Reagan administration had not tried to counter the sloppy estimates of the homeless lobby with equally bad estimates of its own, one wonders whether the question of homelessness would have ever become a "crisis" to be solved by bloating the welfare state.

A Tale of Two Lobbyists

Ten years ago there were homeless in America. Twenty years ago there were homeless. How is it that in the 1980s there is a *homeless crisis?* A close look at what statistics there are reveals that nobody really knows how much—or even whether—the number of homeless is increasing (more on this later). A little more looking, and it becomes clear that homelessness has become an issue in American life largely because of the efforts of two charismatic lobbyists—a Washington adman and a New York City lawyer.

In late 1978, Robert Hayes, an associate at the Wall Street firm of Sullivan and Cromwell, was walking to the subway when he noticed "bums . . . begging for handouts." He began to talk to the homeless and visit shelters. Appalled by what he found, he resolved to do something. Being a lawyer, he resolved to file a class-action lawsuit. He got Robert Callahan, a former short-order cook he'd met in the Bowery, to agree to be the plaintiff. In October 1979, Hayes sued New York Mayor Edward Koch and New York

Governor Hugh Carey to compel the city and state government to provide shelter for the homeless.

In December 1979, New York's supreme court granted a preliminary injunction in *Callahan* v. *Carey* in favor of Callahan—and Hayes. New York City residents now had a "right to shelter"; the court ordered New York City to provide food, shelter, and showers to any resident. Shelters also had to be large enough so that no homeless person has to be bused from one shelter to another.

Callahan v. *Carey* has been a costly decision for New York City's taxpayers. In 1978, the city budgeted $6.8 million for the homeless; by 1983, the figure had risen to $38 million. (While the numbers of people using the shelters rose from about 600 in 1978 to 4,235 in 1983, whether the rise was due to an increase in homelessness or whether people left temporary housing for free beds and food is a question intensely debated by sociologists.). . .

While Hayes was fencing with New York City lawyers, Mitch Snyder was beginning to acquire his notoriety. Snyder was an adman who, in the early 1970s, founded the Community for Creative Non-Violence (CCNV), a Washington, D.C., commune dedicated to opposing the Vietnam war. Snyder widened his range in the late '70s engaging in a series of hunger strikes and demonstrations (usually "tent cities") in Lafayette Park, across the street from the White House. While some of these strikes were antiwar, an increasing number were devoted to the homeless.

Snyder began to acquire a local reputation as an expert on homelessness. If he had lived in Los Angeles or Philadelphia, the state legislature would have asked to hear him; but because he lived in Washington, Snyder was asked to testify before the D.C. equivalent of a statehouse—the House District Committee. The congressional committee asked Snyder and his associates at CCNV to compile an estimate of the number of homeless people in the United States.

In December 1980, Snyder delivered his report. There were, he declared, 2.2 million homeless Americans—or one percent of the population. Snyder then attacked the congressmen who asked for the report. "We have tried to satisfy your gnawing curiosity for a number," he said, carping about "Americans with little Western minds that have to quantify everything in sight."

Two years later, with homelessness increasingly in the news, the Community for Creative Non-Violence published *Homelessness in America*, a revised version of Snyder's 1980 testimony. "We have learned nothing that would cause us to lower our original estimate," wrote Snyder and coauthor Mary Ellen Hombs. "In fact, we would increase it, since we are convinced that the number of homeless people in the United States could reach 3 million or more during 1983."

These two sentences are the strongest "evidence" ever provided by the Community for Creative Non-Violence on the size of the homeless population. Snyder and Hombs chose to prove their claim, not by providing evidence but by listing dozens of horror stories about individual homeless people. . . . 11

Newspaper Stories

Most of the major newspapers in America had a story about national homelessness in 1982 or 1983, and most of these stories had one point in common—they all reported Mitch Snyder's estimate of two million homeless (which Robert Hayes also adopted) as a hard fact: 12

• "1982's Homeless: Americans Adrift in Tents, Autos," *Washington Post*, front page, August 14, 1982: "'From coast to coast, signs of the 1930s reverberate,' says Robert M. Hayes, . . . attorney for the National Coalition for the Homeless, which estimates at least two million people are without shelter in the United States. He notes, "The soup lines grow. The flophouses fill to overflowing. . . . The newest token of a failed American dream is a cardboard box."'" 13

• "Millions Hit Bottom in the Streets," *Los Angeles Times*, front page, December 26, 1982: "According to testimony two weeks ago at a congressional subcommittee hearing on the subject, there may be as many as 2.5 million citizens without a place to stay for the holidays." The unnamed provider of testimony was Mitch Snyder. . . . 14

• It was up to *Newsweek* reporter Jonathan Alter to provide the most florid statement of what by now was everywhere dubbed a crisis. "The tattered ranks of America's homeless are swelling," Alter wrote in a January 3, 1984, cover story, "and the economic recovery that made this Christmas merrier than last for most Americans has not brought them even a lump of coal." . . . 15

The HUD Report

Needless to say, the government was not sitting around letting social activists monopolize the limelight. In 1983, Secretary of Housing and Urban Development Samuel Pierce ordered his 16

Office of Policy Development and Research to produce an estimate of the size and nature of the homeless population. *A Report
to the Secretary on the Homeless and Emergency Shelters* was released
in May 1984—to howls of outrage from Snyder, Hayes, and the
homeless lobby. It was, scoffed Snyder, "a political document."

The HUD report presented four estimates of the homeless   17
population, ranging from 192,000 to 586,000. The authors concluded that "as best as can be determined from all available data,
the most reliable range is 250,000 to 350,000 homeless persons.
This represents the total number of people, nationally, who were
homeless on an average night in December 1983 or January
1984." It was a meager 10 percent of the 2–3 million figure popularized by Snyder and Hayes.

HUD had tried four ways to come up with some homeless es-   18
timates. The highest figure of 586,000 was determined by collecting local newspaper stories, magazine articles, and a few reports
by state and local welfare agencies, dividing the total into the
population of those areas, and so deriving a national estimate
that .25 percent of the population was homeless. HUD's analysts
did not question their source material and relied on news reports
written as much as two years before the December 1983 "snap-
shot" date. For example, estimates for Minneapolis and Philadelphia were derived from 1981 newspaper articles, while Tucson
and Pittsburgh figures were taken from 1982 newspaper stories.

HUD's other estimates deserve closer attention. Consider the   19
number derived from the opinions of operators of shelters for the
homeless.

Shelter operators are not as knowledgeable about the num-   20
bers of homeless in their area as one might expect. As Eugene Er-
icksen, a professor of sociology at Temple University, told a
congressional committee in December 1985, "the shelter operators and other providers are so busy running their facilities and
taking care of the local clientele that they have little time or motivation to learn about the problem as a whole. Knowing how
many homeless people there are in the New York area will not
help you run your shelter in the Bowery when your beds are full
every night and you have to turn people away." . . .

The estimates HUD did receive varied widely. In New York,   21
for example, estimates ranged from 12,000 to 50,000 homeless
people; in Los Angeles, from 19,500 to 39,000.

"Some of these responses may have been wild guesses," Er-   22
icksen testified. "In other cases, respondents may have given the
number of public shelter beds; estimates may also have been

1. Fabricant and Driscoll-Kelly believe that "up to 3 million people now live without a home in the United States" (para. 2). They attribute this rise in the homeless population to changes in the treatment of the mentally ill, inflation, the increase in joblessness among young minority males, and the rise of single-parent, AFDC-dependent families.

2. Wooster questions the statistical methods used by lobbyists, government agencies, and other researchers in determining the number of homeless people. Because their arguments often depend on the "rise" in homelessness, this approach allows Wooster to question the validity of their arguments.

3. Several issues are associated with homelessness:

—Officials debate whether or not more money is necessary to help the homeless.

—The exact number of homeless people is difficult, if not impossible, to determine.

—The causes and remedies of homelessness are hotly debated by different political parties seeking to make homelessness an important political issue.

—Differences of opinion exist on where and how the money to help the homeless should be spent.

1. Responses to this question will vary.

2. Welfare and social support systems were established in the late 1930s and early 1940s to help the poor. Because of recent changes in political control, Fabricant and Driscoll-Kelly perceive a threat to the welfare system as well as to other traditional resources available to the disadvantaged. They believe "expansion or redefinition" (para. 21) of these services is necessary to help those who remain unrepresented in the political system.

given of the number of persons staying in shelters, missions, or hotels and apartments vouchered for the homeless." . . .

In short, what HUD did was not to count the number of homeless people or to rely on counts compiled by others. It simply collected opinions. Some of the opinions may be better than others, but as Richard Applebaum, a professor of sociology at the University of California at Santa Barbara, points out, most of HUD's research was "subjective opinion. . . . I don't think it matters if it is a shelter operator or a member of the Coalition on the Homeless, it is just a guess. It may be a somewhat more informed guess than my guess, but it is still a guess because of the monumental problem [in counting the homeless]." 23

Numbers Too High

The homeless lobby obviously didn't care for HUD's huge deflation of their own numbers. But two recent studies suggest that HUD's estimate were *too high.* Peter Rossi, director of the Social and demographic Research Institute at the University of Massachusetts at Amherst, conducted a study for the National Opinion Research Center to determine the number of homeless people in Chicago. Rossi and his researchers counted homeless people on 245 blocks in downtown Chicago (including "super blocks" such as train, bus, and subway stations that have a large number of homeless people). They concluded that there were between 2,000 and 3,000 homeless on the nights surveyed (in September/October 1985 and February/March 1986). Rossi estimated that 5,000 people were without homes at some point during the year. HUD, by contrast, estimates Chicago's homeless at 12,000–25,000—three times Rossi's figures. 24

In a subsequent article in *Science,* Rossi and his researchers reveal that they have "never been able to locate any data from which [HUD's] numbers were derived." They note that "empirically credible attempts to estimate the size of the homeless population have a produced numbers well below the expectations of the advocacy community." . . . 25

Martha Hicks, president of the Skid Row Development Corp., a nonprofit community agency, discounts HUD's estimate that there are up to 50,000 homeless people in Los Angeles. "They'd be falling all over each other if we had that many people here." Hicks told the *Washington Post* recently. "I think there are some people who think there is some money to be made from homelessness." . . . 26

Politicians and homeless advocates, in trying to "solve" the 27 problem of homelessness by the well-worn method of throwing money at it, underestimate the amount of federal aid already flowing to the homeless. For example, a "fact sheet" put out by the House Select Committee on Hunger claims that only five federal programs serve the homeless.

In fact, as a modest amount of poking around Washington reveals, there are at least *20* federal programs for the homeless, ranging from conversion of surplus buildings to Urban Mass Transit Administration research grants (yes, UMTA is in on the action to figure out how homeless people can use public transportation).

The total amount targeted for homelessness in fiscal year 1986 was between $170 and $200 million. At least $60 million—and as much as $560 million—will be added to this total in fiscal year 1987. And that's just for programs within agencies designated specifically for homeless people; this doesn't count welfare benefits such as food stamps or veterans' benefits for the 25 percent of the homeless population who have served in the armed forces. . . . Calculating *all* federal benefits for homeless people is impossible, since most social welfare programs do not earmark money specifically for the homeless even when that's how it's spent . . . .

Questions

Could the current cornucopia of federal aid—free food, free housing, free electricity—"solve" the homeless problem? Some experts argue that, as the amount of aid increases, the number of people eager to use it increases.

When Thomas Main analyzed New York homeless statistics, he found that 19 percent of the people staying in shelters over a long-term period were "economic-only" clients—men who entered shelters not because of drugs, mental illness, or disability but because life in a shelter is more attractive than either a life on welfare or a life in a minimum-wage job. Main believes that minority youth with "tenuous family ties" may find a shelter more attractive than living with unfriendly relatives.

In an interview, Main said he would like to have lawmakers think about several questions before contributing to the budget crisis by responding to the "homeless crisis" with more and more tax dollars. "Is the best way to approach this problem by building more shelters? Is a national right to shelter the approach that makes the best sense?"

And here's an additional question. Given the vast number of programs already serving the homeless and given the at-best

3. The numbers of homeless are used by politicians to "prove" the need for more money in the welfare system. Because the government is already expending a sizable amount of welfare money, the demonstration of a new clientele is necessary to elicit more money. This money serves to bring more people into the welfare system but not to bring more or better services to those already receiving assistance.

28

ANSWERS TO QUESTIONS: DISCOVERING RHETORICAL STRATEGIES (p. 498)

1. In addition to argument, Fabricant and Driscoll-Kelly use the example of Mitch Snyder, who experienced city shelters as a homeless person, to prove the need for assistance for the homeless. They increase the effectiveness of their argument by including a section on the various causes of the rise in homelessness, which they divide into distinct categories or types of homeless people. They also compare the living conditions several years ago to those faced by homeless people today.

29

Like Fabricant and Driscoll-Kelly, Wooster uses the examples of several prominent people—who, in his opinion, exaggerate the problem of homelessness; in fact, he narrates the story of Mitch Snyder's involvement with the movement to help the homeless, although Wooster presents a rather different picture than Fabricant and Driscoll-Kelly do. Wooster also divides his essay into categories of people and organizations who are exaggerating and exploiting the plight of the homeless. He uses many examples of newspaper stories based on questionable figures of homelessness discovered by "researchers." In his conclusion, Wooster also suggests some possible causes for the rise in homelessness: "as the amount of aid increases, the number of people eager to use it increases" (para. 30).

30

31

32

2. The goal of the argument Fabricant and Driscoll-Kelly present is to convince others that an increase in funding and reorganization of services is required to serve homeless people adequately in the United States. Beyond this point, student opinions will vary.

33

3. Wooster's final questions appeal to his specific audience: mostly educated, professional, taxpaying readers who undoubtedly vote and are politically aware. These questions suggest that increasing aid to the homeless will raise taxes, that building more shelters may actually increase the number of homeless, and that all the steps suggested to change the situation may be an overreaction to an exaggerated problem. Beyond this point, student opinions will vary.

PREWRITING

In preparation for the writing assignments, the Preparing to Write questions ask students to reconsider their thoughts on homelessness in the United States before they write an essay on a related topic. See pages 16–23 for suggestions on generating ideas in response to these questions.

ADDITIONAL DISCUSSION/WRITING TOPIC

What special groups in America (other than the homeless) should receive extra financial assistance from the government? Native Americans? African Americans? Hispanics? Other minority groups? Drug addicts? Artists? Students? The unemployed? The chronically ill? Choose one special group and write an argumentative essay either for or against increased government financial support.

REVISING STRATEGY

Although one rhetorical mode may be dominant, a combination of modes plays a part in all essays. In one of your persuasive essays, identify the rhetorical modes you use to support your argument. Decide whether other rhetorical modes should replace or be used in addition to the strategies you have already incorporated into your essay. Then revise your paper, concentrating on the effectiveness of your rhetorical modes in helping you achieve your purpose with a specific audience.

sketchy evidence offered by the homeless lobby, why should taxpayers believe there *is* a "homeless crisis"?

UNDERSTANDING DETAILS

1. According to Fabricant and Driscoll-Kelly, how many homeless people are there in America? How has the homeless population changed in recent years?
2. What approach does Wooster use to prove that homelessness is not a crisis in America?
3. Based on both of these essays, what are the main issues connected with the problem of homelessness?

ANALYZING MEANING

1. Which argument is most convincing to you? What examples or details persuade you most effectively? Explain your answer.
2. What do Fabricant and Driscoll-Kelly mean when they say, "The homeless crisis reflects the unraveling of many of the advances of the last fifty years" (paragraph 21)?
3. How are homelessness and welfare connected? Why might politicians use one to help raise support for the other?

DISCOVERING RHETORICAL STRATEGIES

1. What principal rhetorical modes do the authors of both of these essays use to support their arguments? How effective are these modes? Give examples of each in your answer.
2. What is the primary focus of Fabricant and Driscoll-Kelly's argument? Do you find this focus effective in terms of what the authors are trying to prove?
3. Wooster ends his essay with a series of questions. Are these questions particularly well chosen? Is this approach an effective way to end the essay? Why or why not?

IDEAS FOR DISCUSSION/WRITING

Preparing to Write

Write freely about your thoughts on homelessness in the United States: Has your opinion on the seriousness of this problem changed since you read these two essays? How serious do you think the problem is? What brings you to this conclusion? What are some signs of its size and severity? What effects does homelessness have on society? How do you think America should approach this problem as a nation? How involved should the federal government be in the solution? The state government? How could we best deal with this problem on the local level?

Choosing a Topic

1. Fabricant and Driscoll-Kelly claim that "if the needs of the homeless, chronically unemployed, or temporarily unemployed are to be met, then economic entitlement must be expanded or advanced, not diminished. This expansion or redefinition must begin with the economic right of citizens to housing and a job at a livable wage" (paragraph 21). Direct an essay to your classmates in which you agree or disagree with this assertion. Be sure to explain your reasoning carefully.

2. In your opinion, how serious is the problem of homelessness in your community? What types of people are homeless? In a coherent essay, persuade your friends that homelessness is or is not a serious problem that should be solved in your community.

3. In an essay written for a group of local representatives to Congress, present a proposal for controlling the homeless situation in your city. First, find out what is currently being done about the problem. Then, explain the details of your plan, including its implementation and its likely effects.

FURTHER READING

Arnold, Craig Anthony. "Beyond Self-Interest—Policy Entrepreneurs and Aid to the Homeless." *Policy Studies Journal* 18 (Fall 1989): 47–66.

Bassuk, Ellen L. "Who Are the Homeless Families: Characteristics of Sheltered Mothers and Children." *Community Mental Health Journal* 26 (October 1990): 425–434.

Goldfinger, Stephen M. "Perspectives on the Homeless Mentally Ill." *Community Mental Health Journal* 26 (October 1990): 387–390.

Hier, Sally J., Paula J. Korboot, and Robert D. Schweitz. "Social Adjustment and Symptomatology in Two Types of Homeless Adolescents—Runaways and Throwaways." *Adolescence* 25 (Winter 1990): 761–771.

Kelly, Elinor, J. Clyde Mitchell, and Susan J. Smith. "Factors in the Length of Stay of Homeless Families in Temporary Accommodation." *Sociological Review* 38 (November 1990): 621–633.

Solarz, Andrea and G. Anne Bogat. "When Social Support Fails—The Homeless." *Journal of Community Psychology* 18 (January 1990): 79–96.

CHAPTER 10

DOCUMENTED ESSAYS
■ ■ ■
Reading and Writing from Sources

Using Sources

We use sources every day in both informal and formal situations. We explain the source of a phone message, for example, or we refer to an instructor's comments in class. We use someone else's opinion in an essay, or we quote an expert to prove a point. We cite sources both in speaking and in writing through summary, paraphrase, and direct quotation. Most of your college instructors will ask you to write papers using sources so they can see how well you understand the course material. The use of sources in academic papers requires you to process what you have read and integrate this reading material with your own opinions and observations—a process that requires a high level of skill in thinking, reading, and writing.

Defining Documented Essays

Documented essays provide you with the opportunity to perform sophisticated and exciting exercises in critical thinking; they draw on the thinking, reading, and writing abilities you have built up over the course of your academic career, and they often require you to put all the rhetorical modes to work at their most analytical level. Documented essays demonstrate the process of

INTRODUCTORY NOTES

This chapter introduces your students to an exciting and interesting advanced form of critical thinking: **documented essays**. The two essays in this chapter demonstrate a high level of reasoning along with the two main styles of documentation, including citations and bibliography. The first, an article on teenage pregnancy by Betty Gittman, relies on careful, thorough research to reveal the seriousness of the high rate of teenage pregnancy in America; it illustrates the Modern Language Association (MLA) form of documentation, which is used principally in such humanities courses as English, philosophy, history, and fine arts. The second, an essay on group violence by John Langone, is an example of the American Psychological Association (APA) style of documentation, which is appropriate for such science and behavioral science courses as biology, chemistry, physics, sociology, anthropology, and psychology. Because some instructors require their own variations on these two forms of documentation, you should explain to your students which style you prefer.

In responding to the essays in this chapter, your students must be able to think clearly and independently in order to follow the authors' reasoning, complete the questions, and write their own essays. Each argument is furnished with a list of "Further Reading," two class activities, and two small group suggestions so you can use the essays in several different pedagogical contexts. The writing assignments following the essays include both argument/persuasion tasks and questions that require library work. In addition, we have designed several assignments so you can have your students either respond in essay form or generate longer papers based on library research, depending on your course objectives. The material in this chapter is flexible enough, then, to be used in several different ways—from more advanced work on argument/persuasion to full-fledged practice on library papers, including documentation and bibliographies.

analytical thinking at its best in different disciplines.

In the academic world, documented essays are also called "research papers," "library papers," and "term papers." Documented essays are generally written for one of three reasons: (1) to **report,** (2) to **interpret,** or (3) to **analyze.**

The most straightforward, uncomplicated type of documented essay **reports** information, as in a survey of problems children have in preschool. The second type of documented essay both presents and **interprets** its findings. It will examine a number of different views on a specific issue and weigh these views as it draws its own conclusions. A topic that falls into this category would be whether children who have attended preschool are more sociable than those who have not. After considering evidence on both sides, the writer would draw his or her own conclusions on this topic. A documented essay that **analyzes** a subject presents a hypothesis, tests the hypothesis, and analyzes or evaluates its conclusions. This type of essay calls for the most advanced form of critical thinking. It might look, for example, at the reasons preschool children are more or less socially flexible than nonpreschool children. At its most proficient, this type of writing requires a sophisticated degree of evaluation that forces you to judge your reading, evaluate your sources, and ultimately scrutinize your own reasoning ability as the essay takes shape.

Each of these types of documented essays calls for a higher level of thinking, and each evolves from the previous category. In other words, interpreting requires some reporting, whereas analyzing draws on both reporting and interpreting.

In the following paragraph, a student reports, interprets, analyzes, and uses sources to document the problem of solid waste in America. Notice how the student writer draws her readers into the essay with a commonly used phrase about America and then questions the validity of its meaning. The student's opinions give shape to the paragraph, while her use of sources helps identify the problem and support her contentions.

"America the Beautiful" is a phrase used to describe the many wonders of nature found throughout our country. American's natural beauty will fade, however, if solutions to our solid waste problems are not found. America is a rich nation socially, economically, and politically. But these very elements may be the cause of Americans' wastefulness. Americans now generate approximately 160 million tons of solid waste a year—3½ pounds per person per day. We live in a consumer society where "convenience," "ready to use," and "throwaway" are words that spark the consumer's attention (Cook

60). However, many of the products associated with these words create a large part of our problem with solid waste (Grossman 39). We are running out of space for our garbage. The people of America are beginning to produce responses to this problem. Are we too late? A joint effort between individuals, businesses, government industries, and local, state, and federal governments is necessary to establish policies and procedures to combat this waste war. The problem requires not one solution, but a combination of solutions involving technologies and people working together to provide a safe and healthy environment for themselves and future generations.

Reading and Writing Documented Essays

Reading and writing documented essays involves the skillful integration of two complex operations: research and writing. Reading documented essays critically means understanding the material and evaluating the sources as you proceed. Writing documented essays includes reading and understanding sources on the topic you have chosen and then combining this reading with your own conclusions. The two skills are, essentially, mirror images of one another.

HOW TO READ DOCUMENTED ESSAYS

Preparing to Read. You should approach a documented essay in much the same way that you approach any essay. First, take a few minutes to look at the preliminary material for each selection: What does Betty Gittman's title, "Pregnant Teenagers: A Challenge," prepare you to read? What can you learn from scanning John Langone's essay, "Group Violence," and reading its synopsis in the Rhetorical Contents?

Also, you should learn as much as you can from the authors' biographies: What is Gittman's background? Does she have the proper qualifications to write about the social challenge of pregnant teenagers? What is Langone's interest in group violence? What biographical details prepare us for his approach to this topic? Who was the original audience for Langone's essay?

Another important part of preparing to read a documented essay is surveying the sources cited. Turn to the end of the essay, and look at the sources cited. Do you recognize any of the authorities that Gittman quotes? What publications does Langone draw from? Are these books and magazines well respected?

Last, before you read these essays, try to generate some ideas

TEACHING THE DOCUMENTED ESSAY: ONE INSTRUCTOR'S COMMENTS

The process of the research paper is as important as its content, for it stresses evaluating sources and authorities, paraphrasing and summarizing, problem solving, and collecting and interpreting data within the context of persuasion and argument. Emphasizing first the overview, I have students begin their research in the reference room by comparing their general topics in three encyclopedias. They learn how to use encyclopedias as a means, rather than as an end, to research. (They do not include the encyclopedias in their reference lists.) For their topics, they identify important characteristics, highlighting any different information, which often helps them focus their topics. They also list and check all cross references, identify experts through the articles' authors, and use the entries' bibliographies to create their own preliminary bibliographies. Armed with this information, students move to CD-ROM sources, specialized dictionaries, guides, and indices. The card catalogue is their last stop only after they have exhausted the reference room's sources. In the classroom, an effective technique is to show students the evolution of my research by using bibliography cards, notes, drafts, etc. through to the finished essay.

Judith C. Kohl
Dutchess Community College
Poughkeepsie, New York

The research paper is generally required in the freshman English sequence. It is used to teach research skills and to teach the synthesis and ethical use of information, ideas, and language within an argumentative (or other) context.

Students choose general topics during in-class conferences with me. These conferences take time but prevent students from trying to cover too much. After preliminary research, students write a paragraph in which they explain what they have found and propose a specific topic. If students do not yet have a focus, the proposal paragraph quickly reveals the lack of focus and shows which students need help at this stage. It's useful to have the proposal paragraphs reviewed in peer groups; classmates can make very insightful, constructive comments.

The research writer should be a processor and creative synthesizer of ideas, not a compiler or clerk simply moving words from various sources into one document. To make sure that students don't merely compile others' words, I limit quotations to 10 percent of the length of papers on non-literary topics. I also require students to take careful notes the old-fashioned way, on notecards. To make sure that careful notes are taken systematically, I check selected source and note cards against their sources (submitted as photocopies) before students begin writing the first draft. Time spent at this stage prevents problems later.

Through careful note-taking, students accomplish two desirable objectives: They avoid plagiarism, and they assimilate essential ideas, enabling themselves to think more thoroughly and write better about their topics. By not looking at others' words so much that those words spontaneously reappear during writing, students avoid unintentional plagiarism. By reading carefully, evaluating, and summarizing, students assimilate the ideas better than they would if they just looked at a stack of photocopies. They get the ideas into their heads where they can use them. A valuable by-product of improved assimilation of ideas is decreased incidence of writer's block: Students in con-

on each topic so you can participate as fully as possible in your reading. The Preparing to Read questions will get you ready for this task. Then, try to speculate further on the topic of each essay: What do you want to know from Gittman about teenage pregnancy? Why do you think this topic has become such an enormous social issue in America? Why has group violence gained so much momentum in the United States? How do you think group violence differs from acts of violence performed by individuals?

Reading. As you react to the material in this chapter, you should respond to both the research and the writing. Record your responses as you read the essay for the first time: What are your reactions to the information you are reading? Are the sources appropriate? How well do they support the author's point? Use the preliminary material before each essay to help you create a framework for your responses to it: Who was Gittman's primary audience when her essay was first published? In what ways is the tone of her essay appropriate for that audience? What motivated Langone to publish his argument on group violence? Do you find it convincing? Your main job at this stage is to determine each author's primary assertion (thesis statement), note the sources the author cites to support this thesis, and begin to ask yourself questions so you can respond critically to your reading. In addition, take a look at the questions after each selection to make certain you are comprehending the major ideas of the essay.

Rereading. As you reread these documented essays, take some time to become aware of the difference between fact and opinion, to weigh and evaluate the evidence brought to bear on the arguments, to consider the sources the writers use, to judge the interpretation of the facts cited, to determine what the writers omitted, and to confirm your own views on the issues at hand. All these skills demand the use of critical thinking strategies at their most sophisticated level. You need to approach this type of argument with an inquiring mind, asking questions and looking for answers as you read the essays. Also, be aware of your own thought processes as you sort facts from opinions. Know where you stand personally in relation to each side of the issues here.

For a list of guidelines for the entire reading process, see the checklists on pages 15–16 of the Introduction.

HOW TO WRITE DOCUMENTED ESSAYS

Preparing to Write. Just as with any writing assignment, you should begin the task of writing a documented essay by exploring and limiting your topic. In this case, however, you draw on other sources to help you with this process. You should seek out both primary and secondary sources related to your topic. **Primary sources** are works of literature, historical documents, letters, diaries, speeches, eyewitness accounts, and your own experiments, observations, and conclusions; **secondary sources** explain and analyze information from other sources. Any librarian can help you search for both types of sources related to your topic.

After you have found a few sources on your general topic, you should scan and evaluate what you have discovered so you can limit your topic further. Depending on the required length of your essay, you want to find a topic broad enough to be researched, established enough that you can find sources on it in the library, and significant enough to demonstrate your abilities to grapple with ideas and draw conclusions. The Preparing to Write questions can help you generate and focus your ideas.

Once you have established these limitations, you might try writing a tentative thesis. At this point, asking a question and attempting to find an answer is productive. But you should keep in mind that your thesis is likely to be revised several times as the range of your knowledge changes and as your paper takes different turns while you write. Then, decide on a purpose and audience for your essay.

Once your tentative thesis is formed, you should read your sources for ideas and take detailed notes on your reading. These notes will probably fall into one of four categories: (1) summary—a condensed statement of someone else's thoughts or observations; (2) paraphrase—a restatement in your own words of someone else's ideas or observations; (3) direct quotations from sources; or (4) a combination of these forms. As you gather information, you should consider keeping a "research journal" where you can record your own opinions, interpretations, and analyses in response to your reading. This journal should be separate from your notes on sources and is the place where you can make your own discoveries in relation to your topic by jotting down thoughts and relationships among ideas you are exposed to, by keeping a record of sources you read and others you want to pursue, by tracking and developing your own ideas and theories, and by clarifying your thinking on an issue.

Finally, before you write your first draft, you might want to write an informal working outline for your own information. Such an exercise can help you check the range of your coverage

trol of their material are unlikely to feel that they don't know what to say.

A five-minute oral presentation of the paper, before the final draft is prepared, helps students sharpen the paper's focus and shows students how research writing fits into the overall context of communication.

Peter Harris
West Virginia Institute of Technology
Montgomery, West Virginia

and the order and development of your ideas. With an outline, you can readily see where you need more information, less information, or more solid sources. Try to be flexible, however. This outline might change dramatically as your essay develops.

Writing.   Writing the first draft of a documented essay is your chance to discover new insights and see important connections between ideas that you might not be aware of yet. This draft is your opportunity to demonstrate that you understand the issue at hand and your sources on three increasingly difficult levels—literal, interpretive, and analytical; that you can organize your material effectively; that you can integrate your sources (in the form of summaries, paraphrases, or quotations) with your opinions; and that you can document your sources.

To begin this process, look again at your thesis statement and your working outline, and adjust them to represent any new discoveries you have made as you read your sources and wrote in your research journal. Then, organize your research notes and information in some logical fashion.

When you begin to draft your paper, write the sections of the essay that you feel most comfortable about first. Throughout the essay, feature your own point of view and integrate summaries, paraphrases, and quotations from other sources into your own analysis. Each point you make should be a section of your paper consisting of your own conclusion and your support for that conclusion (in the form of facts, examples, summaries, paraphrases, and quotations). Remember that the primary reason for doing such an assignment is to let you demonstrate your ability to synthesize material, draw your own conclusions, and analyze your sources and your own reasoning.

A documented paper usually blends three types of material:

1. *Common knowledge, such as the places and dates of events (even if you have to look them up).*
   EXAMPLE: Neil Armstrong and Edwin Aldrin first walked on the moon on July 20, 1969.
2. *Your own thoughts and observations.*
   EXAMPLE: Armstrong and Aldrin's brief walk on the moon's surface was the beginning of a new era in the U.S. space program.
3. *Someone else's thoughts and observations.*
   EXAMPLE: President Richard Nixon reacted to the moonwalk in a telephone call to the astronauts: "For one priceless moment in the history of man all the people on this earth are truly one—one in their pride in what you have done and one in our prayers that you will return safely to earth."

Of these three types of information, you must document or cite your exact source only for the third type. Negligence in citing your sources, whether purposeful or accidental, is called *plagiarism*, which comes from a Latin word meaning "kidnapper." Among student writers, it usually takes one of three forms: (1) using words from another source without quotation marks; (2) using someone else's ideas in the form of a summary or paraphrase without citing your source; and (3) using someone else's term paper as your own.

Avoiding plagiarism is quite simple: You just need to remember to acknowledge the sources of ideas or words that you are using to support your own contentions. Acknowledging your sources also gives you credit for the reading you have done and for the ability you have developed to use sources to support your observations and conclusions.

Documentation styles vary from discipline to discipline. Ask your instructor about the particular documentation style he or she wants you to follow. The most common styles are the Modern Language Association (MLA) style, used in humanities courses, and the American Psychological Association (APA) style, used in behavioral sciences and science courses. (See any writing handbook for more details on documentation formats.)

Even though documentation styles vary somewhat from one discipline to another, the basic concept behind documentation is the same in all disciplines: You must give proper credit to other writers by acknowledging the sources of the summaries, paraphrases, and quotations that you use to support the topics in your documented paper. Once you grasp this basic concept and accept it, you will have no trouble avoiding plagiarism.

Rewriting. To rewrite your documented essay, you should play the role of your readers and impartially evaluate your argument and the sources you have used as evidence in that argument. To begin with, revise your thesis to represent all the discoveries you made as you wrote your first draft. Then, look for problems in logic throughout the essay: Are the essay's assertions clear? Are they adequately supported? Does your argument flow smoothly? Are other points of view recognized and examined? Does the organization of your paper further your assertions/argument? Are all explanations in your paper clear? Have you removed irrelevant material? Have you added information to underdeveloped portions of your paper? Next, look carefully at specific words and sentences: Do the words say what you mean? Do your supporting sentences clearly amplify your main ideas?

Then, check your documentation style: Is your source material (either summarized, paraphrased, or quoted) presented fairly and accurately? Have you rechecked the citations for all the sources in your paper? Do you introduce the sources in your paper when appropriate? Are your sources in the proper format according to your instructor's guidelines (MLA, APA, or another)? Then, proofread carefully. Finally, prepare your paper to be submitted to your instructor: Does your title page follow the assignment's regulations? Have you prepared your paper with the proper margins? Are your page numbers in the proper place? If you have tables and abstracts in your paper, have you consulted the instructor and followed the appropriate rules? Have you prepared an alphabetical list of your sources for the end of your paper? Have you followed all your instructor's directions?

Any additional guidance you may need as you write and revise your documented essays is furnished on pages 27–28 of the Introduction.

Student Essay: Documentation at Work

The following student essay uses documented sources to support its conclusions and observations about our eating habits today. First, the writer creates a profile of carnivorous species in contrast to human beings. She then goes on to discuss the harsh realities connected with eating meat. After recognizing and refuting some opposing views, this student writer ends her paper with her own evaluation of the situation and a list of some famous vegetarians. Throughout the essay, the student writer carefully supports her principal points with summaries, paraphrases, and quotations from other sources. Notice that she uses the MLA documentation style and closes the paper with an alphabetical list of "Works Cited."

Food for Thought

The next time you sit down to a nice steak dinner, pause for a moment to consider whether you are biologically programmed to eat meat. Unlike carnivores, such as lions and tigers, with claws and sharp front teeth allowing them to tear and eat raw flesh, humans are omnivores, with fingers that can pluck fruits and grains and flat teeth that can grind these vegetable foods. To digest their meals, carni-

Back-ground informa-tion

vores have an acidic saliva and a very strong hydrochloric acid digestive fluid. In contrast, we humans have an alkaline saliva, and our digestive fluids are only one-tenth as potent as those of carnivores. Moreover, carnivores have an intestinal tract barely three times their body length, which allows for faster elimination of rotting flesh; humans have an intestinal tract eight to twelve times our body length, better enabling us to digest plant nutrients. These marked physiological distinctions clearly suggest that carnivorous animals and humans are adapted to very different kinds of foods (Diamond and Diamond, <u>Fit for Life II</u> 239). What happens, then, when we eat flesh? <u>The effects of a meat-based diet are far-reaching: massive suffering of the animals killed and eaten, a myriad of diseases in humans, and a devastating effect on world ecology.</u>

Common knowledge

Common knowledge

Paraphrase of secondary source

Thesis

Citation (MLA form)

<u>The atrocities committed daily to provide meat should be enough to make a meat-based diet completely unconscionable.</u> According to Peter Singer, of People for the Ethical Treatment of Animals (PETA), every year several hundred million cattle, pigs, and sheep and three billion chickens are slaughtered to provide food for humans (92). That is equal to 6,278 animals every minute of every day—and those are just the ones that make it to the slaughterhouse. Over 500,000 animals die in transit each year (Singer 150).

Student's first conclusion

Summary of secondary source

Support for conclusion #1

A slaughterhouse is not a pretty sight. Anywhere from 50 to 90 percent of the cattle are slaughtered in a "kosher" manner (Robbins 142). "Kosher" sounds innocent enough, but what it actually means is that the animal must be "healthy and moving" at the time of death. This requires the animals to be fully conscious as "a heavy chain is clamped around one of their rear legs; then they are jerked off their feet and hang upside down" for anywhere from two to five minutes, usually twisting in agony with a broken leg, while they are moved down the conveyer belt to be slaughtered (Robbins 140-1).

Paraphrase of secondary source (fact)

Summary of secondary source

The pain doesn't start at the time of slaughter, however, for most of these animals, but rather at birth. An in-depth look at the animal most slaughtered by people, the chicken, reveals particularly horrendous treatment. Chickens are used in two ways—for their flesh as well as their eggs. For egg

Student's opinion

manufacturers, the one-half million male chicks born every day are useless, so they are immediately thrown into garbage bags and left to suffocate. When you consider the life of their female counterparts, however, perhaps such brutal treatment is a blessing (Robbins 54).

Opinion from secondary source

Examples to support opinion

Chickens naturally belong to a flock with a specific pecking order. They seem to enjoy open spaces to stretch their wings as they scratch around, dust-bathe, and build nests for their eggs (Singer 109). Today, however, chickens are housed in wire-mesh cages suspended over a trench to collect droppings. The typical cage is 12- by 18-inches holding four or five hens for their entire productive lives, which is at least a year or more (Mason in Singer, *Defense* 91). This overcrowding results in such high levels of stress that the hens resort to pecking each other's feathers out and to cannibalism (Singer 98). Rather than incur the expense of increasing space to alleviate these conditions, chicken farmers have routinely adopted the practice of de-beaking the hens by slicing a hot knife through their highly sensitive beak tissue (Singer 99). Another result of this overcrowding is that the hens' toenails get tangled in the bottom wires of the cages; after some time the flesh grows onto the wire. The solution to this problem has become to cut off the chick's toes within a day or two of birth (Robbins 61). Conditions for other farm animals are equally despicable (Singer, *Defense*).

Para-phrase of secondary source (facts)

Para-phrase of secondary source (facts)

Analysis from secondary source

Para-phrase of secondary sources (facts)

Opinion from secondary source

While we would like to assume the animals we eat are healthy at the time of butchering, this is often not the case. Most veal calves, for example, are near death from anemia when sent to the butcher (Diamond and Diamond, *Fit for Life II* 238). Inspections have revealed leukosis (cancer) in 90% of the chickens (Robbins 67), pneumonia rates of 80%, and stomach ulcers of 53% in pigs (Robbins 94). Salmonellosis is found in 90% of the chickens dressed and ready to be purchased (Robbins 303).

Student's opinion

Examples from secondary sources

How can the factory farming industry justify its behavior? The answer boils down to money, for factory farming has become an incredibly huge business, and meat producers can't afford to be sentimental. As shown by USDA Economic Indicators for the Farm Sector, in 1988 the United States had cash receipts totaling over $150 billion from farm

Student's opinion

Para-
phrase of
secondary
sources
(fact)

marketing (State Financial Summary 151) and nearly $80 billion from livestock and livestock products (153). As Fred Haley, head of a poultry farm with nearly 250,000 hens, has stated, "The object of producing eggs is to make money. When we forget this objective, we have forgotten what it is all about" (qtd. in Robbins 67). Cattle auctioneer Henry Pace has a similar comment about the treatment of cattle: "We believe we can be most efficient by not being emotional. We are a business, not a humane society, and our job is to sell merchandise at a profit. It's no different from selling paper clips or refrigerators" (qtd. in Robbins 104).

Quotation
from
secondary
source

Quotation
from
secondary
source

Student's
second
conclusion

Even if we, like the industry leaders, could turn a cold heart to the plight of our fellow creatures, we would still find many reasons to warrant a vegetarian diet, beginning with our own health. Recapping just a few of the hundreds of studies that link diet to disease, we might consider the following:

Para-
phrase of
secondary
sources
(facts)

—A study of nearly 90,000 American women published in the New England Journal of Medicine reports that daily pork, lamb, or beef eaters have a 250 percent greater likelihood of developing colon cancer than people who consume these foods once a month or less ("Red Meat Alert").

Support for
conclusion
#2

—The Journal of the American Medical Association stated that a vegetarian diet could prevent 97 percent of coronary occlusions (Robbins 247).

—Scientists now routinely screen cattle workers for BIV, a disease that "shares about 35 percent of its genetic makeup with HIV," the human AIDS retrovirus ("Cattle's Link with AIDS" 19).

Summary
of
secondary
source

Other equally shocking residual health problems associated with a meat diet are also being documented. For instance, people tend to think that vegetarians are at high risk for pesticide poisoning, but according to the EPA's Pesticides Monitoring Journal, most pesticides in the American diet come from foods originating from animals. Studies have shown that 95 to 99 percent of toxic chemicals in the American diet come from meat, fish, and animal products (Robbins 315). These same pesticides are ending up in the milk of lactating mothers. A similar study in the New England Journal of Medicine showed that the breast milk of vegetarian mothers has contamination levels only 1 to 2 per-

Para-
phrase of
secondary
sources
(facts)

cent of the average (Robbins 345). Not only does vegetarian breast milk have strikingly lower levels of contamination, it also has higher levels of essential elements, such as selenium (Debski et al. 215).

Student's question

But don't we need a lot of protein to be strong and healthy? The RDA for protein is 56 grams (just under two ounces) per day (Diamond and Diamond, Fit for Life 88). People seem to think that meat is the best (or the only) way to get protein, but think about this: Some of the world's strongest animals—elephants, horses, gorillas—eat principally fruits, grain, or grass (Diamond, Fit for Life 89-90). Lest you believe that humans must eat meat to be strong and healthy, consider the following: Edwin Moses, undefeated in the 400-meter hurdles for eight years, is a vegetarian; Andreas Cahling, 1980 Mr. International Body Builder, is a vegetarian (Robbins 160-1); and Dave Scott, Ironman Triathlon winner four times (no one else has won it more than once), is a vegetarian (Robbins 158). In study after study, the consumption of protein is linked not with health but with such diseases as heart disease, hypertension, various forms of cancer, arthritis, and osteoporosis (Diamond and Diamond, Fit for Life 87).

Paraphrase of secondary source (fact)

Examples to answer protein question

Paraphrase of secondary source (fact)

Examples to answer protein question

The effects of meat diets go beyond causing human disease and death. Perhaps the most frightening legacy being left by America's dietary ritual is just now being realized, and that is the profound ecological impact factory farming is having on our planet. Every five seconds, one acre of forest is cleared in America, and one estimate is that 87 percent is cleared for either livestock grazing or growing livestock feed (Robbins 361). According to Christopher Uhl of the Pennsylvania State University Department of Biology and Geoffrey Parker of the Institute of Ecosystem Studies, 55 square feet of forest in Central America is lost for each hamburger eaten (642).

Student's third conclusion

Support for conclusion #3

Paraphrase of secondary sources (facts)

Forests are not all that we are sacrificing. Local governments are constantly calling for water conservation, yet over 50 percent of all water used in America goes into grain production for livestock (Robbins 367). According to one study, the water required to feed a meat eater for one day is 4,000 gallons, but it is only 1,200 gallons for a lacto-ovo (dairy and egg eating) vegetarian and 300 gallons

Student's opinion

Paraphrase of secondary sources (facts)

for a vegan (one who consumes no animal-derived products) (Robbins 367). Not only is the vast amount of water wasted through a meat-based diet outrageous, but the added cost of controlling animal waste must also be taken into account. One cow produces sixteen times as much waste as one human (Robbins 372), and cattle waste produces ten times the water pollution that human waste does (Robbins 373).

A third loss is even more serious than the losses of forests and water. This year, 60 million people will die of starvation, yet in America, we feed 80 percent of our corn and 95 percent of our oats to farm animals. The feed given to cattle alone, excluding pigs and chickens, would feed double the population of humans worldwide (Robbins 352). Three and one-quarter acres of farmland are needed to provide meat for one person per year. A lacto-ovo vegetarian can be fed from just one-half acre per year; a vegan needs only one-sixth of an acre. This means twenty vegans can eat a healthy diet for the same acreage needed to feed just one meat eater. Cutting our meat habit by only 10 percent would provide enough food for all of the 60 million people worldwide who will starve this year (Robbins 352-3).

As John Robbins, who relinquished his inheritance of the largest ice cream company in America, Baskin-Robbins, said, "We live in a crazy time, when people who make food choices that are healthy and compassionate are often considered weird, while people are considered normal whose eating habits promote disease and are dependent on enormous suffering" (305).

With all the devastation the average American diet is creating, we must begin to take responsibility for the consequences of our actions. Let us follow in the footsteps of such famous vegetarians as Charles Darwin, Leonardo da Vinci, Albert Einstein, Sir Isaac Newton, Plato, Pythagoras, Socrates, and Tolstoy (Parham 185). Every time we sit down to eat, we can choose either to contribute to or to help put an end to this suffering and destruction. Only one vote matters, and that is the one we make with our forks.

Works Cited

Alphabetical list of sources

Modern Language Association form

"Cattle's Link with AIDS." New Scientist 8 Oct. 1987: 19.

Debski, Bogdan, et al. "Selenium Content and Glutathione Peroxidase Activity of Milk from Vegetarian and Nonvegetarian Women." Journal of Nutrition 119 (1989): 215-20.

Diamond, Harvey, and Marilyn Diamond. Fit for Life. New York: Warner, 1985.

———. Fit for Life II, Living Health. New York: Warner, 1987.

Parham, Barbara. What's Wrong with Eating Meat? Denver: Ananda Marga, 1981.

"Red Meat Alert." New Scientist 22/29 Dec. 1990.

Robbins, John. Diet for a New America. Walpole: Stillpoint, 1987.

Singer, Peter. Animal Liberation: A New Ethics for Our Treatment of Animals. New York: Hearst, 1975.

Singer, Peter, ed. In Defense of Animals. New York: Basil Blackwell, 1985.

Snowdon, David A., and Roland L. Phillips. "Does a Vegetarian Diet Reduce the Occurrence of Diabetes?" Journal of Public Health 75 (1985): 507-11.

State Financial Summary, 1988. Washington: Economic Indicators for the Farm Sector, 1988.

Uhl, Christopher, and Geoffrey Parker. "Our Steak in the Jungle." Bio Science 36 (1986): 642.

Student Writer's Comments

From the moment this essay was assigned, I knew my topic would be vegetarianism, because I felt the key to a convincing argument was to select a topic I was passionate about. I was undertaking the task of speaking out against an American way of life, so I needed to approach the topic in as nonthreatening a manner as possible. I wanted to be graphic as I appealed to the emotions, concerns, and ethics of my audience so my message would not easily be forgotten, yet I had to strike a careful balance so I would not alienate my readers by appearing preachy or accusatory. While I wrote, I kept in mind that I would be successful only if my words caused my readers to make a change, however small, in their behavior. The only frustration was my difficulty in tracking down a number of key sources. Otherwise, writing this essay was a pleasure.

Some Final Thoughts on Documented Essays

The two essays that follow are vigorous exercises in critical thinking. They both use a combination of the three different types of persuasive appeals we studied in Chapter 9 (logical, emotional, and ethical) and draw on a wealth of rhetorical modes that we have studied throughout the book. In the first essay, on teenage pregnancy, Betty Gittman uses sources to support her thesis in favor of sex education and low-cost, easily accessible contraceptive services; it demonstrates the MLA documentation style. In the next essay, John Langone illustrates the APA documentation format as he dissects and analyzes the notion of mob violence. As you read these essays, be aware of the combination of appeals at work, the various rhetorical modes each author uses to further his or her argument, and the way each author uses sources to support the topics within the argument.

BETTY GITTMAN
(1945–   )

■ ■ ■

Pregnant Teenagers: A Challenge

Betty Gittman grew up in New York City and Long Island and earned a B.S. at New York University, an M.S. at Queens College, and a Ph.D. in Educational Research and Evaluation at Hofstra University. She is currently Coordinator of the Office of Institutional Research and Evaluation for the Board of Cooperative Educational Services in Nassau County, New York, where she prepares grant applications and evaluates educational programs—especially those that keep young students from dropping out of school. She is also a consultant to the Office for Substance Abuse Prevention of the U.S. Department of Health and Human Services and an adjunct professor at Long Island University, where she teaches classes in educational research. An "avid reader with a wide variety of tastes," Gittman enjoys writing fiction and poetry, working on computers, and playing with her Labrador retriever. Her advice to students using *The Prose Reader* is to "keep writing. Becoming a good writer," she explains, "means you must keep revising your work till you are satisfied with it. Writing is a process; you're never finished till you stop revising."

PREREADING

The purpose of this Preparing to Read material is to encourage students to think about the rising rate of teenage pregnancies in America. To help your students focus their attention on teenage pregnancies before responding to the questions here, have them close their eyes and imagine they are unmarried teenagers expecting a baby: What will they tell their parents? Will they keep the baby? What changes will occur in their lives? Guide them through part of the exercise, and then let them visualize the rest of the scenario in silence. See pages 3–6 for other ways to generate thoughts on these questions.

Preparing to Read

The following essay on teenage pregnancy was originally published in *The Educational Forum* (Winter 1986), a journal for members of Kappa Delta Pi, a national education honor society. The statistics were abstracted from a grant proposal Gittman had written earlier; the citations demonstrate current MLA (Modern Language Association) documentation form. As you prepare to read this article, take a few minutes to think about its central topic: Why do you think teenage pregnancy has attracted so much attention in America recently? What various social problems do teenage pregnancies reflect? What moral problems? What are the most serious consequences to the mother? To the father? To the rest of the teenager's family? To society? What can we do to prevent teenage pregnancies?

A recent comparative study concluded that the lowest rates of teenage pregnancy are found in countries where there are comprehensive programs in sex education, as well as low-cost and easily accessible contraceptive services for young people without parental notification (Jones et al. 53–63). Thus, contrary to the general assumption held by Americans, the ready availability of welfare and support for young mothers does not appear to be a motive for childbearing.

Teenage birth rates in the United States are much higher than in other industrialized nations. The contrast between the United States and other nations that are considered to be similar in socioeconomic and cultural characteristics (Sweden, the Netherlands, Great Britain, France and Canada) is particularly striking: "With more than 5 births per 1000 girls aged 14, the United States rate is about 4 times that of Canada, the only other country with as much as 1 birth per 1000 girls of comparable age" (Jones et al. 53–63).

In fact, ours is the only highly industrialized country where teenage pregnancy has been increasing in recent years. Of the babies born in 1982, 14 percent, or 523,531, belonged to adolescent mothers (Brozan 48). The U.S. Department of Labor statistics indicate that 25 percent of females, aged 16 to 19, from low income families are mothers. Only 1 in 20 of these young mothers are or have been married ("Lack of Education, Jobs, Costly for Teenage Mothers" 353–355).

These statistics translate into large numbers of frightened youngsters with few resources, saddled with adult responsibilities. The cost to society is reflected in a multitude of consequences.

Educational Consequences. Of pregnant girls, 2 out of 3 drop out of school. Of those who first gave birth at age 18, 50 percent earned a high school diploma, while 1.6 percent of them completed college ("Legacy of Teen Pregnancy" 216). The failure to complete high school results in reduced employment prospects and earning potential and in welfare dependency (Waxman; Wilson).

Economic Consequences. A 1981 study established that teenage pregnancy costs American taxpayers about $8.3 billion annually in welfare and related expenses. Two-thirds of the families with young children headed by women ages 14 to 25 are living below the poverty level (Edelman 109–116). Early childbirth is often associated with a lifetime of poverty and welfare dependency (McGee).

BACKGROUND INFORMATION

In this essay, Betty Gittman first describes the frightening statistics associated with teenage pregnancies. Then, she explains the cost of this problem for America in five specific areas: education, economics, medicine, psychology, and society in general. She argues in her conclusion that public schools should play a larger role in coordinating support services and in educating students about the responsibilities of raising illegitimate children.

READABILITY LEVEL

18.3

toxemia (para. 7): a condition in which toxic substances are spread by the bloodstream, resulting in headaches, swelling, visual impairment, and sometimes convulsions.
anemia (para. 7): a condition in which the blood is deficient in red blood cells or hemoglobin.
congenital malformity (para. 7): a physical deformity inherent at birth.
Hempstead (para. 13): a small town on Long Island, in New York State.

Medical Consequences. The association between medical complications and teenage pregnancy and birth has been established. The average teenager is in an intense growth state with its own requirements, while poor eating habits, inadequate rest, smoking, alcohol, and other drug abuses may degenerate the health of a teenager. Complications which are likely to affect the teenage mother include toxemia, anemia, and prolonged labor (Westoff; "Adolescent Pregnancy"). Babies born to adolescents are more likely to be of low birth weight. If 5½ pounds or less, the newborn encounters decreased chance for survival in the first year of life, and lessened prospects for healthy development beyond the first year, often suffering from immature organ systems, difficulty in controlling body temperature and blood sugar levels, mental retardation, congenital malformity, and a risk of dying that is 17 to 20 times higher than among babies heavier at birth ("Adolescent Pregnancy"; New Jersey Board of Education; Talan 14). 7

Psychological Consequences. Faced with problems of caring for a newborn child, as well as with worries of money, schooling, employment, housing, adequate food, and medical care, the young mothers, whose parents do not assume the responsibilities, often become desperate and alienated. Indeed, teenage pregnancy is a major factor in high adolescent suicide rates (*Facts of Life*; Wilson). 8

Social Consequences. Research has indicated that the social climate created by the teenage mother is potentially adverse, and especially so for the child who is reared by one who is isolated from adults (Anastasiow 396–401). It is likely that an association exists between child abuse and an adverse social climate (Garbarino and Stocking). 9

The Need to Act

Adolescent pregnancy is a problem of many dimensions, of which the ramifications may surface immediately or years later in welfare, social service, and child abuse statistics. The Children's Defense Fund takes the position that the best way to help a child is by providing services to the families of unborn or newborn infants. A child is far more likely to be raised in a safe and wholesome environment when the parents feel that they have the "power, confidence, and ability" to "act effectively" for their children ("Legacy of Teen Pregnancy" 216). 10

Continuance in school; education in prenatal, infant, and child care; coordination of support services; heightened awareness and sensitivity of teenagers' families and communities to the needs of adolescent mothers—these are the priorities in long-term planning that would improve the quality of life for the adolescent mother and her child at present, and possibly improve the quality of their lives in the future as well. If the family is strengthened and enabled to act for itself and for the child, then future needs for child care services, welfare payments, special education costs, and other related expenses may be lessened. Thus, a program that attempts to deal with the problem in a comprehensive manner, helping the teenager to cope effectively in her situation, may save society money in the long run.

The Role of the Schools.   The challenge to providers of social services is to develop creative ways of maintaining linkages between pregnant adolescents and the schools and to encourage students to meet the obligations associated with parenthood in a responsible manner. Proponents of a strong school role note that the adolescent comes into contact with the schools more than with any other societal institution. Too often, the medical institutions do not serve the adolescent until the pregnancy is well progressed. Of mothers under 15 years of age, 7 out of 10 receive no prenatal care in the first three months of pregnancy. Over 20 percent of these young mothers receive no prenatal care at all, or else they receive the care at the very end of the pregnancy (Edelman 109–116). Whether the cause for avoidance of medical care is fear, ignorance, shame, or denial, the consequence for adolescent mothers is one of medical complications for themselves and, too frequently, for their infants. According to at least one professional in special education, educators must be concerned with this problem because "a disproportionate number of children of young mothers will become future members of the group we refer to as exceptional or handicapped" (Anastasiow 396–401).

Exceptional or not, the children of today's pregnant teenagers will be entering the school systems in five years. The parents and their children, and their problems, do not disappear. However, programs for pregnant adolescents and adolescent mothers are an unpopular cause among local school district administrators. Even when such a program has been developed, a community, shocked by the magnitude of the problem of teenage pregnancy, may blame the school for the very problem. Administrative positions are too political in nature to encourage publication of such

COLLABORATIVE LEARNING:
CLASS ACTIVITY

11 As an entire class, discuss the ramifications of teenage pregnancy on society. Use the material that Gittman provides in this essay as the focal point of your discussion. You may want to point out to your students that since her essay was written in 1986, the rate of teenage pregnancy has declined. Although approximately 95 percent of the teens who give birth annually (about 1,000,000 in 1990) keep their babies, the number of live births is declining. You might consider the implications of these statistics for contemporary society. At this stage, you are simply establishing with your class the extent and seriousness of the problem.

12

COLLABORATIVE LEARNING:
SMALL GROUP ACTIVITY

Divide your class into five groups based on the consequences Gittman discusses: (1) educational, (2) economic, (3) medical, (4) psychological, and (5) social. Then, have your students begin some library work on the

13 subject of teenage pregnancy by finding further information on their assigned set of consequences and relevant solutions. When your students reassemble in their groups, have them compile their information on each subtopic and summarize their findings in a paragraph to be presented to the class. Finally, have one person from each group read the group's paragraph to the rest of the class.

troublesome issues. Few parents are willing to publicize the problems and to demand support from the schools. Furthermore, the program may provoke resentment among some faculty who believe that student pregnancy and parenthood should not be the school's concerns. Thus, those who need them may find a dearth of services in the local district (Zellman 15–21). For instance, in New York state, the town of Hempstead has been identified as having had, between 1978 and 1980, the highest rates of teenage pregnancy, infant deaths, and mothers lacking prenatal care. Yet, in 1980, *no* family planning service existed there (Burton).

Support Services. Finishing high school is recognized as critical to the future well-being of the young mothers, as well as, presumably, of their children. To finish high school and still meet their parental responsibilities, the young mothers need assistance with child care, parenting education, housing, and transportation. A 1980 survey conducted by the New York State Education Department, involving 47,000 students, 600 teachers, and 800 parents, concluded that a program of planning and development be established in order to deal with the need to provide assistance to adolescents and their families who are faced with the issue of pregnancy and parenthood ("Adolescent Pregnancy Project Status Report"). 14

Types of services needed by pregnant teenagers include health services, services for children, basic living needs, life skills training, academic education, counseling, advocacy, employment assistance, emergency help, self-help groups, social and recreational activities, and follow-up. In several cities comprehensive health care clinics have been established on school premises. These clinics offer services to pregnant girls and family planning as well. By May 1985, according to a recent report, "there will be 30 clinics in schools in 17 cities, with 19 more in various stages of planning, including several for New York" (Brozan 48). In contrast, a service delivery approach consists of bringing together a diverse group of religious organizations, family-planning services, potential employers, and health providers to create a network for recruiting and serving pregnant girls. 15

Unfortunately, a 1982 survey found that services, even where available, "are weak: They serve a small percentage of the eligible population; they are disproportionately focused on pregnancy and on crisis intervention; their quality is uneven and their effectiveness mixed; they are not well-coordinated with other services; and many aspects of service delivery limit their accessibility and usefulness" (McGee 55). 16

School Programs. Two basic types may be identified here. 17
The *inclusive* programs provide short-term courses outside the
home school setting, including those in nutrition or prenatal and
infant development. The emphasis is on maintenance, that is to
say, on keeping the girls attending classes so that when they re-
enter their home schools they will not have lost their grade level
standings. The *non-inclusive* programs are academically stronger,
since the girls continue to attend classes in their home school
rather than being requested to attend a special program, where
course offerings are probably quite limited and the coursework is
often far less rigorous. The difficulty with non-inclusive programs is that the pregnant teenagers may be too embarrassed to
be willing to attend classes in their home schools.

The traditional view of the school as an institution responsi- 18
ble primarily for academic education is unsupportable, when one
takes into consideration the fact that the school is the one societal
institution through which children can be reached directly. As society's chief means of contact with adolescents, the schools may
be more successful than other institutions in assisting pregnant
teenagers and their children. Schools can work in partnership
with other state agencies, each agency allowing the others their
full areas of responsibility and each developing its own areas
(academic, medical, social, psychological, etc.), yet all working together to provide the services and support required. Or, schools
can operate as brokers of services, organizing information on the
availability of existing services and then referring the girls to the
appropriate facilities. Or, schools can cooperate with each other
within and between districts to provide pregnant adolescents and
adolescent mothers with one clearly responsible agency and a
centralized site for services.

A centralized approach offers at least one advantage in that it 19
can assume responsibility for coordination and then follow
through by offering the services and evaluating the effectiveness
of service delivery. This approach is highly responsive to students' needs. Another important consideration is that a centralized agency can follow through on long-term evaluation of the
girls' adjustments, thus permitting and possibly encouraging intervention over a long period of time. A centralized agency can
avoid costly duplication of services, ensure coverage of all areas
for service, and eliminate confusion on the part of the pregnant
adolescents and adolescent mothers regarding where and how to
obtain needed assistance.

Whether serving individually, in partnership, as brokers of 20

1. Adolescent pregnancies cause many problems for individual mothers and for society as a whole. Gittman lists five categories of consequences: educational, such as the dropout rate for pregnant high school students; economic, such as the enormous cost to the government in welfare benefits to support teenagers who have minimal job skills; medical, such as the alarming death rate and risk to the health of both the mother and the baby caused by ignoring the need for prenatal care; psychological, such as the depression, frustration, and fear young girls must face, often with little or no assistance; and social, such as unemployment, poverty, and child abuse.

2. Gittman found the lowest teenage pregnancy rates "in countries where there are comprehensive programs in sex education , as well as low-cost and easily accessible contraceptive services" (para. 1).

3. Because the schools have a close link with teenagers, Gittman believes that services for pregnant teenagers, including family planning, should be organized around these institutions so the teenagers' connections with their schools can be maintained. Then, city agencies could coordinate services with high schools to complement the offices already located on individual campuses.

ANSWERS TO QUESTIONS:
ANALYZING MEANING (p. 523)

1. Responses to this question will vary.
2. Responses to this question will vary.
3. Responses to this question will vary.

services, or in a centralized format, the schools would be filling a large and growing need simply by developing administrative policies to cope with the problem through the educational institutions.

Works Cited

"Adolescent Pregnancy." *Leaders Alert Bulletin,* March of Dimes Birth Defects Foundation, 1981.

"Adolescent Pregnancy Project Status Report 1/1/79–1/31/80." New York: State Education Department, Bureau of School Health Education and Services, Oct. 1980.

Anastasiow, Nicholas. "Adolescent Pregnancy and Special Education." *Exceptional Children* 49 (1983): 396–401.

Brozan, Nadine. "Complex Problems of Teenage Pregnancy." *New York Times* 2 March 1985: 48.

Burton, M. C. "A Study of Practices Related to Unwed Mothers in the Local Secondary School Systems of Nassau County, Long Island, New York." New York: Board of Cooperative Educational Services of Nassau County, 1981.

Edelman, Marian Wright. "Who Is for Children?" *American Psychologist* 36 (Feb. 1981): 109–116.

Facts of Life about Teenage Pregnancy in Nassau County. New York: Health Department, Bureau of Family Planning, 1982.

Garbarino, J., and S. H. Stocking. "The Social Context of Child Maltreatment." *Protecting Children from Abuse and Neglect,* ed. J. Garbarino and S. H. Stocking. San Francisco: Jossey-Bass, 1980.

Jones, Elise F., et al. "Teenage Pregnancy in Developed Countries: Determinants and Policy Implications." *Family Planning Perspectives* 17 (1985): 53–63.

"Lack of Education, Jobs, Costly for Teenage Mothers." *Education U.S.A.: National School Public Relations Association Weekly* 15 Jan. 1979: 353–355.

"Legacy of Teen Pregnancy: Dropouts." *Education U.S.A.: National School Public Relations Association Weekly* 1 Mar. 1982: 216.

McGee, Elizabeth A. "Too Little, Too Late: Services for Teenage Parents." New York: Ford Foundation, Oct. 1982.

New Jersey Board of Education. *Educational Services for School-age Parents: Resource Manual.* Washington, D.C.: Bureau of Elementary and Secondary Education, 1974.

Talan, Jamie. "Nutrition for Pregnant Teenagers." *New York Times* 28 Oct. 1984: 14.

Waxman, Rebecca. "Urban Youth in the 80s: Fact Sheets 1–4." ERIC, Jul. 1980: ED 193 409.

Westoff, L. A. "Kids with Kids." *New York Times Magazine* 22 Feb. 1976.

Wilson, Hugh. "Adolescent Pregnancy in Suburbia." New York: Planned Parenthood of Nassau County, 1983.

Zellman, G. L. "Public School Programs for Adolescent Pregnancy and Parenthood: An Assessment." *Family Planning Perspectives* 14 (1982): 15–21.

UNDERSTANDING DETAILS

1. According to Gittman, what are the consequences of the high rate of teenage pregnancy in America?
2. Where were the lowest rates of teenage pregnancy found?
3. According to Gittman, what role should schools play in the prevention of teenage pregnancy?

ANALYZING MEANING

1. Why do you think so many teenagers get pregnant in the United States? How do you think society and family background affect this pregnancy rate?
2. To what extent does Gittman persuade you of "the need to act"? Which of her details were most persuasive to you? Why?
3. Why do you think teenage birth rates are higher in the United States than in other countries?

DISCOVERING RHETORICAL STRATEGIES

1. What principal rhetorical modes does Gittman use in this essay? Give an example of each.
2. Do the subheadings help you understand the essay? In what ways?
3. How do Gittman's sources and statistics help advance her argument? Are they effective? Would the essay be as convincing without this research to support it? Why or why not?

IDEAS FOR DISCUSSION/WRITING

Preparing to Write

Write freely about teenage pregnancy in American society: What do you think are the main causes of the extremely high rate of teenage pregnancy in the United States? Which of the consequences of teenage pregnancy affect you most directly? Which affect your immediate environment? Society in general? What measures should be taken to reduce the number of teenage pregnancies? Who should take charge of solving this problem? How could your proposed solution be implemented? What effects would it have on the problem?

ANSWERS TO QUESTIONS: DISCOVERING RHETORICAL STRATEGIES (p. 523)

1. Gittman uses example, comparison/contrast, and argument/persuasion in her documented essay. Through statistics, she illustrates not only the vast number of teenage mothers, but the number of those mothers who face the consequences she describes. Along with these examples, Gittman compares the pregnancy rates of industrial countries and uses this comparison to support her theory that the best way to keep teenagers from becoming pregnant is to furnish them with frank, useful information and family planning services. By constructing a logical argument that moves from facts to a possible solution (that schools offer services for pregnant teens), Gittman establishes the seriousness of this problem and then attempts to persuade readers to take action to control it.

2. Responses to this question will vary.

3. Without statistics, Gittman's article would be merely an expression of her opinion, and, no matter how valid, her subjective comments would not be as persuasive as the concrete evidence she cites to support her point of view.

PREWRITING

In preparation for the writing assignments, the Preparing to Write questions ask students to consider in detail the consequences of teenage pregnancy before writing an essay on a related topic. See pages 16–23 for suggestions on generating ideas in response to these questions.

ADDITIONAL DISCUSSION/WRITING TOPIC

What do you think the role of the government should be in America's current crisis involving teenage pregnancy. Use Gittman's article as one of your sources, and then read further on the subject in the library. Next, write a clear, well-documented essay suggesting what the government might do to help solve this serious social problem. Should we make the problem more visible? Through what channels? Organize your paper clearly and present your suggestions logically, using proper documentation (citations and bibliography) to support your argument.

REVISING STRATEGY

The types of appeals you choose to persuade your audience make a great deal of difference in the overall effect of your essay. In one of your persuasive papers, underline all your appeals (logical, emotional, and ethical): How many of each type of appeal does your essay contain? Is this an effective proportion for achieving your purpose with your intended audience? In what ways should you adjust this proportion to produce a more effective paper? Also, notice any weaknesses or inconsistencies in these appeals. Then revise your paper, correcting the problems you have identified.

FURTHER READING

Corbett, Margaret-Ann, and Jerrilyn H. Meyer. *The Adolescent and Pregnancy.* Boston: Blackwell Scientific Publications, 1987.

Dash, Leon. *When Children Want Children: An Inside Look at the Crisis of Teenage Parenthood.* New York:Viking Penguin, 1990.

Henshaw, Stanley. *Teenage Pregnancy in the United States: The Scope of the Problem and State Responses.* New York: Alan Guttmacher Institute, 1989.

McCuen, Gary E. *Children Having Children: Global Perspectives on Teenage Pregnancy.* Madison, Wisconsin: Gary E. McCuen Publications, 1988.

Nathanson, Constance. *Dangerous Passage: The Social Control of Sexuality of Women's Adolescence.* Philadelphia: Temple University Press, 1991.

Choosing a Topic

1. Design a feasible solution to the problem of teenage pregnancy that Gittman outlines in this essay. Then, using Gittman's essay as your main source, write an argumentative essay presenting the problem as you understand it and offering a detailed solution to it. Cite Gittman's essay as necessary.

2. What do you think the role of the schools should be in America's current crisis involving teenage pregnancy? Use Gittman's article as one of your sources, and then read further on the subject in the library. Next, write a clear, well-documented argument on what American schools might do to help solve this serious social problem. Should we make the problem more visible? Should we offer more sex education classes? At what levels? Organize your paper clearly and present your suggestions logically, using proper documentation (citations and bibliography) to support your stand.

3. Choose one category of consequences of teenage pregnancy that Gittman discusses in paragraphs 5 through 9 of her essay, and research it further in the library. Then, write a well-documented argument explaining the seriousness of teenage pregnancy in America by discussing and analyzing in depth the consequences you have studied.

JOHN LANGONE
(1929–   )

■ ■ ■

Group Violence

The fifteen books written by scientist/journalist John Langone during the last thirty years have ranged over a fascinating array of topics, including violence, suicide, death and dying, aging, sex education, mental illness, genetic manipulation, drug abuse, and medical ethics. He grew up in Cambridge, Massachusetts, in a family of scientists and spent a great deal of time in the biology and physiology laboratories at Harvard University, where two of his uncles worked. Although he remained interested in science, he pursued educational and employment opportunities that took him in the direction of journalism. Following a B.S. at Boston University, Langone held several newspaper jobs before becoming Rhode Island bureau chief for United Press International, science editor at the *Boston Herald,* and then senior editor of *Discover* magazine. He is currently associate editor for medical news at *Time* magazine. Three academic fellowships have helped the author bring together his dual interests in journalism and science: a Kennedy Fellowship in medical ethics at Harvard, a Fulbright at the University of Tokyo Medical School, and a journalism fellowship at the Center for Advanced Study in the Behavioral Sciences at Stanford. Langone describes himself as "a compulsive writer who has been nurtured in the deadline world of daily newspaper and wire service reporting." His latest book, *Superconductivity: The New Alchemy* (1989), examines the far-reaching implications of research in superconductors—materials that transport electricity without substantial loss of energy. In his private life, the author enjoys gardening, playing ice hockey, reading Shakespeare, and listening to music—particularly Mozart and Liszt.

Preparing to Read

The following essay, taken from *Violence: Our Fastest Growing Public Health Problem* (1984), analyzes the basic causes of mob psychology; its citations and bibliography illustrate proper APA (American Psychological Association) documentation form. Before you read Langone's article, take a few minutes to think about violence in general: How would you define a "violent" action? How many different types of violent acts can you think of? What are the major similarities among these acts? What do individual violence and group violence have in common? How are they different? How could we control violence in America more effectively than we do at present?

▬▬▬▬▬▬▬▬▬▬▬▬▬▬▬▬▬▬▬▬▬▬▬▬▬▬▬▬▬▬▬▬▬

BACKGROUND INFORMATION

John Langone examines the causes and results of crowd violence in several examples throughout history, including the Kent State massacre in 1970 and the bloody Attica prison riot in 1971. In this manner, the author identifies the principal psychological reasons large groups of people become riotous mobs.

READABILITY LEVEL

13.9

RELATED READINGS

Crime

Kimberly Wozencraft, "Notes from the Country Club"   63
Nancy Gibbs, "When Is It Rape?"   345

Societal Problems

Kimberly Wozencraft, "Notes from the Country Club"   63
Judith Wallerstein and Sandra Blakeslee, "Second Chances for Children of Divorce"   264
Nancy Gibbs, "When Is It Rape?"   345
Michael Dorris, "The Broken Cord"   400
Michael Fabricant and Michael Driscoll-Kelly, "The Problem of Homelessness Is Serious"   484
Martin Morse Wooster, "The Problem of Homelessness is Exaggerated"   484
Betty Gittman, "Pregnant Teenagers: A Challenge"   516

Violence can be done by individuals with their own private   1
motives, and by individuals working for the motives of a special group. Many times, when one person assaults another it is for highly personal reasons: A drug dealer murders an undercover agent to escape arrest, a woman kills a lover who has been cheating on her to punish him and the other woman, an irate employee murders the manager who fired him, a young man provokes a brawl to prove he is tough, a woman is raped because her attacker was once spurned by a high school girlfriend and now hates all women.

But quite often, individuals commit violent acts not only to   2
satisfy themselves, but also to gain some benefit for a group of people. They may belong to a lynch mob that takes the law into its own hands and executes a suspect before he or she has had a fair trial; they may be members of a secret society of misguided zealots that uses violence to intimidate; they may be participants in a family feud, a private war waged for generations to avenge the death of one of its members long ago; they may be political terrorists who use violence to force change, or to call attention to their cause, or to avenge some real or imagined or long-past insult or wrong. Some people may not even be members of the group for whom they commit violence: A hired assassin, for instance, might not be at all concerned with the philosophy or actions of the world leader he has been paid to eliminate, nor have any personal grudge against him. But whether such hired killers formally belong to an organization is not all that important; their reasons for maiming and killing are usually to further the aims of that group.

Let us begin our discussion of group violence by looking at   3
what psychologists call crowd behavior, popularly known as mob psychology. Certainly, there are no formal membership requirements, no dues to be paid, to join a lynch mob or a student riot. Unlike some of the other forms of group violence to be discussed later, mob violence is often unplanned and unorganized; a mob's members lose their ability to think rationally, so intent are

they on acting as one; its leadership generally depends on who can shout the loudest or who is strong enough to get to the front of the crowd fastest. Moreover, a mob generally breaks up rather quickly once its purpose has been achieved. Says one sociology textbook, "In crowd behavior, irrational as it always is, the impulse to follow a suggested course of action is obeyed at once; whereas, in any form of rational behavior, there is always delay enough to permit comparisons and evaluations" (Sutherland and Woodward, 1940, p. 317).

Experts in mob psychology say the anatomy of a riot begins with a precipitating event, a trigger. This may be the arrest of someone the crowd believes to be innocent or a scapegoat; an assault on a white by a black or vice versa; a simple official act, like the dedication of a statue of a controversial figure; the parking of a foreign car near an automobile factory that suffered high unemployment because of foreign-car imports; or merely the announcement that a state has approved the construction of a nuclear power plant.

As word of the triggering event spreads, the crowd becomes angrier; finally, violence erupts, escalating from shouting and occasional rock throwing to open street war as the rioters clash with police, others in authority, or those who oppose their views. Such a situation has been compared to the outbreak of a disease epidemic. Dr. John P. Spiegel, who headed the Lemberg Center for the Study of Violence at Brandeis University, once said of mass violence, "You just can't ignore it, isolate it, or hope that it will cure itself" (*Medical World News*, 1967, p. 48).

Often, the common hostility of a crowd has been festering for some time and is not just a sudden eruption. If, for instance, a hostile mob has gathered at a civil rights parade, the concerted action taken when some incident or person ignites the violence is the result of a long-standing racial conflict shimmering in each member of the crowd. Matters are obviously made much worse, and the mob becomes more inflamed, if whatever it is that provokes the riot has not been dealt with fairly, or at all, by authorities.

A mob generally behaves in ways that its individual members would shun if alone: Few members of a riotous crowd would, for example, stand alone in front of a policeman and shout obscenities at him; nor would many people break a store window in broad daylight and help themselves to a television set or a wristwatch; and it is highly unlikely that mob members would, acting alone, attempt to crash a gate at a navy base to

DEFINITIONS

zealots (para. 2): those who vigorously embrace a cause.

Sicily (para. 7): an Italian region west of the southern tip of Italy, the largest island in the Mediterranean Sea.

Angevin French (para. 7): the ruling population of Sicily during the thirteenth century, placed in power by Charles of Anjou in 1266.

Nanking (para. 7): a city in eastern China 150 miles northwest of Shanghai.

White Lotus (para. 8): a Chinese secret society originating around the twelfth century that eventually rose against misgovernment and caused a major rebellion in 1796.

Saint Petersburg (para. 8): the capital of Russia (1712–1917) whose name was changed to Leningrad in 1924 and was changed back in 1991; now the second largest city in the republic of Russia.

Haymarket riot (para. 9): a clash between police and union sympathizers in Chicago (May 4, 1886).

Homestead Strike (para. 9): one of the bitterest labor disputes in American history (July 1892).

Watts (para. 11): a section of Los Angeles whose residents are primarily African-American.

Attica (para. 15): a state prison located in the town of Attica in western New York.

Crispus Attucks (1723?–1770) (para. 16): a sailor of African-American and Native-American heritage who reputedly led the patriots in the Boston Massacre and was one of the first killed.

4

5

6

7

protest the docking of a nuclear submarine. It is the *gathering* of individuals, with their strong, shared feeling, that gives the individuals within the group their sense of courage and power, and allows each to release impulses usually kept under control. Wartime and periods of insurrection contain proof of that. For example, on Easter Monday in 1282, on the island of Sicily, a riot broke out after a French soldier insulted a Sicilian woman in front of a church at the hour of evening worship, or vespers; in what came to be known as the Sicilian Vespers, the riot swelled to a political revolt against the Angevin French who ruled the island, and virtually the entire French population was murdered. In Nanking, China, during World War II, drunken Japanese soldiers and sailors slaughtered 150,000 Chinese and raped some 5,000 women in an outbreak of mob brutality that seems almost inconceivable.

Mob action, like the violence it spawns, is not new. Dissent has a long history, and mobs have gathered since at least the early Roman days—when loud protests were lodged even then against the high cost of living—to air economic, political, and social grievances, or to vent their anger against other groups. In China in 1900, for example, a branch of a sect known as the White Lotus—also called Boxers—rose up against foreigners. Missionaries were murdered, a German official was assassinated, and later some two hundred foreigners were driven to seek refuge in the British legation. They were besieged by the Boxers for two months, and were finally rescued by an expedition of soldiers from America, Great Britain, France, Germany, Russia, and Japan. A few years later, on January 22, 1905, Russian peasant workers marched on Saint Petersburg to present a petition to the czar. They were attacked by the Czar's troops, and hundreds of unarmed workers were killed.

In the United States, mobs turned against immigrants, especially Orientals and Irish Catholics, in the 1800s. Native-born Americans, fearful that the immigrants would gain political power, and angry that they were taking jobs for cheaper pay, regularly attacked the immigrants in the streets. During the same period, bloody labor riots erupted in cities across the United States, and many lives were lost. In 1886, for instance, there was the celebrated Haymarket riot in Chicago. It occurred when police tried to break up a labor protest meeting organized by anarchists—people who believe that all forms of government are unnecessary and undesirable. Someone threw a bomb, killing seven policemen and wounding seventy other people. A few years later, during the so-called Homestead strike at the Carnegie Steel Company plant in Pennsylvania, an armed clash took place between workers and detectives hired by the company; a number of men were killed, and soon after, the state militia had to be sent in to restore order.

Even today, workers are sometimes set upon. In 1983, when a group of independent truckers went on strike, thousands of trucks that defied the strike and kept on rolling were damaged by rocks thrown from bridges, by nails spread on the highways, and by gunfire. Many drivers were injured and one was killed.

Race has also been a factor in mob violence. During World War I (1914–1918), many blacks took jobs in defense factories. The whites were afraid that the blacks would take their jobs and move into white neighborhoods. Several violent incidents occurred—the worst in East Saint Louis in 1917 when some forty blacks and ten whites were killed during a riot. Similar racial violence broke out after World War II (1939–1945) and has continued through the years. Among the worst in recent years were the riots in the Watts section of Los Angeles in 1965, and in Newark and Detroit in 1967.

In the sixties and seventies, mob violence was common during the student protests against the war in Vietnam (1957–1975). In one of the largest such demonstrations, thousands of young people gathered in Chicago during the 1968 Democratic National Convention and battled with police in the streets. Around the same time, militant black students regularly resorted to violence to back up demands for more Afro-American history and culture courses in their colleges.

But of all this mob violence, the two incidents that stand out in recent years, perhaps for the emotional impact they had on Americans, were the tragic student deaths at Kent State University in Ohio in 1970, and the riot at Attica state prison in New York the following year. The two events were unrelated—the Kent State incident came during demonstrations against President Nixon's decision to send U.S. forces into Cambodia, and the Attica uprising stemmed from charges that inmates, most of them black, had been mistreated by white guards. But both places have become unofficial national monuments to the tragic consequences of confrontation.

The Kent State incident began with students throwing rocks, bricks, and bottles at National Guardsmen, and guardsmen firing tear gas. Then, some of the guardsmen knelt and pointed rifles at demonstrators, who shouted, "Shoot, shoot, shoot!" The kneeling

Have each of your students interview someone who has committed an act of violence. Did the person do this alone or as part of a group? Why did he or she commit this act? Set a deadline for bringing the material back to class, and have each student 10 present to the entire class his or her conversations.

11

12

13

Divide your students into 4 or 5 groups. Then, have each group begin some library work on the subject of violence by finding further information on one of the aspects of this problem and its relevant solutions. When your students reassemble in their groups, have them compile information on 14 their particular subtopic and summarize their findings in a paragraph to be presented to the class as a whole. Then, have one person from each group read the group's paragraph to the rest of the class.

guardsmen did not fire. But moments later, it happened. "I heard the first shot," one account quoted a guardsman as saying. "I had my rifle at my shoulder, not sighting, just at my shoulder. I had my finger on the trigger and fired when the others did. I just didn't think about it. It just happened. How can you think at a time like that? Right after the first shot, it sounded like everyone squeezed off one round, like at the range, drawn out. I fired once. I just closed my eyes and shot. I didn't aim at anyone in particular. I just shot at shoulder level toward the crowd." An estimated sixty shots were fired, and thirteen seconds later, when it was over, four of the student demonstrators had been killed, nine wounded. Two reporters who were there that day wrote, "Most of the victims were dressed in bell-bottoms and flowered Apache shirts, and most had Rolling Stone haircuts. Some carried books. The guardsmen wore battle helmets, gas masks, fatigues, and combat boots. The two sides looked, to each other, like the inhabitants of different worlds. . . . Blood shimmered on the grass. Bullet holes marked the trees. A generation of college students said they had lost all hope for the System and the future" (Eszterhas and Roberts, 1970, pp. 8, 163).

The Attica incident was just as chaotic. The revolt involved   15
some one thousand prisoners, who held thirty-eight guards and civilian workers hostage for four days. Faced with the possibility that the convicts would carry out threats to kill the hostages, New York Governor Nelson Rockefeller ordered state troopers to storm the facility. In the assault, which included use of a tear-gas-spraying helicopter, thirty-two prisoners and nine guards and employees were killed. Rockefeller, who had turned down a request that he personally visit the prison during the revolt, defended the action, saying, "There was no alternative but to go in." Adding to the depth of the tragedy were reports that many of the hostages had died of bullet wounds, rather than by knife attacks from convicts—an indication that, as commonly happens in scenes of mob violence, some people were killed unintentionally. Shortly after the riot was quelled, Rockefeller acknowledged that it was possible state troopers had killed some of the hostages. "If you recreate the circumstances of that situation—where the troopers had instructions to shoot the executioners who had been assigned to each of the prisoners [a reference to convicts menacing hostages] and who were standing there with a knife at his throat—then you add to that the helicopter coming in with the gas, and the effect of the gas—which first creates a cloud and then has an effect on the individual—you have a scene of chaos that is

one in which accidents can very well happen" (*New York Times*, 1971, p. 1).

Both the Kent State tragedy and the awful ending to the Attica revolt raise questions about how much force should be used to put down a disturbance. Often, as has been seen, the mob itself loots and burns and kills; other times, however, it is the authorities who lose control and riot. The Boston Massacre of March 5, 1770, is a familiar example of such a situation, and one that is sometimes used when the events at Kent State are being discussed. The stationing of British soldiers in Boston in 1768 had provoked a good deal of anger among the citizens. Matters came to a head when more troops were sent to the city to protect customs commissioners. A mob of men and boys, led by a black named Crispus Attucks, began throwing missiles at the soldiers, who responded by firing into the crowd, killing five. Some witnesses regarded the unfortunate incident as a lawless affair that discredited both soldiers and the crowd; others have seen it as a historically significant event, an important preliminary to the American Revolution. Whatever it was, it lends substance to the old expression that a policeman's lot is not a happy one. "Police often vacillate between brutal suppression and inaction," said Dr. Spiegel. "If they use excessive force, they encourage the use of counterforce. If they do nothing, they encourage rioters and looters" (*Medical World News*, 1967, p. 48).

The Kent State and Attica incidents may also make it somewhat easier to justify the violent explosion of a mob. Many people become angered after being maltreated, as at Attica, or provoked, as were the guardsmen at Kent State, and it is quite natural, although perhaps wrong, to lash out occasionally at the people believed responsible. When nobody listens to a complaint that appears to be legitimate, when nobody tries to rectify a bad situation, a violent act is perhaps the only way left to focus attention on the wrong, and help get something done about it.

References

Eszterhas, J. & Roberts, M. (1970). *Thirteen Seconds: Confrontation at Kent State.* New York: Dodd, Mead & Co.

"Is mass violence an epidemic disease?" *Medical World News*, September 1, 1967, p. 48.

New York Times, September 16, 1971, p. 1.

Sutherland, R. & Woodward, J. (1940). *Introductory sociology.* Philadelphia: J. B. Lippincott.

16

ANSWERS TO QUESTIONS: UNDERSTANDING DETAILS (p. 532)

1. "Mob violence" (para. 3), according to Langone, occurs when a group of people assemble unintentionally and act in ways that would normally be alien to them. They generally share some grievance or complaint that has not been acknowledged, and the idea of being supported by a group releases individuals from the constraints usually governing their actions.

2. A "precipitating event" or "trigger" (para. 4) can take many different forms. Some events trigger deeply held beliefs; some prompt immediate anger over a perceived wrongdoing against the crowd; and others incite people to respond to a cause. The common denominator in all triggering events is that they elicit anger from the crowd.

3. In Langone's view, since World War II racial conflicts have been a major source of mob violence. Racism incites groups to anger based on cultural differences. Because these differences are often the source of a preexisting hatred between groups, any "precipitating event" (para. 4), no matter how small, can set off either side.

ANSWERS TO QUESTIONS: 17 ANALYZING MEANING (p. 532)

1. Group and individual violence differ in their motivation and approach. The individual is likely to commit a violent act because something has been done to him or her on a personal level; group violence, conversely, is usually a response to some wrong that the group feels strongly about whether or not it affects all the individuals in that group. Suprisingly, group violence, according to the information Langone presents, is easier to control than individual violence, because group violence has its source in problems that have been ignored. If addressed and not promoted by a "triggering event" (para. 5), these problems may be averted before they lead to violence.

2. The *"gathering* of individuals, with their strong, shared feeling" (para. 7) enables members of a group to develop a "sense of courage and power" (para. 7). Courage, in this essay, is a brazen feeling that allows the participants to suspend their usual behavior; power is not individual but group power, which is often extremely brutal.

3. Both the Kent State and Attica conflicts were chaotic and unplanned in the sense that neither group planned for the conflict to reach the level of violence it achieved. A second similarity occurred in the way police forces handled each situation—by using violence. In both instances, the rioters wanted to call attention to an issue they thought was being ignored. The differences between these two incidents are fewer than their similarities (a point that supports Langone's assumption), the main one being that the police forces seem to have had less justification for firing at the Kent State students than they did at the Attica prisoners.

ANSWERS TO QUESTIONS: DISCOVERING RHETORICAL STRATEGIES (p. 532)

1. Responses to this question will vary.

2. Langone relies mainly on logic as he builds his case with statistics and examples of group violence. To support his argument, the author compares and contrasts the various types of uprisings that have occurred throughout history. He also uses factual examples to support his conclusions about mob violence. Cause/effect, though, is perhaps the strongest rhetorical mode Langone uses to support his argument. By showing the causes of actual riots and the resulting effects, Langone is able to demonstrate and prove his theory simultaneously.

3. Langone seems to be writing to the general public, because he explains his ideas thoroughly and often defines technical words and phrases. In addition, he avoids the use of scientific or psychological jargon, which he would use if this were intended for professional psychologists.

PREWRITING

In preparation for the writing assignments, the Preparing to Write questions ask students to consider the causes and effects of violence in American society before writing an essay on a related topic. See pages 16–23 for suggestions on generating ideas in response to these questions.

UNDERSTANDING DETAILS

1. What characterizes "mob violence" (paragraph 3) according to Langone?
2. What would qualify as a "precipitating event" or a "trigger" (paragraph 4) for group violence?
3. What role does race frequently play in group violence?

ANALYZING MEANING

1. What are the main differences between group and individual violence? Do these differences give you any clues for controlling either type of violence?
2. According to Langone, what generally gives groups their "sense of courage and power" (paragraph 7)? How would you define "courage" and "power" in this context? What are the consequences of this courage and power?
3. The Kent State and Attica revolts came at approximately the same time in America's history. What were the similarities and differences between these two examples of group violence?

DISCOVERING RHETORICAL STRATEGIES

1. Which events cited by Langone convince you most clearly that group violence exhibits characteristics different from acts of individual violence?
2. What main rhetorical modes does Langone use to state his case? Give examples of each.
3. Who do you think is Langone's intended audience? How did you come to this conclusion?

IDEAS FOR DISCUSSION/WRITING

Preparing to Write

Write freely about violence in general: What characterizes acts of violence? When, in your opinion, is violence justified? When is it not justified? How should group violence be handled once it breaks out? Why do you think violence is so out of control in America? How much force against violent acts is warranted in your opinion? At what point does control of violence become brutality?

Choosing a Topic

1. Langone says, "When nobody listens to a complaint that appears to be legitimate, when nobody tries to rectify a bad situation, a violent act is perhaps the only way left to focus attention on the wrong, and help get something done about it" (paragraph 17). Do you agree or disagree with this statement? Explain your reaction in a clearly reasoned argumentative essay. Cite Langone's selection as necessary.

2. What do you think the role of the police should be in controlling group violence? Use Langone's article as one of your sources, and then read further on the subject in the library. Find specific incidences of crime and violence to support your argument. Next, write a clear, well-documented argumentative essay explaining your opinion on this issue. Organize your paper clearly and present your suggestions logically, using proper documentation (citations and bibliography) to clarify your stand.

3. Use additional library sources to study the circumstances at Kent State and Attica prisons. Then, referring to Langone's explanation of "the anatomy of a riot" (paragraph 4), write a well-documented essay analyzing the similarities and differences between these two situations.

ADDITIONAL DISCUSSION/WRITING TOPIC

Discuss the Los Angeles riots that followed the Rodney King verdict in spring 1992. Using Langone's essay as your main source, present the problem as you understand it, and offer a detailed solution to it in essay form. Cite Langone's essay whenever necessary.

REVISING STRATEGY

The types of appeals you choose in attempting to persuade your audience make a great deal of difference in the overall effect of your essay. In one of your persuasive papers, underline all your appeals (logical, emotional, and ethical): How many of each type of appeal does your essay contain? Is this an effective proportion for achieving your purpose with your intended audience? In what ways should you adjust this proportion to produce a more effective paper? Also, notice any weaknesses or inconsistencies in these appeals. Then revise your paper, avoiding the problems you have identified.

FURTHER READING

Brown, R. M. (1992). *No Duty to Retreat: Violence and Values in American History and Society.* New York: Oxford University Press.

Jankowski, Martin S. (1991). *Islands In the Street: Gangs and American Urban Society.* Berkeley: University of California Press.

Lofland, J. (1985). *Protest: Studies of Collective Behavior and Social Movements.* New Brunswick, N. J.: Transaction Books.

Moscovici, S. (1985). *The Age of the Crowd: A Historical Treatise on Mass Psychology.* Trans. J. C. Whitehouse. Cambridge: Cambridge University Press.

Rule, J. B. (1988). *Theories of Civil Violence.* Berkeley: University of California Press.

CHAPTER 11

ESSAYS ON THINKING, READING, AND WRITING

■ ■ ■

In each of the preceding chapters, we have examined a single rhetorical mode in order to focus attention on how writers use that pattern to organize their thoughts. In this final chapter, five essays on the topics of thinking, reading, and writing demonstrate a combination of rhetorical modes at work in each selection. Our primary purpose in this text has been to show how thinking, reading, and writing work together as fine machinery to help all of us function as intelligent and productive human beings. Our introduction discusses the relationship of thinking, reading, and writing; the text itself illustrates the crucial interdependence of these skills; and this last chapter concludes the book by presenting essays by some of America's best writers on such related topics as listening, reading fiction, understanding the writing process, writing "with style," and using word processors. These essays are intended for you to read and enjoy, letting your mind run freely through the material as you recall in a leisurely way what you have learned in this text.

DEFINITIONS

"Puss in Boots" (c. 1550) (para. 1): a famous tale of an ingenious cat who secures a fortune for his penniless master.
Morris chair (para. 5): an easy chair with an adjustable back and removable cushions, named for the English artist William Morris, who popularized it.
Stoddard's Lectures (1897–1898; 1901) (para. 5): a ten-volume set of reference books by British educator John Stoddard.
Vesuvius (para. 5): a volcano near Naples, Italy.
Venice (para. 5): a city on the northeast coast of Italy famous for its canals.
Victrola Book of the Opera (1921) (para. 5): a reference book published by the Victor Talking Machine Company.
Melba (para. 5): Dame Nellie Melba (1861–1931), an Australian soprano.
Caruso (para. 5): Enrico Caruso (1873–1921), an Italian tenor; one of the greatest opera stars of the twentieth century.
Galli-Curci (para. 5): Amelita Galli-Curci (1882–1963), an Italian soprano.
Geraldine Farrar (1882–1967) (para. 5): an American soprano.
hedonist (para. 6): a person who lives only for pleasure.

EUDORA WELTY
(1909–   )

■ ■ ■

Listening

I learned from the age of two or three that any room in our house, at any time of day, was there to read in, or to be read to. My mother read to me. She'd read to me in the big bedroom in the mornings, when we were in her rocker together, which ticked in rhythm as we rocked, as though we had a cricket accompanying the story. She'd read to me in the diningroom on winter afternoons in front of the coal fire, with our cuckoo clock ending the story with "Cuckoo," and at night when I'd got in my own bed. I must have given her no peace. Sometimes she read to me in the kitchen while she sat churning, and the churning sobbed along with *any* story. It was my ambition to have her read to me while *I* churned; once she granted my wish, but she read off my story before I brought her butter. She was an expressive reader. When she was reading "Puss in Boots," for instance, it was impossible not to know that she distrusted *all* cats.

It had been startling and disappointing to me to find out that story books had been written by *people*, that books were not natural wonders, coming up of themselves like grass. Yet regardless of where they came from, I cannot remember a time when I was not in love with them—with the books themselves, cover and binding and the paper they were printed on, with their smell and their weight and with their possession in my arms, captured and carried off to myself. Still illiterate, I was ready for them, committed to all the reading I could give them.

Neither of my parents had come from homes that could afford to buy many books, but though it must have been something of a strain on his salary, as the youngest officer in a young insurance company, my father was all the while carefully selecting and ordering away for what he and Mother thought we children should grow up with. They bought first for the future.

Besides the bookcase in the livingroom, which was always called "the library," there were the encyclopedia tables and dictionary stand under windows in our diningroom. Here to help us grow up arguing around the diningroom table were the Unabridged Webster, the Columbia Encyclopedia, Compton's Pictured Encyclopedia, the Lincoln Library of Information, and later the Book of Knowledge. And the year we moved into our new house, there was room to celebrate it with the new 1925 of the Britannica, which my father, his face always deliberately turned toward the future, was of course disposed to think better than any previous edition.

In "the library," inside the mission-style bookcase with its three diamond-latticed glass doors, with my father's Morris chair and the glass-shaded lamp on its table beside it, were books I could soon begin on—and I did, reading them all alike and as they came, straight down their rows, top shelf to bottom. There was the set of Stoddard's Lectures, in all its late nineteenth-century vocabulary and vignettes of peasant life and quaint beliefs and customs, with matching halftone illustrations: Vesuvius erupting, Venice by moonlight, gypsies glimpsed by their campfires. I didn't know then the clue they were to my father's longing to see the rest of the world. I read straight through his other love-from-afar: the Victrola Book of the Opera, with opera after opera in synopsis, with portraits in costume of Melba, Caruso, Galli-Curci, and Geraldine Farrar, some of whose voices we could listen to on our Red Seal records.

My mother read secondarily for information; she sank as a hedonist into novels. She read Dickens in the spirit in which she would have eloped with him. The novels of her girlhood that had stayed on in her imagination, besides those of Dickens and Scott and Robert Louis Stevenson, were *Jane Eyre, Trilby, The Woman in White, Green Mansions, King Solomon's Mines.* Marie Corelli's name would crop up but I understood she had gone out of favor with my mother, who had only kept *Ardath* out of loyalty. In time she absorbed herself in Galsworthy, Edith Wharton, above all in Thomas Mann of the *Joseph* volumes.

St. Elmo was not in our house; I saw it often in other houses. This wildly popular Southern novel is where all the Edna Earles in our population started coming from. They're all named for the heroine, who succeeded in bringing a dissolute, sinning roué and atheist of a lover (St. Elmo) to his knees. My mother was able to forgo it. But she remembered the classic advice given to rose growers on how to water their bushes long enough: "Take a chair and *St. Elmo.*"

To both my parents I owe my early acquaintance with a beloved Mark Twain. There was a full set of Mark Twain and a

Dickens (para. 6): Charles Dickens (1812–1870), the English novelist whose works include *A Christmas Carol* (1843) and *A Tale of Two Cities* (1854).

Scott (para. 6): Sir Walter Scott (1771–1832), the Scottish writer who popularized the historical novel; his works include *Old Mortality* (1816) and *Ivanhoe* (1819).

Robert Louis Stevenson (1850–1894) (para. 6): the Scottish novelist and poet best known for *Treasure Island* (1883).

5 *Jane Eyre* (1847) (para. 6): a novel by Charlotte Brontë.

Trilby (1894) (para. 6): a novel by George Du Maurier.

The Woman in White (1860) (para. 6): a mystery novel by Wilkie Collins.

Green Mansions (1904) (para. 6): a novel by William Hudson.

King Solomon's Mines (1885) (para. 6): a novel by Sir Henry Rider Haggard, an English author.

Marie Corelli (para. 6): the pen name of Mary Macay (1885–1924), an English novelist whose works include *A Romance of Two Worlds* (1886) and *Barabbas* (1900).

Ardath (para. 6): *Ardath: The Story of a Dead Self* (1889), a novel by Marie Corelli.

Galsworthy (para. 6): John Galsworthy (1867–1933), an English novelist and

6 playwright who won the 1932 Nobel Prize for Literature; best known for his trilogy *The Forsyte Saga* (1906–1921).

Edith Wharton (1862–1937) (para. 6): an American author whose works include *Ethan Frome* (1911) and *The Age of Innocence* (1920).

Thomas Mann (1875–1955) (para. 6): a German novelist; his works include *The Magic Mountain* (1924) and *Doctor Faustus* (1947).

Joseph volumes (para. 6): a series of four

7 novels by Thomas Mann entitled *Joseph and His Brothers* (1933–1943), an expanded biblical story of Joseph.

St. Elmo (1867) (para. 7): a novel by Augusta Jane Evans.

Edna Earl (para. 7): the heroine of *St. Elmo;* an orphan raised by a widow whose arrogant son falls in love with moralistic Edna.

8 *roué* (para. 7): a man devoted to a life of sensual pleasure, especially with women.

Mark Twain (1835–1910) (para. 8): the pen name of Samuel Clemens, an American author of numerous works, including *The Adventures of Huckleberry Finn* (1855) and *The Adventures of Tom Sawyer* (1876).

Ring Lardner (1885–1933) (para. 8): an American short-story writer whose works include *Gullible's Travels* (1917) and *The Love Nest and Other Stories* (1926).

Thomas Day (1748–1789) (para. 9): an English author and poet best known for his three-volume *History of Sanford and Merton* (1783–1789).

Mary Godolphin (1781–1864) (para. 9): the pseudonym for Lucy Aiken, a British historian, biographer, and writer; the author of a children's version of *Sanford and Merton* (1868).

Grimm (para. 12): a family of two German brothers, Jakob (1785–1863) and Wilhelm (1786–1859), who were authors and scholars; best known for their fairy tales.

Andersen (para. 12): Hans Christian Andersen (1805–1875), Denmark's most famous author; best known for his fairy tales, such as "The Ugly Duckling" and "The Emperor's New Clothes."

"Ali Baba and the Forty Thieves" (para. 12): a popular story of *The Arabian Nights' Entertainment*, a collection of ancient Persian-Indian-Arabian tales (c. 1450).

Aesop (c. 600 B.C.) (para. 12): a Greek slave credited with writing *Aesop's Fables*, a collection of stories about animals who talk and act like humans.

Reynard the Fox (para. 12): a medieval beast fable of unknown origin.

Robin Hood (c. 1300) (para. 12): a legendary English outlaw who stole from the rich and gave to the poor.

King Arthur (para. 12): a legendary king of medieval England; said to have pulled the magic sword Excalibur from a stone.

St. George and the Dragon (para. 12): a medieval fable about George, the legendary Red Cross knight from the *Faerie Queene* (1590) by Edmund Spenser.

Joan of Arc (para. 12): Saint (1412–1431), a French peasant girl who rescued France from defeat during the Hundred Years' War with England; taken prisoner by the English and burned at the stake for witchcraft.

Pilgrim's Progress (1678) (para. 12): an

short set of Ring Lardner in our bookcase, and those were the volumes that in time united us all, parents and children.

9   Reading everything that stood before me was how I came upon a worn old book without a back that had belonged to my father as a child. It was called *Sanford and Merton*. Is there anyone left who recognizes it, I wonder? It is the famous moral tale written by Thomas Day in the 1780s, but of him no mention is made on the title page of *this* book; here it is *Sanford and Merton in Words of One Syllable* by Mary Godolphin. Here are the rich boy and the poor boy and Mr. Barlow, their teacher and interlocutor, in long discourses alternating with dramatic scenes—danger and rescue allotted to the rich and the poor respectively. It may have only words of one syllable, but one of them is "quoth." It ends with not one but two morals, both engraved on rings: "Do what you ought, come what may," and "If we would be great, we must first learn to be good."

10   This book was lacking its front cover, the back held on by strips of pasted paper, now turned golden, in several layers, and the pages stained, flecked, and tattered around the edges; its garish illustrations had come unattached but were preserved, laid in. I had the feeling even in my heedless childhood that this was the only book my father as a little boy had had of his own. He had held onto it, and might have gone to sleep on its coverless face: He had lost his mother when he was seven. My father had never made any mention to his own children of the book, but he had brought it along with him from Ohio to our house and shelved it in our bookcase.

11   My mother had brought from West Virginia that set of Dickens; those books looked, too—they had been through fire and water before I was born, she told me, and there they were, lined up—as I later realized, waiting for *me*.

12   I was presented, from as early as I can remember, with books of my own, which appeared on my birthday and Christmas morning. Indeed, my parents could not give me books enough. They must have sacrificed to give me on my sixth or seventh birthday—it was after I became a reader for myself—the ten-volume set of Our Wonder World. These were beautifully made, heavy books I would lie down with on the floor in front of the diningroom hearth, and more often than the rest volume 5, *Every Child's Story Book*, was under my eyes. There were the fairy tales—Grimm, Andersen, the English, the French, "Ali Baba and the Forty Thieves"; and there was Aesop and Reynard the Fox; there were the myths and legends, Robin Hood, King Arthur, and

St. George and the Dragon, even the history of Joan of Arc; a whack of *Pilgrim's Progress* and a long piece of *Gulliver*. They all carried their classic illustrations. I located myself in these pages and could go straight to the stories and pictures I loved; very often "The Yellow Dwarf" was first choice, with Walter Crane's Yellow Dwarf in full color making his terrifying appearance flanked by turkeys. Now that volume is as worn and backless and hanging apart as my father's poor *Sanford and Merton*. The precious page with Edward Lear's "Jumblies" on it has been in danger of slipping out for all these years. One measure of my love for Our Wonder World was that for a long time I wondered if I would go through fire and water for it as my mother had done for Charles Dickens; and the only comfort was to think I could ask my mother to do it for me.

I believe I'm the only child I know of who grew up with this treasure in the house. I used to ask others, "Did you have Our Wonder World?" I'd have to tell them The Book of Knowledge could not hold a candle to it.

I live in gratitude to my parents for initiating me—and as early as I begged for it, without keeping me waiting—into knowledge of the word, into reading and spelling, by way of the alphabet. They taught it to me at home in time for me to begin to read before starting to school. I believe the alphabet is no longer considered an essential piece of equipment for traveling through life. In my day it was the keystone to knowledge. You learned the alphabet as you learned to count to ten, as you learned "Now I lay me" and the Lord's Prayer and your father's and mother's name and address and telephone number, all in case you were lost.

My love for the alphabet, which endures, grew out of reciting it but, before that, out of seeing the letters on the page. In my own story books, before I could read them for myself, I fell in love with various winding, enchanted-looking initials drawn by Walter Crane at the heads of fairy tales. In "Once upon a time," an "O" had a rabbit running it as a treadmill, his feet upon flowers. When the day came, years later, for me to see the Book of Kells, all the wizardry of letter, initial, and word swept over me a thousand times over, and the illumination, the gold, seemed a part of the word's beauty and holiness that had been there from the start.

allegory by John Bunyan in which people and places represent virtues and vices.
Gulliver (para. 12): *Gulliver's Travels* (1726), an English satire by Jonathan Swift.
"The Yellow Dwarf" (para. 12): a fairy story originating in France in 1698.
Walter Crane (1845–1915) (para. 12): a popular illustrator of children's books.
Edward Lear (1812–1888) (para. 12): an English writer and artist best known for his children's poems, including "The Owl and the Pussy Cat" (1871).
Book of Kells (A.D. 700–800) (para. 15): an illustrated manuscript of the four Gospels of the Bible; considered one of the world's most beautiful books.

COLLABORATIVE LEARNING: CLASS ACTIVITY

13
14 Have your students list their memories of learning to read. Then, have them discuss as a class the various associations they have with those memories. As the discussion takes shape, help your students focus their attention on the relationship between their childhood reading experiences and their reading and writing abilities today.

COLLABORATIVE LEARNING: SMALL GROUP ACTIVITY

15 Divide your students into groups of 3 or 4, and have them list all the associations they make with reading and writing in the following phases of their education: (1) elementary school, (2) junior high and high school, and (3) college. Then, let them discuss freely how these associations have changed in the course of their lives and speculate on reasons for those changes.

DISCUSSION/WRITING TOPIC: NARRATION

Write a narrative for your writing instructor that explains how your childhood environment affected your reading or writing abilities throughout the years.

DISCUSSION/WRITING TOPIC: ANALOGY

For your classmates, write an essay using an analogy to explain what books or reading can do for us.

DONALD HALL
(1928–   )

■ ■ ■

To Read Fiction

BACKGROUND INFORMATION

In this defense of the value of literature from *To Read Fiction* (1987), Donald Hall asserts that fiction is useful for four main reasons: (1) It is an important record of human thought and feelings; (2) it alters and enlarges our minds; (3) it teaches us enduring truths about life that, though less exact and precise than scientific truths, are nonetheless just as valuable; and (4) it makes our minds more sensitive and receptive to the world around us.

READABILITY LEVEL

9.0

... When we learn to read fiction, we acquire a pleasure and 1
a resource we never lose. Although literary study is impractical in one sense—few people make their living reading books—in another sense it is almost as practical as breathing. Literature records and embodies centuries of human thought and feeling, preserving for us the minds of people who lived before us, who were like us and unlike us, against whom we can measure our common humanity and our historical difference. And when we read the stories of our contemporaries they illuminate the world all of us share.

When we read great literature, something changes in us that 2
stays changed. Literature remembered becomes material to think with. No one who has read *The Death of Ivan Ilych* well is quite the same again. Reading adds tools by which we observe, measure, and judge the people and the properties of our universe, we understand the actions and motives of others and of ourselves.

In the fable of the ant and the grasshopper, the wise ant 3
builds his storehouse against winter and prospers; the foolish grasshopper saves nothing and perishes. Anyone who dismisses the study of literature on the ground that it will not be useful—to a chemist or an engineer, to a foreman or an X-ray technician—imitates the grasshopper. When we shut from our lives everything except food and shelter, part of us starves to death. Food for this hunger is music, painting, film, plays, poems, stories, and novels. Much writing in newspapers, magazines, and popular novels is not literature, if we reserve that word for work of high quality. This reading gives us as little nourishment as most television and most fast food. For the long winters and energetic summers of our lives, we require the sustenance of literature.

Reading fiction old and new—taking into ourselves the work 4
of nineteenth-century Russian, contemporary English, Irish, and especially American storytellers—we build a storehouse of knowledge and we entertain ourselves as well. But to take plea-

sure and understanding from fiction we have to learn how to read it. No one expects to walk up to a computer and be able to program it without first learning something about computers. For some reason—perhaps because we are familiar with words from childhood and take them for granted—we tend to think that a quick glance at the written word should reward us, and that if we do not take instant satisfaction the work is beyond us, or not worth it, or irrelevant or boring. But all our lives, in other skills, we have needed instruction and practice—to be able to ride a bicycle, drive a car, play guitar, shoot baskets, typewrite, dance.

The knowledge we derive from literature can seem confusing. Equally great works may contradict each other in the generalizations we derive from them. One work may recommend solitude, another society. One may advise us to seize the moment, another to live a life of contemplation. Or, two good readers may disagree about the implication of a work and each argue convincingly, with detailed references to the writing, in support of contrary interpretations. A complex work of fiction cannot be reduced to a simple, correct meaning. In an elementary arithmetic text, the answers may be printed in the back of the book. There are no answers to be printed in the back of . . . any collection of literature.

Such nebulousness, or ambiguity, disturbs some students. After an hour's class discussion of a short story, with varying interpretations offered, they want to know "But what *does* it mean?" We must admit that literature is inexact, and its truth is not easily verifiable. Probably the story means several things at once, and not one thing at all. This is not to say, however, that it means anything that anybody finds in it. Although differing, equally defensible opinions are common, error is even more common.

When we speak of truth in the modern world, we usually mean something scientific or tautological. Arithmetic contains the truth of tautology; two and two make four because our definitions of *two* and *four* say so. In laboratories we encounter the truth of statistics and the truth of observation. If we smoke cigarettes heavily, it is true that we have one chance in four to develop lung cancer. When we heat copper wire over a Bunsen burner, the flame turns blue.

But there is an older sense of truth, in which statements apparently opposite can be valid. In this older tradition, truth is dependent on context and circumstance, on the agreement of sensible men and women—like the "Guilty" or "Not guilty" ver-

DEFINITIONS

The Death of Ivan Ilyich (1884) (para. 2): a story by Leo Tolstoy about an ordinary man who contemplates life and death upon learning that he is dying and comes to accept death as a part of the natural order of things.

tautological (para. 7): involving or using the needless repetition of an idea, statement, or word.

King James version (1611) (para. 11): an edition of the Bible written by some of the finest scholars in England.

Henry James (1843–1916) (para. 11): the American author of *The American* (1877), *Daisy Miller* (1878) and *The Portrait of a Lady* (1881).

Ernest Hemingway (1899–1961) (para. 11): an American writer who won the 1954 Nobel Prize for Literature and a Pulitzer Prize in 1952 for *The Old Man and the Sea;* some of his other works include *The Sun Also Rises* (1926) and *For Whom the Bell Tolls* (1940).

William Faulkner (1897–1962) (para. 11): an American writer who won the 1949 Nobel Prize for Literature and Pulitzer Prizes in 1955 for *A Fable* and in 1963 for *The Reivers;* some of his other works include *The Sound and the Fury* (1929) and *As I Lay Dying* (1930).

Fyodor Dostoyevsky (1821–1881) (para. 13): a Russian writer whose novels include *Crime and Punishment* (1866) and *The Brothers Karamazov* (1879).

Agatha Christie (1890–1976) (para. 13): an English mystery writer of 67 novels and 16 plays whose works include *The Mousetrap* (1952) and *Witness for the Prosecution* (1953).

Aldous Huxley (1894–1963) (para. 13): an English writer whose works include *Point Counter Point* (1928) and *Brave New World* (1932).

Chekhov (para. 13): Anton Chekhov (1860–1904), a Russian playwright and novelist whose works include *The Sea Gull* (1896) and *The Cherry Orchard* (1904).

Have students individually list any works of fiction they have read in the last five years. In a separate column, have them list other forms of reading they have done during that time, including textbooks, magazines, user manuals, newspapers, or any other printed material. Then, discuss with them ways in which they have channeled their energies into reading. Try to guide them toward discovering why they read what they do and what they learn from it.

In this essay, Hall essentially tells us that reading literature is a way to learn how to live life as effectively as possible. As he puts it, fiction "alters and enlarges our minds, our connections with each other past and present, our understanding of our own feelings" (para. 10); then, at the end of his essay, Hall claims that "as the mind becomes more sensitive and receptive to literature, it may become more sensitive and receptive to all sorts of things" (para. 13). Divide your students into groups of 3 or 4, and have them discuss the validity of these statements from their points of view. What does fiction teach us about living? What do other types of reading teach us about living? Why is fiction more useful in this regard according to Hall? Do your students agree with this assertion?

dict of a jury. Because this literary (or philosophical, or legal, or historical) truth is inexact, changeable, and subject to argument, literature can seem nebulous to minds accustomed to arithmetical certainty.

Let me argue this: If literature is nebulous or inexact; if it is   9 impossible to determine, with scientific precision, the value or the meaning of a work of art, *this inexactness is the price literature pays for representing whole human beings.* Human beings themselves, in their feelings and thoughts, in the wanderings of their short lives, are ambiguous and ambivalent, shifting mixtures of permanence and change, direction and disorder. Because literature is true to life, true to the complexities of human feeling, different people will read the same work with different responses. And the storyteller's art will sometimes affirm that opposite things are both true *because they are.* Such a condition is not tidy; it is perhaps regrettable—but it is human nature.

What's Good, What's Bad

The claims I make for fiction are large: that it alters and en-   10 larges our minds, our connections with each other past and present, our understanding of our own feelings. These claims apply to excellent literature only. This . . . suggests that some fiction is better than other fiction, and that some narratives are not literature at all. Even if judgments are always subject to reversal, even if there is no way we can be certain of being correct, evaluation lives at the center of literary study.

When I was nineteen, I liked to read everything: science fic-   11 tion, Russian novels, mystery stories, great poems, adventure magazines. Then for six months after an accident, sentenced to a hospital bed and a body cast, I set myself a reading list, all serious books I had been thinking about getting to. Of course there was a background to this choice: I had been taught by a good teacher who had directed and encouraged and stimulated my reading. I read through Shakespeare, the Bible in the King James version, novels by Henry James and Ernest Hemingway and William Faulkner. Toward the end of six months, taking physical therapy, I hurried to finish the books I had assigned myself; I looked forward to taking a vacation among private detectives and adventurers of the twenty-fourth century. I thought I would take a holiday of light reading.

When I tried to read the light things, I experienced one of   12 those "turning points in life" we are asked to describe in freshman composition. I remember the dismay, the abject melancholy that crept over me as I realized—restless, turning from book to book in search of entertainment—that these books bored me; that I was ruined for life, that I would never again lose myself to stick-figure characters and artificial suspense. Literature ruined me for light reading. . . .

I don't mean to say that I was able to give reasons why Fyodor Dostoyevsky's novel about a murder was better than Agatha Christie's or why Aldous Huxley's view of the future, though less exciting, was more satisfying than *Astounding Science Fiction*'s. But I began a lifetime of trying to figure out why. What *is* it that makes Chekhov so valuable to us? The struggle to name reasons for value—to evaluate works of art—is lifelong, and although we may never arrive at satisfactory explanations, the struggle makes the mind more sensitive, more receptive to the next work of literature it encounters. And as the mind becomes more sensitive and receptive to literature, it may become more sensitive and receptive to all sorts of things.

DISCUSSION/WRITING TOPIC: EXAMPLE

Use examples to explain to some high school students what you have learned from literature. What is literature from your point of view? What have you learned from this type of reading?

13 **DISCUSSION/WRITING TOPIC: CAUSE/EFFECT**

From your experience, explain the relationship among thinking, reading, and writing. How do these skills affect one another? How does your ability in these skills affect your other academic work?

BACKGROUND INFORMATION

In this essay from her newest book, *The Writing Life* (1989), Annie Dillard uses several building metaphors to explain the process of writing. Although she is referring to an extended writing project here, these same vivid analogies can easily be applied to the daily writing tasks that your students face.

READABILITY LEVEL

6.9

RELATED READINGS

Writing

Russell Baker, "The Saturday Evening Post"   124
Paul Roberts, "How to Say Nothing in Five Hundred Words"   236
Kurt Vonnegut, "How to Write with Style"   546
William Zinsser, "Writing with a Word Processor"   550

DEFINITIONS

epistemological (para. 3): relating to the study of knowledge.
Henry James (1843–1916) (para. 6): the American author of *The American* (1877), *Daisy Miller* (1878), and *The Portrait of a Lady* (1881).
The Spoils of Poynton (1897) (para. 6): a tragic novel by Henry James.
Thoreau (para. 7): (Henry David Thoreau, 1817–1862), an American author, best known for the narrative *Walden*.

COLLABORATIVE LEARNING: CLASS ACTIVITY

Have your students individually list some of the associations they naturally have with writing and the writing process (e.g., coffee, Coke, fear, deadlines, legal pads). Then, have them discuss as a class these various associations. As the discussion takes shape, help your students see the difference between their positive and negative associations and the way in which these connections might affect their current and future writing abilities.

ANNIE DILLARD
(1945–   )

■ ■ ■

When You Write

When you write, you lay out a line of words. The line of words is a miner's pick, a woodcarver's gouge, a surgeon's probe. You wield it, and it digs a path you follow. Soon you find yourself deep in new territory. Is it a dead end, or have you located the real subject? You will know tomorrow, or this time next year. 1

You make the path boldly and follow it fearfully. You go where the path leads. At the end of the path, you find a box canyon. You hammer out reports, dispatch bulletins. 2

The writing has changed, in your hands, and in a twinkling, from an expression of your notions to an epistemological tool. The new place interests you because it is not clear. You attend. In your humility, you lay down the words carefully, watching all the angles. Now the earlier writing looks soft and careless. Process is nothing; erase your tracks. The path is not the work. I hope your tracks have grown over; I hope birds ate the crumbs; I hope you will toss it all and not look back. 3

The line of words is a hammer. You hammer against the walls of your house. You tap the walls, lightly, everywhere. After giving many years' attention to these things, you know what to listen for. Some of the walls are bearing walls; they have to stay, or everything will fall down. Other walls can go with impunity; you can hear the difference. Unfortunately, it is often a bearing wall that has to go. It cannot be helped. There is only one solution, which appalls you, but there it is. Knock it out. Duck. 4

Courage utterly opposes the bold hope that this is such fine stuff the work needs it, or the world. Courage, exhausted, stands on bare reality: This writing weakens the work. You must demolish the work and start over. You can save some of the sentences, like bricks. It will be a miracle if you can save some of the paragraphs, no matter how excellent in themselves or hard-won. You can waste a year worrying about it, or you can get it over with now. (Are you a woman, or a mouse?) 5

The part you must jettison is not only the best-written part; it is also, oddly, that part which was to have been the very point. It is the original key passage, the passage on which the rest was to hang, and from which you yourself drew the courage to begin. Henry James knew it well, and said it best. In his preface to *The Spoils of Poynton*, he pities the writer, in a comical pair of sentences that rises to a howl: "Which is the work in which he hasn't surrendered, under dire difficulty, the best thing he meant to have kept? In which indeed, before the dreadful *done*, doesn't he ask himself what has become of the thing all for the sweet sake of which it was to proceed to that extremity?"

So it is that a writer writes many books. In each book, he intended several urgent and vivid points, many of which he sacrificed as the book's form hardened. "The youth gets together his materials to build a bridge to the moon," Thoreau noted mournfully, "or perchance a palace or temple on the earth, and at length the middle-aged man concludes to build a wood-shed with them." The writer returns to these materials, these passionate subjects, as to unfinished business, for they are his life's work.

COLLABORATIVE LEARNING: SMALL GROUP ACTIVITY

6   Divide your students into groups of 3 or 4, and have each group develop five similes and/or metaphors that accurately describe the process of writing (e.g., writing is like building a house). Then, have each group choose one simile or metaphor to brainstorm and expand in as many different directions as possible. Then, have one person from each group read the group's expanded comparison to the rest of the class.

DISCUSSION/WRITING TOPIC: DEFINITION

7   Write an essay for your English class defining what you mean when you refer to someone as a "good writer." What qualities must this person have to earn this praise from you? Be as specific as possible about the work a writer does—whether you are defining a student or a professional writer.

DISCUSSION/WRITING TOPIC: ARGUMENT AND PERSUASION

Your local newspaper is running a supplement on literacy. Write an essay for this publication encouraging the public to realize the importance of clear, persuasive writing in a literate society.

KURT VONNEGUT
(1922–   )

■ ■ ■

How to Write with Style

BACKGROUND INFORMATION

Kurt Vonnegut's essay on style, from *Palm Sunday* (1981), encourages fledgling authors to use language clearly, simply, and accurately and to write in their own vernacular, in the linguistic idiom they learned as children.

READABILITY LEVEL

8.4

RELATED READINGS

Writing

Russell Baker, "The Saturday Evening Post"   124
Paul Roberts, "How to Say Nothing in Five Hundred Words"   236
Annie Dillard, "When You Write"   544
William Zinsser, "Writing with a Word Processor"   550

DEFINITIONS

James Joyce (1882–1941) (para. 7): an Irish novelist and short-story writer.
Hamlet (para. 7): the title character in a play written by William Shakespeare; a young prince who avenges the murder of his father.
"Eveline" (para. 7): one of James Joyce's stories in a collection entitled *Dubliners* (1916).
Joseph Conrad (1857–1924) (para. 10): an English novelist who wrote such novels as *Lord Jim* (1900) and *Heart of Darkness* (1902).
Pablo Picasso (1881–1973) (para. 15): a Spanish artist who profoundly influenced the direction of art in the twentieth century.
egalitarian (para. 20): based on human equality.

Newspaper reporters and technical writers are trained to reveal almost nothing about themselves in their writings. This makes them freaks in the world of writers, since almost all of the other ink-stained wretches in that world reveal a lot about themselves to readers. We call these revelations, accidental and intentional, elements of literary style. 1

These revelations are fascinating to us as readers. They tell us what sort of person it is with whom we are spending time. Does the writer sound ignorant or informed, crazy or sane, stupid or bright, crooked or honest, humorless or playful—? And on and on. 2

When you yourself put words on paper, remember that the most damning revelation you can make about yourself is that you do not know what is interesting and what is not. Don't you yourself like or dislike writers mainly for what they choose to show you or make you think about? Did you ever admire an empty-headed writer for his or her mastery of the language? No. 3

So your own winning literary style must begin with interesting ideas in your head. Find a subject you care about and which you in your heart feel others should care about. It is this genuine caring, and not your games with language, which will be the most compelling and seductive element in your style. 4

I am not urging you to write a novel, by the way—although I would not be sorry if you wrote one, provided you genuinely cared about something. A petition to the mayor about a pothole in front of your house or a love letter to the girl next door will do. 5

Do not ramble, though. 6

As for your use of language: Remember that two great masters of our language, William Shakespeare and James Joyce, wrote sentences which were almost childlike when their subjects were most profound. "To be or not to be?" asks Shakespeare's Hamlet. The longest word is three letters long. Joyce, when he was frisky, could put together a sentence as intricate and glittering as a neck- 7 lace for Cleopatra, but my favorite sentence in his short story "Eveline" is this one: "She was tired." At that point in the story, no other words could break the heart of a reader as those words do.

Simplicity of language is not only reputable, but perhaps even sacred. The Bible opens with a sentence well within the writing skills of a lively fourteen-year-old: "In the beginning God created the heavens and the earth."

It may be that you, too, are capable of making necklaces for Cleopatra, so to speak. But your eloquence should be the servant of the ideas in your head. Your rule might be this: If a sentence, no matter how excellent, does not illuminate my subject in some new and useful way, scratch it out. Here is the same rule paraphrased to apply to storytelling, to fiction: Never include a sentence which does not either remark on character or advance the action.

The writing style which is most natural for you is bound to echo speech you heard when a child. English was the novelist Joseph Conrad's third language, and much that seems piquant in his use of English was no doubt colored by his first language, which was Polish. And lucky indeed is the writer who has grown up in Ireland, for the English spoken there is so amusing and musical. I myself grew up in Indianapolis, Indiana, where common speech sounds like a band saw cutting galvanized tin, and employs a vocabulary as unornamental as a monkey wrench.

In some of the more remote hollows of Appalachia, children still grow up hearing songs and locutions of Elizabethan times. Yes, and many Americans grow up hearing a language other than English, or an English dialect a majority of Americans cannot understand.

All these varieties of speech are beautiful, just as the varieties of butterflies are beautiful. No matter what your first language, you should treasure it all your life. If it happens not to be standard English, and if it shows itself when you write standard English, the result is usually delightful, like a very pretty girl with one eye that is green and one that is blue.

I myself find that I trust my own writing most, and others seem to trust it most, too, when I sound most like a person from Indianapolis, which is what I am. What alternatives do I have? The one most vehemently recommended by teachers has no doubt been pressed on you, as well: that I write like cultivated Englishmen of a century or more ago.

I used to be exasperated by such teachers, but am no more. I

COLLABORATIVE LEARNING: CLASS ACTIVITY

Have the class as a whole try to come up with a definition of "writing style." In *The Prose Reader* you might refer to pairs of essays that represent different writing styles, such as those of Ray Bradbury and Judith Viorst, John McPhee and Susan Sontag, Maya Angelou and Ellen Goodman, or Garrison Keillor and Germaine Greer. Have your students determine what gives each of these essays a different flavor in its presentation.

Divide your students into groups of four. Then, have them each exchange one paper that they wrote sometime during this course and label the style of that paper. Before the students label the style with appropriate adjectives, have them discuss what qualities they will be looking for to discern the type of style in a particular paper. They should agree upon some general criteria before they do this exercise. If they have participated in the Class Activity for this essay, they will already have a general definition of style from which to form these criteria. Try to give your students a few minutes after they complete this exercise to return the papers to the writers and share some brief insights.

understand now that all those antique essays and stories with which I was to compare my own work were not magnificent for their datedness or foreignness, but for saying precisely what their authors meant them to say. My teachers wished me to write accurately, always selecting the most effective words, and relating the words to one another unambiguously, rigidly, like parts of a machine. The teachers did not want to turn me into an Englishman after all. They hoped that I would become understandable—and therefore understood.

And there went my dream of doing with words what Pablo Picasso did with paint or what any number of jazz idols did with music. If I broke all the rules of punctuation, had words mean whatever I wanted them to mean, and strung them together higgledy-piggledy, I would simply not be understood. So you, too, had better avoid Picasso-style or jazz-style writing, if you have something worth saying and wish to be understood. 15

If it were only teachers who insisted that modern writers stay close to literary styles of the past, we might reasonably ignore them. But readers insist on the very same thing. They want our pages to look very much like pages they have seen before. 16

Why? It is because they themselves have a tough job to do, and they need all the help they can get from us. They have to identify thousands of little marks on paper, and make sense of them immediately. They have to *read*, an art so difficult that most people do not really master it even after having studied it all through grade school and high school—for twelve long years. 17

So this discussion, like all discussions of literary styles, must finally acknowledge that our stylistic options as writers are neither numerous nor glamorous, since our readers are bound to be such imperfect artists. Our audience requires us to be sympathetic and patient teachers, ever willing to simplify and clarify—whereas we would rather soar high above the crowd, singing like nightingales. 18

That is the bad news. The good news is that we Americans are governed under a unique Constitution, which allows us to write whatever we please without fear of punishment. So the most meaningful aspect of our styles, which is what we choose to write about, is unlimited. 19

Also: We are members of an egalitarian society, so there is no reason for us to write, in case we are not classically educated aristocrats, as though we were classically educated aristocrats. 20

For a discussion of literary style in a narrower sense, in a more technical sense, I commend to your attention *The Elements of* 21

Style by William Strunk, Jr., and E. B. White (Macmillan, 1979). It contains such rules as this: "A participial phrase at the beginning of a sentence must refer to the grammatical subject," and so on. E. B. White is, of course, one of the most admirable literary stylists this country has so far produced.

You should realize, too, that no one would care how well or badly Mr. White expressed himself, if he did not have perfectly enchanting things to say.

DISCUSSION/ WRITING TOPIC: DIVISION/CLASSIFICATION

Divide and/or classify the dominant features of your writing style. Then, write an essay explaining to your class these discoveries about your writing.

DISCUSSION/WRITING TOPIC:
22 **PROCESS ANALYSIS**

Write a process analysis essay entitled "How to Read with Understanding." Use Vonnegut's essay as a model.

WILLIAM ZINSSER
(1922–   )

■ ■ ■

Writing with a Word Processor

BACKGROUND INFORMATION

In this essay from *Writing with a Word Processor* (1983) by William Zinsser, the author explains how composing on a word processor can help people strengthen their prose by making it easy for them to (1) prune unnecessary words and phrases from their writing; (2) unify their tone, point of view, pronoun use, and other stylistic matters; (3) create logical progressions from point to point; and (4) simplify their sentence structure.

READABILITY LEVEL

11.2

RELATED READINGS

Writing

Writing is a deeply personal process, full of mystery and surprise. No two people go about it in exactly the same way. We all have little devices to get us started, or to keep us going, or to remind us of what we think we want to say, and what works for one person may not work for anyone else. The main thing is to get something written—to get the words out of our heads. There is no "right" method. Any method that will do the job is the right method for you.

It helps to remember that writing is hard. Most non-writers don't know this; they think that writing is a natural function, like breathing, that ought to come easy, and they're puzzled when it doesn't. If you find that writing is hard, it's because it *is* hard. It's one of the hardest things that people do. Among other reasons, it's hard because it requires thinking. You won't write clearly unless you keep forcing yourself to think clearly. There's no escaping the question that has to be constantly asked: What do I want to say next?

So painful is this task that writers go to remarkable lengths to postpone their daily labor. They sharpen their pencils and change their typewriter ribbon and go out to the store to buy more paper. Now these sacred rituals, as IBM would say, have been obsoleted.

When I began writing this article on my word processor I didn't have any idea what would happen. Would I be able to write anything at all? Would it be any good? I was bringing to the machine what I assumed were wholly different ways of thinking about writing. The units massed in front of me looked cold and sterile. Their steady hum reminded me that they were waiting. They seemed to be waiting for information, not for writing. Maybe what I wrote would also be cold and sterile.

I was particularly worried about the absence of paper. I knew that I would only be able to see as many lines as the screen would hold—twenty lines. How could I review what I had already written? How could I get a sense of continuity and flow? With paper it was always possible to flick through the preceding pages to see where I was coming from—and where I ought to be going. Without paper I would have no such periodic fix. Would this be a major hardship?

The only way to find out was to find out. I took a last look at my unsharpened pencils and went to work.

My particular hang-up as a writer is that I have to get every paragraph as nearly right as possible before I go on to the next paragraph. I'm somewhat like a bricklayer: I build very slowly, not adding a new row until I feel that the foundation is solid enough to hold up the house. I'm the exact opposite of the writer who dashes off his entire first draft, not caring how sloppy it looks or how badly it's written. His only objective at this early stage is to let his creative motor run the full course at full speed; repairs can always be made later. I envy this writer and would like to have his metabolism. But I'm stuck with the one I've got.

I also care how my writing looks while I'm writing it. The visual arrangement is important to me: the shape of the words, of the sentences, of the paragraphs, of the page. I don't like sentences that are dense with long words, or paragraphs that never end. As I write I want to see the design that my piece will have when the reader sees it in type, and I want that design to have a rhythm and a pace that will invite the reader to keep reading. O.K., so I'm a nut. But I'm not alone; the visual component is important to a large number of people who write.

One hang-up we visual people share is that our copy must be neat. My lifelong writing method, for instance, has gone like this. I put a piece of paper in the typewriter and write the first paragraph. Then I take the paper out and edit what I've written. I mark it up horribly, crossing words out and scribbling new ones in the space between the lines. By this time the paragraph has lost its nature and shape for me as a piece of writing. It's a mishmash of typing and handwriting and arrows and balloons and other directional symbols. So I type a clean copy, incorporating the changes, and then I take that piece of paper out of the typewriter and edit it. It's better, but not much better. I go over it with my pencil again, making more changes, which again make it too messy for me to read critically, so I go back to the typewriter for round three. And round four. Not until I'm reasonably satisfied do I proceed to the next paragraph.

This can get pretty tedious, and I have often thought that there must be a better way. Now there is. The word processor is God's gift, or at least science's gift, to the tinkerers and the refin-

COLLABORATIVE LEARNING:
CLASS ACTIVITY

Have the class discuss the pros and cons of the computer age, all the way from ordering merchandise by computer to writing on a word processor. Let them brainstorm aloud about the pros and cons of all facets of the computer, and help them reach some conclusions about whether the computer age currently has more advantages or disadvantages for contemporary society.

Have your class break up into three groups according to whether they compose on a word processor, on a typewriter, or with pen and pencil. Then, have each student draw a picture of his or her writing process from the moment a writing task is assigned to its completion. Next, have students present their drawings to their groups, explaining how they move through their individual writing processes. This should include such prewriting activities as running, taking a shower, washing dishes, washing the car, writing letters, and returning phone calls as well as staying up all night or retyping ten minutes before class. Encourage your students to be open and honest about the procrastination, guilt, and anxiety typically connected with writing tasks. Then, have one person from each group summarize for the entire class the various approaches to writing represented in the group's discussion.

ers and the neatness freaks. For me it was obviously the perfect new toy. I began playing on page 1—editing, cutting and revising—and have been on a rewriting high ever since. The burden of the years has been lifted.

Mostly I've been cutting. I would guess that I've cut at least 11 as many words out of this article as the number that remain. Probably half of those words were eliminated because I saw that they were unnecessary—the sentence worked fine without them. This is where the word processor can improve your writing to an extent that you will hardly believe. Learn to recognize what is clutter and to use the DELETE key to prune it out.

How will you know clutter when you see it? Here's a device I 12 used when I was teaching writing at Yale that my students found helpful; it may be a help here. I would put brackets around every component in a student's paper that I didn't think was doing some kind of work. Often it was only one word—for example, the useless preposition that gets appended to so many verbs (order up, free up), or the adverb whose meaning is already in the verb (blare loudly, clench tightly), or the adjective that tells us what we already know (smooth marble, green grass). The brackets might surround the little qualifiers that dilute a writer's authority (a bit, sort of, in a sense), or the countless phrases in which the writer explains what he is about to explain (it might be pointed out, I'm tempted to say). Often my brackets would surround an entire sentence—the sentence that essentially repeats what the previous sentence has said, or tells the reader something that is implicit, or adds a detail that is irrelevant. Most people's writing is littered with phrases that do no new work whatever. Most first drafts, in fact, can be cut by fifty percent without losing anything organic. (Try it; it's a good exercise.)

By bracketing these extra words, instead of crossing them 13 out, I was saying to the student: "I may be wrong, but I think this can go and the meaning of the sentence won't be affected in any way. But *you* decide: Read the sentence without the bracketed material and see if it works." In the first half of the term, the students' papers were festooned with my brackets. Whole paragraphs got bracketed. But gradually the students learned to put mental brackets around their many different kinds of clutter, and by the end of the term I was returning papers to them that had hardly any brackets, or none. It was always a satisfying moment. Today many of those students are professional writers. "I still see your brackets," they tell me. "They're following me through life."

You can develop the same eye. Writing is clear and strong to the extent that it has no superfluous parts. (So is art and music and dance and typography and design.) You will really enjoy writing on a word processor when you see your sentences growing in strength, literally before your eyes, as you get rid of the fat. Be thankful for everything that you can throw away.

I was struck by how many phrases and sentences I wrote in this article that I later found I didn't need. Many of them hammered home a point that didn't need hammering because it had already been made. This kind of overwriting happens in almost everybody's first draft, and it's perfectly natural—the act of putting down our thoughts makes us garrulous. Luckily, the act of editing follows the act of writing, and this is where the word processor will bail you out. It intercedes at the point where the game can be won or lost. With its help I cut hundreds of unnecessary words and didn't replace them.

Hundreds of others were discarded because I later thought of a better word—one that caught more precisely or more vividly what I was trying to express. Here, again, a word processor encourages you to play. The English language is rich in words that convey an exact shade of meaning. Don't get stuck with a word that's merely good if you can find one that takes the reader by surprise with its color or aptness or quirkiness. Root around in your dictionary of synonyms and find words that are fresh. Throw them up on the screen and see how they look.

Also learn to play with whole sentences. If a sentence strikes you as awkward or ponderous, move your cursor to the space after the period and write a new sentence that you think is better. Maybe you can make it shorter. Or clearer. Maybe you can make it livelier by turning it into a question or otherwise altering its rhythm. Change the passive verbs into active verbs. (Passive verbs are the death of clarity and vigor.) Try writing two or three new versions of the awkward sentence and then compare them, or write a fourth version that combines the best elements of all three. Sentences come in an infinite variety of shapes and sizes. Find one that pleases you. If it's clear, and if it pleases you and expresses who you are, trust it to please other people. Then delete all the versions that aren't as good. Your shiny new sentence will jump into position, and the rest of the paragraph will rearrange itself as quickly and neatly as if you had never pulled it apart.

Another goal that the word processor will help you to achieve is unity. No matter how carefully you write each sentence as you assemble a piece of writing, the final product is bound to

DISCUSSION/WRITING TOPIC: COMPARISON/CONTRAST

14 Compare and/or contrast for your instructor your current writing process in college with your high school writing process. What techniques did/do you use to get yourself going? What tools did/do you write with (e.g., a word processor, a typewriter, paper, pen, or pencil)? If you com-

15 pose on a word processor now, how has this technology changed the way you write? What process did/do you go through when you write? How did/do you handle revising and rewriting? How did/do you feel about writing in general?

DISCUSSION/WRITING TOPIC: DESCRIPTION

Describe for your classmates your general feelings when you face a writing assign-

16 ment. Do some assignments stimulate different feelings than others? How do you handle these feelings? How do you channel these feelings into writing?

17

18

have some ragged edges. Is the tone consistent throughout? And the point of view? And the pronoun? And the tense? How about the transitions? Do they pull the reader along, or is the piece jerky and disjointed? A good piece of writing should be harmonious from beginning to end in the voice of the writer and the flow of its logic. But the harmony usually requires some last-minute patching.

19   I've been writing a book by the bricklayer method, slowly and carefully. That's all very well as far as it goes—at the end of every chapter the individual bricks may look fine. But what about the wall? The only way to check your piece for unity is to go over it one more time from start to finish, preferably reading it aloud. See if you have executed all the decisions that you made before you started writing.

20   One such decision is in the area of tone. I decided, for instance, that I didn't want my book to be a technical manual. I'm not a technician; I'm a writer and an editor. The book wouldn't work if I expected the reader to identify with the process of mastering a new technology. He would have to identify with me. The book would be first of all a personal journey and only parenthetically a manual. I knew that this was a hybrid form and that its unities would never be wholly intact. Still, in going over each finished chapter I found places where the balance could be improved—where instructional detail smothered the writer and his narrative, or, conversely, where the writer intruded on the procedures he was trying to explain. With a word processor it was easy to make small repairs—perhaps just a change of pronoun and verb—that made the balance less uneven.

21   The instructional portions of the book posed a problem of their own—one that I had never faced before. My hope was to try to explain a technical process without the help of any diagrams or drawings. Would this be possible? It would be possible only if I kept remembering one fundamental fact: Writing is linear and sequential. This may seem so obvious as to be insulting: Everybody knows that writing is linear and sequential. Actually everybody doesn't know. Most people under thirty don't know. They have been reared since early childhood on television—a kaleidoscope of visual images flashed onto their brain—and it doesn't occur to them that sentence B must follow sentence A, and that sentence C must follow sentence B, or all the elegant sentences in the world won't add up to anything but confusion.

22   I mention this because word processors are going to be widely used by people who need to impart technical information:

matters of operating procedure in business and banking, science and technology, medicine and health, education and government, and dozens of other specialized fields. The information will only be helpful if readers can grasp it quickly and easily. If it's muddy they will get discouraged or angry, or both, and will stop reading.

You can avoid this dreaded fate for your message, whatever 23 it is, by making sure that every sentence is a logical sequel to the one that preceded it. One way to approach this goal is to keep your sentences short. A major reason why technical prose becomes so tangled is that the writer tries to make one sentence do too many jobs. It's a natural hazard of the first draft. But the solution is simple: See that every sentence contains only one thought. The reader can accommodate only one idea at a time. Help him by giving him only one idea at a time. Let him understand A before you proceed to B.

In writing this article, I was eager to explain the procedures 24 that I had learned, and I would frequently lump several points together in one sentence. Later, editing what I had written, I asked myself if the procedure would be clear to someone who was puzzling through it for the first time—someone who hadn't struggled to figure the procedure out. Often I felt that it wouldn't be clear. I was giving the reader too much. He was being asked to picture himself taking various steps that were single and sequential, and that's how he deserved to get them.

I therefore divided all troublesome long sentences into two 25 short sentences, or even three. It always gave me great pleasure. Not only is it the fastest way for a writer to get out of a quagmire that there seems to be no getting out of; I also like short sentences for their own sake. There's almost no more beautiful sight than a simple declarative sentence. This article is full of simple declarative sentences that have no punctuation and that carry one simple thought. Without a word processor I wouldn't have chopped as many of them down to their proper size, or done it with so little effort. This is one of the main clarifying jobs that your machine can help you to perform, especially if your writing requires you to guide the reader into territory that is new and bewildering.

Not all my experiences, of course, were rosy. The machine 26 had disadvantages as well as blessings. Often, for instance, I missed not being able to see more than twenty lines at a time—to review what I had written earlier. If I wanted to see more lines I had to "scroll" them back into view.

But even this wasn't as painful as I had thought it would be. I 27 found that I could hold in my head the gist of what I had written and didn't need to keep looking at it. Was this need, in fact, still another writer's hang-up that I could shed? To some extent it was. I discovered, as I had at so many other points in this journey, that various crutches I had always assumed I needed were really not necessary. I made a decision to just throw them away and found that I could still function. The only real hardship occurred when a paragraph broke at the bottom of the screen. This meant that the first lines of the paragraph were on one page and the rest were on the next page, and I had to keep flicking the two pages back and forth to read what I was writing. But again, it wasn't fatal. I learned to live with it and soon took it for granted as an occupational hazard.

GLOSSARY
OF USEFUL TERMS

Numbers in parentheses indicate pages in the text where the term is defined and/or examples are given.

Abstract (149, 241–242) nouns, such as "truth" or "beauty," are words that are neither *specific* nor definite in meaning; they refer to *general* concepts, qualities, and conditions that summarize an entire category of experience. Conversely, *concrete* terms, such as "apple," "crabgrass," "computer," and "French horn," make precise appeals to our senses. The word *abstract* refers to the logical process of abstraction, through which our minds are able to group together and describe similar objects, ideas, or attitudes. Most good writers use abstract terms sparingly in their essays, preferring instead the vividness and clarity of *concrete* words and phrases.

Allusion is a reference to a well-known person, place, or event from life or literature. In "Summer Rituals," for example, Ray Bradbury alludes to Herman Melville's great novel *Moby-Dick* when he describes an old man who walks on his front porch "like Ahab surveying the mild mild day."

Analogy (292) is an extended *comparison* of two dissimilar objects or ideas.

Analysis (2, 13, 14, 199, 502) is the examination and evaluation of a topic by separating it into its basic parts and elements and studying it systematically.

Anecdote (87) is a brief account of a single incident.

Argumentation (425–436) is an appeal predominantly to *logic* and reason. It deals with complex issues that can be debated.

Attitude (91, 432) describes the narrator's personal feelings about a particular subject. In "Triple Tragedy in Black Society," Harry Edwards expresses anger and disgust at the manner in which African-American athletes are routinely exploited by the American sports establishment. Attitude is one component of *point of view.*

Audience (22–23, 34, 37–38, 204, 428, 430–433) refers to the person or group of people for whom an *essay* is written.

Cause and effect (385–394) is a form of *analysis* that examines the causes and consequences of events and ideas.

Characterization (92) is the creation of imaginary yet realistic persons in fiction, drama, and *narrative* poetry.

Chronological order (23, 88, 91–92, 153–154, 203) is a sequence of events arranged in the order in which they occurred. George Orwell follows this natural time sequence in his *narrative* essay "Shooting an Elephant."

Classification (251–258) is the analytical process of grouping together similar subjects into a single category or class; *division* works in the opposite fashion, breaking down a subject into many different subgroups. In "Cinematypes," Susan Allen Toth divides movies (and the people who watch them) into several distinct categories; she then classifies her dates according to the movies they prefer.

Clichés (245–246) are words or expressions that have lost their freshness and originality through continual use. For example, "busy as a bee," "pretty as a picture," and "hotter than hell" have become trite and dull because of overuse. Good writers avoid clichés through vivid and original phrasing.

Climactic order (153–154) refers to the *organization* of ideas from one extreme to another—for example, from least important to most important, from most destructive to least destructive, or from least promising to most promising.

Cognitive skills (1–3) are mental abilities that help us send and receive verbal messages.

Coherence (154) is the manner in which an *essay* "holds together" its main ideas. A coherent *theme* will demonstrate such a clear relationship between its *thesis* and its logical structure that readers can easily follow the *argument*.

Colloquial expressions (248) are informal words, phrases, and sentences that are more appropriate for spoken conversations than for written *essays*.

Comparison (291–301) is an *expository* writing technique that examines the similarities between objects or ideas, whereas *contrast* focuses on differences.

Conclusions (26, 431) bring *essays* to a natural close by summarizing the *argument*, restating the *thesis*, calling for some specific action, or explaining the significance of the topic just discussed. If the *introduction* states your *thesis* in the form of a question to be answered or a problem to be solved, then your conclusion will be the final "answer" or "solution" provided in your paper. The conclusion should be approximately the same length as your *introduction* and should leave your reader satisfied that you have actually "concluded" your discussion rather than simply run out of ideas to discuss.

Concrete: See *abstract.*

Conflict is the struggle resulting from the opposition of two strong forces in the plot of a play, novel, or short story.

Connotation and **Denotation** (247–248, 432) are two principal methods of describing the meanings of words. *Connotation* refers to the wide array of positive and negative associations most words naturally carry with them, whereas *denotation* is the precise, literal *definition* of a word that might be found in a dictionary. Alleen Pace Nilsen's "Sexism in English: A 1990s Update" examines the extent to which words such as "mistress," "queen," "matron," and "old maid" betray antifeminist connotations that far outweigh their denotative definitions. See also Judy Brady's "Why I Want a Wife" for further examples.

Content and **Form** (26, 28) are the two main components of an *essay. Content* refers to the subject matter of an *essay,* whereas its *form* consists of the graphic symbols that communicate the subject matter (word choice, spelling, punctuation, paragraphing, etc.).

Contrast: See *comparison.*

Deduction (421–432) is a form of logical reasoning that begins with a *general* assertion and then presents *specific* details and *examples* in support of that *generalization. Induction* works in reverse by offering a number of *examples* and then concluding with a *general* truth or principle.

Definition (337–344) is a process whereby the meaning of a term is explained. Formal definitions require two distinct operations: (1) finding the *general* class to which the object belongs and (2) isolating the object within that class by describing how it differs from other elements in the same category. Marie Winn, for example, defines television addiction as a response to a drug (general class) that results from electronic stimuli (thereby differentiating it from other addictive agents such as alcohol and heroin).

Denotation: See *connotation.*

Description (33–42) is a mode of writing or speaking that relates the sights, sounds, tastes, smells, or feelings of a particular experience to its readers or listeners. Good descriptive writers, such as those featured in Chapter 1, are particularly adept at receiving, selecting, and expressing sensory details from the world around them. Along with *persuasion, exposition,* and *narration,* it is one of the four dominant types of writing.

Development (22–25) concerns the manner in which a *paragraph* of an *essay* expands upon its topic.

Dialect is a speech pattern typical of a certain regional location, race, or social group that exhibits itself through unique word choice, pronunciation, and/or grammatical *usage*. See John McPhee's "The Pines," in which Fred and Bill, two residents of a wilderness area in southern New Jersey, speak in a discernible dialect.

Dialogue is a conversation between two or more people, particularly within a novel, play, poem, short story, or other literary work.

Diction (22–23, 246–248, 432) is word choice. If a vocabulary is a list of words available for use, then good diction is the careful selection of those words to communicate a particular subject to a specific *audience*. Different types of diction include formal (scholarly books and articles), informal (*essays* in popular magazines), *colloquial* (conversations between friends, including newly coined words and expressions), *slang* (language shared by certain social groups), *dialect* (language typical of a certain region, race, or social group), technical (words that make up the basic vocabulary of a specific area of study, such as medicine or law), and obsolete (words no longer in use).

Division: See *classification*.

Documented essay (501–515) is a research or library paper that integrates *paraphrases, summaries,* and quotations from secondary sources with the writer's own insights and conclusions. Such *essays* normally include references within the paper and, at the end, a list of books and articles cited.

Dominant impression (35, 36–37, 37–38) in *descriptive* writing is the principal *effect* the author wishes to create for the *audience*.

Editing (27, 28) is an important part of the *rewriting* process of an *essay* that requires writers to make certain their work observes the conventions of standard written English.

Effect: See *cause and effect*.

Emphasis (88, 429–430) is the stress given to certain words, phrases, sentences, and/or *paragraphs* within an *essay* by such methods as repeating important ideas; positioning *thesis* and *topic sentences* effectively; supplying additional details or *examples;* allocating more space to certain sections of an *essay;* choosing words carefully; selecting and arranging details judiciously; and using certain mechanical devices, such as italics, underlining, capitalization, and different colors of ink.

Essay is a relatively short prose composition on a limited topic. Most essays are 500 to 1,000 words long and focus on a clearly definable question to be answered or problem to be solved. *Formal essays,* such as Germaine Greer's "A Child Is Born," are generally characterized by seriousness of *purpose*, logical *organization,* and dignity of language; *informal essays,* such as Garrison Keillor's "School," are generally brief, humorous, and more loosely structured. Essays in this textbook have been divided into nine traditional *rhetorical* types, each of which is discussed at length in its chapter introduction.

Etymology (340) is the study of the origin and development of words.

Evidence (426, 428, 430–431, 502) is any material used to help support an *argument,* including details, facts, *examples,* opinions, and expert testimony. Just as a lawyer's case is won or lost in a court of law because of the strength of the evidence presented, so too is the effectiveness of a writer's *essay* dependent on the evidence offered in support of its *thesis statement.*

Example (149–156) is an illustration of a *general* principle or *thesis statement.* Harold Krents' "Darkness at Noon," for instance, gives several different examples of prejudice against handicapped people.

Exposition is one of the four main *rhetorical* categories of writing (the others are *persuasion, narration,* and *description*). The principal *purpose* of expository prose is to "expose" ideas to your readers, to explain, define, and interpret information through one or more of the following modes of exposition: *example, process analysis, division/classification, comparison/contrast, definition,* and *cause/effect.*

Figurative language (38–39, 432) is writing or speaking that purposefully departs from the literal meanings of words to achieve a particularly vivid, expressive, and/or imaginative image. When, for example, Joyce Carol Oates refers to a boxing match as a story, she is using figurative language. Other principal figures of speech include *metaphor, simile, hyperbole, allusion,* and *personification.*

Flashback (91–92) is a technique used mainly in *narrative* writing that enables the author to present scenes or conversations that took place prior to the beginning of the story.

Focus (21–25, 38) is the concentration of a *topic* on one central point or issue.

Form: See *content.*

Formal essay: See *essay.*

Free association (17–18) is a process of generating ideas for writing through which one thought leads randomly to another.

General (149, 241–242) words are those that employ expansive categories, such as "animals," "sports," "occupations," and "clothing"; *specific* words are more limiting and restrictive, such as "koala," "lacrosse," "computer programmer," and "bow tie." Whether a word is general or *specific* depends at least somewhat on its context: "Bow tie" is more *specific* than "clothing," yet less *specific* than "the pink and green striped bow tie Aunt Martha gave me last Christmas." See also *abstract.*

Generalization (149, 151, 431–432) is a broad statement or belief based on a limited number of facts, *examples,* or statistics. A product of *in-*

ductive reasoning, generalizations should be used carefully and sparingly in *essays.*

Hyperbole, the opposite of *understatement,* is a type of *figurative language* that uses deliberate exaggeration for the sake of emphasis or comic effect (e.g., "hungry enough to eat a horse").

Hypothesis (389, 502) is a tentative theory that can be proved or disproved through further investigation and *analysis.*

Idiom refers to a grammatical construction unique to a certain people, region, or class that cannot be translated literally into another language.

Illustration (149–150) is the use of *examples* to support an idea or *generalization.*

Imagery (38–39) is *description* that appeals to one or more of our five senses. See, for example, Malcolm Cowley's *description* in "The View from 80" of one of the pleasures of old age: "simply sitting still, like a snake on a sun-warmed stone, with a delicious feeling of indolence that was seldom attained in earlier years." Imagery is used to help bring clarity and vividness to descriptive writing.

Induction: See *deduction.*

Inference (431) is a *deduction* or conclusion derived from *specific* information.

Informal essay: See *essay.*

Introduction (26) refers to the beginning of an *essay.* It should identify the subject to be discussed, set the limits of that discussion, and clearly state the *thesis* or general *purpose* of the paper. In a brief (five-paragraph) *essay,* your *introduction* should be only one *paragraph;* for longer papers, you may want to provide longer introductory sections. A good *introduction* will generally catch the *audience's* attention by beginning with a quotation, a provocative statement, a personal *anecdote,* or a stimulating question that somehow involves its readers in the topic under consideration. See also *conclusion.*

Irony (160) is a figure of speech in which the literal, *denotative* meaning is the opposite of that which is stated. Judy Brady's "Why I Want a Wife" is heavily ironic: What she really wants is for women to be treated as equals to men.

Jargon (244–245) is the special language of a certain group or profession, such as psychological jargon, legal jargon, or medical jargon. When jargon is excerpted from its proper subject area, it generally becomes confusing or meaningless, as in "I have a latency problem with my backhand" or "I hope we can interface tomorrow night after the dance."

Levels of thought (1–2) is a phrase that describes the three sequential stages at which people think, read, and write: literal, interpretive, and analytical.

Logic (426, 431–432) is the science of correct reasoning. Based principally on *inductive* or *deductive* processes, logic establishes a method whereby we can examine *premises* and *conclusions*, construct *syllogisms*, and avoid faulty reasoning.

Logical fallacy (432) is an incorrect conclusion derived from faulty reasoning. See also *post hoc, ergo propter hoc* and *non sequitur*.

Metaphor (38–39, 432) is an implied *comparison* that brings together two dissimilar objects, persons, or ideas. Unlike a *simile*, which uses the words "like" or "as," a metaphor directly identifies an obscure or difficult subject with another that is easier to understand. In George Orwell's "Shooting an Elephant," for example, the author metaphorically describes the great beast as having a "preoccupied grandmotherly air"—a vivid *comparison* that should be of great help to those of us more familiar with grandmothers than with mad elephants.

Mood (91, 432) refers to the atmosphere or *tone* created in a piece of writing. The mood of Mark Mathabane's "Passport to Knowledge," for example, is frantic and exciting; of Jessica Mitford's "Behind the Formaldehyde Curtain," sarcastic and derisive; and of Ellen Goodman's "Putting In a Good Word for Guilt," good-humored and sympathetic.

Narration (87–95) is storytelling: the recounting of a series of events, arranged in a particular order and delivered by a narrator to a specific *audience* with a clear *purpose* in mind. Along with *persuasion, exposition*, and *description*, it is one of the four principal types of writing.

Non sequitur (431–432), from a Latin phrase meaning "it does not follow," refers to a *conclusion* that does not logically derive from its *premises*.

Objective (34, 36) writing is detached, impersonal, and factual; *subjective* writing reveals the author's personal feelings and *attitudes*. Judith Wallerstein and Sandra Blakeslee's "Second Chances for Children of Divorce" is an *example* of objective prose, whereas Mark Mathabane's "Passport to Knowledge" is essentially *subjective* in nature. Most good college-level *essays* are a careful mix of both approaches, with lab reports and technical writing toward the objective end of the scale and personal *essays* in composition courses at the *subjective* end.

Organization (22–23, 26, 88, 91–92, 153–154, 203, 431–432) refers to the order in which a writer chooses to present his or her ideas to the reader. Five main types of organization may be used to develop *paragraphs* or *essays:* (1) *deductive* (moving from *general* to *specific*), (2) *inductive* (from *specific* to *general*), (3) *chronological* (according to time sequence), (4) *spatial* (according to physical relationship in space), and (5) *climactic* (from one extreme to another, such as least important to most important).

Paradox is a seemingly self-contradictory statement that contains an element of truth. In "The View from 80," Malcolm Cowley paradoxically declares that the Ojibwa Indians were "kind to their old people" by killing them when they became decrepit.

Paragraphs are groups of interrelated sentences that develop a central topic. Generally governed by a *topic sentence,* a paragraph has its own *unity* and *coherence* and is an integral part of the logical *development* of an *essay.*

Parallelism (262) is a structural arrangement within sentences, *paragraphs,* or entire *essays* through which two or more separate elements are similarly phrased and developed. Look, for example, at Beth Wald's sequential *description* of her devotion to rock climbing in "Let's Get Vertical!": "I've lived in vans, tepees, tents, and caves; worked three jobs to save money for expenses; driven 24 hours to spend a weekend at a good rock; and lived on beans and rice for months at a time—all of this to be able to climb."

Paraphrase (505) is a restatement in your own words of someone else's ideas or observations.

Parody is making fun of a person, event, or work of literature through exaggerated imitation.

Person (39, 91) is a grammatical distinction identifying the speaker or writer in a particular context: first person (I or we), second person (you), and third person (he, she, it, or they). The person of an *essay* refers to the voice of the narrator. See also *point of view.*

Personification is *figurative language* that ascribes human characteristics to an abstraction, animal, idea, or inanimate object. Consider, for example, Garrison Keillor's *description* of Mrs. Meiers, one of his grade school teachers, in "School": "She was a plump lady with bags of fat on her arms that danced when she wrote on the board: We named them Hoppy and Bob."

Persuasion (425–436) is one of the four chief forms of *rhetoric.* Its main purpose is to convince a reader (or listener) to think, act, or feel a certain way. It involves appealing to reason, to emotion, and/or to a sense of ethics. The other three main *rhetorical* categories are *exposition, narration,* and *description.*

Point of view (39, 91) is the perspective from which a writer tells a story, including *person, vantage point,* and *attitude.* Principal *narrative* voices are first-person, in which the writer relates the story from his or her own *vantage point* ("When I pulled the trigger, I did not hear the bang or feel the kick. . . ."); omniscient, a third-person technique in which the narrator knows everything and can even see into the minds of the various characters; and concealed, a third-person method in which the narrator can see and hear events but cannot look into the minds of the other characters.

Post hoc, ergo propter hoc (387–388), a Latin phrase meaning "after this, therefore because of this," is a *logical fallacy* confusing *cause and effect* with *chronology.* Just because Irving wakes up every morning before the sun rises doesn't mean that the sun rises because Irving wakes up.

Premise (431–432) is a proposition or statement that forms the foundation of an *argument* and helps support a *conclusion.* See also *logic* and *syllogism.*

Prereading (3–6, 15–16) is thoughtful concentration on a topic prior to reading an *essay.* Just as athletes warm up their physical muscles before competition, so too should students activate their "mental muscles" before reading or writing *essays.*

Prewriting (16–23, 27), which is similar to *prereading,* is the initial stage in the composing process during which writers consider their topics, generate ideas, narrow and refine their *thesis statements,* organize their ideas, pursue any necessary research, and identify their *audiences.* Although prewriting occurs principally, as the name suggests, "before" an *essay* is started, writers usually return to this "invention" stage again and again during the course of the writing process.

Process analysis (199–206), one of the seven primary modes of *exposition,* either gives directions about how to do something (directive) or provides information on how something happened (informative).

Proofreading (27, 28), an essential part of *rewriting,* is a thorough, careful review of the final draft of an *essay* to insure that all errors have been eliminated.

Purpose (22–23, 34, 37–38, 428, 432–433) in an *essay* refers to its overall aim or intention: to entertain, inform, or persuade a particular *audience* with reference to a specific topic (to persuade readers of *The Christian Century,* for example, that religion should be taken out of instructional periods in America's high schools, as Donald Drakeman argues in "Religion's Place in Public Schools"). See also *dominant impression.*

Refutation is the process of discrediting the *arguments* that run counter to your *thesis statement.*

Revision (26–27, 28), meaning "to see again," takes place during the entire writing process as you change words, rewrite sentences, and shift *paragraphs* from one location to another in your *essay.* It plays an especially vital role in the *rewriting* stage of the composing process.

Rewriting (26–27, 28) is a stage of the composing process that includes *revision, editing,* and *proofreading.*

Rhetoric is the art of using language effectively.

Rhetorical questions are intended to provoke thought rather than bring forth an answer. See, for example, Shelby Steele's rhetorical questions in "Affirmative Action: The Price of Preference": "Given that unfairness cuts both ways, doesn't it only balance the scales of history that my children now receive a preference over whites? Doesn't this repay, in a small way, the systematic denial under which their grandfather lived out his days?"

Rhetorical strategy is the plan or method whereby an *essay* is organized. Most writers choose from methods discussed in this book, such as *narration, example, comparison/contrast, definition,* and *cause/effect.*

Sarcasm is a form of *irony* that attacks a person or belief through harsh and bitter remarks that often mean the opposite of what they say. Alice Walker's "My Daughter Smokes," in which the author bemoans her father's death from smoking-induced pneumonia as well as her daughter's addiction to cigarettes, ends with the following observation: "I realize now that as a child I sat by, through the years, and literally watched my father kill himself: Surely one such victory in my family, for the rich white men who own the tobacco companies, is enough." See also *satire.*

Satire is a literary technique that attacks foolishness by making fun of it. Most good satires work through a "fiction" that is clearly transparent. Judy Brady claims she wants a wife, for example, yet she obviously does not; she simply uses this satiric "pose" to ridicule the stereotypical male view of wives as docile, obedient creatures who do everything possible to please their husbands.

Setting refers to the immediate environment of a *narrative* or *descriptive* piece of writing: the place, time, and background established by the author.

Simile (38–39, 432) is a *comparison* between two dissimilar objects that uses the words "like" or "as." In "Graduation," Maya Angelou's friends and relatives tell her she looks "like a sunbeam" in her new yellow graduation dress. See also *metaphor.*

Slang (248) is casual conversation among friends; as such, it is inappropriate for use in formal and informal writing, unless it is placed in quotation marks and introduced for a specific *rhetorical* purpose: "Hey dude, ya know what I mean?" See also *colloquial.*

Spatial order (88, 153–154) is a method of *description* that begins at one geographical point and moves onward in an orderly fashion. See, for example, the opening of John McPhee's "The Pines," which first describes the front yard of Fred Brown's house, then moves through the vestibule and into the kitchen, and finally settles on Fred himself, who is seated behind a porcelain-topped table in a room just beyond the kitchen.

Specific: See *general.*

Style is the unique, individual way in which each author expresses his or her ideas. Often referred to as the "personality" of an *essay,* style is dependent on a writer's manipulation of *diction,* sentence structure, *figurative language, point of view, characterization, emphasis, mood, purpose, rhetorical strategy,* and all the other variables that govern written material.

Subjective: See *objective.*

Summary (505) is a condensed statement of someone else's thoughts or observations.

Syllogism (431–432) refers to a three-step *deductive argument* that moves logically from a major and a minor *premise* to a *conclusion.* A traditional example is "All men are mortal. Socrates is a man. Therefore, Socrates is mortal."

Symbol refers to an object or action in literature that metaphorically represents something more important than itself. In George Orwell's "Shooting an Elephant," the stricken beast symbolizes the British Empire, which, despite its immense size, is dying in influence throughout the world.

Synonyms are words with similar or identical *denotative* meanings, such as "aged," "elderly," "older person," and "senior citizen."

Syntax describes the order in which words are arranged in a sentence and the effect that arrangement has on the creation of meaning.

Thesis statement or **thesis** (24) is the principal *focus* of an *essay.* It is usually phrased in the form of a question to be answered, a problem to be solved, or an assertion to be argued. The word derives from a Greek term meaning "something set down," and most good writers find that "setting down" their thesis in writing helps them tremendously in defining and clarifying their topic before they begin to write an outline or a rough draft.

Tone (91, 432) is a writer's *attitude* or *point of view* toward his or her subject. See also *mood.*

Topic sentence is the central idea around which a *paragraph* develops. A topic sentence controls a *paragraph* in the same way a *thesis statement* unifies and governs an entire *essay.* See also *induction* and *deduction.*

Transition (92) is the linking together of sequential ideas in sentences, *paragraphs,* and *essays.* This is accomplished primarily through word repetition, pronouns, parallel constructions, and such transitional words and phrases as "therefore," "as a result," "consequently," "moreover," and "similarly."

Understatement, the opposite of *hyperbole,* is a deliberate weakening of the truth for comic or emphatic purpose. Commenting, for example, on the great care funeral directors take to make corpses look lifelike for their funerals, Jessica Mitford explains in "Behind the Formalde-hyde Curtain," "This is a rather large order, since few people die in the full bloom of health."

Unity (154) exists in an *essay* when all ideas originate from and help support a central *thesis statement.*

Usage (27, 28) refers to the customary rules that govern written and spoken language.

Vantage point (39, 91) is the frame of reference of the narrator in a story: close to the action, far from the action, looking back on the past, or reporting on the present. See also *person* and *point of view.*

CREDITS

INDEX OF AUTHORS
AND TITLES